BIBLIOGRAPHIES OF MODERN AUTHORS

ISSN 0749-470X

Number Twenty-Five

THE WORK OF STEPHEN KING

An Annotated Bibliography & Guide

by

Michael R. Collings
Pepperdine University

Edited by Boden Clarke

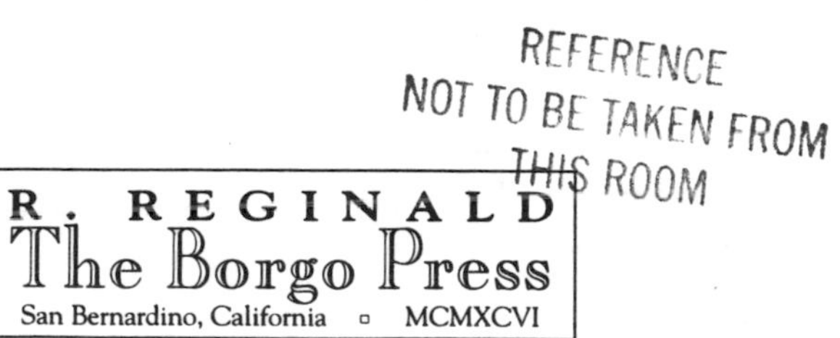

THE BORGO PRESS
Publishers of Fine Books Since 1975
Post Office Box 2845
San Bernardino, CA 92406
United States of America

* * * * * * * *

 Printed in the United States of America by Van Volumes, Ltd. Cover design by Highpoint Type & Graphics.

Library of Congress Cataloging-in-Publication Data

Collings, Michael R.
The work of Stephen King : an annotated bibliography & guide / by Michael R. Collings ; edited by Boden Clarke.
p. cm. — (Bibliographies of modern authors, ISSN 0749-470X ; no. 25)
Includes index.
ISBN 0-8095-0520-7 (cloth). — ISBN 0-8095-1520-2 (pbk.)
1. King, Stephen, 1947- —Bibliography. 2. Horror tales, American—History and criticism—Bibliography. 3. Horror tales, American—Bibliography. I. Clarke, Boden, 1948- . II. Title. III. Series: Bibliographies of modern authors (San Bernardino, Calif.) ; no. 25.
Z8464.47.C65 1996 93-16091
[PS3561.I483]
016.813'54—dc20 CIP

FIRST EDITION

CONTENTS

Dedication

For Judith,
Michael-Brent, Erika,
Ethan, and Kendra

INTRODUCTION

NOT SO MUCH TO TELL, AS TO LET THE STORY FLOW THROUGH

> "I don't understand *any* of this. Why does a story have to be socio-anything? Politics...culture...history...aren't those natural ingredients in any story, if it's told well? I mean...."
>
> —Bill Denbrough, in *IT*

What can one say about Stephen King that will add to the words he has written?

From the bulk of the book that follows, quite a bit has already been said.

The problem may be figuring out something *new* to say—or at least something *else* to say.

That is not actually a problem, of course. Stephen King is nothing if not prolific, often controversial, always true to his inner vision even when that vision is excoriated by critics upset by the fact that King did not write the book they seemed to want him to. With each new novel, each new story, each new project, King provides additional grist for the mills: scholarly, academic, critical, and fan.

Some years ago, Douglas E. Winter noted that King seemed on the verge of suffering because of his high profile. When King went on record referring to his works as the literary equivalents of a "Big Mac and friend," he became, in effect, fair game. Coupled with the at times unbelievable publishing and sales records that he has continued to set over the past decades, his often self-effacing public façade makes him unusually vulnerable to ridicule as well as to admiration (if not adulation).

One consequence is that King has become ubiquitous...and remains enigmatic. Characters on television sitcoms and feature films can refer to "Cujo" and be certain that viewers will immediately catch the in-joke. Cartoons poke fun at the length of King's recent works, especially *IT* and the uncut *Stand*; others make unsubtle references to the Stephen King "novel of the week" or "film of the week." His paperbacks are invariably found on racks in supermarkets, in discount stores, and (in dog-eared, tattered and sometimes coverless manifestations) in used book stores. Bookstores in malls stockpile his latest hardcover editions for the onslaught of eager readers, stacking the books from floor to ceiling until entire sections of a wall become a temporary monument to his storytelling ability. High school students devour his works; parents often worry about them; teachers frequently refuse to allow students to do research projects or term papers based on his novels, considering them little more than commercial hackwork undeserving of critical attention. University professors generally ignore him, professing to have never read him and to having no intentions of altering that condition...or they might devote years to close analytical readings of his works, resulting in studies such as Terrell's or Magistrale's. Even there, however, a kind of literary schizophrenia often surfaces. As with many subjects of scholarly attention, 'Stephen King the storyteller' sometimes submerges, replaced by 'Stephen King, the social critic,' or 'Stephen King, the voice of late 20th Century America,' 'Stephen King, the Freudian' (or Jungian, or whatever), or simply and stereotypically, 'Stephen King, King of Horror' or 'Titan of Terror' or 'Master of the Macabre,' or...well, just fill in the blank with a nicely alliterative phrase.

And in the face of such extraordinary attention, Stephen King just keeps on publishing, keeps on altering the face of the publishing industry, keeps on breaking sales records, keeps on being Stephen King.

Ultimately, perhaps, that is what a bibliography such as the one that follows best illustrates. Stephen King is *sui generis*. Algis Budrys recently considered the phenomenon of Stephen King:

> Do I think he is now in the mainstream of fantasy writers? No, I still don't. For one thing, the readiness with which he shifts in and out of fantasy while continuing to write horror argues against this. Rather, I think he had founded his own genre—and has been followed into it by scores of other writers—and while it overlaps fantasy a lot of the time, what matters is the horror. The little movie-going boy of long ago does not care how you get that special horripilating thrill—it's the thrill that counts. And I think that...this means a new genre *has* been created—"Stephen King," p. 55.

In the next paragraph, however, Budrys demonstrates the bifurcation that often seems endemic to King criticism. What King has achieved is well and good, but in a sense not enough: "I think that trapped inside King is one of the finest writers of our time," submerged beneath the weight of blockbuster bestsellers. Finally, Budrys defines the essence of Stephen King: "he is the first writer, ever, to have truly baffled the critics."

Budrys's essay accompanied two King stories in a special issue of *The Magazine of Fantasy and Science Fiction,* an overtly fan-oriented publication. Yet the same sense of ambivalence persists on other levels as well. In recent scholarly volume published by the Massachusetts Institute of Technology Press, Slavoj Zizek attempts to re-define the philosophy and psychoanalytical theories of Jacques Lacan by combining "Kant with Sade"; *i.e.*, by coupling "the most sublime theoretical motifs of Jacques Lacan together with and through exemplary cases of contemporary mass culture," including not only the works of Alfred Hitchcock, but also "science fiction, dectective novels, sentimental kitsch, and up—or down—to Stephen King" (*Looking Awry*, p. vii). In a work of carefully considered and thoughtfully expressed cultural criticism, the odd phrase "up—or down" echoes Budrys's estimation of King as having baffled the critics. Shortly thereafter, Zizek paraphrases De Quincey with a set of dual and contradictory propositions, the second of which reads:

> If a person renounces Stephen King, soon Hitchcock himself will appear to him dubious, and from here it is just a step to a disdain for psychoanalysis and to a snobbish refusal of Lacan. How many people have entered the way of perdition with some fleeting cynical remark on Stephen King, which at the time was of no great importance to them, and ended by treating Lacan as a phallocentric obscurantist!—p. viii.

An interesting set of juxtapositions, to say nothing of the psychological sequence implied.

Or consider a third example, from an article intended for yet another level of readership. George Will's "Odd, Isn't It, That History's Most Developed Society Has a Deep Craving for Gore" carries a sidebar that reads:

> Eastern Europe,
> be warned:
> First comes capitalism,
> then comes Stephen King
> with razor murderers to
> make it all bearable.

"The fiction of horror and the supernatural has a distinguished pedigree, stretching from Homer (*Ulysses*) through Poe and Henry James," Will rightly assures his readers, even citing the conclusions of Michiko Kakutani that the current interest in horror fiction represent, among other things, "a post-modernist return to traditional storytelling that yields accessible morals." And yet Will remains ambivalent as well-concerned by the content of King's stories, stunned by the unprecedented sales figures (the first printing of *The Dark Half,* if laid end to end, would stretch from Chicago to Cincinnati), uneasy about precisely what King is doing in a novel whose "plot skids along on a sheet of blood and bursts of the bizarre."

As these citations suggest, King *is* a phenomenon. He demands attention but paradoxically not by demanding it. He disclaims interest in academic and popular analyses; similarly, he stands beyond the ability of any reviewer to alter his sales figures up or down.

And yet.

The sheer mass of pages emerging from his imagination, the sheer number of hardcover and paperback books he has created, the seemingly unstoppable flood of film adaptations (ranging from masterful to muddled)—all of these are attested to by the entries in this bibliography. George Beahm claims that more books have been written *about* King than *by* him. A university colleague, hearing about this project and understanding for the first time the extent of materials available by and about King, simply responded with a question that was partly rhetorical but mostly incredulous: "For a *living* author?"

Yes.

The Work of Stephen King attempts to suggest the inordinate extent of contemporary interest in King as writer, as personality, as critic and commentator. While working toward completeness, the bibliography does not claim to be definitive. Information on non-English translations is perforce sketchy. Copies of newspaper reviews and profiles are often difficult to locate, and, because of the nature of the publications, often ephemeral. A number of items probably enjoyed a limited circulation, and many have most likely passed out of general view. But an attempt has been made to locate, identify, and enter as many items as possible.

As with any project of this nature—especially one a decade year in the making—many people have helped beyond all reasonable expectations. My appreciation extends to the following, either for their provocative and insightful discourses on things-King, or more directly for providing essential information about difficult-to-locate items: Neil Barron, George Beahm, Tyson Blue, Barbara Bolan, Algis Budrys, Orson Scott Card, Robert A. Collins, Frank Darabont, William Deese, Ted Dikty, David A. Engebretson, Craig Goden, Mark Graham, Dave

Hinchberger, Gerry Holland, Barry Hoffman, Dan Klamkin, Dean R. Koontz, Stephanie Leonard, Tom Monteleone, Michael Moses, Bill Munster, Sandy Parigan, Virginia Randolph, Rob Reginald, George Slusser, Shirley Sonderegger, Stephen J. Spignesi, Christopher Spruce, Carroll F. Terrell, Marshall B. Tymn, and Douglas E. Winter.

Just before I began writing this introduction, I finished re-reading *The Bachman Books*. Sitting at a booth in a fast-foods restaurant, eating a burger and fries while Ben Richards ran his desperate last against the Network, I was reminded with more force than I might have expected after having immersed myself in King's novels and stories for so many years, of the final acknowledgment that must accompany any discussion of Stephen King:

To the Storyteller,
Stephen King,

with gratitude
for the Stories.

ADDENDUM

Although I have updated the major categories in this book through at least 1994, some of the minor secondary chapters conclude with 1991. This was a period of exploring new directions on the author's part, and of extensive activity on the part of King scholars and others, but there is simply too much material to integrate without delaying this guide even further. I have chosen, therefore, to get this volume out in its present form, and to postpone some updates to a second edition several years hence. I welcome additions, corrections, and changes, sent to me c/o The Borgo Press.

—Michael R. Collings
Thousand Oaks and Malibu, California
July, 1991-September, 1995

A STEPHEN KING CHRONOLOGY

Abbreviations used in this chronology:

(anth.)—Anthology
(coll.)—Collection
(n)—Novel
(s)—Short story
(nonf.)—Non-fiction
(p)—Poem

1947 Stephen Edwin King born on September 21, in Portland, Maine, the second son of Donald and Nellie Ruth (Pillsbury) King (King's older brother, David Victor King, was adopted two years before King's birth).

1949 Donald King walks out the door and is never heard from again. Over the next nine years, the King family lives in Scarborough, New York; Croton-on-Hudson, New York; Chicago, Illinois, West De Pere, Wisconsin; Fort Wayne, Indiana; and Stratford, Connecticut (see David King's "Growing Up With the Boogeyman," in *The Shape Under the Sheet,* by Stephen J. Spignesi, p. 31-38).

1957 In October, when King first hears that the Russians orbited Sputnik, he is struck by the implicit terror in the announcement, initiating a life-long concern for the blending of horror and technology.

1958 King, his mother, and his brother move to Durham, Maine, in the fall of 1958; King remains there until he completes his college education. King meets Chris Chesley.

1960 Publishes *People. Places, Things* (coll., with Chris Chesley; self-published through Triad Publishing Company).

1963 Publishes a second printing of *People, Places, Things* (coll., with Chris Chesley). Begins study at the Lisbon Falls High School.

1964 Publishes "The Star Invaders" (s; self-published through Triad, Inc.).

1965 Publishes "I Was a Teenage Grave Robber" (s), his first semi-professional publication.

1966 King begins study as a freshman at the University of Maine, Orono, majoring in English. "I Was A Teenage Grave Robber" reprinted as "In a Half-World of Terror" (s).

1967 Publishes "The Glass Floor" (s), in *Startling Mystery Stories*—his first professional sale. Completes the manuscript for *The Long Walk* (published in 1979).

1968 Publishes "Here There Be Tygers" (s), "Cain Rose Up" (s), "Strawberry Spring" (s); "Harrison State Park '68" (p). Begins work on a novel-length manuscript, *Sword in the Darkness*.

1969 Publishes "Night Surf" (s), "The Reaper's Image" (s), "Stud City"; "Garbage Truck" columns (nonf., through 1970); "The Dark Man" (p).

1970 Graduates from UMO with a B.Sc. degree in English. Begins work in a number of menial jobs, including laborer in an industrial laundry and pumping gas at a filling station. Publishes "Slade" (s), "Graveyard Shift" (s); "A Possible Fairy Tale" (nonf.); "Donovan's Brain" (p), "Silence" (p). Completes manuscript for *Blaze*, an unpublished novel.

1971 Marries Tabitha Spruce, a fellow student at UMO, on January 2, 1971. Birth of first child, Naomi Rachel. Begins teaching English at Hampden Academy. Publishes "The Blue Air Compressor" (s), "I Am the Doorway" (s); Untitled poem, "Brooklyn August" (p), "The Hardcase Speaks" (p). Completes the manuscript for *The Running Man* (published 1981), his fourth novel manuscript. Begins teaching at Hampden Academy, a position he holds for two years. Begins submitting novels to Doubleday.

1972 Publishes "Suffer the Little Children" (s), "The Fifth Quarter" (s, as 'JOHN SWITHEN'), "Battleground" (s), "The Mangler" (s). Begins work on a short story that would ultimately evolve into *Carrie* (published 1974).

1973 Birth of first son, Joseph Hill. Publishes "The Boogeyman" (s), "Trucks" (s), "Gray Matter" (s), "It Grows on You" (s); "The Horror Marker Writer and the Ten Bears" (nonf.). In March, submits *Carrie* to Doubleday; the novel is accepted. Begins work on *Second Coming,* an early version of *'Salem's Lot* (published 1975). Nellie King (Stephen's mother) dies of cancer.

1974 Publishes *Carrie* (n); "Sometimes They Come Back" (s). Completes work on *'Salem's Lot* and *Roadwork* (published 1981). Moves to Boulder, CO and begins writing *The Stand* and *The Shining*.

1975 The King family returns to Maine. King publishes *'Salem's Lot* (n); "The Lawnmower Man" (s), "The Revenge of Lardass Hogan" (s); "Writing a First novel" (nonf.). Completes the manuscript for *The Stand*.

1976 Publishes "Weeds" (s), "The Ledge" (s), "I Know What You Need" (s); "Not Guilty" (nonf.). *Carrie* released as a feature-length film directed by Brian de Palma, giving King's novels increased visibility and interest.

1977 Publishes *The Shining* (n); *Rage* (n, as 'RICHARD BACHMAN'); "The Cat from Hell," (s), "Children of the Corn" (s), "One for the Road" (s), "The Man Who Loved Flowers" (s). Completes drafts of *The Dead Zone,*

Firestarter, and *Cujo.* Travels to England and meets Peter Straub; first discussions of a collaboration that would lead to *The Talisman.*

1978 Birth of second son, Owen Phillip. Publishes *The Stand* (n), a difficult book that he has described as his "own little Vietnam"; *Night Shift* (coll.); *Stephen King* (coll.); "The Night of the Tiger" (s), "The Gunslinger" (s), "Man With a Belly" (s), "Nona" (s), "The Fright Report" (nonf.); "The Doll Who Ate His Mother" (nonf.). Serves as Writer-in-Residence, UMO. Judge for the 1977 World Fantasy Awards.

1979 Publishes *The Dead Zone* (n); *The Long Walk* (n, as 'RICHARD BACHMAN'); "The Crate" (s); "How to Scare a Woman to Death" (nonf.); "The Writing Life" (nonf.); "The Horrors of '79" (nonf.). Completes drafts for *Christine, Pet Sematary,* and *Danse Macabre*; completes screenplay for *Creepshow.* Guest of Honor, World Fantasy Convention. Receives World Fantasy Award nominations for *The Stand, Night Shift. 'Salem's Lot* airs as a three-night mini-series for television.

1980 The King family moves to Bangor, ME, where they purchase a Victorian mansion. Publishes *Firestarter* (n; first limited edition publication); "The Way Station" (s), "The Wedding Gig" (s), "Big Wheels: A Tale of the Laundry Game" (s), "The Monkey" (s), "Crouch End" (s), "The Mist" (s); "A Pilgrim's Progress" (nonf.); "On Becoming a Brand Name" (nonf.), "Books" (nonf.), "Imagery and the Third Eye" (nonf.), "Some Notes on *Tales of the Vampyre"* (nonf.). Completes first draft of *IT.*
Becomes the first American writer to have three books on the national best-sellers lists simultaneously: *Firestarter, The Dead Zone,* and *The Shining.* Release of Stanley Kubrick's film adaptation of *The Shining.*

1981 Publishes *Cujo* (n); *Roadwork* (n, as 'RICHARD BACHMAN'); *Stephen King's Danse Macabre* (nonf.); "The Oracle and the Mountain" (s), "The Jaunt" (s), "The Slow Mutants" (s), "The Monster in the Closet" (excerpt from *Cujo*), "The Bird and the Album" (excerpt from *IT*), "Do the Dead Sing?" (s), "The Gunslinger and the Dark Man," (s), "The Man Who Would Not Shake Hands" (s); "When Is TV Too Scary for Children" (nonf.), "The Cannibal and the Cop" (nonf.), "The Sorry State of TV Shows" (nonf.).
Receives Career Alumni Award from the University of Maine, Orono. Cameo appearance in George A. Romero's *Knightriders.* Publication of Edward J. Zagorski's *Teacher's Manual: Stephen King.*

1982 Publishes *The Dark Tower: The Gunslinger* (coll.); *The Running Man* (n, as 'RICHARD BACHMAN'); *The Plant* (excerpt from novel-in-progress); *Creepshow* (coll.); *Different Seasons* (coll.); "The Raft" (s), "Before the Play" (s), "Skybar" (s), "Survivor Type" (s); "Between Rock and a Hard Place" (nonf.), "Visit With an Endangered Species" (nonf.), "The Ludlum Attraction" (nonf.); "Mentors" (nonf.); "Favorite Films" (nonf.), "Digging the Boogens" (nonf.), "On *The Shining* and Other Perpetrations" (nonf.), "Peter Straub: An Appreciation" (nonf.), "Horrors!" (nonf.), "The Evil Dead: Why You Haven't Seen It Yet...And Why You Ought To" (nonf.), "My High School Horrors" (nonf.). Begins work on *The Talisman,* with Peter Straub, and *The Cannibals.* Completes work on *Thinner* (published 1984).

Receives the Hugo award for best nonfiction of the year, for *Danse Macabre*. Receives the World Fantasy Award for "Do the Dead Sing?" Named Best Fiction Writer of the Year in a poll by *Us Magazine*. Writes screenplay for *Creepshow*. Release of *Creepshow*, directed by George A. Romero; King has a cameo appearance. Publication of Tim Underwood and Chuck Miller's *Fear Itself: The Horror Fiction of Stephen King*. Publication of Douglas E. Winter's critique, *Stephen King*.

1983 Publishes *Christine* (n); *Cycle of the Werewolf* (n); *Pet Sematary* (n); *The Plant, Part Two* (excerpt from novel-in-progress); "The Word Processor" (s), "Uncle Otto's Truck" (s), "The Return of Timmy Baterman" (excerpt from *Pet Sematary*); "Don't be Cruel" (nonf.), "Dear Walden People" (nonf.), "Horrors!" (nonf.), "A Profile of Robert Bloch" (nonf.), "Ross Thomas Stirs the Pot" (nonf.), "Berni Wrightson" (nonf.), "Black Magic and Music" (nonf.), "Last Waltz" (nonf.), "Special Makeup Effects and the Writer" (nonf.); "Stephen King," in *A Gift from Maine* (nonf.), "Stephen King's 10 Favorite Horror Books or Short Stories" (nonf.). Completes drafts of three novels: *The Talisman*, *The Tommyknockers*, and *The Napkins* (later retitled *The Eyes of the Dragon*). Completes the screenplay for *Cat's Eye*.

Presents "An Evening with Stephen King at the Billerica, Massachusetts, Public Library." Release of John Carpenter's film adaptation of *Christine*. Release of Lewis Teague's film adaptation of *Cujo*. Release of David Cronenberg's film adaptation of *The Dead Zone*. Release of videocassette versions of "The Boogeyman" and "The Woman in the Room."

1984 Publishes *The Eyes of the Dragon* (n, Philtrum limited edition); *The Talisman* (n), with Peter Straub; *Thinner* (n, as 'RICHARD BACHMAN'); "Gramma" (s), "Mrs. Todd's Shortcut" (s), "The Ballad of the Flexible Bullet" (s), "The Revelations of 'Becka Paulson" (excerpt from *The Tommyknockers*); "The Irish King" (nonf.), "1984: A Bad Year If You Fear Friday the 13th" (nonf.), "Dr. Seuss and the Two Faces of Fantasy" (nonf.), "Why I Am for Gary Hart" (nonf.), "My First Car" (nonf.), articles and reviews.

Presents Guest of Honor Address, "Dr. Seuss and the Two Faces of Fantasy," International Conference on the Fantastic in the Arts, Boca Raton FL, March 24. Appearance in American Express commercial for television. Release of Fritz Kiersch's film adaptation of *Children of the Corn*. Release of Mark Lester's film adaptation of *Firestarter*. Publication of James Van Hise's *Enterprise Incidents Presents Stephen King*. Publication of Douglas E. Winter's *Stephen King: The Art of Darkness*.

1985 Acknowledges that 'RICHARD BACHMAN' is Stephen King. Publishes *Skeleton Crew* (coll.); *Silver Bullet* (coll.); *The Bachman Books* (coll.); *The Plant, Part Three*; *Heroes for Hope: Starring the X-Men;* "Dolan's Cadillac" (s), "Beachworld" (s); "What Went Down When Magyk Went Up" (nonf.), "Theodore Sturgeon" (nonf.), "King Testifies" (nonf.), "Cat from Hell" (nonf.), "The Politics of Limited Editions" (nonf.), "His Creepiest Movies" (nonf.), "Lists That Matter" (nonf.), "Ghostmaster General" (nonf.), "The King Speaks" (nonf.), "Why I Was Bachman" (nonf.), "What Ails the U. S. Male" (nonf.), "My Say" (nonf.), "*Regis Reprimandum*" (nonf.).

Establishes another record with five titles on the national bestsellers lists simultaneously, November 1985-January 1986: *Skeleton Crew* (hardcover), *The Bachman Books* (hardcover), *The Talisman* (mass-market paper), *The Bachman Books* (mass-market paper), *Thinner* (mass-market paper). Writes final screenplays for *Cat's Eye* and *Silver Bullet*. Release of Lewis Teague's *Cat's Eye*, with screenplay by King. Release of Daniel Attias's *Silver Bullet*. Appearance of "The Word Processor of the Gods" on the *Tales from the Darkside* television series. Presents "An Evening with Stephen King," at the University of Massachusettts, Amherst. Guest of Honor, Third Annual World Drive-in Movie Festival and Custom Car Rally. First issue of *Castle Rock: The Stephen King Newsletter* published in January, 1985; newsletter continues through the end of 1989.

Publication of Darrell Schweitzer's *Discovering Stephen King*. Publication of Michael R. Collings and David A. Engebretson's *The Shorter Works of Stephen King*. Publication of Michael R. Collings's *Stephen King as Richard Bachman* and *The Many Facets of Stephen King*.

1986 Publishes *IT* (n); "For the Birds" (s); "Lists that Matter" (nonf.), "Let's Scare Dick and Jane" (nonf.), "Tough Talk and Tootsies" (nonf.), "King Vs. Chalker" (nonf.), "Say 'No' to the Enforcers" (nonf.), "Everything You Need to Know About Writing Successfully—in Ten Minutes" (nonf.), "Stephen King Comments on *IT*" (nonf.), "On the Far Side" (nonf.), "How *IT* Happened" (nonf.), "Write-In" (nonf.), "Big Jim Thompson: An Appreciation," "The Dreaded X" (nonf.), articles about baseball and the Red Sox.

Screenwrites and directs *Maximum Overdrive*. Release of *Maximum Overdrive,* with a cameo appearance by King. Release of Rob Reiner's film adaptation of "The Body," *Stand By Me*. King acts as Guest VJ for MTV, June 27. Appearance of "Gramma" as an episode on the *Twilight Zone* television series. Presents "Banned Books and Other Concerns: The Virginia Beach Lecture," Virginia Beach VA, September 22. Lloyd Elliot Lecturer in English, University of Maine. Publication of Michael R. Collings's *The Films of Stephen King*. Publication of Jesse Horsting's *Stephen King: At the Movies*. Publication of Michael R. Collings's *The Annotated Guide to Stephen King*. Publication of Tim Underwood and Chuck Miller's *Kingdom of Fear: The World of Stephen King*.

1987 Publishes *The Eyes of the Dragon* (n, mass-market edition); *Misery* (n); *The Tommyknockers* (n); *The Dark Tower II: The Drawing of the Three* (coll.); "The Doctor's Case" (s), "Popsy" (s); "Postscript to *Overdrive*" (nonf.), "Whining About the Movies in Bangor" (nonf.), "Turning the Thumbscrews on the Reader" (nonf.), "On John D. MacDonald" (nonf.), "Entering the Rock Zone" (nonf.), articles on baseball and the Red Sox.

Appears on the annual hardcover fiction bestsellers lists with three titles: *The Tommyknockers* (#1), *Misery* (#4), and *The Eyes of the Dragon* (#10). Release of *Creepshow 2,* directed by Michael Gornick and adapted for screen by George A. Romero. Appearance of "Sorry, Wrong Number" as an episode on *Tales from the Darkside*. Release of *Return to Salem's Lot,* a film based loosely on King's novel. Presents lecture, "Friends of the Andre Dubus Library Series, Boston MA, March 1. Delivers Commencement Address, University of Maine, May 6. Publication of Michael R. Collings's *The Stephen King Phenomenon*, Jeff Conner's *Stephen King*

Goes to Hollywood, and Gary Hoppenstand and Ray B. Browne's *The Gothic World of Stephen King*.

1988 Publishes *Nightmares in the Sky* (nonf.); "Night Flier" (s), "The Reploids" (s), "Sneakers" (s), "Dedication" (s); "The Ideal, Genuine Writer: A Forenote" (nonf.), "'Ever Et Raw Meat? and Other Weird Questions" (nonf.), "This Guy is *Really* Scary" (nonf.), "SK Criticized for References to Blacks: Stephen King Replies" (nonf.), "SK Clarifies Gardner Reference" (nonf.), "The Ultimate Catelogue" (nonf.), "Robert Marasco: *Burnt Offerings*" (nonf.), reviews and articles on baseball, etc.
Receives Bram Stoker Award (Horror Writers of America) for *Misery* (co-recipient with Robert R. McCammon). *Carrie* adapted as a stage musical; performed in England and New York. *Rage* adapted as a stage play. Release of Paul Michael Glasser's film adaptation of *The Running Man*. Publication of Joseph Reino's *Stephen King: The First Decade....* Publication of Tony Magistrale's *Landscape of Fear*. Publication of Tim Underwood and Chuck Miller's *Bare Bones*. Publication of Don Herron's *Reign of Fear*.

1989 Publishes *The Dark Half* (n); *Dolan's Cadillac* (s); *My Pretty Pony* (s); "Rainy Season" (s), "Home Delivery" (s). Writes screenplay for *Pet Sematary* film. Release of *Pet Sematary*, with a cameo appearqance by King.
Bram Stoker Award nominations for "Night Flier" and "Dedication." Delivers public lecture, 1989 Authors Series, Pasadena, CA, April 26. Publication of Tyson Blue's *The Unseen King*, Don Herron's *Feast of Fear*, George Beahm's *The Stephen King Companion*, and *Das Stephen King Buch*.

1990 Publishes *The Stand: Complete and Uncut Edition* (n); *Four Past Midnight* (coll.); "The Moving Finger" (s); "The Bear" (s). Release of *Tales of the Darkside: The Movie* [includes "The Cat from Hell" segment based on King's short story]; release of *Stephen King's Graveyard Shift* by Paramount Pictures, October 26, 1990; release of *Misery* by Castle Rock Entertainment, November 30, 1990. The mini-series TV adaptation of *IT* aired, November 18 and November 20, 1990.
Guest, Portland Public Library Centennial, Portland, Maine. March 1990. Publication of Stephen Spignesi's *The Stephen King Quiz Book*, James Van Hise's *Stephen King and Clive Barker: The Illustrated Guide to the Masters of the Macabre*, Carroll F. Terrell's *Stephen King: Man and Artist*.

1991 Publishes *The Dark Tower III: The Waste Lands* (n); *Needful Things* (n). Television presentations of "Sometimes They Come Back" and "Golden Years."
Guest, ABA Convention, June, 1991. Publication of George Beahm's *The Stephen King Story: A Literary Profile*; *Gauntlet 2: Exploring the Limits of Free Expression* (Stephen King Special Issue), edited by Barry Hoffman; Stephen Spignesi's *The Shape Under the Sheet: The Complete Stephen King Encyclopedia*; *The Shining Reader*, edited by Anthony Magistrale; Carroll F. Terrell's *Stephen King: Man and Artist* (revised edition).

1992 Publishes *Gerald's Game* (n). Release of *Stephen King's Sleepwalkers* (film); *The Lawnmower Man* (film), a motion picture so distanced from

King's original story that attempts were made to have his name removed from the credits.

Publication of George Beahm's *The Stephen King Story: A Literary Profile—Updated and Revised*; Anthony Magistrale's *Stephen King: The Second Decade, Danse Macabre to The Dark Half*; Magistrale's *The Dark Descent: Essays Defining Stephen King's Horrorscape*; Anne Saidman's *Stephen King*; Stephen Spignesi's *Second Stephen King Quiz Book*.

1993 Publishes *Dolores Clairborne* (n); *Nightmares & Dreamscapes* (coll.). Release of *The Tommyknockers* (made-for-television film). Publication of Stephen Spignesi's *Stephen King A to Z: A Dictionary of People, Places, and Things in the Works of the King of Horror*; and Spignesi's *The Complete Stephen King Encyclopedia: The Definitive Guide to the Works of America's Master of Horror* (paperback reprint of *The Shape Under the Sheet*).

1994 Publishes *Insomnia* (n). Release of *The Stand* (made-for-television film); *The Shawshank Redemption* (film); *Dolores Claiborne* (film). Publication of *Demon-Driven: Stephen King and the Art of Writing*, edited by George Beahm (signed, limited edition also 1994).

1995 Publishes *Rose Madder* (n). Release of *The Langoliers* (made-for-television film). "The Man in the Black Suit" wins a World Fantasy Award for Best Short Fiction and the O. Henry Award for Best American Short Story.

1996 Publication of Michael R. Collings's *The Work of Stephen King: An Annotated Bibliography & Guide*.

ABOUT MICHAEL R. COLLINGS

DR. MICHAEL R. COLLINGS is a professor of English in the Humanities Division at Pepperdine University, Malibu, California, and director of the Creative Writing Program for the Communication Division. Now in his sixteenth year with the University, he teaches a range of courses, including composition, intermediate and advanced poetry in the Creative Writing Program, and Renaissance literature courses, with an emphasis on John Milton.

He is perhaps best known to Stephen King fans for his multiple volumes in the Starmont Studies in Literary Criticism series, particularly *Stephen King as Richard Bachman*, *The Shorter Works of Stephen King* (with David Engebretson), *The Many Facets of Stephen King*, *The Films of Stephen King*, *The Stephen King Phenomenon*, and the work from which this bibliography grew, *The Annotated Guide to Stephen King*. Since 1989 he has been collating materials for this present bibliography. In addition, he has written reviews and essays on King and other contemporary fantasists, including Dean R. Koontz and Orson Scott Card, with extensive materials published in George Beahm's updated *Stephen King Companion* and elsewhere. In August 1995 he served as Scholar Guest of Honor at the annual Mythopoeic Society Conference, delivering the keynote address on Orson Scott Card, extrapolating from ideas incorporated in *In the Image of God: Theme, Characterization, and Landscape in the Fiction of Orson Scott Card* (1990).

Dr. Collings is also a widely published poet, with his fifth and sixth books of poetry appearing in August 1995—*Matrix* (White Crow Press) and *Haiku* (Zarahemla Motets). Over 500 of his poems have appeared in journals and magazines, as well as in chapbooks and collections of poetry. Recently, he has appeared on a number of internet poetry pages as well.

He is currently working on several other books for The Borgo Press.

PART ONE

PRIMARY SOURCES

A

A.

BOOKS

A1. CARRIE

A1. *Carrie.* Garden City, NY: Doubleday & Co., 1974, 199 p., cloth. [horror novel]

PLOT SUMMARY: *Carrie* details the story of Carrie White, a naive young girl whose first bitter experiences in high school parallel her first awareness of mature sexuality and the onset of frightening psychokinetic powers. An outsider by temperament and upbringing, Carrie attempts to fit in with others her own age and to overcome her mother's repressed, obsessively theological rigidity. Befriended by several students and teachers, Carrie moves closer to acceptance until a series of disastrous events at the high school prom results in her death and the devastation of the small town of Chamberlain.

COMMENTS: Told equally as narration and as pseudo-documentation, *Carrie* was King's first published novel but fifth manuscript. Originally intended as short story, in part to demonstrate that King could write about a female protagonist, it quickly outgrew that form and was submitted as a novel to Bill Thompson at Doubleday.

Continually in print since its appearance, *Carrie* was released as a film by Brian de Palma in 1976; King credits the appearance of the film with helping to establish him as a "Brand Name." A musical version of the novel was also produced.

REPRINTS:

ab. New York: Doubleday, 1990, p., cloth. Issued in conjunction with publication of uncut version of *The Stand*.

b. Garden City, NY: Doubleday & Co. [Science Fiction Book Club edition], [n.d.], 199 p., cloth.

c. London: New English Library, May 1974, 240 p., cloth.

cb. London: New English Library, July 1975, 192 p., paper.

d. New York: A Signet Book, New American Library, April 1975, 245 p., mass-market paperback. 64 printings through 1994.

db. New York: A Plume Book, New American Library, October 1991, 152 p., trade paper. "Collector's Edition," with a new introduction by Tabitha King. Includes a color reproduction of the original hardcover dustjacket.

e. Utrecht, Belgium: De Fontein, 1975, 205 p., trade paperback. Translated by Ingrid Nijkerk. 3rd printing, 1986. [Dutch]
f. as: *Carrie*. Barcelona: Pomaire, 1975. [Spanish]
g. as: *Carrie*. Paris: Gallimard, 1976, 228 p., cloth. [French]
h. as: *Carrie*. Milano: Sonzogno, 1977, 176 p. Translated by B. Gasperini. [Italian]
i. as: *Carrie*. München: Franz Schneekluth Verlag, 1977. Translated by Elisabeth Epple. [German]
j. as: *Carrie*. München: Wilhelm Heyne Verlag (TB 5374), 1977, p., paper. Translated by Elisabeth Epple. [German]
k. as: *Carrie*. Barcelona: Circulo de Lectores, 1978, p. [Spanish]
l. as: *Carrie*. Barcelona: Pomaire, 1978, p. [Spanish]
lb. as: *Carrie*. Barcelona: Pomaire, 1981, p. [Spanish]
m. as: *Carrie*. Paris: J'ai-lu/Epouvante, 1980. [French]
n. as: *Carrie*. Stockholm: Askild and Kärnekull, 1980, 228 p. Translated by G. A. Ericsson. [Swedish]
o. in: *The Shining, 'Salem's Lot, Night Shift, Carrie*. London: Octopus Books, 1981, cloth, p. . See also **A13**.
ob. in: *The Shining, 'Salem's Lot, Carrie*. London: Octopus Books, Heinemann, 1983, cloth, p. .
p. as: *Carrie; El Umbral de la Noche* [*Carrie* and *Night Shift*]. Barcelona: Mundo Actual de Ediciones, 1982, p. [Spanish]
q. Utrecht: Luitingh/Veen, 1983, 205 p., trade paperback. 3rd printing, 1986.
r. as: *Carrie*. Bergisch Gladbach: Bastei-Lübbe Verlag, (Paperback 28111), 1983, 284 p., paper. Translated by Elisabeth Epple. Includes an interview with King and excerpts from other novels. [German]
rb. as: *Carrie*. Bergisch-Gladbach: Bastei-Lübbe (TB 13121, 1987, p., paper. Translated by Elisabeth Epple; edited by Brunhilde Janßen, with an abridged interview with King. [German]
s. as: *Carrie*. Milano: Bompiani, 1984, 176 p., paper. Translated by Brunella Gasperini. [Italian]
sb. as: *Carrie*. Milano: Bompiani, January 1987, 174 p., paper. 4th edition. Translated by Brunella Gasperini. [Italian]
t. as: *Carrie*. Barcelona: Plaza & Janés, 1985, 288 p., paper. Translated by Gregorio Vlastelica. [Spanish]
tb. as: *Carrie*. Esplugas Llobregat (Barcelona), Spain: Plaza & Janés Editores, 1989, p. BIBLIOTECA DE STEPHEN KING ['Stephen King Library'], Vol. 8. [Spanish]
u. as: *Carrie*. Barcelona: Laertes, 1988, p. [Spanish]

SECONDARY SOURCES AND REVIEWS:

1. Alexander, Alex E. "Stephen King's *Carrie*—A Universal Fairy Tale." *Journal of Popular Culture* (Fall, 1979): 282-288. Reprinted: *Contemporary Literary Criticism*, Vol. 26. Detroit: Gale Research, 1983, p. 234-236.
2. Beahm, George, ed. *The Stephen King Companion*. Kansas City, MO: Andrews and McMeel, September 1989, p. 171-175.
3. Blue, Tyson. *The Unseen King*. STARMONT STUDIES IN LITERARY CRITICISM, No. 26. Mercer Island, WA: Starmont House, 1989, p. 1, 16, 27, 46, 104.

4. Bright, David. "Hampden Teacher Hits Jackpot with New Book," in *Bangor Daily News* [Maine] (May 25, 1973): .
5. *Booklist* 70 (July 1, 1974): 1180.
6. *Book World* (June 15, 1975): 4.
7. Callendar, Newgate (pseud.). "Criminals at Large," in *The New York Times Book Review* (May 26, 1974): 17.
8. Clinch, Monty. "Carrie's Mom and Danny's Dad," *Ms London* [England] (April 9, 1979): 10.
9. Collings, Michael R. *The Annotated Guide to Stephen King: A Primary and Secondary Bibliography of the Works of America's Premier Horror Writer*. STARMONT REFERENCE GUIDE, No. 8. Mercer Island, WA: Starmont House, October 1986.
10. Collings, Michael R. *The Many Facets of Stephen King*. STARMONT STUDIES IN LITERARY CRITICISM, No. 11. Mercer Island, WA: Starmont House, 1986.
11. Egan, James. "Apocalypticism in the Fiction of Stephen King," in *Extrapolation* 25:3 (Fall, 1984): 214-227.
12. Egan, James. "Technohorror: The Dystopian Vision of Stephen King," in *Extrapolation* 29:2 (Summer, 1988): 140-152 (esp. p. 149).
13. Ehlers, Leigh A. "*Carrie*: Book and Film," in *Ideas of Order in Literature and Film,* edited by Peter Ruppert and others. Tallahassee, FL: University Presses of Florida, 1980, p. 39-50. Reprinted as: "*Carrie*: Book and Film." *Literature Film Quarterly* (Spring, 1981): 32-39.
14. Gordon, J. S. *New York Times Book Review* (September 11, 1977): 3.
15. Hall, Elizabeth. Review in *Psychology Today* 9 (September, 1975): 76. Reprinted: *Contemporary Literary Criticism, Volume 12, Young Adult Literature,* edited by Dedria Bryfonski. Detroit: Gale Research Co., 1980, cloth, p. 309.
16. Hatlen, Burton. "Alumnus Publishes Symbolic Novel, Shows Promise," in *The Maine Campus* [University of Maine, Orono] (April 12, 1974): .
17. *Kirkus Reviews* 42 (February 1, 1974): 137.
18. *Kirkus Reviews* 42 (March 1, 1974): 257.
19. *Library Journal* 99 (February 15, 1974): 584.
20. *Library Journal* 99 (April 15, 1974): 1150.
21. *Library Journal* 99 (May 15, 1974): 1453.
22. *Library Journal* 99 (December 15, 1974): 3249.
23. Magistrale, Tony. *Landscape of Fear: Stephen King's American Gothic*. Bowling Green, OH: Bowling Green State University Popular Press, 1988.
24. Magistrale, Tony. *The Moral Voyages of Stephen King*. STARMONT STUDIES IN LITERARY CRITICISM, No. 25. Mercer Island, WA: Starmont House, 1989, p. 45-47.
25. Neilson, Keith. "*Carrie*," in *Survey of Modern Fantasy Literature, Volume 5,* edited by Frank N. Magill. Englewood Cliffs, NJ: Salem Press, 1983, p. 197-202.
26. *Publishers Weekly* 205 (February 25, 1974): .
27. Reino, Joseph. *Stephen King: The First Decade,* Carrie *to* Pet Sematary. TWAYNE'S UNITED STATES AUTHORS SERIES (TUSAS

531), edited by Warren French. Boston: Twayne Publishers, February 1988.

28. Schweitzer, Darrell, ed. *Discovering Stephen King*. STARMONT STUDIES IN LITERARY CRITICISM, No. 8. Mercer Island, WA: Starmont House, 1985.
29. Spignesi, Stephen J. "Carrie," in *The Shape Under the Sheet: The Complete Stephen King Encyclopedia*. Ann Arbor, MI: Popular Culture, Ink., May 1991, cloth, p. 152-157.
30. Thompson, Bill. "A Girl Named Carrie: Introduction," in *Kingdom of Fear: The World of Stephen King*, edited by Tim Underwood and Chuck Miller. Columbia, PA: Underwood-Miller, 1986, p. 29-34, cloth. See also **I13.**
31. Underwood, Tim and Chuck Miller, eds. *Fear Itself: The Horror Fiction of Stephen King*. San Francisco: Underwood-Miller, 1982.
32. *Washington Post Book World* (May 26, 1974): 4.
33. *Wilson Library Journal* 48 (June 1974): 802.
34. Wilson, Philip. "Before the Brand Name," in *Castle Rock: The Stephen King Newsletter* 4:5-6 (May-June, 1988): 4.
35. *Kingdom of Fear: The World of Stephen King*. Columbia, PA: Underwood-Miller, April 1986, 267 p., cloth.
36. Winter, Douglas E. *Stephen King*. STARMONT READER'S GUIDE, No. 16. Series editor, Roger Schlobin. Mercer Island, WA: Starmont House, October 1982.
37. Winter, Douglas E. *Stephen King: The Art of Darkness*. New York: New American Library, November 1984.
38. Yarbro, Chelsea Quinn. "Cinderella's Revenge—Twists on Fairy Tale and Mythic Themes in the Work of Stephen King," in *Fear Itself: The Horror Fiction of Stephen King,* edited by Tim Underwood and Chuck Miller. San Francisco: Underwood-Miller, 1982, p.45-55.
39. Zagorski, Edward J. *Teacher's Manual: Stephen King*. New York: New American Library, 1981.

A2. 'SALEM'S LOT

A2. ***'Salem's Lot***. Garden City, NY: Doubleday & Co., 1975, 439 p., cloth. [horror novel]

PLOT SUMMARY: Ben Mears returns to his hometown of Jerusalem's Lot; in confronting the spectres of his own past, he also uncovers the town's secret—that a vampire has settled in the sinister old Marsten House. Mear's struggles for personal integrity and survival parallel those of the town as the vampire systematically takes over the inhabitants of 'Salem's Lot.

COMMENTS: One of King's favorites among his own novels, *'Salem's Lot* is an intense, imaginative treatment of the vampire motif as translated into uniquely American idioms. It shows how a vampire might survive in contemporary American society, and in doing so, becomes a study of isolation, fear, and social fragmentation. Some particularly gruesome passages were edited from King's original manuscript (see Beahm's

The Stephen King Companion for details), but the novel does justice to the tradition defined by Stoker's *Dracula*. King's version has been called the finest treatment of the vampire mythos since Stoker's.

The novel was filmed for television as *Salem's Lot* (1979); an unauthorized sequel to the telefilm, titled *Return to Salem's Lot* (but with few recognizable connections to King narrative), is also available on videocassette.

REPRINTS:

ab. Garden City, NY: Doubleday & Co., 1975, 439 p., cloth. Sixteen printings through September 1989.
ac. New York: Doubleday, 1990, 439 p., cloth. A special reissue to coincide with publication of the uncut version of *The Stand*.
b. Garden City, NY: Doubleday [Science Fiction Book Club edition], [n.d.], 405 p., cloth.
c. New York: A Signet Book, New American Library, August 1976, 428 p., mass-market paper. Front cover with embossed figure and a single drop of red blood; no title or author on cover. 55 printings through 1994.
cb. New York: A Signet Book, New American Library, August 1976, 428 p., mass-market paper. New cover, with no embossing but title and King's name added.
cc. New York, A Plume Book, New American Library, 1991?, p., trade paper. "Collector's Edition." Includes a color reproduction of the original hardcover art.
d. as: *Hora del Vampiro*. Barcelona: Pomaire, 1976, p. [Spanish]
e. London: New English Library, February 1977, 440 p., paper.
f. as: *Hora del Vampiro*. Barcelona: Circulo de Lectores, 1977, p. [Spanish]
g. as: *Bezeten Stad* ["*Possessed City*"]. Utrecht: Luitingh/Veen, 1978, 445 p., Trade paper. Translated by W. van Mancius. 6th printing, 1986. [Dutch]
h. as: *Brennen Muß Salem!* ["*Salem Must Burn*"]. Vienna & Hamburg: Paul Zsolnay, April 1979, 437 p., paper. Translated by Ilse Winger and Christoph Wagner. Abridged edition. [German]
i. as: *Notti di Salem* ["*Night of Salem*"]. Milano: Sonzogno, 1979, 448 p. Translated by C. Brera. [Italian]
j. as: *Bezeten Stad*. Utrecht: Skarabee, 1980 (?), trade paper. [Dutch]
k. in: *The Shining, 'Salem's Lot, Night Shift, Carrie*. London: Octopus Books, 1981, cloth, p. . Omnibus edition; see also **A13**.
kb. in: *The Shining, 'Salem's Lot, Carrie*. London: Octopus Books, Heinemann, 1983, cloth, p. .
l. as: *Brennen Muß Salem*. München: Deutscher Taschenbuchverlag, 1981. DTV PHANTASTICA 1877. Translated by Ilse Winger and Christoph Wagner. Abridged edition. [German]
m. as: *Brennen Muß Salem*. Kornwesterheim, Austria: Europäische Bildungsgemeinschaft; Gütersloh, Austria: Bertelsmann Club; Vienna, Austria: Buchgemeinschaft Donauland; Zug, Switzerland: Buch-und-Schallplattenfreunde, February 1985, 447 p., paper. Book Club Editions. Translated by Iris Winger and Christoph Wagner. [German]
n. as: *Staden som Försvann*. Stockholm: Legende, 1985, 476 p. Translated by Lennart Olafsson. 2nd printing, 1987. [Swedish]

o. as: *Brennen Muß Salem.* München: Wilhelm Heyne Verlag (TB 6478), 1985, p., paper. Translated by Ilse Winger and Christoph Wagner. [German]

p. as: *El Misterio de Salem's Lot* ["*The Mystery of Salem's Lot*"]. Esplugas Llobregat, Barcelona: Plaza & Janés, November 1985, 400 p., paper. Translated by Marta I. Guastavino. [Spanish]

pb. as: *El Misterio de Salem's Lot.* Esplugas Llobregat, Barcelona: Plaza & Janés Editores, 1987. [Spanish]

pc. as: *El Misterio de Salem's Lot.* Esplugas Llobregat (Barcelona), Spain: Plaza & Janés Editores, 1989, p. BIBLIOTECA DE STEPHEN KING, Vol. 6. [Spanish]

q. as: *Brennen Muß Salem.* Gütersloh, Austria: Bertelsmann Lesering, 1986. Translated by Iris [error for 'Ilse'] Winger and Christoph Wagner. [German]

r. as: *La Hora del Vampiro* ["*The Hour of the Vampire*"]. Buenos Aires: Emécé Editores, [1986?], p., paper. [Spanish]

SECONDARY SOURCES AND REVIEWS:

1. Beahm, George, ed. *The Stephen King Companion.* Kansas City, MO: Andrews and McMeel, September 1989, p. 265-267.
2. Blue, Tyson. *The Unseen King.* STARMONT STUDIES IN LITERARY CRITICISM, No. 26. Mercer Island, WA: Starmont House, 1989.
3. Bobbie, Walter. *Best Sellers* 35 (January, 1976): 304. Reprinted: *Contemporary Literary Criticism, Volume 12, Young Adult Literature,* edited by Dedria Bryfonski. Detroit: Gale Research Co., 1980, cloth, p. 309.
4. *Booklist* 72 (January 1, 1976): 613.
5. Collings, Michael R. *The Annotated Guide to Stephen King: A Primary and Secondary Bibliography of the Works of America's Premier Horror Writer.* STARMONT REFERENCE GUIDE, No. 8. Mercer Island, WA: Starmont House, October 1986.
6. Collings, Michael. R. *The Many Facets of Stephen King.* STARMONT STUDIES IN LITERARY CRITICISM, No. 11. Mercer Island, WA: Starmont House, 1986.
7. Collings, Michael. R. *The Stephen King Phenomenon.* STARMONT STUDIES IN LITERARY CRITICISM, No. 14. Mercer Island, WA: Starmont House, 1987.
8. Egan, James. "Technohorror: The Dystopian Vision of Stephen King," in *Extrapolation* 29:2 (Summer, 1988): 140-152 (esp. 149).
9. Hatlen, Burton. "*'Salem's Lot* Critiques American Civilization," in *The Maine Campus* [University of Maine, Orono] (December 12, 1975): .
10. Hicks, James E. "Stephen King's Creation of Horror in *'Salem's Lot:* A Prolegomenon Towards a New Hermeneutic of the Gothic Novel," in *The Gothic World of Stephen King: Landscape of Nightmares,* edited by Gary Hoppenstand and Ray B. Browne. Bowling Green, OH: Bowling Green State University Popular Press, December 1987, p. 75-83.
11. Hoppenstand, Gary and Ray B. Browne, eds. *The Gothic World of Stephen King: Landscape of Nightmares.* Bowling Green, OH: Bowling Green State University Popular Press, December 1987.

12. *Kirkus Reviews* (August 15, 1975): 935. Excerpted: *Contemporary Literary Criticism, Volume 12, Young Adult Literature,* edited by Dedria Bryfonski. Detroit: Gale Research Co., 1980, cloth, p. 309.
13. Magistrale, Tony. *Landscape of Fear: Stephen King's American Gothic.* Bowling Green, OH: Bowling Green State University Popular Press, 1988.
14. Magistrale, Tony. *The Moral Voyages of Stephen King.* STARMONT STUDIES IN LITERARY CRITICISM, No. 25. Mercer Island, WA: Starmont House, 1989.
15. Munster, Bill. "Why and How to Teach Stephen King," in *Castle Rock: The Stephen King Newsletter* 2:8 (August, 1986): 1, 4.
16. *Publishers Weekly* (August 11, 1975): 109.
17. *Publishers Weekly* (June 7, 1976): 73.
18. Reino, Joseph. *Stephen King: The First Decade,* Carrie *to* Pet Sematary. TWAYNE'S UNITED STATES AUTHORS SERIES (TUSAS 531), edited by Warren French. Boston: Twayne Publishers, February 1988.
19. Ryan, Alan. "The Marsten House in *'Salem's Lot,*" in *Fear Itself: The Horror Fiction of Stephen King,* edited by Tim Underwood and Chuck Miller. San Francisco: Underwood-Miller, 1982, p.169-180.
20. Sarrantonio, Al. "Stephen King: *'Salem's Lot,*" by Al Sarrantonio. *Horror: 100 Best Books,* edited by Stephen Jones and Kim Newman. London: Xanadu, 1988, p. 161-162.
21. *School Library Journal* 22 (December, 1975): 70.
22. Schweitzer, Darrell, ed. *Discovering Stephen King.* STARMONT STUDIES IN LITERARY CRITICISM, No. 8. Mercer Island, WA: Starmont House, 1985.
23. Spignesi, Stephen J. "'Salem's Lot," in *The Shape Under the Sheet: The Complete Stephen King Encyclopedia.* Ann Arbor, MI: Popular Culture, Ink., May 1991, cloth, p. 158-164.
24. Underwood, Tim and Chuck Miller, eds. *Fear Itself: The Horror Fiction of Stephen King.* San Francisco: Underwood-Miller, 1982, 255 p., cloth.
25. *Voice of Youth Advocates* 6 (December, 1983): 267.
26. *Village Voice Literary Supplement* (November, 1985): 27.
27. Watson, Christine. "*'Salem's Lot,*" in *Survey of Modern Fantasy Literature, Volume 3,* edited by Frank N. Magill. Englewood Cliffs, NJ: Salem Press, 1983: 1350-1354.
28. Winter, Douglas E. *Stephen King.* STARMONT READER'S GUIDE, No. 16. Series editor, Roger Schlobin. Mercer Island, WA: Starmont House, October 1982, 128 p.
29. Winter, Douglas E. *Stephen King: The Art of Darkness.* New York: New American Library, November 1984, 252 p.
30. Zagorski, Edward J. *Teacher's Manual: Stephen King.* New York: New American Library, 1981, 46 p., paper.

A3. THE SHINING

A3. ***The Shining.*** Garden City, NY: Doubleday & Co., 1977, 447 p., cloth. [horror novel]

PLOT SUMMARY: Jack Torrence, his wife Wendy, and his only child Danny spend the winter alone in an isolated hotel high in the Colorado Rockies. As the winter progresses, Jack descends further into madness as the evil inherent in the Overlook Hotel struggles to possess him and through him the extraordinary gift—the "Shine"—young Danny has.

COMMENTS: A study of hauntings and madness, *The Shining* was influenced by Shirley Jackson's *The Haunting of Hill House*, and stands as one of King's most consciously literary works and one of those most accessible to classroom discussion; in addition, it is most frequently included in lists of King's works that may achieve enduring status in literary canons. Originally structured as a five-act tragedy (see "Before the Play," **B69**), the novel was revised heavily to remove many overt signals of that structure. The Overlook Hotel is a compelling setting for interaction among several of King's strongest characters, including Dick Hallorann, who would reappear later in *IT*.

The novel was adapted to film in 1980 by Stanley Kubrick.

REPRINTS:

ab. New York: Doubleday, 1990, 447 p., cloth. Issued in conjunction with the publication of the uncut version of *The Stand*.
b. London: New English Library, September 1977, 447 p., cloth.
bb. London: New English Library, April 1978, 416 p., paper.
bc. London: New English Library, April 1979, 320 p., paper.
c. New York: A Signet Book, New American Library, January 1978, 447 p., paper. Reflective silver mylar cover in first edition; modified or new covers for later printings. 51 printings by 1994.
cb. New York: A Signet Book, New American Library, January 1978, 447 p., paper. Movie tie-in edition, with new cover.
cc. New York, A Plume Book, New American Library, 1991?, p., trade paper. "Collector's Edition." Includes a color reproduction of the original hardcover art.
d. Garden City, NY: Doubleday [Science Fiction Book Club edition], [n.d.], 447 p., cloth.
e. as: *Het Tweede Gezicht* ["*The Second Shift*"]. Utrecht: De Fontein, 1978, 339 p., trade paper. Translated by Johan Cornelisz. [Dutch]
eb. Utrecht, Netherlands. Book Club Edition.
f. as: *Shining*. Milano: Bompiani, 1978, 429 p., paper. Translated by Adriana Dell'Orte. [Italian]
fb. as: *Shining*. Milano: Bompiani, 1981, 432 p. [Italian]
fc. as: *Shining*. Milano: Bompiani, February 1987, 429 p., paper. Translated by Adriana Dell'Orto. [Italian]
g. as: *Insolito Esplendor*. Barcelona: Pomaire, 1978, p. [Spanish]
h. as: *Shining*. Paris: Williams-Alta, 1979. [French]

i. as: *Insolito Esplendor*. Barcelona: Circulo de Lectores, 1979, p. [Spanish]

j. as: *Drengen der Skinnede*. København: Borgen, 1980, 436 p. Translated by Niels Søndergaard. [Danish]

k. as: *Shining*. Bergish Gladbach: Bastei-Lübbe Verlag (Paperback 28100), 1980, p., paper. Translated by Harro Christensen. [German]

kb. as: *Shining*. Bergisch-Gladbach: Bastei-Lübbe, 1982, 400 p., paper. [German]

kc. as: *Shining*. Bergisch Gladbach: Bastei-Lübbe Verlag (TB 13008), 1985, 528 p., paper. Translated by Harro Christensen. [German]

l. as: *Varsel*. Stockholm: Askild and Kärnekull, 1980, 458 p. Translated by G. A. Ericsson. Rpt. editions in 1981, 1983. [Swedish]

m. as: *Vidovitost*. Zagreb, Yugoslavia: [unknown], 1981, p. [Serbo-Croatian]

n. as: *El Resplandor*. Barcelona: Pomaire, 1981, p. [Spanish]

o. in: *The Shining, 'Salem's Lot, Night Shift, Carrie*. London: Octopus Books, 1981, cloth, p. . Omnibus edition; see also **A13**.

ob. in: *The Shining, 'Salem's Lot, Carrie*. London: Octopus Books, Heinemann, 1983, cloth, p. .

p. as: *El Resplandor*. Esplugas de Llobregat (Barcelona), Spain: Plaza & Janés, January 1982, 509 p., paper. Translated by Marta I. Guastavino. [Spanish]

pb. as: *El Resplendor*. Esplugas Llobregat/Barcelona: Plaza & Janés, 1986, 512 p., paper. Translated by Marta I. Gustavino. 2nd printing, 1986. [Spanish]

pc. as: *El Resplandor*. Esplugas Llobregat (Barcelona), Spain: Plaza & Janés Editores,1987, p. [Spanish]

pd. as: *El Resplandor*. BIBLIOTECA DE STEPHEN KING, Vol. 2. Esplugas Llobregat (Barcelona), Spain: Plaza & Janés Editores, 1989, p. [Spanish]

q. as: *De Shining*. Utrecht: Skarabee, 1983. Distributed by Bruna Books, Utrecht/Antwerp. Movie tie-in; new cover. Second printing, 1987. [Dutch]

r. as: *Shining: L'Enfant Lumiére*. Paris: J'ai-Lu, March 1984, 575 p., paper. Translated by Joan Bernard. [French]

rb. as: *Shining*. Paris: J'ai-Lu/Epouvante, 1988. [French]

s. as: *Shining*. Book Club Editions: Kornwesterheim, Austria: Europäische Bildungsgemeinschaft; Gütersloh, Austria: Bertelsmann Club; Vienna, Austria: Buchgemeinschaft Donauland; Zug, Switzerland: Buch-und-Schallplattenfreunde, November 1985, 477 p., paper. Translated by Harro Christensen. [German]

t. as: *Shyainingu*. Tokyo: Bungei Shunju, 1986. 2 vol. Translated by Fukamachi Mariko. [Japanese]

u. as: *Die Shining*. Utrecht: Luitingh, February 1987, p., paper. [Dutch]

v. as: *Ondskapens Hotel* ["*Hotel of Evil*"]. Norway: Fredhois Verlag, p., . [Norwegian]

w. as: *Shining*. Bergisch Gladbach: Gustav Lübbe Verlag, 1987, 400 p. Translated by Harro Christensen. [German]

x. as: *Pestens Tid*. Höganäs, Sweden: Bra Böcker, 1988, 737 p. Translated by Lennart Olaffson. [Swedish]

y. as: *Pesten Tid*. Stockholm: Legende, 1988, 833 p. Translated by Lennart Olaffson. [Swedish]

z. as: *Shining*. Stuttgart: Deutscher Bücherbund, 1988, p. Translated by Harro Christensen. [German]

SECONDARY SOURCES AND REVIEWS:

1. Beahm, George, ed. *The Stephen King Companion*. Kansas City, MO: Andrews and McMeel, September 1989, p. 268-270.
2. *Best Sellers* (January, 1976): 304.
3. *Best Sellers* (May, 1977): 39.
4. *Booklist* (March 1, 1977): 992.
5. *Best of the Times* [*New York Times*] 3 (August, 1980): 387.
6. *BooksWest* 1:1 (October, 1977): 21.
7. Cohen, Alan. "The Collapse of Family and Language in Stephen King's *The Shining,*" in *The Shining Reader*, edited by Anthony Magistrale. Mercer Island, WA: Starmont House, 1991, p. 47-60.
8. Collings, Michael R. *The Annotated Guide to Stephen King: A Primary and Secondary Bibliography of the Works of America's Premier Horror Writer*. STARMONT REFERENCE GUIDE, No. 8. Mercer Island, WA: Starmont House, October 1986.
9. Collings, Michael R. *The Many Facets of Stephen King*. STARMONT STUDIES IN LITERARY CRITICISM, No. 11. Mercer Island, WA: Starmont House, 1986.
10. Collings, Michael R. *The Stephen King Phenomenon*. STARMONT STUDIES IN LITERARY CRITICISM, No. 14. Mercer Island, WA: Starmont House, 1987.
11. Dickerson, Mary Jane. "The 'Masked Author Strikes Again': Writing and Dying in Stephen King's *The Shining*," in *The Shining Reader*, edited by Anthony Magistrale. Mercer Island, WA: Starmont House, 1991, p. 11-22.
12. Eller, Jackie. "Wendy Torrance, One of King's Women: A Typology of King's Female Characters," in *The Shining Reader*, edited by Anthony Magistrale. Mercer Island, WA: Starmont House, 1991, p. 33-46.
13. *English Journal* 68 (January, 1979): 58.
14. Ferreira, Patricia. "Jack's Nightmare at the Overlook: The American Dream Inverted," in *The Shining Reader*, edited by Anthony Magistrale. Mercer Island, WA: Starmont House, 1991, p. 23-32.
15. Hala, James. "Kubrick's *The Shining:* The Specters and the Critics," in *The Shining Reader*, edited by Anthony Magistrale. Mercer Island, WA: Starmont House, 1991, p. 203-216.
16. Hatlen, Burton. "Good and Evil in Stephen King's *The Shining,*" in *The Shining Reader*, edited by Anthony Magistrale. Mercer Island, WA: Starmont House, 1991, p. 81-104.
17. Hatlen, Burton. "Steve King's Third Novel Shines on," in *The Maine Campus* [University of Maine, Orono] (April 1, 1977): .
18. Harris, Ian. "Two Versions of *The Shining*," in *Castle Rock: The Stephen King Newsletter* 3:1 (December, 1986/January, 1987): 14-15.
19. Hyles, Vernon. "The Dark Side of Childhood: *The 500 Hats of Bartholomew Cubbins* and *The Shining,*" in *The Shining Reader*, edited by Anthony Magistrale. Mercer Island, WA: Starmont House, 1991, p. 169-178.

20. Kent, Brian. "Canaries in a Gilded Cage: Mental and Marital Decline in *McTeague* and *The Shining,*" in *The Shining Reader*, edited by Anthony Magistrale. Mercer Island, WA: Starmont House, 1991, p. 139-154.
21. *Kirkus Reviews* (December 1, 1976): 1277.
22. *Kliatt Paperback Book Guide* 12 (Spring, 1978): 8.
23. Lehman-Haupt, Christopher. *New York Times* (June 24, 1980): C9.
24. Lingeman, Richard R. "Something Nasty in the Tub," in *New York Times [Daily]* (March 1, 1977): 35.
25. *Library Journal* (February 1, 1977): 404.
26. Madigan, Mark. "'Orders From the House': Kubrick's *The Shining* and Kafka's 'The Metamorphosis,'" in *The Shining Reader*, edited by Anthony Magistrale. Mercer Island, WA: Starmont House, 1991, p. 193-202.
27. Magistrale, Tony. *Landscape of Fear: Stephen King's American Gothic*. Bowling Green, OH: Bowling Green State University Popular Press, 1988.
28. Magistrale, Tony. *The Moral Voyages of Stephen King*. STARMONT STUDIES IN LITERARY CRITICISM, No. 25. Mercer Island, WA: Starmont House, 1989.
29. Magistrale, Tony. "Shakespeare in 58 Chapters: *The Shining* as Classical Tragedy," in *The Shining Reader*, edited by Anthony Magistrale. Mercer Island, WA: Starmont House, 1991, p. 155-168.
30. Magistrale, Tony. ed. *The Shining Reader*. Mercer Island, WA: Starmont House, 1991.
31. Meyers, Julia. *"The Shining,"* in *Masterplots II: American Fiction Series, Volume 4,* edited by Frank N. Magill. Englewood Cliffs, NJ: Salem Press, 1986, cloth, p. 1407-1410.
32. Mustazza, Leonard. "The Red Death's Sway: Setting and Character in Poe's 'The Mask of the Red Death' and King's *The Shining*," in *The Shining Reader*, edited by Anthony Magistrale. Mercer Island, WA: Starmont House, 1991, p. 105-120.
33. Neilson, Keith. *"The Shining,"* in *Survey of Modern Fantasy Literature, Volume 3,* edited by Frank N. Magill. Englewood Cliffs, NJ: Salem Press, 1983: 1402-1406.
34. *New Statesman & Society* 3 (December 7, 1990): 34.
35. Patten, Frederick. *Delap's Fantasy and Science Fiction Review* (April, 1977): 6. Excerpted: *Contemporary Literary Criticism, Volume 12, Young Adult Literature,* edited by Dedria Bryfonski. Detroit: Gale Research Co., 1980, cloth, p. 310.
36. *Publishers Weekly* (December 6, 1976): 52.
37. *Publishers Weekly* (November 14, 1977): 64.
38. Reesman, Jeanne Campbell. "Stephen King and the Tradition of American Naturalism in *The Shining*," in *The Shining Reader*, edited by Anthony Magistrale. Mercer Island, WA: Starmont House, 1991, p. 121-138.
39. Reino, Joseph. *Stephen King: The First Decade,* Carrie *to* Pet Sematary. TWAYNE'S UNITED STATES AUTHORS SERIES (TUSAS 531), edited by Warren French. Boston: Twayne Publishers, February 1988.
40. *San Francisco Chronicle* (March 27, 1977): 34.
41. *School Library Journal* (December, 1975): 70.

42. Schweitzer, Darrell, ed. *Discovering Stephen King*. STARMONT STUDIES IN LITERARY CRITICISM, No. 8. Mercer Island, WA: Starmont House, 1985.
43. Smith, James. "Kubrick's or King's—Whose *Shining* Is It?" in *The Shining Reader*, edited by Anthony Magistrale. Mercer Island, WA: Starmont House, 1991, p. 181-192.
44. Spignesi, Stephen J. "The Shining," in *The Shape Under the Sheet: The Complete Stephen King Encyclopedia*. Ann Arbor, MI: Popular Culture, Ink., May 1991, cloth, p. 169-175.
45. Stanton, Michael N. "Once, Out of Nature: The Topiary," in *The Shining Reader*, edited by Anthony Magistrale. Mercer Island, WA: Starmont House, 1991, p. 3-10.
46. Straub, Peter. "Stephen King: *The Shining*," in *Horror: 100 Best Books*. Stephen Jones and Kim Newman, eds. London: Xanadu, 1988, p. 171-172.
47. Sullivan, Jack. "Ten Ways to Write a Gothic," in *New York Times Book Review* (February 20, 1977): 8. Reprinted: *Contemporary Literary Criticism, Volume 12, Young Adult Literature,* edited by Dedria Bryfonski. Detroit: Gale Research Co., 1980, cloth, p. 309-310.
48. *Voice of Youth Advocates* 6 (December, 1983): 267.
49. *Washington Post Book World* 16 (December 7, 1986): 7.
50. Weller, Greg. "The Redrum of Time: A Meditation on Francisco Goya's 'Saturn Devouring His Children' and Stephen King's *The Shining*," in *The Shining Reader*, edited by Anthony Magistrale. Mercer Island, WA: Starmont House, 1991, p. 61-78.
51. *West Coast Review of Books* (May, 1977): 26.
52. Wiater, Stanley. "King's *Shining*—Very Bright," in *The Valley Advocate* [Hatfield, MA] (June 25, 1980): .
53. *Wilson Library Bulletin* (April, 1977): 674.
54. Winter, Douglas E. *Stephen King*. STARMONT READER'S GUIDE, No. 16. Series editor, Roger Schlobin. Mercer Island, WA: Starmont House, October 1982.
55. Winter, Douglas E. *Stephen King: The Art of Darkness*. New York: New American Library, November 1984.
56. Zagorski, Edward J. *Teacher's Manual: Stephen King*. New York: New American Library, 1981.

A4. RAGE

A4. ***Rage***, by "RICHARD BACHMAN." New York: A Signet Book, New American Library, 1977, 211 p., paper. [suspense novel]

PLOT SUMMARY: Charlie Dekker, a high-school student, shoots a teacher and holds his class hostage. As the students confront one another, they open up, revealing their fears and frustrations in cutting indictments of the American educational system, the American family, and each other.

COMMENTS: King's first novel published under the Bachman penname, *Rage* was begun while he was in high school and completed during his first year at the University of Maine, Orono. It is at times a strong novel, but is generally considered by the critics as one of his lesser works. The novel was later adapted as a stage play.

REPRINTS:

b. London: New English Library, January 1983, 224 p., paper.
c. *The Bachman Books: Four Early Novels by Stephen King.* New York: New American Library, October 1985, cloth, p. 1-131. See **A30**.
d. as *Razernij* ["*Rage*"], in: *4 X Stephen King*. Utrecht: Luitingh, 1986, p., trade paper. Translated by Margot Bakker. [Dutch]
e. as: *Raseri*. Stockholm: Legende, 1987, 183 p. Translated by Karl G. Fredriksson and Lilian Fredriksson. [Swedish]
f. Höganäs, Sweden: Bra Böcker, 1987, 183 p. [Swedish]
g. as: *Rabia*. Barcelona: Martínez Roca, 1987, 203 p., paper. Translated by Hernán Sabaté. [Spanish]
h. as: *Razernij,* by Stephen King. Utrecht: Luitingh, 1988, 155 p. Translated by Margot Bakker. [Dutch]
i. as: *Amok*. München: Wilhelm Heyne Verlag, 1988 (TB 7695), , paper. Translated by Joachim Honnef. [German]
j. A Swedish edition published in 1988, bibliographical data unknown. [Swedish]

SECONDARY SOURCES AND REVIEWS:

1. Beahm, George, ed. *The Stephen King Companion*. Kansas City, MO: Andrews and McMeel, September 1989.
2. *Booklist* 74 (October 15, 1977): 353.
3. Brown. Stephen P. "The Life and Death of Richard Bachman: Stephen King's Doppelganger," in *Kingdom of Fear: The World of Stephen King,* edited by Tim Underwood and Chuck Miller. San Francisco: Underwood-Miller, 1986, p. 109-126.
4. Collings, Michael R. *The Annotated Guide to Stephen King: A Primary and Secondary Bibliography of the Works of America's Premier Horror Writer*. STARMONT REFERENCE GUIDE, No. 8. Mercer Island, WA: Starmont House, October 1986.
5. Collings, Michael R. *The Many Facets of Stephen King*. STARMONT STUDIES IN LITERARY CRITICISM, No. 11. Mercer Island, WA: Starmont House, 1986.
6. Collings, Michael R. *Stephen King as Richard Bachman*. STARMONT STUDIES IN LITERARY CRITICISM, No. 10. Mercer Island, WA: Starmont House, 1985.
7. D'Ammassa, Don. "Three by Bachman," in *Discovering Stephen King,* edited by Darrell Schweitzer. STARMONT STUDIES IN LITERARY CRITICISM, No. 8. Mercer Island, WA: Starmont House, 1985.
8. Hatlen, Burton. "Stephen King and the American Dream: Alienation, Competition, and Community in *Rage* and *The Long Walk*," in *Reign of Fear: Fiction and Film of Stephen King,* edited by Don Herron. Los Angeles: Underwood-Miller, 1989, p. 19-50.
9. Herron, Don, ed. *Reign of Fear*. Los Angeles: Underwood-Miller, June 1988.

10. Kesseli, Douglas. "Kentucky Hostage Crisis Sounded Familiar to King," in *Bangor Daily News* [Maine] (September 20, 1989): . As microfiche: *NewsBank: Literature* 16 (November, 1989): Fiche 112, F11. As microfiche: *NewsBank: Names in the News* 11 (October, 1989): Fiche 290, F6.
11. Lowell, Dave. "King Play Is Raging Success," in *Castle Rock: The Stephen King Newsletter* 5:5 (May, 1989): 4.
12. Porteau, Chris. "The Individual and Society: Narrative Structure and Thematic Unity in *Rage*," in *Journal of Popular Culture* 27:1 (Summer, 1993): 171-177.
13. *Publishers Weekly* 212 (July 12, 1977): 69.
14. Spignesi, Stephen J. "Rage," in *The Shape Under the Sheet: The Complete Stephen King Encyclopedia*. Ann Arbor, MI: Popular Culture, Ink., May 1991, cloth, p. 164-169.
15. Underwood, Tim, and Chuck Miller, eds. *Kingdom of Fear: The World of Stephen King*. Columbia, PA: Underwood-Miller, April 1986.
16. *Wilson Library Bulletin* 52 (February, 1978): 467.
17. Winter, Douglas E. *Stephen King: The Art of Darkness*. Expanded and updated edition. New York: A Plume Book, New American Library, June, 1986.

A5. THE STAND

A5. *The Stand*. Garden City, NY: Doubleday & Co., 1978, 823 p., cloth. See also **A40.** [horror novel]

PLOT SUMMARY: In a world devastated and nearly depopulated by the Superflu, survivors struggle not only to restore order, purpose, and civilization to their lives, but also to understand the implications of mystical dreams that threaten to separate the vestiges of humanity into two opposing camps, one focusing on goodness and life, the other dedicated to evil and death. As characters work to restore their lives, they must simultaneously choose whether to follow Abigail Freemantle's group, or to throw their lot with King's archetypal "Dark Man," Randall Flagg (see also "The Dark Man" **[D2]**, *The Eyes of the Dragon* **[A24]**, *The Dark Tower* novels **[A17, A34, A43]**, and *Insomnia* **[A48]**).

COMMENTS: The complex intertwining of characters and subplots gives the novel a surprising depth: King's skill at characterization, as well as his shift from science-fictional disaster motifs into overt fantasy elevates the novel from the usual run-of-the-mill end-of-the-world novels. *The Stand* is frequently mentioned as a favorite among King's novels; with its apocalyptic tone, its minute realism of presentation, and its vastness of scope, the novel is among his most successful, especially within the classroom.

175,000 mass-market paperback copies sold in 1979; the book was #6 on the *Publishers Weekly* annual paperback bestsellers list in 1979. Thirteen hardcover printings had been produced by September, 1989. King later published an uncut version of the novel (see **A40**).

REPRINTS:

ab. New York: Doubleday, 1990, 823 p., cloth. Issued in conjunction with the publication of the uncut version of *The Stand*.
b. London: New English Library, March 1979, 840 p., cloth.
bb. London: New English Library, February 1980, 736 p., paper.
c. Garden City, NY: Doubleday [Science Fiction Book Club edition], [n.d.], 823 p., cloth.
d. New York: A Signet Book, New American Library, January 1980, 817 p., paper. 36 printings by September, 1989.
e. as: *L'Ombra dello Scorpione*. Milano: Sonzogno, 1983, 928 p. Translated by A. Dell'Orta and B. Amato. [Italian]
f. as: *De Beproeving* ["*The Ordeal*"]. Utrecht: Luitingh/Veen, 1984, 520 p., trade paper. Translated by Annelies van Dijck. Slightly abridged. 4th printing, 1986. [Dutch]
g. as: *L'Ombra dello Scorpione*. Milano: Bompiani, 1985, 688 p. Translated by A. Dell'Orta and B. Amato. [Italian]
i. as: *Das Letzte Gefecht*. Bergisch Gladbach: Bastei-Lübbe Verlag (Paperback 28186), 1985, 864 p., paper. Translated by Harro Christensen. [German]
ib. as: *Das Letzte Gefecht*. Bergisch Gladbach: Bastei-Lübbe Verlag (Gebundene Ausgabe), 1986, 763 p. Translated by Harro Christensen. [German]
ic. as: *Das Letzte Gefecht*. Bergish Gladbach: Bastei-Lübbe Verlag (TB 13213), 1989, p., paper. Translated by Harro Christensen. [German]
j. as: *Das Letzte Gefecht*. Gütersloh, Austria: Bertelsmann Lesering, 1989, p., paper. Translated by Harro Christensen. [German]
k. as: *Das Letzte Gefecht*. Stuttgart, Germany: Deutscher Bücherbund, 1989, p. Translated by Harro Christensen. [German]

SECONDARY SOURCES AND REVIEWS:

1. *Analog Science Fiction/Science Fact* 100 (August, 1980): 163.
2. Beahm, George, ed. *The Stephen King Companion*. Kansas City, MO: Andrews and McMeel, September 1989.
3. *Booklist* 75 (December 1, 1978): 601.
4. *The Catalyst* [Salt Lake City, Utah] (1988): .
5. Chanen, Audrey Wolff. *American Holocaust Novels (John Hersey, Leon Uris, Flannery O'Connor, Stephen King)*. Unpublished Ph.D. Dissertation, University of Iowa, 1987, 172 p.
6. Cheever, Leonard. "Apocalypse and the Popular Imagination: Stephen King's *The Stand*," in *RE: Artes Liberales* 8 (Fall, 1981): .
7. Collings, Michael R. "*The Stand:* Science Fiction into Fantasy," in *Discovering Stephen King,* edited by Darrell Schweitzer. STARMONT STUDIES IN LITERARY CRITICISM, No. 8. Mercer Island, WA: Starmont House, 1985, p. 83-90.
8. Collings, Michael R. *The Annotated Guide to Stephen King: A Primary and Secondary Bibliography of the Works of America's Premier Horror Writer*. STARMONT REFERENCE GUIDE, No. 8. Mercer Island, WA: Starmont House, October 1986.

9. Collings, Michael R. *The Many Facets of Stephen King*. STARMONT STUDIES IN LITERARY CRITICISM, No. 11. Mercer Island, WA: Starmont House, 1986.
10. Collings, Michael R. *The Stephen King Phenomenon*. STARMONT STUDIES IN LITERARY CRITICISM, No. 14. Mercer Island, WA: Starmont House, 1987.
11. Collins, Anne. "No Sympathy for the Devil," in *Maclean's Magazine* 91 (December 18, 1978): 51. Excerpted: *Contemporary Literature Criticism, Volume 12, Young Adult Literature,* edited by Dedria Bryfonski. Detroit: Gale Research Co., 1980, cloth, p. 311.
12. Conaty, Barbara. *Library Journal* 103 (November 15, 1978): 2351.
13. Cousins, Diane. "Reader's Pick: *The Stand*," in *Castle Rock: The Stephen King Newsletter* 1:11 (November, 1985): 1, 2.
14. Egan, James. "Apocalypticism in the Fiction of Stephen King," in *Extrapolation* 25 (Fall, 1984): 214-227.
15. Egan, James. "Technohorror: The Dystopian Vision of Stephen King," in *Extrapolation* 29:2 (Summer, 1988): 140-152.
16. Furgeson, Mary. "*The Stand*," in *Survey of Modern Fantasy Literature, Volume IV,* edited by Frank Magill. Englewood Cliffs, NJ: Salem Press, 1983, cloth, p. 1801-1806.
17. Gustainis, J. Justin. *Best Sellers* 38 (March, 1979): 378. Excerpted: *Contemporary Literary Criticism, Volume 12, Young Adult Literature,* edited by Dedria Bryfonski. Detroit: Gale Research Co., 1980, cloth, p. 311.
18. Hatlen, Burton. "The Destruction and Re-Creation of the Human Community in Stephen King's *The Stand*," in *Footsteps* 5 (April, 1985): 56-60.
19. Hatlen, Burton. "Steve King's *The Stand*," in *Kennebec* (April, 1979): .
20. Hoppenstand, Gary and Ray B. Browne, eds. *The Gothic World of Stephen King: Landscape of Nightmares*. Bowling Green, OH: Bowling Green State University Popular Press, December 1987.
21. Indick, Ben P. "Stephen King as an Epic Writer," in *Discovering Modern Horror Fiction, Volume I,* edited by Darrell Schweitzer. STARMONT STUDIES IN LITERARY CRITICISM, No. 4. Mercer Island, WA: Starmont House, July 1985, p. 56-67.
22. *Kirkus Reviews* 46 (September 1, 1978): 965-966. Excerpted: *Contemporary Literary Criticism, Volume 12, Young Adult Literature,* edited by Dedria Bryfonski. Detroit: Gale Research Co., 1980, cloth, p. 309.
23. Laidlaw, Bill. *Nyctalops* 2:7 (1978): 34. Excerpted: *Contemporary Literary Criticism, Volume 12, Young Adult Literature,* edited by Dedria Bryfonski. Detroit: Gale Research Co., 1980, cloth, p. 311.
24. Levin, Martin. "Genre Items," in *New York Times Book Review* (February 4, 1979): 15.
25. *Los Angeles Times Book Review* (December 18, 1978): 51.
26. Magistrale, Tony. "Free Will and Sexual Choice in *The Stand*," in *Extrapolation* 34:1 (Spring, 1993): 30-38.

27. Magistrale, Tony. *Landscape of Fear: Stephen King's American Gothic*. Bowling Green, OH: Bowling Green State University Popular Press, March 1988.

28. Magistrale, Tony. *The Moral Voyages of Stephen King*. STARMONT STUDIES IN LITERARY CRITICISM, No. 25. Mercer Island, WA: Starmont House, 1989.

29. McDonald, J. V. *America* 140 (February 17, 1979): 117.

30. McLellan, Joseph. "Vision of Holocaust," in *Washington Post* (August 30, 1979): .

31. Meyers, Julia. *"The Stand,"* in *Masterplots II: American Fiction Series, Volume 4,* edited by Frank N. Magill. Englewood Cliffs, NJ: Salem Press, 1986, cloth, p. 1532-1535.

32. *New Yorker* 54 (January 15, 1979): 109.

33. Osbourne, Linda B. "The Supernatural Con Man vs. the Hymn-Singing Mother," in *Washington Post* (November 23, 1978): .

34. *Publishers Weekly* 214 (September 25, 1978): 127.

35. *Publishers Weekly* (November 12, 1979): 56.

36. Rathburn, Fran Miller. *Anatomy of a Best Seller: Form, Style, and Symbol in Stephen King's* The Stand. Unpublished M.A. thesis, Stephen F. Austin State University, 1981, 191 p.

37. Reino, Joseph. *Stephen King: The First Decade,* Carrie *to* Pet Sematary. TWAYNE'S UNITED STATES AUTHORS SERIES (TUSAS 531), edited by Warren French. Boston: Twayne Publishers, February 1988.

38. Roraback, Dick. "Gift of Sight: Visions from a Nether World," in *Los Angeles Times Book Review* (August 26, 1979): .

39. Schweitzer, Darrell, ed. *Discovering Stephen King*. STARMONT STUDIES IN LITERARY CRITICISM, No. 8. Mercer Island, WA: Starmont House, 1985.

40. Shiner, Lewis. "A Collision of Good and Evil," in *Dallas Morning News* (November 28, 1978): .

41. Spignesi, Stephen J. "The Stand," in *The Shape Under the Sheet: The Complete Stephen King Encyclopedia*. Ann Arbor, MI: Popular Culture, Ink., May 1991, cloth, p. 204-225.

42. Underwood, Tim and Chuck Miller, eds. *Fear Itself: The Horror Fiction of Stephen King*. San Francisco: Underwood-Miller, 1982.

43. Winter, Douglas E. *Stephen King*. STARMONT READER'S GUIDE, No. 16. Series editor, Roger Schlobin. Mercer Island, WA: Starmont House, October 1982.

44. Winter, Douglas E. *Stephen King: The Art of Darkness*. New York: New American Library, November 1984.

45. Zagorski, Edward J. *Teacher's Manual: Stephen King*. New York: New American Library, 1981.

A6. NIGHT SHIFT

A6. *Night Shift*. Garden City, NY: Doubleday & Co., 1978, xxii+336 p., cloth. 11 hardcover printings by September, 1989. [story collection]

King's first story collection includes a number of his best-known tales.

CONTENTS: "Introduction," by John D. MacDonald; "Foreword," by King (see **C55**); "Jerusalem's Lot" (1978; see **B38**); "Graveyard Shift" (1970; see **B12**); "Night Surf" (1969; see **B8**); "I Am the Doorway" (1971; see **B14**); "The Mangler" (1972; see **B18**); "The Boogeyman" (1973; see **B19**); "Gray Matter" (1973; see **B21**); "Battleground" (1972; see **B17**); "Trucks" (1973; see **B20**); "Sometimes They Come Back" (1974; see **B23**); "Strawberry Spring" (original version 1968; see **B7**); "The Ledge" (1976; see **B28**); "The Lawnmower Man" (1975; see **B24**); "Quitters, Inc." (1978; see **B40**); "I Know What You Need" (1976; see **B29**); "Children of the Corn" (1977; see **B31**); "The Last Rung on the Ladder" (1978; see **B39**); "The Man Who Loved Flowers" (1977; see **B34**); "One For the Road" (1977; see **B32**); "The Woman in the Room" (1978; see **B41**).

REPRINTS:

ab. New York: Doubleday, 1990, 336 p., cloth. Issued in conjunction with the publication of the uncut version of *The Stand*.

b. Garden City, NY: Doubleday [Science Fiction Book Club edition], [n.d.], 336 p., cloth.

c. as: *Una Splendida Festa di Morte* ["*A Splendid Feast of Death*"]. Milano: Sonzogno, 1978, 432 p. Translated by A. Dell'Orto. [Italian]

d. New York: A Signet Book, New American Library, February 1979, 327 p., paper. 44 printings by September, 1989.

e. London: New English Library, 1979?, p., cloth?

f. as: *El Umbro de la Noche* ["*The Shadow of the Night*"]. Barcelona: Pomaire, 1979, 426 p., paper. Translated by Eduardo Goligorsky. 20 stories from *Night Shift*, plus King's "preface" and the introduction by John D. MacDonald. [Spanish]

CONTENTS: "Introducción," de John MacDonald; "Prefacio"; "Los Misterios del Gusano"; "El Ultimo Turno"; "Marejada Nocturna"; "Soy la Puerta"; La Trituradora"; "El Coco"; "Materia Gria"; "Campo de Batalla"; "Camiones"; "A Veces Vuelven"; "La Primavera de Fresa"; "La Cornisa"; "El Hombre de la Cortadora de Césped"; Basta, S.A."; "Sé lo que Necesitas"; "Los Niños del Maiz"; "El Ultimo Peldaño de la Escalera"; "El Hombre que Amaba las Flores"; "Un Trago de Despedida"; "La Mujer de la Habitación."

g. in: *The Shining, 'Salem's Lot, Night Shift, Carrie*. London: Octopus Books, 1981, cloth, p. . Omnibus edition; see also **A13**.

h. as: *De Satanskindern en andere Verholen* ["*Satan's Children and Other Stories*"]. Utrecht: Luitingh/Veen, 1985, 248 p., trade paper. Abridged. Translated by F. J. Bruning. 3rd printing, 1986. [Dutch]

CONTENTS: "Satanskindern" ["Satan's Children"="Children of the Corn"]; "Ratten" ["Rats"="Graveyard Shift"]; "De Boeman" ["The Boogeyman"]; "Doodtij" ["Dead Tide"="Night Surf"]; "De Rozige Lente" ["The Rose Spring"="Strawberry Spring"]; "De Richel" ["The Ledge"]; "De Patiente van Kamer 312" ["The Patient in Room 312"="The Woman in the Room"]; "Een Afzakkertje" ["One for the Road"]; "Twee Mal Vier is Vijf" ["Two Times They Come Back"="Sometimes They Come Back"]; "De Mangel" ["The Mangler"]; "Ik Ben de Toegang" ["I Am the Doorway"]; "Pastorale" ["Pastoral"="The Lawnmower Man"]; "Aspraak met Norman" ["Rendez-vous with Norman"="The Man Who Loved Flowers"].

SECONDARY SOURCES AND REVIEWS: Bertin, Eddy C., "Stephen King in the Lowlands," in *Castle Rock: The Stephen King Newsletter* 1:11 (November, 1985): 7-8.

i. as: *Katzenauge* ["*Cat's Eye*"]. Bergish Gladbach: Bastei-Lübbe Verlag (TB 13088), 1986, p., paper. Translated by Karin Balfer, Harro Christensen, Barbara Heidkamp, Ingrid Herrmann, Wolfgang Holbein, Michael Kubiak, Sabine Kuhn, Ulrike A. Pollay, Bernd Seligman, Stefan Sturm. [German]

CONTENTS: "Geschichten aus den Dunkel—Über des Phänomen des Schriftstellers, Drehbuchautors und Film Regisseurs Stephen King" ["Stories from the Dark—Concerning the Phenomenon of Writers, Screen Writers and Directors for Stephen King's Films"], by Willy Loderhose; "Katzenauge—Wie es zu der Verfilmung kam" ["Cat's Eye: How It Came to be Filmed"], by Willy Loderhose; "Quitters Inc."; "Der Mauervorsprung" ["The Ledge"]; "Trucks—Bemerkungen vor Filmung" ["Trucks: Comments about the Filming"], by Willy Loderhose; "Trucks"; "Kinder des Zorns-Bemerkungen zur Entstehung des Films" ["Children of Wrath: Comments on the Film"], by Willy Loderhose; "Kinder des Mais."

j. as: *It Weet Wat Je Wilt* ["*I Know What You Want*"]. Utrecht: Luitingh/Veen, Autumn 1985, 320 p., trade paper. Abridged edition. Translated by F. J. Brunning and Pauline Moody. 2 printings by 1986. [Dutch]

CONTENTS: Seven stories from *Night Shift* and *Different Seasons,* including: "Quitters' Inc," "Jerusalem's Lot," "Trucks," "I Know What You Want," "The Last Rung on the Ladder," and "The Breathing Method."

k. as: *El Umbral de la Noche*. Esplugas Llobregat/Barcelona: Plaza & Janés, 1985, 519 p. paper. Translated by Eduardo Goligorsky. [Spanish]

kb. as: *El Umbral de la Noche*. Esplugas Llobregat (Barcelona), Spain: Plaza & Janés Editores, 1986, p. [Spanish]

kc. as: *El Umbral de la Noche*. BIBLIOTECA DE STEPHEN KING ['Stephen King Library'], Vol. 3. Esplugas Llobregat (Barcelona), Spain: Plaza & Janés Editores, 1989, p. [Spanish]

l. as: *Im Morgengrauen* ["*In Morning Light*"]. München: Wilhelm Heyne, 1985. [German]

m. as: *Trucks*. Bergisch Gladbach: Bastei-Lübbe, 1986, 185 p., paper. Abridged. Translated by Karin Balfer, Harro Christensen, Barbara Heidkamp, Ingrid Herrmann, Wolfgang Hohlbein, Michael Kubiak, Sabine Kuhn, Ulrike A. Pollay, Bernd Seligman, Stefan Sturm. [German]

CONTENTS: "Geschichten aus dem Dunkel: Über das Phänomen des Schritstellers, Drehbuchautors und Regisserus Stephen King," by Willy Loderhose; "Trucks," "Kinder des Zorns" ("Children of the Corn"), "Der Mauervorsprung" ("The Ledge"), and "Quitters, Inc."

n. as: *De Laatste Laddersport* ["*The Last Rung on the Ladder*"]. Utrecht: Luitingh, 1987, 173 p. Abridged. Translated by F. J. Bruning. [Dutch]

o. as: *Trucks*. Utrecht: Luitingh, 1987, 188 p. Translated by F. J. Bruning. Abridged. [Dutch]

p. as: *Dödsbädden*. Stockholm: B. Wahlström, 1987, 409 p. Translated by Ansis Grinbergs. [Swedish]

q. as: *Nachtschicht: Meistererzählungen. Horror bis zum Morgengrauen* ["*Night Shift: Master Stories. Horror until Morning Light*"]. Bergisch Gladbach: Bastei-Lübbe, 1987, 416 p. [German]

qb. as: *Nachtschicht*. Bergisch Gladbach, West Germany: Bastei-Lübbe, 1988, 340 p. [German]

SECONDARY SOURCES AND REVIEWS:

1. Beahm, George, ed. *The Stephen King Companion*. Kansas City, MO: Andrews and McMeel, September 1989, p. 251-256.
2. *Booklist* 74 (March 15, 1978): 1165.
3. Collings, Michael R. *The Annotated Guide to Stephen King: A Primary and Secondary Bibliography of the Works of America's Premier Horror Writer*. STARMONT REFERENCE GUIDE, No. 8. Mercer Island, WA: Starmont House, October 1986.
4. Collings, Michael R. *The Many Facets of Stephen King*. STARMONT STUDIES IN LITERARY CRITICISM, No. 11. Mercer Island, WA: Starmont House, 1986.
5. Collings, Michael R. *The Stephen King Phenomenon*. STARMONT STUDIES IN LITERARY CRITICISM, No. 14. Mercer Island, WA: Starmont House, 1987.
6. Collings, Michael R. and David A. Engebretson. *The Shorter Works of Stephen King*. STARMONT STUDIES IN LITERARY CRITICISM, No. 9. Mercer Island, WA: Starmont House, June 1985.
7. Crider, Bill. *Best Sellers* 38 (April, 1978): 6-7. Excerpted: *Contemporary Literary Criticism, Volume 12, Young Adult Literature,* edited by Dedria Bryfonski. Detroit: Gale Research Co., 1980, cloth, p. 310-311.
8. *Kirkus Reviews* 45 (December 1, 1977): 1285.
9. *Kliatt's Paperback Book Guide* 13 (Spring, 1979): 27.
10. *Los Angeles Times* "Books" (April 23, 1978): 13.
11. Lyles, W. H. *Library Journal* 103 (February, 1978): 385. Excerpted: *Contemporary Literary Criticism, Volume 12, Young Adult Literature,* edited by Dedria Bryfonski. Detroit: Gale Research Co., 1980, cloth, p. 31+.
12. Magistrale, Tony. *Landscape of Fear: Stephen King's American Gothic*. Bowling Green, OH: Bowling Green State University Popular Press, March 1988.
13. Magistrale, Tony. "Stephen King's Vietnam Allegory: An Interpretation of 'Children of the Corn,'" in *Cuyahoga Review* 2:1 (Spring/Summer, 1984): 61-66. Reprinted: *Footsteps* 5 (April, 1985): 61-65.
14. Mewshaw, Michael. "Novels and Stories," in *New York Times Book Review* (March 26, 1978): 13, 23. Excerpted: *Contemporary Literary Criticism, Volume 12, Young Adult Literature,* edited by Dedria Bryfonski. Detroit: Gale Research Co., 1980, cloth, p. 310.
15. Neilson, Keith. *"Night Shift,"* in *Survey of Modern Fantasy Literature, Volume 3,* edited by Frank N. Magill. Englewood Cliffs, NJ: Salem Press, 1983, cloth, p. 116-120.
16. Nolan, William F. "The Good Fabric: Of Night Shifts and Skeleton Crews," in *Kingdom of Fear: The World of Stephen King*, edited by

Tim Underwood and Chuck Miller. Columbia, PA: Underwood-Miller, 1986, p. 99-106.
17. *Publishers Weekly* 212 (November 28, 1977): 46.
18. Reino, Joseph. *Stephen King: The First Decade,* Carrie *to* Pet Sematary. TWAYNE'S UNITED STATES AUTHORS SERIES (TUSAS 531), edited by Warren French. Boston: Twayne Publishers, February 1988, 162 p., cloth.
19. Schweitzer, Darrell, ed. *Discovering Stephen King*. STARMONT STUDIES IN LITERARY CRITICISM, No. 8. Mercer Island, WA: Starmont House, 1985.
20. Spignesi, Stephen J. "Night Shift," in *The Shape Under the Sheet: The Complete Stephen King Encyclopedia*. Ann Arbor, MI: Popular Culture, Ink., May 1991, cloth, p. 175-203.
21. *Voice of Youth Advocates* 6 (December, 1983): 266.
22. *West Coast Review of Books* 4 (May, 1978): 33.
23. Winter, Douglas E. *Stephen King*. STARMONT READER'S GUIDE, No. 16. Series editor, Roger Schlobin. Mercer Island, WA: Starmont House, October 1982.
24. Winter, Douglas E. *Stephen King: The Art of Darkness*. New York: New American Library, November 1984.
25. Zagorski, Edward J. *Teacher's Manual: Stephen King*. New York: New American Library, 1981.

A7. THE DEAD ZONE

A7. ***The Dead Zone*.** New York: Viking Press, 30 August 1979, 426 p., cloth. [horror novel]

PLOT SUMMARY: Johnny Smith emerges from a years-long, accident-induced coma with the ability to see the future. Increasingly distanced from his own world by his gift and by its enervating effects on him, he attempts to use his visions wisely. When he foresees ultimate disaster, however, he must choose between murdering a single individual or allowing a world to remain under the threat of destruction.

COMMENTS: One of King's most restrained novels—and arguably one of his finest—*The Dead Zone* concentrates on a common man in conflict with his uncommon abilities. The novel's strengths include compassionate characterization, intricate and effective use of symbol and image, and an understated sense of horror within the ordinary.

Adapted for film by David Cronenberg in 1983, the novel provided the basis for one of the two or three most sensitive and intelligent film versions of King's works.

Ranked #6 on the *Publishers Weekly* annual hardcover Bestsellers list for 1979.

REPRINTS:

b. New York: Viking [Science Fiction Book Club edition], [n.d.], 372 p., cloth.
c. London: Macdonald, 1979, 426 p., cloth.

d. New York: A Signet Book, New American Library, August, 1980, 403 p. paper. 30 printings by September, 1989.
db. New York, A Plume Book, New American Library, 1991?, p., trade paper. "Collector's Edition." Includes a color reproduction of the original hardcover art.
e. London: Futura, August 1980, 480 p., paper.
f. as: *Dodelijk Dilemma* ["*Deadly Dilemma*"]. Utrecht: Luitingh/Veen, 1980, 408 p., trade paper. Translated by Margot Bakker; slightly abridged. 8th printing, 1986. [Dutch]
g. as: *Das Attentat* ["*The Assault*"]. München: Arthur Moewig Verlag (Playboy Roman, TB 6110), 1981, 416 p., paper. Translated by Alfred Dunkel. A radically abridged translation. [German]
h. as: *La Zona Morta*. Milano: Sperling & Kupfer, 1981, 464 p. Translated by A. Terzi. [Italian]
i. as: *La Zona Muerta*. Barcelona: Pomaire, 1981, p. [Spanish]
j. as: *La Zone Muerta*. Barcelona: Mundo Actual de Ediciones, 1981. [Spanish]
k. as: *La Zona Muerta*. Panamá: Printer Internacional de Panamá, 1982, p. [Spanish]
l. Anstey, Leicestershire: Charnwood Library Service, Ulversoft Large Print Books, December 1983, 656 p., cloth. Large print edition.
m. Leistershire: Thorpe, 1983, 646 p., cloth. Large print edition.
n. as: *Dead Zone [L'Accident]*. Paris: Jean-Claude Lattes, 1983, 479 p., paper. Translated by Richard Matas. [French]
o. as: *Död Zon* ["*Dead Zone*"]. Stockholm: Askild and Kärnekull, 1983, 508 p. Translated by Jimmy Hofsö. Rpt. 1984. [Swedish]
p. as: *Dodelijk Dilemma* ["*Deadly Dilemma*"]. Utrecht: Skarabee, 1984, 408 p., trade paper. [Dutch]
q. as: *The Dead Zone: Buch zum Film*. Rastatt, West Germany: Arthur Moewig Verlag (TB 2277), 1984, p., paper. Translated by Alfred Dunkel; radically abridged edition. [German]
r. as: *La Zona Meurta*. Esplugas Llobreget/Barcelona: Plaza & Janés, July 1985, 456 p., paper. Translated by Eduardo Goligorsky. [Spanish]
rb. as: La Zona Muerta. Esplugas Llobregat (Barcelona): Plaza & Janés Editores, 1986, [456?] p., paper. [Spanish]
rc. as: *La Zona Muerta*. BIBLIOTECA DE STEPHEN KING, Vol. 5. Esplugas Llobregat (Barcelona), Spain: Plaza & Janés Editores, 1989, [456?] p., paper. [Spanish]
s. as: *Morke Krefter* ["*Dark Forces*"]. Oslo: Hjemmets Bokklubb, 1985?, p. [Norwegian]
t. as: *La Zona Muerta*. Buenos Aires: Eméce Editores, [by 1986], p., paper. [Spanish]
u. as: *Zona Muerta*. Ciudad de México: Edivisión Compañía Editorial, 14 March 1986, 452 p., trade paper. Translated by Eduardo Goligarsky. 15,000 copies. [Spanish]
v. as: *Dead Zone: Das Attentat* ["*Dead Zone: The Assault*"]. München: Wilhelm Heyne (TB 6953), 1987, p., paper. Translated by Joachim Körber. Unabridged translation. [German]
w. as: *La Zona Morta*. Milano: Mondadori, 1987, 464 p. Translated by A. Terzi. [Italian]
x. as: *Das Attentat* ["*The Assault*"]. Gütersloh, Austria: Bertelsmann Lesering, 1988. Translated by Joachim Körber. [German]

y. as: *Dead Zone*. Stuttgart: Deutscher Bücherbund, 1988, p. Translated by Joachim Körber. [German]

SECONDARY SOURCES AND REVIEWS:

1. Beahm, George. *The Stephen King Companion*. Kansas City, MO: Andrews and McMeel, September 1989, paper, p. 201-202.
2. *Best of the Times* [*New York Times*] 2 (August, 1979): 391.
3. *Best Sellers* 39 (October, 1979): 238.
4. Brown, Charles N. "On Books: The Best of 1979," in *Isaac Asimov's Science Fiction Magazine* 27 (May, 1980): 17.
5. *Booklist* 76 (September 1, 1979): 24.
6. Collings, Michael R. *The Annotated Guide to Stephen King: A Primary and Secondary Bibliography of the Works of America's Premier Horror Writer*. STARMONT REFERENCE GUIDE, No. 8. Mercer Island, WA: Starmont House, October 1986.
7. Collings, Michael R. *The Many Facets of Stephen King*. STARMONT STUDIES IN LITERARY CRITICISM, No. 11. Mercer Island, WA: Starmont House, 1986.
8. Collings, Michael R. *The Stephen King Phenomenon*. STARMONT STUDIES IN LITERARY CRITICISM, No. 14. Mercer Island, WA: Starmont House, 1987.
9. Easton, Tom. *Analog Science Fiction/Science Fact* 101:4 (March 30, 1981): 164-165. Excerpted: *Contemporary Literary Criticism, Volume 26,* edited by Jean C. Stine. Detroit: Gale Research Co., 1983, cloth, p. 238.
10. Gault, John. "Not Quite Fright," in *Maclean's Magazine* 93 (September 24, 1979): 56. Excerpted: *Contemporary Literary Criticism*, Volume 26, edited by Jean C. Stine. Detroit: Gale Research Co., 1983, cloth, p. 234.
11. Graham, Mark. "Moral Dilemma in Latest Novel by Stephen King," in *Rocky Mountain News* [Denver, CO] (September 9, 1979): 36.
12. *Kirkus Reviews* 47 (June 15, 1979): 705.
13. Lehman-Haupt, Christopher. *New York Times* (August 17, 1979): C23.
14. *Library Journal* 104 (July, 1979): 1485.
15. *Los Angeles Times Book Review* (August 26, 1979): 1.
16. Magistrale, Tony. *Landscape of Fear: Stephen King's American Gothic*. Bowling Green, OH: Bowling Green State University Popular Press, March 1988.
17. Magistrale, Tony. *The Moral Voyages of Stephen King*. STARMONT STUDIES IN LITERARY CRITICISM, No. 25. Mercer Island, WA: Starmont House, 1989.
18. Murphy, Patrick D. "The Realities of Unreal Worlds: King's *The Dead Zone,* Schmidt's *Kensho,* and Lem's *Solaris*," in *Spectrum of the Fantastic: Selected Essays from the Sixth International Conference on the Fantastic in the Arts,* edited by Donald Palumbo. CONTRIBUTIONS TO THE STUDY OF SCIENCE FICTION AND FANTASY, Number 31. Series editor, Marshal Tymn. Westport, CT: Greenwood Press, 1988, cloth, p. 175-183.

19. Neilson, Keith. *"The Dead Zone,"* in *Magill's Literary Annual 1980, Volume 1,* edited by Frank N. Magill. Englewood Cliffs, NJ: Salem Press, 1980, cloth, p. 205-209.
20. Ott, Bill. *Booklist* 78:21 (July, 1982): 1394. Excerpted: *Contemporary Literary Criticism, Volume 26,* edited by Jean C. Stine. Detroit: Gale Research Co., 1983, cloth, p. 240.
21. *Publishers Weekly* 215 (June 11, 1979): 97.
22. *Publishers Weekly* 217 (June 13, 1980): 72.
23. Reino, Joseph. *Stephen King: The First Decade,* Carrie *to* Pet Sematary. TWAYNE'S UNITED STATES AUTHORS SERIES (TUSAS 531), edited by Warren French. Boston: Twayne Publishers, February 1988.
24. Schweitzer, Darrell, ed. *Discovering Stephen King.* STARMONT STUDIES IN LITERARY CRITICISM, No. 8. Mercer Island, WA: Starmont House, 1985.
25. Spignesi, Stephen J. "The Dead Zone," in *The Shape Under the Sheet: The Complete Stephen King Encyclopedia.* Ann Arbor, MI: Popular Culture, Ink., May 1991, cloth, p. 241-247.
26. Underwood, Tim and Chuck Miller, eds. *Fear Itself: The Horror Fiction of Stephen King.* San Francisco: Underwood-Miller, 1982.
27. Watson, Christine. *"The Dead Zone,"* in *Survey of Modern Fantasy Literature, Volume 1,* edited by Frank N. Magill. Englewood Cliffs, NJ: Salem Press, 1983, cloth, p. 350-354.
28. *Wilson Library Bulletin* 54 (January, 1980): 323.
29. Winter, Douglas E. *Stephen King.* STARMONT READER'S GUIDE, No. 16. Series editor, Roger Schlobin. Mercer Island, WA: Starmont House, October 1982.
30. Winter, Douglas E. *Stephen King: The Art of Darkness.* New York: New American Library, November 1984.
31. Zagorski, Edward J. *Teacher's Manual: Stephen King.* New York: New American Library, 1981.

A8. THE LONG WALK

A8. ***The Long Walk***, by "RICHARD BACHMAN." New York: A Signet Book, New American Library, July 1979, 244 p., paper. [science-fiction novel]

PLOT SUMMARY: Ray Garraty and ninety-nine other young men begin a non-stop walk from northern Maine toward Boston. The goal: to walk as long as possible without stopping, since walkers who drop out are killed. The reward: anything the survivor wants. The walkers' physical and mental tortures provide the structure for this strong, at times psychologically gruelling novel.

COMMENTS: The second "Bachman" novel, *The Long Walk* was written essentially as published while King was still in college. It presents the incremental horror of the walkers as they move through a landscape that is simultaneously physical and symbolic, real and illusory, naturalistic and surrealistic. King's foray into marginal science-fiction allows him to critique—albeit obliquely—contemporary American society. At the same time, the novel acknowledges King's debt to Shirley Jackson and others.

REPRINTS:

b. in: *The Bachman Books: Four Early Novels by Stephen King*. New York: New American Library, October 1985, cloth, p. 133-322. See **A30**.

c. as: *De Marathon* ["*The Long Walk*"], in: *4 X Stephen King*. Utrecht: Luitingh, 1986, p., paper. Translated by Mariella de Kuyper-Snel. [Dutch]

d. as: *Todesmarch* ["*Death-March*"]. München: Wilhelm Heyne Verlag, , p., paper. [German]

e. as: *La Larga Marcha*, by Stephen King, "escribiendo como Richard Bachman." Barcelona: Martínez Roca, 1986, 286 p., paper. Translated by Hernán Sabaté. [Spanish]

f. as: *La Lunga Marcia: L'Uomo in Fuga*. Milano: Mondadori, 1986, 412 p. Translated by M. Tropea. [Italian]

g. as: *Maratonmarschen*. Stockholm: Legende, 1987, 275 p. Translated by Karl G. Fredriksson and Lilian Fredriksson. 2nd printing, 1988. [Swedish]

h. as: *De Marathon*, by Stephen King. Utrecht: Luitingh, 1988, 263 p. Translated by Mariëlla de Kuyper-Snel. [Dutch]

SECONDARY SOURCES AND REVIEWS:

1. Beahm, George, ed. *The Stephen King Companion*. Kansas City, MO: Andrews and McMeel, September 1989.
2. Brown. Stephen P. "The Life and Death of Richard Bachman: Stephen King's Doppelganger," in *Kingdom of Fear: The World of Stephen King*, edited by Tim Underwood and Chuck Miller. San Francisco: Underwood-Miller, 1986, p. 109-126.
3. Collings, Michael R. *The Annotated Guide to Stephen King: A Primary and Secondary Bibliography of the Works of America's Premier Horror Writer*. *STARMONT* REFERENCE GUIDE, No. 8. Mercer Island, WA: Starmont House, October 1986.
4. Collings, Michael R. *The Many Facets of Stephen King*. STARMONT STUDIES IN LITERARY CRITICISM, No. 11. Mercer Island, WA: Starmont House, 1986.
5. Collings, Michael R. *Stephen King as Richard Bachman*. STARMONT STUDIES IN LITERARY CRITICISM, No. 10. Mercer Island, WA: Starmont House, 1985.
6. D'Ammassa, Don. "Three by Bachman," in *Discovering Stephen King*, edited by Darrell Schweitzer. STARMONT STUDIES IN LITERARY CRITICISM, No. 8. Mercer Island, WA: Starmont House, 1985, p. 123-130.
7. Gallagher, Steve. "Standing by Jericho," in *Science Fiction Review* 12:1 (February, 1983): 35-36. Excerpted: *Contemporary Literary Criticism, Volume 37*, edited by Daniel G. Marowski. Detroit: Gale Research Co., 1986, cloth, p. 201.
8. Hatlen, Burton. "Stephen King and the American Dream: Alienation, Competition, and Community in *Rage* and *The Long Walk*," in *Reign of Fear: Fiction and Film of Stephen King*, edited by Don Herron. Los Angeles: Underwood-Miller, 1988, cloth, p. 19-50.
9. Herron, Don, ed. *Reign of Fear*. Los Angeles: Underwood-Miller, June 1988.

10. Schweitzer, Darrell, ed. *Discovering Stephen King*. STARMONT STUDIES IN LITERARY CRITICISM, No. 8. Mercer Island, WA: Starmont House, 1985.
11. Spignesi, Stephen J. "The Long Walk," in *The Shape Under the Sheet: The Complete Stephen King Encyclopedia*. Ann Arbor, MI: Popular Culture, Ink., May 1991, cloth, p. 231-241.
12. Underwood, Tim, and Chuck Miller, eds. *Kingdom of Fear: The World of Stephen King*. Columbia, PA: Underwood-Miller, April 1986.
13. Winter, Douglas E. *Stephen King: The Art of Darkness*. Expanded and updated edition. New York: A Plume Book, New American Library, June 1986.

A9. FIRESTARTER

A9. *Firestarter.* Huntington Woods, MI: Phantasia Press, 1980, 428 p., cloth. [horror novel]

PLOT SUMMARY: The product of parents who had participated in a scientific experiment, Charlie McGee is gifted/cursed with psychokinetic powers—specifically, the ability to start fires through her mental power. Fleeing from the government agency that has killed her mother, hounded her father, and now wants to control her powers, she is finally forced to develop those powers beyond the limits even the Shop directors might have imagined.

COMMENTS: By restricting himself to a science-fictional rationale for horror, King allows *Firestarter* to move more directly as a narrative than occurs in some of his later novels. The story is unencumbered by multiple subplots, depending for its momentum upon strength of characterization and visualization.

The novel was adapted for screen and released in 1984. Although produced by Frank Capra, Jr., based almost verbatim on King's text, and featuring such fine actors as Drew Barrymore, George C. Scott, Art Carney, Martin Sheen and others, the resulting film is a uniquely lifeless production.

REPRINTS:

b. New York: Viking, 29 September 1980, 428 p., cloth. The first trade edition; 285,000 copies were sold in 1980; ranked #4 on the *Publishers Weekly* annual hardcover Bestsellers List.
c. London: Macdonald Futura, October 1980, 428 p., cloth.
d. New York: Viking [Science Fiction Book Club edition], [n.d.], 371 p., cloth.
e. New York: A Signet Book, New American Library, August 1981, 403 p., paper. 21 printings by September, 1989.
eb. New York, A Plume Book, New American Library, October 1994, 382 p., trade paper. "Collector's Edition." Introduction by John Grisham. Includes a color reproduction of the original hardcover art.
f. London: Futura, August 1981, 512 p., paper.

g. as: *Eldfödd.* Stockholm: Askild and Kärnekull, 1981, 439 p. Translated by Jimmy Hofsö. Reprinted in 1983. [Swedish]

h. as: *Ogen van Vuur* ["*Eyes of Fire*"]. Utrecht: Luitingh/Veen, 1981, 413 p., trade paper. Translated by Margot Bakker. 7th printing, 1986; 9th printing, 1988. [Dutch]

hb. as: *Ogen van Vuur: Firestarter* ["*Eyes of Fire: Firestarter*"]. Utrecht: Luitingh/Veen, 1988, 413 p., trade paper. Translated by Margot Bakker. Movie tie-in edition. [Dutch]

i. as: *Feuerkind* ["*Firechild*"]. Bergish Gladbach: Bastei-Lübbe, (Paperback 28103), 1981, 393 p., paper. Translated by Harro Christensen. [German]

ib. as: *Feuerkind: Das Buch zum Film 'Feuerteufel'* ["*Fire-Child: The Book for the Film Firedevil*"]. Bergisch Gladbach: Bastei-Lübbe (TB13001), 1984, 393 p.(?), paper. Translated by Harro Christensen. [German]

j. as: *Ojos de Fuego* ["*Eyes of Fire*"]. Barcelona: Pomaire, 1981. [Spanish]

k. Anstey, Leicestershire: Charnwood Library Services/Ulversoft Large Print Books, December 1982, 633 p., cloth. Large print edition.

l. as: *L'Incendiaria.* Milano: Sperling & Kupfer, 1982, 408 p. Translated by M. G. Prestini. [Italian]

m. as: *Ojos de Fuego.* Panamá: Printer Internacional de Panamá, 1982, p. [Spanish]

n. as: *Charlie.* Paris: Albin Michel, 1984, 435 p., cloth. Translated by F. M. Lennox. [French]

o. as: *Ojos de Fuego.* Barcelona: Mundo Actual de Ediciones, 1982, p. [Spanish]

p. as: *Feuerkind.* Gütersloh, Austria: Bertelsmann Lesering, 1983, p . Translated by Harro Christensen. [German]

q. as: *Feuerkind.* Book Club Editions-Stüttgart, West Germany: Europäische Bildungsgemeinschaft; Gütersloh, Austria: Bertelsmann Club; Vienna, Austria: Buchgemeinschaft Donauland; Zug, Switzerland: Buch-und-Schallplattenfreunde, 1984, 413 p. Translated by Harro Christensen. [German]

r. as: *Ojos de Fuego.* Espluga Llobregat/Barcelona: Plaza & Janés, 1985, 432 p., paper. Translated by Eduardo Goligorsky. [Spanish]

rb. as: *Ojos de Fuego.* Esplugas Llobregat/Barcelona: Plaza & Janés Editores, 1987, 432 p. (?), paper. [Spanish]

rc. as: *El Ojos de Fuego.* BIBLIOTECA DE STEPHEN KING, Vol. 4. Esplugas Llobregat/Barcelona: Plaza & Janés Editores, 1989, 432 p. (?), paper. [Spanish]

s. as: *Charlie.* Paris: Epouvante/J'ai-Lu, October 1986, 466 p., paper. Translated by F. M. Lennox. [French]

t. as: *L'Occhio del Male* ["*The Eyes of Evil*"]. Milano: Sonzogno, 1986, 280 p. Translated by F. Brera. [Italian]

u. as: *Ojos de Fuego.* Buenos Aires, Argentina: Emece, 1986, 463 p. Translated by Eduardo Goligorsky. [Spanish]

v. as: *Ildbarnet* ["*Child of Fire*:]. Oslo, Norway: Hjemmets Bokklubb. No further information. [Norwegian]

SECONDARY SOURCES AND REVIEWS:

1. Barkham, John. "A Story Fired with Imagination, Protest," in *Philadelphia Inquirer* (August 31, 1980): .
2. Beahm, George, ed. *The Stephen King Companion*. Kansas City, MO: Andrews and McMeel, September 1989, p. 214-234.
3. *Best of the Times* [*New York Times*] 3 (November, 1980): 541.
4. *Best Sellers* 40 (November, 1980): 273.
5. Brosnahan, John. "Firestarter," in *Booklist* 76 (June 15, 1980): 1464. Excerpted: *Contemporary Literary Criticism, Volume 26,* edited by Jean C. Stine. Detroit: Gale Research Co., 1983, cloth, p. 237.
6. Budrys, Algis. "King's *Firestarter:* It's Hot Stuff, All Right," in *Chicago Sun-Times* (September 21, 1980): .
7. Clark, Jeff. *Library Journal* 105 (August, 1980): 1660.
8. Collings, Michael R. *The Annotated Guide to Stephen King: A Primary and Secondary Bibliography of the Works of America's Premier Horror Writer.* STARMONT REFERENCE GUIDE, No. 8. Mercer Island, WA: Starmont House, October 1986.
9. Collings, Michael R. *The Many Facets of Stephen King*. STARMONT STUDIES IN LITERARY CRITICISM, No. 11. Mercer Island, WA: Starmont House, 1986.
10. Collings, Michael R. *The Stephen King Phenomenon*. STARMONT STUDIES IN LITERARY CRITICISM, No. 14. Mercer Island, WA: Starmont House, 1987.
11. Demarest, Michael. "Hot Moppet," in *Time* 116 (September 15, 1980): K12, K18.
12. Egan, James. "Technohorror: The Dystopian Vision of Stephen King," in *Extrapolation* 29:2 (Summer, 1988): 140-152, esp. 147.
13. Graham, Mark. "New King Novel Will Frighten You," in *Rocky Mountain News* [Denver, CO] (September 14, 1980): 31.
14. Granger, Bill. "Stephen King Strikes Again," in *Chicago Tribune Book World* (August 24, 1980): .
15. Hoppenstand, Gary and Ray B. Browne, eds. *The Gothic World of Stephen King: Landscape of Nightmares*. Bowling Green, OH: Bowling Green State University Popular Press, December 1987.
16. *Kirkus Reviews* 48:14 (July 15, 1980): 930. Excerpted: *Contemporary Literary Criticism, Volume 26,* edited by Jean C. Stine. Detroit: Gale Research Co., 1983, p. 237.
17. Lehmann-Haupt, Christopher. *New York Times* (September 8, 1980): III, 15.
18. *Los Angeles Times Book Review* (September 28, 1980): 4.
19. Magistrale, Tony. *Landscape of Fear: Stephen King's American Gothic*. Bowling Green, OH: Bowling Green State University Popular Press, March 1988.
20. Neilson, Keith. "*Firestarter*," in *Survey of Modern Fantasy Literature, Volume 2,* edited by Frank N. Magill. Englewood Cliffs, NJ: Salem Press, 1983, cloth, p. 553-556.
21. *The New Republic* 184 (February 21, 1981): 38.
22. Prescott, P. S. "Hot Tot," in *Newsweek* 96 (October 6, 1980): 96.
23. *Publishers Weekly* 218 (July 25, 1980): 147.
24. *Publishers Weekly* 219 (June 12, 1981): 53.

25. Reino, Joseph. *Stephen King: The First Decade,* Carrie *to* Pet Sematary. TWAYNE'S UNITED STATES AUTHORS SERIES (TUSAS 531), edited by Warren French. Boston: Twayne Publishers, February 1988.
26. *San Francisco Chronicle* (August 25, 1980): 45.
27. *School Library Journal* 27 (November 1980): 93.
28. Schweitzer, Darrell, ed. *Discovering Stephen King.* STARMONT STUDIES IN LITERARY CRITICISM, No. 8. Mercer Island, WA: Starmont House, 1985.
29. Spignesi, Stephen J. "Firestarter," in *The Shape Under the Sheet: The Complete Stephen King Encyclopedia.* Ann Arbor, MI: Popular Culture, Ink., May 1991, cloth, p. 247-252.
30. Stuewe, Paul. "American Thrillers: *Firestarter, Brass Diamonds, Brain 2000,*" in *Quill and Quire* 46 (October, 1980): p. 40-41. Excerpted: *Contemporary Literary Criticism, Volume 26,* edited by Jean C. Stine. Detroit: Gale Research Co., 1983, cloth, p. 237.
31. Underwood, Tim and Chuck Miller, eds. *Fear Itself: The Horror Fiction of Stephen King.* San Francisco: Underwood-Miller, 1982.
32. Underwood, Tim and Chuck Miller, eds. *Kingdom of Fear: The World of Stephen King.* Columbia, PA: Underwood-Miller, April 1986.
33. *Voice of Youth Advocates* 3 (February, 1981): 31.
34. *Voice of Youth Advocates* 6 (December, 1983): 266.
35. *Wall Street Journal* 196 (September 4, 1980): 26.
36. *Washington Post Book World* (August 26, 1980): 1.
37. *Wilson Library Journal* 55 (February, 1981): 456.
38. Winter, Douglas E. "Shadowings: *Firestarter* by Stephen King," in *Fantasy Newsletter* (November, 1980): .
39. Winter, Douglas E. *Stephen King.* STARMONT READER'S GUIDE, No. 16. Series editor, Roger Schlobin. Mercer Island, WA: Starmont House, October 1982.
40. Winter, Douglas E. *Stephen King: The Art of Darkness.* New York: New American Library, November 1984.
41. Zagorski, Edward J. *Teacher's Manual: Stephen King.* New York: New American Library, 1981.

A10. ROADWORK

A10. ***Roadwork: A Novel of the First Energy Crisis***, by "RICHARD BACHMAN." New York: A Signet Book, New American Library, April (?) 1981, 247 p., mass-market paper. [suspense novel]

PLOT SUMMARY: When the city decides to construct a freeway through George Dawes's home, he fights back—in the process losing his wife, his job, his sense of identity, and finally his life.

COMMENTS: The third "Bachman" novel, this powerful study of psychological fragmentation under stress retains King's unique touch without depending upon supernatural horror; its horrors are cancer and isolation and impersonality. Based upon and written during the oil crisis of 1974, it is a mature, topical work that retains its interest well.

REPRINTS:

b. London: New English Library, June 1983, 282 p., paper.
c. in: *The Bachman Books: Four Early Novels by Stephen King*. New York: New American Library, October 1985, p. 323-530. See **A30.**
d. as: *Werk in Uitvoering*, in: *4 X Stephen King*, by Stephen King. Utrecht: Luitingh, 1986, p. , paper. Translated by Hugo Kuipers. [Dutch]
e. as: *Sprengstoff* ["*Explosive*"], by RICHARD BACHMAN. München: Wilhelm Heyne Verlag (TB 6762), 1986, p., paper. Translated by Nora Jensen. [German]
f. as: *Carretera Maldita*, by Stephen King, ["escribiendo como Richard Bachman"]. Barcelona: Martínez Roca, 1987, 256 p., trade paper. Translated by Joseph M. Apfelbaüme. [Spanish]
g. as: *Vägbygge*. Höganäs, Sweden: Bra Böcker, 1988, 305 p. Translated by Jimmy Hofsö. [Swedish]
h. Stockholm: Legende, 1988, 305 p. Translated by Jimmy Hofsö. [Swedish]
i. as: *Werk in Uitvoering*, by Stephen King. Utrecht: Luitingh, 1988, 271 p. Translated by Hugo Kuipers. [Dutch]

SECONDARY SOURCES AND REVIEWS:

1. Beahm, George, ed. *The Stephen King Companion*. Kansas City, MO: Andrews and McMeel, September 1989.
2. Brown. Stephen P. "The Life and Death of Richard Bachman: Stephen King's Doppelganger," in *Kingdom of Fear: The World of Stephen King*, edited by Tim Underwood and Chuck Miller. San Francisco: Underwood-Miller, 1986, p. 109-126.
3. Collings, Michael R. *The Annotated Guide to Stephen King: A Primary and Secondary Bibliography of the Works of America's Premier Horror Writer*. STARMONT REFERENCE GUIDE, No. 8. Mercer Island, WA: Starmont House, October 1986.
4. Collings, Michael R. *The Many Facets of Stephen King*. STARMONT STUDIES IN LITERARY CRITICISM, No. 11. Mercer Island, WA: Starmont House, 1986.
5. Collings, Michael R. *Stephen King as Richard Bachman*. STARMONT STUDIES IN LITERARY CRITICISM, No. 10. Mercer Island, WA: Starmont House, 1985.
6. Spignesi, Stephen J. "*Roadwork*," in *The Shape Under the Sheet: The Complete Stephen King Encyclopedia*. Ann Arbor, MI: Popular Culture, Ink., May 1991, cloth, p. 252-262.
7. Winter, Douglas E. *Stephen King: The Art of Darkness*. Expanded and updated edition. New York: A Plume Book, New American Library, June 1986.

A11. STEPHEN KING'S DANSE MACABRE

A11. ***Stephen King's Danse Macabre.*** New York: Everest House, July (?) 1981, 400 p., cloth. [nonfiction]

CONTENTS: Forenote; "I. October 4, 1957, and an Invitation to Dance"; "II. Tales of the Hook"; "III. Tales of the Tarot"; "IV. An Annoying Autobiographical Pause"; "V. Radio and the Set of Reality"; "VI. The Modern American Horror Movie—Text and Subtext"; "VII. The Horror Movie as Junk Food"; "VIII. The Glass Teat, or, This Monster Was Brought to You by Gainsburgers"; "IX. Horror Fiction"; "X. The Last Waltz—Horror and Morality, Horror and Magic"; "Afterword," by King; "Appendix I. The Films"; "Appendix 2. The Books"; Index.

COMMENTS: *Danse Macabre* reads as much like a novel as it does criticism, since King relies on his personal vision and trademark colloquial style in analyzing dark fantasy from 1953 (Jack Arnold's *It Came From Outer Space*) through 1978 (John Carpenter's *Halloween* and David Lynch's *Eraserhead*). King discusses major films; television series such as *Thriller, Outer Limits,* and *Twilight Zone*; and fiction, with particular attention to Peter Straub's *Ghost Story*, Anne Rivers Siddons's *The House Next Door*, Shirley Jackson's *The Haunting of Hill House*, Ira Levin's *Rosemary's Baby*, Jack Finney's *The Invasion of the Body Snatchers*, Ray Bradbury's *Something Wicked This Way Comes*, Richard Matheson's *The Shrinking Man*, and works by Ramsey Campbell and James Herbert. In the final chapter, King connects the imagined worlds of dark fantasy to external reality, then concludes by defending the magic underlying both fantasy and imagination. As criticism, *Danse Macabre* is valuable and entertaining; as a reflection of King's beliefs, it illuminates his own fiction and screenplays.

REPRINTS:

ab. New York: Everest House, 1981, 400 p., cloth. Limited edition; lettered state.

ac. New York: Everest House, 1981, 400 p., cloth. Limited edition; numbered state, plain tissue dust jacket and slipcase, 250 copies.

ad. New York: Everest House, 1981, 400 p., cloth. Limited edition; Publisher's state, limited to 35 copies not originally for sale. No dust jacket or slipcase.

b. New York: Book of the Month Club [n.d.], cloth.

c. London: Macdonald Futura, July 1981, 448 p., cloth.

d. London: Futura, July 1981, 480 p., paper.

e. New York: Berkley Books, May 1982, xiv+400 p., trade paper.

eb. New York: Berkley Books, December 1983, 437 p., mass-market paper. 20 printings by September, 1989.

f. as: *Danse Macabre*. Paris: J'ai-Lu/Epouvante, 1982, 412 p. paper. [French]

g. as: *Danse Macabre*. Italy: Theoria, 1985, 176 p. Translated by E. Turchetti. [Italian]

h. as: *Danse Macabre*. Amsterdam: Loeb, 1986, 397 p., paper. Translated by Mariëlla de Kuyper. Second printing, 1988. [Dutch]

i. as: *La Danza de la Muerte*. Esplugas Llobregat/Barcelona: Plaza & Janés, 1986, 616 p., paper. Translated by Eduardo Goligorsky. 2nd printing, 1986. Rpt. 1989. [Spanish]

ib. as: *La Danza de la Muerte*. Esplugas Llobregat/Barcelona: Plaza & Janés Editores, 1989, 616 p. (?). [Spanish]

j. as: *Danse Macabre.* München: Wilhelm Heyne Verlag (Sachbuch 2), 1988, p., paper. Translated by Joachim Körber, following the expanded, corrected U.S. edition of 1982. [German]

SECONDARY SOURCES AND REVIEWS:

1. Adams, Michael. "*Danse Macabre*," in *Magill's Literary Annual, Book of 1981, Volume 1,* edited by Frank N. Magill. Englewood Cliffs, NJ: Salem Press, 1982, p. 171-174.
2. Beahm, George, ed. *The Stephen King Companion.* Kansas City, MO: Andrews and McMeel, September 1989, p. 192-194.
3. *Best of the Times* [*New York Times*] 4 (July, 1981): 296.
4. *Book World* 11 (April 12, 1981): 4.
5. *Book World* 12 (June 6, 1982): 12.
6. *Booklist* 77 (January 15, 1981): 651.
7. *Choice* 19 (September, 1981): 80.
8. Collings, Michael R. *The Annotated Guide to Stephen King: A Primary and Secondary Bibliography of the Works of America's Premier Horror Writer.* STARMONT REFERENCE GUIDE, No. 8. Mercer Island, WA: Starmont House, October 1986.
9. Egan, James. "Technohorror: The Dystopian Vision of Stephen King," in *Extrapolation* 29:2 (Summer, 1988): 140-152.
10. *English Journal* 76 (March, 1987): 72.
11. Graham, Mark. "An Dance into Horror with Stephen King," in *Rocky Mountain News* [Denver, CO]: .
12. Hemesath, J. B. *Library Journal* 106 (April 1, 1981): 797.
13. Kendrick, Walter. "Stephen King Gets Eminent," in *The Village Voice* 26:18 (April 29-May 5, 1981): 45. Excerpted: *Contemporary Literary Criticism, Volume 37,* edited by Daniel G. Marowski. Detroit: Gale Research Co., 1986, p. 197-198.
14. *Kirkus Reviews* 49 (March 1, 1981): 332.
15. Klavan, Andrew. *Saturday Review* 8 (April, 1981): 80.
16. *Kliatt Paperback Book Guide* 16 (Fall, 1982): 24.
17. Lehmann-Haupt, Christoher. *New York Times* (April 14, 1981): C11.
18. Magistrale, Tony. *Landscape of Fear: Stephen King's American Gothic.* Bowling Green, OH: Bowling Green State University Popular Press, March 1988.
19. Magistrale, Tony. *The Moral Voyages of Stephen King.* STARMONT STUDIES IN LITERARY CRITICISM, No. 25. Mercer Island, WA: Starmont House, 1989.
20. Morrison, Michael. "*Carrie* on Screaming," in *Times Educational Supplement* (August 21, 1981): 18. Excerpted: *Contemporary Literary Criticism, Volume 37,* edited by Daniel G. Markowski. Detroit: Gale Research Co., 1986, p. 199-200.
21. *New York Times Book Review* 87 (May 23, 1982): 39.
22. *Publishers Weekly* 219 (February 27, 1981): 144.
23. *Quill & Quire* 47 (July, 1981): 66.
24. Rockett, W. H. "The Door Ajar: Structure and Convention in Horror Films That Would Terrify," in *Journal of Popular Film and Television* (Fall, 1981): 130-136.
25. *School Library Journal* 28 (September, 1981): 147.

26. Schweitzer, Darrell, ed. *Discovering Stephen King*. STARMONT STUDIES IN LITERARY CRITICISM, No. 8. Mercer Island, WA: Starmont House, 1985.
27. *Science Fiction Review* 10 (August, 1981): 26.
28. Slung, Michelle. "Scare Tactics," in *New York Times Book Review* 86 (May 10, 1981): 15, 27. Excerpted: *Contemporary Literary Criticism, Volume 37,* edited by Daniel G. Marowski. Detroit: Gale Research Co., 1986, p. 198-199.
29. Spignesi, Stephen J. "A Look at *Danse Macabre,* Stephen King's Only Book-Length Work of Non-Fiction," in *The Shape Under the Sheet: The Complete Stephen King Encyclopedia.* Ann Arbor, MI: Popular Culture, Ink., May 1991, cloth, p. 266-267.
30. *Top of the News* 39 (Fall, 1982): 98.
31. *Voice of Youth Advocates* 6 (December, 1983): 266.
32. Wiater, Stanley. "Stephen King's *Danse Macabre,*" in *The Valley Advocate* [Hatfield, MA] (May 27, 1981): .
33. *Wilson Library Bulletin* 55 (June, 1981): 775.
34. Winter, Douglas E. *Stephen King*. STARMONT READER'S GUIDE, No. 16. Series editor, Roger Schlobin. Mercer Island, WA: Starmont House, October 1982.
35. Winter, Douglas E. *Stephen King: The Art of Darkness*. New York: New American Library, November 1984.

A12. CUJO

A12. *Cujo*. New York: New York: Viking Press, 8 September 1981, 319 p., cloth. [horror novel]

PLOT SUMMARY: The internal, systematic breakdown of a marriage is paralleled externally by the separation of a husband from his family. When the family car breaks down, Donna Trenton and her son Tad are isolated and threatened by a rabid St. Bernard dog, Cujo. The Trentons remain in the car for several days; when help finally arrives, it is too late.

COMMENTS: Closer to mainstream fiction than most of King's works, *Cujo* seems originally intended as a "Richard Bachman" novel. In the second draft, King incorporated the cross-references to Frank Dodd and the Castle Rock mystique, as well as the supernatural elements of the monster in the closet, in order to bring the novel closer to those published under his name. It demonstrates the incremental horrors of daily life as love is betrayed and trust leads to death.

The novel was adapted for film in 1983, directed by Lewis Teague.

350,000 copies sold in 1981; the novel ranked #3 on the *Publishers Weekly* annual hardcover Bestsellers List, 1981.

REPRINTS:

b. New York: Mysterious Press, 1981, 319 p., cloth. Lettered state (limited to 26 copies?); not for sale when originally published.
bb. New York: Mysterious Press, 1981, 319 p., cloth. Signed, numbered limited edition; mylar cover and slipcase; 750 copies.

c. London: Macdonald, February 1982, 320 p., cloth.
d. New York: A Signet Book, New American Library, August 1982, 305 p., mass-market paperback. 28 printings by 1994.
db. New York, A Plume Book, New American Library, October 1994, 277 p., trade paper. "Collector's Edition." Introduction by Dan Simmons. Includes a color reproduction of the original hardcover art.
e. London: Futura, August 1982, 352 p., paper.
f. New York: Viking [Science Fiction Book Club edition.], [n.d.], 309 p., cloth.
g. as: *Cujo*. Barcelona: Ediciones Grijalba, 10 November 1982, 414 p., paper. Translated by María Antonia Menini. [Spanish]
h. as: *Cujo*. Paris: Albin Michel, 1982, 360 p., cloth. [French]
i. as: *Cujo*. Stockholm: Askild and Kärnekull, 1982, 342 p. Translated by Jimmy Hofsö. Rpt. 1984. [Swedish]
j. as: *Cujo*. Utrecht: Luitingh/Veen, 1982, 288 p., trade paper. Translated by Margot Bakker. 5th printing, 1986. [Dutch]
k. as: *Cujo*. Miguel Hidalgo, México: Editorial Grijalbo (Bestsellers Oro), February 1983, 416 p., paper. Translated by María Antonia Menini. First edition of 5,000 copies. [Spanish]
l. Anstey, Leicestershire: Charnwood Library Services/Ulversoft Large Print Books, June 1983, 476 p., cloth. [Large print edition]
m. as: *Cujo*. Milano: Mondadori, 1983, 376 p. Translated by T. Dobner. [Italian]
mb. as: *Cujo*. Milano: Mondadori, 1986, 380 p. Translated by T. Dobner. [Italian]
n. as: *Cujo*. Paris: J'ai-Lu/Epouvante, 1983, paper. [French]
o. as: *Cujo*. Bergisch Gladbach: Bastei-Lübbe (Paperback 2109), 1983, p, paper. Translated by Harro Christensen. [German]
ob. as: *Cujo*. Bergisch Gladbach: Bastei-Lübbe (TB13035), 368 p., paper, 1986. Translated by Harro Christensen. [German]
p. as: *Cujo*. Barcelona: Circulo de Lectores, 1983, p. [Spanish]
q. as: *Cujo*. Panamá: Printer Internacional de Panamá, 1983, p. [Spanish]
r. as: *Cujo: Spaendingsroman*. Valby, Denmark: Borgen, 1984, 317 p. Translated by Niels Søndergaard. [Danish]
s. as: *Cujo*. Stockholm: Legenda, 1985, 342 p., paper. Translated by Jimmy Hofsö. [Swedish]
t. as: *Cujo*. Book Club Editions-Kornwesterheim, Austria: Europäische Bildungsgemeinschaft; Gütersloh, Austria: Bertelsmann Club; Zug, Switzerland: Buch-und-Schallplattenfreunde. August 1986, 383 p., paper. Translated by Harro Christensen. [German]
u. as: *Cujo*. Gütersloh, Austria: Bertelsmann Lesering, 1986, p. Translated by Harro Christensen. [German]
v. as: *Cujo*. Barcelona: Grijalbo, 1986, 419 p., cloth. Translated by Mariá Antonia Menini. [Spanish]
vb. as: *Cujo*. Barcelona: Grijalbo, 1986, 419 p., paper. 2nd edition. Translated by Mariá Antonia Menini Pagés. [Spanish]
vc. as: *Cujo*. Barcelona: Ediciones Grijalbo, 1989, 419 p. (?). [Spanish]
w. as: *Faresonen* ["*Danger Zone*"]. Oslo, Norway: Hjemmets Bokklubb. No further information. [Norwegian]

SECONDARY SOURCES AND REVIEWS:

1. Beahm, George, ed. *The Stephen King Companion*. Kansas City, MO: Andrews and McMeel, September 1989, p. 184-185.
2. Bishop, Michael. "Mad Dogs...and Englishmen," in *Washington Post Book World* 11 (August 23, 1981): 1-2.
3. Bishop, Michael. "The Saint Bernard That Becomes an Engine of Madness and Death," in *San Francisco Chronicle* "Review" (September 20, 1981): 3. Excerpted: *Contemporary Literary Criticism, Volume 26,* edited by Jean C. Stine. Detroit: Gale Research Co., 1983, cloth, p. 238-239.
4. *Booklist* 77 (May 15, 1981): 1213.
5. Broderick, Dorothy M. *Voice of Youth Advocates* 4:4 (October, 1981): 34.
6. Budrys, Algis. "A Doggy New Novel from Stephen King," in *Chicago Sun-Times* (September 6, 1981): .
7. Chute, David. "King Gives Second-Best Horror Effort in *Cujo,*" in *Los Angeles Herald Examiner* (September 9, 1981): .
8. Collings, Michael R. *The Annotated Guide to Stephen King: A Primary and Secondary Bibliography of the Works of America's Premier Horror Writer*. STARMONT REFERENCE GUIDE, No. 8. Mercer Island, WA: Starmont House, October 1986.
9. Collings, Michael R. *The Many Facets of Stephen King*. STARMONT STUDIES IN LITERARY CRITICISM, No. 11. Mercer Island, WA: Starmont House, 1986.
10. Collings, Michael R. *The Stephen King Phenomenon*. STARMONT STUDIES IN LITERARY CRITICISM, No. 14. Mercer Island, WA: Starmont House, 1987.
11. Davis, L. J. "A Shabby Dog Story from Stephen King," in *Chicago Tribune Book World* (August 16, 1981): .
12. *English Journal* 72 (January, 1983): 79.
13. Graham, Mark. "Mouth Foaming for Good Scare?" in *Rocky Mountain News* [Denver, CO] (September 6, 1981): 32.
14. Green, Michael. *Saturday Review* 8 (September, 1981): 59.
15. Hall, Melissa Mia. "Stephen King Thinks It's Fun to 'Get the Reader'," in *Fort Worth Star-Telegram* (August 23, 1981): .
16. Hatlen, Burton. "The Mad Dog and Maine," in *Shadowings,* edited by Douglas E. Winter. Mercer Island, WA: Starmont House, 1983, p. 33-38.
17. Hoppenstand, Gary and Ray B. Browne, eds. *The Gothic World of Stephen King: Landscape of Nightmares*. Bowling Green, OH: Bowling Green State University Popular Press, December 1987.
18. *Kirkus Reviews* 49 (July 1, 1981): 825.
19. *Kirkus Reviews* 49 (July 15, 1981): 878.
20. Lehmann-Haupt, Christopher. *New York Times* (August 14, 1981): C2.
21. Magistrale, Tony. *Landscape of Fear: Stephen King's American Gothic*. Bowling Green, OH: Bowling Green State University Popular Press, March 1988.
22. Pascal, Sylvia. *School Library Journal* 28:2 (October, 1981): 162.
23. *Publishers Weekly* 220:3 (July 17, 1981): 80.
24. *Publishers Weekly* 221 (June 11, 1982): 61.

25. Reino, Joseph. *Stephen King: The First Decade,* Carrie *to* Pet Sematary. TWAYNE'S UNITED STATES AUTHORS SERIES (TUSAS 531), edited by Warren French. Boston: Twayne Publishers, February 1988.
26. *San Francisco Chronicle* (August 21, 1981): 59.
27. *Science Fiction Review* 11 (May, 1982): 47.
28. Schweitzer, Darrell, ed. *Discovering Stephen King*. STARMONT STUDIES IN LITERARY CRITICISM, No. 8. Mercer Island, WA: Starmont House, 1985.
29. Spignesi, Stephen J. "Cujo," in *The Shape Under the Sheet: The Complete Stephen King Encyclopedia*. Ann Arbor, MI: Popular Culture, Ink., May 1991, cloth, p. 262-265, 268-271.
30. *Starship* 18 (Summer, 1981): 5.
31. Strouse, Jean. "Beware of the Dog," in *Newsweek* 98 (August 31, 1981): 64.
32. Stump, Debra. "A Matter of Choice: King's *Cujo* and Malamud's *The Natural*," in *Discovering Stephen King,* edited by Darrell Schweitzer. STARMONT STUDIES IN LITERARY CRITICISM, No. 8. Mercer Island, WA: Starmont House, 1985, p. 131-140.
33. Thompson, Thomas. "King's Latest a Shaggy Rabid Dog Story," in *Los Angeles Times Book Review* (September 6, 1981): 5. Reprinted as: "*Cujo:* Tale About a Mad Dog Ought to be Put to Sleep," in *Baltimore News American* (September 6, 1981): .
34. Winter, Douglas E. "King's *Cujo*: 'Nope, Nothing Wrong Here'," in *Fantasy Newsletter* (November, 1981): 9-11.
35. Winter, Douglas E. *Stephen King*. STARMONT READER'S GUIDE, No. 16. Series editor, Roger Schlobin. Mercer Island, WA: Starmont House, October 1982, p. 90-96.
36. Winter, Douglas E. *Stephen King: The Art of Darkness*. New York: New American Library, November 1984.
37. Yamamoto, Judith. *Library Journal* 106 (July, 1981): 1442.

A13. THE SHINING, 'SALEM'S LOT, NIGHT SHIFT, CARRIE

A13. ***The Shining, 'Salem's Lot, Night Shift, Carrie.*** London: Octopus Books, September 1981, 991 p., cloth. [omnibus collection]

CONTENTS: *The Shining* (1977, see **A3**]); *'Salem's Lot* (1975, see **A2**); *Night Shift* (1978, see **A6**); *Carrie* (1974, see **A1**).

REPRINTS:

b. as: ***The Shining, 'Salem's Lot, Carrie.*** London: Octopus Books, Heinemann, July 1983, 747 p., cloth. Drops *Night Shift*.
c. Peerage Books, 1986, 1991 p., cloth. Restores the original text of the 1981 version; issued in one slipcase with the omnibus editions, *Isaac Asimov* and *Robert Ludlow*.

A14. THE RUNNING MAN

A14. ***The Running Man***, by "RICHARD BACHMAN." New York: A Signet Book, New American Library, May 1982, 219 p., mass-market paperback. [science-fiction novel]

PLOT SUMMARY: Unemployed and desperate in the business-controlled America of 2025, Ben Richards becomes a contestant on the TV program, *The Running Man*, hoping to earn enough money to rescue his wife and daughter from poverty—ironically, they are killed by thieves looking for the money that the network sends them. Richards eludes capture long enough to return to network headquarters and extract his vengeance.

COMMENTS: The fourth "Bachman" novel, *The Running Man* was written in a weekend while King was a student at the University of Maine, Orono, and subsequently published almost unrevised. The novel has a distinctive science-fictional basis, allowing King to explore extrapolative satire based on the media, television game shows, and American culture in general.

The novel was adapted for film in 1988 as a strictly action-adventure narrative, starring Arnold Schwarzenegger in a radically altered characterization of Ben Richards (see **G14**).

REPRINTS:

ab. New York: A Signet Book, New American Library, 1988, 219 p., movie tie-in edition. 7 printings by September, 1989.
b. London: New English Library, December 1983, 219 p., paper.
c. in: *The Bachman Books: Four Early Novels by Stephen King*. New York: New American *Library,* October 1985, cloth, p. 531-692. See **A30**.
d. as: *El Fugitivo*. Barcelona: Martínez Roca, 1986, 258 p., cloth. Translated by Hernán Sabaté. [Spanish]
db. as: *El Fugitivo*. Barcelona: Martínez Roca, 1986, 258 p., paper. Translated by Hernán Sabaté. [Spanish]
e. as: *Vlucht Naar de Top*, in: *4 X Stephen King*. Utrecht: Luitingh, 1986, p., paper. Translated by Frank de Groot. [Dutch]
f. as: *Menschenjagd* ["*Manhunt*"], by RICHARD BACHMAN. München: Wilhelm Heyne Verlag (TB 6687), 1986, p., paper. Translated by Nora Jensen. Cover includes the note that "Bachman est King" [Stephen King is Bachman]. [German]
g. as: *Den Flyende Mannen*, by "Stephen King alias Richard Bachman." Stockholm: Legenda, 1986, 226 p. Translated by Jimmy Hofsö. 2nd printing, 1988. [Swedish]
h. as: *El Fugitivo*. Barcelona: Circulo de Lectores, 1987, p. [Spanish]
i. as: *Vlucht Naar de Top*, by Stephen King. Utrecht: Luitingh, 1988, 199 p. Translated by Frank de Groot. [Dutch]

SECONDARY SOURCES AND REVIEWS:

1. Beahm, George, ed. *The Stephen King Companion*. Kansas City, MO: Andrews and McMeel, September 1989.
2. Brown. Stephen P. "The Life and Death of Richard Bachman: Stephen King's Doppelganger," in *Kingdom of Fear: The World of Stephen King*, edited by Tim Underwood and Chuck Miller. San Francisco: Underwood-Miller, 1986, p. 109-126.
3. Collings, Michael R. *The Annotated Guide to Stephen King: A Primary and Secondary Bibliography of the Works of America's Premier Horror Writer*. STARMONT REFERENCE GUIDE, No. 8. Mercer Island, WA: Starmont House, October 1986.
4. Collings, Michael R. *The Many Facets of Stephen King*. STARMONT STUDIES IN LITERARY CRITICISM, No. 11. Mercer Island, WA: Starmont House, 1986.
5. Collings, Michael R. *Stephen King as Richard Bachman*. STARMONT STUDIES IN LITERARY CRITICISM, No. 10. Mercer Island, WA: Starmont House, 1985.
6. Donovan, Diane C. *Voice of Youth Advocates* 6:1 (April, 1983): 44. [No reference to King as author]. Excerpted: *Contemporary Literary Criticism*, Volume 37, edited by Daniel G. Marowski. Detroit: Gale Research Co., 1986, p. 201.
7. D'Ammassa, Don. "Three by Bachman," in *Discovering Stephen King*, edited by Darrell Schweitzer. STARMONT STUDIES IN LITERARY CRITICISM, No. 8. Mercer Island, WA: Starmont House, 1985, p. 123-130.
8. Spignesi, Stephen J. "*The Running Man*," in *The Shape Under the Sheet: The Complete Stephen King Encyclopedia*. Ann Arbor, MI: Popular Culture, Ink., May 1991, cloth, p. 276-280.
9. Winter, Douglas E. *Stephen King: The Art of Darkness*. Expanded and updated edition. New York: A Plume Book, New American Library, June 1986, paper.

A15. CREEPSHOW

A15. ***Stephen King's Creepshow: A George A. Romero Film***, artwork by Berni Wrightson. New York: A Plume Book, New American Library, July 1982, [64] p., oversized trade paper. [comic-book collection of horror short stories]

CONTENTS: "Father's Day" (1982; see **B65**); "The Lonesome Death of Jordy Verrill" (as "Weeds," 1976; see **B66** and **B27**); "The Crate" (1979; see **B43**); "Something to Tide You Over" (1982; see **B67**); "They're Creeping Up on You" (1982; see **B68**).

COMMENTS: A comic-book adaptation of the King-Romero film, *Creepshow*, the book was published in softcover format, with frames suggesting E.C. Comics originals. "The Crate" and "The Lonesome Death of Jordy Verrill" (as "Weeds") had been published previously; the remaining tales are original to the film and the collection. The book deletes the framing tale that opens and closes the film.

REPRINTS:

b. as: *Creepshow*. Amsterdam: W. L. Beck, 1983, 64 p., cloth. Printed in Spain; translated by professional translation studio. [Dutch]
c. as: *Creepshow*. Paris: Albin Michel, 1983?, [64?] p., cloth. The only hardcover edition of the book to date. [French]
d. Garden City, NY: A Plume Book, New American Library [Science Fiction Book Club], [n.d.], 64 p. paper.
e. Garden City, NY: Mystery Guild Book Club, [n.d.], paper.
f. as: *Creepshow*. Bergish Gladbach: Bastei-Lübbe (Paperback 71202), 1989, p., paper.

SECONDARY SOURCES AND REVIEWS:

1. Ansen, David. "The Roaches Did It," in *Newsweek* 100:21 (November 22, 1982): 118A. A review of the movie *Creepshow*. Excerpted: *Contemporary Literary Criticism, Volume 26,* edited by Jean C. Stine. Detroit: Gale Research Co., 1983, p. 243.
2. Beahm, George, ed. *The Stephen King Companion*. Kansas City, MO: Andrews and McMeel, September 1989, p. 179-183.
3. Collings, Michael R. *The Annotated Guide to Stephen King: A Primary and Secondary Bibliography of the Works of America's Premier Horror Writer*. STARMONT REFERENCE GUIDE, No. 8. Mercer Island, WA: Starmont House, October 1986.
4. Collings, Michael R. *The Many Facets of Stephen King*. STARMONT STUDIES IN LITERARY CRITICISM, No. 11. Mercer Island, WA: Starmont House, 1986.
5. Collings, Michael R., and David A. Engebretson. *The Shorter Works of Stephen King*. STARMONT STUDIES IN LITERARY CRITICISM, No. 9. Mercer Island, WA: Starmont House, June 1985.
6. Corliss, Richard. "Jolly Contempt," in *Time* 120:21 (November 22, 1982): 108-110. Excerpted: *Contemporary Literary Criticism, Volume 26,* edited by Jean C. Stine. Detroit: Gale Research Co., 1983, p. 243.
7. *Los Angeles Times Book Review* (August 29, 1982): 6.
8. *Science Fiction Review* 12 (November, 1983): 47.
9. Spignesi, Stephen J. "*Creepshow*," in *The Shape Under the Sheet: The Complete Stephen King Encyclopedia*. Ann Arbor, MI: Popular Culture, Ink., May 1991, cloth, p. 271-276.
10. *Village Voice Literary Supplement* (September, 1982): 6.
11. Winter, Douglas E. "Collecting King," in *Twilight Zone Magazine* 5:6 (February, 1986): 32-33, 97.
12. Winter, Douglas E. *Stephen King*. STARMONT READER'S GUIDE, No. 16. Series editor, Roger Schlobin. Mercer Island, WA: Starmont House, October 1982.
13. Winter, Douglas E. *Stephen King: The Art of Darkness*. New York: New American Library, November 1984.

A16. DIFFERENT SEASONS

A16. ***Different Seasons.*** New York: Viking Press, 27 August 1982, 527 p., cloth. [novella collection]

CONTENTS (all original): "Hope Springs Eternal: Rita Hayworth and Shawshank Redemption" (see **B61**); "Summer of Corruption: Apt Pupil" (see **B62**); "Fall from Innocence: The Body" (see **B63**); "A Winter's Tale: The Breathing Method" (see **B64**); "Afterword," by King (see **C96**).

The book sold 270,264 copies in 1982, and was ranked #7 on the *Publishers Weekly* annual hardcover Bestsellers List for 1982, an unusual feat for a collection of short fiction.

REPRINTS:

b. London: Macdonald, October 1982, 468 p., cloth.

c. New York: A Signet Book, New American Library, August 1983, 507 p., mass-market paperback. 33 printings by September, 1989.

cb. New York: A Signet Book, New American Library, 1986, 507 p., mass-market paperback. Movie tie-in with the film, *Stand by Me*; new cover, includes blurb: "*Stand by Me*—now a smash movie based on *The Body*, a novella in *DIFFERENT SEASONS*."

cc. as: *Stephen King: The Shawshank Redemption—Different Seasons*. New York, A Signet Book, Viking Penguin, 1994, 507 p., mass-market paperback. Movie tie-in with the film, *The Shawshank Redemption*. Despite the title, the contents are the same.

d. London: Futura, September 1983, 560 p., paper.

f. partial translation as: *Sommerdad: Tva Berättelser*. Stockholm: Askild and Kärnekull, 1983, 305 p. Translated by Martin Edlund. [Swedish]

g. excerpted as: *Verano de Corrupción*. Barcelona: Ediciones Grijalbo, 1983, p., paper? [Spanish]

gb. excerpted as: *Verano de Corrupción*. Barcelona: Grijalbo, 1986, 356 p., paper. 2nd edition. Translated by J. N. Peréz and Angela Peréz. [Spanish]

gc. excerpted as: *Verano de Corrupción*. Barcelona: Ediciones Grijalbo, 1989, p. [Spanish]

h. excerpted as: *El Cuerpo* ["*The body*"]. Barcelona: Ediciones Grijalbo, 1983, p., paper? [Spanish]

hb. excerpted as: *El Cuerpo* ["*The body*"]. Barcelona: Gribaljo, 1987, 296 p., paper. 3rd edition. Translated by J. M. Perez and Angela Perez. [Spanish]

i. as: *Frühling, Sommer, Herbst und Tod* ["*Spring, Summer, Autumn, and Death*"]. Bergish Gladbach: Bastei-Lübbe Verlag (Paperback 28120), 1984, 560 p., paper. Translated by Harro Christensen. [German]

j. partial translation as: *Vinterverk: [Tva Berättelser]*. Stockholm: Askild and Kärnekull, 1984, 252 p. Translated by Jimmy Hofsö. [Swedish]

k. partial translation as: *De Leerling* ["*The Pupil*"]. Utrecht: Veen, 1984, 271 p., trade paper. Translated by Pauline Moody. Second printing, 1988. [Dutch]

CONTENTS: "The Leerling" ["The Pupil"] and "De Ontnapping" ("The Escape" = "Rita Hayworth and Shawshank Redemption")].

l. excerpted as: *Verano de Corrupción. El Cuerpo*. Barcelona: Mundo Actual de Ediciones, 1984, p. [Spanish]

m. partial translation as: *It Weet Wat Je Wilt* ["*I Know What You Want*"]. Utrecht: Luitingh/Veen, Autumn 1985, 320 p., trade paper. Translated by F. J. Brunning and Pauline Moody. 2 printings by 1986. [Dutch]

CONTENTS: Seven stories from *Night Shift* and *Different Seasons,* including "De Laaste Laddersport" ["The Last Ladder Game" = "The Last Rung on the Ladder"]; "Ik Weet Wat Je Wilt" ["I Know What You Want" = "I Know What You Need"]; "Stop Ermee, B.V." ["Stop It, Inc." = "Quitters, Inc."]; "Jerusalem's Lot"; "Trucks"; "Het Lijk" ["The Corpse" = "The Body"]; "De Ademhalingsmethode" ["The Breathing Method"].

n. as: *Différent Saisons*. Paris: Albin Michel, 1986, 529 p., cloth. Translated by Pierre Allen. [French]

o. as: *Stagioni Diverse*. Milano: Sperling & Kupfer, 1987, 588 p. Translated by B. Amato, P. Formenti, and M. B. Piccioli. [Italian]

p. excerpted as: *Jahreszeiten: Herbst und Winter* ["*The Seasons: Fall and Winter*"]. Bergisch Gladbach: Bastei-Lübbe (TB 13114), 1987, 331 p., paper. Translated by Harro Christensen. [German]

CONTENTS: "Herbstsonate: Die Leiche" ["Autumn Sonata: The Body" = "The Body"] and "Ein Winter Märchen: Atemtechnik" ["The Breathing Method"]; "Nachwort" ["Afterword"].

q. excerpted as: *De Leerling* ["*The Pupil*"]. Utrecht: Luitingh, 1987, 271 p. Translated by Pauline Moody. [Dutch]

r. excerpted as: *Jahreszeiten: Frühling & Sommer* ["*Seasons: Spring and Summer*"]. Bergish Gladbach: Bastei-Lübbe Verlag, (TB 13115), 1988, p., paper. Translated by Harro Christensen. [German]

SECONDARY SOURCES AND REVIEWS:

1. Atchity, Kenneth. "Stephen King: Making Burgers with the Best," in *Los Angeles Times Book Review* (August 29, 1982): 7. Excerpted: *Contemporary Literary Criticism Volume 26*, edited by Jean C. Stine. Detroit: Gale Research Co., 1983, p. 241.
2. Beahm, George. *The Stephen King Companion*. Kansas City, MO: Andrews and McMeel, September 1989, paper, p. 203-206.
3. Bertin, Eddy C. "Stephen King in the Lowlands: An Annotated Bibliography of His Works as Published in the Netherlands (Holland and Belgium)," in *Castle Rock: The Stephen King Newsletter* 1:11 (November, 1985): 7-8.
4. Bertin, Eddy C. "Additions to 'Stephen King in the Lowlands'," a letter in an unknown publication.
5. *Best Sellers* 42 (October, 1982): 259.
6. Blue, Tyson. *The Unseen King*. STARMONT STUDIES IN LITERARY CRITICISM, No. 26. Mercer Island, WA: Starmont House, 1989.
7. Budrys, Algis. *The Magazine of Fantasy & Science Fiction* 64 (February 1983): 61.
8. Cheuse, Alan. "Horror Writer's Holiday," in *New York Times Book Review* (August 29, 1982): 10, 17. Excerpted: *Contemporary Lit-*

erary Criticism, Volume 26, edited by Jean C. Stine. Detroit: Gale Research Co., 1983, cloth, p. 242.

9. Collings, Michael R. *The Annotated Guide to Stephen King: A Primary and Secondary Bibliography of the Works of America's Premier Horror Writer.* STARMONT REFERENCE GUIDE, No. 8. Mercer Island, WA: Starmont House, October 1986.
10. Collings, Michael R. *The Many Facets of Stephen King.* STARMONT STUDIES IN LITERARY CRITICISM, No. 11. Mercer Island, WA: Starmont House, 1986.
11. Collings, Michael R. *The Stephen King Phenomenon.* STARMONT STUDIES IN LITERARY CRITICISM, No. 14. Mercer Island, WA: Starmont House, 1987.
12. Collings, Michael R., and David A. Engebretson. *The Shorter Works of Stephen King.* STARMONT STUDIES IN LITERARY CRITICISM, No. 9. Mercer Island, WA: Starmont House, June 1985.
13. *English Journal* 72 (December, 1983): 69.
14. Gifford, Thomas. "Stephen King's Quartet," in *Washington Post Book World* 12 (August 22, 1982): 1-2. Excerpted: *Contemporary Literary Criticism, Volume 26*, edited by Jean C. Stine. Detroit: Gale Research Co., 1983, p. 240-241.
15. Graham, Mark. "Stephen King Shows Another Grisly Side," in *Rocky Mountain News* [Denver, CO] (September 19, 1982): 22N.
16. Grant, Charles L., and others. "Different Writers on *Different Seasons*," in *Fantasy Newsletter* (February, 1983): .
17. Gray, Paul. "Master of Postliterate Prose," in *Time* 120 (August 20, 1982): 87. Excerpted: *Contemporary Literary Criticism, Volume 26,* edited by Jean C. Stine. Detroit: Gale Research Co., 1983, p. 242-243.
18. Hard, Anette. "King: Novellas from a Consummate Story Teller," in *Houston Chronicle* (September 12, 1982): .
19. Heldreth, Leonard. "Viewing 'The Body': King's Portrait of the Artist as Survivor," in *The Gothic World of Stephen King: Landscape of Nightmares,* edited by Gary Hoppenstand and Ray B. Browne. Bowling Green, OH: Bowling Green State University Popular Press, December 1987, p. 64-74.
20. *Kirkus Reviews* 50:12 (June 15, 1982): 693. Excerpted: *Contemporary Literary Criticism, Volume 26,* edited by Jean C. Stine. Detroit: Gale Research Co., 1983, cloth, p. 240.
21. Lehmann-Haupt, Christopher. *New York Times* [Daily] 131 (August 11, 1982): III, 22.
22. Magistrale, Tony. *The Moral Voyages of Stephen King.* STARMONT STUDIES IN LITERARY CRITICISM, No. 25. Mercer Island, WA: Starmont House, 1989.
23. McCoy, W. Keith. *Library Journal* 107 (August, 1982): 1481.
24. Neilson, Keith. "*Different Seasons*," in *Magill's Literary Annual, Book of 1983, Volume 1,* edited by Frank Magill. Englewood Cliffs, NJ: Salem Press, 1984, p. 189-193.
25. *Publishers Weekly* (June 18, 1982): 64.
26. *Publishers Weekly* 223 (June 24, 1983): 56.
27. Reed, Glenn. "*Different Seasons*," in *Science Fiction & Fantasy Book Review* (January/February, 1983): 29-30.

28. Schweitzer, Darrell, ed. *Discovering Stephen King*. STARMONT STUDIES IN LITERARY CRITICISM, No. 8. Mercer Island, WA: Starmont House, 1985.
29. *Science Fiction Review* 12 (February, 1983): 28.
30. Seelye, John. "Wizard of Ooze with Four Novellas Makes Poe a Piker," in *Chicago Tribune Bookworld* (August 22, 1983): .
31. Spignesi, Stephen J. "*Different Seasons*," in *The Shape Under the Sheet: The Complete Stephen King Encyclopedia*. Ann Arbor, MI: Popular Culture, Ink., May 1991, cloth, p. 284-294.
32. Underwood, Tim, and Chuck Miller, eds. *Kingdom of Fear: The World of Stephen King*. Columbia, PA: Underwood-Miller, April 1986.
33. *Voice of Youth Advocates* 5 (December, 1982): 33.
34. Waters, Kate. *School Library Journal* 29 (November, 1982): 106.
35. *Wilson Library Bulletin* 57 (December, 1982): 336.
36. Winter, Douglas E., ed. *Shadowings: The Reader's Guide to Horror Fiction, 1981-1982*. STARMONT STUDIES IN LITERARY CRITICISM, No. 1. Mercer Island, WA: Starmont House, 1983, p. 38-43.
37. Winter, Douglas E. *Stephen King*. STARMONT READER'S GUIDE, No. 16. Series editor, Roger Schlobin. Mercer Island, WA: Starmont House, October 1982.
38. Winter, Douglas E. *Stephen King: The Art of Darkness*. New York: New American Library, November 1984.

A17. THE DARK TOWER: THE GUNSLINGER

A17. ***The Dark Tower: The Gunslinger.*** West Kingston, RI: Donald M. Grant Publisher, August (?) 1982, 224 p., cloth. Illustrations by Michael Whelan. Limited edition; lettered state and publisher's state. [fantasy novel]

CONTENTS: "The Gunslinger" (1978; see **B36**); "The Way Station" (1980; see **B44**); "The Oracle and the Mountain" (1981; see **B51**); "The Slow Mutants" (1981; see **B53**); "The Gunslinger and the Dark Man" (1981; see **B57**); Afterword, by King (see **C124**).

COMMENTS: One of King's most controversial texts because of its initial very limited print run, *The Dark Tower* collects five stories that originally appeared in *The Magazine of Fantasy & Science Fiction*. In these stories, King transcends horror to suggest instead the opening of an epic quest. The narratives are more static than usual for King, and the characters less rounded—as befits the alteration in genre. Yet the narrative is compelling, particularly as an introduction to the epic quest. The cycle was continued in *The Drawing of the Three* (see also **A34**), *The Waste Lands* (see also **A43**), and beyond.

REPRINTS:

ab. West Kingston, RI: Donald M. Grant, Publisher, 1982, 224 p., cloth. Limited edition, numbered and signed by author and artist, 500 copies.

ac. West Kingston, RI: Donald M. Grant, Publisher, 1982, 224 p., cloth. Trade edition, 20,000 copies.
ad. West Kingston, RI: Donald M. Grant, Publisher, 1984, 224 p., cloth. Second trade edition, 10,000 copies.
b. New York: A Plume Book, New American Library, September 1988, 224 p, trade paperback. Illustratons by Michael Whelan.
bb. New York: A Signet Book, New American Library, July 1989, 315 p., mass-market paper. No illustrations.
bc. New York: A Plume Book, New American Library, n.d., 224 p., trade paperback. A boxed set issued with *The Dark Tower II: The Drawing of the Three*.
bd. New York: A Signet Book, New American Library, n.d., 315 p., mass-market paper. A boxed set issued with *The Dark Tower II: The Drawing of the Three*.
c. London: Sphere, 1988, p., cloth.
cb. London: Sphere, 1989, p., paper.
d. as: *De Donkere Toren: 1. De Scherpschutter* ["*The Dark Tower: 1. The Sharpshooter*"]. Utrecht: Luitingh, 1988, 206 p. Translated by Hugo Timmerman. [Dutch]
e. as: *Schwarz* ["*Black*"]. München: Wilhelm Heyne Verlag (Jumbo Paperback 41/11), 1988, p., paper. Translated by Joachim Körber. [German]
f. as: *Schwarz* ["*Black*"]. Gütersloh, Austria: Bertelsmann Lesering, 1989, p. Translated by Joachom Körber. [German]

SECONDARY SOURCES AND REVIEWS:

1. *Analog Science Fiction/Science Fact* 109 (June, 1989): 185.
2. Beaulieu, Janet C. "King Excels in Quest for Dark Tower," in *Bangor Daily News* [Maine] (January 10, 1989): . As microfiche: *NewsBank: Literature* 16 (February, 1989): Fiche 19: B6-B7. Reprinted: *Castle Rock: The Stephen King Newsletter* 5:3 (March, 1989): 1, 6.
3. Beaulieu, Janet C. "*Gunslinger* Stalks Darkness in Human Spirit," in *Castle Rock: The Stephen King Newsletter* 5:3 (March, 1989): 1, 3.
4. Beahm, George, ed. *The Stephen King Companion*. Kansas City, MO: Andrews and McMeel, September 1989.
5. Bertin, Eddy C. "DT Books Make Dutch Appearance," in *Castle Rock: The Stephen King Newsletter* 5:12 (December, 1989): .
6. Blue, Tyson. "Mass Market Edition of *Gunslinger* Released," in *Castle Rock: The Stephen King Newsletter* 4:10 (October, 1988): 5.
7. Blue, Tyson. *The Unseen King*. STARMONT STUDIES IN LITERARY CRITICISM, No. 26. Mercer Island, WA: Starmont House, 1989.
8. *Booklist* 84 (July, 1988): 1755.
9. Collings, Michael R. *The Annotated Guide to Stephen King: A Primary and Secondary Bibliography of the Works of America's Premier Horror Writer*. STARMONT REFERENCE GUIDE, No. 8. Mercer Island, WA: Starmont House, October 1986.
10. Collings, Michael R. *The Many Facets of Stephen King*. STARMONT STUDIES IN LITERARY CRITICISM, No. 11. Mercer Island, WA: Starmont House, 1986.

11. Collings, Michael R. *The Stephen King Phenomenon*. STARMONT STUDIES IN LITERARY CRITICISM, No. 14. Mercer Island, WA: Starmont House, 1987.
12. Collings, Michael R., and David A. Engebretson. *The Shorter Works of Stephen King*. STARMONT STUDIES IN LITERARY CRITICISM, No. 9. Mercer Island, WA: Starmont House, June 1985.
13. Egan, James. "*The Dark Tower:* Stephen King's Gothic Western," in *The Gothic World of Stephen King: Landscape of Nightmares,* edited by Gary Hoppenstand and Ray B. Browne. Bowling Green, OH: Bowling Green State University Popular Press, December 1987, p. 95-106.
14. *Emergency Librarian* 16 (March, 1989): 47.
15. Fuller, Richard. *New York Times Book Review* (January 8, 1989): 22-23.
16. Graham, Mark. "*Dark Tower* Shows King in Different Light," in *Rocky Mountain News* [Denver, CO] (August 1, 1982): .
17. *Guardian Weekly* 137 (November 1, 1987): 27.
18. Hoppenstand, Gary and Ray B. Browne, eds. *The Gothic World of Stephen King: Landscape of Nightmares*. Bowling Green, OH: Bowling Green State University Popular Press, December 1987.
19. *Kirkus Reviews* 56 (July 15, 1988): 1019.
20. Mehegan, S. L. "*The Dark Tower: The Gunslinger*," in *Castle Rock: The Stephen King Newsletter* 2:5 (May, 1986): 3.
21. *Publishers Weekly* 234 (July 29, 1988): 227.
22. Reino, Joseph. *Stephen King: The First Decade,* Carrie *to* Pet Sematary. TWAYNE'S UNITED STATES AUTHORS SERIES (TUSAS 531), edited by Warren French. Boston: Twayne Publishers, February 1988.
23. *San Francisco Chronicle* "Reviews" (August 15, 1982): 10.
24. Schweitzer, Darrell, ed. *Discovering Stephen King*. STARMONT STUDIES IN LITERARY CRITICISM, No. 8. Mercer Island, WA: Starmont House, 1985.
25. *Science Fiction Chronicle* 10 (December, 1988): 45.
26. Spignesi, Stephen J. "The Dark Tower: The Gunslinger," in *The Shape Under the Sheet: The Complete Stephen King Encyclopedia*. Ann Arbor, MI: Popular Culture, Ink., May 1991, cloth, p. 280-284.
27. *West Coast Review of Books* 13:3 (1987): 60.
28. Winders, Glenda. "King Takes a Browning Poem, and Sets 'Gunfighter' in Future," in *San Diego Union* (December 4, 1988): . As microfiche: *NewsBank: Literature* 16 (January, 1989): Fiche 6, G13.
29. Winter, Douglas E. *Stephen King*. STARMONT READER'S GUIDE, No. 16. Series editor, Roger Schlobin. Mercer Island, WA: Starmont House, October 1982.
30. Winter, Douglas E. *Stephen King: The Art of Darkness*. New York: New American Library, November 1984.
31. Woods, Larry D. *Science Fiction & Fantasy Book Review* (January/February, 1983): 28-29.

A18. THE PLANT

A18. ***The Plant.*** Bangor, ME: Philtrum Press, December (?) 1982, 32 p., paper. Limited to 226 copies, all signed by King, 26 copies lettered from A-Z, and the rest numbered from 1. [horror pamphlet]

COMMENTS: The first installment of a novel-in-progress, privately published by King and sent as Christmas greetings. See also the sequels (**A23**, **A31**).

SECONDARY SOURCES AND REVIEWS:

1. Beahm, George. *The Stephen King Companion.* Kansas City, MO: Andrews and McMeel, September 1989, paper, p. 111-113.
2. Blue, Tyson. *The Unseen King.* STARMONT STUDIES IN LITERARY CRITICISM, No. 26. Mercer Island, WA: Starmont House, 1979, p. v-vii, 70-71, 88-100, 174.
3. Blue, Tyson. "The Plant: The Unseen King," in *Castle Rock: The Stephen King Newsletter* 2:6 (June 1986): 1, 3.
4. Collings, Michael R., and David A. Engebretson. *The Shorter Works of Stephen King.* STARMONT STUDIES IN LITERARY CRITICISM, No. 9. Mercer Island, WA: Starmont House, 1985, p. 173, 178.
5. Spignesi, Stephen J. "The Plant," in *The Shape Under the Sheet: The Complete Stephen King Encyclopedia.* Ann Arbor, MI: Popular Culture, Ink., May 1991, cloth, p. 498-505.
6. Winter, Douglas E. *Stephen King: The Art of Darkness.* New York: New American Library, November 1984, p. 176.

A19. CHRISTINE

A19. ***Christine: A Novel.*** West Kingston, RI: Donald M. Grant, Publisher, 1983, 544 p., cloth. Limited edition, letter state; not originally for sale. [horror novel]

PLOT SUMMARY: When Arnie Cunningham buys a dilapidated old car—Christine—his life suddenly changes. But gradually the car begins intruding into his life and the lives of those around him, with deadly results. Both haunted and haunting, Christine seeks to possess Arnie at all costs.

COMMENTS: *Christine* is King's response to America's love-affair with the automobile, as epitomized by a 1958 Plymouth Fury with a mind of her own. Interwoven with the horror motifs are considerations of youth and maturity, the role of parents (which is, in the words of Arnie Cunningham, to kill their children), deficiencies in the American school system, and the frustrations of being young in American society. One of King's few first-person novel-length narratives (and even that interrupted by a long passage in the third-person), *Christine* evokes the difficulties of growing up, a theme important in his novels as early as *Carrie* and *Rage*.

Adapted for film by John Carpenter in 1983.

The book sold 303,589 hardcover copies in 1983, and was ranked #5 on the *Bowkers Annual* hardcover fiction bestsellers list for 1983. King was also represented on the list by *Pet Semetary*, the first time since 1972 that an author had had two books on the list simultaneously.

REPRINTS:

ab. West Kingston, RI: Donald M. Grant, Publisher, 1983, 544 p., cloth. Limited edition, numbered, with dustjackets and slipcases; 1000 copies. Signed by the author and artist.
ac. West Kingston, RI: Donald M. Grant, Publisher, 1983, 544 p., cloth. Limited, lettered A-Z, with dustjackets and slipcases; 26 copies. Signed by author and artist.
b. New York: Viking, 29 April 1983, viii+526 p., cloth.
c. London: Hodder and Stoughton, May 1983, 482 p., cloth.
d. as: *Christine.* Barcelona: Gran Parade, Plaza & Janés, October 1983, 416 p., paper. Translated by Adolfo Martín. [Spanish]
db. as: *Christine.* Esplugas Llobregat (Barcelona), Spain: Plaza & Janés Editores, 1989, p. BIBLIOTECA DE STEPHEN KING, Vol. 9. [Spanish]
e. as: *Christine.* Utrecht: Luitingh/Veen, 1983, 446 p., trade paper. Translated by Margot Bakker; slightly abridged. 3rd printing, 1986. [Dutch]
f. New York: Viking [Science Fiction Book Club edition], [n.d.], 471 p., cloth.
g. Garden City, NY: Mystery Guild Book Club, [n.d.], cloth.
h. New York: A Signet Book, New American Library, December 1983, 505 p., mass-market paper. 21 printings by 1994.
i. as: *Christine.* Bergish Gladbach: Bastei-Lübbe (Paperback 28118), 496 p., paper. Translated by Harro Christensen. [German]
ib. as: *Christine.* Bergisch Gladbach: Bastei-Lübbe, 1984, 496 p., paper. Translated by Harro Christensen. [German]
ic. as: *Christine.* Bergisch Gladbach: Bastei-Lübbe (TB 13054), 1986, 620 p., paper. Translated by Harro Christensen. [German]
j. London: New English Library, March 1984, 608 p., paper.
k. as: *Christine.* México: Edivision, 1984, p., paper. [Spanish]
l. as: *Christine.* Panamá: Printer Internacional de Panamá, 1984, 528 p., cloth. Translated by Adolfo Martín. [Spanish]
m. as: *Christine.* Paris: Albin Michel, 1984, 351 p. cloth. [French]
n. as: *Christine.* Milano: Sperling & Kupfer, 1984, 634 p. Translated by T. Dobner. [Italian]
o. as: *Christine.* Buenos Aires: Emece, 1984, 415 p. Translated by César Aira. [Spanish]
p. as: *Christine.* Book Club Editions-Stüttgart, Germany: Europäische Bildungsgemeinschaft; Gütersloh, Austria: Bertelsmann Club; Vienna, Austria: Buchgemeinschaft Donauland; Zug, Switzerland: Buch-und-Schallplattenfreunde, April 1985, 607 p., paper. Translated by Bato Bauman. [German]
q. as: *Christine.* Paris: J'ai-Lu/Epouvante, 1985, 380 p. paper. Translated by Marie Allpois. [French]
r. as: *Christine.* Stockholm: Legenda, 1986, 679 p., cloth. Translated by Jimmy Hofsö. [Swedish]

rb. as: *Christine*. Stockholm: Legenda, 1987, 679 p., pocket paper. Translated by Jimmy Hofsö. [Swedish]

SECONDARY SOURCES AND REVIEWS:

1. Aig, M. R. "Buying a Used Car From Stephen King," in *St. Louis Globe-Democrat* [Missouri] (April 30-May 1, 1983): . As microfiche: *NewsBank: Literature* 9 (June, 1983): Fiche 97, D12.
2. Aig, M. R. "A Neurotic Car?" in *Minneapolis Tribune* (May 1, 1983): . As microfiche: *NewsBank: Literature* 9 (June, 1983): Fiche 97, D10.
3. Anders, Smiley. "Youthful Exuberance in King's Horror Tale," in *Morning Advocate* [Baton Rouge, LA] (May 15, 1983): . As microfiche: *NewsBank: Literature* 9 (June, 1983): Fiche 97, D8.
4. Barry, Dave. "*Christine* Is Demon for Punishment," in *Philadelphia Inquirer* (March 27, 1983): .
5. Beahm, George. *The Stephen King Companion*. Kansas City, MO: Andrews and McMeel, September 1989, paper, p. 176-178.
6. Bean, Covey. "Even King Fans Won't Buy This," *Daily Oklahoman* [Oklahoma City, OK] (July 3, 1983): . As microfiche: *NewsBank: Literature* 10 (August, 1983): Fiche 11, B11.
7. *Best Sellers* 43 (July, 1983): 123.
8. Blue, Tyson. *The Unseen King*. STARMONT STUDIES IN LITERARY CRITICISM, No. 26. Mercer Island, WA: Starmont House, 1989.
9. Boesch, Barry. "King Tale More Than Boy-Meets-Car Story," *Dallas Morning News* (July 3, 1983): . As microfiche: *NewsBank: Literature* 10 (August, 1983): Fiche 11, B12.
10. *Booklist* 79 (February 1, 1983): 697.
11. *Books and Bookmen* (July, 1983): 32.
12. Chandler, Randy. "Horror Master Tells Motor-Vating Tale," in *Atlanta Journal-Constitution* [Georgia] (April 17, 1983): .
13. Chelton, Mary K. *Voice of Youth Advocates* 6 (August, 1983): 146.
14. Collings, Michael R. *The Annotated Guide to Stephen King: A Primary and Secondary Bibliography of the Works of America's Premier Horror Writer*. STARMONT REFERENCE GUIDE, No. 8. Mercer Island, WA: Starmont House, October 1986.
15. Collings, Michael R. *The Many Facets of Stephen King*. STARMONT STUDIES IN LITERARY CRITICISM, No. 11. Mercer Island, WA: Starmont House, 1986.
16. Collings, Michael R. *The Stephen King Phenomenon*. STARMONT STUDIES IN LITERARY CRITICISM, No. 14. Mercer Island, WA: Starmont House, 1987.
17. Egan, James. "Technohorror: The Dystopian Vision of Stephen King," in *Extrapolation* 29:2 (Summer, 1988): 140-152, esp. p. 144.
18. *English Journal* 73 (December, 1984): 66.
19. Gorner, Peter. "King Drives at Horror with Less-Than-Usual Fury," in *Chicago Tribune* (April 6, 1983): .
20. Graham, Mark. "Stephen King Causes a 'Fury' of a Monster, 1958 Vintage," in *Rocky Mountain News* [Denver, CO] (May 8, 1983): .

21. Henderson, Randi. "A Boy, a Car, and a Horror," in *Sun* [Baltimore, MD] (May 1, 1983): . As microfiche: *NewsBank: Literature* 9 (June, 1983): Fiche 97, D9.
22. "King Tries to Make Novel Wheel Scary," in *Houston Post* (May 15, 1983): . As microfiche: *NewsBank: Literature* 9 (June, 1983): Fiche 97, E1.
23. *Kirkus Reviews* 51 (February 1, 1983): 138.
24. *Kliatt Paperback Book Guide* 18 (Spring, 1984): 19.
25. Lamott, Anne. "A Boy, a Girl, and Christine," in *San Francisco Chronicle* (April 7, 1983): 55. As microfiche: *NewsBank: Literature* 9 (May, 1983): Fiche 87, B14.
26. Landgarter, Steven. "*Christine*," in *Tulsa World* [Oklahoma] (May 22, 1983): . As microfiche: *NewsBank: Literature* 9 (June, 1983): Fiche 97, D14.
27. Lehmann-Haupt, Christopher. *New York Times Daily* 132 (April 12, 1983): III, 15.
28. Lewis, Don. "The Horror King Rules the Road," in *Milwaukee Journal* (April 24, 1983): . As microfiche: *NewsBank: Literature* 9 (May, 1983): Fiche 87, C4.
29. Lyons, Gene. "King of High-School Horror," in *Newsweek* 101 (May 2, 1983): 76.
30. *The Magazine of Fantasy & Science Fiction* 65 (August, 1983): 15.
31. Magistrale, Tony. *Landscape of Fear: Stephen King's American Gothic*. Bowling Green, OH: Bowling Green State University Popular Press, March 1988.
32. Magistrale, Tony. *The Moral Voyages of Stephen King*. STARMONT STUDIES IN LITERARY CRITICISM, No. 25. Mercer Island, WA: Starmont House, 1989.
33. Pautz, Peter J. *Science Fiction & Fantasy Book Review* [Science Fiction Research Association] no. 16 (July-August, 1983): 35.
34. Pendergast, Lolo. "'Christine' is Wild, Wonderful Adventure and Subsequent Love Affair With the Car," in *Clarion-Ledger* [Jackson, MS] (April 24, 1983): . As microfiche: *NewsBank: Literature* 9 (May, 1983): Fiche 87, C1-C2.
35. Potter, Chuck. "Killer Car's Not So Silly As It Sounds," in *Wichita Eagle* [Kansas] (April 24, 1983): . As microfiche: *NewsBank: Literature* 9 (June, 1983): Fiche 97, D7.
36. *Publishers Weekly* 223 (February 25, 1983): 80. Excerpted: *Contemporary Literary Criticism, Volume 26,* edited by Jean C. Stine. Detroit: Gale Research Co., 1983, cloth, p. 244.
37. *Publishers Weekly* 224 (October 7, 1983): 93.
38. Reino, Joseph. *Stephen King: The First Decade,* Carrie *to* Pet Sematary. TWAYNE'S UNITED STATES AUTHORS SERIES (TUSAS 531), edited by Warren French. Boston: Twayne Publishers, February 1988.
39. Riggenbach, Jeff. "Suspense Accelerates in King's *Christine,*" in *San Jose Mercury News* [California] (May 1, 1983): . As microfiche: *NewsBank: Literature* 9 (June, 1983): Fiche 97, D6.
40. Schleier, Curt. "King Covers Terror-tory in Story of Murderous Car," in *Kansas City Star* [Missouri] (May 22, 1983): . As microfiche: *NewsBank: Literature* 9 (June, 1983): Fiche 97, D11.

41. Schweitzer, Darrell, ed. *Discovering Stephen King*. STARMONT STUDIES IN LITERARY CRITICISM, No. 8. Mercer Island, WA: Starmont House, 1985.
42. *Science Fiction Review* 12 (November, 1983): 39.
43. See, Carolyn. "A Bumper Crop of Horror," in *Los Angeles Times Book Review* (May 8, 1983): 3. As microfiche: *NewsBank: Literature* 9 (June, 1983): Fiche 97, D4-D5.
44. Shea, Jeremy C. "Scary Ride in a Spooky Car," in *St. Louis Post-Dispatch* [Missouri] (May 8, 1983): . As microfiche: *NewsBank: Literature* 9 (June, 1983): Fiche 97, D13.
45. Shestak, George. "Tale to Please King Fans, Auto Buffs," in *Omaha World-Herald* [Nebraska] (April 17, 1983): . As microfiche: *NewsBank: Literature* 9 (May, 1983): Fiche 87, C3.
46. Silva, Mary. *Horn Book Magazine* 59 (August, 1983): 479.
47. Spignesi, Stephen J. "*Christine*," in *The Shape Under the Sheet: The Complete Stephen King Encyclopedia*. Ann Arbor, MI: Popular Culture, Ink., May 1991, cloth, p. 295-300.
48. Stasio, Marilyn. "High Suspense," in *Penthouse* (July, 1983): 56.
49. Steuwe, Paul. *Quill and Quire* (June, 1983): 37.
50. Van Rjndt, Phillipe. "The Other Woman Was a Car," in *New York Times Book Review* 88 (April 3, 1983): 12.
51. Walther, Jim. "Novel Lulls Readers into Trap," in *Montgomery Advertiser* [Alabama] (May 8, 1983): . As microfiche: *NewsBank: Literature* 9 (June, 1983): Fiche 97, D3.
52. Ward, Frank. *Library Journal* 108 (March 1, 1983): 517.
53. *Washington Post Book World* (March 23, 1983): 1.
54. *West Coast Review of Books* 9 (May, 1983): 36.
55. Winter, Douglas E. *Stephen King*. STARMONT READER'S GUIDE, No. 16. Series editor, Roger Schlobin. Mercer Island, WA: Starmont House, October 1982.
56. Winter, Douglas E. *Stephen King: The Art of Darkness*. New York: New American Library, November 1984.
57. Winter, Douglas E. "Stephen King's *Christine*: Where Innocence Peels Away Like Burnt Rubber and Death Rides Shotgun," in *Fantasy Newsletter* (February, 1983): .

A20. RITA HAYWORTH AND SHAWSHANK REDEMPTION

A20. ***Rita Hayworth and Shawshank Redemption***. Thorndike, ME: Thorndike Press, 1983, 181 p., cloth. Large print edition. [short novel]

COMMENTS: *Castle Rock: The Stephen King Newsletter* (May, 1986) reported this title as *Hope Springs Eternal*; a representative of Thorndike Press, however, indicated that the book was issued as noted above. Originally published as part of the collection, *Different Seasons* (see **A16**).

A21. CYCLE OF THE WEREWOLF

A21. *Cycle of the Werewolf.* Westland, MI: The Land of Enchantment, Christopher Zavisa, 1983, 114 p., cloth. Artwork by Berni Wrightson. A limited edition consisting of eight presentation copies. See also **A29**. [horror novella]

PLOT SUMMARY: Marty Coslaw becomes convinced that there is a werewolf in Tarker's Mills, a belief bolstered by the incremental terror resulting from monthly depredations by the creature. Although confined to a wheelchair, Marty convinces his sister and uncle to help him combat the werewolf.

COMMENTS: Beginning as an idea for a calendar with vignettes written specifically for each month, *Cycle of the Werewolf* quickly evolved into King's first extended treatment of the werewolf motif. The vignettes expanded to become the skeleton of a novel, further enfleshed by King's screenplay for *Silver Bullet* (1985; see **A29**).

REPRINTS:

ab. Westland, MI: The Land of Enchantment, Christopher Zavisa, 1983, 114 p., cloth. Collector's state, with artwork by Wrightson tipped in.
ac. Westland, MI: The Land of Enchantment, Christopher Zavisa, 1983, 114 p., cloth. Deluxe limited, with portfolio of Wrightson's artwork.
ad. Westland, MI: The Land of Enchantment, Christopher Zavisa, 1983, 114 p., cloth. Deluxe limited without the portfolio.
ae. Westland, MI: The Land of Enchantment, Christopher Zavisa, 1983, 114 p., cloth. Limited trade edition of 7,500 copies.
b. New York: A Plume Book, New American Library, April 1985, 128 p., trade paperback.
c. London: New English Library, October 1985, 128 p., paper.
d. in: *Silver Bullet*. New York: A Plume Book, New American Library, October 1985, p. 17-138, trade paperback. [See **A29**.]
e. as: *Das Jahr des Werwolfs* ["*The Year of the Werewolf*"]. Bergish Gladbach: Bastei-Lübbe Verlag (Paperback 28135), 1985, p., paper. Translated by Herro Christensen. Includes "Von Carrie bis Christine—Stephen King, der Meister des Makabren," by Douglas E. Winter. Translated by Helmut W. Pesch. [German]
eb. as: *Das Jahr des Werwolfs* ["*The Year of the Werewolf*"]. Bergisch Gladbach: Bastei-Lübbe Verlag (TB 25007), 1988, 200 p., paper. Translated by Harro Christensen. Issued without the translation of Winter's article (see above). [German]
f. as: *L'Année du Loup-Garou*. Paris: Albin Michel, 1986, 126 p., cloth. Translated by François Lasquin. [French]
g. as: *El Ciclo del Hombre Lobo* ["*Cycle of the Man Wolf*"]. Barcelona: Planeta, January 1986, 160 p., paper. Translated by Joaquín María Adsuar Ortega. [Spanish]
h. as: *Unico Indizio: La Luna Piena* (?). Italy: Longanesi, 1986, 144 p. Translated by C. Brera. [Italian]

i. as: *Varulvens År*. Stockholm: B. Wahlström, [1986], 127 p. Translated by Britt-Marie Thieme. [Swedish]
j. as: *Silver Bullet: Het Uur van de Weerwolf*. Utrecht: Luitingh, 1987, 127 p. Translated by Margot Bakker. [Dutch]

SECONDARY SOURCES AND REVIEWS:

1. Beahm, George, ed. *The Stephen King Companion*. Kansas City, MO: Andrews and McMeel, September 1989, p. 186-191.
2. Blue, Tyson. "Prolific Author Produces a 'Werewolf'," in *Courier Herald* [Dublin, GA]: .
3. Blue, Tyson. *The Unseen King*. STARMONT STUDIES IN LITERARY CRITICISM, No. 26. Mercer Island, WA: Starmont House, 1989.
4. *Book Report* 6 (September, 1987): 30. Review of *El Ciclo Del Hombre Lobo*. [Spanish translation]
5. Collings, Michael R. *The Annotated Guide to Stephen King: A Primary and Secondary Bibliography of the Works of America's Premier Horror Writer*. STARMONT REFERENCE GUIDE, No. 8. Mercer Island, WA: Starmont House, October 1986.
6. Collings, Michael R. *The Many Facets of Stephen King*. STARMONT STUDIES IN LITERARY CRITICISM, No. 11. Mercer Island, WA: Starmont House, 1986.
7. Collings, Michael R. *The Stephen King Phenomenon*. STARMONT STUDIES IN LITERARY CRITICISM, No. 14. Mercer Island, WA: Starmont House, 1987.
8. Collings, Michael R., and David A. Engebretson. *The Shorter Works of Stephen King*. STARMONT STUDIES IN LITERARY CRITICISM, No. 9. Mercer Island, WA: Starmont House, June 1985.
9. Klein, Jeanne. "King Recycles a Chilling Tale," in *Seattle Post-Intelligencer* [Washington] (May 6, 1985): B-12.
10. Larson, Randall. "*Cycle of the Werewolf* and the Moral Tradition of Horror," in *Discovering Stephen King,* edited by Darrell Schweitzer. STARMONT STUDIES IN LITERARY CRITICISM, No. 8. Mercer Island, WA: Starmont House, 1985, p. 102-108.
11. Magistrale, Tony. *Landscape of Fear: Stephen King's American Gothic*. Bowling Green, OH: Bowling Green State University Popular Press, March 1988.
12. Munster, Bill. "50% of the Cycle: Berni Wrightson," in *Footsteps VI* (December, 1985): 47-54.
13. Reino, Joseph. *Stephen King: The First Decade,* Carrie *to* Pet Sematary. TWAYNE'S UNITED STATES AUTHORS SERIES (TUSAS 531), edited by Warren French. Boston: Twayne Publishers, February 1988.
14. *San Francisco Chronicle* "Reviews" (June 9, 1985): 5.
15. Schweitzer, Darrell, ed. *Discovering Stephen King*. STARMONT STUDIES IN LITERARY CRITICISM, No. 8. Mercer Island, WA: Starmont House, 1985.
16. *Science Fiction Chronicle* 7 (January, 1986): 34.
17. *Science Fiction Review* 14 (November, 1985): 5.
18. *Science Fiction Review* 15 (February, 1986): 26.
19. Sherman, David. "Nightmare Library," in *Fangoria* No. 35 (1984): 37.

20. Spignesi, Stephen J. "*Cycle of the Werewolf*," in *The Shape Under the Sheet: The Complete Stephen King Encyclopedia.* Ann Arbor, MI: Popular Culture, Ink., May 1991, cloth, p. 322-325.
21. Stamm, Michael E. "Not for the Average King Fan," in *Fantasy Review* No. 65 (March, 1984): 32. Excerpted: *Contemporary Literary Criticism, Volume 37,* edited by Daniel G. Marowski. Detroit: Gale Research Co., 1986, cloth, p. 17-198.
22. *Voice of Youth Advocates* 8 (August, 1985): 185.
23. *West Coast Review of Books* 11 (May, 1986): 46.
24. Winter, Douglas E. *Stephen King: The Art of Darkness.* New York: New American Library, November 1984.

A22. PET SEMATARY

A22. ***Pet Sematary.*** Garden City, NY: Doubleday & Co., 14 November 1983, 373 p., cloth. [horror novel]

PLOT SUMMARY: Louis Creed and his family move to a small town in Maine. At the back of their property is a children's "Pet Sematary"; further back in the forest lies another, older, darker cemetery—one with the power to restore the dead to life. Louis first buries his daughter's cat, Church, in the Indian cemetery; and even though Church returns changed and frightening, Louis repeats his actions when his son Gage is accidentally killed.

COMMENTS: King himself has noted that this novel is darker than most of his others, exploring deeper and darker motives. Based loosely on W. W. Jacob's classic story, "The Monkey's Paw," *Pet Sematary* directly confronts the reality of death and its role in human life. Each major character must discover what death is, why it is important, how it must be reconciled with life. The novel methodically recreates an unendurable tension as it moves toward what still stands as King's most chilling final sentence.

King did not originally intend the novel for publication; contractual disputes with Doubleday forced him to release the manuscript, but he refused to promote the book actively. The story was adapted as a screenplay by King, and released in summer of 1989 as *Pet Sematary* (see **G15**).

The book sold 657,741 hardcover copies in 1983, King's highest year-end sales to that date, and was ranked #3 on the *Bowkers Annual* hardcover fiction bestsellers list for 1983. Appearing with *Christine* (#5), this marked the first time since 1972 that an author had had two books on the list simultaneously.

Over 750,000 hardcover copies had been sold in 11 hardcover printings by September, 1989. The novel appeared for more than thirty weeks on the *New York Times* bestsellers list.

REPRINTS:

b. London: Hodder & Stoughton, February 1984, 368 p., cloth.
c. New York: A Signet Book, New American Library, November 1984, 413 p., mass-market paperback. 25 printings by September, 1989.

d. Bath, England: Chivers Press, November 1984, 648 p., cloth. Large print edition.
e. Garden City, NY: Doubleday [Science Fiction Book Club edition], [n.d.], 374 p., cloth.
f. Garden City, NY: Mystery Guild Book Club, [n.d]., cloth.
g. as: *Cemetario de Animales* ["*Cemetery of the Animals*"]. Valencia, Spain: Circulo de Lectores, 1984, 304 p., paper. Translated by Anna María de las Fuente. [Spanish]
gb. as: *Cemetario de Animales* ["*Cemetery of the Animals*"]. Valencia, Spain: Circulo de Lectores, 1986, 304 p., cloth. Translated by Anna María de las Fuente. Smaller format. [Spanish]
h. as: *Cemetario de Animales* ["*Cemetery of the Animals*"]. Barcelona: Plaza & Janés, November 1984, 304 p., paper. Translated by Anna María de la Fuente. [Spanish]
hb. as: *Cemetario de Animales*. Esplugas Llobregat/Barcelona: Plaza & Janés, 1987, 304 p., paper. Translated by Anna María de la Fuente. [Spanish]
hc. as: *Cemetario de Animales*. Esplugas Llobregat (Barcelona), Spain: Plaza & Janés Editores, 1989, 304 p., paper. BIBLIOTECA DE STEPHEN KING, Vol. 1. [Spanish]
i. as: *Cemetario de Animales* ["*Cemetery of the Animals*"]. Buenos Aires: Emece, 1984, 343 p. Translated by César Aira. [Spanish]
j. as: *Dodenwake* ["*Deathwatch*"]. Utrecht: Luitingh/Veen, 1984, 368 p., trade paper. Translated by Margot Bakker. 4th printing, 1986. [Dutch]
k. as: *Jurtiyrkogården*. Höganäs, Sweden: Bra Böcker, 1984, 493 p. Translated by Lennart Olafsson. [Swedish]
l. Boston: G. K. Hall & Co., 1984, x+634 p., cloth. Large print edition.
m. as: *Semetario de Mascotas*. México: Edivisión, 1985, 395 p. Translated by Angelika Scherp. [Spanish]
n. London: New English Library, February 1985, 432 p., paper.
o. as: *Friedhof der Kuscheltiere*. Hamburg, West Germany: Hoffman and Campe Verlag, 1985, 381 p., cloth. Translated by Christel Wiemken. [German]
p. excerpted as: "Friedhof der Kuscheltiere," in *Der Stern* No. 19-No. 33 (1985). In 15 parts.
q. as: *Simetierre*. Paris: Albin Michel, 1985, 480 p, cloth?. [French]
r. as: *Jurtiyrkogården*. Stockholm: Legenda, 1986, 493 p., pocket paper. Translated by Lennart Olaffson. [Swedish]
s. as: *Friedhof der Kuscheltiere*. Book Club Editions-Kornwesterheim, Austria: Europäische Bildungsgemeinschaft; Gütersloh, Austria: Bertelsmann Club; Vienna, Austria: Buchgemeinschaft Donauland; Zug, Switzerland: Buch-und-Schallplattenfreunde, April 1987, 379 p., paper. Translated by Christel Wiemken. [German]
t. as: *Friedhof der Kuscheltiere*. Gütersloh, Austria: Bertelsmann Lesering, 1987, p. Translated by Chrisetl Wiemken. [German]
u. as: *Simetierre*. Paris: J'ai-Lu/Epouvante, 1987, 572 p., paper. Translated by François Lasquin. [French]
v. as: *Dyrekirkegården*. Copenhagen, Denmark: Gode Bφger, 1987, 298 p. Translated by Elsebeth Eskestad. [Danish]
w. as: *Friedhof der Kuscheltiere*. München: Wilhelm Heyne Verlag (TB 7627), 1988, p., paper. Translated by Christel Wiemkin. [German]

x. as: *Friedhof der Kuscheltiere*. Stuttgart: Deutscher Bücherbund, 1988, p. Translated by Christel Wiemkin. [German]

SECONDARY SOURCES AND REVIEWS:

1. *Analog Science Fiction/Science Fact* 104 (September, 1984): 169.
2. Anders, Smiley. "Scaring Readers Silly," in *Morning Advocate* [Baton Rouge, LA] (November 6, 1983): . As microfiche: *NewsBank: Literature* 10 (December, 1983): Fiche 44, E9.
3. Beahm, George. *The Stephen King Companion*. Kansas City, MO: Andrews and McMeel, September 1989, paper, p. 257-264.
4. *Best Sellers* 43 (January, 1984): 360.
5. Bleiler, Richard. "Burial Grounds Disturb Family," in *Columbus Evening Dispatch* [Ohio] (November 20, 1983): . As microfiche: *NewsBank: Literature* 10 (December, 1983): Fiche 44, E13.
6. Blue, Tyson. "King Deals Directly with Death," in *Courier Herald* [Dublin, GA] (November 12, 1983): .
7. *Booklist* 80 (September 15, 1983): 114.
8. Chelton, Mary K. *Voice of Youth Advocates* 7 (April, 1984): 32.
9. Clark, Roxanne. "'Pet Sematary' a Top King Novel, But Don't Read It Before Bed!" in *Indianapolis Star* [Indiana] (November 20, 1983): . As microfiche: *NewsBank: Literature* 10 (December, 1983): Fiche 44, E8.
10. Collings, Michael R. *The Annotated Guide to Stephen King: A Primary and Secondary Bibliography of the Works of America's Premier Horror Writer*. STARMONT REFERENCE GUIDE, No. 8. Mercer Island, WA: Starmont House, October 1986.
11. Collings, Michael R. *The Many Facets of Stephen King*. STARMONT STUDIES IN LITERARY CRITICISM, No. 11. Mercer Island, WA: Starmont House, 1986.
12. Collings, Michael R. *The Stephen King Phenomenon*. STARMONT STUDIES IN LITERARY CRITICISM, No. 14. Mercer Island, WA: Starmont House, 1987.
13. Dickerson, James. "King's Book of Pet Horrors," in *Commercial Appeal* [Memphis, TN] (December 18, 1983): . As microfiche: *NewsBank: Literature* 10 (January, 1984): Fiche 51, E7.
14. *The Ecphorizer* [Sunnyvale, CA] (December, 1984): .
15. *English Journal* 73 (December, 1984): 66.
16. Garner, Jack. "America's Boogeyman Is Raising Hair Again, Including His Own," in *Rochester Democrat and Chronicle* [New York] (October 30, 1983): . As microfiche: *NewsBank: Literature* 10 (December, 1983): Fiche 44, E11-E12.
17. Gottlieb, Anne. "Something Lurks in Ludlow," in *New York Times Book Review* 88 (November 6, 1983): 15. Excerpted: *Contemporary Literary Criticism, Volume 37,* edited by Daniel G. Marowski. Detroit: Gale Research Co., 1986, p. 203.
18. Graham, Mark. "Macabre Master," in *Rocky Mountain News* [Denver, CO] (December 4, 1983): 38M.
19. Henderson, Randi. "More of the Same Sort of Spooky Shenanigans," in *Sun* [Baltimore, MD] (November 6, 1983): . As microfiche: *NewsBank: Literature* 10 (December, 1983): Fiche 44, E9.

20. Herron, Don, ed. *Reign of Fear*. Los Angeles: Underwood-Miller, June 1988.
21. Hoppenstand, Gary and Ray B. Browne, eds. *The Gothic World of Stephen King: Landscape of Nightmares*. Bowling Green, OH: Bowling Green State University Popular Press, December 1987.
22. "Horror King Stumbles Again," in *Chicago Tribune* (November 10, 1983): . As microfiche: *NewsBank: Literature* 10 (December, 1983): Fiche 44, E7.
23. *Kirkus Reviews* 51 (September 1, 1983): 968.
24. Lehmann-Haupt, Christopher. *New York Times* 133 (October 21, 1983): III, 31.
25. Lewis, Don. "A Few Stones Unturned in King's '*Pet Sematary*'!" in *Milwaukee Journal* [Wisconsin] (November 6, 1983): . As microfiche: *NewsBank: Literature* 10 (December, 1983): Fiche 44, E14.
26. Libertore, Karen. "Gruesome and Gross," in *San Francisco Examiner* (November 6, 1983): . As microfiche: *NewsBank: Literature* 10 (December, 1983): Fiche 44, E6
27. Magistrale, Tony. *Landscape of Fear: Stephen King's American Gothic*. Bowling Green, OH: Bowling Green State University Popular Press, March 1988.
28. Magistrale, Tony. *The Moral Voyages of Stephen King*. STARMONT STUDIES IN LITERARY CRITICISM, No. 25. Mercer Island, WA: Starmont House, 1989.
29. Magistrale, Tony. "Stephen King's *Pet Sematary*: Hawthorne's Woods Revisited," in *The Gothic World of Stephen King: Landscape of Nightmares,* edited by Gary Hoppenstand and Ray B. Browne. Bowling Green, OH: Bowling Green State University Popular Press, December 1987, p. 126-134.
30. Maychick, Diana. "Unearthing the Origins of Stephen King's '*Pet Sematary*,'" in *New York Post* (April 16, 1989): . As microfiche: *NewsBank: Names in the News* 11 (May 1989): Fiche 134, C4-C5. As microfiche: *NewsBank: Film and Television* 16 (May, 1989): Fiche 53, 2-B3.
31. Miller, Ronnie. "'*Pet Sematary*' Is King's Latest Journey into Horror," in *Oregon Statesman* [Salem, OR] (December 11, 1983): . As microfiche: *NewsBank: Literature* 10 (January, 1984): Fiche 51, E6.
32. Pharr, Mary Ferguson. "A Dream of New Life: Stephen King's *Pet Sematary* as a Variant of *Frankenstein*," in *The Gothic World of Stephen King: Landscape of Nightmares*, edited by Gary Hoppenstand and Ray B. Browne. Bowling Green, OH: Bowling Green State University Popular Press, December 1987, p. 115-125.
33. *Publishers Weekly* 224 (September 23, 1983): 61.
34. *Publishers Weekly* 226 (September 28, 1984): 111.
35. Reino, Joseph. *Stephen King: The First Decade,* Carrie *to* Pet Sematary. TWAYNE'S UNITED STATES AUTHORS SERIES (TUSAS 531), edited by Warren French. Boston: Twayne Publishers, February 1988.
36. Rosenbaum, Mary Helene. "Pet Sematary," in *Christian Century* 101 (March 21-28, 1984): 316.

37. Sales, Grover. "King Rules over Scare-Fiction," in *Los Angeles Times Book Review* (November 20, 1983): 17. As microfiche: *NewsBank: Literature* 10 (December, 1983): Fiche 44, E5.
38. *San Francisco Chronicle* "Reviews" (November 6, 1983): 7.
39. Schaefer, Stephen. "Stephen King Philosophizes From the Grave," in *Record* [Hackensack, New Jersey] (April 21, 1989): . As microfiche: *NewsBank: Names in the News* 11 (July, 1989): Fiche 203, C13-C14.
40. Schleier, Curt. "'*Sematary*' Frightening Even to King of Horror," in *Kansas City Star* [Missouri] (December 18, 1983): . As microfiche: *NewsBank: Literature* 10 (January, 1984): Fiche 51, E5.
41. *School Library Journal* 30 (August, 1984): 38.
42. Schroeder, Natalie. "'Oz the Gweat and Tewwible' and 'The Other Side': The Theme of Death in *Pet Sematary* and *Jutterbug Perfume*," in *The Gothic World of Stephen King: Landscape of Nightmares,* edited by Gary Hoppenstand and Ray B. Browne. Bowling Green, OH: Bowling Green State University Popular Press, December 1987, p. 135-141.
43. Schweitzer, Darrell, ed. *Discovering Stephen King*. STARMONT STUDIES IN LITERARY CRITICISM, No. 8. Mercer Island, WA: Starmont House, 1985.
44. *Science Fiction Review* 13 (February, 1984): 42.
45. Slifkin, Irv. "Occupation: Offending," in *Philadelphia Inquirer* (October 12, 1989): . As microfiche: *NewsBank: Names in the News* 11 (November, 1989): Fiche 315, D10-D11.
46. Spignesi, Stephen J. "*Pet Sematary*," in *The Shape Under the Sheet: The Complete Stephen King Encyclopedia*. Ann Arbor, MI: Popular Culture, Ink., May 1991, cloth, p. 301-304.
47. Stamm, Michael R. "*Pet Sematary:* Opposing Views...Flawed, Unsatisfying," in *Fantasy Review* 64 (January, 1984): 49.
48. Stamm, Michael R. *Science Fiction & Fantasy Book Review* No. 20 (December, 1983): 35-36. Excerpted: *Contemporary Literary Criticism, Volume 37,* edited by Daniel G. Marowski. Detroit: Gale Research Co., 1986, cloth, p. 204.
49. "Stephen King on *Pet Sematary*," in *The Blood Review: The Journal of Horror Criticism* 1:1 (October 1989): 49.
50. Stuewe, Paul. *Quill and Quire* 50 (Fall, 1984): 41.
51. *Top of the News* 42 (Fall, 1985): 96.
52. Underwood, Tim, and Chuck Miller, eds. *Kingdom of Fear: The World of Stephen King*. Columbia, PA: Underwood-Miller, April 1986.
53. Ward, Frank. *Library Journal* 108 (October 15, 1983): 1973.
54. *Washington Post Book World* (October 2, 1983): 6.
55. *Wilson School Journal* 202 (October 28, 1983): 28.
56. Winter, Douglas E. *Stephen King: The Art of Darkness*. New York: New American Library, November 1984.
57. Winter, Douglas E. *Washington Post Book World* 13 (November 13, 1983): 1. Excerpted: *Contemporary Literary Criticism, Volume 37,* edited by Daniel G. Marowski. Detroit: Gale Research Co., 1986, p. 203-204.

58. Zizek, Slavoj. *Looking Awry: An Introduction to Jacques Lacan Through Popular Culture.* Cambridge, MA: MIT Press, 1991, cloth, p. 23-26.

A23. THE PLANT [PART 2]

A23. ***The Plant [Part 2].*** Bangor, ME: Philtrum Press, December (?) 1983, 36 p., paper. Limited edition consisting of 26 lettered copies signed by King plus 200 numbered copies. [horror pamphlet]

COMMENTS: The second installment of a novel-in-progress, privately published by King and sent as Christmas greetings. See also the other two parts (**A18**, **A31**).

SECONDARY SOURCES AND REVIEWS:

1. Beahm, George. *The Stephen King Companion.* Kansas City, MO: Andrews and McMeel, September 1989, paper, p. 111-113.
2. Blue, Tyson. *The Unseen King.* STARMONT STUDIES IN LITERARY CRITICISM, No. 26. Mercer Island, WA: Starmont House, 1979, p. v-vii, 70-71, 88-100, 174.
3. Blue, Tyson. "The Plant: The Unseen King," in *Castle Rock: The Stephen King Newsletter* 2:6 (June 1986): 1,3.
4. Collings, Michael R., and David A. Engebretson. *The Shorter Works of Stephen King.* STARMONT STUDIES IN LITERARY CRITICISM, No. 9. Mercer Island, WA: Starmont House, 1985, p. 173, 178.
5. Spignesi, Stephen J. "The Plant," in *The Shape Under the Sheet: The Complete Stephen King Encyclopedia.* Ann Arbor, MI: Popular Culture, Ink., May 1991, cloth, p. 498-505.
6. Winter, Douglas E. *Stephen King: The Art of Darkness.* New York: New American Library, November 1984, p. 176.

A24. THE EYES OF THE DRAGON

A24. ***The Eyes of the Dragon.*** Bangor, ME: Philtrum Press, 1984, 314 p., cloth. Illustrations by Kenneth R. Linkhäuser [Linkhaus]. Limited edition of 1250 copies, numbered in black (1000) or red (250) ink, with slipcase. [fantasy novel]

DEDICATION: "This story is for my great friend Ben Straub, and for my daughter, Naomi King."

PLOT SUMMARY: In the kingdom of Delain, the death of the reigning king brings disorder and disruption, orchestrated by the malevolent Flagg. The usurping younger brother, Thomas, falls under Flagg's spell; only the true king, Peter, who has been falsely imprisoned for his father's murder, can restore the peace and order to the realm.

COMMENTS: An engaging children's fantasy (that also touches adult readers) as it relates the fairy-tale story of the kingdom of Delain, the novel first appeared in a limited edition from King's Philtrum press.

REPRINTS:

ab. Bangor, ME: Philtrum Press, 1984, 314 p., cloth. Signed limited edition; numbered in red ink, slipcase.
ac. Bangor, ME: Philtrum Press, 1984, 314 p., cloth. Numbered in black ink, slipcase.
b. New York: Viking, 2 February 1987, 326 p., cloth. Illustrations by David Palladini. COMMENTS: First printing: 1,000,000 copies; sold 525,000 copies by the end of 1987; ranked #10 on the annual fiction hardcover bestsellers list.
c. London: Macdonald, April 1987, 336 p., cloth. Illustrations by David Palladini.
d. as: *Ogen van de Draak.* Utrecht: Luitingh, 1987, 311 p. Translated by Margot Bakker. [Dutch]
e. as: *Los Ojos de Dragon.* Buenos Aires: Emece, 1987, 463 p. Translated by Rosa S. Corgatelli. [Spanish]
f. as: *Die Auge des Drachen.* München: Wilhelm Heyne Verlag, 1987, paper. Translated by Joachim Körber. [German]
g. as: *Die Augen des Drachen.* Gütersloh, Austria: Bertelsmann Lesering (Gebundene Ausgabe), 1988. Translated by Joachim Körber. Unchanged reprint of preceding issue. [German]
h. New York: A Signet Book, New American Library, January 1988, 380 p., mass-market paper. Illustrations by David Palladini. 7 printings by September, 1989.
i. Bath, England: Windsor Selection Series/Chivers Press, May 1988, 456 p., cloth. Large print edition.
j. Boston: G. K. Hall & Co., 1988, 443 p., cloth. Large print edition.
k. as: *Drakens Ögen.* Stockholm: Legenda, 1988, 352 p. Translated by Karl G. Fredriksson and Lilian Fredriksson. [Swedish]
l. Book-of-the-Month Club selection.
m. London: Futura, 1988, 427 p., paper.
n. as: *Los Ojos del Dragon.* Esplugas Llobregat (Barcelona), Spain: Plaza & Janés, 1988, p. Reprinted in 1989. [Spanish]
o. as: *Die Augen des Drachen.* Stuttgart: Deutscher Bücherband, 1989. Translated by Joachim Körber. [German]
p. as: *Los Ojos del Dragon.* Barcelona: Circulos de Lectores, 1989, p. [Spanish]

SECONDARY SOURCES AND REVIEWS:

1. Alpert, Michael. "Designing *The Eyes of the Dragon*," in *Castle Rock: The Stephen King Newsletter* 1:8 (August, 1985): 1, 4, 6.
2. *Atlanta Journal-Constitution* [Georgia] (February 1, 1987): .
3. Beahm, George. *The Stephen King Companion.* Kansas City, MO: Andrews and McMeel, September 1989, paper, p. 209-213.
4. Blue, Tyson. "Editing *Eyes*: An Interview with Deborah Brodie," in *Castle Rock: The Stephen King Newsletter* 3:3 (March, 1987): 5, 8.
5. Blue, Tyson. "King's New Novel a Captivating Fantasy," in *Macon Telegraph & News* [Macon, GA] (January 18, 1987): .
6. Blue, Tyson. "Review: *The Eyes of the Dragon*," in *Castle Rock: The Stephen King Newsletter* 3:2 (February, 1987): 4-5.

7. Blue, Tyson. *The Unseen King*. STARMONT STUDIES IN LITERARY CRITICISM, No. 26. Mercer Island, WA: Starmont House, 1989.
8. *Book Report* 6 (September, 1987): 39.
9. *Booklist* 83 (November 1, 1986): 370.
10. *Booklist* 85 (November 15, 1988): 568.
11. Carlton, Michael. "Stephen King Delivers a Fantasy for Adolescents," in *Denver Post* [Colorado] (February 15, 1987): . As microfiche: *NewsBank: Literature* 13 (March, 1987): Fiche 75, C11.
12. Cassada, Jackie. *Library Journal* 111 (December 1986): 141.
13. Chalker, Jack L. "On Specialty Presses: The State of the Art," in *Fantasy Review* No. 85 (November, 1985): 11-12, 40.
14. Chandler, Randy. "King's '*Eyes of the Dragon*' a Grim Fairy Tale," in *Atlanta Journal-Constitution* [Georgia] (February 1, 1987): . As microfiche: *NewsBank: Literature* 13 (March, 1987): Fiche 75, C12.
15. Clayton, Walnum. "The 'Eyes' Have It," in *Fantasy Review* (May, 1986): 40.
16. Collier, Cynthia. "'*Eyes of the Dragon*' an Alluring Fairy Tale," in *San Diego Union* [California] (February 22, 1987): . As microfiche: *NewsBank: Literature* 13 (March, 1987): Fiche 75, C8.
17. Collings, Michael R. *The Annotated Guide to Stephen King: A Primary and Secondary Bibliography of the Works of America's Premier Horror Writer*. STARMONT REFERENCE GUIDE, No. 8. Mercer Island, WA: Starmont House, October 1986.
18. Collings, Michael R. *The Many Facets of Stephen King*. STARMONT STUDIES IN LITERARY CRITICISM, No. 11. Mercer Island, WA: Starmont House, 1986.
19. Collins, Robert A. "The Editor's Notebook: Read the Letters First, Friends," in *Fantasy Review* (May, 1986): 4.
20. de Camp, L. Sprague. "The Glass-Eyed Dragon," in *Reign of Fear: Fiction and Film of Stephen King*, edited by Don Herron. Los Angeles: Underwood-Miller, June 1988, p. 63-68.
21. de Lint, Charles. "Privately Printed Fantasy King's Best," in *Fantasy Review* No. 81 (July, 1985): 19.
22. Dockery, Bill. "King's '*Dragon*' Has Fluff, Puff, but Not a Lot of Fire," in *Knoxville News Sentinel* [Tennessee] (February 8, 1987): . As microfiche: *NewsBank: Literature* 13 (March, 1987): Fiche 75, D3.
23. Donovan, Mark. Review in "Picks & Pans," in *People Weekly* (April 13, 1987): .
24. Dugherty Marianne. "Stephen King's '*Dragon*' an Imaginative Fairy Tale," in *Pittsburgh Press* [Pennsylvania] (February 15, 1987): . As microfiche: *NewsBank: Literature* 13 (March, 1987): Fiche 75, D1.
25. *Fantasy Review* 9 (July, 1986): 28.
26. *English Journal* 78 (April, 1989): 89.
27. Freeman, Mark. "*The Eyes of the Dragon:* New King, Old King," in *Castle Rock: The Stephen King Newsletter* 3:6 (June, 1987): 5.
28. Graham, Mark. "Stephen King's Fairy Tale Come True," in *Rocky Mountain News* [Denver, CO] (February 7, 1987): 33-M.
29. Gustavons-Larsen, Anita. "Stephen King's '*Dragon*' to Charm Young Readers," in *St. Paul Pioneer Press-Dispatch* [Minnesota]

(February 7, 1987): . As microfiche: *NewsBank: Literature* 13 (March, 1987): Fiche 75, C14.

30. Kenny, Kevin. *Voice of Youth Advocates* (August/September 1987): 121.
31. *Kirkus Reviews* 54 (November 1, 1986): 1606.
32. Lawhorn, Jonelle. "King's Regal Fairy Tale," in *Boston Herald* (February 8, 1987): . As microfiche: *NewsBank: Literature* 13 (March, 1987): Fiche 75, C13.
33. Leonard, Stephanie. "And Now, the Publisher's Apprentice," in *Fantasy Review* 91 (May, 1986): 40.
34. Lewis, Don. "Stephen King Puts the Horror on Hold," in *Milwaukee Journal* [Wisconsin] (February 15, 1987): . As microfiche: *NewsBank: Literature* 13 (March, 1987): Fiche 75, D4.
35. Liberatore, Karen. "The Triumph of Good in a Fairy Tale by King," in *San Francisco Examiner* (January 25, 1987): . As microfiche: *NewsBank: Literature* 13 (March, 1987): Fiche 75, C9-C10.
36. *Macleans* 100 (July 20, 1987): 51.
37. Miller, G. Wayne. "A Pretty Fair Fantasy from King of Horror," in *Journal* [Providence, RI] (February 8, 1987): . As microfiche: *NewsBank: Literature* 13 (March, 1987): Fiche 75, D2.
38. Penny, Karl. *School Library Journal* (June/July 1987): 116.
39. *Publishers Weekly* 230 (December 5, 1986): 63.
40. *School Library Journal* 33 (February, 1987): 99.
41. *School Library Journal* 33 (June, 1987): 116.
42. Schweitzer, Darrell. "Book Review: *The Eyes of the Dragon*," in *Castle Rock: The Stephen King Newsletter* 3:9 (September, 1987): 5.
43. Schweitzer, Darrell, ed. *Discovering Stephen King*. STARMONT STUDIES IN LITERARY CRITICISM, No. 8. Mercer Island, WA: Starmont House, 1985.
44. *Science Fiction Chronicle* 8 (May, 1987): 46.
45. Spignesi, Stephen J. "The Eyes of the Dragon," in *The Shape Under the Sheet: The Complete Stephen King Encyclopedia*. Ann Arbor, MI: Popular Culture, Ink., May 1991, cloth, p. 403-406.
46. Taub, K. Deborah. "Science Fiction and Fantasy: Two Outdo King's Try," in *Washington* [D.C.] *Times* (March 30, 1987): . As microfiche: *NewsBank: Literature* 13 (April, 1987): Fiche 86, A7-A8.
47. *Time* 129 (February 23, 1987): 79.
48. Tritel, Barbara. *The New York Times Book Review* 92 (February 22, 1987): VII, 12.
49. Turner, Billy. "Stephen King: Horror Master Changes Style," in *Clarion-Ledger* [Jackson, MS] (March 6, 1987): . As microfiche: *NewsBank: Literature* 13 (April, 1987): Fiche 86, A6.
50. Underwood, Tim, and Chuck Miller, eds. *Kingdom of Fear: The World of Stephen King*. Columbia, PA: Underwood-Miller, April 1986.
51. *Village Voice* 32 (March 3, 1987): 46.
52. *Voice of Youth Advocates* 10 (August, 1987): 121.
53. *Washington Post Book World* 17 (December 6, 1987): 19.
54. *Washington Post Book World* 17 (February 15, 1987): 8.
55. *West Coast Review of Books* 12:5 (1987): 26.

56. *Wilson School Journal* 209 (February 3, 1987): 30.
57. Winter, Douglas E. *Stephen King: The Art of Darkness*. New York: New American Library, November 1984.

A25. THE BREATHING METHOD

A25. ***The Breathing Method***. Bath, Avon, England: A Lythway Book, Chivers Press, September 1984, 106 p., cloth. Large print edition. [short novel]

Originally published as part of the collection, *Different Seasons* (see **A16**).

REPRINTS:

b. as: *De Ademhalingsmethode* ["*The Breathing Method*"]. Utrecht: Luitingh, 1987, 214 p. Translated by Pauline Moody. Second printing, 1988. [Dutch]

A26. THE TALISMAN

A26. ***The Talisman***, by Stephen King and Peter Straub. New York: Viking, G. P. Putnam's Sons, 8 November 1984, x+646 p., cloth. [fantasy novel]

PLOT SUMMARY: Young Jack Sawyer must travel westward—through the heartland of America as well as through its analogue in the Territories—in order to discover the Talisman that will save his mother's life. Alone and apparently without external supports, Jack confronts physical and psychological horrors in both landscapes as he moves from the objective world of America to the fantastical one of the Territories; he overcomes each obstacle and along the way alters the lives of those he contacts as well as his own.

COMMENTS: A collaborative effort between two bestselling fantasists, *The Talisman* was highly touted before its publication and frequently excoriated afterward. The narrative is more epic quest than straightforward horror; the style reflects neither King's distinctive colloquialism nor Straub's controlled academic tone. Instead, a new, third voice emerges, one unexpected by either King's readership or Straub's; readers anticipating another *Pet Sematary* or *Floating Dragon* were disappointed. *The Talisman* is long, complex, convoluted, and at times oddly static; still, given the increasingly epic dimensions of the narrative, King and Straub remain true to their subject and treatment.

The novel sold 880,207 hardcover copies in 1984. Its first printing of 600,000 hardcover copies was the largest of any King title to that date, buttressed by a $500,000 advertising campaign.

REPRINTS:

b. West Kingston, RI: Donald M. Grant, Publisher, 1984, 2 vol., cloth. Artist's presentation state; two volumes, slipcased, signed by both authors and all artists, lettered.

bb. West Kingston, RI: Donald M. Grant, Publisher, 1984, 2 vol., cloth. Artist's presentation state; 70 numbered copies, signed by both authors and all artists, two volumes, slipcased.

bc. West Kingston, RI: Donald M. Grant, Publisher, 1984, 2 vol., cloth. Deluxe limited edition; 1200 numbered copies, two volumes, slipcased, signed by King and Straub.

bd. West Kingston, RI: Donald M. Grant, Publisher, 1984, 2 vol., cloth. Trade edition; 1200 numbered copies, two volumes, slipcased.

c. London: Viking Penguin, October 1984, 646 p., cloth.

d. as: *El Talisman*. Barcelona: Planeta, 1984. [Spanish]

e. New York: Berkley Books, March 1985, 770 p., mass-market paper.

f. London: Penguin Books, August 1985, 784 p., paper.

g. as: *De Talisman*. Utrecht: Luitingh/Veen, 1985, 470 p., trade paper. Translated by Margot Bakker; a substantial abridgement, with around 100 pages deleted from descriptions. 3rd printing, 1986. [Dutch]

h. as: *Der Talisman*. Hamburg, West Germany: Hoffman & Campe Verlag, 1986, 716 p., cloth. Translated by Christel Wiemken. [German]

i. as: *Il Talismano*. Milano: Sperling & Kupfer, 1986, 635 p. Translated by T. Dobner. [Italian]

j. as: *Le Talisman des Territoires*. Lyon, France: Laffont, 1986, 645 p. cloth. Translated by Béatrice Gartenberg and Isabelle Delord. [French]

k. as: *Le Talisman*. Paris: LGF, 1987, 1084 p. paper. Translated by Béatrice Gartenberg and Isabelle Delord. [French]

l. as: *Der Talisman*. Stuttgart: Deutscher Bücherbund, 1987, p. Translated by Cristel Wiemkin. [German]

m. as: *Der Talisman*. Gütersloh, Austria: Bertelsmann Lesering, 1987. Translated by Cristel Wiemken. [German]

n. as: *Talismann*. Stockholm: Legenda/Norstadt, 1987, 798 p. Translated by Lennart Olaffson. [Swedish]

nb. as: *Talismann*. Stockholm: Legenda/Norstadt, 1988, 798 p., paperback. Translated by Lennart Olaffson. [Swedish]

o. Höganäs, Sweden: Bro Böcker, 1987, 798 p. Translated by Lennart Olaffson. [Swedish]

p. as: *Der Talisman*. München: Wilhelm Heyne Verlag (TB 7662), 1988, p., paper. Translated by Cristel Wiemken. [German]

SECONDARY SOURCES AND REVIEWS:

1. Adler, Constance. "Prince of Darkness: In His Reign of Best-selling Terror, Author Stephen King Remains Absolute Master of the Scary Story," in *Philadelphia Magazine* 76 (August, 1985): 85+. [3-page article]
2. Amantia, A. M. B. *Library Journal* 109 (November 1, 1984): 2080.
3. Anders, Smiley. "Blockbuster of a Fantasy Tale Gets Guidance from Twain," in *Morning Advocate* [Baton Rouge, LA] (November 18, 1984): . As microfiche: *NewsBank: Literature* 11 (December, 1984): Fiche 58, A8-A9.
4. Beagle, Peter. "King Plus Straub Equals Pure Cliché," in *San Jose Mercury News* [California] (October 28, 1984): . As microfiche: *NewsBank: Literature* 11 (November, 1984): Fiche 45, G14-46, A1.

5. Beahm, George. *The Stephen King Companion*. Kansas City, MO: Andrews and McMeel, September 1989, paper, p. 280-283.
6. Blue, Tyson. "Collaboration of Two Masterful Authors Produces a Suspenseful '*The Talisman*'," in *Courier Herald* [Dublin, GA] (November 10, 1984): .
7. Blue, Tyson. "*Talisman* Limited Review," in *Castle Rock: The Stephen King Newsletter* 3:1 (December, 1986-January, 1987): 6.
8. *Book World* 14 (October 14, 1984): 1.
9. *Booklist* 81 (January 15, 1985): 686.
10. Bosky, Bernadette. "Stephen King and Peter Straub: Fear and Friendship," in *Discovering Stephen King,* edited by Darrell Schweitzer. STARMONT STUDIES IN LITERARY CRITICISM, No. 8. Mercer Island, WA: Starmont House, 1985, p. 55-82.
11. Cheuse, Alan. "A Sci-Fi Quest Novel from King and Straub," in *Los Angeles Herald Examiner* (November 18, 1984): . As microfiche: *NewsBank: Literature* 11 (December, 1984): Fiche 57, G12-G14.
12. Clark, Theresa J. *Saturday Review* (November/December 1984): 85.
13. Collings, Michael R. *The Annotated Guide to Stephen King: A Primary and Secondary Bibliography of the Works of America's Premier Horror Writer.* STARMONT REFERENCE GUIDE, No. 8. Mercer Island, WA: Starmont House, October 1986.
14. Collings, Michael R. *The Many Facets of Stephen King*. STARMONT STUDIES IN LITERARY CRITICISM, No. 11. Mercer Island, WA: Starmont House, 1986.
15. Collings, Michael R. *The Stephen King Phenomenon*. STARMONT STUDIES IN LITERARY CRITICISM, No. 14. Mercer Island, WA: Starmont House, 1987.
16. Cortland, Will. "The King of Bump in the Night," in *Dodge Adventurer* (Spring, 1985): 17-18. As: "The Adventurer Looks at Stephen King," in *Castle Rock: The Stephen King Newsletter* 1:6 (June, 1985): 11.
17. D'Angelo, John. "'*Talisman*' Tells of Modern-Day Huckleberry Finn," in *Pittsburgh Press* (December 2, 1984): . As microfiche: *NewsBank: Literature* 11 (December, 1984): Fiche 58, A14.
18. Eaglen, Audrey. *Voice of Youth Advocates* (April 1985): 49.
19. *English Journal* 74 (December, 1985): 57.
20. *Esquire* 102 (November, 1984): 231.
21. Fazell, Daryl. "King and Straub Weave a Snug Yarn," in *St. Petersburg Times* [Florida] (October 28, 1984): . As microfiche: *NewsBank: Literature* 11 (November, 1984): Fiche 46, A2.
22. Goldstein, William, interviewer. "A Coupl'a Authors Sittin' Around Talkin'," in *Publishers Weekly* (May, 11, 1984): . Reprinted: *The Stephen King Companion,* edited by George Beahm. Kansas City, MO: Andrews and McMeel, September 1989, paper, p. 283-287.
23. Graham, Mark. "Masters of the Macabre," in *Rocky Mountain News* [Denver, CO] (October 7, 1984): 34M.
24. Grooms, Roger. "'*Talisman*' Not Without Macabre Charm," in *Cincinnati Enquirer* [Ohio] (October 21, 1984): . As microfiche: *NewsBank: Literature* 11 (November, 1984): Fiche 46, A10.
25. Harvey, L. J. "Unlucky '*Talisman*' Defeats Horror King," in *Kansas City Star* [Missouri] (November 4, 1984): . As microfiche: *NewsBank: Literature* 11 (November, 1984): Fiche 46, A5.

26. Herron, Don, ed. *Reign of Fear*. Los Angeles: Underwood-Miller, June 1988.
27. Kernan, Michael. "Kindred Spirits: Horror Pros Stephen King and Peter Straub Put Their Skills Together for a Best Seller," in *Washington Post* 107 (November 27, 1984): C1.
28. "King Rejects Book Club Offer for *The Talisman*," in *Science Fiction Chronicle* 6:4 (January, 1985): 1.
29. Kirk, Robin. "King and Straub, Masters of Horror, Team Up for Highly Derivative Yawner," in *Tribune* [Oakland, CA] (November 18, 1984): . As microfiche: *NewsBank: Literature* 11 (December, 1984): Fiche 58, A1.
30. *Kirkus Reviews* 52 (August 15, 1984): 771.
31. *Kliatt Young Adult Paperback Book Guide* 20 (Spring, 1986): 22.
32. Leerhsen, Charles. "The Titans of Terror," in *Newsweek* (December 24, 1984): 61-62.
33. Lehmann-Haupt, Christopher. *New York Times Daily* (November 8, 1984): III, 27.
34. Lewis, Don. "'*Talisman*' Good, But No Supernovel," in *Milwaukee Journal* [Wisconsin] (November 11, 1984): . As microfiche: *NewsBank: Literature* 11 (December, 1984): Fiche 58, B4.
35. Liberatore, Karen. "Jack Sawyer in Fantasyland," in *San Francisco Examiner* (October 7, 1984): . As microfiche: *NewsBank: Literature* 11 (November, 1984): Fiche 45, G12-G13.
36. Lileks, James. "A Horror Novel That's a Splatter Version of '*The Wizard of Oz*,'" in *Minnesota Star and Tribune* (November 25, 1984): . As microfiche: *NewsBank: Literature* 11 (December, 1984): Fiche 58, A10.
37. *The Magazine of Fantasy & Science Fiction* 68 (March, 1985): 16.
38. Magistrale, Tony. *Landscape of Fear: Stephen King's American Gothic*. Bowling Green, OH: Bowling Green State University Popular Press, March 1988.
39. Magistrale, Tony. *The Moral Voyages of Stephen King*. STARMONT STUDIES IN LITERARY CRITICISM, No. 25. Mercer Island, WA: Starmont House, 1989.
40. McC.Dresser, Sheila. "One Good Book by Two Masters of the Best-Seller List," in *Sun* [Baltimore, MD] (November 4, 1984): . As microfiche: *NewsBank: Literature* 11 (November, 1984): Fiche 46, A3.
41. McLaurin, Preston. "Epic Tale from Masters of Macabre," in *State* [Columbia, SC] (November 11, 1984): . As microfiche: *NewsBank: Literature* 11 (December, 1984): Fiche 58, B1.
42. Merritt, Robert. "Horrors! King, Straub Turn to Fantasy," in *Richmond Times-Dispatch* [Virginia] (October 28, 1984): . As microfiche: *NewsBank: Literature* 11 (November, 1984): Fiche 46, A11.
43. Millhiser, Marlys. "When Nit Comes to Grit," in *Denver Post* [Colorado] (November 18, 1984): . As microfiche: *NewsBank: Literature* 11 (December, 1984): Fiche 58, A3.
44. Nathan, Paul S. "*The Talisman* and the Clubs," in *Publishers Weekly* (November 23, 1984): 28.
45. Perry, Pamela M. "Lack of Structure Main Weakness of '*Talisman*,'" in *Atlanta Journal-Constitution* [Georgia] (November 4, 1984): .

As microfiche: *NewsBank: Literature* 11 (December, 1984): Fiche 58, A6.

46. Pollack, Dale. "Fantasy Quest for the Reel Thing," in *Los Angeles Times Book Review* (November 18, 1984): 13.
47. *Publishers Weekly* 226 (September 7, 1984): 73.
48. *Publishers Weekly* 228 (September 20, 1985): 107.
49. Reino, Joseph. *Stephen King: The First Decade,* Carrie *to* Pet Sematary. TWAYNE'S UNITED STATES AUTHORS SERIES (TUSAS 531), edited by Warren French. Boston: Twayne Publishers, February 1988.
50. Reuter, Madalynne. "502,000 Copies of *Talisman* Shipped in One Day," in *Publishers Weekly* (October 26, 1984): 25.
51. Richmond, Peter. "Striking Out With King (and Straub)," in *Miami Herald* [Florida] (November 25, 1984): . As microfiche: *NewsBank: Literature* 11 (December, 1984): Fiche 58, A4-A5.
52. Rothenstein, Richard. "Two Terror Titans Team Up," in *Daily News* [New York] (October 14, 1984): . As microfiche: *NewsBank: Literature* 11 (November, 1984): Fiche 45, G10-G11.
53. Sanders, Joe. "Vigorous, Messy, Untidy—And Compulsively Readable," in *Fantasy Review* 76 (February, 1985): 17-18.
54. *Saturday Review* 10 (November, 1984): 85.
55. Schachtsiek-Freitag, Norbert. "Horror and Fantasy: Stephen Kings und Peter Straubs *Der Talisman*," in *Frankfurter Rundschau* [West Germany] (August 12, 1986): .
56. Schulte, Jean. "Two Grim Reapers Predictably Macabre in Modern Dark Ages," in *Columbus Dispatch* [Ohio] (November 4, 1984): . As microfiche: *NewsBank: Literature* 11 (December, 1984): Fiche 58, A12.
57. Schweitzer, Darrell, ed. *Discovering Stephen King*. STARMONT STUDIES IN LITERARY CRITICISM, No. 8. Mercer Island, WA: Starmont House, 1985.
58. Schweitzer, Darrell. "Epic Fantasy in Modern Dress," in *Philadelphia Inquirer* (November 11, 1984): . As microfiche: *NewsBank: Literature* 11 (December, 1984): Fiche 58, A13.
59. *Science Fiction Review* 14 (February, 1985): 41.
60. Shapiro, Anna. *New York Times Book Review* 89 (November 4, 1984): 24. Excerpted: *Contemporary Literary Criticism, Volume 37,* edited by Daniel G. Marowski. Detroit: Gale Research Co., 1986, cloth, p. 205-206.
61. Sherman, David. "Nightmare Library," in *Fangoria* no. 44 (1985): 39-40.
62. Shestak, George. "King/Straub Tale Overloads to a Point of Numbness," in *Omaha World-Herald* [Nebraska] (November 4, 1984): . As microfiche: *NewsBank: Literature* 11 (December, 1984): Fiche 58, A11.
63. Skow, John. *Time* 124 (November 5, 1984): 88.
64. Slay, Jack, Jr. "'The Road Laid Its Mark on You': Jack's Metamorphosis in *The Talisman* (or, Beyond Boy-Wonderdom)," in *Castle Rock: The Stephen King Newsletter* 4:7 (July, 1988): 1, 4-5.
65. Small, Michael. "Peter Straub & Stephen King Team Up for Fear," in *People Weekly* (January 28, 1985): 50-52.
66. Smithers, Susan L. *School Library Journal* 31 (January, 1985): 92.

67. Somerville, Richard. "Huck Meets Hobbit," in *Des Moines Register* [Iowa] (November 4, 1984): . As microfiche: *NewsBank: Literature* 11 (December, 1984): Fiche 58, A7.
68. Spignesi, Stephen J. "*The Talisman*," in *The Shape Under the Sheet: The Complete Stephen King Encyclopedia*. Ann Arbor, MI: Popular Culture, Ink., May 1991, cloth, p. 304-317.
69. Straub, Peter. "Straub Talks About *Talisman*," in *Castle Rock: The Stephen King Newsletter* 1:7 (July, 1985): 1, 3.
70. Stuewe, Paul. *Quill and Quire* 50 (December 24, 1984): 37.
71. Terrell, Carroll F. *Stephen King: Man and Artist*. Orono, ME: Northern Lights Publications, 1990, cloth, p. 219-238.
72. Toepfer, Susan. "'*The Talisman*': A Classic," in *Daily News* [New York] (October 14, 1984): . As microfiche: *NewsBank: Literature* 11 (November, 1984): Fiche 46, A6-A7.
73. Tucker, Ken. "Boo! Ha-Ha, You Sap!" in *The Village Voice* 29:43 (October 23, 1984): 53. Excerpted: *Contemporary Literary Criticism, Volume 37*, edited by Daniel G. Marowski. Detroit: Gale Research Co., 1986, cloth, p. 205.
74. Turner, Billy. "King-Straub Combo Pleases, But Fails to Horrify," in *Clarion-Ledger* [Jackson, MS] (October 21, 1984): . As microfiche: *NewsBank: Literature* 11 (November, 1984): Fiche 46, A4.
75. Underwood, Tim, and Chuck Miller, eds. *Kingdom of Fear: The World of Stephen King*. Columbia, PA: Underwood-Miller, April 1986.
76. *USA Today* 3 (October 19, 1984): 3D.
77. Wallace, Gail Smith. "Happy Halloween Horrors to You!" in *News and Observer* [Raleigh, NC] (October 28, 1984): . As microfiche: *NewsBank: Literature* 11 (November, 1984): Fiche 46, A8-A9.
78. *West Coast Review of Books* 11 (January, 1985): 33.
79. Winter, Douglas E. *Stephen King: The Art of Darkness*. New York: New American Library, November 1984.

A27. THINNER

A27. ***Thinner***, by "RICHARD BACHMAN." New York: An NAL Book, New American Library, 19 November 1984, 309 p. cloth. [horror novel]

PLOT SUMMARY: Billy Halleck, an overweight lawyer, accidentally kills an old gypsy woman. He is exonerated by a friendly court, but nevertheless punished when the old woman's son touches his cheek and whispers, "Thinner." Halleck begins losing weight—rapidly and frighteningly. He can only save his life by having the curse removed.

COMMENTS: The novel that finally revealed the "RICHARD BACHMAN" pen-name, *Thinner* is vintage King in tone, style, diction, plot structure, characterization, and atmosphere. The incursion of the supernatural is direct and fatal in this tale, and the deterioration of the central character both inexorable and externalized; we see overtly the consequences of guilt as they play through the lives of Halleck, Halleck's friends, his family, and the gypsies themselves.

The first printing was 26,000, with a total of 208,000 cloth copies in the first four printings. The book sold 28,000 copies before the Bachman pseudonym was finally revealed, and almost immediately sold 280,000 more copies when King acknowledged his authorship. The book sold 300,000 hardcover copies in 1985.

REPRINTS:

b. London: New English Library, August 1985, 310 p., cloth.
bb. London: New English Library, February 1986, 288 p., paper.
c. *Thinner,* by Stephen King. New York: A Signet Book, New American Library, September 1985, 318 p., mass-market paperback. 21 printings by 1994.
d. Garden City, NY: The Mystery Guild, [n.d.], cloth.
e. Garden City, NY: New American Library [Science Fiction Book Club], [n.d.], cloth.
f. as: *De Vervloeking* ["*The Curse*"], by RICHARD BACHMAN. Utrecht/ Aartselaar: A. W. Bruna and Zoons, Summer 1985, 272 p., trade paper with plasticized cover. Translated by Thomas Nicholaas. Third printing, 1987. Includes a wrap-around band stating: "Stephen King writing as Richard Bachman." [Dutch]
g. as: *Der Fluch* ["*The Curse*"], by RICHARD BACHMAN. München: Wilhelm Heyne (TB 6001), 1985, p., paper. Translated by Nora Jensen. Note under the by-line indicates that "Bachman est King—Stephen King is Bachman." [German]
h. Bath, England: Chivers Press, June 1986, 408 p., cloth. Large print edition.
i. as: *Maleficio,* by Stephen King "(con el nombre de Richard Bachman)." Buenos Aires: Eméce Editores, September 1986, 301 p., trade paper. Translated by Lorenzo Cortina. [Spanish]
ib. as: *Maleficio*, con el nombre de RICHARD BACHMAN. Buenos Aires: Emece, 1986, 297 p., paper. [Spanish]
j. as: *Thinner,* by RICHARD BACHMAN. Boston: G. K. Hall & Co., 1986, 397 p., cloth. Also published in trade paper. Large print edition.
k. as: *Förbannelse*, by Stephen King alias Richard Bachman. Stockholm: Legenda, 1986, 304 p. Translated by Love Kellberg. Rpt. 1988. [Swedish]
kb. Höganäs, Sweden: Bra Böcker, 1987, 304 p. Translated by Love Kellberg. [Swedish]
kc. Stockholm: Legenda, 1988, 304 p., mass-market paper. Translated by Love Kellberg. [Swedish]
l. as: *Maleficio*. Esplugas Llobregat/Barcelona: Plaza & Janés, 1986, 256 p., paper. Rpt. 1989. Translated by Lorenzo Cortina. [Spanish]
lb. as: *Maleficio*. Esplugas Llobregat (Barcelona), Spain: Plaza & Janés Editores, 1989, 256 p. (?), paper. BIBLIOTECA DE STEPHEN KING, Vol. 7. [Spanish]
m. as: *Maleficio*. Barcelona: Circulo de Lectores, 1989, p. [Spanish]

SECONDARY SOURCES AND REVIEWS:

1. Adler, Constance. "Prince of Darkness: In His Reign of Best-selling Terror, Author Stephen King Remains Absolute Master of the Scary

Story," in *Philadelphia Magazine* 76 (August, 1985): 85+. [3-page article]
2. *Bangor Daily News* [Maine] (February 9, 1985): .
3. Barron, Neil. "'Bachman' Indeed Reads Like Stephen King," in *Fantasy Review* 77 (March, 1985): 15.
4. Beahm, George, ed. *The Stephen King Companion*. Kansas City, MO: Andrews and McMeel, September 1989, p. 170.
5. Blue, Tyson. "Richard Bachman's '*Thinner*' is a Thriller of the First Magnitude," in *Courier Herald* [Dublin, GA] (February, 1985): .
6. Brown. Stephen P. "The Life and Death of Richard Bachman: Stephen King's Doppelganger," in *Kingdom of Fear: The World of Stephen King*, edited by Tim Underwood and Chuck Miller. San Francisco: Underwood-Miller, 1986, p. 109-126.
7. Collings, Michael R. *The Annotated Guide to Stephen King: A Primary and Secondary Bibliography of the Works of America's Premier Horror Writer*. STARMONT REFERENCE GUIDE, No. 8. Mercer Island, WA: Starmont House, October 1986.
8. Collings, Michael R. *The Many Facets of Stephen King*. STARMONT STUDIES IN LITERARY CRITICISM, No. 11. Mercer Island, WA: Starmont House, 1986.
9. Collings, Michael R. *Stephen King as Richard Bachman*. STARMONT STUDIES IN LITERARY CRITICISM, No. 10. Mercer Island, WA: Starmont House, 1985.
10. Eidus, Janice. *The New York Times Book Review* (April 14, 1985): 27. Excerpted: *Contemporary Literary Criticism, Volume 37*, edited by Daniel G. Marowski. Detroit: Gale Research Co., 1986, p. 206.
11. *Fantasy Mongers* 13 (Winter, 1984/1985): 5.
12. Graham, Mark. "Fit for a King," in *Rocky Mountain News* [Denver, CO] (December 23, 1984): 26M.
13. *Kirkus Reviews* 52 (September 15, 1984): 864. [A review of the novel by 'Richard Bachman'].
14. Pepper, Michael. "The Growing Optimism of Stephen King: Bachman's Pessimism Gets Thinner," in *Castle Rock: The Stephen King Newsletter* 3:7 (July, 1987): 1, 4.
15. *Publishers Weekly* 226 (September 28, 1984): 99. [A review of the novel by 'Richard Bachman'].
16. *Publishers Weekly* (March 22, 1985): 43.
17. Rousch, Matt. "Bachman's Best Seller," in *USA Today* 4 (October 18, 1985): .
18. Sallee, Wayne Allen. "*Thinner*: A Thinly Disguised King Novel," in *Castle Rock: The Stephen King Newsletter* 1:5 (May, 1985): 2.
19. Shestack, George. "You Win, Lose With a Pair of Kings," in *Omaha World-Herald* [Nebraska] (May 26, 1985): . As microfiche: *NewsBank: Literature* 11 (June, 1985): Fiche 110, A3.
20. Spignesi, Stephen J. "*Thinner*," in *The Shape Under the Sheet: The Complete Stephen King Encyclopedia*. Ann Arbor, MI: Popular Culture, Ink., May 1991, cloth, p. 317-322.
21. Timpone, Anthony. *Fangoria* No. 52 (1986): 55.
22. *Washington Post Book World* (April 9, 1985): C1-C2.
23. "Weird Reviews," in *Fan Plus* 2:2 (1985): .

24. Winter, Douglas E. *Stephen King: The Art of Darkness*. Expanded and updated edition. New York: A Plume Book, New American Library, June, 1986.

A28. SKELETON CREW

A28. *Skeleton Crew*. New York: G. P. Putnam's Sons, 21 June 1985, 512 p., cloth.

CONTENTS: "Introduction," by King (see **C132**); "The Mist" (1980; see **B50**); "Here There Be Tygers" (1968; see **B5**); "The Monkey" (1980; see **B48**); "Cain Rose Up" (1968; see **B6**); "Mrs. Todd's Shortcut" (1984; see **B77**); "The Jaunt" (1981; see **B52**); "The Wedding Gig" (1980; see **B46**); "Paranoid: A Chant" (poem; see **D9**); "The Raft" (1982; see **B60**); "Word Processor of the Gods" (1983; see **B72**); "The Man Who Would Not Shake Hands" (1982; see **B58**); "Beachworld" (1985; see **B82**); "The Reaper's Image (1969; see **B9**); "Nona" (1978; see **B42**); "For Owen" (poem; see **D8**); "Survivor Type (1982; see **B71**); "Uncle Otto's Truck (1983; see **B73**); "Morning Deliveries (Milkman #1)" (1985; see **B83**); "Big Wheels: A Tale of the Laundry Game (Milkman #2)" (1980; see **B47**); "Gramma" (1984; see **B76**); "The Ballad of the Flexible Bullet" (1984; see **B78**); "The Reach" (as "Do the Dead Sing?," 1981; see **B56**); "Notes," by King (see **C133**).

COMMENTS: *Skeleton Crew* is the most comprehensive collection of King's short fiction to that date. More extensive than *Night Shift*, with greater breadth and depth than *The Dark Tower: The Gunslinger* or *The Dark Tower II: The Drawing of the Three*, it represents the range of King's career through 1985. His second professional sale is included ("The Reaper's Image"), as well as a story first published sixteen years later, "Beachworld." The collection opens with what some critics consider one of King's most sustained explorations of the terror of the unknown, "The Mist"; and it concludes with "The Reach," an exquisitely crafted tale of ghosts and love, of death and life that may represent King at his finest.

The book sold 600,000 copies in 1985, and was ranked #5 on the *Bowker Annual* hardcover fiction bestsellers list for 1985. Nominated as Best Anthology/Collection, World Fantasy Convention, 1986.

REPRINTS:

b. as: *Stephen King's Skeleton Crew*. Santa Cruz, CA: Scream/Press, 1985, xxiv+545 p., cloth. Illustrated by J. K. Potter. Includes: "The Revelations of 'Becka Paulson" (from *The Tommyknockers* [1984; see **B79**]). Deluxe lmited edition of 69 leather-bound and zippered copies, 17 presentation copies and 52 lettered copies. [horror story collection]

bb. as: *Stephen King's Skeleton Crew*. Santa Cruz, CA: Scream/Press, 1985, xxiv+545 p., cloth. Limited edition of 1,000 copies, numbered in silver ink and signed by author and artist Potter.

c. London: Macdonald, June 1985, 700 p., cloth.

d. as: *Im Morgengrauen: Unheimlische Geschichten* [*Skeleton Crew*, part 1]. München: Wilhelm Heyne Verlag (TB 6553), 1985, p., paper. Translated by Alexandra von Reinhardt. [German]

CONTENTS: "Der Mann, der Niemandem die Hand Geben Wollte" ["The Man Who Would Not Shake Hands"]; "Achtung—Tiger!" ["Here There Be Tygers"]; "Omi" ["Gramma"]; "Der Nebel" ["The Mist"].

e. excerpted as: *Nona und die Ratten* ["*Nona and the Rats*"]. München: Wilhelm Heyne Mini-bücher (Mini TB 2), 1985, p. paper. Translated by Alexandra von Reinhardt. [German]

f. New York: A Signet Book, New American Library, June 1986, 573 p. mass-market paper. 12 printings by September, 1989.

g. London: Futura, July 1986, 624 p., paper.

h. as: *Nebel* ["*The Mist*"]. Linkenheim, Germany: Edition Phantasia, 1986, p., cloth. Illustrated by Herbert Brandmeier. Limited numbered edition of 500 numbered copies (I-XXX) and 30 presentation copies; most were seized by U.S. Customs Officers and only about 50 copies exist.

i. as: *Duistere Krachten: Verhalen van de Meester van de Horror* ["*Dark Forces: Stories by the Master of Horror*"]. Utrecht: Luitingh, 1986, 413 p., paper. Translated by Margot Bakker. Second printing, 1988. 21 stories and poems from *Skeleton Crew*, excluding "The Mist." [Dutch]

CONTENTS: "Vorwoord" ["Foreword"], by King; "Er Zit Dar een Tijger" ["Here There Be Tigers"]; "De Aap" ["The Monkey"]; "Kain Stond Tegen Zijn Broeder Op" ["Cain Stood up Against His Brother"="Cain Rose Up"]; "Mevrouw Todd Gaat Binnendoor" ["Mrs. Todd's Shortcut"]; "De Jaunt" ["The Jaunt"]; "De Schnabbel" ["The Wedding Gig"]; "Paranoide: Een Bezwering" ["Paranoid: A Chant"]; "Het Vlot" ["The Raft"]; "Duistere Kraften" ["Dark Forces"="The Word Processor of the Gods"]; "De Man Die Geen Hand Wilde Geven" ["The Man Who Would Not Shake Hands"]; "Strandleven" ["Beach Life"="Beachworld"]; "Het Spiegelbeeld van de Maaier" ["The Reaper's Image"]; "Nona"; "Voor Owen" ["For Owen"]; "Overleven" ["Survival"="Survivor Type"]; "De Vrachtauto van Oom Otto" ["Uncle Otto's Truck"]; "Vroege Bestellingen (Melkman 1)"; ["Early Deliveries"="Morning Deliveries: (Milkman 1)"]; "Zwaren Wielen: Een Vertelling Rondom de Wasserij (Melkman 2)"; ["Heavy Wheels"="Big Wheels: A Tale of the Laundry Game (Milkman 2)"]; "Grootma" ["Gramma"]; "De Ballade van de Flexible Kogel" ["The Ballad of the Flexible Bullet"]; "Het Rak" ["The Reach"].

j. as: *Dichte Mist* ["*Heavy Mist*"]. Utrecht: Luitingh, 1986, 160 p., paper. Translated by Pauline Moody. [Dutch]

CONTENTS: "Dichte Miste" (p. 5-150); "Stephen King," by Kim Foltz and Penelope Wang (p. 151-156); plus four pages of black-and-white reproductions of King's books translated in Dutch.

k. as: *Den Förskräckliga Apan och Andra Berättelser*. Stockholm: Legenda, 1986, 597 p., paper?. Translated by Karl G. Fredriksson and Lilian Fredriksson. Rpt. 1987. [Swedish]

l. excerpted as: *Der Fornit* (*Skeleton Crew*, part 3). München: Wilhelm Heyne (TB 6888), 1986, p., paper. Translated by Monika Hahn, Joachim Körber, and Alexandra von Reinhardt. [German]

CONTENTS: "Der Affe" ["The Monkey"]; "Paranoid: Ein Gesang" ["Paranoid: A Chant"]; "Der Textcomputer der Götter" ["The

Word Processor of the Gods"]; "Für Owen" ["For Owen"]; Überlebenstyp" ["Survivor Type"]; "Der Milchman Schlägt Wieder zu" ["The Milkman Leaves a Bonus Again"="Big Wheels: A Tale of the Laundry Game"]; "Der Fornit" ["The Ballad of the Flexible Bullet"]; "Der Dünenplanet" ["Beachworld"].

m. as: *Der Gesang der Toten* ["*The Song of the Dead*"; *Skeleton Crew*, part 2]. München: Wilhelm Heyne Verlag (TB 6705), 1986, p., paper. Translated by Matrin Bliesse, Rolf Jurkeit, and Alexandra von Reinhardt. [German]

CONTENTS: "Mrs. Todd's Abkürzung" ["Mrs. Todd's Shortcut"]; "Der Hochzeit Empfang" ["The Wedding Gig"]; "Travel" ["The Jaunt"]; "Kains Aufbegehren" ["Cain Rose Up"]; "Das Floß" ["The Raft"]; "Der Gesang der Toten" ["Do the Dead Sing?"]; "Der Sensenmann" ["The Reaper's Image"]; "Nona"; "Onkel Ottos Lastwagen" ["Uncle Otto's Truck"].

n. excerpted as: *La Niebla* ["*The Mist*"]. Barcelona: Grijalbo, 1986, 320 p., paper. Translated by Antonio Samons. [Spanish]

o. as: *Historias Fantásticas* ["*Fantastic Stories*"]. Barcelona: Plaza & Janés, February 1987, 189 p., paper. Translated by Rosa S. de Naveira. Thirteen stories and poems from *Skeleton Crew*, plus King's "Notes"; "The Mist" deleted. [Spanish]

CONTENTS: "Hay Tigres"; "Apareció Caín"; "Zarabanda Nupcial"; "Paranoia: Un Canto"; "El Procesador de Palabras de los Dioses"; "El Hombre Que no Quería Estrechar Manos"; "La Playa"; "La Imagen de la Muerte"; "Para Owen"; "El Camión de Tío Otto"; "Reparto Matutino (El Lechero, 1)"; "Ruedas: Un Cuento de Lavandería (El Lechero, 2)"; "El Brazo."

ob. as: *Historias Fantásticas*. Esplugas de Llobregat (Barcelona), Spain: Plaza & Janés, 1989, 189 p. (?), paper. [Spanish]

p. excerpted as: *De Aap* ["*The Monkey*"]. Utrecht: Luitingh, 1987, 197 p., paper. Translated by Margot Bakker. Second printing, 1988. [Dutch]

q. excerpted as: *De Ballade van de Flexibele Kogel* ["*The Ballad of the Flexible Bullet*"]. Utrecht: Luitingh, 1987, 197 p. Translated by Margot Bakker. [Dutch]

r. as: *Brume: Nouvelles* ["*Fog: Novellas*"]. Paris: Albin Michel, 1987, 643 p. cloth. Translated by Michele Pressé. [French]

s. excerpted as: *Der Fornit*. München: Wilhelm Heyne, 1987. [German]

t. excerpted as: *Het Spiegelbeeld van de Maaier* ["*The Reaper's Image*"]. Utrecht: Luitingh, 1987, 176 p. Translated by Margot Bakker. Second printing, 1988. [Dutch]

u. excerpted as: *La Expedición*. Barcelona: Grijalbo, 1987, 206 p. Translated by Francisco Blanco. [Spanish]

v. Stockholm: Legenda, 1988, 596 p., pocket paperback. Translated by Karl G. Fredrikkson and Lilian Fredriksson. [Swedish]

w. excerpted as: *La Niebla* ["*The Mist*"]. Barcelona: Ediciones Grijalbo, 1989, p. [Spanish]

x. as: *Historicas Fantásticas*. Madrid: Plaza Jovan, 1989, p. [Spanish]

SECONDARY SOURCES AND REVIEWS:

1. Adler, Constance. "Prince of Darkness: In His Reign of Best-selling Terror, Author Stephen King Remains Absolute Master of the Scary

Story," in *Philadelphia Magazine* 76 (August, 1985): 85+. [3-page article]

2. Alley, Jerry. "Tasteless, Tame, Silly," in *Virginian-Pilot* [Norfolk, VA] (June 23, 1985): . As microfiche: *NewsBank: Literature* 12 (July, 1985): Fiche 4, F7.
3. Beahm, George. *The Stephen King Companion*. Kansas City, MO: Andrews and McMeel, September 1989, paper, p. 271-275.
4. Bentkowski, Kent Daniel. "A Skeleton Crew Inside King's Closet," in *Castle Rock: The Stephen King Newsletter* 1:4 (April, 1985): 2.
5. Bertin, Eddy C. *SF Gids* [Belgium] (1986): 20. [Dutch review]
6. Bertin, Eddy C. "Stephen King in the Lowlands," in *Castle Rock* 1:11 (November, 1985): 7-8.
7. Bertin, Eddy C. "Additions to 'Stephen King in the Lowlands.'" Letter.
8. *Best Sellers* 45 (August, 1985): 168.
9. Blue, Tyson. "Stephen King's Short Stories Sure to Please His Many Fans," in *Courier Herald* [Dublin, GA] (June 22, 1985): .
10. Boesch, Barry. "Wide-Ranging '*Skeleton Crew*' Looks at Internal, External Monsters," in *Dallas Morning News* [Texas] (August 4, 1985): . As microfiche: *NewsBank: Literature* 12 (September, 1985): Fiche 23, G9-G10.
11. Bolotin, Susan. *New York Times Book Review* 90 (June 9, 1985): VII, 1.
12. *Booklist* 81 (December 15, 1984): 538.
13. Brocale, Carla. "Stories in '*Skeleton Crew*' Are Vintage King," in *Kansas City Star* [Missouri] (July 14, 1985): . As microfiche: *NewsBank: Literature* 12 (August, 1985): Fiche 12, D3.
14. Brown, Stephen. "Secretly Hidden Behind the Pen Name of Richard Bachman was Stephen King," in *Daily News* [New York] (May 19, 1985): . As microfiche: *NewsBank: Literature* 11 (June, 1985): Fiche 110, A1-A2.
15. Chute, David. "Chilling Horror from Stephen King," in *Los Angeles Herald Examiner* (June 16, 1985): . As microfiche: *NewsBank: Literature* 12 (July, 1985): Fiche 4, E11-E12.
16. Collings, Michael R. "King Collection Worth Waiting For," in *Fantasy Review* 8:6 [whole #80] (June, 1985): 22.
17. Collings, Michael R. *The Annotated Guide to Stephen King: A Primary and Secondary Bibliography of the Works of America's Premier Horror Writer*. STARMONT REFERENCE GUIDE, No. 8. Mercer Island, WA: Starmont House, October 1986.
18. Collings, Michael R. *The Many Facets of Stephen King*. STARMONT STUDIES IN LITERARY CRITICISM, No. 11. Mercer Island, WA: Starmont House, 1986.
19. Collings, Michael R. *The Stephen King Phenomenon*. STARMONT STUDIES IN LITERARY CRITICISM, No. 14. Mercer Island, WA: Starmont House, 1987.
20. Collings, Michael R., and David A. Engebretson. *The Shorter Works of Stephen King*. STARMONT STUDIES IN LITERARY CRITICISM, No. 9. Mercer Island, WA: Starmont House, June 1985.
21. Graham, Mark. "Stephen King Stories Never Seem to Die," in *Rocky Mountain News* [Denver, CO] (June 16, 1985): .

22. Halford, Celia C. "Boo! New Stephen King Anthology," in *News and Courier* [Charleston, SC] (July 28, 1985): . As microfiche: *NewsBank: Literature* 12 (August, 1985): Fiche 12, D5.
23. Hartwell, David G. Headnote to "The Monkey," in *The Dark Descent*, edited by David G. Hartwell. New York: Tor, A Tom Doherty Associates Book, October 1988, cloth, p. 382.
24. Hartwell, David G. Headnote to "The Reach," in *The Dark Descent*, edited by David G. Hartwell. New York: Tor, A Tom Doherty Associates Book, October 1988, cloth, p. 15.
25. Hornbaker, Alice. "King Courts Royal Set of Scary Stories," in *Cincinnati Enquirer* (June 2, 1985): . As microfiche: *NewsBank: Literature* 12 (July, 1985): Fiche 4, F3.
26. *Illustrated London News* 273 (August, 1985): 65.
27. *Illustrated London News* 273 (October, 1985): 107.
28. Keller, Scott A. "Latest King Collection a Bit Disappointing," in *Atlanta Journal-Constitution* (July 14, 1985): . As microfiche: *NewsBank: Literature* 12 (August, 1985): Fiche 12, D1.
29. *Kirkus Reviews* 53 (May 1, 1985): 386.
30. *Kliatt Young Adult Paperback Book Guide* 20 (Fall, 1986): 38.
31. Kloer, Phil. "'*Skeleton Crew*': The Bare Bones of Stephen King," in *Florida Times-Union* [Jacksonville, FL] (June 30, 1985): . As microfiche: *NewsBank: Literature* 12 (July, 1985): Fiche 4, E13-E14.
32. Lehmann-Haupt, Christopher. *New York Times* (July 11, 1985): III, 21.
33. *Library Journal* 110 (May 1, 1985): 78.
34. *Los Angeles Times* "Books" (August 25, 1985): 4.
35. McCaffrey, Larry. "It's Time for King to Desert Treadmill," in *San Diego Union* [California] (August 4, 1985): . As microfiche: *NewsBank: Literature* 12 (September, 1985): Fiche 23, G8.
36. *The Magazine of Fantasy & Science Fiction* 69 (November, 1985): 12.
37. Magistrale, Tony. *Landscape of Fear: Stephen King's American Gothic*. Bowling Green, OH: Bowling Green State University Popular Press, March 1988.
38. Merritt, Robert. "Collection Displays King's Childlike Mischief," in *Richmond Times-Dispatch* [Virginia] (June 30, 1985): . As microfiche: *NewsBank: Literature* 12 (July, 1985): Fiche 4, F8.
39. Moss, Chuck. "Multiple Shivers from a Champion of the Game," in *The Detroit News* (June 16, 1985): 2K. Excerpted: *Contemporary Literary Criticism, Volume 37,* edited by Daniel G. Marowski. Detroit: Gale Research Co., 1986, p. 207-208.
40. *New Statesman* 112 (September 12, 1986): 30.
41. *New York Times* [Daily] 134 (June 11, 1985): 17.
42. *New York Times Book Review* 91 (June 29, 1986): 38.
43. Nicholls, Peter. "Beach Blanket Books: *Skeleton Crew*," in *Washington Post Book World* 15 (June 16, 1985): 1, 13. Excerpted: *Contemporary Literary Criticism, Volume 37,* edited by Daniel G. Marowski. Detroit: Gale Research Co., 1986, p. 206-207.
44. Nolan, William F. "The Good Fabric: Of Night Shifts and Skeleton Crews," in *Kingdom of Fear: The World of Stephen King*, edited by

Tim Underwood and Chuck Miller. Columbia, PA: Underwood-Miller, 1986, p. 99-106.

45. Potter, Chuck. "Out of '*The Mist*' a Stephen King '*Skeleton Crew*,'" in *Wichita Eagle-Beacon* [Kansas] (June 23, 1985): . As microfiche: *NewsBank: Literature* 12 (August, 1985): Fiche 12, D2.
46. *Publishers Weekly* 227 (April 19, 1985): 72.
47. *Publishers Weekly* 229 (April 18, 1986): 66.
48. Rickard, Dennis. "Horror Without Limits: Looking into *The Mist*," in *Reign of Fear: Fiction and Film of Stephen King*, edited by Don Herron. Los Angeles: Underwood-Miller, June 1988, p. 177-192.
49. Sallee, Wayne Allen. "No Bones About It," in *Castle Rock: The Stephen King Newsletter* 1:8 (August, 1985): 2.
50. *San Francisco Chronicle* (June 24, 1985): 55.
51. Schleier, Curt. "Stephen King's Stories Offer Evidence of Pact with the Devil," in *Chicago Tribune* (June 9, 1985): . As microfiche: *NewsBank: Literature* 12 (June, 1985): Fiche 118, E8.
52. Schweitzer, Darrell, ed. *Discovering Stephen King*. STARMONT STUDIES IN LITERARY CRITICISM, No. 8. Mercer Island, WA: Starmont House, 1985.
53. *Science Fiction Chronicle* (October, 1985): 43.
54. *Science Fiction Review* 15 (February, 1986): 24.
55. Shestak, George. "You Win, Lose With a Pair of Kings," in *Omaha World-Herald* [Nebraska] (May 26, 1985): . As microfiche: *NewsBank: Literature* 11 (June, 1985): Fiche 110, A3.
56. Spignesi, Stephen J. "*Skeleton Crew*," in *The Shape Under the Sheet: The Complete Stephen King Encyclopedia*. Ann Arbor, MI: Popular Culture, Ink., May 1991, cloth, p. 325-331, 335-360.
57. *Time* 125 (July 1, 1985): 59.
58. Turner, Billy. "Stephen King's Newest Is Recycled Old Stuff," in *Clarion-Ledger* [Jackson, MS] (June 16, 1985): . As microfiche: *NewsBank: Literature* 12 (July, 1985): Fiche 4, F1.
59. Vicarel, Jo Ann. "Horror, Science Fiction Meet Horror-Story Mold," in *Cleveland Plain Dealer* [Ohio] (July 13, 1985): . As microfiche: *NewsBank: Literature* 12 (August, 1985): Fiche 12, D4.
60. *Voice of Youth Advocates* 10 (April, 1987): 53.
61. *West Coast Review of Books* 11 (July, 1985): 28.
62. Winter, Douglas E. "The King of Storytelling Is Back Again," in *Philadelphia Inquirer* (June 30, 1985): . As microfiche: *NewsBank: Literature* 12 (July, 1985): Fiche 4, F4-F6.
63. Winter, Douglas E. *Castle Rock: The Stephen King Newsletter* 1:9 (September, 1985): 1-2.
64. Winter, Douglas E. *Stephen King: The Art of Darkness*. Expanded and updated edition. New York: A Plume Book, New American Library, June, 1986.
65. York, John. "King Collection Goes Back to the Beginning," in *Charlotte Observer* [North Carolina] (June 30, 1985): . As microfiche: *NewsBank: Literature* 12 (July, 1985): Fiche 4, F2.

A29. SILVER BULLET

A29. ***Silver Bullet.*** New York: A Signet Book, New American Library, October 1985, 255 p., trade paper. Illustrations by Berni Wrightson. [horror collection]

CONTENTS: "Foreword," by King (see **C142**); *Cycle of the Werewolf* (1983; see **A21**); *Silver Bullet* (screenplay).

REPRINTS:

b. as: *Der Werewolf von Tarker Mills*. Bergisch Gladbach: Bastei-Lübbe Verlag (Paperback 28146), 1986, p., paper. Translated by Helmut W. Pesch and Harro Christensen. [German]
CONTENTS: "Vorwort" ("Foreword"); *Das Jahr des Werwolfs* ["*The Year of the Werewolf*" =*Cycle of the Werewolf*]; *Der Werwolf von Tarker Mill* ["*The Werewolf of Tarker Mill*" =*Silver Bullet*].

c. Utrecht: Luitingh. [Dutch]

SECONDARY SOURCES AND REVIEWS:

1. Blue, Tyson. "*Silver Bullet*—Book Review," in *Castle Rock: The Stephen King Newsletter* 2:1 (January, 1986): 5.
2. *Booklist* 82 (February 15, 1986): 843.
3. Collings, Michael R. *The Annotated Guide to Stephen King: A Primary and Secondary Bibliography of the Works of America's Premier Horror Writer*. STARMONT REFERENCE GUIDE, No. 8. Mercer Island, WA: Starmont House, October 1986.
4. Collings, Michael R. *The Many Facets of Stephen King*. STARMONT STUDIES IN LITERARY CRITICISM, No. 11. Mercer Island, WA: Starmont House, 1986.
5. Winter, Douglas E. *Stephen King: The Art of Darkness*. Expanded and updated edition. New York: A Plume Book, New American Library, June 1986.

A30. THE BACHMAN BOOKS

A30. ***The Bachman Books: Four Early Novels: Rage, The Long Walk, Roadwork, The Running Man.*** New York: An NAL Book, New American Library, October 1985, x+692 p., cloth. [novel collection]

CONTENTS: Introduction, "Why I Was Bachman" (see **C141**); *Rage* (1977; see **A4**); *The Long Walk* (1979; see **A8**); *Roadwork* (1981; see **A10**); *The Running Man* (1982; see **A14**).

REPRINTS:

ab. New York: A Plume Book, New American Library, October 1985, x+692 p., trade paperback.
ac. New York: A Signet Book, New American Library, November 1986, xiii+923 p., mass-market paperback. 10 printings by 1994.
b. London: New English Library, July 1986, x+692 p., cloth.
bb. London: New English Library, August 1987, xiii+865 p., paper.
c. as: *4 X Stephen King*. Utrecht: Luitingh, 1986, p., paper. Includes: *Razernij* ["*Rage*"], translated by Margot Bakker; *De Marathon* ["*The Long Walk*"], translated by Mariella de Kuyper-Snel; *Werk in Uitvoering* ["*Roadwork*"], translated by Hugo Kuipers; *Vlucht Naar de Top* ["*The Running Man*"], translated by Frank de Groot. [Dutch]
d. as: *La Larga Marcha*. Barcelona: Martínez Roca, 1986, 288 p., paper. Translated by Hernán Sabaté. [Spanish]
e. as: *La Larga Marcha*. Barcelona: Circulo de Lectores, 1987, 288 p. (?). [Spanish]
f. as: *Todesmarsch* ["*Death March*"]. München: Wilhelm Heyne Verlag (TB 6848), 1987, p., paper. Translated by Nora Jensen. [German]

SECONDARY SOURCES AND REVIEWS:
[see also the reviews listed separately under each book in this collection]

1. Beahm, George. *The Stephen King Companion*. Kansas City, MO: Andrews and McMeel, September 1989, paper, p. 167-170.
2. *Best Sellers* 46 (April, 1986): 6.
3. Blue, Tyson. "King Re-releases Novels Published by 'Bachman,'" in *Courier Herald* [Dublin, GA] (September 28, 1985): . As: "Bachman Books are Interesting Trip," in *Castle Rock: The Stephen King Newsletter* 1:12 (December, 1985): 5.
4. *Booklist* 82 (October 1, 1985): 191.
5. Collings, Michael R. *The Annotated Guide to Stephen King: A Primary and Secondary Bibliography of the Works of America's Premier Horror Writer*. STARMONT REFERENCE GUIDE, No. 8. Mercer Island, WA: Starmont House, October 1986.
6. Collings, Michael R. "New King, Vintage King," in *Fantasy Review* no. 84 (October, 1985): 18.
7. Collings, Michael R. *The Stephen King Phenomenon*. STARMONT STUDIES IN LITERARY CRITICISM, No. 14. Mercer Island, WA: Starmont House, 1987.
8. Costello, William J. "'Bachman Books' Is a Collection of Four King Novels," in *Forum* [Fargo, ND] ([unknown], 1986): . As microfiche: *NewsBank: Literature* 12 (May, 1986): Fiche 74, F3.
9. Field, Ben. "Bachman Isn't Vintage King," in *Seattle Post-Intelligencer* [Washington] (November 7, 1985): .
10. *Kirkus Reviews* 53 (September 15, 1985): 968.
11. Lawson, John. *School Library Journal* 32 (April, 1986): 105.
12. *Publishers Weekly* 228 (September 6, 1985): 59.
13. Rousch, Matt. "King Can't Hide Behind Bachman," in *USA Today* 4 (October 17, 1985): 2D.
14. *Science Fiction Chronicle* 7 (February, 1986): 34.

15. Smith, Gene. "King's Early Work," in *Topeka Capital-Journal* [Kansas] (April 20, 1986): . As microfiche: *NewsBank: Literature* 12 (May, 1986): Fiche 93, C12.
16. *Voice of Youth Advocates* 10 (June 1987): 103.
17. Winter, Douglas E. *Stephen King: The Art of Darkness*. Expanded and updated edition. New York: A Plume Book, New American Library, June 1986, p. 174-188.

A31. THE PLANT [PART 3]

A31. ***The Plant [Part 3]***. Bangor, ME: Philtrum Press, December (?) 1985, 56 p., paper. Limited edition of 26 lettered copies signed by King plus 200 numbered copies. [horror pamphlet]

COMMENTS: The third installment of a novel-in-progress (see **A18** and **A23**), privately published by King and sent as Christmas greetings.

SECONDARY SOURCES AND REVIEWS:

1. Beahm, George. *The Stephen King Companion*. Kansas City, MO: Andrews and McMeel, September 1989, paper, p. 111-113.
2. Blue, Tyson. *The Unseen King*. STARMONT STUDIES IN LITERARY CRITICISM, No. 26. Mercer Island, WA: Starmont House, 1979, p. v-vii, 70-71, 88-100, 174.
3. Blue, Tyson. "The Plant: The Unseen King," in *Castle Rock: The Stephen King Newsletter* 2:6 (June 1986): 1, 3.
4. Collings, Michael R., and David A. Engebretson. *The Shorter Works of Stephen King*. STARMONT STUDIES IN LITERARY CRITICISM, No. 9. Mercer Island, WA: Starmont House, 1985, p. 173, 178.
5. Spignesi, Stephen J. "The Plant," in *The Shape Under the Sheet: The Complete Stephen King Encyclopedia*. Ann Arbor, MI: Popular Culture, Ink., May 1991, cloth, p. 498-505.
6. Winter, Douglas E. *Stephen King: The Art of Darkness*. New York: New American Library, November 1984, p. 176.

A32. IT

A32. *ES*. Linkenheim, West Germany: Edition Phantasia, [May] 1986, p., cloth. Translated by Alexandra von Reinhardt. Limited edition of 280 numbered copies, bound in leather, red velvet slipcase; 30 copies numbered I-XXX were not offered for sale. This German-language edition is the true first appearance of the novel better known in the United States as *IT*. [horror novel]

PLOT SUMMARY: *IT* focuses on the interactions of seven characters, both as children and as adults, as they discover the secrets of the horror that lives beneath the sewers of Derry, Maine.

COMMENTS: King considered *IT* a culmination as well as a completion; certainly the novel represents the climax of over a decade of working with monsters (physical and psychological) and threatened children. The novel integrates the fears of childhood with the fears of adulthood and attempts a final resolution. Responses to *IT* varied from acknowledgments of the book as King's masterwork to date, to scathing denunciations of the novel as overly long, pretentious, and numbingly pat in its final imagery and resolution.

The Viking hardcover sold 1,206,200 copies in 1986; the novel ranked #1 on the *Bowker Annual* hardcover fiction bestsellers list for 1985. This novel was one of the few King books to receive an award, receiving the British Fantasy Award for Best Novel.

REPRINTS:

ab. as: *ES*. München: Wilhelm Heyne Verlag (Jumbo Bände), 1986, 859 p., paper. Translated by Alexandra von Reinhardt. [German]
b. as: *IT*. London: Hodder & Stoughton, August 1986, 912 p., cloth.
c. as: *IT*. New York: Viking, 15 September 1986, x+1138 p., cloth.
d. as: *IT*. New York: Book-of-the-Month-Club], [n.d.], cloth.
e. as: *Es*. Gütersloh, Austria: Bertelsmann Lesering, 1986, 859 p., cloth (?). Translated by Alexandra von Reinhardt. [German]
f. as: *Het*. Utrecht: Luitingh, October 1986, 576 p., paper. Translated by Margot Bakker. 20,000 copies in first printing. [Dutch]
g. excerpted: *Book-of-the-Month Club News* (October, 1986): 4. The opening paragraphs of the novel.
h. as: *IT*. New York: A Signet Book, New American Library, September 1987, 1093 p., mass-market paper. 13 printings by September, 1989.
i. as: *IT*. London: New English Library, October 1987, 1116 p., paper.
j. as: *Det*. Stockholm: Legenda, 1987, 1189 p. in 2 v. Translated by Roland Adlerberth. [Swedish]
jb. as: *Det*. Stockholm: Legenda, 1988, 1187 p. in 2 v. Translated by Roland Adlerberth. [Swedish]
k. as: *Eso*. Barcelona: Plaza y Janés, 1987, 1026 p., paper. Translated by Edith Zilli. [Spanish]
kb. as: *It*. Esplugas Llobregat (Barcelona): Plaza & Janés, 1989, 1026 p. (?), paper. [Spanish]
l. as: *It*. Milano: Sperling & Kupfer, 1987, 1238 p. paper. Translated by Tullio Dobner. [Italian]
m. as: *Es*. Book Club Editions-Kornwesterheim, Austria: Europäische Bildungs-gemeinschaft; Gütersloh, Austria: Bertelsmann Club; Vienna, Austria: Buchgemeinschaft Donauland; Zug, Switzerland: Buch-und-Schallplattenfreunde, December 1988, 859 p., paper. [German]
n. excerpted: *Diamonds Are Forever: Writers and Artists on Baseball*. Washington: Smithsonian Institute.
o. as: *Ça*. Paris: Albin Michel, 1988. Listed as the 7th best-selling French-language book. [French]
p. excerpted as: "Es," in *Die Jumbos von Heyne*. München: Wilhelm Heyne Verlag (Jumbo Paperback o. Nr.), 1989, paper, p. Translated by Alexandra von Reinhardt. [German]
q. as: *Eso*. Barcelona: Circulo de Lectores, 1989, p. [Spanish]

SECONDARY SOURCES AND REVIEWS:

1. Beahm, George, ed. *The Stephen King Companion*. Kansas City, MO: Andrews and McMeel, September 1989, 365 p., paper.
2. Bennet, Ron. *Christian Science Monitor* 78 (September, 19, 1986): 21.
3. Bertin, Eddy C. "*IT* in the Netherlands, or: The Rape of Stephen King," in *Castle Rock: The Stephen King Newsletter* 3:9 (September, 1987): 7.
4. Bleiler, E. F. "Books," in *Twilight Zone Magazine* 6:6 (February, 1987): 8-9.
5. Blue, Tyson. "*IT:* A Journey into the Darkside," in *Castle Rock: The Stephen King Newsletter* 2:11 (November, 1986): 1, 3.
6. Blue, Tyson. "*IT* Marks a Turning Point in King's Career," in *Macon Telegraph & News* [Macon, GA] (August 31, 1986): .
7. Blue, Tyson. "The Truth about '*IT*,'" in *Twilight Zone Magazine* 6:5 (December, 1986): 48-49.
8. *Booklist* 82 (June 15, 1986): 1474.
9. Bryant, Edward. "*Twilight Zone* Review 1986," in *Twilight Zone Magazine* 6:6 (February, 1987): 56.
10. *Boston Globe* (August 23, 1987): .
11. Collings, Michael R. *The Annotated Guide to Stephen King: A Primary and Secondary Bibliography of the Works of America's Premier Horror Writer*. STARMONT REFERENCE GUIDE, No. 8. Mercer Island, WA: Starmont House, October 1986, cloth.
12. Collings, Michael R. "*IT:* Stephen King's Comprehensive Masterpiece," in *Castle Rock: The Stephen King Newsletter* 2:7 (July 1986): 1, 4-6.
13. Collings, Michael R. *The Many Facets of Stephen King*. STARMONT STUDIES IN LITERARY CRITICISM, No. 11. Mercer Island, WA: Starmont House, 1986.
14. Collings, Michael R. *Stephen King as Richard Bachman*. STARMONT STUDIES IN LITERARY CRITICISM, No. 10. Mercer Island, WA: Starmont House, 1985.
15. Collings, Michael R. *The Stephen King Phenomenon*. STARMONT STUDIES IN LITERARY CRITICISM, No. 14. Mercer Island, WA: Starmont House, 1987, p. 13-25.
16. Edwards, Thomas R. "Gulp!" in *The New York Review of Books* (December 18, 1986): 58-59.
17. *English Journal* 77 (January, 1988): 101.
18. *Fangoria* (March, 1987): .
19. Gates, David. "The Creature That Refused to Die," in *Newsweek* (September 1, 1986): 84.
20. Goldberg, Whoopi. *Los Angeles Times Book Review* (October 5, 1986): B, 2.
21. Graham, Mark. "Awakening Childhood Nightmares," in *Rocky Mountain News* [Denver, CO] (October 12, 1986): 34-M.
22. Grant, Charles L. "It Wasn't a Half Bad Year," in *Amazing Stories* (September, 1987): .
23. Herron, Don. "Ravening Beast Meets Losers," in *Newsday* [Long Island, NY] (August 31, 1986): . As microfiche: *NewsBank: Literature* 13 (September, 1986): Fiche 23, A10-A11.

24. Herron, Don. "Summation," in *Reign of Fear: Fiction and Film of Stephen King*, edited by Don Herron. Los Angeles: Underwood-Miller, June 1988, p. 209-240.
25. Hoffman, Barry. "*IT* an ABC Mini-Series: I Shudder at the Thought," in *Castle Rock: The Stephen King Newsletter* 3:11 (November, 1987): 7-8.
26. Hoffman, Barry. "King's Kids...Less than Meets the Eye," in *Castle Rock: The Stephen King Newsletter* 4:7 (July, 1988): 3.
27. Hoppenstand, Gary, and Ray B. Browne, eds. *The Gothic World of Stephen King: Landscape of Nightmares*. Bowling Green, OH: Bowling Green State University Popular Press, December 1987.
28. Johnson, Eric W. *Library Journal* 111 (August, 1986): 171.
29. Johnson, Kimball. "Letter," in *Castle Rock: The Stephen King Newsletter* 3:11 (December, 1986/January, 1987): 7.
30. Kanfer, Stefan. "King of Horror: The Master of Pop Dread Writes on...and on...and on...and on...," in *Time* 128 (October 6, 1986): 74-83.
31. Kaveney, Roz. *Times Literary Supplement* [London] (December 5, 1986): 1368.
32. Kimberly, Judy. "Horror 'Wonderland,'" in *Fantasy Review* no. 93 (July/August, 1986): 28-29.
33. King, Stephen. "Stephen King Comments on *It*," in *Castle Rock: The Stephen King Newsletter* 2:7 (July 1986): 1, 5.
34. King, Stephen. "How *IT* Happened," in *Book-of-the-Month-Club News* (October 1986): .
35. "King's Latest Much More Than a Horror Novel," in *Asbury Park Press* [Neptune, NJ] (September 7, 1986): . As microfiche: *NewsBank: Literature* 13 (December, 1986): Fiche 30, G11.
36. *Kirkus Reviews* 54 (June 1, 1986): 811.
37. *Kliatt Young Adults Paperback Book Guide* 22 (January, 1988): 11.
38. Koontz, Dean R. "The Specter of Death Shadows Stephen King's '*It*,'" in *San Jose Mercury News* [California] (August 31, 1986): . As microfiche: *NewsBank: Literature* 13 (December, 1986): Fiche 30, G8.
39. Lai, Jill. "Stephen King's Newest is Creepingly Sinister," in *Seattle Post-Intelligencer* (August 30, 1986): .
40. Lehmann-Haupt, Christopher. *The New York Times* 135 (August 21, 1986): .
41. Liberatore, Karen. "Another Ride on the Nightmare Roller Coaster," in *San Francisco Examiner* (August 24, 1986): . As microfiche: *NewsBank: Literature* 13 (October, 1986): Fiche 30, G6-G7.
42. *Locus* (August, 1986): .
43. *The Magazine of Fantasy & Science Fiction* 71 (November, 1986): 18.
44. Magistrale, Tony. *Landscape of Fear: Stephen King's American Gothic*. Bowling Green, OH: Bowling Green State University Popular Press, 1988.
45. Magistrale, Tony. *The Moral Voyages of Stephen King*. STARMONT STUDIES IN LITERARY CRITICISM, No. 25. Mercer Island, WA: Starmont House, 1989.
46. Moses, Michael. "Stanley Uris: World's Smallest Adult," in *Castle Rock: The Stephen King Newsletter* 5:7 (July, 1989): 3, 10-11.

47. Moss, Chuck. "This is 'It,' a Scary Book with Real Merit," in *Detroit News* (August 24, 1986): . As microfiche: *NewsBank: Literature* 13 (September, 1986): Fiche 23, A7.
48. *New Statesman* 112 (December 12, 1986): 31.
49. Norris, Gloria. "The October Selection: *IT*," in *Book-of-the-Month Club News* (October, 1986): 2, 4. An introduction to the novel.
50. Perry, Roy E. "King's '*It*' the 'War and Peace' of Horror Stories," in *Nashville Banner* [Tennessee] (August 30, 1986): . As microfiche: *NewsBank: Literature* 13 (September, 1986): Fiche 23, A12-A13.
51. Podhoretz, John. "An Encounter with the Horror King," in *Washington* [D.C.] *Times* (August 25, 1986): . As microfiche: *NewsBank: Literature* 13 (September, 1986): Fiche 23, A14-B1. As: "Stopping '*It*' Before It's Too Late," in *Insight* (August 25, 1986): 68-69.
52. *Publishers Weekly* 229 (June 27, 1986): 74.
53. Reese, Kathleen. "'*It*' Performs Feats of King-ly Magic," in *Dallas Times Herald* (September 7, 1986): . As microfiche: *NewsBank: Literature* 13 (December, 1986): Fiche 30, G12-G13.
54. Ringel, Faye. "Some Notes on *It*," in *Castle Rock: The Stephen King Newsletter* 3:9 (September, 1987): 1, 4.
55. Rousch, Matt. *USA Today* (1986): .
56. Rose, Lloyd. *Atlantic Monthly* 258 (September, 1986): 102.
57. Sallee, Wayne Allen. "And So It Goes," in *Castle Rock: The Stephen King Newsletter* 2:11 (November, 1986): 1, 5.
58. *San Francisco Chronicle* (August 23, 1986): .
59. Sarrantonio, Al. *Night Cry* 2:3 (Spring, 1987): 184-185.
60. *Science Fiction Chronicle* 8 (March, 1987): 34.
61. *Science Fiction Chronicle* 8 (March, 1987): 43.
62. Spignesi, Stephen J. "*IT*," in *The Shape Under the Sheet: The Complete Stephen King Encyclopedia.* Ann Arbor, MI: Popular Culture, Ink., May 1991, cloth, p. 360-395.
63. Terrell, Carroll F. *Stephen Kng: Man and Artist* Orono, ME: Northern Lights Publishing, 1990, cloth, p. 239-269.
64. Thompson, Don C. "This Is '*It*,' The Real King: Long-Awaited Book Is Huge and Worth the Wait," in *Denver Post* [Colorado] (September 7, 1986): . As microfiche: *NewsBank: Literature* 13 (December, 1986): Fiche 30, G9-G10.
65. Tucker, Ken. "King of Macabre," in *Louisville Globe-Democrat* [Missouri] (August 23, 1986): . As microfiche: *NewsBank: Literature* 13 (September, 1986): Fiche 23, A8-A9.
66. Tucker, Ken. "Literature or Pop Fiction? What's the Difference, Eh?" in *Birmingham News* [Alabama] (August 31, 1986): . As microfiche: *NewsBank: Literature* 13 (December, 1986): Fiche 45, B2-B4.
67. *Village Voice* 32 (March 3, 1987): 35.
68. Wager, Walter. "More Evil Than a 15-Foot Spider," in *New York Times Book Review* 91 (August 24, 1986): VII, 9.
69. *Washington Post Book World* 16 (August 24, 1986): 1.
70. *Washington Post Book World* 17 (December 6, 1987): 19.
71. *West Coast Review of Books* 12:4 (1986): 35.
72. *Wilson School Journal* 208 (October 13, 1986): 11.

73. Winter, Douglas E. *Stephen King: The Art of Darkness*. New York: New American Library, November 1984.

A33. MISERY

A33. *Misery*. New York: Viking, 8 June 1987, 310 p., cloth. [horror novel]

PLOT SUMMARY: Severely injured in a car accident, novelist Paul Sheldon finds himself at the mercy of his rescuer—a former nurse named Annie Wilkes, who is obsessed with Sheldon's fictional creation, Misery Chastain. Annie's insane determination to keep Sheldon to herself and to force him to resurrect Misery in one final story parallels Sheldon's equally desperate need to escape from Annie's control.

COMMENTS: A sparse, sharply defined treatment of the horrors of being a public figure, *Misery* is the stronger for its focus on only two characters and its examination of the horrors of real life. The most frightening thing about the novel is the realization that Annie Wilkes may be only a pale reflection of people who actually live among us.

819,486 hardcover copies were sold in 1987; the novel ranked #4 on the *Bowker Annual* hardcover fiction bestseller list. King was represented on that list by *The Tommyknockers* (#1) and *The Eyes of the Dragon* (#10)—the titles appearing simultaneously. The novel tied with Robert McCammon's *Swan Song* for the Bram Stoker Award [Horror Writers of America], June 1988, one of the few awards King has won. King has noted that *Misery* was originally intended to be published as a "RICHARD BACHMAN" book.

REPRINTS:

b. London: Stodder & Houghton, September 1987, 320 p., cloth.
c. as: *Misery*. Utrecht: Luitingh, 1987, 352 p. Translated by Margot Bakker. [Dutch]
d. as: *Sie* ["*She*"]. München: Wilhelm Heyne Verlag, 1987, p. paper. JUMBO BÄNDE 7500, 41/2. Translated by Joachim Körber. [German]
e. as: *Sie* ["*She*"]. Book Club Editions-Kornwesterheim, Austria: Europäische Bildungsgemeinschaft; Gütersloh, Austria: Bertelsmann Club; Vienna, Austria: Buchgemeinschaft Donauland; Zug, Switzerland: Buch-und-Schallplattenfreunde, May 1988, 400 p., paper. Translated by Joachim Körber. [German]
f. New York: A Signet Book, New American Library, June 1988, 339 p., mass-market paper. 30 printings by 1994.
g. Bath: Windsor Selection Services/Chivers Press, September 1988, 504 p., cloth. Large print edition.
h. London: New English Library, November 1988, 384 p., paper.
i. Boston: G. K. Hall & Co., 1988, 491 p., cloth. Large print edition.
j. as: *Lida*. Stockholm: Höganäs: Bra Böcker, 1988, 352 p. Translated by Lennart Olofsson. [Swedish]
k. as: *Kida*. Stockholm: Legenda, 1988. 352 p. Translated by Lennart Olofsson. [Swedish]

l. as: *Sie* ["*She*"]. Stuttgart: Deutscher Bücherbund, 1988, p. Translated by Joachim Körber. [German]
m. Quality Paperback Book Club edition.
n. as: *Misery*. Esplugas Llobregat (Barcelona), Spain: Plaza & Janés Editores, 1989, p., paper. [Spanish]

SECONDARY SOURCES AND REVIEWS:

1. Allen, Jerry. "The Master of Disaster Hits Rock Bottom," in *Virginian-Pilot* [Norfolk, VA] (May 31, 1987): . As microfiche: *NewsBank: Literature* 13 (June, 1987): Fiche 110, D9.
2. Amantia, A. M. B. *Library Journal* (May 1, 1987): 83.
3. *Booklist* 83 (April 1, 1987): 1153.
4. Beahm, George, ed. *The Stephen King Companion*. Kansas City, MO: Andrews and McMeel, September 1989, p. 245-250.
5. Beaulieu, Janet C. "A Book, and an Author to Be Taken Seriously," in *Bangor Daily News* [Maine] (June 9, 1987): . As microfiche: *NewsBank: Literature* 14 (July 1987): Fiche 7, B10.
6. Blue, Tyson. "*Misery* King's Most Horrifying Tale Yet," in *Telegraph and News* "Books/The Arts" [Macon, GA] (May 3, 1987): 10E, 14E.
7. *Books* (September, 1987): 11.
8. *Book Report* 6 (March, 1988): 34.
9. *Book World* (14 June 1987): 1.
10. Brown, Jerry Earl. "Serious as Well as Scary," in *Denver Post* [Colorado] (July 5, 1987): . As microfiche: *NewsBank: Literature* 14 (August, 1987): Fiche 20, B11-B12.
11. Budrys, Algis. "Stephen King Bares His Soul (Maybe) in '*Misery*,'" in *Chicago Sun Times* (June 21, 1987): . As microfiche: *NewsBank: Literature* 14 (August, 1987): Fiche 20, B13-B14.
12. Card, Orson Scott. "Books to Look for," in *The Magazine of Fantasy & Science Fiction* (November 1987): 34-38.
13. *Christian Science Monitor* (July 3, 1987): B4.
14. Collings, Michael R. *The Annotated Guide to Stephen King: A Primary and Secondary Bibliography of the Works of America's Premier Horror Writer*. STARMONT REFERENCE GUIDE, No. 8. Mercer Island, WA: Starmont House, October 1986, 179 p., cloth.
15. Craig, Paul. "Stephen King Does It Again," in *Sacramento Bee* [California] (June 21, 1987): . As microfiche: *NewsBank: Literature* 14 (August, 1987): Fiche 20, B9-B10.
16. Dailey, Janet. "Book-Within-a-Book Lets Reader Get Inside Creative Writer's Mind," in *Chicago Tribune* (May 17, 1987): Section 14, 3. As microfiche: *NewsBank: Literature* 13 (June, 1987): Fiche 110, D8.
17. de Lint, Charles. "Urban Thrills: Reviews of Short Horror and Contemporary Fantasy Fiction," in *Short Form* 1:3/4 (1989): 56-70. Includes *Misery* on the "Best of the Year" list.
18. Duffy, Thom. "One Writer's '*Misery*' Is Sure-Fire Horror," in *Orlando Sentinel* [Florida] (June 7, 1987): . As microfiche: *NewsBank: Literature* 14 (July 1987): Fiche 7, B8.
19. Flewelling, Lynn. "King Working on Book He Believes Could Be His Best," in *Bangor Daily News* [Maine] (September 11, 1990): .

As Microfiche: *NewsBank: Names in the News* 12 (October, 1990): Fiche 272, B9.

20. Geoghegan, Bill. "Stephen King's Latest Not for the Squeamish," in *Washington* [D.C.] *Times* (July 6, 1987): . As microfiche: *NewsBank: Literature* 14 (July 1987): Fiche 7, C3-C4.
21. Graham, Mark. "King Shares '*Misery*,' and Reader Grimaces," in *Rocky Mountain News* [Denver, CO] (June 21, 1987): 28-M.
22. Harris, Ian. "*Misery* on Stage?" in *Castle Rock: The Stephen King Newsletter* 3:10 (October, 1987): 3, 6.
23. Hogan, Patricia. "*Misery*...No Way!" in *Castle Rock: The Stephen King Newsletter* 3:4 (April/May, 1987): 5.
24. Katzenbach, John. *The New York Times Book Review* 92 (May 31, 1987): VII, 20.
25. Keller, Scott A. "'*Misery*' Is Stephen King at His Terrifying Best," in *Atlanta Journal-Constitution* (June 7, 1987): . As microfiche: *NewsBank: Literature* 14 (July 1987): Fiche 7, B9.
26. Kies, Cosette. *Voice of Youth Advocates* (February 10, 1988): 281.
27. King, Tabitha. "Co-Miser-A-Ting with Stephen King," in *Castle Rock: The Stephen King Newsletter* 3:8 (August, 1987): 1, 5.
28. *Kirkus Reviews* 55 (April 1, 1987): 502.
29. Krim, Seymour. "Forced to Compose at Blowtorch-Point," in *Newsday* [Long Island, NY] (July 5, 1987): . As microfiche: *NewsBank: Literature* 14 (July 1987): Fiche 7, B12-13.
30. Lehmann-Haupt, Christopher. *New York Times* 136 (June 8, 1987): III, 17.
31. Lehmann-Haupt, Christopher. "A King of Mystery Makes a Masterpiece of '*Misery*,'" in *Fairbanks Daily News-Miner* [Alaska] (June 21, 1987): . As microfiche: *NewsBank: Literature* 14 (July 1987): Fiche 7, B6-B7.
32. Liberatore, Karen. "King Whines and Oinks All the Way to the Bank," in *San Francisco Examiner* (May 29, 1987): . As microfiche: *NewsBank: Literature* 13 (June, 1987): Fiche 110, D5.
33. *Listener* 118 (September 24, 1987): 22.
34. *London Review of Books* 10 (April 21, 1988): 22.
35. *Los Angeles Times Book Review* (May 10, 1987): 8.
36. Lowell, David M. "A KING-size Remedy That Worked!" in *Castle Rock: The Stephen King Newsletter* 3:9 (September, 1987): 3.
37. Macknee, Salem. "King Serves Up His Own Nightmare," in *The News and Observer* [Raleigh, NC] (July 19, 1987): . As microfiche: *NewsBank: Literature* 14 (August, 1987): Fiche 20, C1.
38. *The Magazine of Fantasy & Science Fiction* 73 (October, 1987): 27.
39. *The Magazine of Fantasy & Science Fiction* 73 (October, 1987): 36.
40. Magistrale, Anthony. *The Moral Voyages of Stephen King*. STARMONT STUDIES IN LITERARY CRITICISM, No. 25. Mercer Island, WA: Starmont House, 1989.
41. Miller, G. Wayne. "'*Misery*' Will Take Good Care of King's Horror Fans," in *Journal* [Providence, RI] (June 14, 1987): . As microfiche: *NewsBank: Literature* 14 (July 1987): Fiche 7, C2-C3.
42. Moore, J. R. T. "The Writer and His Shadow," in *SFRA Newsletter* No. 182 (November, 1990): 38-39.

43. Morrison, Michael A. "The Year in Horror, 1987," in *Science Fiction & Fantasy Book Review Annual,* edited by Robert A. Collins and Robert Latham. Westport, CT: Meckler, 1988, cloth, p.30-31.
44. *New Statesman & Society* 3 (December 7, 1990): 34.
45. Newman, Kim. *New Statesman* (September 11, 1987): 30.
46. *The New York Times Book Review* 93 (June 12, 1988): 38.
47. Paul, Steve. "A New Conquest for King Bibliophiles," in *Kansas City Star* [Missouri] (June 7, 1987): . As microfiche: *NewsBank: Literature* 14 (July 1987): Fiche 7, B11.
48. Perry, Vern. "King's Latest Is Trip Down Thriller Lane," in *Orange County Register* [Santa Ana, CA] (May 24, 1987): . As microfiche: *NewsBank: Literature* 13 (June, 1987): Fiche 110, D6-D7.
49. Pluto, Terry. "'*Misery*' Loves Company," in *Akron Beacon Journal* [Ohio] (June 28, 1987): . As microfiche: *NewsBank: Literature* 14 (July 1987): Fiche 7, B14.
50. *Publishers Weekly* 231 (May 1, 1987): 52.
51. *Publishers Weekly* 233 (March 25, 1988): 63.
52. Sarrantonio, Al. "Horrors Red," in *Mystery Scene* No. 10 (1987): 35-36.
53. Smith, Wendy. "King King of Popular Novelists," in *Cleveland Plain Dealer* [Ohio] (May 24, 1987): . As microfiche: *NewsBank: Literature* 14 (July 1987): Fiche 7, C1.
54. Spignesi, Stephen J. "*Misery*," in *The Shape Under the Sheet: The Complete Stephen King Encyclopedia.* Ann Arbor, MI: Popular Culture, Ink., May 1991, cloth, p. 406-413.
55. Streitfield, David. "Stephen King's No. 1 Fans," in *Washington Post* "Style" (May 8, 1987): .
56. *Time* 129 (June 8, 1987): 82.
57. *Washington Post Book World* 17 (June 14, 1987): 1.
58. *Washington Post Book World* 17 (December 6, 1987): 19.
59. *Wilson School Journal* 209 (June 23, 1987): 28.

A34. THE DARK TOWER II: THE DRAWING OF THE THREE

A34. ***The Dark Tower II: The Drawing of the Three.*** Illustrated by Phil Hale. West Kingston, RI: Donald M. Grant, Publisher, 1987, 400 p., cloth. [fantasy novel]

COMMENTS: The second volume in King's epic-quest-in-progress, *The Dark Tower* (see also **A17** and **A43**).

REPRINTS:

ab. West Kingston, RI: Donald M. Grant, Publisher, 1987, 400 p., cloth. Lettered state, perhaps 52 copies (A-Z, AA-ZZ).
ac. West Kingston, RI: Donald M. Grant, Publisher, 1987, 400 p., cloth. Limited edition, 850 copies; dust jacket and slipcase.
ad. West Kingston, RI: Donald M. Grant, Publisher, 1987, 400 p., cloth. Trade edition of 30,000 copies.

b. excerpted in: *Castle Rock: The Stephen King Newsletter* 3:4 (April/May, 1987): 1, 8-9, 11, 13.
c. London: Sphere, September 1988, 224 p., paper.
d. New York: A Plume Book, New American Library, March 1989, 399 p., trade paper. Illustrated by Phil Hale.
db. New York: A Signet Book, New American Library, January 1990, 463 p., mass-market paper. No illustrations.
dc. New York: A Plume Book, New American Library, n.d., 399 p., trade paperback. A boxed set issued with *The Dark Tower: The Gunslinger*.
dd. New York: A Signet Book, New American Library, n.d., 463 p., mass-market paper. A boxed set issued with *The Dark Tower: The Gunslinger*.
e. Book-of-the-Month Club selection.
f. as: *Drei* ["*Three*"]. München: Wilhelm Heyne Verlag, 1989, p., paper. "Jumbo" Paperback 41/14. Translated by Joachim Körber. [German]
g. as: *Drei* ["*Three*"]. Gütersloh, Austria: Bertelsmann Lesering, 1989, p. Translated by Joachim Körber. [German]
h. Dutch edition. Further information unknown.

SECONDARY SOURCES AND REVIEWS:

1. Beahm, George, ed. *The Stephen King Companion*. Kansas City, MO: Andrews and McMeel, September 1989, p. 198-200.
2. Beaulieu, Janet C. "Road to *Dark Tower* Powerful, Intense," in *Bangor Daily News* [Maine] (July 11, 1989): . As microfiche: *NewsBank: Literature* 16 (August, 1989): Fiche 80, C14-D1.
3. Bertin, Eddy C. "DT Books Make Dutch Appearance," in *Castle Rock: The Stephen King Newsletter* 5:12 (December, 1989): .
4. Blue, Tyson. "Review: *The Dark Tower II: The Drawing of the Three*," in *Castle Rock: The Stephen King Newsletter* 3:7 (July, 1987): 1, 7, 8.
5. *Booklist* 85 (December 15, 1988): 666.
6. Condon, Garrett. "King's 'Other' Publisher Well-Kept Collector's Secret," in *Hartford Courant* [Connecticut] (August 28, 1987): . As microfiche: *NewsBank: Literature* 13 (October, 1987): Fiche 41, E4-E5.
7. Coven, Laurence. "King Draws a Bead on New York City," in *Daily News* [Los Angeles, CA] (July 16, 1989): . As microfiche: *NewsBank: Literature* 16 (August, 1989): Fiche 80, C12-13.
8. de Lint, Charles. *Science Fiction & Fantasy Book Review Annual*, edited by Robert A. Collins and Robert Latham. Westport, CT: Meckler, 1988, cloth, p. 226-227.
9. Fuller, Richard. *The New York Times* (January 8, 1989): VII, 18.
10. *Inside Books: The Bestseller Magazine* (March 1989): .
11. *Kirkus Reviews* 57 (January 1, 1989): 8.
12. *Locus* 22 (May 1989): 48.
13. *Publishers Weekly* 235 (January 13, 1989): 86.
14. Ruiz, Estelle. "The King/Roland Quest," in *Castle Rock: The Stephen King Newsletter* 3:12/4:1 (December, 1987-January 1988): 3, 13.
15. *Science Fiction Chronicle* 9 (October, 1987): 39.
16. Spignesi, Stephen J. "*The Dark Tower II: The Drawing of the Three*," in *The Shape Under the Sheet: The Complete Stephen King*

Encyclopedia. Ann Arbor, MI: Popular Culture, Ink., May 1991, cloth, p. 395-401.
17. *Voice of Youth Advocates* 13 (June, 1990): 138.
18. *West Coast Review of Books* 13:3 (1987): 60.
19. *West Coast Review of Books* 14:4 (1989): 25.

A35. THE TOMMYKNOCKERS

A35. ***The Tommyknockers***. New York: G. P. Putnam's Sons, 10 November 1987, 558 p., cloth. [science-fiction horror novel]

PLOT SUMMARY: When an ancient alien spacecraft is unearthed near a small town, the inhabitants are gradually transformed physically and psychologically into something not quite human, something not quite alien.

COMMENT: An exercise in science-fiction-*cum*-horror, *The Tommyknockers* clearly illustrates King's strengths and weaknesses. His self-referential treatment of earlier novels and characters can be seen either as summational (suggesting that *Tommyknockers*, like *IT*, represents a turning point for King), or as self-indulgent. References to topical issues have been similarly interpreted as King touching on his own times, or as King indulging in lecturing for a captive audience. Regardless of interpretations, the novel does tend to static portrayals, while also incorporating striking imagery, characters, and episodes.

Advance orders for the hardcover totaled 900,000 copies, with 1,405,000 hardcover copies sold in 1987, King's highest sales total to that date, placing King in the #1 spot on the hardcover fiction BestSeller List for the second consecutive year (the last time an author had appeared in consecutive years was 1973/1974). With *Misery* and *The Eyes of the Dragon* also on the list, King appeared a total of three times.

REPRINTS:

b. London: Hodder & Stoughton, February 1988, 563 p., cloth.
c. New York: A Signet Book, New American Library, November 1988, 747 p., mass-market paper. 4 printings by September, 1989.
d. serialized in: *Australian Women's Day Magazine*. [Cited in *Castle Rock: The Stephen King Newsletter* 4:7 (July, 1988): 6].
e. as: *De Gloed*. Utrecht: Luitingh, 1988, 560 p. Translated by Margot Bakker. Second printing, 1988. [Dutch]
f. as: *Das Monstrum/Tommyknockers*. Hamburg, West Germany: Hoffman and Campe, 1988, 688 p., cloth. Translated by Joachim Körber. [German]
g. London: New English Library, 15 October 1989, [704] p., paper.
h. as: *Los Tommyknockers*. Esplugas Llobregat (Barcelona), Spain: Plaza & Janés Editores, 1989, p. [Spanish]

SECONDARY SOURCES AND REVIEWS:

1. Auerbach, Nina. *New York Times Book Review* 92 (December 5, 1987): VII, 8.

2. Beahm, George, ed. *The Stephen King Companion*. Kansas City, MO: Andrews and McMeel, September 1989, paper.
3. Beaulieu, Janet C. "A Slow Start, But Rousing Finish," in *Bangor Daily News* [Maine] (December 8, 1987): . As microfiche: *NewsBank: Literature* 15 (January, 1988): Fiche 8, C11.
4. *Booklist* 84 (October 1, 1987): 170.
5. *Books* (February, 1988): 18.
6. Card, Orson Scott. "Books to Look for," in *The Magazine of Fantasy & Science Fiction* 75 (July, 1988): 30.
7. Cobb, Anne. "King's Latest Doesn't Raise Many Hairs," in *Buffalo News* [New York] (December 6, 1987): . As microfiche: *NewsBank: Literature* 15 (January, 1988): Fiche 8, C13.
8. Collings, Michael R. *The Annotated Guide to Stephen King: A Primary and Secondary Bibliography of the Works of America's Premier Horror Writer*. STARMONT REFERENCE GUIDE, No. 8. Mercer Island, WA: Starmont House, October 1986.
9. Collings, Michael R. *The Many Facets of Stephen King*. STARMONT STUDIES IN LITERARY CRITICISM, No. 11. Mercer Island, WA: Starmont House, 1986.
10. Collings, Michael R. "The Revelations of 'Becka Paulson," in *The Shorter Works of Stephen King,* by Michael R. Collings and David A. Engebretson. STARMONT STUDIES IN LITERARY CRITICISM, No. 9. Mercer Island, WA: Starmont House, June 1985, p. 173-181.
11. Collings, Michael R. *The Stephen King Phenomenon*. STARMONT STUDIES IN LITERARY CRITICISM, No. 14. Mercer Island, WA: Starmont House, 1987, cloth.
12. Collings, Michael R. "Stephen King, Sci-Fi, and *The Tommyknockers*," in *Castle Rock: The Stephen King Newsletter* 3:11 (November, 1987): 1, 4-5.
13. Collings, Michael R. *SFRA Newsletter* No. 152 (October, 1987): 34-35. Reprinted as: *"The Tommyknockers,"* in *Science Fiction & Fantasy Book Review Annual,* edited by Robert A. Collins and Robert Latham. Westport, CT: Meckler, 1988, cloth, p. 228-229.
14. Connolly, Sherryl. "You Scared? Well, I'm Not," in *Daily News* [New York] (November 29, 1987): . As microfiche: *NewsBank: Literature* 14 (December, 1987): Fiche 64, D8.
15. Dougherty, Marianne. "'*Tommyknockers*' Finds Stephen King as His Scary Best," in *Pittsburgh Press* (December 13, 1987): . As microfiche: *NewsBank: Literature* 15 (January, 1988): Fiche 8, D1.
16. Flick, Arend. "Stephen King as Nerd's Best Friend," in *Los Angeles Times Book Review* (December 20, 1987): B1, B12.
17. Frazell, Daryl. "Horror Turns to Disgust: Stephen King Lets Us Down When He Holds Human Spirit in Low Regard," in *St. Petersburg Times* [Florida] (December 6, 1987): . As microfiche: *NewsBank: Literature* 15 (January, 1988): Fiche 8, C9.
18. Gorner, Peter. "King Foregoes Horror for Gore in '*The Tommyknockers*," in *Chicago Tribune* (November 22, 1987): Section 14, 5. As microfiche: *NewsBank: Literature* 14 (December, 1987): Fiche 64, D5-D6.
19. Graham, Mark. "King Epic Complex, Incongruous," in *Rocky Mountain News* [Denver, CO] (February 1, 1988): 53.

20. Hauser, Jerald. "Stephen King's Latest Horror Lives Underground," in *Milwaukee Journal* (December 13, 1987): . As microfiche: *NewsBank: Literature* 15 (January, 1988): Fiche 8, D4.
21. Hemesath, James B. *Library Journal* 113:1 (January, 1988): 99.
22. Hermann, Spring. "New King Novel a Good Read Despite Structural Flaws," in *Hartford Courant* [Connecticut] (December 20, 1987): . As microfiche: *NewsBank: Literature* 15 (January, 1988): Fiche 8, C7-C8.
23. Hoppenstand, Gary, and Ray B. Browne, eds. *The Gothic World of Stephen King: Landscape of Nightmares*. Bowling Green, OH: Bowling Green State University Popular Press, December 1987.
24. Indick, Ben P. "H. P. Lovecraft and Those *Tommyknockers*," in *Castle Rock: The Stephen King Newsletter* 4:8 (August, 1988): 4, 12.
25. Johnson, George. "New and Noteworthy," in *New York Times Book Review* (November 13, 1988): 66.
26. *Kliatt Paperback Book Guide* 23 (January 1989): 10.
27. Kloer, Phil. "King's Latest Has Mind-Warping Bogeymen from Space," in *Atlanta Journal-Constitution* (December 6, 1987): . As microfiche: *NewsBank: Literature* 15 (January, 1988): Fiche 8, C10.
28. Krolczyk, Gregory N. "'*Tommyknockers*': People Get Knocked Off, But Who Cares," in *Sun* [Baltimore, MD] (December 27, 1987): . As microfiche: *NewsBank: Literature* 15 (January, 1988): Fiche 8, C12.
29. Larson, Susan. "Not Your Backyard, Garden-Variety UFO," in *Houston Post* (November 29,1987): . As microfiche: *NewsBank: Literature* 15 (January, 1988): Fiche 8, D2-D3.
30. Lehmann-Haupt, Christopher. *New York Times* 137 (November 5, 1987): III, 33.
31. *London Review of Books* 10 (April 21, 1988): 22.
32. Morrison, Michael A. "The Year in Horror, 1987," in *Science Fiction & Fantasy Book Review Annual,* edited by Robert A. Collins and Robert Latham. Westport, CT: Meckler, 1988, cloth, p.21-36.
33. *New York Times Book Review* 93 (November 13, 1988): 66.
34. *Publishers Weekly* 232 (October 9, 1987): 79.
35. *Publishers Weekly* 234 (August 26, 1988): 83.
36. Reese, Kathleen. "Stephen King Mixes Movies and Monsters in '*The Tommyknockers*,'" in *Dallas Times Herald* [Texas] (November 22, 1987): . As microfiche: *NewsBank: Literature* 14 (December, 1987): Fiche 64, D9-D10.
37. Sarrantonio, Al. "Horrors Red," in *Mystery Scene* No. 14 (1988): 48.
38. Schleier, Curt. "Newest King Thriller Isn't Up to His Previous Books," in *Grand Rapids Press* [Michigan] (November 22, 1987): . As microfiche: *NewsBank: Literature* 14 (December, 1987): Fiche 64, D7.
39. Schleier, Curt. "A Spaceship Gives 'Em Hell," in *Newsday* [Long Island, NY] (January 3, 1988): . As microfiche: *NewsBank: Literature* 15 (January, 1988): Fiche 8, C14.
40. *School Library Journal* 34 (February, 1988): 95.

41. Schweitzer, Darrell. "Fear and the Future: King as a Science-Fiction Writer," in *Castle Rock: The Stephen King Newsletter* 3:11/4:1 (December, 1987-January, 1988): 1, 6-8. Reprinted: *Reign of Fear: Fiction and Film of Stephen King,* edited by Don Herron. Los Angeles: Underwood-Miller, June 1988, cloth, p. 193-208.
42. Schweitzer, Darrell. "Schweitzer on TK, SK, and Science Fiction," in *Castle Rock: The Stephen King Newsletter* 4:5-6 (May-June, 1988): 9.
43. *Science Fiction Chronicle* 9 (February, 1988): 42.
44. Spignesi, Stephen J. "*The Tommyknockers*," in *The Shape Under the Sheet: The Complete Stephen King Encyclopedia.* Ann Arbor, MI: Popular Culture, Ink., May 1991, cloth, p. 413-427.
45. *Washington Post Book World* 17 (November 29, 1987): 9.
46. *West Coast Review of Books* 13:4 (1988): 28.
47. White, Sarah J. "Second *Tommyknockers* Quite Different," in *Castle Rock: The Stephen King Newsletter* 4:5-6 (May-June, 1988): 5. [Comparative review of King's novel and *The Tommyknockers,* by Alan E. Leisk, 1987].

A36. NIGHTMARES IN THE SKY

A36. ***Nightmares in the Sky: Gargoyles and Grotesques.*** New York: Viking Studio Books, November 1988, 128 p., cloth. Text by Stephen King (35 p.); photographs by f-Stop Fitzgerald. [photo-essay]

REPRINTS:

b. excerpted in: *Penthouse* (September, 1988): . [See **C191**.]
c. as: *Nachtgesichter* ["*Night Faces*"]. München: Wilhelm Heyne Verlag (Gebundene Ausgabe), 1989, p. Translated by Joachim Körber. [German]
d. Germany: Droemer/Knaur Verlag, 1989, p., cloth. [German]

SECONDARY SOURCES AND REVIEWS:

1. Blue, Tyson. "Of New Frontiers and Gargoyles," in *Castle Rock: The Stephen King Newsletter* 4:11 (November, 1988): 3.
2. *Book World* 18 (December 4, 1988): 19.
3. *Booklist* 85 (November 1, 1988): 442.
4. Indick, Ben P. "Looking for Trouble: Nightmares in Daylight," in *Castle Rock: The Stephen King Newsletter* 5:1 (January, 1989): 1, 7.
5. *Washington Post Book World* 18 (December 4, 1988): 19.

A37. DOLAN'S CADILLAC

A37. ***Dolan's Cadillac.*** Northridge, CA: Lord John Press, 1989, 64 p., cloth. Lettered state of 26 copies (A-Z), half-bound, in slipcase, signed by King. See also **B80**. [horror novella]

COMMENTS: The story originally appeared as a serial in *Castle Rock: The Stephen King Newsletter*, from February through June 1985 [See **B80**]. As did "The Blue Air Compressor" and "Crouch End," the story suggests the depths of King's debt to a previous writer—in this case Poe and "The Cask of Amontillado." King updates the story, amplifying his protagonist's motivation and suffering. Not among King's strongest works, it tends to lengthy explication that obscures the narrative movement.

REPRINTS:

ab. Northridge, CA: Lord John Press, 1989, 64 p., cloth. Deluxe edition; 250 numbered copies, quarter-bound, signed by King.
ac. Northridge, CA: Lord John Press, 1989, 64 p., cloth. Limited, signed edition, 1000 numbered copies, signed by King.
b. in: *Nightmares & Dreamscapes*. New York: Viking, 1993, cloth, p. 11-66. [See **A47**, **B80**].

SECONDARY SOURCES AND REVIEWS:

1. Beahm, George. *The Stephen King Companion*. Kansas City, MO: Andrews and McMeel, September 1989, p. 109.
2. Blue, Tyson. *The Unseen King*. STARMONT STUDIES IN LITERARY CRITICISM, No. 26. Mercer Island, WA: Starmont House, 1989, p. 120-123.
3. Collings, Michael R., and David A. Engebretson. *The Shorter Works of Stephen King*. STARMONT STUDIES IN LITERARY CRITICISM, No. 9. Mercer Island, WA: Starmont House, June 1985, p. 182-183.
4. Indick, Ben P. "A Cadillac for King's Used Car Lot," in *Castle Rock: The Stephen King Newsletter* 5:5 (May, 1989): 8.
5. Indick, Ben P. *"Dolan's Cadillac,"* in *The Blood Review: The Journal of Horror Criticism* 1:1 (October 1989): 68.
6. Spignesi, Stephen J. *"Dolan's Cadillac,"* in *The Shape Under the Sheet: The Complete Stephen King Encyclopedia*. Ann Arbor, MI: Popular Culture Ink, May 1991, cloth, p. 507-509.

A38. MY PRETTY PONY

A38. ***My Pretty Pony.*** New York: Library Fellows of the Whitney Museum, Whitney Museum of Art, Artists and Writers series, September (or October) 1989, [64] p., cloth. Illustrated by Barbara Kruger (all illustrations in the limited edition are lithographed). Bound in stainless steel jacket with digital clock inset. Limited printing of 280 copies; 150 offered for sale; list price of $2,200. See **B104**. [short story]

REPRINTS:

b. New York: Alfred A. Knopf, Random House, September 1989, [64] p., oversized cloth. A limited printing of 15,000 copies, with a list price of $50.00. Red and white covers in slipcase.

c. In: *Nightmares & Dreamscapes*. New York: Viking, 1993, cloth, p. 437-466. [See **A47**, **B104**].

SECONDARY SOURCES AND REVIEWS:

1. Beahm, George. *The Stephen King Companion.* Kansas City, MO: Andrews and McMeel, September 1989, paper, p. 106-108.
2. Blue, Tyson. "*My Pretty Pony*: A Treat for the Eye," in *Castle Rock: The Stephen King Newsletter* 4:12 (December, 1988): 1, 8.
3. Blue, Tyson. "Affordable 'My Pretty Pony' Published by Whitney Museum," in *Castle Rock: The Stephen King Newsletter* 5:12 (December, 1989): .
4. *Booklist* 86 (December 1, 1989): 724.
5. de la Ree, Gerry. [Letter] in *Castle Rock: The Stephen King Newsletter* 5:9-10 (September-October 1989): 9.
6. de Lint, Charles. "Night Journeys—Reviews of Horror," in *Mystery Scene* No. 26 (June, 1990): 111.
7. Indick, Ben P. "*My Pretty Pony*: An Odd Couple Produces a Work of Art," in *Castle Rock: The Stephen King Newsletter* 5:4 (April, 1989): 1, 9.
8. *Library Journal* 114 (December, 1989): 118.
9. *Locus* 23 (November, 1989): 56.
10. "*Mystery Scene* Horror Bestseller List," in *Mystery Scene* No. 24 (January, 1990): 96.
11. Streitfeld, David. "Long Live the King," in *Washington Post Book World* (August 20, 1989): 15.
12. Spignesi, Stephen J. "*My Pretty Pony*," in *The Shape Under the Sheet: The Complete Stephen King Encyclopedia*. Ann Arbor, MI: Popular Culture Ink, May 1991, cloth, p. 529-532.
13. Tallman, Susan. "Counting Pretty Ponies: Barbara Kruger and Stephen King Make a Book," in *Arts Magazine* 63 (March 1989): 19-20.
14. Williams, Gene. "Short Story Is Something New for King," in *Cleveland Plain Dealer* [Ohio] (April 22, 1990): . As microfiche: *NewsBank: Literature* (May, 1990-August, 1990): Fiche 48, A10.
15. *West Coast Review of Books* 15:2 (1989): 50.
16. Winter, Douglas E. "Venturing a Bit into the Magical," in *Washington* [D.C.] *Times* (November 29, 1989): . As microfiche: *NewsBank: Literature* 16 (December, 1989): Fiche 126, A11.

A39. THE DARK HALF

A39. *The Dark Half.* London: Hodder & Stoughton, 19 October 1989, 413 p., cloth. [horror novel]

AUTHOR'S NOTE: "I'm indebted to the late Richard Bachman for his help and inspiration. This novel could not have been written without him."

PLOT SUMMARY: Thad Beaumont's pseudonym, George Stark—officially "dead and buried"—comes to life and demands that his character be resurrected. To indicate the strength of his demands, Stark begins the systematic destruction of everyone involved in his "demise."

COMMENTS: *The Dark Half* set a record of 1.5 million copies of the first hardcover edition. The Hodder & Stoughton publication packet announces *The Dark Half* as the first novel in a four-book sale. The book is the second in what has been called King's "writer's trilogy," comprising *Misery, The Dark Half,* and "Secret Window, Secret Garden" (in *Four Past Midnight*).

REPRINTS:

b. New York: Viking, 1989, 431 p., cloth.
c. as: *Stark: The Dark Half*. Hamburg, West Germany: Hoffmann und Campe, 1989, p., cloth. Translated by Christel Wiemken. [German]
d. as: . West Germany: Droemer/Knaur Verlag, 1989, 475 p., cloth. [German]
e. New York: A Signet Book, October 1990, 484 p., mass-market paper.
f. as: *Le Part des Ténèbres: Roman*. Paris: Albin Michel, 1990, 461 p., cloth. Translated by William Olivier Desmond. [French]
g. as: *La Mitad Siniestra*. México, D.F.: Editorial Grijalbo, 1990, 475 p., paper? Translated by María Elisa Moreno Canaleja. [Spanish]

SECONDARY SOURCES AND REVIEWS:

1. Alderman, John R. "Story of Two Novelists Is Not King at His Best," in *Richmond News Leader* [Virginia] (February 14, 1990): . As microfiche: *NewsBank: Literature* 17 (March, 1990): Fiche 27, D2.
2. Beaulieu, Janet C. "'*The Dark Half*' Brings Pseudonyms to Life," in *Bangor Daily News* "Books in Review" [Maine] (November 14, 1989): . As microfiche: *NewsBank: Literature* 16 (December, 1989): Fiche 126, A7-A8.
3. Blue, Tyson. "The Misery of Pseudonyms," in *The Blood Review: The Journal of Horror Criticism* 1:1 (October 1989): 53-54.
4. Blue, Tyson. "New Novel Puts SK Back on Track," in *Castle Rock: The Stephen King Newsletter* 5:11 (November, 1989): .
5. *Booklist* 85 (August, 1989): 1922.
6. Chandler, Randy. "The Story of King's Alter Ego Inspires Frightening '*Dark Half*,'" in *Atlanta Journal-Constitution* [Georgia] (October 15, 1989): . As microfiche: *NewsBank: Literature* 16 (November, 1989): Fiche 112, F14.
7. *Christian Science Monitor* 82 (January 22, 1990): 13.
8. Collings, Michael R. "Transforms Frankenstein Mythos," in *The Blood Review: Journal of Horror Criticism* 1:2 (January, 1990): 53.
9. Coltrera, Francesca. "When An Evil Alter Ego Takes Over," in *Boston Herald* (November 12, 1989): . As microfiche: *NewsBank: Literature* 16 (December, 1989): Fiche 126, A9.
10. Connelly, Sherryl. "Stephen King is Back: Scared Yet?" in *Daily News* [New York] (October 22, 1989): . As microfiche: *NewsBank: Literature* 16 (November, 1989): Fiche 112, G2.

11. Costello, Matthew J. "Trying to Unlock the Secret," in *The Blood Review: Journal of Horror Criticism* 1:2 (January, 1990): 52.
12. de Lint, Charles. "Night Journeys—Reviews of Horror: Installment #9," in *Mystery Scene* No. 24 (January, 1990): 87-88.
13. de Lint, Charles. "Night Journeys—Reviews of Horror," in *Mystery Scene* No. 25 (March, 1990): 78. *The Dark Half* is listed as one of the top fifteen titles of 1989.
14. de Lint, Charles. "Night Journeys—Reviews of Horror," in *Mystery Scene* No. 28 (January, 1991): 96.
15. Donaldson, Stanley. "Doctors Find Man's Twin Inside His Head," in *National Examiner* (August 20, 1991): 9. While this article contains no reference to *The Dark Half*, the medical condition described is startlingly similar to Thad Beaumont's in the novel, and thus provides an interesting sidelight to King's fiction.
16. Foster, Prudence. "Suspenseful, Intriguing, Irritating," in *The Blood Review: Journal of Horror Criticism* 1:2 (January, 1990): 52.
17. Gagliani, William D. "Danger Within: New King Novel Hits Close to Home," in *Milwaukee Journal* [Wisconsin] (October 22, 1989): . As microfiche: *NewsBank: Literature* 16 (November, 1989): Fiche 112, G4.
18. Hall, Melissa Mia. "An Experiment for King," in *The Blood Review: Journal of Horror Criticism* 1:2 (January, 1990): 53.
19. Hautala, Rick. "Wrote from the Gut on This One," in *The Blood Review: Journal of Horror Criticism* 1:2 (January, 1990): 53.
20. *Kirkus Reviews* 57 (July 15, 1989): 1020.
21. Krolczyk, Gregory N. "End of Latest King Novel Doesn't Convince," in *Sun* [Baltimore, MD] (October 29, 1989): . As microfiche: *NewsBank: Literature* 16 (November, 1989): Fiche 112, G1.
22. Lehmann-Haupt, Christopher. "From Stephen King, a Writer's Demon," in *New York Times* "Word and Image" (October 23, 1989): C20.
23. Leonard, Stephanie. "Editor's Column," in *Castle Rock: The Stephen King Newsletter* 4:11 (November, 1988): 2. [Notes that King has written a book under this title, "But at this time he has no plans to publish it."]
24. Liberatore, Karen. "The 'Endsville' in the Horror Writer's Mind," in *San Francisco Examiner* (October 19, 1989): . As microfiche: *NewsBank: Literature* 16 (November, 1989): Fiche 112, F12-13.
25. Lileks, James. "The More You Think About It, The Scarier It Gets," in *St. Paul Pioneer Press-Dispatch* (November 12, 1989): . As microfiche: *NewsBank: Literature* 16 (December, 1989): Fiche 126, A10.
26. *Locus* 23 (September, 1989): 17.
27. *Locus* 23 (September, 1989): 25.
28. *Los Angeles Times Book Review* (September 30, 1990): 14. [Publication notice for paperback edition].
29. Massie, Elizabeth. "The Book Is a Success," in *The Blood Review: Journal of Horror Criticism* 1:2 (January, 1990): 52.
30. *MacLean's* 102 (December 18, 1989): 57.

31. Miller, G. Wayne. "The Pleasure/Pain of Being a Writer," in *The Blood Review: Journal of Horror Criticism* 1:2 (January, 1990): 53.
32. Moore, J. R. T. "The Writer and His Shadow," in *SFRA Newsletter* [Science Fiction Research Association] No. 182 (November, 1990): 398.
33. *New Statesman & Society* 3 (December 7, 1990): 34.
34. *New York Times* [late edition] 139 (October 23, 1989): C20.
35. *New York Times Book Review* (October 29, 1989): . [Half-page favorable review].
36. *Publishers Weekly* 236 (September 1, 1989): 76.
37. *Publishers Weekly* 237 (August 31, 1990): 60.
38. *Science Fiction Chronicle* 11 (Fall, 1990): 34.
39. Stabiner, Karen. "Storytellers: New in November," in *Los Angeles Times Book Review* (October 15, 1989): 14.
40. Spignesi, Stephen J. "*The Dark Half*," in *The Shape Under the Sheet: The Complete Stephen King Encyclopedia*. Ann Arbor, MI: Popular Culture, Ink., May 1991, cloth, p. 427-437.
41. Streitfeld, David. "Long Live the King," in *Washington Post Book World* (August 20, 1989): 15.
42. Stumpf, Edna. "In Stephen King's Tale, a Writer's Alter Ego Is Out of Control," in *Philadelphia Inquirer* [Pennsylvania] (October 29, 1989): . As microfiche: *NewsBank: Literature* 16 (November, 1989): Fiche 112, G3.
43. *Time* 134 (November 20, 1990): 105.
44. Vander Putten, Joan. "Another Masterpiece of Horror," in *The Blood Review: Journal of Horror Criticism* 1:2 (January, 1990): 52.
45. Will, George. "Odd, Isn't It, That History's Most Developed Society Has a Deep Craving for Gore," in *Philadelphia Inquirer* [Pennsylvania] (December 11, 1989): .
46. Winter, Douglas E. "Venturing a Bit into the Magical," in *Washington* [D.C.] *Times* (November 29, 1989): . As microfiche: *NewsBank: Literature* 16 (December, 1989): Fiche 126, A11.

A40. THE STAND: THE COMPLETE & UNCUT EDITION

A40. ***The Stand: The Complete & Uncut Edition.*** New York: Doubleday, 1990, xix+1153 p., cloth. Illustrated by Berni Wrightson. Limited edition of 1250 copies ($325), with 52 lettered copies not for sale. Both states signed by King and Wrightson. See also **A5**. [horror novel]

CONTENTS: "Author's Note" (see also **C199**); "A Preface in Two Parts"—"Part 1: To Be Read Before Purchase"; "Part 2: To Be Read After Purchase" (see also **C200**); *The Stand.*

COMMENTS: More than merely an augmented edition, the 1991 *Stand* represents not only a restoration of materials deleted from the original edition (adding some 150,000 words and increasing the chapter count by ten), but an updating of the story as well, bringing it into the 1990s.

REPRINTS:

b. New York: Doubleday, May 1990, 1153 p., cloth. A trade edition of 400,000 copies.
c. London: Houghton & Stoughton, 1990, 1007 p., cloth.
d. as: *Apocalipsis*. Barcelona: Plaza y Janés, 1990, 1299 p., paper. Translated by Lorenzo Cortina. [Spanish]
e. Camp Hill, PA: Quality Paperback Club, [n.d.], p., trade paper.
f. New York: A Signet Book, May 1991, xxv+1141 p., mass-market paper.
fb. New York: A Signet Book, Fall 1994, 1142 p., mass-market paper. Movie tie-in edition for the made-for-TV film.

SECONDARY SOURCES AND REVIEWS:

1. Beaulieu, Janet. "Uncut '*Stand*' a Wonderful Read," in *Bangor Daily News* [Maine] (May 8, 1990): . As microfiche: *NewsBank: Literature* (May, 1990): Fiche 48, A5-7.
2. Blue, Tyson. "Needful Kings," in *The Blood Review: Journal of Horror Criticism* 1:2 (January, 1990): 11.
3. *Book Watch* 11 (August, 1990): 3.
4. *Booklist* 86 (March 15, 1990): 1394.
5. Collings, Michael R. *Mystery Scene* No. 27 (October, 1990): 132.
6. Collings, Michael R. "Considering *The Stands*," in *Gauntlet* No. 2 (April, 1991): 179-188. Reprinted: *Gauntlet 2*, edited by Barry Hoffman. Baltimore, MD: Borderlands Press, May, 1991, p. 129-134.
7. Castello, William. "King's Longer '*Stand*' Is Better Saga," in *Reno Gazette-Journal* [Nevada] (July 1, 1990): . As microfiche: *NewsBank: Literature* (May, 1990-August, 1990): Fiche 82, C1.
8. de Lint, Charles. *Mystery Scene* no. 27 (October, 1990): 138.
9. Girard, James P. "King's 1978 Cult Classic Refurbished, Improved," in *Wichita Eagle* [Kansas] (June 10, 1990): . As microfiche: *NewsBank: Literature* (May, 1990): Fiche 71, D14-E1.
10. "It Appears This IS the End of the World—Death Can Only Come as a Kindness," in *Dayton Daily News/Journal Herald* [Ohio] (June 24, 1990): . As microfiche: *NewsBank: Literature* (May, 1990-August, 1990): Fiche 71, E3.
11. Kiely, Robert. "Armageddon: Complete and Uncut," in *New York Times Book Review* (May 13, 1990): 3. [Full-page review article].
12. *Kirkus Reviews* 58 (February 15, 1990): 210.
13. Krolczyk, Gregory N. "King's Restoration Strengthens '*The Stand*,'" in *Sun* [Baltimore, MD] (May 6, 1990): . As microfiche: *NewsBank: Literature* (May, 1990-August, 1990): Fiche 59, D9.
14. *Locus* 24 (June, 1990): 19.
15. Martin, Sue. "'*Stand*' Corrected," in *Los Angeles Times Book Review* (July 15, 1990): 12.
16. McDowell, Edwin. "Reissuing a King Novel with 150,000 Words of Cuts Restored," in *The New York Times* [New York] 139 (January 31, 1990): B2+.
16. Moss, Chuck. "The King's Last '*Stand*' Is a Winner," in *Detroit News* (May 9, 1990): . As microfiche: *NewsBank: Literature* (May, 1990-August, 1990): Fiche 59, D10.

17. Nash, Jesse. "King Fans Take a New '*Stand*,'" in *Times-Picayune* [New Orleans, LA] (June 3, 1990): . As microfiche: *NewsBank: Literature* (May, 1990): Fiche 71, E2.
18. Phillips, Rhonda. "Longer '*Stand*' Still Rich Reading Experience," in *Arkansas Democrat* [Little Rock] (July 1, 1990): . As microfiche: *NewsBank: Literature* (May, 1990-August, 1990): Fiche 71, E3.
19. *Publishers Weekly* 237 (March 16, 1990): 60.
20. Sanders, Joe. "*The Stand* in All Its Glory," in *SFRA Newsletter* No. 181 (October, 1990): 38-39.
21. Spignesi, Stephen J. "Addendum: *The Stand*—The Complete & Uncut Edition," in *The Shape Under the Sheet: The Complete Stephen King Encyclopedia*. Ann Arbor, MI: Popular Culture, Ink., May 1991, cloth, p. 225-231.
22. Williams, Gene. "Best-Seller Reissued with Cuts Restored," in *Cleveland Plain Dealer* [Ohio] (April 22, 1990): . As microfiche: *NewsBank: Literature* (May, 1990): Fiche 48, A9.
23. *Wilson Library Journal* 65 (October, 1990): 111.

A41. FOUR PAST MIDNIGHT

A41. ***Four Past Midnight***. New York: Viking, 1990, xvi+763 p., cloth. [novella collection]

CONTENTS: "Straight Up Midnight: An Introductory Note" (see **C202**); "One Past Midnight: A Note on 'The Langoliers'" (see **C203**); "The Langoliers" (1990; see **B96**); "Two Past Midnight: A Note on 'Secret Window, Secret Garden'" (see **C204**); "Secret Window, Secret Garden" (1990; see **B97**); "Three Past Midnight: A Note on 'The Library Policeman'" (see **C205**); "The Library Policeman" (1990; see **B98**); "Four Past Midnight: A Note on 'The Sun Dog'" (see **C206**); "The Sun Dog" (1990; see **B99**).

REPRINTS:

b. London: Hodder & Stoughton, 1990, p., cloth. Released in Australia prior to Viking's U.S. edition; however, the British edition was not released until October, 1990.
c. "The Langoliers" reprinted with *Get Shorty* by Elmore Leonard and *The Wings of Morning* by Thomas Tryon in *Book Digest*. Richmond, VA: T-L Books, 1990, 511 p., cloth.
d. Boston: G. K. Hall & Co., 1990, 2 vol., cloth? Large print edition.
e. New York: A Signet Book, September 1991, xvi+744 p., mass-market paper.
f. London: New English Library, 1991, 930 p., mass-market paper.

SECONDARY SOURCES AND REVIEWS:

1. Belden, Elizabeth A., and Judith M. Beckman. *English Journal* 80:4 (April, 1991): 84.

2. Blue, Tyson. "Needful Kings," in *The Blood Review: Journal of Horror Criticism* 1:2 (January, 1990): 11.
3. Bodart, Joni. *Wilson Library Journal* 69:7 (March, 1991): BT3.
4. *Bookworld* 20 (August 26, 1990): 9.
5. *Booklist* 86 (June 15, 1990): 1932.
6. Cameron, June. "'*Four Past Midnight*' More of the Unusual from King," in *Pittsburgh Press* (October 7, 1990): . As microfiche: *NewsBank: Literature* (October, 1990): Fiche 103, B9-B10.
7. Flewelling, Lynn. "'*Midnight*' Eyes Supernatural," in *Bangor Daily News* [Maine] (September 11, 1990): . As microfiche: *NewsBank: Literature* (October, 1990): Fiche 103, B2-3.
8. Gottlieb, Anne. "Three-Dimensional Characters Missing in King's Newest Thriller," in *Denver Post* [Colorado] (September 2, 1990): . As microfiche: *NewsBank: Literature* (September, 1990): Fiche 93, D10.
9. Hard, Annette. "Stephen King and the Monsters of the Mind: Four Horror Novellas," in *Houston Chronicle* [Texas] (October 14, 1990): . As microfiche: *NewsBank: Literature* (November, 1990): Fiche 112, D11.
10. Hauser, Jerald. "King Serves Up a 4-Course Feast of Chilling Horror," in *Milwaukee Journal* [Wisconsin] (August 26, 1990): . As microfiche: *NewsBank: Literature* (September, 1990): Fiche 93, D14.
11. Johnson, Dean. "The King Is Back, Horror Fans," in *Orlando Sentinel* [Florida] (September 9, 1990): . As microfiche: *NewsBank: Literature* (October, 1990): Fiche 103, A14.
12. *Kirkus Reviews* 58 (June 15, 1990): 825.
13. Kloer, Phil. "King's Novella Collection," in *Atlanta Journal-Constitution* [Georgia] (August 12, 1990): . As microfiche: *NewsBank: Literature* (September, 1990): Fiche 93, D11.
14. Ladd, Susan. "Collection of Novellas Proves King Hasn't Lost His Touch," in *Greensboro News and Record* [North Carolina] (September 16, 1990): . As microfiche: *NewsBank: Literature* (October, 1990): Fiche 103, B8.
15. Moore, J. R. T. "The Writer and His Shadow," in *SFRA Newsletter* No. 182 (November, 1990): 38-39. A brief review of *FPM* embedded in the last paragraph of a review of *The Dark Half*.
16. Murphy, Ray. "Two Tales Stand Out in New King Quartet," in *Boston Globe* (September 11, 1990): . As microfiche: *NewsBank: Literature* (October, 1990): Fiche 103, B4-B5.
17. *New Statesman & Society* 3 (December 7, 1990): 34.
18. Persico, Joyce J. "Time to Take a Whirlwind to Hell," in *Times* [Trenton, NJ] (October 28, 1990): . As microfiche: *NewsBank: Literature* (November, 1990): Fiche 112, D9-D10.
19. *Publishers Weekly* 237 (June 20, 1990): 48.
20. Purvis, Kathleen. "King's a Writer, All Right, But He Worries," in *Charleston Observer* [North Carolina] (September 23, 1990): . As microfiche: *NewsBank: Literature* (October, 1990): Fiche 103, B7.
21. Ray, Keith. "King's '*Midnight*' May Disappoint Some Fans," in *Arizona Daily Star* [Tucson] (September 30, 1990): . As microfiche: *NewsBank: Literature* (November, 1990): Fiche 112, D7.

22. Schrodt, Anita. "King Reveals How His Tales Started, But Not How They End," in *Wichita Eagle* [Kansas] (September 23, 1990): . As microfiche: *NewsBank: Literature* (October, 1990): Fiche 103, B1.
23. Schubert, Gail. "Stephen King Serves up New Tales of Terror," in *Boston Globe* (September 30, 1990): . As microfiche: *NewsBank: Literature* (November, 1990): Fiche 112, D8.
24. Slater, Libby. "Sampler Is Vintage King," in *Tulsa World* [Oklahoma] (August 26, 1990): . As microfiche: *NewsBank: Literature* (September, 1990): Fiche 93, D12.
25. Solomon, Andy. "Scared But Safe," in *New York Times Book Review* (September 2, 1990): 14.
26. Spignesi, Stephen J. "*Four Past Midnight*," in *The Shape Under the Sheet: The Complete Stephen King Encyclopedia*. Ann Arbor, MI: Popular Culture, Ink., May 1991, cloth, p. 437-456.
27. Stamm, Michael. "King's Title as Horror Fiction Master Remains Secure with Latest Release," in *The Register Guard* [Eugene, OR] (November 25, 1990): . As microfiche: *NewsBank: Literature* (1990): Fiche 4, C14.
28. Stumpf, Edna. "Four Novellas the Products of the King Horror Factory," in *Philadelphia Inquirer* (August 26, 1990): . As microfiche: *NewsBank: Literature* (September, 1990): Fiche 93, D13.
29. *Time* 136 (October 15, 1990): 89.
30. *Tribune Books* [Chicago] (June 15, 1990): 4.
31. *Tribune Books* [Chicago] (August 26, 1990): 3.
32. Wilson, Shirley. "Horror Returns in 4 King Tales," in *The Detroit News and Free Press* (September 9, 1990): . As microfiche: *NewsBank: Literature* (October, 1990): Fiche 103, B6.

A42. NOUVELLES

A42. *Nouvelles*. Paris: Presses Pocket, 1990, 223 p., paper. [bilingual story collection]

A bilingual edition of King's previously-published short stories, intended for schools, with the French-language versions translated by Michael Oriano.

A43. THE DARK TOWER III: THE WASTE LANDS

A43. ***The Dark Tower III: The Waste Lands.*** Hampton Falls, NH: Donald M. Grant Publisher, August 1991, 509 p., cloth. A limited edition. Illustrated by Ned Dameron with 12 color illustrations. [fantasy novel]

PLOT SUMMARY: Having successfully "drawn" two others into his alternate world, Roland continues his quest for the Dark Tower. As the small company comes nearer to the center of an ancient Kingdom, they are joined by the boy Jake, likewise drawn by magic from his own world into Roland's. After safely negotiating the perils of a decaying city and its even more decadent inhabitants, the four set out across the waste lands in search of the Tower.

COMMENTS: The third and longest volume to date in *The Dark Tower* series (see also **A17**, **A34**), *The Waste Lands* is much less a collection of individual stories than the two previous books, and more a coherent novel-in-progress. Images and scenes from *The Waste Lands* recur in *Insomnia*, providing an important link between the two novels, and a sense of progression to the Dark Tower Tales. The fourth volume in the series, *Wizard in Glass*, is tentatively scheduled for publication in 1996.

REPRINTS:

ab. Hampton Falls, NH: Donald M. Grant, Publisher, August 1991, 509 p., cloth. Trade edition.
b. New York: A Plume Book, January 1992, 422 p., trade paper. Illustrated by Ned Dameron.
bb. New York: A Plume Book, January 1992, 422 p., trade paper. A boxed set with the first two books in the series.
bc. New York: A Signet Book, January 1993, 590 p., mass-market paper.
bd. New York: A Signet Book, January 1993, 590 p., mass-market paper. A boxed set with the first two books in the series.
c. as: *Tot*. München: Wilhelm Heyne Verlag, 1992, 453 p., paper? Translated by Joachim Körber. [German]

SECONDARY SOURCES AND REVIEWS:

1. *Analog Science Fiction/Science Fact* 112 (June, 1992): 162+.
2. *Booklist* 88 (October 15, 1991): 382.
3. *Booklist* 88 (January 15, 1992): 870.
4. *Bloomsbury Review* 11 (December, 1991): 27.
5. *Bookwatch* 12 (October, 1991): 3.
6. *Kirkus Reviews* 59 (September 15, 1991): 1176.
7. *Kliatt Young Adult Paperback Book Guide* 26 (April, 1992): 14+.
8. *Locus* 27 (November, 1991): 21.
9. *Locus* 27 (November, 1991): 56.
10. *Locus* 28 (January, 1992): 57.
11. Nicholls, Richard E. *New York Times Book Review* 96 (September 29, 1991): 14.
12. *Publishers Weekly* 238:49 (November 8, 1991): 60-61.
13. *Rapport: West Coast Review of Books, Art & Entertainment* 16 (May 5, 1992): 21.
14. *Science Fiction Chronicle* 13 (October, 1991): 42.
15. *School Library Journal* 38 (August, 1992): 195.
16. *Voice of Young Advocates* 15 (June, 1992): 110.

A44. NEEDFUL THINGS

A44. *Needful Things*. New York: Viking, Fall 1991, 690 p., cloth. [horror novel]

PLOT SUMMARY: The citizens of Castle Rock, Maine are curious and excited when a new store opens: the proprietor, Leland Gaunt, seems to know just what each of them needs...or, at least, what each of them wants. More remarkably, he also seems able to fill those needs for surprisingly little money and the promise of a small prank to be played on someone else. Only gradually does it become clear that Gaunt is orchestrating the pranks, playing one person's greed off against another's obsession, until the souls of Castle Rock's inhabitants are literally at stake.

COMMENTS: In what King has called the last Castle Rock story, he gathers a number of strands, including his trademark references to past characters and stories; at the same time, he also creates his clearest, most successful direct confrontation between the White and the Dark, connecting this novel implicitly with the restored *The Stand* and with the Dark Tower series.

REPRINTS:

b. London: Hodder & Stoughton, 1991, 698 (or 672) p., cloth.
c. New York: A Signet Book, New American Library, July 1992, 736 p., mass-market paper.
d. Boston: G. K. Hall & Co., 1992, p., cloth. Large print edition.
e. as: *K'aesullok ui Pimil*. Soul: Toesong, 1992, 3 vol., paper. [Korean]
f. as: *La Tienda*. Barcelona: Ediciones B, 1992, 772 p., cloth? Translated by Hernán Sabaté. [Spanish]
g. as: *Bazaar: Roman*. Paris: A. Colin, 1992, 678 p., cloth. Translated by William Olivier Desmond. [French]
h. as: *Neobkhodimye Veshchi: Poslednaia Naibolee Polnaia Istoriia Kastl Roka*. L'vov: Khronos, 1993, 573 p., paper? Translated by L. A. Gridin, O. V. Beimuk, and E. IU. Kharitonova. [Ukrainian]
i. London: New English Library, 1994, 790 p., mass-market paper.

SECONDARY SOURCES AND REVIEWS:

1. Blue, Tyson. "Needful Kings," in *The Blood Review: Journal of Horror Criticism* 1: 2 (January, 1990): 11.
2. *Booklist* 87 (June 15, 1991): 1907.
3. *Booklist* 88 (March 15, 1992): 1398.
4. *Books* (March, 1994): 16.
5. *Bookworld* 21 (September 29, 1991): 9.
6. Collings, Michael R. *Mystery Scene* No. 31 (October, 1991): 51-52.
7. Kanfer, Stefan. *Time* 138:19 (November 11, 1991): GT12.
8. *Kirkus Reviews* 59 (July 1, 1991): 813.
9. *Kliatt Young Adult Paperback Book Guide* 26 (November, 1992): 9.
10. *Locus* 27 (July, 1991): 23.
11. *Locus* 27 (August, 1991): 29.
12. *Locus* 27 (December, 1991): 53.
13. *Locus* 28 (August, 1992): 53.
14. *Los Angeles Times Book Review* (October 20, 1991): 6.
15. *Magazine of Fantasy & Science Fiction* 82 (January, 1992): 45+.
16. *New York Times* [late edition] 141 (October 3, 1991): C23.
17. *Newsweek* 118 (September 16, 1991): 60.
18. *Observer* [London] (November 17, 1991): 64.

19. *Publishers Weekly* 238:32 (July 25, 1991): 36.
20. Queenan, Joe. *New York Times Book Review* (September 29, 1991): 13.
21. Schwartz, Gil. *Fortune* 124:15 (December 30, 1991): 137.
22. *Science Fiction Chronicle* 13 (March, 1992): 20+.
23. Sutherland, John. *Times Literary Supplement* No. 4624 (November 15, 1991): 6.
24. *Voice of Youth Advocates* 15 (December, 1992): 293.
25. *Voice of Youth Advocates* 16 (April, 1993): 16.

A45. GERALD'S GAME

A45. ***Gerald's Game.*** New York: Viking, 1992, 332 p., cloth. Illustrated by Bill Russell. [suspense novel]

PLOT SUMMARY: When Gerald Burlingame's marital bondage-game gets out of hand, his wife Jessie demands that he release her. He refuses; she kicks him in the chest and the groin, and Gerald dies...leaving Jessie handcuffed to the headboard of the bed in their isolated lakeside cabin. Jessie struggles to free herself from the handcuffs and simultaneously from the weight of the emotional and psychological baggage she has carried for most of her life.

COMMENTS: There is little of the supernatural or of horror in *Gerald's Game*, and those few elements are either explained away or left largely undeveloped. More than any other recent King work, this novel seems driven by a need to respond to a particular social agenda.

REPRINTS:

b. London: Hodder and Stoughton, 1992, 342 p., cloth.
c. Hingham, MA: Wheeler Publishing, 1992, 447 p., cloth? Large print edition.
d. New York: A Signet Book, July 1993, 445 p., mass-market paper.
e. as: *El Juego de Gerald*. México, D.F.: Editorial Grijalbo, 1993, 452 p., paper? Translated by María Vidal. [Spanish]
f. as: *Gra Geralda*. Warszawa: Prima, 1994, 302 p., paper? Translated by Tomasz Wyzynski. [Polish]

SECONDARY SOURCES AND REVIEWS:

1. *Book World (Washington Post)* 22 (July 19, 1992): 7.
2. *Booklist* 88 (May 1, 1992): 1563.
3. *Books* 7 (May, 1993): 20.
4. Doniger, Wendy. *New York Times Book Review* (August 16, 1992): 3.
5. *Entertainment Weekly* (July 16, 1993): 53.
6. Gates, David. *Newsweek* 120:1 (July 6, 1992): 56.
7. *Kirkus Reviews* 60 (April 15, 1992): 487.
8. *Locus* 29 (July, 1992): 50.
9. *Locus* 29 (August, 1992): 53.

10. *Locus* 29 (September, 1992): 21.
11. *Locus* 30 (August, 1993): 46.
12. *Magazine of Fantasy & Science Fiction* 83 (December, 1992): 31+.
13. *New York Magazine* 26 (August 2, 1993): 21.
14. *New York Times* [late edition] 141 (June 29, 1992): C13.
15. *Publishers Weekly* 239:24 (May 25, 1992): 38.
16. *Rapport: West Coast Review of Books, Art & Entertainment* 17 (January, 1992): 26.
17. Schwartz, Gil. *Fortune* 126:4 (August 24, 1992): 148-149.
18. *Science Fiction Chronicle* 13 (August, 1992): 49.
19. *Time* 140:2 (July 13, 1992): 81.

A46. DOLORES CLAIBORNE

A46. ***Dolores Claiborne***. New York: Viking, 1993, 305 p., cloth. Illustrated by Bill Russell. [novel]

PLOT SUMMARY: Dolores Claiborne appears late one evening at the Little Tall Island police station to clear herself of suspicion in one murder by admitting to another. Her only hope of convincing the authorities (and the other islanders) that she did not kill her employer is by giving a detailed account of her relationship with Vera Donovan and of the circumstances that led to the death of Joe St. George years before.

COMMENTS: While dealing with issues raised in *Gerald's Game*, particularly spouse and child abuse, *Dolores Claiborne* is remarkable for King's decision to tell the tale in a single block of uninterrupted, first-person narration. The strength of the novel relates directly to King's uncompromising portrait of Claiborne as wife, mother, and woman.

REPRINTS:

ab. New York: Viking, 1993, 332 p., paper? Large print edition.
b. London: Hodder & Stoughton, 1993, 241 p., cloth.
c. New York: A Signet Book, December 1993, 372 p., mass-market paper.
d. Sevenoaks, Kent: New English Library, 1993, 307 p., mass-market paper.
e. as: *Dolores Claiborne*. México, D.F.: Editorial Grijalbo, 1993, 291 p., paper? Translated by Irving Roffe. [Spanish]
f. as: *Dolores Claiborne*. Barcelona: Ediciones B, 1993, 307 p., paper? Translated by Enrique de Heriz. [Spanish]
g. as: *Dolores Claiborne: Roman*. Paris: Albin Michel, 1993, 324 p., cloth? Translated by Dominique Dill. [French]
h. as: *Dolores Claiborne*. Budapest: Európa, 1994, 260 p., paper? Translated by Endre Greskovits. [Hungarian]
i. with *Misery* as: *Dolores Kleiborn; Mizori: Romany*. L'vov: "Kameniar," 1995, 605 p., paper? Translated by E. Kharitonova. [Ukrainian]

SECONDARY SOURCES AND REVIEWS:

1. Blue, Tyson. "Needful Kings," in *The Blood Review: Journal of Horror Criticism* 1:2 (January, 1990): 11. A brief mention of the then work-in-progress.
2. *Booklist* 89 (September 15, 1992): 100.
3. *Book World* [*Washington Post*] 22 (December 13, 1992): 5.
4. *Book Watch* 14 (February, 1993): 7.
5. *Books* 7 (January, 1993): 15.
6. Johnson, Eric W. *Library Journal* 117:18 (November 1, 1992): 117.
7. Kent, Bill. *New York Times Book Review* (December 27, 1992): 15.
8. *Kirkus Reviews* 60 (September 1, 1992): 1081.
9. *Locus* 29 (November, 1992): 19+.
10. *Locus* 30 (January, 1993): 46.
11. *Locus* 30 (February, 1993): 55.
12. *New York Times* [late edition] 142 (November 16, 1992): C15.
13. *Observer* [London] (January 31, 1993): 57.
14. *Publishers Weekly* 239 (October 12, 1992): 64.
15. *Rapport: West Coast Review of Books, Art & Entertainment* 17 (March, 1993): 20.
16. Skow, John. *Publishers Weekly* 239:53 (December 7, 1992): 28.
17. Steinhauer, Heidi M. *School Library Journal* 39:4 (April, 1993): 149.
18. *Time* 140 (December 7, 1992): 81.

A47. NIGHTMARES & DREAMSCAPES

A47. *Nightmares & Dreamscapes*. New York: Viking, 1993, 816 p., cloth. [horror story collection]

CONTENTS: "Introduction: Myth, Belief, Faith, and *Ripley's Believe It or Not!*" by King; "Dolan's Cadillac" (1985; see **A37**, **B80**); "The End of the Whole Mess" (1992; see **B85**); "Suffer the Little Children" (1972; see **B15**); "The Night Flier" (1988; see **B89**); "Popsy" (1987; see **B88**); "It Grows on You" (1973; see **B22**); "Chattery Teeth" (1992; see **B103**); "Dedication" (1988; see **B92**); "The Moving Finger" (1990; see **B100**); "Sneakers" (1988; see **B91**); "You Know They Got a Hell of a Band" (1992; see **B102**); "Home Delivery" (1989; see **B95**); "Rainy Season" (1989; see **B93**); "My Pretty Pony" (1989; see **A38**, **B104**); "Sorry, Right Number" (screenplay, 1987; see **E5**); "The Ten O'Clock People" (1993; see **B105**); "Crouch End" (1980; see **B49**); "The House on Maple Street" (1993; see **B106**); "The Fifth Quarter" (1972; see **B16**); "The Doctor's Case" (1987; see **B87**); "Umney's Last Case" (1993; see **B107**); "Head Down" (nonfiction, 1990; see **C197**); "Brooklyn August" (poem, 1971; see **D6**); "Notes," by Stephen King (see **C222**); "The Beggar and the Diamond" (1993; see **B108**).

REPRINTS:

ab. Issued with commemorative dustjacket, cover art by John Mercer, plus postcard set. Overlook Connection, 1994.
b. London: Hodder & Stoughton, 1993, 593 p., cloth.
c. New York: A Signet Book, September 1994, x+692 p., mass-market paper.
d. Thorndike, MA: G. K. Hall & Co., 1994, 1062 p., paper? Large print edition.

SECONDARY SOURCES AND REVIEWS:

1. *Book Report* 12 (March, 1994): 40.
2. *Book World* (*Washington Post*) 23 (October 10, 1993): 4.
3. *Booklist* 89 (July, 1993): 1918.
4. *Books* 7 (November, 1993): 12.
5. *Bookwatch* 14 (December, 1993): 6.
6. *Entertainment Weekly* (October 1, 1993): 48+.
7. *Kirkus Reviews* 61 (July 1, 1993): 807.
8. *Locus* 31 (October, 1993): 29+.
9. *Locus* 31 (December, 1993): 48.
10. *Locus* 32 (1994): 39.
11. Nicholls, Richard E. *New York Times Book Review* (October 24, 1993): 22.
12. *Publishers Weekly* 240:31 (August 2, 1993): 62.
13. *Publishers Weekly* 241 (July 25, 1994): 47+.
14. *Science Fiction Chronicle* 15 (March, 1994): 33.
15. *Tribune Books* [Chicago] (November 7, 1993): 9.

A48. INSOMNIA

A48. ***Insomnia: A Novel***. Shingletown, CA: Mark V. Ziesing Books, June 1994, 591 p., cloth. Illustrated by Phil Hale; cover art by Arnie Fenner. Signed, limited edition of 1250 copies. [horror novel]

PLOT SUMMARY: Following the death of his wife, Ralph Roberts is afflicted with progressive insomnia, until finally he is sleeping only an hour or so each night. As his insomnia (and the accompanying fatigue and depression) increases, he also begins seeing things that cannot possibly exist, including brilliant auras surrounding people. When he starts seeing what appear to be aliens—little men in doctor's suits—he also becomes aware that he and a few others have become players in a game of cosmic significance.

COMMENTS: Although *Insomnia* begins rather slowly, it gradually builds its own rhythms of plot, narrative, and image, until King abruptly connects this story with the wider explorations of the Dark Tower novels.

REPRINTS:

ab. Shingletown, CA: Mark V. Ziesing Books, June 1994, 591 p., cloth. Illustrated by Phil Hale. Gift Edition of 3,750 copies, slipcased with jacket by Arnie Fenner.
b. New York: Viking, 1994, 787 p., cloth. Illustrated by David Johnson.
c. London: Hodder & Stoughton, 1994, 787 p., cloth.
d. as: *Schlaflos: Roman*. München: Wilhelm Heyne Verlag, 1994, 815 p., paper? Translated by Joachim Körber. [German]
e. New York: A Signet Book, 1995, 663 p., mass-market paper.
f. Thorndike, MA: G. K. Hall & Co., 1995, p., paper? Large print edition.
g. London: New English Library, 1995, 760 p., mass-market paper.

SECONDARY SOURCES AND REVIEWS:

1. *Kirkus Reviews* 62 (July 15, 1994): 938.
2. *Publishers Weekly* 241:31 (August 1, 1994): 69.

A49. ROSE MADDER

A49. ***Rose Madder***. New York: Viking, 1995, 420 p. cloth. [fantasy novel]

PLOT SUMMARY: After suffering through fourteen years of physical abuse at the hands of her policeman husband, Rose Daniels abruptly walks out of her house, and takes a bus to another town. There she spends time in a halfway house, and rebuilds her life, finding a job as an audio book reader. One day in a pawn shop she buys a curious painting labeled "Rose Madder," depicting a barbarian woman gazing upon the ruins of a decayed temple. Over time the picture seems almost to evolve, and Rose experiences a "dream" in which she goes through the painting into another world. Meanwhile, Norman Daniels is determined to punish his wayward wife, using his skills as a cop to trace her path to her apartment. There he kills several of her friends, and threatens Rose and her new boyfriend, Bill Steiner, with torture and death. But Rose Madder, the woman from the other reality, intervenes, and Norman comes to a very bad end.

COMMENTS: In the third book of a loose trilogy of "women's issues" novels, King returns to fantasy, evoking an atmosphere similar to that in David Lindsay's *The Haunted Woman*. Compelling and original, ***Rose Madder*** represents a further evolution of King's skills as a writer.

REPRINTS:

b. Boston: Compass Press, 1995, p., cloth. Large print edition.

A50. LOS LANGOLIERS

A50. *Los Langoliers*. New York: A Signet Book, 1995, 317 p., paper. A Spanish-language edition of the short novel that originally appeared in *Four Past Midnight* (see **A41** and **B96**). [horror novel]

B.

SHORT FICTION

INCLUDING PUBLISHED EXCERPTS FROM LONGER WORKS

For additional reprint appearances of collected stories, see general entries for King's several short-fiction collections in Section A. General sources of secondary information about the short fiction include the following:

Blue, Tyson. *The Unseen King*. STARMONT STUDIES IN LITERARY CRITICISM, No. 26. Mercer Island, WA: Starmont House, 1989, cloth, 200 p.

Collings, Michael R. "Acorns to Oaks: Explorations of Theme, Image, and Character in the Early Works of Stephen King, Part I," in *Castle Rock: The Stephen King Newsletter* 5:8 (August, 1989): 1.

Collings, Michael R. *The Annotated Guide to Stephen King: A Primary and Secondary Bibliography of the Works of America's Premier Horror Writer*. Mercer Island, WA: Starmont House, October 1986, 179 p., cloth.

Collings, Michael R. *The Many Facets of Stephen King*. Mercer Island, WA: Starmont House, 1985, 190 p., cloth.

Collings, Michael R., and David A. Engebretson. *The Shorter Works of Stephen King*. Mercer Island, WA: Starmont House, June 1985, 202 p., cloth.

Reino, Joseph. *Stephen King: The First Decade,* Carrie *to* Pet Sematary. TWAYNE'S UNITED STATES AUTHORS SERIES (TUSA 531). Boston: Twayne, February 1988, 162 p., cloth.

Schweitzer, Darrell, ed. *Discovering Stephen King*. STARMONT STUDIES IN LITERARY CRITICISM, No. 8. Mercer Island, WA: Starmont House, 1985, 219 p., cloth.

Spignesi, Stephen J. "Uncollected Works," in *The Shape Under the Sheet: The Complete Stephen King Encyclopedia*. Ann Arbor, MI: Popular Culture, Ink., May 1991, cloth, p. 467-542.

Spignesi, Stephen J. "The Unwritten King: Stories Stephen King Has Thought of But Just Hasn't Written Down (Yet)," in *The Shape Under the Sheet: The Complete Stephen King Encyclopedia*. Ann Arbor, MI: Popular Culture, Ink., May 1991, cloth, p. 773-775.

Van Hise, James. *Enterprise Incidents Presents Stephen King*. Tampa, FL: New Media, 1984, 58 p., paper.

Van Hise, James. *Stephen King and Clive Barker: The Illustrated Guide to the Masters of the Macabre,* by James Van Hise. Las Vegas NV: Pioneer Books, 1990, 152 p., paper.

Winter, Douglas E. *The Art of Darkness*. New York: New American Library, November 1984, 252 p., cloth.

SECTION B. SHORT FICTION

B1. "People, Places, Things," by Stephen King and Chris Chesley. Triad Publishing Company, 1960, 18 p. typescript booklet.

ab. Second printing, 1963.

CONTENTS: "The Hotel at the End of the Road" (by King); "I've Got to Get Away" (by King); "The Dimension Warp" (by King); "The Thing at the Bottom of the Well" (by King); "The Stranger" (by King); "I'm Falling" (by King); "The Cursed Expedition" (by King); "The Other Side of the Fog" (by King); "Never Look Behind You" (by King and Chesley); "Genius" (by Chesley); "Top Forty, News, Weather and Sports" (by Chesley); seven other stories by Chesley.

COMMENTS: Along with "The Star Invaders" (see **B2**), these stories are perhaps best categorized as juvenilia, considering that they were written when King was twelve or thirteen. In approach, content, theme, and treatment, however, they suggest directions the mature King would explore in greater detail, and, since they were in fact published (even though by King himself), they represent his earliest extant attempts at reaching a specific readership. He has indicated that these stories, along with "The Star Invaders," "King's Garbage Truck," "Slade," "The Glass Floor," and others, are sufficiently flawed that he feels uncomfortable about allowing them to be reprinted.

The booklet contained eighteen stories, eight by King, nine by Chesley, and one collaborative effort. All copies of the booklet were thought to have disappeared until one was discovered in a box of papers in King's home in 1985.

SECONDARY SOURCES AND REVIEWS:

1. Blue, Tyson. *The Unseen King*. Mercer Island, WA: Starmont House, 1989, cloth, p. 4-13. Blue provides brief annotations for each of King's stories, based on an incomplete xerox of the single copy in King's possession.
2. Spignesi, Stephen J. "People, Places, and Things: Volume I," in *The Shape Under the Sheet: The Complete Stephen King Encyclopedia*. Ann Arbor, MI: Popular Culture, Ink., May 1991, cloth, p. 467-470.

B2. "The Star Invaders." Durham, ME: Triad, Inc. and Gaslight Books, 1964, 17 p., paper. Typed and stapled mimeographed half-sheets plus front matter.

Among King's earliest extant short fiction, the story consists of seventeen typed, double-spaced half-sheets, stapled together, with a hand-drawn cover page complete with artistically arranged title and publisher's logo. The story is derivative, concerning aliens who nearly conquer the Earth but are destroyed at the last moment by Jed Pearce and his ray-gun. Although self-consciously science-fictional in content, the story has an odd sense of horror about it (primarily in the descriptions of the aliens), as well as hints of motifs King would incorporate into *Carrie* and other stories over a decade later. Its primary value is biographical and historical—an early work on a par with C. S. Lewis's published Boxen stories. King has indicated that he does not intend to allow the story to be republished.

SECONDARY SOURCES AND REVIEWS:

1. Blue, Tyson. *The Unseen King*. Mercer Island, WA: Starmont House, 1989, cloth, p. 13-17.
2. Collings, Michael R. "Acorns to Oaks: Explorations of Theme, Image, and Character in the Early Works of Stephen King, Part I," in *Castle Rock: The Stephen King Newsletter* 5:8 (August, 1989): 1.
3. Collings, Michael R. *The Many Facets of Stephen King*. Mercer Island, WA: Starmont House, 1985, cloth, p.17-18, 95.
4. Collings, Michael R., and David A. Engebretson. *The Shorter Works of Stephen King*. Mercer Island, WA: Starmont House, 1985, cloth, p. 8, 9, 10-12, 17, 21, 150.
5. Collings, Michael R. "The Star Invaders," in *The Shape Under the Sheet: The Complete Stephen King Encyclopedia*. Ann Arbor, MI: Popular Culture, Ink., May 1991, cloth, p. 470-471.
6. Winter, Douglas E. *The Art of Darkness*. New York: New American Library, November 1984, cloth, p. 19, 159, 180.

B3. **"I Was a Teenage Grave Robber,"** in *Comics Review* (1965): .

b. as: "In a Half-World of Terror," in *Stories of Suspense* (1966): 1-12.

In Marvin Wolfman's publication, the story covers twelve typed pages, poorly mimeographed and stapled together. Heralding King's first public appearance as a writer, the story concerns an unlikely hero, his improbable loss of a family fortune, and his subsequent involvement with a stereotypical mad scientist whose experiments with corpses result in gigantic maggots roaming the counterside.

B4. **"The Glass Floor,"** in *Startling Mystery Stories* 1 (Fall, 1967): 23-29.

b. *Weird Tales* No. 298 (Fall, 1990): .

King's first professional sale. Until 1990 the story had never been reprinted, nor did King wish to permit it to be reprinted. Superior to his other early stories, it nonetheless promises more than it delivers. The story is static and lacks internal logic; settings and characters echo Poe much too closely. The final image, however, strengthens the story and points to King's increasing command of genre and language.

B5. **"Here There Be Tygers,"** in *Ubris* [University of Maine, Orono] (Spring, 1968): 8, 10.

b. *Skeleton Crew*. New York: G. P. Putnam's Sons, 1985, cloth, p. 135-139. See **A28**.

B6. **"Cain Rose Up,"** in *Ubris* [University of Maine, Orono] (Spring, 1968): 33-35.

b. *Skeleton Crew*. New York: G. P. Putnam's Sons, June 1985, cloth, p. 175-180. See **A28**

Written during King's junior year at the University of Maine, Orono, and published in the university literary magazine, the story reflects the frustration endemic in student life. The story parallels *Rage*, *The Long Walk*, and *Roadwork* in the intensity of thematic development; the sense of entrapment by depression and frustration that explodes into violence equally parallels King's perceptions of Charles Whitman's shooting spree in Texas. King's revisions of the story for the *Skeleton Crew* reprint highlight Curt Garrish's sexual repression and obsession with death and amplify the graphic violence implicit in the original version.

B7. **"Strawberry Spring,"** in *Ubris* [University of Maine, Orono] (Fall, 1968): 13-15.

b. *Cavalier* (November, 1975): .
c. *Gent* (February, 1977): .
d. *Night Shift*. Garden City, NY: Doubleday & Co., 1978, cloth, p. 176-185. See **A6.**
e. *An International Treasury of Mystery & Suspense*, edited by Marie R. Reno. Garden City, NY: Doubleday & Co., 1983, cloth, p. 111-119.

One of the central stories in *Night Shift,* this is a tight treatment of psychological terror overlaid with an eerie atmosphere perfectly reflecting the story's content. In spite of stereotypically dismembered corpses, the story works, primarily through implication and indirection, suggesting that true horror extends beyond surface terror. The *Night Shift* version represents an intensive re-working of the original; King adds flashbacks that give the later version an unnerving strength. What began as a moody atmosphere piece coalesces around King's altered purposes; his narrator emerges as an unknowing participant in the horrors he describes.

B8. **"Night Surf,"** in *Ubris* [University of Maine, Orono] (Spring, 1969): 6-10.

b. *Cavalier* (August, 1974): .
c. *Cavalier Annual* (1976): 28-30.
d. *Night Shift*. Garden City, NY: Doubleday & Co., 1978, cloth, p. 54-62. See **A6**.

B9. **"The Reaper's Image,"** in *Startling Mystery Stories* 2 (Spring, 1969): 22-29.

b. *The Seventeenth Fontana Book of Great Ghost Stories,* edited by R. Chetwynd-Hayes. London: Fontana/Collins, 1981, paper, p. 15-22.
c. *Skeleton Crew*. New York: G. P. Putnam's Sons, June 1985, cloth, p. 321-338. See **A28**.
d. *Realms of Darkness,* edited by Mary Danby. London: Octopus Books, 1985, cloth, p. 476-482.
db. *Realms of Darkness,* edited anonymously by Mary Danby. New York: Chartwell, 1988, cloth, p. 476-482.

B10. **"Stud City,"** in *Ubris* [University of Maine, Orono] (Fall, 1969): .

b. as: "'Stud City,' by Gordon Lachance. Originally published in *Greenspun Quarterly* No. 45 (Fall, 1970). Used by Permission" [sic], as part of: "The Body: Fall from Innocence," in *Different Seasons*. New York: Viking, 1982, cloth, p. 322-334. See also **A16, B63**.

B11. **"Slade,"** in *The Maine Campus* [University of Maine, Orono] (June 11, 1970): 4; (June 18, 1970): 4; (June 25, 1970): 5; (July 2, 1970): 5, 7; (July 9, 1970): 5, 7; (July 23, 1970): 5; (July 30, 1970): 6; (August 6, 1970): 5.

"Slade" is in some ways the most revealing of King's uncollected early works, especially as it shows King reveling in the joy of storytelling. It is an engaging explosion of off-the-wall humor, literary pastiche, and cultural criticism masquerading as a Western—the adventures of Slade and his quest for Miss Molly Peachtree of Paduka. The three final installments were published during the summer following his graduation from UMO.

SECONDARY SOURCES AND CRITICISM:

1. Blue, Tyson. *The Unseen King*. Mercer Island, WA: Starmont House, 1989, cloth, p. 34-38.
2. Collings, Michael R. "Acorns to Oaks: Explorations of Theme, Image, and Character in the Early Works of Stephen King, Part I," in *Castle Rock: The Stephen King Newsletter* 5:8 (August, 1989): 1, 8.
3. Collings, Michael R. *The Annotated Guide to Stephen King*. Mercer Island, WA: Starmont House, 1986, cloth, p. 45.
4. Collings, Michael R. *The Many Facets of Stephen King*. Mercer Island, WA: Starmont House, 1985, cloth, p.25, 47-48.
5. Collings, Michael R., and David A. Engebretson. *The Shorter Works of Stephen King*. Mercer Island, WA: Starmont House, 1985, cloth, p. 9, 17-22, 105-106.
6. Spignesi, Stephen J. "Slade," in *The Shape Under the Sheet: The Complete Stephen King Encyclopedia*. Ann Arbor, MI: Popular Culture, Ink., May 1991, cloth, p. 475-478.
7. Winter, Douglas E. *The Art of Darkness*. New York: New American Library, November, 1984, cloth, p. 178, 200.

B12. **"Graveyard Shift,"** in *Cavalier* (October, 1970): .

b. *Night Shift*. Garden City, NY: Doubleday & Co., 1978, p. 36-53. See **A6**.

c. *The 21st Pan Book of Horror Stories*, edited by Herbert van Thal. London & Sydney: Pan Books, 1980, paper, p. 104-121.

The short story was used as a basis for the full-length film, *Graveyard Shift* (1990), which has, with *Children of the Corn*, been considered among the least successful film adaptations of King's works.

B13. **"The Blue Air Compressor,"** in *Onan* [University of Maine, Orono] (January, 1971): p. 70-79.

b. *Heavy Metal* (July, 1981): 31-33. Revised.

Written during King's student days at the University of Maine, Orono, the story indicates his early debt to Poe, as well as developing the twin (and recurring) themes of deadly machines and deadly "monstrous" women. The original version, in a UMO literary magazine, was heavily revised for its appearance a decade later (for a discussion of the revisions, see Collings and Engebretson. *The Shorter Works of Stephen King*, p. 25).

B14. **"I Am the Doorway,"** in *Cavalier* (March, 1971): .

b. *Night Shift*. Garden City, NY: Doubleday & Co., 1978, cloth, p. 63-75. See **A6.**

c. as: "Ich Bin das Tor," in *Dämonengeschenk Gespensterbuch,* edited by Michael Görden. Bergisch Gladbach: Bastei-Lübbe Verlag (TB 72505), 1985, paper, p. . Translated by Harro Christensen. [German]

d. as: "Ich Bin das Tor," in *Das Große Ferienbuch*, edited by Ilse Walter. Gütersloh, Austria: Bertelsmann Lesering, 1989, p. . Translated by Harro Christensen. [German]

B15. **"Suffer the Little Children,"** in *Cavalier* (February, 1972): 35-38, 90-94.

b. *Nightmares,* edited by Charles L. Grant. Chicago: Playboy Paperbacks, September 1979, 256 p., paper, p. 11-23. Second printing, November, 1979.

c. *The Evil Image: Two Centuries of Gothic Short Fiction and Poetry*, edited by Patricia L. Skarda and Nora Crow Jaffe. New York: A Meridian Book, New American Library, June 1981, trade paper, p. 465-475.

d. *65 Great Spine Chillers*, edited by Mary Danby. London, New York: Octopus Books, 1982, cloth, p. 397-406.

db. *65 Great Spine Chillers*, edited by Mary Danby. New York, London: Octopus Books, 1986, paper, p. 397-406.

e. as: "Laat de Kinderkens Tot Mÿ Komen" ["Let the Little Children Come to Me"], in *Duistere Machten* ["*Dark Powers*"]. Amsterdam: Loeb, 1983. [Dutch]

f. *Treasury of Great Short Stories*. New York: Exeter Books, 1986, cloth, p. .

g. *Nightmares & Dreamscapes*. New York: Viking, 1993, cloth, p. 95-108. See **A47.**

gb. *Nightmares & Dreamscapes*. New York: A Signet Book, September 1994, paper, p. 81-92.

B16. **"The Fifth Quarter,"** by "JOHN SWITHEN," in *Cavalier* (April, 1972): 52-60, 90-94.

b. as: "The Fifth Quarter," by Stephen King, in *Twilight Zone Magazine* (February, 1986): 24-28, 96.

c. *Nightmares & Dreamscapes*. New York: Viking, 1993, cloth, p. 633-650. See **A47**.

cb. *Nightmares & Dreamscapes*. New York: A Signet Book, September 1994, paper, p. 535-550.

Other than the Bachman novels, this is King's only pseudonymous work. It is more strictly crime fiction than horror, but the characteristic King overtones are present nonetheless. Characterization, plotting, and the puzzling title engage the reader's interest.

B17. **"Battleground,"** in *Cavalier* (September, 1972): .

b. *Cavalier Annual* (Fall, 1983): 58-60.

c. *Night Shift*. Garden City, NY: Doubleday & Co., 1978, cloth, p. 120-129. See **A6.**

In the mode of *Maximum Overdrive* and *The Tommyknockers,* this story concentrates on the terrors of mechanization, on a society enamored with gadgets that ultimately turn on their creators. The story explores the potentials for horror in normally neutral or positive objects, as well as the circularity (and ultimately the uselessness) of revenge.

B18. **"The Mangler,"** in *Cavalier* (December, 1972): .

b. *Night Shift*. Garden City, NY: Doubleday & Co., 1978, cloth, p. 76-95. See **A6.**

c. *The 21st Pan Book of Horror Stories,* edited by Herbert van Thal. London & Sydney: Pan Books, 1980, paper, p. 122-141.

d. *The Arbor House Celebrity Book of Horror Stories*, edited by Martin H. Greenberg and Charles Waugh. New York: Arbor House, 1982, cloth, p. 79-100.

db. *The Arbor House Celebrity Book of Horror Stories,* edited by Martin H. Greenberg and Charles Waugh. New York: Priam, 1982, paper, p. 79-100.

e. *Tales of Dungeons and Dragons*, edited by Peter Haining. London: Century Publishing, 1986, cloth, p. 112-134.

f. *Demons!* edited by Jack Dann. New York: Ace Books, July 1987, paper, p. 74-92.

g. *Dark Voices: The Best from the Pan Book of Horror Stories*, edited by Stephen Jones and Clarence Paget. London & Sydney: Pan Books, 1990, paper, p. 19-40.

h. *Young Blood*, edited by Mike Baker. New York: A Zebra Book, Kensington Publishing Corp., 1994, paper, p. 99-120.

B19. **"The Boogeyman,"** in *Cavalier* (March, 1973): . See also **GE4**.

b. *Gent* (December, 1975): .

c. *Night Shift*. Garden City, NY: Doubleday & Co., 1978, cloth, p. 96-107. See **A6.**

d. *The 25th Pan Book of Horror Stories*, edited by Herbert van Thal. London & Sydney: Pan Books, 1984, paper, p. 107-118.

e. as: "Das Schreckgespenst," in *Mal Gänsehaut*, edited by Jason Dark. Bergisch Gladbach: Bastei-Lübbe Verlag (TB 13052), 1986, paper, p. . Translated by Harro Christensen. [German]

f. *House Shudders*, edited by Martin Harry Greenberg and Charles G. Waugh. New York: DAW Books, Sept. 1987, paper, p. 220-232.

B20. "Trucks," in *Cavalier* (June, 1973): .

b. *Night Shift*. Garden City, NY: Doubleday & Co., 1978, cloth, p. 130-146. See **A6.**

c. *Mysterious Motoring Stories*, edited by William Pattrick (i.e., Peter Haining). London: W. H. Allen & Co., 1987, cloth, p. 193-210.

cb. *Duel and Other Horror Stories of the Road*, edited by William Pattrick (i.e., Peter Haining). London: A Star Book, W. H. Allen & Co., 1987, paper, p. 193-210.

Print original for the central narrative of King's screenplay and film, *Maximum Overdrive*. See also **E4, G11, GE16.**

B21. "Gray Matter," in *Cavalier* (October, 1973): .

b. *Cavalier Annual* (1975): 4-6.

c. *Night Shift*. Garden City, NY: Doubleday & Co., 1978, cloth, p. 108-120. See **A6.**

d. *The Arbor House Necropolis: Voodoo! A Chrestomathy of Necromany; Mummy! A Chrestomathy of Cryptoology; Ghoul! A Chrestomathy of Ogrery,* edited by Bill Pronzini. New York: Arbor House, 1981, paper, p. 702-716.

db. *Tales of the Dead*, edited by Bill Pronzini. New York: Bonanza Books, 1986, cloth, p. 689-702.

e. *The 28th Pan Book of Horror Stories*, edited by Clarence Paget. London & Sydney: Pan Books, 1987, paper, p. 70-81.

B22. "It Grows on You," in *Marshroots* (Fall, 1973): 63-72.

b. *Whispers* (August, 1982): 59-65.

c. *Death*, edited by Stuart David Schiff. New York: Playboy Paperbacks, 1982, paper, p. 215-225.

d. *Weird Tales* No. 301 (Summer, 1991): 65-71.

e. *Nightmares & Dreamscapes*. New York: Viking, 1993, cloth, p. 161-178. See **A47.**

eb. *Nightmares & Dreamscapes*. New York: A Signet Book, September 1994, paper, p. 139-154.

B23. "Sometimes They Come Back," in *Cavalier* (March, 1974): .

b. *Night Shift*. Garden City, NY: Doubleday & Co., 1978, cloth, p. 147-175. See **A6.**

c. as: "Manchmal Kommen Sie Wieder," in *Nachtspuk: Gespensterbuch 1*, edited by Michael Görden. Bergisch Gladbach: Bastei-Lübbe Verlag (TB 72501), 1984, paper, p. . Translated by Barbara Heidkamp. [German]

Print original for a made-for-television movie (1991; see **GB7**); the story was altered radically to meet the time requirements for the film. King's use of the occult and his originally pessimistic conclusion were abandoned.

B24. **"The Lawnmower Man,"** in *Cavalier* (May, 1975): .

b. *Night Shift*. Garden City, NY: Doubleday & Co., 1978, cloth, p. 203-212. See **A6.**
c. *Bizarre Adventures* 29 (October, 1981): 21. A comic-book adaptation.
d. *The 30th Pan Book of Horror Stories*, edited by Clarence Paget. London & Sydney: Pan Books, 1989, paper, p. 7-16.

Another story later adapted into a poor motion picture version.

B25. **"The Revenge of Lardass Hogan,"** in *The Maine Review* (July, 1975 [?]): 37-51.

b. as: "From 'The Revenge of Lardass Hogan,' by Gordon Lachance. Originally published in *Cavalier* magazine, March, 1975. Used by permission" [sic], incorporated into "The Body: Fall From Innocence," in *Different Seasons*. New York: Viking, 1982, cloth, p. 380-388. See also **A16, B63.**

B26. **"'Salem's Lot,"** in *Cosmopolitan* (March, 1976): . A twenty-page excerpt from the novel. See **A2.**

B27. **"Weeds,"** in *Cavalier* (May, 1976): .

b. *Nugget* (April, 1979): .
c. as: "The Lonesome Death of Jordy Verrill," in *Creepshow*. New York: A Plume Book, New American Library, July 1982, trade paper, unpaginated. A comic-book adaptation; see also **A15, B66.**

As "The Lonesome Death of Jordy Verrill," the story became an episode in George Romero's film adaptation, *Creepshow*, with King portraying the title role.

B28. **"The Ledge,"** in *Penthouse* (July, 1976): 146-148, 166, 172-182.

b. *Night Shift*. Garden City, NY: Doubleday & Co., 1978, cloth, p. 186-202. See **A6.**
c. as: "Wer im Penthouse Sitzt Sollte Nicht um Liebe Spielen" ["One Who Sits in a Penthouse Should Not Play Around with Love"], in *Lui* No. 5 (May, 1981): . [German]
d. *The 29th Pan Book of Horror Stories*, edited by Clarence Paget. London & Sydney: Pan Books, 1988, paper, p. 72-88.

Print original for an episode in King's screenplay, *Cat's Eye* (see **G9**).

B29. **"I Know What You Need,"** in *Cosmopolitan* (September, 1976):

b. *Night Shift.* Garden City, NY: Doubleday & Co., 1978, cloth, p. 234-256. See **A6**.
c. *Spells: Isaac Asimov's Magical Worlds of Fantasy #4,* edited by Isaac Asimov, Martin H. Greenberg, and Charles G. Waugh. New York: A Signet Book, New American Library, May 1985, paper, p. 259-281.
d. as: "Ich Weiß, Was Du Brauchst," in *Schattenhochzeit: Gespensterbuch 7,* edited by Michael Görden. Bergisch Gladbach: Bastei-Lübbe Verlag (TB 72507), 1985, paper, p. . Translated by Ingrid Herrmann. [German]
e. *The 27th Pan Book of Horror Stories*, edited by Clarence Paget. London & Sydney: Pan Books, 1986, paper, p. 101-122.
f. as: "Ich Weiß, Was Du Brauchst," in *Märschenwelt der Fantasy*, edited by isaac Asimov, Martin H. Greenberg, and Charles G. Waugh. Bergisch Gladbach: Bastei-Lübbe Verlag (TB 28152), 1987, paper, p. . Translated by Ingrid Herrmann. [German]

B30. **"The Cat from Hell,"** in *Cavalier* (March, 1977): . Partial publication of the first 500 words.

ab. *Cavalier* (June, 1977): . The complete story (see below).
c. *Second Book of Unknown Tales of Horror*, edited by Peter Haining. London: Sidgwick & Jackson, 1978, p. 132-143.
cb. *Tales of Unknown Horror*, edited by Peter Haining. London: New English Library, 1978, paper, p. 132-143.
cc. *Tales of Unknown Horror*, edited by Peter Haining. New York: A Signet Book, New American Library, 1978, paper, p. .
d. *Year's Finest Fantasy,* edited by Terry Carr. New York: Berkley Publishing Corp., 1978, cloth, p. 55-69.
db. *Year's Finest Fantasy,* edited by Terry Carr. New York: Berkley Books, July 1979, paper, p. 55-69.
e. *Magicats!*, edited by Jack Dann and Gardner Dozois. New York: Ace Books, 1984, paper, p. 33-49.
eb. *Kats*, edited by Jack Dann and Gardner Dozois. Amsterdam: Meulenhoff, 1987, paper, p. . Translated by Jaime Martijn. [Dutch]
f. *New Bern Magazine* (March-April, 1984): .
g. *Top Horror: de Beste Griezelverhalen* ["*Top Horror: The Best Horror Stories*"], edited by Josh Pachter. Amsterdam: Loeb, 1985, 366 p. Translated by W. H. M. van den Hout. [Dutch]
gb. *Top Horror,* edited by Josh Pachter. München: Heyne Verlag (Die Unheimliche Bücher 20), 1986, paper, p. . [German]

Originally published as part of a competition sponsored by *Cavalier*, the story was begun by King, with an invitation to the magazine's readers to complete it. The winning story was published in the magazine, as was King's entire version. George Beahm's *The Stephen King Companion* discusses the genesis of the story.

The story served as the print original for an episode in *Tales from the Darkside—The Movie* (1990; see **G16**).

B31. **"Children of the Corn,"** in *Penthouse* (March, 1977): 65-68, 124-126, 141-148.

b. *Night Shift*. Garden City, NY: Doubleday & Co., 1978, cloth, p. 257-286. See **A6.**
c. *The Year's Best Horror Stories: Series VI*, edited by Gerald W. Page. New York: DAW Books, 1978, paper, p. 131-159.
d. as: "De Maiskindern," in *Griezel-Omnibus: Het Verschrikkelijke Geheim (E. A. Verhalen)* ["The Corn Children," in "*The Horror-Omnibus: The Terrible Secret and Other Stories*"]. Amsterdam/Brussels: Elsevier, 1982, p. . Apollo Series [book club]. [Dutch]
e. *Cults!: An Anthology of Secret Societies, Sects, and the Supernatural*, edited by Martin H. Greenberg and Charles C. Waugh. New York: Beaufort Books, 1983, cloth, p. 227-254.
g. as: "Kinder des Zorns" ["Children of Wrath"], in *Totentanz: Gespensterbuch 3*, edited by Michael Görden. Bergisch Gladbach: Bastei-Lübbe Verlag (TB 72503), 1984, paper, p. . Translated by Wolfgang Holbein. [German]
g. *A Treasury of American Horror Stories*, edited by Charles Waugh, Martin H. Greenberg, and Frank D. McSherry Jr. New York: Bonanza Books, 1985, cloth, p. 345-368.
h. as: " ," in *Las Mejores Historias del Terror V*, edited by Gerald Page (?). Barcelona: Ediciones Martinez Roca, [1986?], paper, p. . [Spanish]

This concise tale of religion, fanaticism, and inexplicable horror has generated a number of interpretations, including Anthony Magistrale's reading of the story as paralleling America's distress during the Vietnam period (see Collings and Engebretson. *The Shorter Works of Stephen King*, p. 71-72). The story is enigmatic, concise, taut, fast-paced, and oppressively pessimistic, unlike the subsequent movie version, *Children of the Corn* (almost unanimously accepted as the single worst transformation of a King story to film to date).

SECONDARY SOURCES AND REVIEWS:

1. Magistrale, Anthony S. "Stephen King's Vietnam Allegory: An Interpretation of 'Children of the Corn,'" in *Cuyahoga Review* (Spring/Summer, 1984): 61-66. Reprinted: *Footsteps V* (April, 1985): 61-65.

B32. **"One for the Road,"** in *Maine* (March/April, 1977): .

b. *Night Shift*. Garden City, NY: Doubleday & Co., 1978, cloth, p. 306-322. See **A6.**
c. *Young Monsters*, edited by Isaac Asimov, Martin H. Greenberg, and Charles G. Waugh. New York: Harper & Row, 1985, cloth, p. 190-215.
cb. *Asimov's Monsters*, edited by Isaac Asimov, Martin H. Greenberg, and Charles G. Waugh. London: Dragon Books, 1986, paper, p. .
cc. *Asimov's Ghosts & Monsters*, edited by Isaac Asimov, Martin H. Greenberg, and Charles G. Waugh. London: Armada, 1988, paper, p. . An omnibus of *Young Monsters* and *Young Ghosts*.
d. *Strange Maine*, edited by Charles Waugh, Martin Greenberg, and Frank D. McSherry Jr. Augusta, ME: Lance Tapley, 1986, paper, p. 77-92.

e. *Vamps: An Anthology of Female Vampire Stories*, edited by Martin Greenberg and Charles Waugh. New York: DAW Books, 1987, paper, p. 12-30.

eb. as: "Einen auf den Weg," in *Vampire!*, edited by Martin H. Greenberg and Charles G. Waugh. Bergisch Gladback: Bastei-Lübbe Verlag, 1988, paper, p. . Translated by Stefan Sturm. [German]

B33. **"The Shining,"** in *Ramada Reflections* (June, 1977): . An excerpt from *The Shining*. See **A3**.

B34. **"The Man Who Loved Flowers,"** in *Gallery* (August, 1977): 68-70, 82.

b. *Night Shift*. Garden City, NY: Doubleday & Co., 1978, cloth, p. 299-305. See **A6.**

c. as: "Der Mann, der Blumen Liebte," in *Phantastische Literatur 84,* edited by Michael Görden. Bergisch Gladbach: Bastei-Lübbe Verlag (TB 72033), 1983, paper, p. . Translated by Bernd Seligmann. [German]

B35. **"The Night of the Tiger,"** in *The Magazine of Fantasy & Science Fiction* 54 (February, 1978): 82-93.

b. *More Tales of Unknown Horror,* edited by Peter Haining. London: New English Library, 1979, paper, p. 127-140.

c. *The Year's Best Horror Stories, Series VII,* edited by Gerald W. Page. New York: DAW Books, 1979, paper, p. 20-33.

d. *The Third Book of Unknown Tales of Horror*, edited by Peter Haining. London: Sidgwick & Jackson, 1980, cloth, p. 161-175.

e. *Chamber of Horrors*, anonymously edited by Emma Blackley. London: Octopus Books, 1984, cloth, p. 179-189.

f. *The Best Horror Stories from the Magazine of Fantasy & Science Fiction*, edited by Edward L. Ferman and Anne Jordan. New York: St. Martin's Press, 1988, cloth, p. 81-93.

fb. *The Best Horror Stories from the Magazine of Fantasy & Science Fiction, Volume 1*, edited by Edward L. Ferman and Anne Jordan. New York: St. Martin's Press, 1989, mass market paper, p. 104-119.

fc. as: "Die Nacht des Tigers," in *Die Besten Horrorstories,* edited by Edward L. Ferman. München: Droemer Knaur Verlag (Paperback 1835), 1989, paper, p. . [German]

fd. *The Best of Modern Horror*, edited by Edward L. Ferman and Anne Jordan. London: Viking, 1989, cloth, p. 81-93.

g. *Horrorstory, Volume Three: The Year's Best Horror Stories VII; The Year's Best Horror Stories VIII; The Year's Best Horror Stories IX*, edited by Karl Edward Wagner and Gerald W. Page. Novato, CA, Lancaster, PA: Underwood-Miller, 1992, cloth, p. 11-22.

B36. **"The Gunslinger,"** in *The Magazine of Fantasy & Science Fiction* 55 (October, 1978): .

b. *The Year's Finest Fantasy, Volume 2*, edited by Terry Carr. New York: Berkley Publishing Corp., July 1979, cloth, p. 91-140.

c. *The Dark Tower: The Gunslinger*. West Kingston, RI: Donald M. Grant, 1984, cloth, p. 11-66. See **A17**.

d. as: "Der Revolvermann," in *Sterbliche Götter (Die Besten Geschichten aus* The Magazine of Fantasy & Science Fiction, *55. Folge)*, edited by Manfred Kluge. München: Wilhelm Heyne Verlag (TB 3718), 1980, paper, p. . Translated by Marvel Bieger. [German]

B37. **"Man with a Belly,"** in *Cavalier* (December, 1978): 35, 77-81.

b. *Gent* (November/December, 1979): .

B38. **"Jerusalem's Lot,"** in *Night Shift*. Garden City, NY: Doubleday & Co., 1978, cloth, p. 1-35. See **A6**; for a related narrative, see also **A2.**

b. *World Fantasy Awards, Volume Two*, edited by Stuart David Schiff and Fritz Leiber. Garden City, NY: Doubleday & Co., 1980, cloth, p. 20-56.
c. as: "Briefe aus Jerusalem" ["Letters from Jerusalem"], in *Phantastische Literature 84*. Bergisch Gladbach: Bastei-Lübbe Verlag, 1983, paper, p. . Translated by Barbara Heidkamp. [German]
d. *Baker's Dozen: 13 Short Horror Novels*, edited by Martin H. Greenberg and Charles G. Waugh. New York: Bonanza Books, 1987, cloth, p. 1-38.
e. *Tales of the Cthulhu Mythos*, edited anonymously by August Derleth and James Turner. Sauk City, WI: Arkham House, 1989, cloth, p. 468-502.

B39. **"The Last Rung on the Ladder,"** in *Night Shift*. Garden City, NY: Doubleday & Co., 1978, cloth, p. 287-298. See **A6** and **GE18**.

B40. **"Quitters, Inc.,"** in *Night Shift*. Garden City, NY: Doubleday & Co., 1978, cloth, p. 213-233. See **A6** and **G9**.

b. *Best Detective Stories of the Year,* edited by Edward D. Hoch. New York: E. P. Dutton, 1979, cloth, p. .
c. *The Science Fiction Weight-Loss Book,* edited by Isaac Asimov, George R. R. Martin, and Martin H. Greenberg. New York: Crown Publishers, 1983, cloth, p. 231-249.

The print original for an episode in King's film, *Cat's Eye* (see **G9**).

B41. **"The Woman in the Room,"** in *Night Shift*. Garden City, NY: Doubleday & Co., 1978, cloth, p. 323-336. See **A6**.

b. *The 25th Pan Book of Horror Stories*, edited by Herbert van Thal. London & Sydney: Pan Books, 1984, paper, p. 139-152.
c. *The Complete Masters of Darkness,* edited by Dennis Etchison. Novato, CA, Lancaster, PA: Underwood-Miller, 1991, cloth, p. 727-740.
d. *Masters of Darkness III,* edited by Dennis Etchison. New York: Tor, A Tom Doherty Associates Book, May 1991, paper, p. 303-319.

"The Woman in the Room" is unique among the stories in *Night Shift* for its autobiographical sense, its emotional intensity, and its carefully realized, frightening realism. Lacking in supernatural elements, the story concentrates on a painful decision—whether or not to assist in a terminally ill mother's suicide. See also **GE9**.

B42. **"Nona,"** in *Shadows*, edited by Charles L. Grant. Garden City, NY: Doubleday & Co., 1978, cloth, p. 151-182.

ab. *Shadows*, edited by Charles L. Grant. New York: Playboy Paperbacks, 1980, paper, p. 187-223.
ac. *Shadows II*, edited by Charles L. Grant. London: Headline, 1987, cloth, p. .
b. *The Dodd, Mead Gallery of Horror,* edited by Charles L. Grant. New York: Dodd, Mead, 1983, cloth, p. 333-365.
bb. *A Gallery of Horror*, edited by Charles L. Grant. London: Robson, 1983, cloth, p. 333-365.
c. *Skeleton Crew*. New York: G. P. Putnam's Sons, June 1985, cloth, p. 329-358. See **A28**.
d. as: "Nona," in *Das Große Bruselkabinett*, edited by Charles L. Grant. München: Wilhelm Heyne Verlag (Die Unheimliche Bücher 16), 1984, paper, p. . Translated by Rolf Jurkeit. [German]

B43. **"The Crate,"** in *Gallery* (July, 1979): .

b. *Fantasy Annual III,* edited by Terry Carr. New York: A Timescape Book, Pocket Books, May 1981, paper, p. 1-32.
c. *The Arbor House Treasury of Horror and the Supernatural,* edited by Bill Pronzini, Barry N. Malzberg, and Martin H. Greenberg. New York: Arbor House, 1981, cloth, p. 570-599.
cb. *The Arbor House Treasury of Horror and the Supernatural,* edited by Bill Pronzini, Barry N. Malzberg, and Martin H. Greenberg. New York: Priam Books/Arbor House, 1981, trade paper, p. 570-599.
cc. *Great Tales of Horror and the Supernatural*, edited by Bill Pronzini, Barry N. Malzberg, and Martin H. Greenberg. New York: A&W/Galahad Books, 1985, cloth, p. 568-597.
d. *Creepshow*. New York: A Plume Book, New American Library, July 1982, trade paper, [no pagination]. Comic book format; illustrated by Berni Wrightson. See **A15**.
e. as: "Die Kiste," in *Unheimliches*, edited by Bill Pronzini, Barry N. Malzberg, and Martin H. Greenberg. München: Wilhelm Heyne Verlag (Jubiläumsband 9), 1985, paper, p. . Translated by Sonja Hauser and Bernd Lenz. [German]

The early prose version of the story succeeds without the visual overlay of E.C. comics in the published *Creepshow* version, or the serio-comic performances by Adrienne Barbeau and Hal Holbrook in the film adaptation. The narrative begins in the middle of crisis, with flashbacks and explication to set the stage. The monster is fleetingly compared to the Tasmanian Devil (appropriate for the comic-book ancestry of the story), but only generally described; King's text relies on evocation of the unknown for its primary impact. Print original for an episode in the film, *Creepshow* (**G9**).

B44. **"The Way Station,"** in *The Magazine of Fantasy & Science Fiction* 58 (April, 1980): .

b. *The Dark Tower: The Gunslinger.* West Kingston, RI: Donald M. Grant, 1984, cloth, p. 71-113. See **A17**.

c. as: "Das Rasthaus," in *Grenzstreifzüge (Die Besten Geschichten aus* The Magazine of Fantasy & Science Fiction, *58. Folge)*, edited by Manfred Kluge. München: Wilhelm Heyne Verlag (TB 3792), 1981, paper, p. . Translated by Wolfgang Schrader. [German]

B45. **"Firestarter,"** in *Omni* 2 (July, 1980): . An excerpt from the novel. See **A9**.

B46. **"The Wedding Gig,"** in *Ellery Queen's Mystery Magazine* (December 1, 1980): 127-139.

b. *Skeleton Crew.* New York: G. P. Putnam's Sons, June 1985, cloth, p. 227-240. See **A28**.

c. as: "Der Hochzeitempfang," in *Heyne Jubiläumsbuch*, edited by Günther Fetzer. München: Wilhelm Heyne Verlag (TB 6700), 1988, paper, p. . Translated by Alexandra von Reinhardt. [German]

d. *Great Tales of Madness & the Macabre*, edited by Charles Ardai. New York: Galahad Books, 1990, cloth, p. 269-281.

B47. **"Big Wheels: A Tale of the Laundry Game,"** in *New Terrors 2*, edited by Ramsey Campbell. London & Sydney: Pan Books, 1980, paper, p. 177-188.

ab. *New Terrors*, edited by Ramsey Campbell. New York: Pocket Books, October 1982, paper, p. 250-262.

c. as: "Big Wheels: A Tale of the Laundry Game (Milkman #2)," in *Skeleton Crew.* New York: G. P. Putnam's Sons, June 1985, cloth, p. 401-414. See **A28**.

d. as: "Der Milchmann Schlägt Wieder Zu" ["The Milkman Gives a Bonus Again"], in *Das Ferien-lesebuch*, edited by Günther Fetzer. München: Wilhelm Heyne Verlag (TB 7834), 1989, paper, p. . Translated by Alexandra von Reinhardt. [German]

In "Beach Blanket Books" Peter Nicholls refers to the story as "Something out of the way for King: a piece of true-blue surrealism, beautifully judged and paced....The horror in this one bubbles up through the beer cans that are central to its imagery, and the reader discovers more about the soft white underbelly of blue-collar life than he could conceivably want to know" (p. 13); in *The Dark Descent,* David G. Hartwell similarly points to the surrealistic nature of the story, noting that this story, "Mrs. Todd's Shortcut," and "Crouch End" represent King's most intensive "concern with alterations in base or consensus reality" (p. 690). Douglas Winter describes both "Big Wheels" and "Morning Deliveries" as part of an unfinished novel, "Milkman" (*Art of Darkness*, p. 161).

B48. **"The Monkey,"** in *Gallery* (November, 1980): .

b. *Modern Masters of Horror*, edited by Frank Coffey. New York: Coward, McCann & Geoghegan, 1981, cloth, p. 13-56.

bb. *Modern Masters of Horror*, edited by Frank Coffey. New York: Ace Books, 1982, paper, p. 13-56.

bc. *Modern Masters of Horror*, edited by Frank Coffey. New York: Berkley Books, July 1988, paper, p. 13-56.

c. *The Year's Best Horror Stories, Series IX,* edited by Karl Edward Wagner. New York: DAW Books, August 1981, paper, p. 15-53.

d. *Horrors*, edited by Charles L. Grant. New York: Playboy Paperbacks, October 1981, paper, p. 186-223. 2nd printing, November, 1981.

db. as: *Horrors!* Barcelona: Martinéz Roca, 1986, paper, p. . [Spanish]

e. *Fantasy Annual IV,* edited by Terry Carr. New York: A Timescape Book, Pocket Books, November 1981, paper, p. 1-40.

eb. *Fantasy Annual IV,* edited by Terry Carr. New York: A Timescape Book, Pocket Books, [n.d.], cloth, p. 3-39. [Book Club edition].

f. *Skeleton Crew*. New York: G. P. Putnam's Sons, June 1985, cloth, p. 141-174. See **A28**.

g. *Heyne Jahresband 1986* ["*Heyne Yearbook 1986*"]. München: Wilhelm Heyne Verlag (TB 6600), 1986, paper, p. . Translated by Alexandra von Reinhardt. [German]

h. *The Dark Descent*, edited by David G. Hartwell. New York: Tor, A Tom Doherty Associates Book, October 1987, cloth, p. 382-409.

hb. *The Dark Descent 2: The Medusa in the Shield*, edited by David G. Hartwell. London: Grafton, 1990, cloth, p. .

hc. *The Medusa in the Shield: The Dark Descent, Volume 3*, edited by David G. Hartwell. New York: Tor Horror, 1991, paper, p. 146-185.

i. *The Mammoth Book of Short Horror Novels,* edited by Mike Ashley. London: Robinson, 1988, paper, p. 1-34.

ib. *The Mammoth Book of Short Horror Novels,* edited by Mike Ashley. New York: Carroll & Graf, 1988, paper, p. 1-34.

j. *Horrorstory, Volume Three: The Year's Best Horror Stories VII; The Year's Best Horror Stories VIII; The Year's Best Horror Stories IX*, edited by Karl Edward Wagner and Gerald W. Page. Novato, CA, Lancaster, PA: Underwood-Miller, 1992, cloth, p. 369-400.

B49. "**Crouch End,**" in *New Tales of the Cthulhu Mythos,* edited by Ramsey Campbell. Sauk City, WI: Arkham House, 1980, cloth, p. 3-32.

b. *The Dark Descent*, edited by David G. Hartwell. New York: Tor, A Tom Doherty Associates Book, October 1987, cloth, p. 690-711.

bb. *The Dark Descent 3: A Fabulous, Formless Darkness*, edited by David G. Hartwell. London: Grafton, 1991, cloth, p. 78-100.

bc. *A Fabulous, Formless Darkness: The Dark Descent, Vol. 3*, edited by David G. Hartwell. New York: Tor, 1992, paper, p. 107-138.

c. *Nightmares & Dreamscapes*. New York: Viking, 1993, cloth, p. 559-592. See **A47**.

cb. *Nightmares & Dreamscapes*. New York: A Signet Book, September 1994, paper, p. 476-503.

The story demonstrates King's awareness of and debt to Lovecraft's unique vision and world view; it is also unique in King's canon for its exclusively English atmosphere and milieu.

B50. **"The Mist,"** in *Dark Forces: New Stories of Suspense and Supernatural Horror,* edited by Kirby McCauley. New York: Viking Press, August 1980, cloth, p. 419-550.

ab. *Dark Forces: New Stories of Suspense and Supernatural Horror,* edited by Kirby McCauley. New York: Viking Press [Science Fiction Book Club], November 1980, cloth, p. 374-492.

ac. *Dark Forces: New Stories of Suspense and Supernatural Horror,* edited by Kirby McCauley. Toronto, New York: Bantam Books, December 1981, paper, p. 1-130.

b. as: *De Mist*, in *Macaber Carnaval* ["*Macabre Carnival*"]. Amsterdam: Loeb, 1983. [Dutch]

c. *Skeleton Crew*. New York: G. P. Putnam's Sons, June 1985, cloth, p. 21-134. See **A28**.

d. as: *Nebel* ["*Fog*"]. Linkenheim, Germany: Edition Phantasia, 1986, cloth. [German]

e. as: *Dichte Mist* ["*Thick Mist*"]. Utrecht: Luitingh, 1986, p., paper. Translated by Pauline Moody. [Dutch]

f. as: "Der Nebel" ["The Fog"] in *Horror*. München: Wilhelm Heyne Verlag (Jubiläumsband 21), 1987, paper, p. . Translated by Alexandra von Reinhardt. [German]

B51. **"The Oracle and the Mountain,"** in *The Magazine of Fantasy & Science Fiction* 60 (February, 1981): .

b. *The Dark Tower: The Gunslinger*. West Kingston, RI: Donald M. Grant, 1984, cloth, p. 117-144. See **A17**.

c. as: "Das Orakel und die Berge," in *Cyrion in Bronze (Die Besten Geschichten aus* The Magazine of Fantasy & Science Fiction, *65. Folge)*, edited by Ronald M. Hahn. München: Wilhelm Heyne Verlag (TB 3965), 1983, paper, p. . Translated by Wolfgang Schrader. [German]

B52. **"The Jaunt,"** in *The Twilight Zone Magazine* 1 (June, 1981): .

b. *Gallery* (December, 1981): .

c. *Great Stories from Rod Serling's The Twilight Zone Magazine, 1983 Annual*, edited by T. E. D. Klein. New York: TZ Publications, 1982, paper, p. 22-34.

d. as: "Travel," in *Schattenlicht,* edited by Rolf Jurkeit. München: Wilhelm Heyne Verlag (TB 6428), 1984, paper, p. . Translated by Rolf Jurkeit. [German]

e. *Skeleton Crew*. New York: G. P. Putnam's Sons, June 1985, cloth, p. 203-225. See **A28.**

B53. **"The Slow Mutants,"** in *The Magazine of Fantasy & Science Fiction* 61 (July, 1981): .

b. *The Dark Tower: The Gunslinger*. West Kingston, RI: Donald M. Grant, 1984, cloth, p. 149-192. See **A17**.

c. as: "Die Geistermutanten" ["The Spirit-Mutants"], in *Im Fünften Jahr der Reise: Die Besten Geschichten aus* The Magazine of Fantasy & Science Fiction, *66. Folge*, edited by Ronald M. Hahn. München: Wilhelm

Heyne Verlag (TB 4005), 1983, paper, p. . Translated by Jürgen Langowski. [German]

B54. **"The Monster in the Closet,"** in *Ladies' Home Journal* (October, 1981): . An excerpt from *Cujo*. See **A12**.

B55. **"The Bird and the Album,"** in *A Fantasy Reader: The Seventh World Fantasy Convention Program Book,* edited by Jeff Frane and Jack Rems. Berkeley, CA: The Seventh World Fantasy Convention, October 30, 1981, p. 79-85. An excerpt from the opening of chapter 13 of the manuscript *IT*. 1,000 copies printed.

b. incorporated into: *IT*. New York: Viking, 1986, cloth, p. 701-707.

"The Bird and the Album" constitutes an early version of "Part 4: July of 1958" and "Chapter 14: The Album"—Parts 1, and 2 [partial]. The passage has been substantially revised, including a shift of verb tense from past to present. See **A32**.

B56. **"Do the Dead Sing?"** in *Yankee* (November, 1981): 139-143, 238-264.

b. *The Best of Yankee, 1935-1985*, edited by Jud Hale. 1985.
c. as: "The Reach," in *Skeleton Crew*. New York: G. P. Putnam's Sons, June 1985, cloth, p. 487-505. See **A28**.
d. as: "Der Gesang der Toten" ["The Song of the Dead"], in *Das Winterlesebuch*, edited by Manfred Kluge. München: Wilhelm Heyne Verlag (TB 6759), 1986, paper, p. . Translated by Alexandra von Reinhardt. [German]
e. as: "The Reach," in *The Dark Descent*, edited by David G. Hartwell. New York: Tor, A Tom Doherty Associates Book, October 1987, cloth, p. 15-30.
eb. as: "The Reach," in *The Dark Descent 1: The Colour of Evil*, edited by David G. Hartwell. London: Grafton, 1990, cloth, p. .
ec. as: "The Reach," in *The Color of Evil: The Dark Descent, Vol. 1*, edited by David G. Hartwell. New York: Tor, 1991, paper, p. 18-42.
f. as: "The Reach," in *The Horror Hall of Fame*, edited by Robert Silverberg and Martin H. Greenberg. New York: Carroll & Graf, 1991, cloth, p. 380-401.

Winner of the World Fantasy Award, 1981, this story appeared in *Skeleton Crew* with King's original title. "Do the Dead Sing?" is a gentle story that, as David G. Hartwell notes, carefully distances the horrific to concentrate on the human; the result is "a work of unusual subtlety and sentiment, a ghost story of love and death, a virtuoso performance..." (*The Dark Descent*, p. 15). The story of Stella Flanders and her ninety-six years of life on Goat Island, and of her journey across the frozen Reach, modulates from stark realism into a meditation on life and death, fear and love. Justly applauded by most readers, it concludes *Skeleton Crew* and stands among King's best stories.

B57. **"The Gunslinger and the Dark Man,"** in *The Magazine of Fantasy & Science Fiction* 61 (November, 1981): .

b. *The Dark Tower: The Gunslinger*. West Kingston, RI: Donald M. Grant, 1984, cloth, p. 197-216. See **A17**.

c. as: "Der Revolvermann und der Mann in Schwarz," in *Mythen der Nahen Zukunft (Die Besten Geschichten aus* The Magazine of Fantasy & Science Fiction, *68. Folge)*, edited by Ronald M. Hahn. München: Wilhelm Heyne Verlag (TB 4062), 1984, paper, p. . Translated by Andreas Decker. [German]

B58. **"The Man Who Would Not Shake Hands,"** in *Shadows 4*, edited by Charles L. Grant. Garden City, NY: Doubleday & Co., 1981, cloth, p. 1-17.

ab. *Shadows 4*, edited by Charles L. Grant. New York: Berkley Books, 1985, paper, p. 1-20.

ac. *Shadows*, edited by Charles L. Grant. London: Headline, 1987, cloth, p.

b. *Skeleton Crew*. New York: G. P. Putnam's Sons, June 1985, cloth, p. 289-304. See **A28**.

c. as: "Der Mann, der Niemandem die Hand Geben Wollte," in *Mordslust, Band 2* ["*Bloodthirst*," Vol. 2], edited by Viragilio Iafrate. München: Westarp Verlag, 1987, p. . Translated by Alexandra von Reinhardt. [German]

d. *The Best of Shadows,* edited by Charles L. Grant. New York, London: A Foundation Book, Doubleday, October 1988, cloth, p. 63-82.

B59. **"Cujo,"** in *Science Fiction Digest* 1 (January/February, 1982): . An excerpt from the novel. See **A12**.

B60. **"The Raft,"** in *Gallery* (November, 1982): . See **G13**.

b. *Twilight Zone Magazine* 3 (May/June, 1983): 32-46.

c. *Skeleton Crew*. New York: G. P. Putnam's Sons, June 1985, cloth, p. 245-270. See **A28**.

d. as: "Das Floß," in *Dämmerlight* ["*Twilight*"], edited by Rolf Jurkheit. München: Wilhelm Heyne Verlag (TB 7498), 1985, paper, p. . Translated by Rolf Jurkeit. [German]

e. Unauthorized reprint in a college publication in Arkansas.

The print original for an episode in George Romero's, *Creepshow II*. See **G13**.

SECONDARY SOURCES AND REVIEWS:

1. Rhodes, Wayne. "Cut Adrift in a Plagiarized Raft," in *Castle Rock: The Stephen King Newsletter* 5:12 (December, 1989): .

B61. **"Rita Hayworth and Shawshank Redemption,"** in *Different Seasons*. New York: Viking Press, 1982, cloth, p. 1-101. See also **A16** and **G23**.

B62. **"Apt Pupil: Summer of Corruption,"** in *Different Seasons*. New York: Viking Press, 1982, cloth, p. 103-296. See also **A16.**

"Apt Pupil" is one of King's most intense psychological explorations of horror within consensus reality; without recourse to monsters or denizens of the dark, King's straightforward narrative of corruption and disillusionment is compelling in its starkness and simplicity. The increasingly (and reciprocally) deadly relationship between an archetypally clean-cut American boy and a Nazi war criminal in hiding illuminates several of King's persistent themes, most remarkably intergenerational conflict, lack of family unity, and the failure of the American educational system.

B63. **"The Body: Fall From Innocence,"** in *Different Seasons*. New York: Viking Press, 1982, cloth, p. 299-451. See also **A16.** Incorporates "Stud City" and "The Revenge of Lardass Hogan."

As the print original for Rob Reiner's superlative film, *Stand by Me,* "The Body" has established itself as one of King's finest—and also most autobiographical—short stories. His re-creation of the frustrations of childhood-verging-on-adulthood is accurate, penetrating, and moving. The story is important symbolically and thematically for its variations on the theme of the sacrificial child, as represented in different ways by each of the four central characters, coupled with the quest and the search for meaning in death. The narrative is heavily autobiographical as well; one of King's childhood friends was killed while playing on railroad tracks, and the short stories credited to Gordon Lachance were early works of King's own. King recognizes the centrality of the story when he states that *IT,* arguably his most extensive exploration of childhood and adulthood and the rites of transition between the two states, is "The Body" extended and transformed into myth (Letter, 3 March 1986). With its sharp evocation of time and place, largely accomplished through King's (and Reiner's) deft inclusion of cultural icons from the early sixties, "The Body" resonates whether experienced as short fiction or as film. See also **B10**, **G12**, and **GE17**.

SECONDARY SOURCES AND REVIEWS:

1. Terrell, Carroll F. "The Body," in *Stephen King: Man and Artist.* Orono, ME: Northern Lights Publishing, 1990, cloth, p. 191-217.

B64. **"The Breathing Method: A Winter's Tale,"** in *Different Seasons*. New York: Viking Press, 1982, cloth, p. 453-518. See also **A16.**

King creates an eerie atmosphere in this climax story to the *Different Seasons* collection by combining the disparate traditions of the winter's tale, at least as old as Shakespeare; the men's club tale, including the inscrutable and mysteriously knowledgeable butler (see also King's "The Man Who Would Not Shake Hands" and Peter Straub's *Ghost Story*); and the ghost story proper.

B65. **"Father's Day,"** in *Creepshow*. New York: A Plume Book, New American Library, July 1982, paper, unpaginated. See **A15**.

B66. **"The Lonesome Death of Jordy Verrill,"** in *Creepshow*. New York: A Plume Book, New American Library, July 1982, paper, unpaginated. See **A15**.

B67. **"Something to Tide You Over,"** in *Creepshow*. New York: A Plume Book, New American Library, July 1982, paper, unpaginated. See **A15**.

B68. **"They're Creeping Up on You,"** in *Creepshow*. New York: A Plume Book, New American Library, July 1982, paper, unpaginated. See **A15**.

B69. **"Before the Play,"** in *Whispers* (August, 1982): 19-47.

Deleted from the final version of *The Shining* (see **A3**), these episodes reinforce the original five-act dramatic/tragic structure King envisioned for the novel. While not critical to a fully satisfactory reading of the novel, the passages provide interesting insights into key characters, including Jack Torrance, and into the history of the Overlook itself.

The segment was originally slated to be included in Stephen Spignesi's *The Shape Under the Sheet: The Complete Stephen King Encyclopedia* (May 1991), but King later reconsidered and withdrew it from further publication.

B70. **"Skybar,"** in *The Do-It-Yourself Bestseller,* edited by Tom Silberkleit and Jerry Biederman. Garden City, NY: Doubleday & Co., 1982, cloth, p. .

b. New York: Dolphin, 1982, paper, p. 15-16, 20.

King wrote the first four paragraphs and the conclusion of this partial tale, leaving the body for aspiring writers to complete. The piece suggests *IT,* as well as demonstrating traditional King stylistics and techniques: brand names and a painfully precise realism as backdrop for fear.

B71. **"Survivor Type,"** in *Terrors,* edited by Charles L. Grant. New York: Playboy Paperbacks, July 1982, paper, p. 203-222.

b. as: "Das Überlebenstyp," in *Das Weißbuch des Schwarzen Humors* ["*The White Book of Black Humor*"], edited by Hans Gamber. München: Wilhelm Heyne Verlag (TB 6351), 1984, paper, p. . Translated by Monika Hahn. [German]
c. *Skeleton Crew*. New York: G. P. Putnam's Sons, June 1985, cloth, p. 361-378. See **A28**.

B72. **"The Word Processor,"** in *Playboy* (January, 1983): 173, 217-226.

ab. as: "Taste des Todes" ["Touch of Death"], in *Playboy* No. 11 (November, 1984): . Translator unknown. [German]
ac. as: "De Tekstverwerker," in *Playboy* (June, 1985). [Dutch]
b. as: "The Word Processor of the Gods," in *Skeleton Crew*. New York: G. P. Putnam's Sons, June 1985, cloth, p. 271-288. Restores King's original title. See **A28**.
c. as: "Der Textcomputer der Götter," in *Das Ferien-lesebuch*, edited by Günther Fetzer. München: Wilhelm Heyne Verlag (TB 6678), 1986, paper, p. . Translated by Alexandra von Reinhardt. [German]
d. as: "The Word Processor of the Gods," in *Tales from the Darkside, Volume One,* edited by Mitchell Galin and Tom Allen. New York: Berkley Books, October 1988, mass-market paper, p. 17-36.

With "The Word Processor" and "The Reach," King explores the possibility of order and justice in an unjust, disordered universe. Stella Flanders discovers truth at the end of her long life; Richard Hagstrom does not have to wait so long to find self-fulfillment and happiness. Although based partially on W. W. Jacobs's "The Monkey's Paw," "The Word Processor of the Gods" avoids the darkness of *Pet Sematary*, bringing the traditional three wishes to a satisfying conclusion. Read in the context of *IT*, "The Reach" and "The Word Processor of the Gods" prefigure the mythic order King creates at the conclusion of that novel.

The print original for a *Tales From the Dark Side* episode (see **GB2**).

B73. **"Uncle Otto's Truck,"** in *Yankee* (October, 1983): .

b. *The Year's Best Horror Stories, Series XII*, edited by Karl Edward Wagner. New York: DAW Books, 1984, paper, p. 17-35.

bb. as: "Onkel Ottos Lastwagen," in *Die Gruselgeschichten des Jahres*, edited by Karl Edward Wagner. München: Wilhelm Heyne Verlag (TB 6614), 1986, paper, p. . Translated by Martin Bliesse. [German]

c. *Skeleton Crew*. New York: G. P. Putnam's Sons, June 1985, cloth, p. 379-394. See **A28**.

d. as: "Onkel Ottos Lastwagen," in *Phantastische Weltliteratur 1986*, edited by Michael Görden. Bergisch Gladbach: Bastei-Lübbe Verlag (TB 72044), 1986, paper, p. . Translator unknown. [German]

e. *Horrorstory, Volume Four: The Year's Best Horror Stories X; The Year's Best Horror Stories XI; The Year's Best Horror Stories XII*. Novato, CA, Lancaster, PA: Underwood-Miller, 1990, cloth, p. 447-462.

B74. **"Cycle of the Werewolf,"** in *Heavy Metal* (December, 1983): . An excerpt from *Cycle of the Werewolf*. See **A21**.

B75. **"The Return of Timmy Baterman,"** in *Satyricon II Program Book*, edited by Rusty Burke. Knoxville TN: Satyricon II/DeepSouthCon XXI, 1983, paper, p. . An excerpt from *Pet Sematary*. See **A22**.

B76. **"Gramma,"** in *Weirdbook* No. 19 (Spring, 1984): 3-16.

b. *Skeleton Crew*. New York: G. P. Putnam's Sons, June 1985, cloth, p. 415-441. See also **A28**.

c. as: "Omi," in *Hexengeschichten* ["*Witch Stories*"], edited by Ernst M. Frank. München: Wilhelm Heyne Verlag (TB 7701), 1988, paper, p. . Translated by Alexandra von Reinhardt. [German]

d. *Tales of Witchcraft*, edited by Richard Dalby. London: Michael O'Mara Books, 1991, cloth, p. 137-164.

e. *The Television Late Night Horror Omnibus*, edited by Peter Haining. London: Orion, 1993, cloth, p. 502-530.

The story combines third-person narrative with interior monologue approaching stream-of-consciousness to evoke incremental, Lovecraftian horror. Gramma is one of King's most obsessive and oppressive "monstrous women," and Georgie one of his most intensive sacrificial children. The story integrates the Lovecraftian elements more subtly than did Harlan Ellison's otherwise fine screenplay for *Twilight Zone* (February 1986; see **GB3**).

B77. **"Mrs. Todd's Shortcut,"** in *Redbook* (May, 1984): 56, 58, 178-188.

b. *Skeleton Crew*. New York: G. P. Putnam's Sons, June 1985, cloth, p. 181-202. See **A28**.

c. *The Year's Best Horror Stories, Series XIII*, edited by Karl Edward Wagner. New York: DAW Books, 1985, paper, p. 13-40.

cb. as: "Mrs. Todds Abkürzung," in *Die Gruselgeschichten des Jahres 2*, edited by Karl Edward Wagner. München: Wilhelm Heyne Verlag (TB 6793), 1987, paper, p. . Translated by Alexandra von Reinhardt. [German]

d. *Horrorstory, Volume Five: The Year's Best Horror Stories XIII; The Year's Best Horror Stories XIV; The Year's Best Horror Stories XV*. Novato, CA, Lancaster, PA: Underwood-Miller, 1989, cloth, p. 5-28.

B78. **"The Ballad of the Flexible Bullet,"** in *The Magazine of Fantasy & Science Fiction* 66 (June, 1984): 6-48.

b. *Skeleton Crew*. New York: G. P. Putnam's Sons, June 1985, cloth, p. 443-486. See also **A28**.

c. *The Best Fantasy Stories from the Magazine of Fantasy & Science Fiction*, edited by Ed Ferman. London: Octopus Books, 1985, cloth, p. 459-503.

B79. **"The Revelations of 'Becka Paulson,"** in *Rolling Stone* (July 19-August 2, 1984): 82-85, 110. An early version of portions of *The Tommyknockers* (see **A35**).

b. *Skeleton Crew*. Santa Barbara, CA: Scream/Press, 1985, cloth, p. . Included in the limited edition only. See **A28**.

c. *I Shudder at Your Touch*, edited by Michele Slung. New York: A Roc Book, Penguin Books, May 1991, cloth, p. 1-21.

SECONDARY SOURCES AND REVIEWS:

1. LaFaille, Gene. *Wilson Library Journal* 66:2 (October, 1991): 111.
2. Schwartz, Gil. *Fortune* 124:5 (1991?): .

B80. **"Dolan's Cadillac,"** in *Castle Rock: The Stephen King Newsletter* 1:2 (February, 1985): 2-6; and 1:3 (March, 1985): 2-6; and 1:4 (April, 1985): 2-9; and 1:5 (May, 1985): 1, 4; and 1:6 (June, 1985): 1-2, 5.

b. as: *Dolan's Cadillac*. Northridge, CA: Lord John Press, 1989, 64 p., cloth. See **A37**.

B81. **"Heroes for Hope: Starring the X-Men,"** in *Marvel Comics* (1985): 10-12. [comic book]

As part of a campaign for famine relief and recovery in Africa, King joined over a dozen other writers—including Harlan Ellison, George Martin, and

Stan Lee—to create an adventure based on hunger, guilt, and human responsibility. Each writer contributed from one to three pages of text, each segment drawn, inked, lettered, and colored by different artists. King's contribution includes the ghoulishly skeletal figure of Hunger and the image of food melting into a putrescent slush. All proceeds from the magazine were donated to famine relief.

B82. **"Beachworld,"** in *Weird Tales* (1985): .

b. *Skeleton Crew*. New York: G. P. Putnam's Sons, June 1985, cloth, p. 305-320. See **A28**.

One of King's closest approximations to strict science fiction, "Beachworld" uses a traditional SF motif of human explorers stranded on an alien world—this one composed of sand dunes. The world is controlled by a planetary sentience, on the order of the world-ocean of Stanislaw Lem's *Solaris*, that is ultimately unknowable, inimical to humanity, and, on its own terms, horrific.

B83. **"Morning Deliveries (Milkman #1),"** in *Skeleton Crew*. New York: G. P. Putnam's Sons, June 1985, cloth, p. 395-400. See **A28**.

A companion piece to "Big Wheels: a Tale of the Laundry Game (Milkman #1)." Both are excerpts from a longer manuscript, both share a surrealistic quality, and both deal with an abrupt intrusion of the irrational into the rational. "Morning Deliveries" is more immediately accessible, but paradoxically more disturbing in its suggestion of mindless, purposeless death set against a pastoral setting.

B84. **"For the Birds,"** in *Bred Any Good Rooks Lately?*, edited by James Charlton. Garden City, NY: Doubleday & Co., October (?) 1986, trade paper, p. .

B85. **"The End of the Whole Mess,"** in *Omni* 9 (October, 1986): .

b. *Nightmares & Dreamscapes*. New York: Viking, 1993, cloth, p. 67-94. See **A47**.

bb. *Nightmares & Dreamscapes*. New York: A Signet Book, September 1994, paper, p. 57-80.

B86. **"The Dark Tower: The Drawing of the Three,"** excerpted in *Castle Rock: The Stephen King Newsletter* 3:4 (April/May, 1987): 1, 8-9, 11, 13. See **A34.**

B87. **"The Doctor's Case,"** in *The New Adventures of Sherlock Holmes: Original Stories by Eminent Mystery Writers*, edited by Martin Harry Greenberg and Carol-Lynn Rössel Waugh. New York: Carroll & Graf, 1987, cloth, p. 303-334.

b. as: "Der Fall des Doktors," in *Heyne Krimi Jahresband zum Jubiläums-Jahr 1988*. München: Wilhelm Heyne Verlag, 1988, paper, p. .

Translated by Joachim Körber (given incorrectly in text as Körleer). [German]

c. as: "Der Fall des Doktors," in *Die Neuen Abenteur des Sherlock Holmes,* edited by Martin H. Greenberg and Carol-Lynn Rössel-Waugh. Bergisch Gladbach: Bastei-Lübbe Verlag (Paperback 28179), 1988, paper, p . Translated by Joachim Körber. [German]

d. *Nightmares & Dreamscapes*. New York: Viking, 1993, cloth, p. 651-686. See **A47**.

db. *Nightmares & Dreamscapes*. New York: A Signet Book, September 1994, paper, p. 551-581.

B88. **"Popsy,"** in *Masques II: All-New Stories of Horror and the Supernatural*, edited by J. N. Williamson. Baltimore: Maclay & Associates, 1987, cloth, p. 13-24. A limited edition of 300 copies.

ab. *Masques II: All-New Stories of Horror and the Supernatural*, edited by J. N. Williamson. Baltimore: Maclay & Associates, 1987, cloth, p. 13-24. Trade edition.

b. *The Best of Masques*, edited by J. N. Williamson. New York: Berkley Books, June 1988, mass-market paper, p. 209-220.

c. *Karl Edward Wagner Presents The Year's Best Horror Stories XVI,* edited by Karl Edward Wagner. New York: DAW Books, 1988, paper, p. 15-30.

d. *Popsy und 25 Weitere Geschichten nach Mitternacht* [*"Popsy and 25 More Stories Past Midnight"*], edited by J. N. Williamson. Bergisch Gladbach: Bastei-Lübbe Verlag (TB 13150), 1988, paper, p. . Translated by Ingrid Herrmann. This is probably adapted from one of Williamson's *Masque* anthologies. [German]

e. *Nightmares & Dreamscapes*. New York: Viking, 1993, cloth, p. 147-160. See **A47**.

eb. *Nightmares & Dreamscapes*. New York: A Signet Book, September 1994, paper, p. 126-138.

B89. **"The Night Flier,"** in *Prime Evil: New Stories by the Masters of Modern Horror,* edited by Douglas E. Winter. West Kingston, RI: Donald M. Grant, Publisher, April 1988, cloth, p. 13-47. Limited to 1000 copies.

b. *Prime Evil,* edited by Douglas E. Winter. New York: NAL Books, New American Library, June 1988, cloth, p. 13-47.

bb. *Prime Evil,* edited by Douglas E. Winter. New York: A Signet Book, New American Library, April 1989, paper, p. 25-63.

bc. *Prime Evil,* edited by Douglas E. Winter. New York: New American Library [Science Fiction Book Club edition], [n.d.], p. 3-33.

c. as: "Der Nachtflieger," in *Horror vom Feinsten* [*"Horror from the Finest"*], edited by Douglas E. Winter. München: Wilhelm Heyne Verlag (Jumbo Paperback 41/17), Fall 1989, paper, p. . Translated by Joachim Körber. [German]

d. *Nightmares & Dreamscapes*. New York: Viking, 1993, cloth, p. 109-146. See **A47**.

db. *Nightmares & Dreamscapes*. New York: A Signet Book, September 1994, paper, p. 93-125.

King's exploration of the vampire motif, translated into uniquely American, 1980s' idiom. The story not only remains true to vampire lore, but expands it to include many levels of American society as well. Psychologically at least, King's vampire ("Dwight Renfield") shares much with the story's protagonist and by extension with the millions of Americans who satisfy their sublimated bloodlust by following the most recent horrific headlines in tabloid newspapers. The vampire literally consumes blood; the rest do so figuratively, but just as obsessively.

SECONDARY SOURCES AND REVIEWS:

1. Enfantino, Peter. "Quick Chills," in *The Scream Factory* no. 3 (Summer 1989): 29-32. This review of *Prime Evil* notes that, except for King's story and Dennis Etchison's "The Blood Kiss," the anthology was lackluster and unoriginal. Its success was "100% due to the name Stephen King on the cover" (p. 29).
2. Holman, Curt. "Horrors: New Books Fall Short of Mark," in *Nashville Banner* [Tennessee] (August, 1988): . As microfiche: *Newsbank: Literature* 15 (September, 1988): Fiche 102, D5.
3. Schweitzer, Darrell. "Anthology of New Horror Tales: Interviews with Stephen King," in *Philadelphia Inquirer* (July 24, 1988): . As microfiche: *Newsbank: Literature* 15 (September, 1988): Fiche 102, D4.

B90. "**The Reploids,**" in *Night Visions 5*, edited by Douglas E. Winter. Arlington Heights, IL: Dark Harvest, 1988, cloth, p. 19-34. A limited edition illustrated by Ron Lindahm.

ab. *Night Visions 5*, edited by Douglas E. Winter. Arlington Heights, IL: Dark Harvest, 1988, cloth, p. 19-34. Trade edition.
ac. *The Skin Trade*, edited by Douglas E. Winter. New York: Berkley Books, 1990, paper, p. 11-29.

B91. "**Sneakers,**" in *Night Visions 5*, edited by Douglas E. Winter. Arlington Heights, IL: Dark Harvest, 1988, cloth, p. 35-58. A limited edition illustrated by Ron Lindahm.

ab. *Night Visions 5*, edited by Douglas E. Winter. Arlington Heights, IL: Dark Harvest, 1988, cloth, p. 35-58. Trade edition.
ac. *The Skin Trade*, edited by Douglas E. Winter. New York: Berkley Books, 1990, paper, p. 31-57.
b. *Nightmares & Dreamscapes*. New York: Viking, 1993, cloth, p. 303-332. See **A47**.
bb. *Nightmares & Dreamscapes*. New York: A Signet Book, September 1994, paper, p. 259-283.

B92. "**Dedication,**" in *Night Visions 5*, edited by Douglas E. Winter. Arlington Heights, IL: Dark Harvest, 1988, p. 59-100. A limited edition illustrated by Ron Lindahm.

ab. *Night Visions 5*, edited by Douglas E. Winter. Arlington Heights, IL: Dark Harvest, 1988, cloth, p. 59-100. Trade edition.

ac. *The Skin Trade*, edited by Douglas E. Winter. New York: Berkley Books, 1990, paper, p. 59-110.

b. *Nightmares & Dreamscapes*. New York: Viking, 1993, cloth, p. 215-262. See **A47**.

bb. *Nightmares & Dreamscapes*. New York: A Signet Book, September 1994, paper, p. 186-225.

B93. **"Rainy Season,"** in *Midnight Graffiti* No. 3 (Spring, 1989): 14-24.

b. *Midnight Graffiti*, edited by Jessica Horsting and James Van Hise. New York: Warner Books, 1992, paper, p. 5-29.

c. *Nightmares & Dreamscapes*. New York: Viking, 1993, cloth, p. 413-436. See **A47**.

cb. *Nightmares & Dreamscapes*. New York: A Signet Book, September 1994, paper, p. 351-371.

B94. **"The Dark Half,"** in *Fear: Fantasy and Science Fiction* [England] (October, 1989): . An excerpt from the novel of the same name (see **A39**), with Stephen King cover illustration.

B95. **"Home Delivery,"** in *Book of the Dead,* edited by John Skipp and Craig Spector. Willimantic, CT: Mark V. Ziesing, 1989, cloth, p. 33-58. A limited edition.

ab. *Book of the Dead,* edited by John Skipp and Craig Spector. Willimantic, CT: Mark V. Ziesing, 1989, cloth, p. 33-58. Trade edition.

ac. *Book of the Dead,* edited by John Skipp and Craig Spector. New York: Bantam Books, 1989, paper, p. 51-79.

b. excerpted in: *Midnight Graffiti* No. 2 (Fall, 1988): .

c. *Nightmares & Dreamscapes*. New York: Viking, 1993, cloth, p. 381-412. See **A47**.

cb. *Nightmares & Dreamscapes*. New York: A Signet Book, September 1994, paper, p. 324-350.

SECONDARY SOURCES AND REVIEWS:

1. Cupp, Scott A. "Penny Dreadfuls," in *Mystery Scene* No. 23 (October, 1989): 75-76.
2. Graham, Mark. "Skipp & Spector's *Book of the Dead*: Gross, Shocking, Darkly Humorous," in *The Blood Review: The Journal of Horror Criticism* 1:1 (October 1989): 18.

B96. **"The Langoliers,"** in *Four Past Midnight*. New York: Viking, 1990, p. 3-246. See also **A41**.

Dedication: "This is for Joe, Another White-Knuckle Flier."

B97. **"Secret Window, Secret Garden,"** in *Four Past Midnight*. New York: Viking, 1990, p. 253-399. See also **A41**.

Dedication: "This is for Chuck Verrill."

B98. **"The Library Policeman,"** in *Four Past Midnight*. New York: Viking, 1990, p. 407-604. See also **A41**.

Dedication: "This is for the staff and patrons of the Pasadena Public Library."

B99. **"The Sun Dog,"** in *Four Past Midnight*. New York: Viking, 1990, p. 613-763. See also **A41**.

DEDICATION: "This is in memory of John D. MacDonald. I miss you, old friend—and you were right about the tigers."

King notes that this story provides a narrative link between *The Dark Half* and *Needful Things*, his "final" Castle Rock novel.

B100. **"The Moving Finger,"** in *The Magazine of Fantasy & Science Fiction* 79:6 (December, 1990): 8-43. A Special Stephen King issue.

c. *Nightmares & Dreamscapes*. New York: Viking, 1993, cloth, p. 263-302. See **A47**.

cb. *Nightmares & Dreamscapes*. New York: A Signet Book, September 1994, paper, p. 226-258.

B101. **"The Bear,"** in *The Magazine of Fantasy & Science Fiction* 79:6 (December, 1990): 61-88. An excerpt from *The Dark Tower III: The Waste Lands* (see **A43**). A Special Stephen King issue.

B102. **"You Know They Got a Hell of a Band,"** in *Shock Rock*, edited by Jeff Gelb. New York: Pocket Books, January 1992, mass-market paper, p. 1-45.

b. *Kingpins*, edited by Cynthia Manson and Charles Ardai. New York: Carroll & Graf, 1992, cloth, p. .

c. *Nightmares & Dreamscapes*. New York: Viking, 1993, cloth, p. 330-380. See **A47**.

cb. *Nightmares & Dreamscapes*. New York: A Signet Book, September 1994, paper, p. 284-323.

B103. **"Chattery Teeth,"** in *Cemetery Dance* 4:4 (Fall, 1992): 4-22.

b. *Nightmares & Dreamscapes*. New York: Viking, 1993, cloth, p. 179-214. See **A47**.

bb. *Nightmares & Dreamscapes*. New York: A Signet Book, September 1994, paper, p. 155-185.

B104. **"My Pretty Pony,"** in *Nightmares & Dreamscapes*. New York: Viking, 1993, cloth, p. 437-466. See also **A38** and **A47**.

ab. *Nightmares & Dreamscapes*. New York: A Signet Book, September 1994, paper, p. 372-395.

B105. **"The Ten O'Clock People,"** in *Nightmares & Dreamscapes*. New York: Viking, 1993, cloth, p. 501-558. See also **A47**.

ab. *Nightmares & Dreamscapes*. New York: A Signet Book, September 1994, paper, p. 427-475.

B106. **"The House on Maple Street,"** in *Nightmares & Dreamscapes*. New York: Viking, 1993, cloth, p. 593-632. See also **A47**.

ab. *Nightmares & Dreamscapes*. New York: A Signet Book, September 1994, paper, p. 504-536.

B107. **"Umney's Last Case,"** in *Nightmares & Dreamscapes*. New York: Viking, 1993, cloth, p. 687-741. See also **A47**.

ab. *Nightmares & Dreamscapes*. New York: A Signet Book, September 1994, paper, p. 582-626.

SECONDARY SOURCES AND REVIEWS:

1. "King Work to Be Offered Only on Internet Network," in *Wall Street Journal* (September 17, 1993): B3 (W), B6 (E).

B108. **"The Beggar and the Diamond,"** in *Nightmares & Dreamscapes*. New York: Viking, 1993, cloth, p. 813-816. See also **A47**.

ab. *Nightmares & Dreamscapes*. New York: A Signet Book, September 1994, paper, p. 689-692.

B109. **"Jhonathan and the Witches,"** in *First Words: Earliest Writing from Favorite Contemporary Authors*, edited by Paul Mandelbaum. Chapel Hill, NC: Algonquin Books of Chapel Hill, 1993, cloth, p. 286-288.

The first publication of the earliest story King wrote (at age nine), in an anthology featuring early works by authors such as Isaac Asimov and Joyce Carol Oates.

B110. **"Killer,"** in *Famous Monsters of Filmland* (1994): .

The story was sent to Forrest J Ackerman in the mid-1960s, but not published until now.

B111. **"The Man in the Black Suit,"** in *The New Yorker* (October 31, 1994): .

B112. **"Lucky Quarter,"** in *USA Weekend* (June 30-July 2, 1995): 4-7. Distributed in newspapers throughout the United States as a Sunday supplement.

B113. **"Lunch at the Gotham Café,"** in *Dark Love*, edited by Nancy A. Collins, Edward E. Kramer, and Martin Harry Greenberg. New York: A Roc Book, November 1995, cloth, p. 17-54.

C.

SHORT NONFICTION

King's nonfiction ranges from formal criticism to fan appreciation and political statements, from serious cultural appraisals to semicomic statements on a variety of subjects. His voice is unique, whether speaking through criticism or narrative—everything he writes is tinged with a sense of the novelist, even when he defines current trends in culture, society, politics, baseball, or rock and roll music.

The following list identifies King's published utterances in many circumstances: introductions and afterwords to his own works, introductions to works by other writers, and speculations on the nature of American society. Yet each illuminates his own fiction through comments made in other contexts.

C1. "**King's Garbage Truck,**" by "STEVE KING," in *The Maine Campus* (February 20, 1969): 9.

The first issue of King's weekly column for the student publication at the University of Maine, Orono. The columns are uneven but fascinating, giving at times unusual insight into the young King. For detailed discussions of each column, see Collings's *The Stephen King Phenomenon* (**I15**).

SECONDARY SOURCES AND REVIEWS:

1. Blue, Tyson. *The Unseen King*. STARMONT STUDIES IN LITERARY CRITICISM, No. 26. Mercer Island, WA: Starmont House, 1989, cloth, p. 22-34.
2. Collings, Michael R. *The Many Facets of Stephen King*. STARMONT STUDIES IN LITERARY CRITICISM, No. 11. Mercer Island, WA: Starmont House, cloth, 1986.
3. Collings, Michael R., and David A. Engebretson. *The Shorter Works of Stephen King*. STARMONT STUDIES IN LITERARY CRITICISM, No. 9. Mercer Island, WA: Starmont House, cloth, 1985.
4. Collings, Michael R. *Stephen King in* The Maine Campus, *1969-1970.* Thousand Oaks, CA: Privately Printed, 25 July 1985, typescript, 126 p. Indexed. A typed and bound transcription of all "King's Garbage Truck" columns and "Slade" columns; done in two copies, one of which was sent to King.
5. Collings, Michael R. *The Stephen King Phenomenon*. STARMONT STUDIES IN LITERARY CRITICISM, No. 14. Mercer Island, WA. Starmont House, 1987, cloth, p. 107-123. A column-by-column synopsis and discussion.
6. Winter, Douglas E. *Stephen King: The Art of Darkness*. New York: New American Library, November 1984, cloth.

C2. **"King's Garbage Truck,"** by "STEVE KING," in *The Maine Campus* (February 27, 1969): 7.

C3. **"King's Garbage Truck,"** by "STEVE KING," in *The Maine Campus* (March 6, 1969): 9.

C4. **"King's Garbage Truck,"** by "STEVE KING," in *The Maine Campus* (March 13, 1969): 7.

C5. **"King's Garbage Truck,"** by "STEVE KING," in *The Maine Campus* (March 20, 1969): 7.

C6. **"King's Garbage Truck,"** by "STEVE KING," in *The Maine Campus* (March 27, 1969): 7.

C7. **"King's Garbage Truck,"** by "STEVE KING," in *The Maine Campus* (April 10, 1969): 6.

C8. **"King's Garbage Truck,"** by "STEVE KING," in *The Maine Campus* (April 17, 1969): 7, 13.

C9. **"King's Garbage Truck,"** by "STEVE KING," in *The Maine Campus* (April 24, 1969): 11.

C10. **"King's Garbage Truck,"** by "STEVE KING," in *The Maine Campus* (May 1, 1969): 7.

C11. **"King's Garbage Truck,"** by "STEVE KING," in *The Maine Campus* (May 8, 1969): 6.

C12. **"King's Garbage Truck,"** by "STEVE KING," in *The Maine Campus* (May 15, 1969): 7.

C13. **"King's Garbage Truck,"** by "STEVE KING," in *The Maine Campus* (May 22, 1969): 7.

C14. **"King's Garbage Truck,"** by "STEVE KING," in *The Maine Campus* (June 12, 1969): 4.

C15. **"King's Garbage Truck,"** by "STEVE KING," in *The Maine Campus* (June 20, 1969): 6.

C16. **"King's Garbage Truck,"** by "STEVE KING," in *The Maine Campus* (June 27, 1969): 5, 6.

C17. **"King's Garbage Truck,"** by "STEVE KING," in *The Maine Campus* (July 4, 1979): 4.

C18. **"King's Garbage Truck,"** by "STEVE KING," in *The Maine Campus* (July 11, 1969): 5.

C19. **"King's Garbage Truck,"** by "STEVE KING," in *The Maine Campus* (July 18, 1969): 7.

C20. **"King's Garbage Truck,"** by "STEVE KING," in *The Maine Campus* (July 27, 1969): 5, 6.

C21. **"King's Garbage Truck,"** by "STEVE KING," in *The Maine Campus* (August 1, 1969): 4, 7.

C22. **"King's Garbage Truck,"** by "STEVE KING," in *The Maine Campus* (August 8, 1969): 4.

C23. **"King's Garbage Truck,"** by "STEVE KING," in *The Maine Campus* (September 18, 1969): 7.

C24. **"King's Garbage Truck,"** by "STEVE KING," in *The Maine Campus* (September 25, 1969): 5.

C25. **"King's Garbage Truck,"** by "STEVE KING," in *The Maine Campus* (October 3, 1969): 5.

C26. **"King's Garbage Truck,"** by "STEVE KING," in *The Maine Campus* (October 9, 1969): 5.

C27. **"King's Garbage Truck,"** by "STEVE KING," in *The Maine Campus* (October 16, 1969): 4, 6.

C28. **"King's Garbage Truck,"** by "STEVE KING," in *The Maine Campus* (October 23, 1969): 6.

C29. **"King's Garbage Truck,"** by "STEVE KING," in *The Maine Campus* (October 30, 1969: 5.

C30. **"King's Garbage Truck,"** by "STEVE KING," in *The Maine Campus* (November 6, 1969): 5.

C31. **"King's Garbage Truck,"** by "STEVE KING," in *The Maine Campus* (November 13, 1969): 5.

C32. **"King's Garbage Truck,"** by "STEVE KING," in *The Maine Campus* (December 4, 1969): 5.

C33. **"King's Garbage Truck,"** by "STEVE KING," in *The Maine Campus* (December 11, 1969): 5.

C34. **"King's Garbage Truck,"** by "STEVE KING," in *The Maine Campus* (December 18, 1969): 6.

C35. **"King's Garbage Truck,"** by "STEVE KING," in *The Maine Campus* (January 8, 1970): 5.

C36. **"King's Garbage Truck,"** by "STEVE KING," in *The Maine Campus* (January 15, 1970): 5.

C37. **"King's Garbage Truck,"** by "STEVE KING," in *The Maine Campus* (February 5, 1970): 10.

C38. **"King's Garbage Truck,"** by "STEVE KING," in *The Maine Campus* (February 12, 1970): 5.

C39. **"King's Garbage Truck,"** by "STEVE KING," in *The Maine Campus* (February 19, 1970): 8.

C40. **"King's Garbage Truck,"** by "STEVE KING," in *The Maine Campus* (February 26, 1970): 5.

C41. **"King's Garbage Truck,"** by "STEVE KING," in *The Maine Campus* (March 19, 1970): 5.

C42. **"King's Garbage Truck,"** by "STEVE KING," in *The Maine Campus* (March 26, 1970): 5.

C43. **"King's Garbage Truck,"** by "STEVE KING," in *The Maine Campus* (April 4, 1970): 5.

C44. **"King's Garbage Truck,"** by "STEVE KING," in *The Maine Campus* (April 16, 1970): 5.

C45. **"King's Garbage Truck,"** by "STEVE KING," in *The Maine Campus* (April 30, 1970): 5.

C46. **"King's Garbage Truck,"** by "STEVE KING," in *The Maine Campus* (May 7, 1970): 5.

C47. **"A Possible Fairy Tale,"** in *The Paper* (May 8, 1970): 5.

An account of a fictional anti-war demonstration by American students against the continuing war in Cambodia, beginning with a UMO (University of Maine, Orono) student strike on May 8 and ending with Nixon withdrawing US troops from Cambodia on May 18.

SECONDARY SOURCES AND REVIEWS:

1. Spignesi, Stephen J. *The Shape Under the Sheet: The Complete Stephen King Encyclopedia*. Ann Arbor, MI: Popular Culture, Ink., May 1991, cloth, p. 90-91. A summary and paraphrase.

C48. **"King's Garbage Truck,"** by "STEVE KING," in *The Maine Campus* (May 21, 1970): 5.

b. *Maine* [Alumni Magazine, University of Maine, Orono] (1989): .

C49. **"The Horror Market Writer and the Ten Bears,"** in *Writer's Digest* (November, 1973): 10-13.

b. as: "The Horror Writer and the Ten Bears: Foreword," in *Kingdom of Fear: The World of Stephen King*, edited by Tim Underwood and Chuck Miller. San Francisco, CA, Columbia, PA: Underwood-Miller, 1986, cloth, p. 11-19. See **I11**.

A discussion of the ten fears that readers respond most readily to. The 1986 reprint is presented essentially unchanged from the 1973 version, resulting in a number of out-of-date or by then inaccurate items.

SECONDARY SOURCES AND REVIEWS:

1. Spignesi, Stephen J. *The Shape Under the Sheet: The Complete Stephen King Encyclopedia.* Ann Arbor, MI: Popular Culture, Ink., May 1991, cloth, p. 3-4.

C50. **"Writing a First Novel,"** in *The Writer* 88:6 (June, 1975): 25-27. The fourth and final segment in a series by new novelists.

ab. excerpted in: *The Writer* 100:4 (April, 1987): 15.

C51. **"Not Guilty,"** in *The New York Times Book Review* (October 24, 1976): 55.

In this response to criticism, King comments on *'Salem's Lot* as an "accessible" novel, written with the author's intention of doing the best job he could. King compares his advance for the book with the $15,000 received by David Madden for *Bijou*; although not assertively great literature, *'Salem's Lot*, says King, justly earned what it received.

C52. **[Title unknown],** in *Coda: Poets and Writers Newsletter* 4:2 (November/December, 1976): 20.

A discussion of the impact movies have on reading audiences.

C53. **"The Fright Report,"** in *Oui* (January, 1978): 76-78, 107-108.

b. portions incorporated as: "An Annoying Autobiographical Pause, Part 4," in *Stephen King's Danse Macabre*. New York: Everest House, 1981, cloth, p. 103-110. See **A11**.

A critical and autobiographical essay outlining the rise of horror films from the 1930s through the 1970s.

C54. **"The Doll Who Ate His Mother,"** in *Whispers* No. 11/12 (October, 1978): 63.

b. incorporated into: *Stephen King's Danse Macabre*. New York: Everest House, 1981, cloth. See **A11**.

A review of Ramsey Campbell as horror writer.

C55. **"Foreword,"** in *Night Shift*. Garden City, NY: Doubleday & Co., 1978, cloth, p. xi-xxii. See **A6**.

b. excerpted as: "Warum Lesen Wir Phantastische Geschichten?" in *Phantastische Literatur 83,* edited by Michael Görden. Bergisch Gladbach: Bastei-Lübbe Verlag (TB 72022), 1983, paper, p. . Translated by Michael Görden. [German]

An early attempt at articulating the nature of horror, beginning with the memorable lines, "Let's talk you and I. Let's talk about fear." King discusses his belief in horror fiction as therapeutic, adaptive, and spellbinding, as well as the literary and cultural influences on his early works.

C56. **"How to Scare a Woman to Death,"** in *Murderess Ink: The Better Half of the Mystery,* edited by Dilys Winn. New York: Bell, 1979, cloth, p. 173-175. Published simultaneously in trade paperback.

Tips on "throwing a jolt into what some of us still refer to as the fairer sex" (p. 173).

C57. **"Introduction,"** in *Frankenstein, Dracula, Dr. Jekyll and Mr. Hyde,* by Mary Shelley, Bram Stoker, and Robert Louis Stevenson. New York: A Signet Book, New American Library, 1978, paper, p. v-viii.

b. as: "Inleidung" ["Introduction"], in *Die Grote Horror-Omnibus* ["*The Big Horror Omnibus*"]. Amsterdam: Loeb, 1983, paper (?), p. 5-14. [Dutch]

An extensive discussion of the merits and weaknesses of three classic horror tales.

SECONDARY SOURCES AND REVIEWS:

1. Zagorski, Edward J. *The Novels of Stephen King*. New York: New American Library, 1981, paper.

C58. **"Introduction" to "The Cat from Hell,"** in *Top Horror,* edited by Josh Pachter. München: Wilhelm Heyne Verlag (Die Unheimliche Bücher 20), 1986, paper, p. . Translated by Rolf Jurkeit. [German]

This short introduction to the story was commissioned specifically for this volume, and has appeared only in the German translation. See **B30**.

C59. **"The Writing Life: An Interview with Myself,"** in *Writer's Digest* (January, 1979): 16-17.

King answers questions about writing in general, and horror writing in particular.

C60. **"The Horrors of '79,"** in *Rolling Stone* (December 27, 1979-January 10, 1980): 17-21.

A discussion of the strongest films of 1979, including *Breaking Away, Rocky II, The Deer Hunter, Apocalypse Now, Phantasm, Nightwing, Prophecy, Alien, Lord of the Rings, Watership Down,* and *Dawn of the Dead* ("the finest horror film of the year, perhaps of the decade").

C61. **"A Pilgrim's Progress,"** in *American Bookseller* (January, 1980): .

C62. **"On Becoming a Brand Name,"** in *Adelina* (February, 1980): 40-45, 82-83.

b. as: "Foreword—On Becoming a Brand Name," in *Fear Itself: The Horror Fiction of Stephen King,* edited by Tim Underwood and Chuck Miller. San Francisco CA: Underwood-Miller, 1982, cloth, p. 15-44. See **I2.**

The essay covers King's career as a novelist to date, with some intentional inaccuracies to protect the "BACHMAN" pseudonym.

C63. **"Books: The Sixties Zone,"** in *Adelina* (June, 1980): 12.

A review of Leslie Waller's *The Brave and the Free,* with mention of Robert Marasco's *Burnt Offerings*; the review defends "another BIG NOVEL OF THE SIXTIES," and critiques reviewers who miss the power of long novels.

C64. **"Books: Critic Critique,"** in *Adelina* (July, 1980): 9.

A continuation of the Waller review (**C63**), and a critique of contemporary reviewers who insist on separating popular literature from "great literature," an approach King sees as dangerous.

C65. **"Books: Two for Terror,"** in *Adelina* (August, 1980): 12.

A review of Thomas H. Block's *Mayday* and Michael McDowell's *The Amulet,* one of "the best paperback original horror fiction[s] to be found over the last four or five years."

C66. **"Imagery and the Third Eye,"** in *The Writer* (October, 1980): 11-14, 44.

b. *Maine Alumnus* (December, 1981): .
c. *The Writer's Handbook,* edited by Sylvia Burack. Boston: The Writer Inc., 1984, cloth, p. .
d. incorporated into: *Stephen King's Danse Macabre.* New York: Everest House, 1981, cloth. See **A11.**

C67. **"Some Notes on *Tales of the Vampyre,*"** in *Opera New England of Northern Maine* (Fall, 1980): [unpaged].

Two-page program notes to a production of *Tales of the Vampyre*; text by Wohlbrück, music by Marschner.

C68. **"Introduction,"** in *The Shapes of Midnight,* by Joseph Payne Brennan. New York: Berkley Books, October 1980, paper, p. ix-xvi.

C69. **"Books: Love Those Long Novels,"** in *Adelina* (November, 1980): 12.

A discussion of negative reactions to long novels, including *The Dead Zone* and *The Stand*. Contemporary critics tend to judge such novels negatively on their length, not their merit.

C70. **"Why We Crave Horror Movies,"** in *Playboy* (January, 1981): 150-154, 237-246. Excerpts from *Danse Macabre*, p. 131-175. See **A11**.

b. *The St. Martin's Guide to Student Writing,* edited by Rise B. Axelrod and Charles R. Cooper. Short 2nd ed. New York: St. Martin's Press, 1988, paper, p. 294-96.

c. *Literature: The Human Experience, Shorter Fifth Edition with Essays*, edited by Richard Abcarian and Marvin Klotz. New York: St. Martin's Press, November 1991, paper, p. .

C71. **"Scare Movies,"** in *Cosmopolitan* (April, 1981): .

C72. **"Guilty Pleasures,"** in *Film Comment* (May-June, 1981): .

C73. **"Notes on Horror,"** in *Quest* (June 1981): 28-31, 87. Illustrated by Robert Pryor.

Excerpts from *Danse Macabre* (see **A11**), concluding that horror is not a dance of death at all, but a "dance of dreams that arouses the child inside" (p. 87).

C74. **"When Is TV Too Scary for Children?"** in *TV Guide* (June 13-19, 1981): .

C75. **[Untitled—opening line: "I don't have many dreams"],** in *Dreamworks* (Summer, 1981): .

A repeating dream/nightmare described by King.

C76. **"Danse Macabre,"** in *Book Digest* (September, 1981): . A 24-page excerpt from *Danse Macabre*. See **A11**.

C77. **"The Healthy Power of a Good Scream,"** in *Self* (September, 1981): . An excerpt from *Danse Macabre*. See **A11**.

C78. **"The Cannibal and the Cop,"** in *Washington Post Book World* (November 1, 1981): 1-3.

b. *Shadowings*, edited by Douglas E. Winter. Mercer Island, WA: Starmont House, 1983, cloth, p. 27-29. Published simultaneously in trade paper.

A review of Thomas Harris's *Red Dragon,* "probably the best popular novel to be published in America since *The Godfather*." King takes critics to task for ignoring the novel merely because it enjoys huge sales potentials.

C79. **"The Sorry State of TV Shows: You Gotta Put on the Gruesome Mask and Go Booga-Booga,"** in *TV Guide* (December 5-11, 1981): 65-68.

An excerpt from *Danse Macabre,* with heavily edited passages selected from "The Glass Teat" (especially p. 216-238). See **A11**.

C80. **"Forenote,"** in *Danse Macabre*. New York: Everest House, 1981, cloth, p. 9-12. See **A11**.

Outlines the genesis of *Danse Macabre,* from King's teaching a course in supernatural literature at the University of Maine, Orono, through discussions with Bill Thompson about publishing the study. Autobiographical emphasis.

C81. **"Afterword,"** in *Danse Macabre*. New York: Everest House, 1981, cloth, p. 381-382. See **A11**.

C82. **"Foreword,"** in *Tales from the Nightside,* edited by Charles L. Grant. Sauk City, WI: Arkham House, 1981, cloth, p. vii-xii.

An appreciation of Grant as writer: "The man is a pro."

C83. **"Introduction,"** in *The Arbor House Treasury of Horror and the Supernatural,* compiled by Bill Pronzini, Barry Malzberg, and Martin H. Greenberg. New York: Arbor House, 1981, cloth, p. 11-19.

ab. New York: Arbor House/Priam, 1981, trade paper, p. 11-19.
ac. *Great Tales of Horror and the Supernatural,* edited by Bill Pronzini, Barry N. Malzberg, and Martin H. Greenberg. New York: Galahad Books, 1988, cloth, p. 11-19.
b. as: "Einführung," in *Unheimliches,* edited by Bill Pronzini, Barry N. Malzberg, and Martin H. Greenberg. München: Wilhelm Heyne Verlag (Jubiläumsband 9), 1985, paper?, p. . Translated by Sonja Hauser and Bernd Lenz. [German]

A discussion of horror as not only an outward escape "into a kind of never-never-land," but an escape "*inward,* toward the very center of our perceived humanity."

C84. **"Introduction,"** in *When Michael Calls,* by John Farris. New York: Pocket Books, 1981, paper, p. [i-iv].

C85. **"Between Rock and a Hard Place,"** in *Playboy* (January, 1982): 120-122, 238-242.

C86. **"Visit with an Endangered Species,"** in *Playboy* (January, 1982): 122, 244.

A tribute to hard-rock Disc jockey "Mighty John" Marshall of station WAZC, Bangor, Maine.

C87. **"The Ludlum Attraction,"** in *Washington Post Book World* (March 7, 1982): 1, 10.

A review of Ludlum's *The Parsifal Mosaic* in the form of a letter from Reed Smalley (of Smalley, Hally, and Polly) to Theodore Smoot (of Smoot, Hoot, Doot, and Foot); the reviews analyzes Ludlum's audience and techniques, as well as the book's ability to "keep you occupied without engaging you or troubling you or removing your mind for more than one second after the bookmark has been placed and the book closed" (p. 10).

C88. **"Mentors,"** in *Rolling Stone College Papers* (April 15, 1982): .

A tribute to Burton Hatlen, one of King's college professors at the University of Maine, Orono.

C89. **"Favorite Films,"** in *Washington Post* (June 24, 1982): .

King's listing of his favorite films.

C90. **"Digging *The Boogens*,"** in *Twilight Zone Magazine* (July, 1982): 9-10.

An extensive essay-review of James L. Conway's film, *The Boogens*. Ultimately the piece becomes more a definition of horror as genre than an analytical or critical discussion of the specific film.

C91. **"On *The Shining* and Other Perpetrations,"** in *Whispers* No. 17/18 (August, 1982): 11-16.

A discussion of the genesis of *The Shining* in its original conception as five-act narrative based on Shakespearean tragedy. Many of the points discussed are illustrated in "Before the Play" (see **B69**).

C92. **"Peter Straub: An Informal Appreciation,"** in *World Fantasy Convention '82*, edited by Kennedy Poyser. New Haven, CT: The Eighth World Fantasy Convention, 1982, paper, p. .

C93. **"Horrors!"** in *TV Guide* (October 30-November 5, 1982): 54-58.

King's annotated listing of the ten best videocassettes available for Halloween, 1982: *Night of the Living Dead, An American Werewolf in London, Invasion of the Body Snatchers, The Thing, The Shining, Rabid, Wolfen, Dead of Night, The Fog,* and *The Toolbox Murders*.

C94. **"*The Evil Dead*: Why You Haven't Seen It Yet...And Why You Ought To,"** in *Twilight Zone Magazine* 2 (November, 1982): 20-22.

An assessment of Steve Raini's film as the "most ferociously original horror film of 1982"; it has the "simple stupid power of a good campfire story," yet is a "black rainbow" of horror that defines the extremes of the genre.

C95. **[Title unknown]**, in *Playboy Guide: Electronic Entertainment* (Fall/Winter, 1982): .

A discussion of films King would like to see preserved on videocassette.

C96. **"Afterword,"** in *Different Seasons*. New York: G. P. Putnam's Sons, 1982, cloth, p. 519-527. See **A16.**

C97. **"Afterword,"** in *Firestarter*. New York: A Signet Book, New American Library, 1982, paper, p. 402-403. See **A9**.

C98. **"Foreword,"** in *Stalking the Nightmare*, by Harlan Ellison. Huntington Woods MI: Phantasia Press, 1982, cloth, p . Limited edition.

b. New York: Berkley Books, 1984, paper, p. .

King's evaluation of Ellison as a "ferociously talented writer, ferociously in love with the job of writing stories and essays, ferociously dedicated to the craft of it as well as its art."

C99. **"Introduction"** to Ramsey Campbell's "The Companion," in *The Arbor House Celebrity Book of Horror Stories,* edited by Charles G. Waugh and Martin H. Greenberg. New York: Arbor House, 1982, cloth, p. 131-132.

King identifies key stories that influenced him as a writer: H. P. Lovecraft's "Pickman's Model," "The Rats in the Walls," and "The Colour Out of Space"; Robert Bloch's "Sweets to the Sweet"; and Ramsey Campbell's "The Companion."

C100. **"My High School Horrors,"** in *Sourcebook: The Magazine for Seniors* (1982): 30-33.

b. as: "High School Horrors," in *Castle Rock: The Stephen King Newsletter* 2:2 (February, 1986): 8.

A semi-comic treatment of classroom "horrors" based on King's experience as a high-school teacher. The listing includes "the thing that wouldn't shut up," "the classroom of the living dead," and "the smell from hell."

C101. **"Introduction: *The Importance of Being Forry,*"** in *Mr. Monster's Movie Gold,* by Forrest J Ackerman. Virginia Beach, Norfolk, VA: Donning Company, 1982, trade paper, p. 8-12.

An autobiographical account of King's discovering Ackerman's *Famous Monsters of Filmland*. Ackerman "stood up for a generation of kids who understood that if [horror] was junk, it was *magic* junk" (p. 12).

C102. "Special Make-Up Effects and the Writer," in *Grande Illusions: A Learn-by-Example Guide to the Art and Technique of Special Make-Up Effects,* by Tom Savini. Pittsburgh, PA: Imagine Inc., January 1983, trade paper, p. 6-7.

b. *Bizarro*, by Tom Savini. New York: Crown Publishers, 1983, paper, p. .

An appreciation of Savini's work and reminiscences of filming *Creepshow*.

C103. "Don't Be Cruel," in *TV Guide* (April 30-May 6, 1983): A-1.

A letter commenting favorably on Dave Marsh's article on Elvis Presley (*TV Guide*, April 9, 1983), and clarifying further King's interest in and responses to rock 'n' roll.

C104. "Dear Walden People," in *Waldenbooks Book Notes* (August, 1983): .

b. *Bare Bones: Conversations on Terror With Stephen King*, edited by Tim Underwood and Chuck Miller. San Francisco, CA: Underwood-Miller, 1988; New York: McGraw-Hill, 1988, p. 123-124. See **I20**.

c. *The Stephen King Companion,* by George Beahm. Kansas City, MO: Andrews and McMeel, 1989, paper, p. 207-208. See **I24**.

C105. "Horrors!" in *Games* (October, 1983): .

b. *Castle Rock: The Stephen King Newsletter* 1:5 (May, 1985): 6.

A crossword puzzle, with clues by King, grid by Mike Shenk.

C106. "A Profile of Robert Bloch," in *World Fantasy Convention 1983*, edited by Robert Weinberg. Oak Forest, IL: Weird Tales Ltd., 1983, paper, p. 11-14.

C107. "Ross Thomas Stirs the Pot," in *Washington Post Book World* (October 16, 1983): 1-2.

A review of Thomas's *Missionary Stew*.

C108. "Berni Wrightson: An Appreciation," in *Cycle of the Werewolf*. Westland, MI: Land of Enchantment, 1983, portfolio. A signed and limited edition of 300 copies.

C109. "Black Magic and Music: A Novelist's Perspective on Bangor." Bangor, ME: Bangor Historical Society, 1983, paper, p. .

ab. A later reprint without advertisements.

C110. "Introduction," in *Tales by Moonlight,* edited by Jessica Amanda Salmonson. Chicago: Robert T. Garcia, 1983, cloth, p. .

ab. New York: Tor, A Tom Doherty Associates Book, 1985, paper, p. xii-xviii.

King begins with an overview of the fiction of the 1980s, decrying the dangerous position of the short story and poetry (the latter now the "sole property of college eggheads and groaning, discontented high school students" (p. xii), the disappearance of the pulps and slicks, and the current threat to the novel from "junky *romans à clef*" and nonfiction books on Rubik's cubes and faddish dressing. Popular literature is "withdrawing in a long and melancholy roar," but *Tales by Moonlight* and other anthologies are valuable markets for short fiction. Horror fiction comes from the jungle; parents don't want children in that jungle, and "serious critics acknowledge that jungle only reluctantly, but it is there, in all its ripe-rotten mystery" (p. xviii).

C111. **"Introduction to the Marvel Edition of *Frankenstein*,"** in *Frankenstein; or, The Modern Prometheus,* by Mary Shelley, illustrated by Berni Wrightson. New York: Dodd, Mead & Co., 1983, cloth, p. 6-9. Limited edition.

ab. New York: Dodd, Mead & Co., 1983, trade paper, p. 6-9.

C112. **"Last Waltz: Horror and Morality, Horror and Magic,"** in *1983/1984 Fiction Writer's Market,* edited by Jean M. Fredette. Cincinnati, OH: Writer's Digest, 1983, cloth, p. 172-195.

C113. **"Stephen King,"** in *A Gift From Maine*, by Maine's Foremost Artists and Writers and James Plummer's Sixth Grade Class. Portland, ME: Gannet, 1983, trade paper, p. 91.

An autobiographical sketch mentioning King's education and family, and the fact that he has written novels and short stories.

C114. **"Stephen King's 10 Favorite Horror Books or Short Stories,"** in *The Book of Lists #3*, compiled by Amy Wallace, David Wallechinsky, and Irving Wallace. New York: William Morrow, 1983, cloth, p. 237-238.

Includes Peter Straub's *Ghost Story*, Bram Stoker's *Dracula,* Shirley Jackson's *The Haunting of Hill House,* Robert Louis Stevenson's *Dr. Jekyll and Mr. Hyde,* Robert Marasco's *Burnt Offerings,* M. R. James's "Casting the Runes," Lord Dunsany's "Two Bottles of Relish," Arthur Machen's "The Great God Pan," H. P. Lovecraft's "The Colour Out of Space," and Marion Crawford's "The Upper Berth."

C115. **"Letter,"** in *Fantasy Review* (January, 1984): 45.

A brief discussion of anthologies and reprint publishing.

C116. **"The Irish King,"** in *New York Daily News* (March 16, 1984): .

A discussion of King's Irish family roots.

C117. **"1984: A Bad Year If You Fear Friday the 13th,"** in *New York Times* (April 12, 1984): .

b. as: "The Triple Whammy," in *Castle Rock: The Stephen King Newsletter* 3:11 (November, 1987): 1, 8.

An overview of lore surrounding Friday the 13th and the fear of the number thirteen—*triskadekaphobia*.

C118. **"Dr. Seuss and the Two Faces of Fantasy,"** in *Fantasy Review* No. 68 (June, 1984): 10-12.

A Guest of Honor address presented to the International Conference on the Fantastic in the Arts, March 24, 1984, Boca Raton, Florida, featuring King's personal reminiscences on fantasy. The author discusses the sources and forms of horror, childhood influences, relationships between children's fiction and his adult-oriented tales.

C119. **"Why I Am for Gary Hart,"** in *The New Republic* (June 4, 1984): 14-16.

Comments on King's support for Hart's 1984 Presidential campaign.

C120. **"My First Car,"** in *Gentleman's Quarterly* (July, 1984): 147.

A description of King's 1964 Ford Galaxie, with mention of *Cujo*, and photograph of King with his second car, a 1956 Plymouth that resembles Christine.

C121. **[Title unknown],** in *Twilight Zone Magazine* 4 (August, 1984): .

King discusses the film of *Firestarter*. See **G8**.

C122. **[Title unknown],** in *Money!* (September, 1984): .

King discusses word processors.

C123. **"Childress Debut with 'World' Shows Uncanny Style and Eye for Detail",** in *Atlanta Journal-Constitution* [Georgia] (October 21, 1984 [or November 5, 1984]): .

A review of *A World Made of Fire,* by Mark Childress.

C124. **"Afterword,"** in *The Dark Tower: The Gunslinger*. West Kingston, RI: Donald M. Grant, Publisher, 1984, cloth, p. 219-224. See **A17**.

C125. **"Introduction,"** in *The Blackboard Jungle,* by Evan Hunter. New York: Arbor House, Library of Contemporary Americana, 1984, paper, p. v-x.

A discussion of the novel as exemplifying "American naturalism," with its author a "*brave* voice speaking out suddenly and with surprising vigor from the literary horse latitudes of the mid-fifties" (p. x).

C126. **"Basic Bread/Lunchtime Goop/Egg Puff"** [recipe], in *The Famous New Englanders Cookbook.* Dublin, NH: __, 1984, paper, p. .

C127. **"What Went Down When the Magyk Went Up,"** in *New York Times Book Review* (February 10, 1985): 7.

A review of Elmore Leonard's *Glitz,* perhaps "the best crime novel of the year."

C128. **[Letter]**, in *Fangoria* No. 45 (1985): .

C129. **"Theodore Sturgeon—1918-1985,"** in *Washington Post Book World* (May 26, 1985): 11.

b. *Locus* (1985): .
c. *SFWA Bulletin* 19:2 (Summer, 1985): 14-15.
d. as: "Viewpoint: Theodore Sturgeon—1918-1985," in *Isaac Asimov's Science Fiction Magazine* (January, 1986): 33-35.

C130. **"King Testifies,"** in *Fantasy Review* (May, 1985): 11.

Repudiation of a hoax-review by "Helen Purcell" of an erotic novel, *Love Lessons,* by "John Wilson" but credited to King in the April *Fantasy Review* column. King denies authorship of that or any other erotic novel and warns would-be collectors against buying copies.

C131. **"Cat From Hell,"** in *Castle Rock: The Stephen King Newsletter* 1:6 (June, 1985): 9.

A discussion of how King wrote "The Cat from Hell." See **B30**.

C132. **"Introduction,"** in *Skeleton Crew.* New York: G. P. Putnam's Sons, June 1985, cloth, p. 13-18.

An anecdotal essay giving backgrounds to several of the stories and introducing the critical thematic motif repeated throughout the collection, "Do you love?" See **A28**.

C133. **"Notes,"** in *Skeleton Crew.* New York: G. P. Putnam's Sons, June 1985, cloth, p. 507-512.

Annotations for several stories, particularly "The Mist" and "The Raft." See **A28**.

C134. **"The Politics of Limited Editions,"** in *Castle Rock: The Stephen King Newsletter* 1:6 (June, 1985): 3-4, 6; and 1:7 (July, 1985): 1-2, 5.

King's response to readers frustrated by limited printings of *The Dark Tower, The Eyes of the Dragon,* and *Cycle of the Werewolf,* with a justification of allowing limited printings of certain works.

C135. **"His Creepiest Movies,"** in *USA Today* (August 27, 1985): .

One of King's "lists that matter."

C136. **"Lists That Matter (Number 7),"** in *Castle Rock: The Stephen King Newsletter* 1:8 (August, 1985): 6.

Lists King's best-of-all-time films: *Casablanca, E.T., The Godfather Part II, West Side Story, The Haunting, Psycho, Stagecoach, Sorcerer, Cool Hand Luke*, and *The Wizard of Oz*.

C137. **"Lists That Matter (Number 8),"** in *Castle Rock: The Stephen King Newsletter* 1:9 (September, 1985): 7.

Lists the ten worst movies of all time: *Blood Feast, Plan Nine from Outer Space, Teenage Monster, Old Yeller, Missing in Action, Children of the Corn, Bring Me the Head of Alfredo Garcia, Love Story, The Gauntlet,* and *Oceans Eleven.*

C138. **"Lists That Matter (Number 14),"** in *Castle Rock: The Stephen King Newsletter* 1:10 (October, 1985): 7.

King's ten worst fears, including reaching the point of no return on a transatlantic flight and knowing you're doomed if something happens; checking the circuit breakers in a dark cellar; taking a shower in a strange motel; driving on a deserted street late at night and hearing breathing in the back seat; and being in a tall building on a windy day and wondering "if skyscrapers ever tip over." Number ten is left blank, for the reader to fill in.

C139. **"Ghostmaster General,"** in *Castle Rock: The Stephen King Newsletter* 1:10 (October, 1985): 1, 7.

A Halloween article, telling how to enjoy safe Trick-or-Treating.

C140. **"The King Speaks,"** in *Twilight Zone Magazine* 5:4 (October, 1985): 8.

A letter responding to the *Fantasy Review* hoax review.

C141. **"Why I Was Bachman,"** in *The Bachman Books: Four Early Novels by Stephen King*. New York: New American Library, October 1985, p. v-x. See **A30**.

b. as: "Warum Ich Richard Bachman War," in *Phantistiche Zeiten* 5:4/88 (1988): . Translated by Nora Jensen. [German]

A discussion of the reasons why King assumed the "RICHARD BACHMAN" pseudonym. See **A30**.

C142. **"Foreword,"** in *Silver Bullet*. New York: A Plume Book, New American Library, October 1985, trade paper, p. 7-16. See **A29**.

Backgrounds to King's relationship with Christopher Zavisa, the publisher responsible for *Cycle of the Werewolf*, and Dino De Laurentiis, who helped transform the book into a film.

C143. **"What Ails the U.S. Male: Fire and Ice Cream,"** in *Mademoiselle* 91 (November, 1985): 137.

Men feel vulnerable because there are "certain things we don't want to admit to women."

C144. **"My Say: Stephen King,"** in *Publishers Weekly* 226 (December 20, 1985): 60.

b. *The Stephen King Companion,* edited by George Beahm. Kansas City, MO: Andrews & McMeel, September 1989, cloth, p. 103-105.

A discussion of the declining paperback market.

C145. ***"Regis Reprimandum,"*** in *Fantasy Review* (December, 1985): 40.

b. as: "Fie on Fantasy," in *Castle Rock* 2:1 (January, 1986): 2.

King's reply to Jack L. Chalker's article on specialty presses and to the errors that have plagued references to King in *Fantasy Review*, with special focus on *The Eyes of the Dragon* and Philtrum Press.

C146. **"Lists That Matter,"** in *Castle Rock: The Stephen King Newsletter* 2:1 (January, 1986): 7.

King's chronological list of the ten "Best Things in Life," ranging from an ice-cream cone" (age 7) to "being alive, healthy, and fully functional" (age 70).

C147. **[Title unknown],** in *Twilight Zone Magazine* (February 1986): .

An article on *Firestarter* the film. See **G8**.

C148. **[Title unknown],** in *Albacon III Program Book* (Glasgow, Scotland, March 28-31, 1986).

b. as: "Introduction," in *The Inhuman Condition,* by Clive Barker. New York: Poseidon Press, August 1986, cloth, p. .

bb. Also issued as a separate promotional booklet distributed to booksellers.

An appreciation of horror writer Clive Barker.

C149. **"Hello Mary Lou, Goodbye Rick,"** in *Spin* (April, 1986): .

On the death of Ricky Nelson.

C150. **"Let's Scare Dick and Jane,"** in *Washington Post Book World* (May 11, 1986): 1, 18.

b. revised: *The Creative Child and Adult Quarterly* 13:2 (1988): .

Response to *The Day After* as "a sanitized and fairly unrealistic television film"; also a discussion of children's adaptability to horror and dependence upon storytelling. Notes that *Bambi* was "one of the scariest movies ever made."

C151. **"Red Sox Fan Crows About Team, But May Have to Eat Chicken,"** in *Bangor Daily News* [Maine] (May 17, 1986): 17.

King's response to Bob Haskell's column criticizing the Boston Red Sox during the 1986 season; the article ends with a bet on the team's standings by July 1, the loser to eat a chicken dinner on the lawn of the *Bangor Daily News* office in his underwear. King won.

C152. **"Tough Talk and Tootsies, Just 25 Cents,"** in *USA Today* (May 23, 1986): 4D. Original title: "Escape for a Quarter."

A discussion of paperback originals of the 1950s, refering to John D. MacDonald's *The Executioners*, as well as works by Elmore Leonard, Kate Wilhelm, Evan Hunter, Richard Matheson, and Louis L'Amour.

C153. **"King vs. Chalker: One Last Round,"** in *Fantasy Review* (May, 1986): 6, 40.

In this final installment in King's exchange with Jack L. Chalker over publication of *The Eyes of the Dragon*, King refutes nine charges made by Chalker.

C154. **"Say 'No' to the Enforcers,"** in *Maine Sunday Telegram* [Portland, ME] (June 6, 1986): .

b. *Castle Rock: The Stephen King Newsletter* 2:8 (August, 1986): 7.

An argument against a proposed anti-pornography law before the Maine electorate; the proposal was later defeated.

C155. **"King Awaits His Chicken and Haskell Should Shop for Shorts,"** in *Bangor Daily News* [Maine] (June __, 1986): .

A guest columnist follow-up to King's Boston Red Sox bet. See **C151**.

C156. **"Everything You Need to Know About Writing Successfully—In Ten Minutes,"** in *The Writer* 99:7 (July, 1986): 7-10, 46.

b. *The Writer's Handbook,* edited by Sylvia K. Burrack. Boston: The Writer Inc., 1989, cloth, p. 15-21.

C157. **"All American Love Story,"** in *Washington Post Book World* (June 6, 1986): .

A review of Thomas Williams's novel.

C158. **"Stephen King Comments on *IT*,"** in *Castle Rock: The Stephen King Newsletter* 2:7 (July, 1986): 1, 5.

A letter-response to an article by Michael R. Collings.

C159. **"Red Sox Stretch Out to the World Series,"** in *Bangor Daily News* [Maine] (September 12, 1986): .

C160. **"On the Far Side,"** a Foreword to *The Far Side Gallery 2,* by Gary Larson. Kansas City, MO: Andrews and McMeel, September 1986, trade paper, p. 5-6.

b. Book-of-the-Month Club selection.

C161. **"How *IT* Happened,"** in *Book-of-the-Month Club News* (October, 1986): 3, 5.

b. as: "Writing the #1 Bestseller...How *IT* Happened," in *The Writer* 100:4 (April, 1987): 14-15.

C162. **[Title unknown],** *in Bangor Daily News* [Maine] (1986): .

A Halloween advertisement cited in Blue (p. 182).

C163. **"86 Is Just the Ticket,"** in *Boston Globe* (October 6, 1986): .

b. *The Red Sox Reader: 30 Years of Musings on Baseball's Most Amusing Team,* edited by Dan Riley. Thousand Oaks, CA: Ventura Arts, March 1987, trade paper, p. 200-202.

C164. **"The Opera Ain't Over...,"** in *Bangor Daily News* [Maine] (October 14, 1986): .

C165. **"Why I Chose Batman,"** an Introduction in *Batman Comics* #400 (October 1986): .

C166. **"Write-in,"** in *Writing!* (October 1986 [?]): .

C167. **"How Much am I Hurting?"** in *Bangor Daily News* "Maine Weekend" [Maine] (November 1-2, 1986): 12.

An article on the Boston Red Sox.

C168. **"Big Jim Thompson: An Appreciation,"** in *Now and On Earth*, by Jim Thompson. Belem, NM: Dennis Macmillan Publications, 1986, cloth, p. .

A four-page introduction to a limited edition of 400 copies.

C169. **"The Dreaded X,"** in *Castle Rock: The Stephen King Newsletter* 3:1 (December, 1986/January, 1987): 1, 4-5, 9, 10.

b. *Gauntlet: Exploring the Limits of Free Expression* No. 2 (April, 1991): 69-84.

c. *Gauntlet 2*, Edited by Barry Hoffman. Baltimore, MD: Borderlands Press, May 1991, p. 45-59.

A fervent discussion of the rating system for films, with special attention to *Maximum Overdrive* and the threat of an "X" rating because of several scenes in King's screenplay. See **E4** and **G11**.

C170. **"Postscript to 'Overdrive,'"** in *Castle Rock: The Stephen King Newsletter* 3:2 (February, 1987): 1, 5.

Additional thoughts on the film industry's rating system. See **E4** and **G11**.

C171. **"Why I Wrote *The Eyes of the Dragon*,"** in *Castle Rock: The Stephen King Newsletter* 3:2 (February, 1987): 1, 6.

A discussion of the genesis of the novel as a bedtime story for King's daughter Naomi. See **A24**.

C172. **"What's Scaring Stephen King?"** in *Omni* 9 (February 1987): 16.

An article on censorship, with photograph.

C173. **"A Look at the Red Sox on the Edge of '87,"** in *Bangor Daily News* [Maine] (March 28-29, 1987): .

b. *Castle Rock: The Stephen King Newsletter* 3:7 (July, 1987): 5.

C174. **"Whining About the Movies in Bangor: Take That 'Top Gun,'"** in *Bangor Daily News* [Maine] (April 9, 1987): .

C175. **"Turning the Thumbscrews on the Reader,"** in *Book-of-the-Month Club News* (June, 1987): 5.

An article on writing *Misery*. See **A33**.

C176. **"On John D. MacDonald,"** in *The Mystery Scene Reader: A Special Tribute to John D. MacDonald,* edited by Ed Gorman. Cedar Rapids, IA: Fedora, August (?) 1987, paper, p. 26-29.

King's tribute to MacDonald as a writer and as a person, with backgrounds on why MacDonald agreed to write the introduction to *Night Shift* and how that affected King's career.

C177. **"Entering the Rock Zone; or, How I Happened to Marry a Rock Station from Outer Space,"** in *Castle Rock: The Stephen King Newsletter* 3:10 (October, 1987): 1, 5.

A discussion of King's involvement with WZON, a rock station in Bangor, Maine.

C178. **"Introduction,"** in *Transylvania Station: A Mohonk Mystery,* by Donald and Abby Westlake. MOHONK MYSTERY SERIES. Miami Beach, FL: Dennis McMillan Publications, October 1987, paper, p. .

Includes participation by King, Peter Straub, Gahan Wilson, and others.

SECONDARY SOURCES AND REVIEWS:

1. King, Naomi. "Mystery Weekend Is Novelized," in *Castle Rock: The Stephen King Newsletter* 4:3 (March, 1988): 8.

C179. **"The Ideal, Genuine Writer: A Forenote,"** in *The Ideal, Genuine Man,* by Don Robertson. Bangor, ME: Philtrum Press, October 1987, cloth, p. .

An introduction to the second full-length book produced by King's press.

SECONDARY SOURCES AND REVIEWS:

1. Blue, Tyson. "The Ideal, Genuine Novel," in *Castle Rock* 3:10 (October, 1987): 3, 6.

C180. **"'Ever Et Raw Meat?' and Other Weird Questions,"** in *New York Times Book Review* (December 6, 1987): .

b. as: "Who Ever Et Raw Meat," in *Twilight Zone Magazine* (June, 1988): .
c. *The Writer* 101 (July, 1988): 7-8.
d. as: "Letters From Hell." Northridge, CA: Lord John Press, September 1988, 18" x 24" broadsheet, printed in three colors. Limited edition of 500 copies signed by King. Discussion of fan's letters and questions.
e. reprint of the Lord John Press broadsheet in reduced format, in *Castle Rock: The Stephen King Newsletter* 4:12 (December, 1988): 11. An advertisement for the broadsheet, with all of the original text reproduced.
f. *Book Talk* (Winter, 1989): .

SECONDARY SOURCES AND REVIEWS:

1. Beahm, George. *The Stephen King Companion.* Kansas City, MO: Andrews and McMeel, September 1989, paper, p. 109-110.

C181. **"This Guy is *Really* Scary,"** introduction to *Joe Bob Goes to the Drive-in,* by Joe Bob Briggs (pseud. of John Bloom). New York: Delacorte Press, 1987, trade paper, p. .

C182. **"Afterword,"** in *The Dark Tower II: The Drawing of the Three.* West Kingston, RI: Donald M. Grant, 1987, cloth, p. 400. See also **A34**.

b. New York: A Plume Book, New American Library, March 1989, trade paper, p. 400.

C183. **"SK Criticized for References to Blacks: Stephen King Replies,"** in *Castle Rock: The Stephen King Newsletter* 4:3 (March, 1988): 1, 5.

C184. "***Quinn's Book*,"** in *Times Union* [Albany, NY] (April 24, 1988): .

A review of the book by William Kennedy.

C185. **[Title unknown],** in *The Register* [Bangor, ME] (May 11, 1988): .

King discusses drunk driving.

C186. **[Title unknown],** in *The Register* [Bangor, ME] (May 18, 1988): .

King discusses tabloids.

C187. **[Title unknown],** in *The Register* [Bangor, ME] (May 25, 1988): .

King discusses cocaine.

C188. **"SK Clarifies Gardner Reference,"** in *Castle Rock: The Stephen King Newsletter* 4:5-6 (May-June, 1988): 3.

King discusses literary and personal sources for the "'Sunshine' Gardner" character in *The Talisman*. See **A26**.

C189. **[Title unknown],** in *The Register* [Bangor, ME] (June 1, 1988): .

King discusses Elvis Presley.

C190. **"The Ultimate Catalogue,"** in *Bangor Daily News* [Maine] (June 1988): .

b. *Castle Rock: The Stephen King Newsletter* 5:6 (June, 1989): 3.

C191. **[Title unknown],** in *Penthouse* (September, 1988): . An excerpt from *Nightmares in the Sky*. See **A36**.

C192. **"Why Red Sox Fans Believe...,"** in *USA Today* (October 4, 1988): .

C193. **"Introduction"** to *The Killer Inside Me*, by Jim Thompson. Los Angeles, CA: Blood & Guts Press, October 1988, cloth, p. . A limited edition of 350 copies, signed by King.

C194. **"Robert Marasco: *Burnt Offerings*,"** in *Horror: 100 Best Books*, edited by Stephen Jones and Kim Newman. London: Xanadu, 1988, cloth, p. 156-161. Limited edition of 300 copies.

ab. London: Xanadu, 1988, cloth, p. 156-161. Trade edition.
ac. New York: Carroll & Graf, 1988, cloth, p. 156-161.

C195. **"Remembering John,"** in *Bangor Daily News* [Maine] (1988): . (Cited in Blue, p. 183.)

C196. **"Introduction"** to *The Collector*, by John Fowles. New York: Book-of-the-Month Club, 1988?, cloth, p. .

SECONDARY SOURCES AND REVIEWS:

1. Indick, Ben P. "Here's An Unusual King Collectible," in *Castle Rock: The Stephen King Newsletter* 5:11 (November, 1989): .

C197. **"Head Down: The Sporting Scene [Little League],"** in *The New Yorker* (April 16, 1990): .

b. *Nightmares & Dreamscapes*. New York: Viking, 1993, cloth, p. 741-794. See **A47**.

C198. **"What Stephen King Does for Love,"** in *Seventeen* 49:4 (April, 1990): 240+.

C199. **"Author's Note,"** in *The Stand: The Complete & Uncut Edition."* New York: Doubleday, May 1990, cloth, p. [vii]. See also **A40**.

C200. **"A Preface in Two Parts—Part I: To Be Read Before Purchase; Part 2: To Be Read After Purchase,"** in *The Stand: The Complete & Uncut Edition*. New York: Doubleday, May 1990, cloth, p. ix-xii. See also **A40**.

C201. **"Stephen King's Desert Island,"** in *Condé Nast Traveler* (July,1990): .

C202. **"Straight Up Midnight: An Introductory Note,"** in *Four Past Midnight*. New York: Viking, 1990, p. xi-xvi. See also **A41**.

C203. **"One Past Midnight: A Note on 'The Langoliers,'"** in *Four Past Midnight*. New York: Viking, 1990, p. 3-5. See also **A41**.

C204. **"Two Past Midnight: A Note on 'Secret Window, Secret Garden,'"** in *Four Past Midnight*. New York: Viking, 1990, p. 249-251. See also **A41**.

C205. **"Three Past Midnight: A Note on 'The Library Policeman,'"** in *Four Past Midnight*. New York: Viking, 1990, p. 403-405. See also **A41**.

C206. **"Four Past Midnight: A Note on 'The Sun Dog,'"** in *Four Past Midnight*. New York: Viking, 1990, p. 607-611. See also **A41**.

King refers to the story "The Sun Dog" as the "connective tissue" between *The Dark Half* and *Needful Things*.

C207. **"Introduction" to "The Glass Floor,"** in *Weird Tales* No. 298 (Fall, 1990): .

C208. **"Scare Tactics,"** in *Reader's Digest* 137:832 (November, 1990): 20. A brief excerpt from *Bare Bones*.

C209. **"My New Year's Resolution (or, Look What Dave's Got Us Doing Now),"** in *The Overlook Connection* (Winter, 1990): 22.

A three-paragraph New Year's Resolution with accompanying photo of King on a motorcycle.

C210. **"King on *Firestarter*: Who's to Blame,"** in *Cinefantastique* 21:4 (February 1991): 35.

A letter response to the Mark Lester's comments about King's published criticisms of the film. See **G8**.

C211. **"Author's Note"** to "The Woman in the Room," in *Masters of Darkness III,* edited by Dennis Etchison. New York: Tor, A Tom Doherty Associates Book, May 1991, paper, p. 319-320.

C212. **"From Stephen King,"** in *Mystery Scene* No. 30 (July-August, 1991): iv.

An open letter to Barry R. Levin, in which King criticizes the bookdealer for offering the pirated German edition of *The Mist*, which was "produced in arrant violation" of King's copyright. King urges Levin to "pass on any future acquisitions not covered by an original copyright."

C213. **"How I Created *Golden Years*...and Spooked Dozens of TV Executives,"** in *Entertainment Weekly* No. 77 (August 2, 1991): 28-32.

An overview of the genesis of the TV series, with photos. See **GB8**.

C214. **"A Warning from Stephen King,"** in *Disney Adventures* (October, 1991): 118.

A one-page introduction to King's choice as the winning entry in a children's "scary stories" contest: Aaron M. Carmichael's "Mr. Tilmore" (printed on p. 119-121).

C215. **[Title Unknown],** in *Bangor Daily News* [Maine] (March 29, 1992): .

A guest editorial discussing censorship.

C216. **"Introduction,"** in *Graven Images: The Best of Horror, Fantasy, and Science Fiction Film Art from the Collection of Ronald V. Borst and Margaret A. Borst*, edited by Ronald V. Borst, Keith Burns, and Leith Adams. New York: Grove/Atlantic, 1992, cloth, p. .

Includes reminiscences by Clive Barker, Harlan Ellison, Peter Straub, and Forrest J Ackerman.

SECONDARY SOURCES AND REVIEWS:

1. Letofsky, Irv. *The Los Angeles Times Book Review* (December 20, 1992): 11.

C217. **"Son of Best Seller Stalks the Moors,"** in *The New York Times Book Review* (June 6, 1993): 59.

Includes a list of ten rules for packaging blockbuster bestsellers.

C218. **"A Guy to Have in Your Corner,"** in *Time* 142:13 (September 27, 1993): 95.

King defends Scott Smith's first novel, *A Simple Plan*.

C219. **"A Satiric Punch,"** in *Time* 142:15 (October 11, 1993): 12.

C220. **"Stephen King on Censorship,"** in *War of Worlds: The Censorship Debate*, edited by George Beahm. Kansas City, MO: Andrews & McMeel, 1993, trade paper, p. 31.

Excerpted from a videotaped interview conducted by New American Library for its sales personnel in 1989; King argues that censorship has no place in "public institutions and libraries," and urges people to support books that have been censored.

C221. **"Introduction: Myth, Belief, Faith, and *Ripley's Believe It or Not!*,"** in *Nightmares & Dreamscapes*. New York: Viking, 1993, cloth, p. 1-9. See **A47**.

ab. *Nightmares & Dreamscapes*. New York: A Signet Book, 1994, paper, p. 1-8.

C222. **"Notes,"** in *Nightmares & Dreamscapes*. New York: Viking, 1993, cloth, p. 797-812. See **A47**.

ab. *Nightmares & Dreamscapes*. New York: A Signet Book, 1994, paper, p. 675-688.

C223. **"Stephen King on the Internet."** October 6, 1994.

An internet posting by King (?) in conjunction with his appearance at Cornell University. The memo, with King's name on it, discusses some points about *Rose Madder* and the next Dark Tower novel. See **A49**.

D.

POETRY

Since King has written little published poetry—most of that quite early in his career—there is an equivalent dearth of substantive criticism or analysis of it. The poems are, however, treated specifically in the following works:

Blue, Tyson. *The Unseen King*. STARMONT STUDIES IN LITERARY CRITICISM, No. 26. Mercer Island, WA: Starmont House, 1989, cloth. Includes the first authorized reprint of "Brooklyn August."

Collings, Michael R. "Acorns to Oaks: Explorations of Theme, Image, and Character in the Early Works of Stephen King, Part I," in *Castle Rock* 5:8 (August, 1989): 1, 8.

Collings, Michael R. *The Annotated Guide to Stephen King: a Primary and Secondary Bibliography of the Works of America's Premier Horror Writer*. STARMONT REFERENCE GUIDE, No. 8. Mercer Island, WA: Starmont House, 1986, cloth.

Collings, Michael R. "The Radiating Pencils of His Bones: The Poetry of Stephen King," in *The Shape Under the Sheet: The Complete Stephen King Encyclopedia,* edited by Stephen Spignesi. Ann Arbor, MI: Popular Culture, Ink., May 1991, cloth, p. .

Collings, Michael R., and David A. Engebretson. *The Shorter Works of Stephen King*. STARMONT STUDIES IN LITERARY CRITICISM, No. 8. Mercer Island, WA: Starmont House, 1985, cloth.

D1. **"Harrison State Park '68,"** in *Ubris* [University of Maine, Orono] (Fall, 1968): 25-26.

The earliest extant published poem to date; the free verse stanzas, theme (a murder victim found in a nearby park), characterization, and vocabulary are all consistent with directions King would follow in subsequent poems and in his more substantive body of prose.

D2. **"The Dark Man,"** in *Ubris* [University of Maine, Orono] (Spring 1969): [n.p.].

b. *Moth* (1970): [n.p.]. Published as by Steve King

This is one of three poems attributed to "Steve King" in the 1970 issue of *Moth*. It suggests the powerful and threatening Dark-Man motif that recurs throughout King's fiction, particularly in *The Stand*, *The Eyes of the Dragon*, and *The Dark Tower* novels.

D3. **"Donovan's Brain,"** by Steve King, in *Moth* (1970): [n.p.].

E.

SCREENPLAYS

PRODUCED SCREENPLAYS

E1. ***Creepshow.*** Produced by Warner Brothers, 1982. Directed by George A. Romero. See **G3**.

E2. ***Cat's Eye*.** MGM/United Artists, April 1985. Directed by Lewis Teague. See **G9**.

E3. ***Silver Bullet*.** Produced by Paramount/North Carolina Film Corporation (Dino de Laurentiis), 1985. Directed by Daniel Attias. See **G10**.

E4. ***Maximum Overdrive*.** Produced by North Carolina Film Corporation (Dino de Laurentiis), July 1986. Directed by Stephen King. See **G11**.

E5. **"Sorry, Right Number,"** for *Tales of the Darkside*, November 21, 1987. Directed by John Sutherland. See **GB4**.

b. *Nightmares & Dreamscapes*. New York: Viking, 1993, cloth, p. 465-500. See **A47**.
bb. *Nightmares & Dreamscapes*. New York: A Signet Book, Sept. 1994, paper, p. 396-426.

E6. ***Pet Sematary.*** Produced by Paramount. June 1989. Directed by Mary Lambert. See **G15**.

E7. ***Stephen King's Golden Years*.** CBS. Series began July 1991. See **GB8**.

E8. ***Stephen King's Sleepwalkers*.** Produced by Columbia Pictures, 1992. Directed by Mick Garris. See **G19**.

E9. ***Stephen King's The Stand*.** ABC, Greengrass and Laurel/Spelling. May 1994. See **GB10**.

UNPRODUCED SCREENPLAYS

EB1. ***Battleground.***

EB2. ***Children of the Corn.***

EB3. ***Cujo.***

EB4. ***The Dead Zone.***

EB5. ***Night Shift.***

EB6. ***The Shotgunners.***

EB7. ***The Shining.***

EB8. ***Something Wicked This Way Comes***, based on the novel of the same name by Ray Bradbury.

F.

PUBLIC AND SCREEN APPEARANCES

PUBLIC APPEARANCES AND SPEECHES

F1. **"An Evening With Stephen King at the Billerica, Massachusetts, Public Library."** 1983.

b. in: *Bare Bones: Conversations on Terror With Stephen King*, edited by Tim Underwood and Chuck Miller. San Francisco, CA: Underwood-Miller, 1988; New York: McGraw-Hill, 1988, cloth, p. 1-24. See **I20**.

SECONDARY SOURCES AND REVIEWS:

1. "Stephen King Tells Library Audience: 'I'm Warped'," in *American Libraries* 14 (July-August, 1983): 489.

F2. **"Dr. Seuss and the Two Faces of Fantasy,"** Guest of Honor Address, presented to the International Conference on the Fantastic in the Arts, 24 March 1984, Boca Raton, FL. See **C118.**

F3. **"Now in Paperback,"** speech by King, April 1984. Three-minute excerpt carried on local cable television channel.

F4. **"An Evening with Stephen King,"** University of Massachusetts, Amherst, MA, 1985. Distinguished Visitors Program.

SECONDARY SOURCES AND REVIEWS:

1. Mayer, Sheryl. "An Evening with Stephen King at Amherst," in *Castle Rock: The Stephen King Newsletter* 1:5 (May, 1985): 1, 6.

F5. **Guest of Honor, Third Annual World Drive-in Movie Festival and Custom Car Rally**, Dallas, TX, 1985.

SECONDARY SOURCES AND REVIEWS:

1. Ellis, Ray, and Katalin Ellis. "The Night of the Horror King," in *Cinefantastique* (May, 1985): 20.

F6. **"Banned Books and Other Concerns: The Virginia Beach Lecture,"** Virginia Beach Public Library, Virginia Beach, VA, 22 September 1986.

b. as videocassette: *Stephen King at the Pavilion*, Virginia Beach Library, March 1987. 90 Minutes. Recording of the Virginia Beach Lecture.

c. *The Stephen King Companion*, edited by George Beahm. Lecture transcribed by Beahm and edited by Howard Wornom. Kansas City, MO: Andrews & McMeel, September 1989, paper, p. 51-61.

SECONDARY SOURCES AND REVIEWS:

1. Beahm, George. *The Stephen King Companion.* Kansas City, MO: Andrews and McMeel, September, 1989, p. 46-51.
2. Blue, Tyson. "Virginia Beach Lecture Available," in *Castle Rock: The Stephen King Newsletter* 3:6 (June, 1987): 4.
3. Freeman, Mark. "King Goes to the Beach," in *Castle Rock: The Stephen King Newsletter* 3:1 (December, 1986/January, 1987): 10.

F7. **Lloyd Elliot Lecturer in English,** University of Maine, Fall Semester, 1986.

F8. **Public Lecture,** University of Maine, 6 November 1986.

SECONDARY SOURCES AND REVIEWS:

1. Spruce, Sarah. "Kings Deliver UM Lectures," in *Castle Rock: The Stephen King Newsletter* 3:1 (December, 1986/January, 1987): 1, 12.

F9. **Lecture,** YMCA, Camden, ME. 3 February 1987.

F10. **Lecture and Reading, Friends of the Andre Dubus Literary Series,** Boston, MA, 1 March 1987.

F11. **Lecture, Boston University**, 1 April 1987.

b. *Castle Rock: The Stephen King Newsletter* 3:6 (June, 1987): 6.

SECONDARY SOURCES AND REVIEWS:

1. Vail, Tiffany. "King Discusses His Creepy Craft," in *Daily Free Press* [Boston University]:

F12. **Commencement Address, University of Maine,** 6 May 1987.

SECONDARY SOURCES AND REVIEWS:

1. Beahm, George. *The Stephen King Companion.* Kansas City, MO: Andrews and McMeel, September 1989, p. 296, 298. Photographs of Stephen and Tabitha King at the Commencement.

F13. **Seminar,** Harvard University Writing Exposition. 27 February 1989.

F14. **Lecture,** 1989 Authors Series, Pasadena, CA. 26 April 1989.

F15. **Guest,** Portland Public Library Centennial, Portland, ME. March 1990. King addressing 2300 fans and library patrons.

SECONDARY SOURCES AND REVIEWS:

1. Lovell, John. "King Horrifies His Audience: Author Jams Dark City Hall," in *Portland Press Herald* [Portland, ME] (March 7, 1990): . As microfiche: *NewsBank: literature* 17 (April, 1990): Fiche 38, D2.

F16. ***Graveyard Shift* Press Conference.** October 1990.

F17. **Guest,** American Booksellers Association Convention, June 1991.

F18. **Library Promotional**, July 18, 1991. Commercial-length film with King extoll the virtues of libraries and reading.

F19. **National Press Club Library**, October 1993. 1 hour.

F20. **Speech**, Cornell University, Ithaca, NY, October 6, 1994.

F21. **Stephen King's Insomnia Tour**, October 1994. King drove 4,609 miles on his Harley, from Maine to California, stopping at ten independent bookstores across the country in conjuction with the release of *Insomnia*.

APPEARANCES IN FILMS AND VIDEOCASSETTES

FB1. ***Knightriders.*** Laurel Productions, 1981. Directed by George A. Romero. Cameo appearance by Stephen and Tabitha King.

FB2. ***Creepshow.*** Laurel, 1982. Directed by George A. Romero. King portrays Jordy Verrill in "The Lonesome Death of Jordy Verrill" segment. See **G3**.

FB3. **American Express commercial.** September 1984. Produced by Ogilvy & Mather agency.

SECONDARY SOURCES AND REVIEWS:

1. Beahm, George. *The Stephen King Companion*. Kansas City, MO: Andrews & McMeel, September 1989, paper, p. 15.
2. Brook, Dr. Barry M. "Stephen King on Television," in *Castle Rock: The Stephen King Newsletter* 2:11 (November, 1986): 5, 6.
3. Underwood, Tim, and Chuck Miller, eds. *Bare Bones: Conversations on Terror with Stephen King*. Los Angeles: Underwood-Miller, 1988.

FB4. **Guest VJ,** MTV, 27 June 1986. King playing and commenting on his favorite music videos.

FB5. **Trailer for *Maximum Overdrive.*** King stands in front of the Green Goblin truck to talk about the film.

FB6. ***Maximum Overdrive.*** MGM, 1986. Directed by Stephen King. King has an early cameo appearance as customer of an ATM.

FB7. ***Stephen King at the Pavilion.*** Virginia Beach Library, Virginia Beach, VA, March 1987. 90 Minutes. Recording of the Virginia Beach Lecture.

SECONDARY SOURCES AND REVIEWS:

1. Blue, Tyson, "Virginia Beach Lecture Available," in *Castle Rock: The Stephen King Newsletter* 3:6 (June, 1987): 4.

FB8. ***Creepshow II.*** New World, 1987. Directed by George A. Romero. King has a cameo appearance as truck driver. See G13.

FB9. ***Land of Confusion,*** by Genesis. Videocassette, 1988. Cameo by Stephen King.

FB10. ***Pet Sematary.*** Paramount, 1989. Directed by Mary Lambert. King has a cameo appearance as a minister at a grave-side service. See **G15**.

FB11. ***This Is Horror.*** 1990, 95 minutes. King, Clive Barker, Wes Craven, John Carpenter, and others discuss the horror genre.

FB12. ***The Rock Bottom Remainders.*** 1992. Videocassette, 40 minutes. On May 25, 1992 King toured with this band, composed of fifteen authors, including Dave Barry and Matt Groenig. The cassette features eleven numbers by the band, along with interviews and additional footage. King sings "Teen Angel" and reads additional lyrics to "Louie, Louie."

b. *The Rock Bottom Remainders.* Reissue, with two songs deleted due to legal action.

FB13. ***Stephen King's Sleepwalkers.*** Columbia, 1992. King has a cameo appearance as a cemetery caretaker. See **G19**.

FB14. ***The Stand.*** ABC, May 1994. King makes several appearances as one of the survivors assembling at Boulder. See **GB10**.

FB15. ***The Langoliers.*** ABC/Laurel Entertainment, February 1995. King has a minor role in Part II as a businessman. See **GB11**.

G.

VISUAL ADAPTATIONS OF KING MATERIALS

FILMS, TELEPLAYS, MUSICALS STAGE PLAYS, VIDEOCASSETTES

King is among the most visible of writers in that many of his novels and stories have been widely adapted for film, television, videocassette, audiocassette, and computer games. The adaptations vary greatly in quality, but have helped make King's name a household phenomenon. Many of the non-print adaptations have been discussed in full-length studies. The following include extensive discussions of King's films (for full bibliographies of each, see also entries in appropriate "About The Author" sections):

Beahm, George. *The Stephen King Companion*. Kansas City, MO: Andrews and McMeel, September 1989, paper, p. 331-339.

Blue, Tyson. "Stephen King on Videocassette," in *Castle Rock: The Stephen King Newsletter* 2:7 (July, 1986): 8-9.

Collings, Michael R. *The Annotated Guide to Stephen King: A Primary and Secondary Bibliography of the Works of America's Premier Horror Writer*. STARMONT REFERENCE GUIDE, No. 28. Mercer Island, WA: Starmont House, 1986, cloth. Includes filmography.

Collings, Michael R. *The Films of Stephen King*. STARMONT STUDIES IN LITERARY CRITICISM, No. 12. Mercer Island, WA: Starmont House, 1986, cloth.

Collings, Michael R. *Stephen King und Seine Filme*. HEYNE FILMBIBLIOTHEK, no. 32/112. Translated by Norbert Stresau. München, Germany: Wilhelm Heyne Verlag, 1987. Updated. [German]

Conner, Jeff. *Stephen King Goes to Hollywood: A Lavishly Illustrated Guide to All the Films Based on Stephen King's Fiction*, produced by Tim Underwood and Chuck Miller. New York: New American Library, August 1987, paper.

Hoffman, Barry. "...And the Critics be Damned," in *Castle Rock: The Stephen King Newsletter* 4:8 (April, 1988): 8.

Horsting, Jessie. *Stephen King: At the Movies*. New York: Starlog/Signet, August 1986, paper.

Hunt, Robert. "King of Horror," in *St. Louis* (August, 1986): 40-41.

Lentz, Harris M. III. *Science Fiction, Horror, and Fantasy Film and Television Credits*. Jefferson, NC: MacFarland & Co., 1983, 2 vol., cloth.

Lentz, Harris M. III. *Science Fiction, Horror and Fantasy Film and Television Credits Supplement: Through 1987*. Jefferson, NC: MacFarland & Co., 1989, cloth.

Limbacher, James L., ed. *Feature Films: A Directory of Feature Films on 16 mm and Videotape Available for Rental, Sale, and Lease.* New York: R. R. Bowker Co., 1985, cloth.

Magistrale, Anthony, ed. *The Shining Reader.* Mercer Island, WA: Starmont House, 1991, cloth.

Martin, Mick, and Marsha Porter. *Video Movie Guide.* New York: Ballentine Books, December 1988, mass-market paper.

Miller, Chuck. "Stephen King Goes to the Movies," in *Kingdom of Fear: The World of Stephen King,* edited by Tim Underwood and Chuck Miller. Columbia, PA: Underwood-Miller, April 1986, cloth.

Murphy, Tim. "The Power of the Unseen," in *Castle Rock: The Stephen King Newsletter* 4:8 (April, 1988): 3-4.

Nash, Jay Robert, and Stanley Ralph Ross. *The Motion Picture Guide.* Chicago: Cinebooks Inc., 1985.

Seligsohn, Leo. "The King of Horror," in *Newsday* [Long Island, NY] (May 6, 1984): . As microfiche: *NewsBank: Film and Television* 10 (June, 1984): Fiche 111, C14-D1.

Spignesi, Stephen. "Motion Picture Adaptations," in *The Shape Under the Sheet: The Complete Stephen King Encyclopedia.* Ann Arbor, MI: Popular Culture, Ink., May 1991, cloth, p. 543-622.

Warren, Bill. "The Movies and Mr. King," in *Fear Itself: The Horror Fiction of Stephen King*, edited by Tim Underwood and Chuck Miller. San Francisco: Underwood-Miller, 1982, cloth.

Warren, Bill. "The Movies and Mr. King, Part II," in *Reign of Fear: Fiction and Film of Stephen King*, edited by Don Herron. Los Angeles: Underwood-Miller, June 1988, p. 123-148.

Willis, Donald C. *Horror and Science Fiction Films II.* Metuchen, NJ: Scarecrow Press, 1982, cloth.

Winter, Douglas E. *Stephen King: The Art of Darkness.* New York: New American Library, November 1984, cloth.

Wood, Gary. "King's Boxoffice Bits," in *Cinefantastique* 21:4 (February, 1991): 38.

Wood, Gary. "Stephen King and Hollywood: King and His Adaptors Tell What Went Wrong on the Horror Assembly Line," in *Cinefantastique* 21:4 (February, 1991): 24-51.

Wood, Gary. "Stephen King: On Moviemaking with Dino de Laurentiis," in *Cinefantastique* 21:4 (February, 1991): 40-41.

Wright, Gene. *Horrorshows: The A to Z of Horror in Film, TV, Radio and Theater.* New York: Facts on File Publication, 1986, cloth. Multiple references.

FEATURE-LENGTH FILMS

G1. *Carrie*. United Artists, 1976. Produced by Paul Monash; directed by Brian De Palma; screenplay by Lawrence D. Cohen. 97 minutes. Rating: R. See **A1** and **GE1**.

CAST: Sissy Spacek, Piper Laurie, Amy Irving, William Katz, Nancy Allen, John Travolta.

SECONDARY SOURCES AND REVIEWS:

1. Babington, Bruce. "Twice a Victim: Carrie Meets the BFI" [British Film Institute]. *Screen* 23 (September/October 1982): .
2. Bathrick, S. K. *Jump Cut* 14 (1977): 9.
3. Bowers, S. *Film Information* 7:12 (December, 1976): 3.
4. Childs, Mike, and Alan Jones. "De Palma Has the Power," in *Cinefantastique* 6:1 (Summer, 1977): 4.
5. Citron, M. *Jump Cut* 14 (1977): 10.
6. Coleman, J. *New Statesman* [England] 93:2391 (January 14, 1977): 63.
7. Combs, R. *BFI: Monthly Film Bulletin* [England] 44:516 (January, 1977): 3.
8. Crist, Judith. *The Saturday Review* 4:6 (December 11, 1976): 78.
9. Ebert, Roger. *Roger Ebert's Movie Home Companion, 1988 Edition.* Kansas City, MO: Andrews, McMeel & Parker, 1987, cloth, p. 98.
10. *Film & BroadCasting Review* 41:23 (December 15, 1976): 132.
11. *Film Bulletin* 45 (1976): 43.
12. Goldstein, P. *Creem* 8:10 (March, 1977): 56.
13. Greenspun, Roger. "Carrie and Sally and Leatherface Among the Film Buffs," in *Film Comment* 13:1 (January/February, 1977): 16.
14. *Hollywood Reporter* (November 1, 1976): 4.
15. *Independent Film Journal* 78 (November 26, 1976): .
16. Jameson, R. T. *Film Comment* 16:2 (March/April, 1980): 13.
17. Kael, Pauline. *The New Yorker* 52:39 (November 15, 1976): 177. Reprinted: *5001 Nights at the Movies: A Guide from A to Z.* New York: Holt, Rinehart & Winston, 1982, cloth, p. 95.
18. Kelley, B. *Cinefantastique* 5:3 (1976): 20.
19. Lorenz, Janet. "*Carrie,*" in *Magill's Survey of Cinema, 2nd Series, Volume 1,* edited by Frank N. Magill. Englewood Cliffs, NJ: Salem Press, 1981, cloth, p. 408-411.
20. *Los Angeles Times* (November 17, 1976): IV, 23.
21. Mack, __. *Variety* 284:13 (November 3, 1976): 27.
22. Maslin, J. *Newsweek* 88:21 (November 22, 1976): 113.
23. Matusa, P. *Film Quarterly* 31:1 (Fall, 1977): 31.
24. Miller, E. *Seventeen* 36:2 (1977): 61.
25. Minton, L. *McCall's* 104:5 (February 1977): 78.
26. *Motion Picture Herald Product Digest* (November 24, 1976): 50.
27. Nash, Robert Jay, and Stanley Ralph Moss. "*Carrie,*" in *The Motion Picture Guide, 1927-1983, Vol II.* Chicago: Cinebooks, 1985, cloth, p. 364.
28. *The New York Times* (September 17, 1976): II, 6.
29. *The New York Times* (December 12, 1976): II, 13.
30. *The New York Times* (December 5, 1976): II, 13.
31. Pirie, David. *Movie* [England] 25 (Winter, 1977-1978): 20.
32. *Playboy* 24:2 (February, 1977): 26.
33. Rainer, P. *Mademoiselle* 83:2 (February, 1977): 173.
34. Ripp, J. *Parents* 52:1 (January, 1977): 16.
35. Rosen, D. *Cinefantastique* 8:1 (1977): 37.
36. Sarris, A. *The Village Voice* 21:48 (November 29, 1976): 53.
37. Schenker, S. *Take One* [Canada] 5:6 (January, 1977): 37.
38. Schickel, R. *Variety* 284:13 (November 3, 1976): 27.

39. Schow, David J. "Return of the Curse of the Son of Mr. King: Book Two," in *Whispers* No. 17/18 (August, 1982): 49-56.
40. *Sight and Sound* [England] 46:2 (Spring, 1977): 132.
41. Stainer, K. *Mother Jones* 2:1 (January, 1977): 59.
42. Stein, R. *Audience* 100 (January 19, 1977): 3.
43. Stoop, N. M. *After Dark* 9:9 (January, 1977): 89.
44. Swires, S. *Films in Review* 28:1 (January, 1977): 59.
45. *Time* 108:19 (November 8, 1976): 110.
46. Timpone, Anthony. "Amy Irving's DePalma Days," in *Fangoria* 52 (1986): 46-47.
47. Turan, K. *The Progressive* 41:1 (January, 1977): 47.
48. *The Village Voice* (December 6, 1976): 59-60.
49. Vertlieb, S. *Black Oracle* 10 (Spring, 1977): 31.

G2. ***The Shining.*** Warner Brothers/Hawks Films, 1980. Produced and directed by Stanley Kubrick; screenplay by Stanley Kubrick and Diane Johnson. Rating: R. See **A3** and **GE3**.

CAST: Jack Nicholson, Shelley Duvall, Danny Lloyd, Scatman Crothers, Barry Nelson. Critics generally consider Kubrick's adaptation a brilliant film when taken on its own, but flawed when considered against King's novel. The film shifts emphasis from an overtly, externally haunted "Bad Place" to a study of internal madness.

SECONDARY SOURCES AND REVIEWS:

1. Alberton, Jim, and Peter S. Perakos. "The Shining," in *Cinefantastique* 7:3/4 (1978): .
2. Allen, T. *The Village Voice* 25:22 (June 2, 1980): 41.
3. Anderson, P. *Films in Review* 16:4 (August/September, 1980): 438.
4. Asahina, Robert. "Summer Doldrums," in *New Leader* 63:13 (June 14, 1980): 19-20.
5. *Audio Video Review Digest* 2:1 (May, 1990): 180.
6. Blake, R. A. *America* 142:23 (June 14, 1980): 504.
7. Blakemore, Bill. "Kubrick's 'Shining' Secret," in *The Washington Post* (July 12, 1987): .
8. Blue, Tyson. "'The Shining' Comes to Local Theater," in *The Courier Herald* [Dublin, GA] (July 6, 1980): .
9. Brodsky, Allen. "Reflection and Desire: *The Shining,*" in *Cinemacabre* (Summer, 1984): [9-page article].
10. Bromell, Henry. "The Dimming of Stanley Kubrick," in *The Atlantic* 246:2 (August, 1980): 80-83.
11. Brown, Garrett. "The Steadicam and *The Shining*," in *American Cinematographer* (August, 1980): 786.
12. Christensen, Dan. "Stephen King: Living in 'Constant Deadly Terror,'" in *Bloody Best of Fangoria* (1982): 30-33.
13. Caldwell, Larry W., and Samuel J. Umland. "'Come and Play With Us': The Play Metaphor in Kubrick's *The Shining*," in *Literature/Film Quarterly* 14:2 (1986): 106-111.
14. Ciment, Michel, translated by Gilbert Adair. *Kubrick*. New York: Holt, Rinehart & Winston, 1983, cloth.

15. Coleman, J. *New Statesman* [England] 100:2584 (October 3, 1980): 30.
16. Combs, R. *Monthly Film Bulletin* [England] 47:562 (November, 1980): 222.
17. Cook, D. A. *Literature Film Quarterly* 12:1 (January, 1984): 2+.
18. Crist, Judith. "This Week's Movies," in *TV Guide* (April 30-May 6, 1983): A5-A6.
19. Denby, D. *New York Magazine* 13:23 (June 9, 1980): 60.
20. Edwards, Phil. "The Shining," in *Starburst* [England] (1980): 24-27.
21. *Fangoria* No. 7 (1980?): . Cover article.
22. *Fangoria* No. 33 (1993): . Pullout poster.
23. *Film* [England] 91 (November, 1980): 12.
24. *Film BroadCasting Review* 45:12 (June 15, 1980): 70.
25. *Film Comment* 16:4 (July/August, 1980): 28.
26. Flatley, G. *Cosmopolitan* 189:2 (August, 1980): 18.
27. Geduld, Harry. M. "Mazes and Murders," in *The Humanist* 40:5 (September/October, 1980): 49-50.
28. Hala, James. "Kubrick's *The Shining:* The Specters and the Critics," in *The Shining Reader*, edited by Anthony Magistrale. Mercer Island, WA: Starmont House, 1989, cloth, p. 203-216.
29. Harvey, S. *Saturday Review* 7:11 (July, 1980): 64.
30. Hatch, R. *The Nation* 230:23 (June 14, 1980): 732.
31. Hofsess, John. "Kubrick: Critics Be Damned," in *Soho News* [New York] (May 28, 1980): .
32. Hofsess, John. "The Shining Example of Kubrick," in *Los Angeles Times* "Calendar" (June 1, 1980): 1.
33. Hogan, D. J. *Cinefantastique* 10:2 (Fall, 1980): 38.
34. Hoile, C. *Literature Film Quarterly* 12:1 (January, 1984): 5+.
35. Jameson, Richard T. "Kubrick's Shining," in *Film Comment* (July/August, 1980): 28-32.
36. Kael, Pauline. *The New Yorker* 56:16 (June 9, 1980): 130-147.
37. Kael, Pauline. *5001 Nights at the Movies: A Guide from A to Z.* New York: Holt, Rinehart and Winston, 1982, cloth, p. 528.
38. Kauffmann, Stanley. "The Dulling," in *New Republic* 182:24 (June 14, 1980): 26-27.
39. Keeler, Greg. "The Shining: Ted Kramer Has a Nightmare," in *Journal of Popular Film and Television* (Winter, 1981): 2-8.
40. Kennedy, Harlan. "Kubrick Goes Gothic," in *American Film* 5:8 (June, 1980): 49+ [4-page article].
41. Kroll, Jack. "Stanley Kubrick's Horror Show," in *Newsweek* 95:21 (May 26, 1980): 96-99.
42. Leibowitz, F., and L. Jeffress. *Film Quarterly* 34:3 (Spring, 1981): 45.
43. *Library Journal* 114 (October 15, 1989): 46.
44. Lightman, Herb. "Photographing Stanley Kubrick's *The Shining*: An Interview with John Alcott," in *American Cinematographer* (August, 1980): 760.
45. Macklin, Anthony F. "Understanding Kubrick: *The Shining*," in *Journal of Popular Film and Television* 9:2 (Summer, 1981): 93-95.

46. Madigan, Mark. "'Orders From the House': Kubrick's *The Shining* and Kafka's 'The Metamorphosis,'" in *The Shining Reader*, edited by Anthony Magistrale. Mercer Island, WA: Starmont House, 1989, cloth, p. 193-202.
47. Magistrale, Anthony, ed. *The Shining Reader*. Mercer Island, WA: Starmont House, 1989, cloth.
48. Malpezzi, Frances M., and William M. Clements. "*The Shining*," in *Magill's Survey of Cinema, 2nd Series, Vol. 5,* edited by Frank N. Magill. Englewood Cliffs, NJ: Salem Press, 1981: 2175-2178.
49. Mayersberg, Paul. "Overlook Hotel," in *Sight and Sound* [England] 50:1 (Winter, 1980/1981): 54-55.
50. Miller, E. *Seventeen* 39:8 (August, 1980): 81.
51. Minton, L. *McCall's* 107:11 (August, 1980): 136.
52. Molina, Vincente. "An Interview with Stanley Kubrick," in *Cahiers du Cinema* No. 319 (1981): 5-11.
53. *Monthly Film Bulletin* 47:562 (November, 1980): 228.
54. Munroe, D. *Film Bulletin* 49:3 (May/June, 1980): .
55. Nash, Jay Robert, and Stanley Ralph Ross. "*The Shining*," in *The Motion Picture Guide, 1927-1983, Vol VII*. Chicago: Cinebooks, 1987, cloth, p. 2886.
56. Nelson, Thomas Allen. "*The Shining*: Remembrance of Things Forgotten," in *Kubrick: Inside a Film Artist's Maze*. Bloomington, IN: Indiana University Press, 1982, paper, p. 197-231.
57. Norton, M. J. *Creem* 12:4 (September, 1980): 47.
58. Otis, G. *Cinefantastique* 10:3 (Winter, 1980): 16.
59. Pearce, Howard D. "*The Shining* as *Lichtung:* Kubrick's Film, Heidegger's Clearing," in *Forms of the Fantastic: Selected Essays from the Third International Conference on the Fantastic in Literature and Film*, edited by Jan Nolanson and Howard Pearce. Westport, CT: Greenwood Press, 1986, cloth, p. 49-57.
60. Powell, D. *Punch* [England] 279:7301 (October 8, 1980): 611.
61. Rainer, P. *Mademoiselle* 86:8 (August, 1980): 64.
62. Rothenbuecher, B. *Christian Century* 97:2 (July 30-August 6, 1980): 771.
63. Sarris, A. *The Village Voice* 25:45 (November 5, 1980): 49.
64. Sarris, A., and T. Allen. *The Village Voice* 28:19 (May 10, 1983): 59.
65. Schickel, Richard. "Red Herrings and Refusals," in *Time* 115:22 (June 2, 1980): 69.
66. Schiff, S. *Glamour* 78:8 (August, 1980): 40.
67. Schow, David J. "Return of the Curse of the Son of Mr. King: Book Two," in *Whispers* No. 17/18 (August, 1982): 49-56.
68. Simon, J. *National Review* 32:13 (June 27, 1980): 795.
69. Smith, James. "Kubrick's or King's—Whose *Shining* Is It?" in *The Shining Reader*, edited by Anthony Magistrale. Mercer Island, WA: Starmont House, 1989, cloth, p. 181-192.
70. Snyder, S. *Film Criticism* 7:1 (Fall, 1982): 4.
71. Stoop, N. M. *After Dark* 1:4 (August, 1980): 25.
72. Schillaci, P. *Mass Media* 17:4 (July 14, 1980): 7.
73. Titterington, P. L. "Kubrick and *The Shining*," in *Sight and Sound* [England] 50:2 (Spring, 1981): 117-121.
74. *Variety* 299:4 (May 28, 1980): 14.

75. *Video Choice* 2 (October, 1989): 2.
76. Wells, J. *Films in Review* 16:4 (August/September, 1980): 438.
77. Westerbeck, Collin. L., Jr. "The Waning of Stanley Kubrick," in *Commonweal* 107:14 (August 1, 1980): 438-440.
78. Williamson, B. *Playboy* 27:9 (September 1980): 28.
79. Wilson, William. "Riding the Crest of the Horror Craze," in *New York Times Magazine* (May 11, 1980): 42+.
80. Wynorski, Jim. "A New Definition for Ultimate Horror: *The Shining*," in *Fangoria* (August, 1980): .

G3. *Creepshow*. Warner Brothers, Laurel Films, United Film Distribution, October 1982. Produced by Richard Rubinstein; directed by George A. Romero; screenplay by Stephen King. 120 minutes. Rating: R. See **A15** and **GE5**.

CAST: Viveca Lindfors, Carrie Nye, Ed Harris, Stephen King, Leslie Nelson, Ted Danson, Gaylen Ross, Hal Holbrook, Adrienne Barbeau, Fritz Weaver, E. G. Marshall, Joe King.

EPISODES: "Prologue"; "Father's Day" [17 minutes]; "The Lonesome Death of Jordy Verrill" [14 minutes]; "Something to Tide You Over" [25 minutes]; "The Crate" [37 minutes]; "They're Creeping Up On You" [14 minutes]; "Epilogue."

SECONDARY SOURCES AND REVIEWS:

1. *American Film* 7:9 (July/August, 1982): 79.
2. "Are These The Scariest Men in America," in *Cinefantastique* 13:1 (September, October, 1982): .
3. Blue, Tyson *The Courier Herald* [Dublin, GA] (November 6, 1982):.
4. Chute, D. *Film Comment* 18:5 (September/October, 1982): 13+.
5. "'Creepshow' Horrifies Viewers by Playing on Human Phobias," in *Arkansas Gazette* [Little Rock, AR] (December 5, 1982): . As microfiche: *NewsBank: Film and Television* 9 (January, 1983): Fiche 60, G7.
6. "'Creepshow' Isn't Just Another Slice-and-Dice Horror Movie," in *Concord Monitor* [New Hampshire] (December 2, 1982): . As microfiche: *Newsbank: Film and Television* 9 (January, 1983): Fiche 60, G9.
7. "'Creepshow': It's Awful Times Two," in *Bulletin & Advertiser* [Honolulu, HI] (November 15, 1982): . As microfiche: *Newsbank: Film and Television* 9 (January, 1983): Fiche 60, G8.
8. Ebert, Roger. *Roger Ebert's Movie Home Companion, 1988 Edition.* Kansas City, MO: Andrews, McMeel & Parker, 1987, p. 126.
9. Everitt, David. "Of Roaches and Snakes," in *Fangoria* No. 20 (1982): 13-16.
10. Everman, Welch D. "TZ Video," in *Twilight Zone Magazine* (February, 1986): 88-91.
11. *Famous Monsters Film Fantasy Yearbook, 1983*, [4-page article].
12. "Front Row Seats at the *Creepshow*," in *Twilight Zone* (May, 1982): .
13. *Fangoria* 37 ( ): . Article and pull-out poster.
14. *Fangoria* 45 ( ): . King portrayed in a pull-out poster.
15. Gagne, Paul R. *Cinefantastique* 12:1 (February, 1982): 6.

16. Gagne, Paul R. "*Creepshow*: Five Jolting Tales of Horror! from Stephen King and George Romero," in *Cinefantastique* 12:2/3 (April, 1982): 16+.
17. Gagne, Paul R. "*Creepshow*: It's an $8 Million Comic Book, from George Romero and Friends," in *Cinefantastique* 13:1 (September/October, 1982): 17-35.
18. Gagne, Paul R. *Cinefantastique* 13:2/3 (November/December, 1982): 10+.
19. Gagne, Paul R. *The Zombies That Ate Pittsburgh: The Films of George A. Romero.* New York: Dodd, Mead, 1987, 236 p., paper.
20. Gilbert, R. *New York Magazine* 15:37 (September 20, 1982): 36.
21. Hansen, Ron. "*Creepshow*: The Dawn of a Living Horror Comedy," in *Esquire* (January, 1982): 72-73, 76. Excerpted: *Contemporary Literary Criticism, Volume 26,* edited by Jean C. Stine. Detroit: Gale Research Co., 1983, cloth, p. 239-240.
22. Hoberman, J. *The Village Voice* 27:47 (November 23, 1982): 62.
23. Hogan, David J. "Creepshow: Romero, King Bring Back the Gory Glory Days of E.C. Comics," in *Cinefantastique* 13:4 (April/May, 1983): .
24. "Horrors! Romero and King Tap the Funny Bone in 'Creepshow,'" in *Des Moines Register* [Iowa] (November 18, 1985): . As microfiche: *Newsbank: Film and Television* 9 (February, 1983): Fiche 73, B5.
25. Lundegaard, Bob. "Have No Fear, 'Creepshow' Is Hardly Crawling with Horror," in *Minneapolis Star and Tribune* [Minnesota] (November 19, 1985): . As microfiche: *Newsbank: Film and Television* 9 (February, 1983): Fiche 73, B6.
26. Mahar, Ted. "Horror Anthology 'Creepshow' Creeps on Much Too Long," in *The Oregonian* [Portland, OR] (November 20, 1982): . As microfiche: *Newsbank: Film and Television* 9 (January, 1983): Fiche 60, G10.
27. Martin, Robert H. [Bob]. "TZ Screen Preview: *Creepshow*," in *Twilight Zone Magazine* (September, 1982): .
28. Martin, Robert H. [Bob]. "A Casual Chat with Mr. George A. Romaro," in *Fangoria* (October, 1982): .
29. Martin, Robert H. [Bob]. "On (and Off) the Set of *Creepshow*: Tom Savini at Work; Stephen King at Home," in *Fangoria* 20 (1982): 40-43.
30. McDonnell, David, and John Sayers. "*Creepshow*: The First Look Inside George Romero's New Bestiary," in *Mediascene Prevue* (May, 1982): 61-63.
31. Milne, T. *Monthly Film Bulletin* [England] 49:586 (November, 1982): 260.
32. Mitchell, Blake, and Jim Ferguson. "Director George Romero Talks About *Creepshow*," in *Fantastic Films* No. 32 (February, 1983): .
33. Naha, Ed. "Fritz Weaver and *Creepshow*," in *Fangoria* (May, 1982): 43.
34. Naha, Ed. "Front Row Seats at the *Creepshow*," in *Twilight Zone Magazine* (May, 1982): 46-50.
35. Nash, Jay Robert, and Stanley Ralph Ross. "*Creepshow*," in *The Motion Picture Guide, 1927-1983, Vol II.* Chicago: Cinebooks, 1985, cloth, p. 512.

36. Rambeau, Catharine. "Zombies Carry Director into Limelight," in *Detroit Free Press* (August 11, 1985): . As microfiche: *Newsbank: Film and Television* 12 (September, 1985): Fiche 31, E2-E3.
37. "Reel Comic Book," in *Arizona Republic* [Phoenix] (November 29, 1982): . As microfiche: *Newsbank: Film and Television* 9 (January, 1983): Fiche 60, G6.
38. *San Francisco Chronicle* "Reviews" (December 19, 1982): 6.
39. Sragow, Michael. "Stephen King's *Creepshow*: The Aesthetics of Gross-Out," in *Rolling Stone* 383 (November 25, 1982): 48, 54. Excerpted: *Contemporary Literary Criticism, Volume 26,* edited by Jean C. Stine. Detroit: Gale Research Co., 1983, cloth, p. 243-244.
40. Stein, J. "*Creepshow,*" in *Fantastic Films* (November, 1982): .
41. Taggart, Patrick. "'Creepshow'—Director Aims for More Visibility," in *American-Statesman* [Austin, TX] (November 21, 1982): . As microfiche: *Newsbank: Film and Television* 9 (January, 1983): Fiche 60, G11.
42. *Variety* 307:4 (May 26, 1982): 17.
43. *Voice of Youth Advocates* 6 (December, 1983): 266.
44. Wiater, Stanley. "Stephen King and George Romero: Collaboration in Terror," in *Bloody Best of Fangoria* (1982): 28-29.
45. Williamson, B. *Playboy* 29:11 (November, 1982): 42.
46. Winter, Douglas E. "I Want My Cake!: Thoughts on *Creepshow* and E.C. Comics," in *Fantasy Newsletter* (February, 1983). Revised: *Shadowings,* edited by Douglas E. Winter. Mercer Island, WA: Starmont House, 1983, cloth, p. 135-138.

G4. ***Christine.*** Columbia Pictures, Polar Film Corp., December 1983. Produced by Richard Kobritz; directed by John Carpenter; screenplay by Bill Phillips. 110 minutes. Rating: R. See **A19** and **GE6**.

CAST: Keith Gordon, John Stockwell, Alexandra Paul, Robert Prosky, Harry Dean Stanton.

SECONDARY SOURCES AND REVIEWS:

1. Anderson, P. *Films in Review* 35:2 (February, 1984): 109.
2. Ansen, D. *Newsweek* 105:25 (December 19, 1983): 66.
3. Blue, Tyson. "Fury is Furious," in *The Courier Herald* [Dublin, GA] (January 21, 1984): .
4. Corliss, Richard. *Time* 122:26 (December 19, 1983): 74.
5. Ebert, Roger. *Roger Ebert's Movie Home Companion, 1988 Edition.* Kansas City, MO: Andrews, McMeel & Parker, 1987, cloth, p. 104.
6. Harper, L. Christine. "Christine," in *Mile High Futures* (January 22, 1984): 22.
7. Hogan, David J. "Carpenter Borrowed King's Car, But Doesn't Know How to Drive," in *Cinefantastique* 14:3 (May, 1984): 56.
8. Johnson, Kim. "*Christine:* Stephen King and John Carpenter Take a Joy Ride into Terror," in *Mediascene Prevue* (1983): 24-26.

9. Kelley, Bill. "Effects Man Roy Arbogast Was in Charge of the Film's Amazing Automotive Star," in *Cinefantastique* 14:3 (May, 1984): .
10. Kelley, Bill. "John Carpenter's *Christine:* Bringing Stephen King's Best Seller to the Screen," in *Cinefantastique* 13:6/14:1 (August/September, 1983): 8.
11. Kilbourne, Dan. *"Christine,"* in *Magill's Cinema Annual 1984,* edited by Frank N. Magill. Englewood Cliffs, NJ: Salem Press, 1984, cloth, p. .
12. Lofficier, Randy. "Stephen King Talks About *Christine,*" in *Twilight Zone Magazine* 3:6 (February, 1984): 73-74.
13. Martin, Robert H. [Bob]. "Keith Gordon and Christine," in *Fangoria* 32 (1983): 19-22.
14. Martin, Robert H. [Bob]. "Richard Kobritz and Christine," in *Fangoria* 32 (1983): 14-17.
15. Nash, Robert Jay, and Stanley Ralph Ross. *"Christine,"* in *The Motion Picture Guide, 1927-1983, Vol II.* Chicago: Cinebooks, 1985, cloth, p. 422.
16. *People Weekly* (January 9, 1984): . On Keith Gordon and review of film.
17. Radburn, Barry. "Stephen King and John Carpenter: Cruisin' with Christine," in *Footsteps V* (April, 1985): 47-49.
18. *San Francisco Chronicle* (December 10, 1983): 34.
19. Stein, E. *The Village Voice* 268:51 (December 20, 1983): 82.
20. *Variety* 313:6 (December 7, 1983): 14.
21. Vernier, James. *"Christine,"* in *Twilight Zone Magazine* (February, 1984): 69-74.

G5. *Cujo*. Warner Communications, Sunn Classic Pictures, Taft Entertainment Co., 1983. Produced by Daniel H. Blatt and Robert Singer; directed by Lewis Teague; screenplay by Don Carlos Dunaway and Lauren Currier [Barbara Turner]. 93 minutes. Rating: R. See **A12** and **GE7**.

CAST: Dee Wallace, Daniel Hugh-Kelly, Christopher Stone, Ed Lauter, Danny Pintauro.

SECONDARY SOURCES AND REVIEWS:

1. Blue, Tyson. "King's Novel *Cujo* Is a Motion Picture Delight," in *The Courier Herald* [Dublin, GA] (August 13, 1983): .
2. Coleman, J. *New Statesman* [England] 106:2748 (November 18, 1983): 28.
3. Counts, Kyle. "King's Shaggy Dog Thriller Only Succeeds at the Shock Level," in *Cinefantastique* 14:2 (December, 1983-January, 1984): 50.
4. Everett, David. "*Cujo:* Lewis Teague, *The Alligator* Director, Talks About Bringing Stephen King's Rabid Saint Bernard to the Screen," in *Fangoria* (October, 1983): .
5. "Fantasy Films '83: The Year of Living Langorously," in *Twilight Zone Magazine* 3:6 (January/February, 1984): 49.

6. Horsting, Jessie. "*Cujo:* Director Lewis Teague Reveals the Difficulties of Adapting the Best-Selling Novel for the Screen," in *Fantastic Films* No. 36 (November, 1983): .
7. Horsting, Jessie. "*Cujo*: The Movie," in *Fantastic Films* No. 36 (November, 1983): .
8. Jenkins, S. *Monthly Film Bulletin* 50:598 (November, 1983): 301.
9. Jenkins, S. *Sight and Sound* 52:1 (Winter, 1983/1984): 4.
10. Minton, L. *McCall's* 111:2 (November, 1983): 82.
11. Nash, Jay Robert, and Stanley Ralph Ross. "*Cujo,*" in *The Motion Picture Guide, 1927-1983, Vol II.* Chicago: Cinebooks, 1985, cloth, p. 535.
12. Powell, D. *Punch* 285:7461 (November 23, 1983): 73.
13. *San Francisco Chronicle* (August 15, 1983): 40.
14. *Sight and Sound* 52:1 (Winter, 1983/1984): 76.
15. Spignesi, Stephen J. "Dog (and Cat) Days: An Interview With Lewis Teague," in *The Shape Under the Sheet: The Complete Stephen King Encyclopedia*. Ann Arbor, MI: Popular Culture, Ink, May 1991, cloth, p. 572-574.
16. Stein, F. *The Village Voice* 28:34 (August 23, 1983): 49.
17. *Time* 122:11 (September 12, 1983): 70.
18. *Variety* 312:3 (August 17, 1983): 23.
19. Wood, Gary. "Animal Lovers vs. Pets Run Amuk," in *Cinefantastique* 21:4 (February, 1991): 42.

G6. ***Dead Zone.*** Paramount Pictures, Dino de Laurentiis, October 1983. Produced by Debra Hill; directed by David Cronenberg; screenplay by Jeffrey Boam. Rating: R. See **A7** and **GE8**.

CAST: Christopher Walken, Brooke Adams, Tom Skerrit, Herbert Lom, Anthony Zerbe, Colleen Dewhurst, Martin Sheen. Generally considered among the best King adaptations, *Dead Zone* is a strong film in its own right, entirely consistent with the atmosphere and vision of King's print original.

SECONDARY SOURCES AND REVIEWS:

1. Ansen, D. *Newsweek* 102:19 (November 7, 1983): 128.
2. Ayscough, S. *Cinema Canada* 102 (December, 1983): 18.
3. *Christian Science Monitor* (November 10, 1983): 36.
4. Chute, D. *Rolling Stone* 391 (March 17, 1983): 36.
5. Ebert, Roger. *Roger Ebert's Movie Home Companion, 1988 Edition.* Kansas City, MO: Andrews, McMeel & Parker, 1987, p. 142.
6. *Fangoria* no. 29 (1983?): . An article on the set of *Dead Zone*.
7. *Fangoria* no. 30 (?): .
8. *Fangoria* no. 31 (?): .
9. Handling, Piers, ed. *The Shape of Rage: The Films of David Cronenberg*. Toronto: General Publishing Company, 1983; New York: Zoetrope, 1983.
10. Hoberman, J. *The Village Voice* 28:45 (November 8, 1983): 46.
11. Hogan, David J. "King and Cronenberg: It's the Best of Both Worlds," in *Cinefantastique* 14:2 (December, 1983/January, 1984): 51+.

12. Hubin, Allen J., ed. Novel indexed in *1981-1985 Supplement to Crime Fiction 1749-1980*. New York: Garland, 1988, cloth, p. 68.
13. Jenkins, S. *Monthly Film Bulletin* 51:604 (May, 1984): 147.
14. Lucas, Tim. "*Dead Zone:* David Cronenberg to Direct Stephen King's Chilling ESP Saga for Dino DeLaurentiis," in *Cinefantastique* 13:3 (November/December, 1982): .
15. Lucas, Tim. "David Cronenberg Shuns the Auteur Route To Adapt Stephen King's ESP Novel to the Screen," in *Cinefantastique* 13:5 (June/July, 1983): 17.
16. Lucas, Tim. "David Cronenberg's *The Dead Zone:* Horror Film Auteur David Cronenberg Takes a Brief Hiatus in Stephen King Territory," in *Cinefantastique* 14:2 (December, 1983/January, 1984): 24-31, 60-61.
17. Nash, Robert Jay, and Stanley Ralph Ross. *"The Dead Zone,"* in *The Motion Picture Guide, 1927-1983, Vol II*. Chicago: Cinebooks, 1985, cloth, p. 594-595.
18. Powell, D. *Punch* 286:7484 (May 9, 1984): 67.
19. Sarris, A. *The Village Voice* 28:45 (November 8, 1983): 43.
20. Stric, P. *Sight and Sound* 53:2 (Spring, 1984): 150.
21. Tuchman, Michael. "From Niagara-on-the-Lake, Ontario," in *Film Comment* 19:3 (May-June, 1983): .
22. *Variety* 312:11 (October 12, 1983): 20.
23. Vernier, James. "On the Set of *Dead Zone*," in *Twilight Zone Magazine* (December, 1983): 55.
24. Vernier, James. "A Talk With David Cronenberg," in *Twilight Zone Magazine* (December, 1983): 56-58.
25. Vernier, James. "Zeroing in on the *Dead Zone*," in *Twilight Zone Magazine* (December, 1983): 52-54.
26. Wheen, F. *New Statesman* 107:2773 (May 11, 1984): 30.
27. Williamson, B. *Playboy* 31:1 (January, 1984): 50.

G7. ***Children of the Corn***. New World Pictures, Hal Roach Studios, Gatlin Productions, June 1984. In association with Angeles Entertainment Group, Inverness Productions, Inc. Produced by Donald P. Borchers and Terence Kirby; directed by Fritz Kiersch; screenplay by George Goldsmith. 93 minutes. Rating: R. See also **B31** and **GE11**.

CAST: Peter Horton, Linda Hamilton, R. G. Anthony, John Franklin, Courtenay Gains. Generally considered to be among the worst adaptations of a King property to film.

SECONDARY SOURCES AND REVIEWS:

1. Adams, Jan. "'Children of the Corn' Designed to Be Shocking, Yet Entertaining," in *Manchester Union Leader* [New Hampshire] (May 5, 1984): . As microfiche: *Newsbank: Film and Television* 10 (June, 1984): Fiche 115, A12-A13.
2. Advokat, Stephen. "Shucks, 'Corn' Is a Disappointment," in *Detroit Free Press* (April 29, 1984): . As microfiche: *Newsbank: Film and Television* 10 (May, 1984): Fiche 104, E6.
3. Briggs, Joe Bob [pseud. for John Bloom]. "Gary Hart Is Strange and So Is This Movie About Cornflake Kids," in *Joe Bob Goes to the*

Drive-In. New York: Delacorte Press, 1987. Reprinted: *The Stephen King Companion*, by George Beahm. Kansas City, MO: Andrews and McMeel, September 1989, paper, p. 254-246.

4. Butler, Richard W. "'Corn' Has Less Than a Kernel of Quality," in *Kansas City Star* [Missouri] (April 27, 1984): . As microfiche: *Newsbank: Film and Television* 10 (May, 1984): Fiche 104, E7.
5. Cain, Scott. "A Brisk Chiller Is Harvested from Nebraska's Cornfields," in *Atlanta Journal-Constitution* [Georgia] (April 3, 1984): . As microfiche: *Newsbank: Film and Television* 10 (May, 1984): Fiche 104, E4.
6. "'Children of the Corn' Short on Vulgar Thrills," in *Sun* [Baltimore, MD] (March 13, 1984): . As microfiche: *Newsbank: Film and Television* 10 (April, 1984): Fiche 96, A3.
7. Cosford, Bill. "Kids Get the Upper Hand in King's 'Corn,'" in *Miami Herald* [Florida] (March 19, 1984): . As microfiche: *Newsbank: Film and Television* 10 (April, 1984): Fiche 95, G14.
8. Counts, Kyle. *Cinefantastique* 14:4/5 (September, 1984): 102.
9. Counts, Kyle. *Cinefantastique* 14:4/5 (September, 1984): 108.
10. Drake, Kerry. "'Children' Capitalizes on King's Fame," in *Wyoming State Tribune* [Cheyenne] (April 1, 1984): . As microfiche: *Newsbank: Film and Television* 10 (May, 1984): Fiche 104, E10-E11.
11. Edelstein, D. *The Village Voice* 29:13 (March 27, 1984): 52.
12. "Eerie in Parts, But Stretched Out," in *Grand Rapids Press* [Michigan] (May 1, 1984): . As microfiche: *Newsbank: Film and Television* 10 (June, 1984): Fiche 115, A10.
13. Ehrenstein, David. "Harvest of Schlock in 'Children of the Corn,'" in *Los Angeles Herald Examiner* (March 9, 1984): . As microfiche: *Newsbank: Film and Television* 10 (April, 1984): Fiche 95, G10.
14. Everitt, David. "Stephen King's Children of the Corn," in *Fangoria* No. 35 (1984): 42-45.
15. Fiely, Dennis. "Movie Makers Creamed 'Corn,'" in *Columbus Dispatch* [Ohio] (May 1, 1984): . As microfiche: *Newsbank: Film and Television* 10 (June, 1984): Fiche 115, A14.
16. Fox, Thomas. "Mix in 'Corn' Caters to Taste for the Gory," in *Commercial Appeal* [Memphis, TN] (April 28, 1984): . As microfiche: *Newsbank: Film and Television* 10 (May, 1984): Fiche 104, E9.
17. Gagne, Paul R. *Cinefantastique* 14:3 (May, 1984): 18.
18. Hassor, Alan. "'Corn' Slashflick—Plow It Under," in *Idaho Statesman* [Boise] (March 30, 1984): . As microfiche: *Newsbank: Film and Television* 10 (May, 1984): Fiche 104, E5.
19. Haun, Harry. "Children of the Corn," in *Daily News* [New York] (March 16, 1984): . As microfiche: *Newsbank: Film and Television* 10 (April, 1984): Fiche 96, A4.
20. Johnson, Malcolm. "'Children of the Corn' Silly, Not Chilling," in *Hartford Courant* [Connecticut] (May 2, 1984): . As microfiche: *Newsbank: Film and Television* 10 (June, 1984): Fiche 115, A9.
21. "King's Reign Deserves a Boo in Bloody 'Corn,'" in *Virginian-Pilot* [Norfolk] (March 21, 1984): . As microfiche: *Newsbank: Film and Television* 10 (April, 1984): Fiche 96, A6.

22. Kloer, Phil. "Children Are King in This Horror Movie," in *Florida Times-Union* [Jacksonville, FL] (March 22, 1984): . As microfiche: *Newsbank: Film and Television* 10 (April, 1984): Fiche 95, G13.
23. Loderhose, Willy. "Kinder des Zorns—Bemerkungen zur Entstehung des Films" ["Children of Anger: Comments on the Film"], in *Katzenauge* ["*Cat's Eye*"]. Bergisch Gladbach: Bastei-Lübbe Verlag, 1986, p. .
24. Lyman, Rick. "Film: Cult Worship in Midwest Cornfield," in *Philadelphia Inquirer* (March 10, 1984): . As microfiche: *Newsbank: Film and Television* 10 (April, 1984): Fiche 96, A5.
25. Mahar, Ted. "Corny, Over-Long 'Children of the Corn' Has Mere Kernel of Plot," in *The Oregonian* [Portland, OR] (May 2, 1984): . As microfiche: *Newsbank: Film and Television* 10 (June, 1984): Fiche 115, B1.
26. Matheny, Dave. "'Children of the Corn' Fails to Reap Horror," in *Minneapolis Star and Tribune* (May 11, 1984): . As microfiche: *Newsbank: Film and Television* 10 (June, 1984): Fiche 115, A11.
27. Minton, L. *McCalls* 111:9 (May, 1984): 46.
28. Mueller, Roxanne. "Agri-Flick of Stephen King Short Story Scary But Corny," in *Cleveland Plain Dealer* (April 30, 1984): . As microfiche: *Newsbank: Film and Television* 10 (May, 1984): Fiche 104, E8.
29. Murphy, R. *Monthly Film Bulletin* 512:106 (August, 1984): 238.
30. Sabulis, Tom. "'Children of the Corn': Cheap Production Makes Decent Thriller," in *St. Petersburg Times* [Florida] (March 20, 1984): . As microfiche: *Newsbank: Film and Television* 10 (April, 1984): Fiche 96, A1.
31. Schulman, M. *Punch* 287:7496 (August 1, 1984): 57.
32. Siskel, Gene. "Too Much Gore Overpowers Suspense in 'Children of the Corn,'" in *Chicago Tribune* (March 13, 1984): . As microfiche: *Newsbank: Film and Television* 10 (April, 1984): Fiche 96, A2.
33. Stanley, John. "Aw Shucks, Not a Kernel of Gore," in *San Francisco Chronicle* [March 11, 1984): . As microfiche: *Newsbank: Film and Television* 10 (April, 1984): Fiche 95, G12.
34. *Variety* 314:7 (March 14, 1984): 22.
35. Wheen, F. *New Statesman* 108:2784 (July 27, 1984): 32.
36. Williams, George. "Cornball Story Not Stephen King's Best," in *Sacramento Bee* [California] (March 13, 1984): . As microfiche: *Newsbank: Film and Television* 10 (April, 1984): Fiche 95, G11.
37. Williamson, B. *Playboy* 31:6 (June, 1984): 29.

G8. ***Firestarter.*** Universal Pictures, Dino de Laurentiis, October 1984. Produced by Frank Capra, Jr.; directed by Mark Lester; screenplay by Stanley Mann. 115 minutes. Rating: R. See **A9** and **GE12**.

CAST: David Keith, Drew Barrymore, Freddie Jones, Heather Locklear, Martin Sheen, George C. Scott, Art Carney, Louise Fletcher. A strictly faithful but ultimately static adaptation, which retains the dialogue-framework of King's novel but loses its dynamism.

SECONDARY SOURCES AND REVIEWS:

1. Adler, Andrew. "'Firestarter' Opens at Several Theaters," in *Courier-Journal* [Louisville, KY] (May 12, 1984): . As microfiche: *Newsbank: Film and Television* 10 (June, 1984): Fiche 109, E9.
2. *American Film* 9:7 (May, 1984): 69.
3. Blue, Tyson. "'Firestarter' Is Latest Movie from Novel by Stephen King," in *The Courier Herald* [Dublin, GA] (June 9, 1984): .
4. Boyum, J. G. *Glamour* 82:7 (July, 1984): 107.
5. Briggs, Joe Bob [pseud. for John Bloom]. "Burned-up NOW Bimbos Can't Hold a Candle to *Firestarter,*" in *Joe Bob Goes to the Drive-In.* New York: Delacorte Press, 1987, paper, p . Reprinted as: "A Review of *Firestarter,*" in *The Stephen King Companion,* by George Beahm. Kansas City, MO: Andrews and McMeel, September 1989, paper, p. 222-223.
6. Buckley, M. *Films in Review* 35:7 (August/September, 1984): 434.
7. Butler, Richard. "Actors Glow in Stephen King's Thriller 'Firestarter,'" in *Kansas City Star* [Missouri] (May 13, 1984): . As microfiche: *Newsbank: Film and Television* 10 (June, 1984): Fiche 109, F1.
8. Cain, Scott. "Slapdash 'Firestarter' Burns Out in Spite of Its Powerful Potential," in *Atlanta Journal-Constitution* [Georgia] (May 14, 1984): . As microfiche: *Newsbank: Film and Television* 10 (June, 1984): Fiche 109, E6.
9. Canby, Vincent. "King's Latest Is a Hot Item," in *San Diego Union* [California] (May 12, 1984): . As microfiche: *Newsbank: Film and Television* 10 (June, 1984): Fiche 109, D13.
10. *Christian Science Monitor*. "Arts & Leisure" (May 24, 1984): 24.
11. Cosford, Bill. "'Firestarter' Provides Thrills Without Chills," in *Miami Herald* [Florida] (May 12, 1984): . As microfiche: *Newsbank: Film and Television* 10 (June, 1984): Fiche 109, E3.
12. Curtright, Bob. "'Firestarter' a Mere Comedy of Terrors," in *Wichita Eagle* [Kansas] (May 15, 1984): . As microfiche: *Newsbank: Film and Television* 10 (June, 1984): Fiche 109, E8.
13. Dimeo, Steve. *Cinefantastique* 14:4/5 (September, 1984): 109.
14. Douglas, John A. "Sci-fi Movie with the Right Combustion," in *Grand Rapids Press* [Michigan] (May 15, 1984): . As microfiche: *Newsbank: Film and Television* 10 (June, 1984): Fiche 109, E14.
15. Douglas, John A. "Firestarter," in *Cinefantastique* 15:1 (January, 1985): 48.
16. Edelstein, D. *The Village Voice* 29:21 (May 22, 1984): 61.
17. "*Firestarter,*" in *Magill's Cinema Annual, 1985: A Survey of 1984 Films,* edited by Frank N. Magill. Englewood Cliffs, NJ: Salem Press, 1985, cloth, p. 519.
18. "'Firestarter' Burns Out in Corniness," in *Tallahassee Democrat* [Florida] (May 17, 1984): . As microfiche: *Newsbank: Film and Television* 10 (June, 1984): Fiche 109, E5.
19. Flatley, G. *Cosmopolitan* 197:1 (July, 1984): 26.
20. French, Thomas. "Stephen King's 'Firestarter' Fails to Kindle Interest," in *St. Petersburg Times* [Florida] (May 12, 1984): . As mi-

crofiche: *Newsbank: Film and Television* 10 (June, 1984): Fiche 109, E4.

21. Haun, Harry. "'Firestarter' Flames in Cliches," in *Daily News* [New York] (May 13, 1984): . As microfiche: *Newsbank: Film and Television* 10 (June, 1984): Fiche 109, F2.
22. Healy, Michael. "'Firestarter' Belongs on Burned-out Ash Heap," in *Denver Post* [Colorado] (May 12, 1984): . As microfiche: *Newsbank: Film and Television* 10 (June, 1984): Fiche 109, E2.
23. Hogan, David J. "*Firestarter: ET*'s Drew Barrymore Gets Scary as the Title Character in Stephen King's Bestseller," in *Cinefantastique* 14:3 (May, 1984): 28-30.
24. Hogan, David J. "*Firestarter*," in *Cinefantastique* 14:4/5 (September, 1984): 16-25.
25. Hunter, Stephen. "The Movie 'Firestarter' Is an Incendiary Bomb," in *Sun* [Baltimore, MD] (May 14, 1984): . As microfiche: *Newsbank: Film and Television* 10 (June, 1984): Fiche 109, E10-E11.
26. Jenkins, S. *Monthly Film Bulletin* 51:606 (July, 1984): 202.
27. Kass, Carole. "'Firestarter' Surges, Wanes," in *Richmond Times-Dispatch* [Virginia] (May 12, 1984): . As microfiche: *Newsbank: Film and Television* 10 (June, 1984): Fiche 109, F7.
28. King, Stephen. "King on Firestarter: Who's to Blame?" in *Cinefantastique* 21:4 (February, 1991): 35.
29. Leydon, Joe. "Actors Save Movie from Crash, Burn," in *Houston Post* [Texas] (May 14, 1984): . As microfiche: *Newsbank: Film and Television* 10 (June, 1984): Fiche 109, F4.
30. Lovell, Glen. "'Firestarter' a Burned Out Idea," in *San Jose Mercury* [California] (May 16, 1984): . As microfiche: *Newsbank: Film and Television* 10 (June, 1984): Fiche 109, E1.
31. Martin, Robert H. [Bob]. "Mark Lester Directs *Firestarter*," in *Fangoria* 36 (1984): 12-15.
32. Martin, Robert H. [Bob]. "On the Set of *Firestarter*: Exclusive Scoop! It's Not a Horror Picture," in *Fangoria* 35 (1984): 56-59.
33. McLeod, Michael. "'Firestarter' Kindles Real Emotion," in *Cincinnati Enquirer* [Ohio] (May 14, 1984): . As microfiche: *Newsbank: Film and Television* 10 (June, 1984): Fiche 109, F4.
34. Miller, E. *Seventeen* 43:7 (July, 1984): 71.
35. Mills, Bart. "David Keith: On Fire Over Stephen King," in *Los Angeles Times* 102 (November 20, 1983): C39.
36. Mills, Bart. "'Firestarter' in Thriller Tradition," in *Boston Herald* (May 13, 1984): . As microfiche: *Newsbank: Film and Television* 10 (June, 1984): Fiche 109, E12.
37. Minton, L. *McCalls* 111:11 (August, 1984): 28.
38. *The Movie Magazine* (Spring, 1984): . A two-page article with color photographs.
39. Munster, Bill. "Footsteps in the Dark," in *Footsteps IV* (Summer, 1984): 76-79.
40. Novak, Ralph. "Firestarter," in *People* (May 28, 1984): 12.
41. O'Connor, Bill. "'Firestarter' Top-Heavy with Special Effects," in *Akron Beacon Journal* [Ohio] (May 17, 1984): . As microfiche: *Newsbank: Film and Television* 10 (June, 1984): Fiche 109, F3.
42. Powell, D. *Punch* 287:7493 (July 11, 1984): 43.

43. Rose, Rita. "Drew 'Sizzling' in New Film," in *Indianapolis Star* [Indiana] (May 12, 1984): . As microfiche: *Newsbank: Film and Television* 10 (June, 1984): Fiche 109, E7.
44. Scapperotti, Dan. "Gary Zeller," in *Cinefantastique* 14:4/5 (September, 1984): 22.
45. "Script Puts Damper on 'Firestarter,'" in *Detroit Free Press* (May 13, 1984): . As microfiche: *Newsbank: Film and Television* 10 (June, 1984): Fiche 109, E13.
46. Stack, Peter. "Hollywood Grinds Out Yet Another Stephen King Horror," in *San Francisco Chronicle* (May 12, 1984): . As microfiche: *Newsbank: Film and Television* 10 (June, 1984): Fiche 109, D14.
47. Thomas, Kevin. "'Firestarter': Hot on a Child's Trail," in *Los Angeles Times* (May 11, 1984): . As microfiche: *Newsbank: Film and Television* 10 (June, 1984): Fiche 109, D12.
48. *Variety* 315:2 (May 9, 1984): 10.
49. Vincent, Mal. "Will Someone Please Douse 'Firestarter,' the Latest Stephen King Non-Thriller?" in *Virginian-Pilot* [Norfolk, VA] (May 16, 1984): . As microfiche: *Newsbank: Film and Television* 10 (June, 1984): Fiche 109, F6.
50. Williamson, B. *Playboy* 31:8 (August, 1984): 25.
51. Wood, Gary. "Firestarter: Director Mark Lester Takes off the Gloves to Respond to King's Knock That This Adaptation Is 'The Worst of the Bunch,'" in *Cinefantastique* 21:4 (February, 1991): 34.

G9. *Cat's Eye*. MGM/United Artists, April 1985. Executive producer, Dino de Laurentiis; directed by Martha J. Schumacher; directed by Lewis Teague; screenplay by Stephen King. 94 minutes. Rating: PG-13. See **GE10**.

CAST: Drew Barrymore, James Woods, Alan King, Kenneth McMillan, Robert Hays, Candy Clark, James Naughton.

EPISODES: "Quitter's Inc." [38 minutes; see **B40**]; "The Ledge" [26 minutes; see **B28**]; "The General" [30 minutes].

SECONDARY SOURCES AND REVIEWS:

1. Adams, Jim. "'Cat's Eye' Only 'Mildly Interesting,'" in *Union Leader* [Manchester, NH] (April 19, 1985): . As microfiche: *Newsbank: Film and Television* 11 (May, 1985): Fiche 109, E8.
2. Ansen, Davie. "Cat Calls and Wolf Whistles," in *Newsweek* 105:18 (May 6, 1985): 73. Excerpted: *Contemporary Literary Criticism, Volume 37,* edited by Daniel G. Marowski. Detroit: Gale Research Co., 1986, cloth, p. 206.
3. Baron, David. "King's Latest Chiller Not Up to His Scary Standards," in *Times Picayune* [New Orleans] (April 18, 1985): . As microfiche: *Newsbank: Film and Television* 11 (May, 1985): Fiche 109, E3.
4. Briggs, Joe Bob [pseud. for John Bloom]. "Big Steve Is the Cat's Pajamas," in *USA Today* (May 8, 1985): .
5. Canby, Vincent. "'Cat's Eye' Is a Stylish, Clever Thriller," in *Sacramento Bee* [California] (April 15, 1985): . As microfiche:

Newsbank: Film and Television 11 (May, 1985): Fiche 109, D6-D7.

6. "*Cat's Eye*," in *Take One* (October, 1985): .
7. "*Cat's Eye* Reviews," in *Castle Rock: The Stephen King Newsletter* 1:6 (June, 1985): 5.
8. Cosford, Bill. "Three Thrillers for Feline Fans," in *Miami Herald* [Florida] (April 17, 1985): . As microfiche: *Newsbank: Film and Television* 11 (May, 1985): Fiche 109, D13.
9. Edelstein, D. *The Village Voice* 30:17 (April 23, 1985): 57.
10. Elliot, David. "The Gleam in 'Cat's Eye' Doesn't Hide Blind Spots," in *San Diego Union* [California] (April 23, 1985): . As microfiche: *Newsbank: Film and Television* 11 (May, 1985): Fiche 109, D8.
11. *Fangoria* No. 43 (March, 1985): .
12. Fiely, Dennis. "New King a 'Cat' Above," in *Columbus Dispatch* [Ohio] (April 15, 1985): . As microfiche: *Newsbank: Film and Television* 11 (May, 1985): Fiche 109, F1.
13. French, Lawrence. "Cat's Eye," in *Cinefantastique* 15:4 (October, 1985): 36.
14. "From King, Shivers and Laughs," in *Philadelphia Inquirer* (April 13, 1985): . As microfiche: *Newsbank: Film and Television* 11 (April, 1985): Fiche 98, B1.
15. Hewitt, Tim. "Cat's Eye: Horror Master Stephen King Blends Stories from *Night Shift* with a Dash of Macabre Humor," in *Cinefantastique* 15:2 (May, 1985): 9-11.
16. Hewitt, Tim. "Stephen King's *Cat's Eye*," in *Cinefantastique* 15:4 (October, 1985): 34-39.
17. Horsting, Jessie. "A Director's Eye View of Stephen King's *Cat's Eye*," in *Fantastic Films* (June, 1985): 20-21, 42.
18. Hunter, Stephen. "'Cat's Eye' Raises Questions King Won't Answer," in *Sun* [Baltimore, MD] (April 15, 1985): . As microfiche: *Newsbank: Film and Television* 11 (April, 1985): Fiche 98, A13.
19. Johnson, Malcolm. "Fearless Feline Ties Together Fun Tales of 'Cat's Eye,'" in *Hartford Courant* [Connecticut] (April 17, 1985): . As microfiche: *Newsbank: Film and Television* 11 (May, 1985): Fiche 109, D11.
20. Johnson, Paul. "'Cat's Eye' Relies on Ironic Twist," in *Arkansas Gazette* [Little Rock] (April 26, 1985): . As microfiche: *Newsbank: Film and Television* 11 (May, 1985): Fiche 109, D3.
21. Kelley, B. "Cat's Eye," in *Cinefantastique* 14:3 (July, 1985): 52.
22. Leydon, Joe. "More Fun Than Fright in King's 'Cat's Eye,'" in *Houston Post* [Texas] (April 16, 1985): . As microfiche: *Newsbank: Film and Television* 11 (May, 1985): Fiche 109, F3.
23. Loderhose, Willy. "Geschichten aus dem Dunkel: Über des Phänomen des Schriftstellers, Drehbuchautors und Filmregisserus Stephen King" ["Tales from the Dark: Concerning the Phenomenon of Writers, Screenwriters, and Film Directors for Stephen King Films"], in *Katzenauge* ["*Cat's Eye*"]. Bergisch Gladbach: Bastei-Lübbe Verlag, 1986, p. .
24. Loderhose, Willy. "Katzenauge: Wie es zu der Verfilmung Kam" ["Cat's Eye: How It Came to Be Filmed"], in *Katzenauge* ["*Cat's Eye*"]. Bergisch Gladbach: Bastei-Lübbe Verlag, 1986, p. .

25. Loderhose, Willy. "Trucks: Bermerkungen zur Verfilmung" ["Trucks: Comments on the Filming"], in *Katzenauge* ["*Cat's Eye*"]. Bergisch Gladbach: Bastei-Lübbe Verlag, 1986, p. .
26. Lovell, Glen. "Scares to Give You Pause in 'Cat's Eye,'" in *San Jose Mercury News* [California] (April 13, 1985): . As microfiche: *Newsbank: Film and Television* 11 (May, 1985): Fiche 109, D10.
27. Lucas, W. D., and W. Miedema. *Classical Images* 126 (December, 1985): 19.
28. Lyman, Rick. "'Cat's Eye' Winningly Macabre Horror Trio," in *The Oregonian* [Portland, OR] (April 17, 1985): . As microfiche: *Newsbank: Film and Television* 11 (May, 1985): Fiche 109, F2.
29. Matheny. Dave. "King Writes Screenplay and Produces a Hit in 'Cat's Eye,'" in *Minneapolis Star and Tribune* [Minnesota] (April 19, 1985): . As microfiche: *Newsbank: Film and Television* 11 (May, 1985): Fiche 109, E6.
30. McLeod, Michael. "'Cat's Eye' Works as Comedy, Horror," in *Cincinnati Enquirer* [Ohio] (April 15, 1985): . As microfiche: *Newsbank: Film and Television* 11 (May, 1985): Fiche 109, E13.
31. Minton, L. *McCalls* 112:10 (July, 1985): 50.
32. Morrison, Bill. "Stephen King Leaves Out Terror, Makes 'Cat's Eye' Seem Like TV Movie," in *News and Observer* [Raleigh, NC] (April 25, 1985): . As microfiche: *Newsbank: Film and Television* 11 (May, 1985): Fiche 109, E11.
33. Moynihan, Martin. "King's Pen Crackles to Life in 'Cat's Eye,'" in *Times Union* [Albany, NY] (April 18, 1985): . As microfiche: *Newsbank: Film and Television* 11 (May, 1985): Fiche 109, E9.
34. Mueller, Roxanne T. "Violent Steve King Beats a Dead Horse," in *Cleveland Plain Dealer* [Ohio] (April 16, 1985): . As microfiche: *Newsbank: Film and Television* 11 (May, 1985): Fiche 109, E14.
35. Newman, K. *Monthly Film Bulletin* 52:618 (July, 1985): 211.
36. O'Connor, Bill. "'Cat's Eye' Should've Been TV Show," in *Akron Beacon Journal* [Ohio] (April 19, 1985): . As microfiche: *Newsbank: Film and Television* 11 (May, 1985): Fiche 109, E12.
37. Patton, Charlie. "Stephen King Film Anthology Shows Whimsy of Horror Master," in *Florida Times-Union* [Jacksonville] (April 25, 1985): . As microfiche: *Newsbank: Film and Television* 11 (May, 1985): Fiche 109, D12.
38. *People Weekly* (May 6, 1985): . Review with photographs.
39. Rainer, Paul. "'Cat's Eye': The Latest Model Stephen King," in *Los Angeles Herald Examiner* (April 12, 1985): . As microfiche: *Newsbank: Film and Television* 11 (May, 1985): Fiche 109, D4.
40. Rhetts, JoAnn. "'Cat's Eye': The Latest Film from Stephen King's Work," in *Charlotte Observer* [North Carolina] (April 17, 1985): . As microfiche: *Newsbank: Film and Television* 11 (May, 1985): Fiche 109, E10.
41. Ricky, Carrie. "Tabby with ESP Is the Real Star," in *Boston Herald* (April 12, 1985): . As microfiche: *Newsbank: Film and Television* 11 (April, 1985): Fiche 98, A14.
42. Roddick, N. *Cinema Papers* No. 54 (November, 1985): 74.
43. Rose, Rita. "King Trilogy Is Stomach-Turner," in *Indianapolis Star* (April 16, 1985): . As microfiche: *Newsbank: Film and Television* 11 (May, 1985): Fiche 109, E1.

44. Salamon, Julie. *Wall Street Journal* (April 25, 1985): 34.
45. Shorey, Kenneth. "'Cat's Eye,'" in *Birmingham News* [Alabama] (April 18, 1985): . As microfiche: *Newsbank: Film and Television* 11 (May, 1985): Fiche 109, D2.
46. Siskel, Gene. "King's 'Cat's Eye' Trio Dogged by Limp Pause," in *Chicago Tribune* (April 15, 1985): . As microfiche: *Newsbank: Film and Television* 11 (May, 1985): Fiche 109, D14.
47. Spignesi, Stephen J. "Dog (and Cat) Days: An Interview With Lewis Teague," in *The Shape Under the Sheet: The Complete Stephen King Encyclopedia*. Ann Arbor, MI: Popular Culture, Ink, May 1991, cloth, p. 572-574.
48. Stack, Peter. "'Cat's Eye': Three Tales from Stephen King," in *San Francisco Chronicle* (April 15, 1985): . As microfiche: *Newsbank: Film and Television* 11 (May, 1985): Fiche 109, D9.
49. "Stephen King's Cat's Eye," in *Des Moines Register* [Iowa] (April 18, 1985): . As microfiche: *Newsbank: Film and Television* 11 (May, 1985): Fiche 109, E2.
50. "Stephen King's Latest Effort Isn't a Classic, But Holds Its Own With Some Suspense, Humor," in *Grand Rapids Press* [Michigan] (April 16, 1985): . As microfiche: *Newsbank: Film and Television* 11 (May, 1985): Fiche 109, E4.
51. Strauss, Bob. "Stephen King's *Cat's Eye*," in *Monsterland* (June, 1985): 55-57, 66.
52. Thomas, Kevin. "A Sly Trio of Vignettes from a 'Cat's Eye' View," in *Los Angeles Times* (April 12, 1985): . As microfiche: *Newsbank: Film and Television* 11 (May, 1985): Fiche 109, D5.
53. Trussell, Robert C. "Film Is Entertaining, But Barely Scratches Surface," in *Kansas City Star* [Missouri] (April 15, 1985): . As microfiche: *Newsbank: Film and Television* 11 (May, 1985): Fiche 109, E7.
54. *Variety* 318:12 (April 17, 1985): 10.
55. Vincent, Mal. "'Cat's Eye' Has Been Declawed," in *Virginian-Pilot* [Norfolk] (April 17, 1985): . As microfiche: *Newsbank: Film and Television* 11 (May, 1985): Fiche 109, F4.
56. Wilson, Gahan. "TZ Screen," in *Twilight Zone Magazine* 5:4 (October, 1985): 96-98.
57. Wood, Gary. "Animal Lovers vs. Pets Run Amuk," in *Cinefantastique* 21:4 (February, 1991): 42.
58. "Writer King Is the Attraction of His Homogenized Movies," in *Altanta Journal-Constitution* [Georgia] (April 21, 1985): . As microfiche: *Newsbank: Film and Television* 11 (May, 1985): Fiche 112, G5.

G10. ***Stephen King's Silver Bullet.*** Paramount Pictures, North Carolina Film Corporation (Dino de Laurentiis), October 1985. Produced by Martha Schumacher, with John M. Eckert; directed by Daniel Attias; screenplay by Stephen King. 95 minutes. Rating: R. See **A29** and **GE14**.

CAST: Gary Bussey, Everitt McGill, Corey Haim, Megan Follows.

SECONDARY SOURCES AND REVIEWS:

1. *American Film* 111 (October, 1985): 86.
2. Blank, Ed. "King's 'Silver Bullet' Almost Hits the Mark," in *Pittsburgh Press* (October 12, 1985): . As microfiche: *Newsbank: Film and Television* 12 (November, 1985): Fiche 52, G13.
3. Blue, Tyson. "'Bullet' is SK's Best Screenplay," in *Castle Rock: The Stephen King Newsletter* 2:1 (January, 1986): 6.
4. Blue, Tyson. "'Silver Bullet' a Werewolf Surprise," in *the Courier Herald* [Dublin, GA] (October 12, 1985): .
5. Bunke,Joan. "Werewolf, Godzilla, and Ninja Flicks Rate Only as Halloween 'Nightmares,'" in *Des Moines Register* [Iowa] (October 31, 1985): . As microfiche: *Newsbank: Film and Television* 12 (November, 1985): Fiche 52, G10.
6. *Cinefantastique* 15:1 (January, 1985): 18.
7. Collings, Michael R. "Silver Bullet: Another Opinion," in *Castle Rock: The Stephen King Newsletter* 1:12 (December, 1985): 3.
8. Cosford, Bill. "This 'Silver Bullet' Is a Blank," in *Miami Herald* [Florida] (October 14, 1985): . As microfiche: *Newsbank: Film and Television* 12 (November, 1985): Fiche 52, G9.
9. Crumpler, David. "Stephen King's 'Silver Bullet' Takes Aim, Fires a Blank," in *Florida Union-Times* [Jacksonville] (October 17, 1985): . As microfiche: *Newsbank: Film and Television* 12 (November, 1985): Fiche 52, G8.
10. Dimeo, Steve. "Stephen King Script Little More Than Sheep in Wolf's Clothes," in *Cinefantastique* 16:11 (March, 1986): 43, 54.
11. Ebert, Roger. *Roger Ebert's Movie Home Companion, 1988 Edition.* Kansas City, MO: Andrews, McMeel & Parker, 1987, cloth, p. 552-553.
12. Everitt, David. "Stephen King's *Silver Bullet,*" in *Fangoria* No. 48 (1985): 30-32.
13. Freedman, Richard. "'Silver Bullet' Off Target in Teen's Werewolf Hunt," in *Star-Ledger* [Newark, NJ] (October 11, 1985): . As microfiche: *Newsbank: Film and Television* 12 (November, 1985): Fiche 52, G11.
14. Grody, W. *MD Medical News Magazine* 29:12 (December, 1985): 108.
15. Hewitt, Tim. "*Silver Bullet:* Stephen King's Tale Pits Werewolf Against Wheelchair Hotrodder," in *Cinfantastique* 15:2 (May, 1985): 12.
16. Kagan, Rick. "'Silver Bullet': A Sheep of a Movie in Wolf's Garb," in *Chicago Tribune* (October 16, 1985): . As microfiche: *Newsbank: Film and Television* 12 (December, 1985): Fiche 62, C5.
17. Maeder, Jay. "'Bullet' Should Be Shot," in *Daily News* [New York] (October 11, 1985): . As microfiche: *Newsbank: Film and Television* 12 (October, 1985): Fiche 44, A14.
18. Martin, Robert H. [Bob]. "Interview with a Werewolf," in *Fangoria* 44 (1985): 41-44.
19. McGrady, Mike. "Stephen King Pounds Out Another One," in *Newsday* [Long Island, NY] (October 11, 1985): . As microfiche: *Newsbank: Film and Television* 12 (October, 1985): Fiche 44, A14.
20. Newman, K. *Monthly Film Bulletin* 53:629 (July, 1986): 212.

21. Pettus, David. "Stephen King's Silver Bullet: A Review," in *Castle Rock: The Stephen King Newsletter* 1:11 (November, 1985): 1, 4.
22. Reed, Rex. "King's Werewolf a Howler," in *New York Post* (October 11, 1985): . As microfiche: *Newsbank: Film and Television* 12 (November, 1985): Fiche 52, G12.
23. Spignesi, Stephen J. "The Unfinished King," in *The Shape Under the Sheet: The Complete Stephen King Encyclopedia*. Ann Arbor, MI: Popular Culture, Ink., May 1991, cloth, p. 778-780.
24. Stack, Peter. "Stephen King's Latest Werewolf," in *San Francisco Chronicle* (October 12, 1985): . As microfiche: *Newsbank: Film and Television* 12 (November, 1985): Fiche 52, G7.
25. Turner, N. *Film* 151 (December, 1986): 3.
26. *Variety* 320:12 (October 16, 1985): 10.
27. Williams, Sharon. "Stephen King's *Cycle of the Werewolf* Becomes *Silver Bullet* for the Silver Screen," in *Fantastic Films* (October, 1985): 20-22.
28. Wuntch, Philip. "King Fires a Dud With 'Silver Bullet,'" in *Dallas Morning News* (October 15, 1985): . As microfiche: *Newsbank: Film and Television* 12 (November, 1985): Fiche 52, G14.

G11. ***Maximum Overdrive.*** De Laurentiis Entertainment Group, July 18, 1986. Produced by Martha Schumacher; directed by Stephen King; screenplay by Stephen King. 95 minutes. Rating: R. See **B20** and **GE16**.

CAST: Emilio Estevez, Pat Hingle, Laura Harrington, Yeardley Smith, John Short, Ellen McElduff; with cameo role by King.

SECONDARY SOURCES AND REVIEWS:

1. Ahlgren, Calvin. "King of Horror Finds Directing unnerving," in *San Francisco Chronicle* (July _, 1986): . As microfiche: *Newsbank: Film and Television* 13 (August, 1986): Fiche 14, D8-D9.
2. Blue, Tyson. "King Goes into Overdrive," in *Twilight Zone Magazine* 5 (February, 1986): 30-31.
3. Blue, Tyson. "*Overdrive* Movie Set Relaxed," in *Castle Rock: The Stephen King Newsletter* 1:11 (November, 1985): 3.
4. Blue, Tyson. "*Maximum Overdrive* Video Reviewer," in *Castle Rock: The Stephen King Newsletter* 3:2 (February, 1987): 5, 7.
5. Blue, Tyson. "Stephen King's Debut as Director Is a Maximum Thriller," in *The Courier Herald* [Dublin, GA] (July 26, 1986): .
6. Blue, Tyson. "Stephen King's First Film, *Maximum Overdrive*, as Intense as His Books," in *Macon Telegraph and News* [Macon, GA] (July 25, 1986): .
7. "Castle Rock Readers Comment on *Maximum Overdrive*," in *Castle Rock: The Stephen King Newsletter* 2:9 (September, 1986): 6-7.
8. "Castle Rock Readers Comment on *Maximum Overdrive*," in *Castle Rock: The Stephen King Newsletter* 2:10 (October, 1986): 6.
9. Cosford, Bill. "'Overdrive': A Good Idea Badly Done," in *Miami Herald* [Florida] (July 26, 1986): . As microfiche: *Newsbank: Film and Television* 13 (August, 1986): Fiche 14, E1.
10. Crist, Judith. *Coming Attractions* (January, 1987): . One-page review.

11. *Daily News* "L.A. Life" [Los Angeles, CA] (July 26, 1986): .
12. Denerstein, Robert. "Minimum 'Max,'" in *Rocky Mountain News* [Denver, CO] (July 26, 1986): . As microfiche: *Newsbank: Film and Television* 13 (August, 1986): Fiche 14, D13.
13. "Dress Rehearsal for Death," in *New York Daily News* (April 17, 1989): .
14. Ewing, Darrell, and Dennis Myers. "King of the Road," in *American Film* 11:8 (June, 1986): 44-47.
15. *Fangoria* No. 54 (1986): . Article with photographs.
16. *Fangoria* No. 56 (August, 1986): . King Interview.
17. Garrett, Robert. "'Overdrive': Bodies by King," in *Boston Globe* (July 26, 1986): .
18. Goodman, Walter. *New York Times* (August 3, 1986): II, 17.
19. Harris, Judith P. "*Maximum Overdrive*: Sneak Preview of Rampaging Truck Shocker Shows Stephen King Knows How to Direct," in *Cinefantastique* 16:3 (July, 1986): .
20. Hellman, I. *People Weekly* (August 18, 1986): 10.
21. Hewitt, Tim. "Overdrive," in *Cinefantastique* 16:1 (March, 1986): 9.
22. Hewitt, Tim. "*Maximum Overdrive*: Stephen King Rises from the Ashes of His Latest Adaptation in the Driver's Seat," in *Cinefantastique* 16:4/5 (October, 1987): 96.
23. Johnson, Malcolm. "King Is in High Gear in 'Maximum Overdrive,'" in *Hartford Courant* [Connecticut] (July 26, 1986): . As microfiche: *Newsbank: Film and Television* 13 (August, 1986): Fiche 14, D14.
24. Jones, A. *Cinefantastique* 16:4/5 (October, 1987): 101.
25. "King's Movie Is a Humbling Affair," in *Toronto Globe and Mail* (July 28, 1986): .
26. Kogan, Rick. "King's a Horror at Directing," in *Chicago Tribune* (July 26, 1986): . As microfiche: *Newsbank: Film and Television* 13 (August, 1986): Fiche 14, E2.
27. Lovell, Glen. "King's at Helm of 'Overdrive,'" in *San Jose Mercury News* [California] (July 23, 1986): . As microfiche: *Newsbank: Film and Television* 13 (August, 1986): Fiche 13, G13-G14.
28. Martin, Robert H. [Bob]. "George Romero on *Day of the Dead* and *Pet Sematary*," in *Fangoria* No. 48 (October, 1985): 43-47.
29. "*Maximum Overdrive*," in *Magill's Cinema Annual, 1987: A Survey of the Films of 1986*, edited by Frank N. Magill. Englewood Cliffs, NJ: Salem Press, 1987, cloth, p. 497.
30. Miller, G. Wayne. "King of Horror," in *Journal* [Providence, RI] (August 3, 1986): . As microfiche: *Newsbank: Film and Television* 13 (August, 1986): Fiche 14, A1-A4.
31. Miller, G. Wayne. "Machines Are King's, Violence Reigns in 'Maximum Overdrive,'" in *Journal* [Providence, RI] (July 26, 1986): . As microfiche: *Newsbank: Film and Television* 13 (August, 1986): Fiche 14, E6.
32. Mueller, Roxanne T. "Horror King's Film Is Horrible," in *Cleveland Plain Dealer* [Ohio] (July 29, 1986): . As microfiche: *Newsbank: Film and Television* 13 (August, 1986): Fiche 14, E5.
33. *New York Post* (April 22, 1989): .
34. *Newark Star Ledger* (April 22, 1989): .

35. O'Grady, F. *Cinema Papers* 61 (January, 1987): 51.
36. Pareles, Jon. "Film: By Stephen King, *Maximum Overdrive*," in *The New York Times* (July 25, 1986): III, 17.
37. Ratliff, Larry. "Stephen King's *Maximum Overdrive* Spins its Wheels," in __ [San Antonio, TX]: .
38. Rhetts, Jo Ann. "The Titan of Terror," in *Escondido Times-Advocate*, "North County Magazine" (October 3, 1985): 30-31.
39. Ross, Peter. "Gore Is Still Gore, Even If It's Done by Machines," in *Detroit News* (July 28, 1986): . As microfiche: *Newsbank: Film and Television* 13 (August, 1986): Fiche 14, E3.
40. Schaefer, Stephen. "The King Is Director," in *Film Comment* 22:3 (May/June, 1986): 6-7.
41. Shapiro, Susin. "One Picture Is Worth a Million Words," in *Daily News* [New York] (July 13, 1986): 8-13. As microfiche: *Newsbank: Film and Television* 13 (August, 1986): Fiche 14, D10-D12. Also as microfiche: *NewsBank: Names in the News* 9 (August, 1986): Fiche 5, E12-E14.
42. Treadway, Joseph. "King on Directing *Maximum Overdrive* for Dino De Laurentiis," in *Cinefantastique* 17:2 (March, 1987): 49.
43. Trussell, Robert C. "King Authors a Bad Film," in *Kansas City Star* [Missouri] (July 27, 1986): . As microfiche: *Newsbank: Film and Television* 13 (August, 1986): Fiche 14, E4.
44. *Variety* 324:1 (July 30, 1986): 18.
45. Vincent, Mal. "'Overdrive' Offers Minimal Entertainment," in *Virginian-Pilot* [Norfolk, VA] (August 2, 1986): . As microfiche: *Newsbank: Film and Television* 13 (August, 1986): Fiche 14, E7-E8.
46. Weldon, M. J. *Video Review* 7:12 (March, 1987): 70.
47. Wiater, Stanley. "Stephen King Shifts into High Gear on the Highway to Hell-Driving Horror," in *Mediascene Prevue* (May/July, 1986): 52-55, 71.
48. Wood, Gary. "Stephen King: To Direct or Not to Direct," in *Cinefantastique* 21:4 (February, 1991): 47.
49. Wuntch, Phillip. "Reviews of 'Maximum Overdrive' Don't Faze Author-Turned-Director," in *Dallas Morning News* (July 28, 1986): . As microfiche: *Newsbank: Film and Television* 13 (August, 1986): Fiche 14, A5-A6.

G12. ***Stand By Me.*** Columbia Pictures, August 8, 1986. Produced by Andrew Scheinman, Bruce A. Evans, and Raynold Gideon; directed by Rob Reiner; screenplay by Raynold Gideon and Bruce A. Evans. 110 minutes. Rating: R. See **B63** and **GE17**.

CAST: Wil Wheaton, Richard Dreyfuss, River Phoenix, Corey Feldman, Jerry O'Connell, Kiefer Sutherland.

SECONDARY SOURCES AND REVIEWS:

1. *American Film* 12:6 (April, 1987): 57.
2. Ansen, David. "Growing Up in the '50s," in *Newsweek* 108:8 (August 25, 1986): 63.

3. Blue, Tyson. "*Stand By Me* Is a King-ly Rendition," in *The Courier Herald* [Dublin, GA] (August 8, 1986): .
4. Blue, Tyson. "'Stand By Me': The Best King Film Ever," in *Castle Rock: The Stephen King Newsletter* 2:10 (October, 1986): 1, 4.
5. Brooks, David. "What Is Death, What Is Goofy?" in *Insight* (September 1, 1986): 57.
6. Carroll, Kathleen. "And Along the Way, They All Grow Up," in *Daily News* [New York] (August 8, 1986): 3.
7. Carson, Norman. "*Stand By Me*," in *Magill's Cinema Annual, 1987: A Survey of the Films of 1986*, edited by Frank N. Magill. Englewood Cliffs, NJ: Salem Press, 1987, cloth, p. 413-417.
8. Clark, Mike. "*Stand by Me* Is a Summer Standout," in *USA Today* (August 8, 1986): .
9. Corliss, Richard. "No Slumming in Summertime," in *Time* 128:8 (August 25, 1986): 62.
10. Cunleff, Tom. "Stand By Me," in *People Weekly* "Picks & Pans" (September 1, 1986): 12.
11. Denby, D. *New York Magazine* 19:32 (August 18, 1986): 58.
12. Denby, D. *New York Magazine* 19:50 (December 22-29, 1986): 141.
13. Edelstein, D. *The Village Voice* 31:33 (August 19, 1986): 54.
14. *Fangoria* No. 57 (September, 1986): . Four-page article with photographs.
15. *Films in Review* 37 (November, 1986): 550.
16. Flatley, G. *Cosmopolitan* 201:4 (October, 1986): 62.
17. Floyd, N. *Monthly Film Bulletin* 54:638 (March, 1987): 88.
18. Forshey, G. E. *Christian Century* 103:31 (October 22, 1986): 920.
19. Freedman, Richard. "Boys Will Be Boys in Refreshing *Stand By Me*," in *The Star-Ledger* [Newark, NJ] (August 8, 1986): 49.
20. Goodman, Walter. "Film: Rob Reiner's *Stand by Me*," in *New York Times* 135 (August 8, 1986): C10.
21. Harmetz, A. *New York Times* (September 16, 1987): C17.
22. Holden, Stephen. "At the Movies: Rob Reiner Films Unusual Teen Drama," in *New York Times* 135 (August 8, 1986): C8.
23. Holdship, B. *Creem* 18:4 (December, 1986): 62.
24. Kael, Pauline. *The New Yorker* 62:29 (September 8, 1986): 110.
25. Lally, Kevin. "Here's a Movie to Stand By: Stephen King Adaptation Is a Sleeper," in *The Courier-News* [Bridgewater, NJ] (August 8, 1986): C-1.
26. Levy, M. Z. *Video Review* 8:11 (April 1987): 88.
27. *Los Angeles Times* (August 8, 1986): VI, 1.
28. Maginot, M. *American Cinematographer* 68:3 (March, 1987): 95.
29. *McCalls* 114:2 (November, 1986): 162.
30. *Newsweek* 108 (August 25, 1986): 63.
31. Quart, A. *Cineaste* 15:3 (1987): 48.
32. Rebello, S. *Cinefantastique* 17:1 (January, 1987): 52.
33. Reed, Rex. "*Stand by Me*—A Corny Kids' Caper," in *New York Post* (August 8, 1986): 22.
34. Reed, Susan, and James Grant. "The Child of Flower Children, Actor River Phoenix Rises from a Strange Past to Bloom in *Stand By Me*," in *People* 26:13 (September 26, 1986): 73-74.
35. Rothstein, M. *New York Times* 136:47 (July 19, 1987): H24.

36. Simon, J. *National Review* 38:19 (October 10, 1986): 59.
37. Smith, L. *Classical Images* 136 (October, 1986): 14.
38. Somtow, S. P. "Stand by Stephen King: A Certain Slant of 'I,'" in *Fantasy Review* No. 95 (October, 1986): 11,16.
39. "*Stand By Me*." *Los Angeles Times* "Calendar" (August 31, 1986): 27.
40. *Variety* 324:1 (July 30, 1986): 16.
41. *The Wall Street Journal* 208 (August 7, 1986): 16.
42. *The Washington Post* (August 22, 1986): D1.

G13. ***Creepshow 2***. Laurel Entertainment, New World Pictures, May 2, 1987. Executive producer, Richard P. Rubinstein; produced by David Ball; directed by Michael Gornick; screenplay by George A. Romero. 89 minutes. Rating: R. See **GE21**.

CAST: Lois Chiles, George Kennedy, Dorothy Lamour, Daniel Beer, Jeremy Green, Page Hannah, Don Harvey, David Holbrook, Holt McCallany, Frank S. Salsedo, Paul Satterfield, Tom Wright; cameos by Stephen King, Tom Savini.

EPISODES: Wraparound #1 [5 minutes]; "Old Chief Wood'nhead" [28 minutes]; "Wraparound #2" [1 minute]; "The Raft" [21 minutes; see **B60**]; Wraparound #3 [2 minutes]; "The Hitchhiker" [24 minutes]; Wraparound #4 [6 minutes].

SECONDARY SOURCES AND REVIEWS:

1. "About the Filmmakers: Some *Creepshow II* Notes," in *Castle Rock: The Stephen King Newsletter* 3:6 (June, 1987): 1, 6.
2. Blank, Ed. "Tepid 'Creepshow 2' Trades on Names of Romero, King," in *Pittsburgh Press* [Pennsylvania] (May 29, 1987): . As microfiche: *Newsbank: Film and Television* 14 (July, 1987): Fiche 3, F8.
3. Butler, Robert W. "This Show Is Worse Than Creepy," in *Kansas City Star* [Missouri] (May 31, 1987): . As microfiche: *Newsbank: Film and Television* 14 (July, 1987): Fiche 3, F6.
4. *Cinefantastique* 17:1 (January, 1987): 8.
5. Cotton, Tim. "*Creepshow 2*: Somewhere Between a 5 and a 9," in *Castle Rock: The Stephen King Newsletter* 3:6 (June, 1987): 1, 6.
6. "*Creepshow II*," in *Castle Rock: The Stephen King Newsletter* 3:1 (December, 1986/January,1987): 11-12.
7. "*Creepshow 2*," in *Magill's Cinema Annual, 1988: A Survey of the Films of 1987,* edited by Frank N. Magill. Englewood Cliffs, NJ: Salem Press, 1988, cloth, p. 398.
8. *Fangoria* No. 64 (1987): . Four-page article with photographs.
9. Forrest, W. *Cinefantastique* 17:3/4 (June, 1987): 12.
10. Harris, J. P. *Cinefantastique* 17:5 (September, 1987): 50.
11. Harti, John. "'Creepshow 2': You've Seen It Before," in *Seattle Times* [Washington] (May 30, 1987): . As microfiche: *Newsbank: Film and Television* 14 (July, 1987): Fiche 3, F10.
12. Hemming, R., and G. P. Fagan. *Video Review* 8:6 (September, 1987): 102.

13. Hicks, Christopher. "'Creepshow 2' Is Worse Than the First Time Out," in *Deseret News* [Salt Lake City, UT] (May 22, 1987): . As microfiche: *Newsbank: Film and Television* 14 (July, 1987): Fiche 3, F9.
14. *Marquee* (May, 1987): . One-page article with photographs.
15. Maslin, J. *New York Times* 136:47 (May 4, 1987): C17.
16. Pally, Marcia. "Creepy, Crawly Things Haunt 'Creepshow II,'" in *Boston Herald* (May 22, 1987): . As microfiche: *Newsbank: Film and Television* 14 (July, 1987): Fiche 3, F4-F5.
17. *People Weekly* (December 13, 1982): . On George Romero and King.
18. Pitts, M. *The Village Voice* 32:20 (May 19, 1987): 64.
19. *Premiere* 1:1 (July/August, 1987): 83.
20. Smith, L. *Classical Images* 145 (July, 1987): 33.
21. Smith, Patricia. "'Creepshow 2' Beats Formula to a Pulp," in *Chicago Sun Times* (May 4, 1987): . As microfiche: *Newsbank: Film and Television* 14 (July, 1987): Fiche 3, F3.
22. "A Stephen King Kind of Creep Show," in *Newsday* [Long Island, NY] (May 2, 1987): . As microfiche: *Newsbank: Film and Television* 14 (July, 1987): Fiche 3, F7.
23. Strissel, Jodi. "Another Look at *Creepshow 2,*" in *Castle Rock: The Stephen King Newsletter* 3:8 (August, 1987): 2.
24. *Variety* 327:3 (May 13, 1987): 19.

G14. ***The Running Man.*** Tri-Star/Taft Entertainment, November 13, 1987. Executive producers, Keith Barish, Rob Cohen; produced by Tim Zinneman, George Linder; directed by Paul Michael Glasser; screenplay by Steven E. de Souza. 101 minutes. Rating: R. See **A14** and **GE22**.

CAST: Arnold Schwarzenegger, Maria Conchita Alonso, Yaphet Kotto, Jim Brown, Richard Dawson.

SECONDARY SOURCES AND REVIEWS:

1. Blue, Tyson. "'Running Man': Fun for Arnie," in *Castle Rock: The Stephen King Newsletter* 4:2 (February, 1988): 5.
2. Collings, Michael R. "*The Running Man* and Stephen King: Not a Bad Film," in *Castle Rock: The Stephen King Newsletter* 4:2 (February, 1988): 1, 4.
3. *Fangoria* No. 69 (December, 1987): . Four-page article with photographs.
4. Harris, Ian. "Arnold Who?" in *Castle Rock: The Stephen King Newsletter* 2:6 (June, 1986): 2.
5. McGuigan, C., and J. Huck. *Newsweek* 110:23 (December 7, 1987): 84.
6. Magid, R. *American Cinematographer* 68:12 (December, 1987): 70.
7. "More Comments on *The Running Man,*" in *Castle Rock: The Stephen King Newsletter* 4:2 (February, 1988): 4-5. Reader-response reviews to the film.
8. Scapperotti, D. *Cinefantastique* 17:5 (September, 1987): 17.

9. Schweitzer, Darrell. "*The Running Man* and Stephen King: *The Running Man* Is Fundamentally Dishonest," in *Castle Rock: The Stephen King Newsletter* 4:2 (February, 1988): 1, 4.
10. *Starlog* (December, 1987): .

G15. ***Pet Sematary***. Paramount Pictures, April 14, 1989. Produced by Richard Rubenstein; directed by Mary Lambert; screenplay by Stephen King. Filmed entirely in the Ellsworth/Bangor area of Maine. 95 minutes. Rated: R. See **A22**, **E6**, **GE23**.

CAST: Dale Midkiff, Fred Gwynne, Denise Crosby, Blaze Berhahl, Miko Hughes, Brad Greenquist, Susan J. Blommaert, Michael Lombard; with cameo role by King. According to Gary Wood, the project was rejected by Universal, United Artists, and twice by Paramount, but *Pet Sematary* is still the "most profitable Stephen King adaptation to [that] date," earning Paramount "over $26 million in domestic theatrical film rentals alone in 1989."

SECONDARY SOURCES AND REVIEWS:

1. Armstrong, David. "King's 'Pet Sematary'—Stylish But a Bit of a Stiff," in *San Francisco Examiner* (April 21, 1989): . As microfiche: *Newsbank: Film and Television* 16 (May, 1989): Fiche 55, E1.
2. Burke-Block, Candace. "Master of Ghouls Fears Loss of a Child," in *Washington* [DC] *Times* (May 9, 1989): . As microfiche: *Newsbank: Film and Television* 16 (May, 1989): Fiche 65, A13.
3. Canby, __. *New York Times* (April 22, 1989): A16.
4. Carr, Jay. "'Pet Sematary' Doesn't Live Up to Previous King Film Adaptations," in *Denver Post* [Colorado] (April 23,1989): . As microfiche: *Newsbank: Film and Television* 16 (May, 1989): Fiche 55, E2.
5. *Chicago Tribune* (April 24, 1989): V, 2.
6. *Cinefantastique* 19 (March, 1989): 4.
7. Collings, Michael R. "Resting in Pieces: *Pet Sematary* Offers Grounds for Intense Horror Scenes," in *The Blood Review: The Journal of Horror Criticism* 1:1 (October 1989): 46-49.
8. *Courier-News* [New Jersey] (April 22, 1989): .
9. Degan, Anne. "*Pet Sematary*: Moviemaking Next Door Can Really Change Scenes," in *Maine Sunday Telegram* [Portland, ME] (October 2, 1988): 10E-11E, 13E. As microfiche: *Newsbank: Film and Television* 15 (October, 1988): Fiche 159, D8-D10.
10. Draheim, Tom. "*Pet Sematary* Doesn't Draw Raves in Boston," in *Boston Globe* (April 21, 1989): 46. Reprinted: *Castle Rock: The Stephen King Newsletter* 5:6 (June, 1989): 1, 12.
11. Edelstein, David. "Grave Doings," in *New York Post* (April 22,1989): . As microfiche: *Newsbank: Film and Television* 16 (May, 1989): Fiche 55, E9-E10.
12. *Fangoria* No. 80 (1988): . One-page article.
13. *Fangoria* No. 81 (1988): . Four-page article with photographs.
14. Freedman, Richard. "'Pet Sematary' Unearths Deadly Secrets in Stephen King's Fast-Paced Shocker," in *Star-Ledger* [Newark, NJ]

(April 22,1989): . As microfiche: *Newsbank: Film and Television* 16 (May, 1989): Fiche 55, E8.

15. Gadberry, Greg. "'Pet Sematary' Continued King Tradition," in *Maine Sunday Telegram* [Portland, ME] (October 2, 1988): 11E.
16. Gadberry, Greg. "Two Maine Actresses Put Their Scare into 'Pet Sematary,'" in *Maine Sunday Telegram* [Portland, ME] (April 16, 1989): . As microfiche: *Newsbank: Film and Television* 16 (May, 1989): Fiche 55, D13.
17. Garner, Jack. "It's a Grave New World in King's Disturbingly Real 'Pet Sematary,'" in *Detroit News* (April 24, 1989): . As microfiche: *Newsbank: Film and Television* 16 (May, 1989): Fiche 55, E7.
18. *Gruezone* No. 8 (July, 1989): . Cover article.
19. "King's 'Pet Sematary': A Grave Mistake," in *Washington* [DC] *Times* (April 24,1989): . As microfiche: *Newsbank: Film and Television* 16 (May, 1989): Fiche 55, E12-E13.
20. Klein, Andy. "The Horrors of 'Pet Sematary,'" in *Los Angeles Examiner* (April 24, 1989): . As microfiche: *Newsbank: Film and Television* 16 (May, 1989): Fiche 55, D14.
21. Johnson, Malcolm. "'Pet Sematary' Unable to Resurrect King's Terror," in *Hartford Courant* [Connecticut] (April 22,1989): . As microfiche: *Newsbank: Film and Television* 16 (May, 1989): Fiche 55, E3-E4.
22. *Los Angeles Times* (April 24, 1989): VI, 5.
23. Martin, Robert H. [Bob]. "George Romero on *Day of the Dead* and *Pet Sematary*," in *Fangoria* No. 48 (October, 1985): 43-47.
24. McGarrigle, Dale. "Audience at 'Pet Sematary' Debut Praises Film's Faithfulness to Book," in *Bangor Daily News* [Maine] (April 11, 1989): . As microfiche: *Newsbank: Film and Television* 16 (May, 1989): Fiche 55, D12.
25. McKibben, Robert. "On Location: Maine's Not Profiting from Hollywood as Much as It Might," in *Maine Times* [Topsham, ME] (September 23, 1988): . As microfiche: *Newsbank: Film and Television* 15 (October, 1988): Fiche 159, D11-D13.
26. Mulay, James. "*Pet Sematary*," in *The Motion Picture Guide, 1990 Annual.* Evanston, IL: Cinebooks, 1990, cloth, p. 175-176.
27. *People Weekly* 31 (May 15, 1989): 13.
28. "'Pet Sematary' Is Strong Shocker, One of Best from Stephen King," in *Seattle Times* [Washington] (April 21, 1989): . As microfiche: *Newsbank: Film and Television* 16 (May, 1989): Fiche 55, E11.
29. Rambeau,Catharine. "Zombies Carry Director into Limelight," in *Detroit Free Press* (August 11, 1985): . As microfiche: *Newsbank: Film and Television* 12 (September, 1985): Fiche 31, E2-E3.
30. Roeper, Richard. "'Pet Sematary' Should Have Been Interred, Not Released," in *Chicago Sun Times* (April 25, 1989): . As microfiche: *Newsbank: Film and Television* 16 (May, 1989): Fiche 55, E5.
31. Rosenthal, Donna. "In 'Pet Sematary,' Stephen King Replays the Horror on Film," in *Daily News* [New York] (April 17, 1989): . As microfiche: *Newsbank: Film and Television* 16 (May, 1989): Fiche 53, A14-A15.

32. Schaefer, Stephen. "King Digs Horror in 'Pet Sematary,'" in *Boston Herald* (April 16, 1989): . As Microfiche: *Newsbank: Film and Television* 16 (June, 1989): Fiche 65, A10-A12. Also as microfiche: *NewsBank: Names in the News* 11 (May, 1989): Fiche 134, C1-C3.
33. "SK Brings Hollywood to Maine," in *Maine* (September/October, 1989): . Cover article.
34. Spruce, Christopher. "Do You Know Where Your Kid Is Tonight?" in *Castle Rock: The Stephen King Newsletter* 5:5. (May, 1989): 1, 12.
35. *Us* 3 (May 29, 1989): 62.
36. *Variety* 135 (April 26, 1989): 26.
37. Verniere, James. "'Pet Sematary' Dogged by Copycat Horror Plot," in *Boston Herald* (April 21, 1989): . As microfiche: *Newsbank: Film and Television* 16 (May, 1989): Fiche 55, E6.
38. *Washington Post* (April 22, 1989): C1.
39. Welsh, James M. "Pet Sematary," in *Magill's Cinema Annual, 1990: A Survey of the films of 1989,* edited by Frank N. Magill. Englewood Cliffs, NJ: Salem Press, 1990, p. 271-274.
40. "What the Newspaper Critics Said...," in *The Blood Review: The Journal of Horror Criticism* 1:1 (October 1989): 49.
41. Wood, Gary. "Stephen King Strikes Back!" in *Cinefantastique* 20:3 (January, 1990): .
42. Wood, Gary. "Pet Sematary: More Creative Control over His Own Screenplay Translated into One of the Author's Biggest Success Stories at the Movies," in *Cinefantastique* 21:4 (February, 1991): 39.

G16. ***Tales from the Darkside: The Movie*** [includes "The Cat from Hell"]. Paramount Pictures, May 1990. Produced by Richard P. Rubinstein; directed by John Harrison; screenplay for "The Cat from Hell," by George A. Romero. 93 minutes. Rated: R. See **GE24**.

CAST ["The Cat From Hell']: David Johansen, Paul Greeno, William Hickey, Alice Drummond, Delores Sutton, Mark Margolis.

EPISODES: "The Wraparound Story"; "Lot 249"; "The Cat From Hell" (see **B30**); "Lover's Vow."

SECONDARY SOURCES AND REVIEWS:

1. Bernard, Jami. *New York Post* (May 5, 1990): .
2. Boonstra, John. *Advocate* [New Haven, CT] (May 14, 1990): .
3. *New York Daily News*. (May 15, 1990): .

G17. ***Stephen King's Graveyard Shift.*** Paramount Pictures, October 26, 1990. Produced by William J. Dunn and Ralph S. Singleton; executive producers, Bonnie and Larry Sugar; directed by Ralph S. Singleton; screenplay by John Esposito. Based on the short story, "Graveyard Shift." 88 minutes. Rated: R. See **B12** and **GE26**.

CAST: David Andrews, Kelly Wolf, Stephen Macht, Andrew Divoff, Vic Polizos, Brad Dourif, Robert Alan Beuth, Ilona Margolis, Jimmy Woodward, Jonathan Emerson.

SECONDARY SOURCES AND REVIEWS:

1. Burden, Martin. "Gross Graveyard," in *New York Post* (October 27, 1990): . As microfiche: *Newsbank: Film and Television* 17 (December, 1990): Fiche 131, E3.
2. Dollar, Steve. "In 'Graveyard Shift,' Bare-bones King Rules," in *Atlanta Journal-Constitution* (October 29, 1990): . As microfiche: *Newsbank: Film and Television* 17 (December, 1990): Fiche 131, D13.
3. *Entertainment Weekly* (June 7, 1991): 67-68. The film received a "D+".
4. Freedman, Richard. "'Graveyard Shift' a Yawn from Beginning to End," in *Star-Ledger* [Newark, NJ] (October 27, 1990): . As microfiche: *Newsbank: Film and Television* 17 (December, 1990): Fiche 131, E2.
5. Freedman, Richard. "Rats! 'Graveyard Shift' Is Monument to Movie Clichés," in *San Francisco Examiner* (October 29, 1990): . As microfiche: *Newsbank: Film and Television* 17 (December, 1990): Fiche 131, D12.
6. "'Graveyard Shift' Digs Up a Lurking Menace," in *Washington* [D.C.] *Post* (October 29, 1990): . As microfiche: *Newsbank: Film and Television* 17 (December, 1990): Fiche 131, E5.
7. Leayman, Charles. "Graveyard Shift: With Numbing Mediocrity, Hollywood Makes Laborious and Incoherent What King Implied with a Few Well Chosen Words," in *Cinefantastique* 21:4 (February, 1991): 50.
8. Leayman, Charles. "Shooting It in Maine: Bangor's Own Best-Selling Author Has Been a Boon to the State's Filmmaking Economy," in *Cinefantastique* 21:4 (February, 1991): 45.
9. Mahar, Ted. "The Rat Patrol Stars in 'Graveyard Shift': Stephen King Tale Is Simplistic, Scary, and Slimy," in *The Oregonian* [Portland, OR] (October 31, 1990): . As microfiche: *Newsbank: Film and Television* 17 (December, 1990): Fiche 131, E4.
10. McGarrigle, Dale. "Bangor-Area Filming of Stephen King Story Begins," in *Bangor Daily News* [Maine] (June 14, 1990): . As microfiche: *Newsbank: Film and Television* 17 (July, 1990): Fiche 83, G9.
11. Sachs, Lloyd. "Rats! 'Stephen King's Graveyard Shift' Has No Bite," in *Chicago Sun Times* (October 30, 1990): . As microfiche: *Newsbank: Film and Television* 17 (December, 1990): Fiche 131, D14.
12. Sherman, Paul. "Headed for Early Grave: 'Graveyard Shift' Is Dead on Arrival," in *Boston Herald* (October 27, 1990): . As microfiche: *Newsbank: Film and Television* 17 (December, 1990): Fiche 131, E1.
13. Strauss, Bob. "You Can Always Smell a Rat in a King Movie," in *Daily News* [Los Angeles, CA] (October 27, 1990): . As microfiche: *Newsbank: Film and Television* 17 (December, 1990): Fiche 131, D11.
14. Wood, Gary. "Stephen King's *Graveyard Shift*," in *Cinefantastique* 21:3 (February, 1990): .

G18. *Misery*. Castle Rock Entertainment Association with Nelson Entertainment/Columbia. November 30, 1990. Produced by Andrew Scheinman, Rob Reiner; directed by Rob Reiner; screenplay by William Goldman. Released for holiday audiences. 105 minutes. Rated R. See **A33** and **GE27**.

CAST: James Caan, Cathy Bates, Richard Farnsworth, Frances Sternhagen, Lauren Bacall.

The film earned an Academy Award for Best Supporting Actress for Cathy Bates. The film marks Reiner as the first filmmaker to direct two films from King's stories; both *Misery* and *Stand by Me* received wide popular and critical acclaim.

SECONDARY SOURCES AND REVIEWS:

1. Beahm, George. "It Is the Tale *and* He Who Tells It," in *The Shape Under the Sheet: The Complete Stephen King Encyclopedia*. Ann Arbor, MI: Popular Culture, Ink, May 1991, cloth, p. 612.
2. Bernard, Jami. "The Joys of 'Misery,'" in *New York Post* (November 30, 1990): .
3. Caan, James. Interview in *Details Magazine* (December, 1990): .
4. Carroll, Kathleen. "'Misery' Checks in at Kathy Bates' Motel," in *New York Daily News* (November 30, 1990): .
5. Clark, Mike. "Reiner's 'Misery' Makes Scary Company," in *USA Today* (November 30, 1990): .
6. Ebert, Roger. "'Misery' Works, But King's Tale Holds Director Back," in *Chicago Sun Times* (November 30, 1990): . As microfiche: *Newsbank: Film and Television* 18 (January, 1991): Fiche 6, D1.
7. Falk, Sally. "Novelist Is Terrorized by Fan," in *Indianapolis Star* [Indiana] (November 30, 1990): . As microfiche: *Newsbank: Film and Television* 17 (December, 1990): Fiche 134, B14-C1.
8. Farber, Stephen. *Movieline* (December, 1990): .
9. Gleiberman, Owen. *Entertainment Weekly* (November 30, 1990): .
10. Graham, Mark. "Horror Writer Revisits State in 'Misery,'" in *Rocky Mountain News* [Denver, CO] (November 29, 1990): . As microfiche: *Newsbank: Film and Television* 18 (January, 1991): Fiche 5, E5.
11. Johnson, Malcolm. "Makers Add Depth to 'Misery,'" in *Hartford Courant* [Connecticut] (November 30, 1990): . As microfiche: *Newsbank: Film and Television* 17 (December, 1990): Fiche 134, B10-B11.
12. Johnson, Malcolm. "'Misery' Chilling Mix of Terror, Humor," in *Hartford Courant* [Connecticut] (November 30, 1990): . As microfiche: *Newsbank: Film and Television* 17 (December, 1990): Fiche 134, B12.
13. "The Joys of 'Misery,'" in *Detroit News* (November 30, 1990): . As microfiche: *Newsbank: Film and Television* 17 (December, 1990): Fiche 134, C7.
14. Klinghoffer, David. "'Misery' Just Doesn't Get to Heart of Matters," in *Washington* [D.C.] *Times* (November 30, 1990): . As mi-

crofiche: *Newsbank: Film and Television* 17 (December, 1990): Fiche 134, C8.

15. Mahar, Ted. "This Love Isn't a Novel Idea," in *The Oregonian* [Portland, OR] (November 30, 1990): . As microfiche: *Newsbank: Film and Television* 18 (January, 1991): Fiche 6, D2.
16. Movshowitz, Howie. "'Misery' Loves Erratic Fan's Company," in *Denver Post* [Colorado] (November 30, 1990): . As microfiche: *Newsbank: Film and Television* 18 (January, 1991): Fiche 6, C14.
17. Ringel, Eleanor. "Getting a Kick Out of 'Misery,'" in *Atlanta Journal-Constitution* (November 30, 1990): . As microfiche: *Newsbank: Film and Television* 17 (December, 1990): Fiche 134, B13.
18. Schickel, Richard. "Deadly Game of Nursing Care," in *Time* (December 10, 1990): .
19. Sharkey, Betsy. "'Misery's' Company Loves a Good Time: Filming the Stephen King Thriller Is Serious Business with Time Out for a Laugh," in *The New York Times* 139 (June 17, 1990): H13.
20. Stark, Susan. "Tender, Loving Cruelty," in *Detroit News* (November 30, 1990): . As microfiche: *Newsbank: Film and Television* 17 (December, 1990): Fiche 134, C5-C6.
21. Strauss, Bob. "Going for the Scare Diminishes 'Misery,'" in *Daily News* [Los Angeles, CA] (November 30, 1990): . As microfiche: *Newsbank: Film and Television* 18 (January, 1991): Fiche 6, C11.
22. Strauss, Bob. "What Scares Stephen King?" in *Daily News* [Los Angeles, CA] (November 29, 1990): . As microfiche: *Newsbank: Film and Television* 17 (December, 1990): Fiche 134, B8-B9.
23. Sragow, Michael. "Not-So-Sweet Misery," in *San Francisco Examiner* (November 30, 1990): . As microfiche: *Newsbank: Film and Television* 18 (January, 1991): Fiche 6, C12-C13.
24. Verniere, James. "Menacing 'Misery,'" in *Boston Herald* (November 30, 1990): . As microfiche: *Newsbank: Film and Television* 17 (December, 1990): Fiche 134, C2-C4.
25. Wood, Gary. "Directing the Blood and Gore: 'Misery,'" in *Cinefantastique* 21:4 (February, 1991): .
26. Wood, Gary. "Hard Hitting Makeup Effects," in *Cinefantastique* 21:4 (February 1991): 23.
27. Wood, Gary. "Rob Reiner on Stephen King," in *Cinefantastique* 21:4 (February, 1991): 21.
28. Wood, Gary. "Stephen King's *Misery*," in *Cinefantastique* 21:3 (February, 1990): .
29. Wood, Gary. "To Splatter or Not to Splatter: Rob Reiner Sounds as Tortured as Lady Macbeth," in *Cinefantastique* 21:4 (February, 1991): 16-22.
30. Wuntsch, Philip. "Adding 'Misery' to Holiday Cheer," in *Dallas Morning News* (November 39, 1990): . As mircofiche: *Newsbank: Film and Television* 18 (January, 1991): Fiche 6, D3.

G19. ***Stephen King's Sleepwalkers***. Columbia Pictures, 1992. Produced by Mark Victor, Michael Grais, and Nabeel Zahid; directed by Mick Garris; screenplay by Stephen King. Executive producers, Dimitri Logothetis and Joseph Medawar. Co-producer, Richard Stenta. 89 minutes. Rated: R. See **E8** and **GE29**.

CAST: Brian Krause, Mädchen Amick, Alice Krige, Stephen King.

SECONDARY SOURCES AND REVIEWS:

1. Cohn, Lawrence. *Variety* 347:1 (April 29, 1992): 47.
2. Floyd, Nigel. *Sight and Sound* 2:4 (August, 1992): 62.

G20. *The Dark Half*. Orion Pictures, 1992. Produced by Declan Baldwin. Director, executive producer, and screenwriter George A. Romero. Associate producer, Christine Romero. 122 minutes. Rated: R. See **A39** and **GE31**.

CAST: Timothy Hutton, Amy Madigan, Julie Harris, Michael Rooker.

SECONDARY SOURCES AND REVIEWS:

1. Porton, Richard. *Cineaste* 20:1 (Winter, 1993): 64.
2. Travers, Peter. *Rolling Stone* No. 656 (May 13, 1993): 113.
3. Van Gelder, Lawrence. "A Writer's Dark Side," in *The New York Times* 140 (November 30, 1992): B5.
4. Wood, Gary. "*The Dark Half*: George Romero Tries His Hand at Adapting a King Best-Seller," in *Cinefantastique* 21:4 (February, 1991): 26.

G21. *Needful Things*. Columbia/Castle Rock Entertainment/New Line Cinema, 1993. Produced by Jack Cummins; directed by Fraser C. Heston; screenplay by W. D. Richter. Executive producer, Peter Yates. 121 minutes. Rated: R. See **A44** and **GE32**.

CAST: Ed Harris, Max von Sydow, Bonnie Bedelia, J. T. Walsh, Valri Bromfield, Ray McKinnon, Amanda Plummer.

G22. *The Lawnmower Man*. Allied Vision Lane Pringle Productions/Fuji Eight Co., 1993. Produced by Gimel Everett; directed by Brett Leonard; screenplay by Brett Leonard and Gimel Everett. Executive producers: Edward Simons, Steve Lane, Clive Turner, Robert Pringle; associate producers: Peter McRae, Masao Takiyama; co-producer: Milton Subotsky. "Based on a story by Stephen King." Rated: R. See **B24**, **GE19**, **GE30**.

CAST: Pierce Brosnan, Jeff Fahey, Geoffrey Lewis, Jenny Wright, Mark Bringleson, Jeremy Slate. While many film adaptations of King work vary markedly from the original print source, the sole connections between this film and King's story seem to be the title and the fact that someone uses a lawnmower. This tale of virtual reality and a stereotypic mad scientist bears no resemblance whatever to King's blend of horror, fantasy, and oddly resonant myth.

SECONDARY SOURCES AND REVIEWS:

1. Cox, Dan. "New Line Raked over 'Lawn'," in *Variety* 352:9 (April 4, 1994): 15.

2. O'Steen, Kathleen. "King Wants Name Off 'Lawnmower'," in *Variety* 347:8 (June 8, 1992): 18.

G23. ***The Shawshank Redemption***. October 1994. Directed and screenplay by Frank Darabont. See **B61**.

CAST: Tim Robbins, Morgan Freeman. By November 1994 the film had reached tenth place in box office earnings; its gross to that date exceeded $10 million.

G24. ***Dolores Claiborne***. 1994/95. See **A46**.

CAST: Kathy Bates, Jennifer Jason Leigh.

FILMS OPTIONED OR UNDER PRODUCTION

GA1. ***Apt Pupil***. Produced by Richard Kobritz and William Frye; directed by Alan Bridges; screenplay by Jim Wheat and Ken Wheat (an earlier unused screenplay was completed by B. J. Nelson). Filming abandoned in 1988, after about ten weeks of shooting, reportedly only eleven days from completion. See **B62**.

Cast: Ricky Schroeder, Nicol Williamson, Richard Masur. According to Kobritz, the film "may very well have been the definitive translation of Stephen King into film" (Wood, 36). Reviving work on the film was discussed in January, 1988 and January, 1989; Kobritz, however, denies the possibility of completing the film.

SECONDARY SOURCES AND REVIEWS:

1. *Twilight Zone* (October, 1988): .
2. Wood, Gary. "Apt Pupil: The Story Behind the Filming of King's Novella from 'Different Seasons,' Never to be Seen," in *Cinefantastique* 21:4 (February, 1991): 36-37.

GA2. ***Creepshow 3.*** In production with Richard Rubinstein, Laurel Entertainment.

The film may include a story by King that was not used for *Creepshow 2,* "Pinfall," with a preliminary script by George A. Romero; Blue reports the episodes as: "Dolan's Cadillac," "Popsy," "The Rainy Season," "Pinfall."

SECONDARY SOURCES AND REVIEWS:

1. Blue, Tyson. "Needful Kings," in *The Blood Review: Journal of Horror Criticism* 1:2 (January, 1990): .
2. Spignesi, Stephen J. "The King of Bowling: An Introduction to 'Pinfall,'" in *The Complete Stephen King Encyclopedia.* Ann Arbor, MI: Popular Culture, Ink, May 1991, cloth, p. 594-598.
3. Wood, Gary. "Upcoming Horrors, Thinner & Others," in *Cinefantastique* 21:4 (February, 1991): 31.

GA3. ***The Mangler.*** Reported as complete in September 1994, with director Tobe Hooper looking for a distributor. See **B18**.

GA4. ***The Night Flyer.*** In production with Richard Rubinstein, Laurel Entertainment. Second revised script draft completed, Fall 1994. See **B89**.

SECONDARY SOURCES AND REVIEWS:

1. Wood, Gary, "Upcoming Horrors, *Thinner* & Others," in *Cinefantastique* 21:4 (February, 1991): 31.

GA5. ***The Shotgunners.*** Directed by Sam Peckinpah from an original script by Stephen King. Peckinpah died during pre-production in 1984.

SECONDARY SOURCES AND REVIEWS:

1. Wood, Gary. "Shotgunners: King & Peckinpah," in *Cinefantastique* 21:4 (February, 1991): 43.

GA6. ***Thinner.*** In production with Richard Rubinstein, Laurel Entertainment, 1991. Preliminary screenplay by Michael McDowell. See **A27**.

SECONDARY SOURCES AND REVIEWS:

1. Wood, Gary. "Upcoming Horrors, *Thinner* & Others," in *Cinefantastique* 21:4 (February, 1991): 31.

GA7. ***Training Exercises.*** North Carolina Film Corporation (Dino de Laurentiis). From a treatment by Stephen King.

GA8. ***The Talisman.*** Optioned for film by Steven Spielberg. See **A26**.

GA9. ***The Long Walk.*** Optioned for film. See **A8**.

TELEPLAYS AND TELEVISION PROGRAMS BASED ON KING'S NOVELS AND STORIES

GB1. **"Salem's Lot."** Warner Brothers, 1979. Produced by Richard Kobritz; directed by Tobe Hooper; teleplay by Paul Monash. CBS. November 17, 24, 1979. 210 minutes [edited movie, 157 minutes]. See **A2**, **GE2**.

CAST: David Soul, James Mason, Lance Kerwin, Bonnie Bedelia, Lew Ayres, Reggie Nalder, Ed Flanders.

SECONDARY SOURCES AND REVIEWS:

1. Casey, Susan. "On the Set of *'Salem's Lot,*" in *Fangoria* 4 (1980): 38-41, 45.
2. *Fangoria* 38: . Includes *Salem's Lot* pullout poster.
3. Kelley, Bill. "*'Salem's Lot*: Filming Horror for Television," in *Cinefantastique* 9:2 (Winter, 1979): .

4. Leishman, Katie. "When Is Television Too Scary for Children," in *TV Guide* (January 10, 1981): 5-8.
5. Schow, David J. "Return of the Curse of the Son of Mr. King: Book Two," in *Whispers* No. 17/18 (August, 1982): 49-56.
6. Spignesi, Stephen. "A Stop at the Marsten House: An Interview with Tobe Hooper," in *The Shape Under the Sheet: The Complete Stephen King Encyclopedia.* Ann Arbor, MI: Popular Culture, Ink, May 1991, cloth, p. 561-566.

GB2. **"The Word Processor of the Gods,"** on *Tales from the Darkside.* Laurel Entertainment, Inc. November 19, 1985. Executive Producer, David E. Vogel; produced by William Teitler; directed by Michael Gornick; teleplay by Michael McDowell. 30 minutes. See **B72** and **GE15**.

CAST: Bruce Davidson, Karen Schallo, Bill Cain, Jonathan Matthews, Patrick Piccininni, Miranda Beeson, Paul Sparer.

SECONDARY SOURCES AND REVIEWS:

1. Harris, Judith P. "Timid, One-Note Stories Need Padding to Fill Even 30 Minutes," in *Cinefantastique* (July, 1985): .
2. Scapperotti, Dan. "Tales from the Darkside," in *Cinefantastique* (January, 1985): 15, 52.

GB3. **"Gramma,"** on *The New Twilight Zone* series. CBS. February 14, 1986. Produced by Harvey Fraud; directed by Bradford May; teleplay by Harlan Ellison. 30 minutes. See **B76**.

CAST: Barrett Oliver, Darl Anne Fluegel, Frederick Long.

SECONDARY SOURCES AND REVIEWS:

1. Bentkowski, Kent Daniel. "King's 'Gramma' Makes Her Small Screen Debut," in *Castle Rock: The Stephen King Newsletter* 2:4 (April, 1986): 5, 8.
2. Blue, Tyson. "Gramma Update," in *Castle Rock: The Stephen King Newsletter* 2:3 (March, 1986): 4.
3. Blue, Tyson. "Praise for Ellison's 'Gramma'," in *Castle Rock: The Stephen King Newsletter* 2:4 (April 1986): 1, 5.
4. Herndon, Ben. "Real Tube Terror: The Secretaries Were Afraid to Type 'Gramma'," in *Twilight Zone Magazine* (December, 1985): 10A-11A.
5. Herndon, Ben. "The Twilight Zone," in *Cinefantastique* (March, 1986): 22-23, 58-59.
6. Rebeaux, Max. "Twilight Zone," in *Cinefantastique* 15 (October, 1985): 13, 53.

GB4. **"Sorry, Right Number."** *Tales from the Darkside.* November 20, 1987. Executive producers, Richard P.Rubinstein, George A. Romero, Jerry Golod; produced by Anthony Santa Croce; directed by John Sutherland; teleplay by Stephen King. 30 minutes. See **E5**.

CAST: Arthur Taxier, Deborah Harmon, Rhonda Dotson, Katherine Britton, Brandon Stewart, Nichold Huntington, Catherine Battistone, Paul Sparer.

SECONDARY SOURCES AND REVIEWS:

1. Blue, Tyson. "Sorry, Right Number," in *Castle Rock: The Stephen King Newsletter* 3:10 (October, 1987): 5.

GB5. ***Stephen King's World of Horror***, three-part television special.

GB6. ***It.*** Konigsberg/Sanitsky Company In Association with Lorimar Television. ABC. Executive producers, Jim Green and Allen Epstein. Supervising producer, Matthew O'Connor; directed by Tommy Lee Wallace; teleplay by Lawrence D. Cohen, Tommy Lee Wallace [Part 2]. ABC-TV four-hour mini-series. Sunday, November 18, 1990, 9:00-11:00 pm; Tuesday, November 20, 1990, 9:00-11:00 pm. See **A32**.

CAST: Harry Anderson, Tim Curry, Richard Masur, Annette O'Toole, Tim Reid, John Ritter, Richard Thomas, Dennis Christopher, Olivia Hussey, Jonathan Brandis, Brandon Crane, Adam Faraizi, Seth Green, Ben Heller, Emily Perkins, Marlon Taylor.

SECONDARY SOURCES AND REVIEWS:

1. "At Least 'It' is Different," in *Austin American-Statesman* [Texas] (November 18, 1990): . As microfiche: *Newsbank: Film and Television* 17 (December, 1990): Fiche 137, E11.
2. "The Best and Worst [of 1990-1991]," in *TV Guide* 39:27 (#1997) (July 6, 1991): 7. "Best horror thriller: 'Stephen King's It.' (ABC)."
3. Bianculli, David. "Bozo's Evil Twin," in *New York Post* (November 15, 1990): . As microfiche: *Newsbank: Film and Television* 17 (December, 1990): Fiche 137, E8.
4. "A Clown as Killer? 'It' Is a Horrible Film," in *Washington* [D.C.] *Times* (November 16, 1990): . As microfiche: *Newsbank: Film and Television* 17 (December, 1990): Fiche 137, E13.
5. Farrell, Peter. "Gripping 'It' a Pure Horror Story," in *The Oregonian* [Portland, OR] (November 18, 1990): . As microfiche: *Newsbank: Film and Television* 17 (December, 1990): Fiche 137, E9-E10.
6. Gerber, Eric. "'It' Should Be Scarier," in *Houston Post* (November 17, 1990): . As microfiche: *Newsbank: Film and Television* 17 (December, 1990): Fiche 137, E12.
7. "Hazard Ye Not Unto the Depths of 'It'!" in *Boston Globe* (November 17, 1990): . As microfiche: *Newsbank: Film and Television* 17 (December, 1990): Fiche 137, E7.
8. Millman, Joyce. "Stephen King Lets Them Have 'IT,'" in *San Francisco Examiner* (November 19, 1990): . As microfiche: *Newsbank: Film and Television* 17 (December, 1990): Fiche 137, E5-E6.

9. "Play It Again, Steff," in *Castle Rock: The Stephen King Newsletter* 2:8 (August, 1986): 6.
10. Richmond, Ray. "'It': 'Stand By Me' Meets 'Godzilla,'" in *Orange County Register* (November 16, 1990): . Reprinted: *Register* [New Haven, CT] (November 16, 1990): .
11. "Specials," in *TV Guide* (September 9, 1989): 6. An announcement of the schedule for the mini-series.
12. Spignesi, Stephen J. "The Art of Adaptation: A Synoptic Comparison of 'IT' and *IT*," in *The Shape Under the Sheet: The Complete Stephen King Encyclopedia*. Ann Arbor, MI: Popular Culture, Ink, May 1991, cloth, p. 615-622.
13. Tucker, Ken. *Entertainment Weekly* (November 16, 1990): .
14. *TV Guide* (November, 1990): .
15. Wood, Gary. "IT: Burbank's Fantasy 2 Effects Met the Task of Enlivening the Novel's Horrors, Including Its Shape-shifting Giant Spider," in *Cinefantastique* 21:4 (February, 1991): 48-49.
16. Wood, Gary. "Stephen King's *IT*," in *Cinefantastique* (February, 1990): .
17. Zurawik, David. "ABC's 'It': This One Isn't for the Kiddies," in *Sun* [Baltimore, MD] (November 18, 1990): . As microfiche: *Newsbank: Film and Television* 18 (January, 1991): Fiche 8, B2-B3.

GB7. ***Stephen King's "Sometimes They Come Back."*** Paradise Films, 1991. Executive producer, Dino De Laurentiis; produced by Michael S. Murphey; co-producer, Milton Subotsky; directed by Tom McLoughlin; teleplay by Lawrence Konner and Mark Rosenthal. CBS. 2 hours.

CAST: Tim Matheson, Brooke Adams, Robert Rusler, Chris Demetral, Robert Hy Corman, William Sanderson, Nicholas Sadler, Bentley Mitchum. See **B23**.

SECONDARY SOURCES AND REVIEWS:

1. "The Best and Worst [of 1990-1991]," in *TV Guide* 39:27 (#1997) (July 6, 1991): 7. "Worst horror thriller: 'Stephen King's Sometimes They Come Back.' (ABC). Sometimes they shouldn't bother."

GB8. ***Stephen King's Golden Years.*** CBS; directed by Ken Fink, teleplay by Stephen King. Episode 1, July 16, 1991, 9:00-11:00, 2 hours; Episode 2, July 18, 1991, 10:00-11:00, 1 hour; Episode 3, July 25, 1991, 10:00-11:00, 1 hour. See **E7** and **GE28**.

CAST: Keith Szarabajka, Frances Sternhagen, Felicity Huffman, Bill Raymond, Ed Lauter, R. D. Call, Stephen Root, J. R. Horne, Graham Paul, Phil Lenkjowsky, Kathleen Piche, Tim Guinee, Brad Greenquist, Mert Hatfield.

SECONDARY SOURCES AND REVIEWS:

1. Beck, Marilyn. "Insider Grapevine: Glad About Being Golden," in *TV Guide* 39:29 (#1999) (July 20, 1991): 18-19.

2. Droesch, Paul. "This Week on TV: Stephen King, New '50s Sitcom, Working Women," in *TV Guide* 39:28 (#1998) (Jule 13-19, 1991): .
3. King, Stephen. "How I Created *Golden Years*...and Spooked Dozens of TV Executives," in *Entertainment Weekly* No. 77 (August 2, 1991): 28-32.
4. Sharbutt, Jay. "Fountain of Youth Stephen King Style," in *News Chronicle* [Thousand Oaks, CA] (July 16, 1991): C6.
5. "Stephen King 'Golden Years' Drama to Debut July 16 on CBS," in *News Chronicle* [Thousand Oaks, CA] (June 19, 1991): C8.
6. "Stephen King's 'Golden Years'," in *Variety* 344:1 (July 15, 1991): 42.
7. Zoglin, Richard. *Time* 138:3 (July 22, 1991): 56.

GB9. ***The Tommyknockers***. ABC, 1993. Produced by Jayne Bieber and Jane Scott; directed by John Power; teleplay by Lawrence D. Cohen. Executive producers: Frank Konigsberg and Larry Sanitsky. Co-producer: Lawrence D. Cohen. See **A35** and **GE33**.

CAST: Jimmy Smits, Marg Helgenberger, John Ashton, Allyce Beasley, Robert Carradine, Joanna Cassidy, Annie Corley, Cliff DeYoung, Traci Lords, E. G. Marshall.

SECONDARY SOURCES AND REVIEWS:

1. Leonard, John. "Stephen King's *The Tommyknockers*," in *New York* 26:19 (May 10, 1993): 64.
2. *USA Today* (July 22, 1991): .

GB10. ***Stephen King's The Stand***. ABC, 1994; Greengrass and Laurel/Spelling. Executive producers: Richard P. Rubenstein and Stephen King. Associate producer: Michael Gornick. Directed by Mick Garris; teleplay by Stephen King. Part I, Episode 1, May 8, 1994, 89 minutes; Part I, Episode 2, The Dreams, May 9, 1994, 89 minutes; Part II, Episode 3, The Betrayal, May 11, 1994, 89 minutes; Part II, Episode 4, The Stand, May 12, 1994, 93 minutes. See **A5**, **E9**, and **GE34**.

CAST: Gary Sinise, Adam Storke, Rob Lowe, Molly Rinwald, Corin Nemec, Jamey Sheridan, Miguel Ferrer, Laura San Giacomo, Ruby Dee, Bill Fagerbakke, Ray Walston, Ed Harris, Ossie Davis, Matt Frewer, Kareem Abdul-Jabbar, Kathy Bates. Promotional brochure includes "The Making of *The Stand*" and a short interview with King; some copies also include a four-color card from ABC signed by director Garris.

SECONDARY SOURCES AND REVIEWS:

1. Everett, Tod. "*The Stand*," in *Variety* 355:1 (May 2, 1994): 42.
2. Giles, Jeff. "*The Stand*," in *Newsweek* 123:19 (May 9, 1994): 70.
3. Jarvis, Jeff. "The Couch Critic: *Stephen King's The Stand*," in *TV Guide* 42:19 (#2145) (May 7, 1994): 7.
4. Leonard, John. *New York* 27:19 (May 9, 1994): 84.
5. O'Connor, John J. "*Stephen King's The Stand*," in *The New York Times* 143 (May 6, 1994): B12 (N), D17 (L).

6. Wood, Gary. "*The Stand*: The Filming of King's Masterpiece Has Been a Movie Deal More Than Ten Years in the Making," in *Cinefantastique* 21:4 (February, 1991): 28-29.
7. Zoglin, Richard. *Time* 143:19 (May 9, 1994): 83.

GB11. *The Langoliers*. ABC/Laurel Entertainment. Aired as a two-part miniseries beginning February 25, 1995. Produced by Robert Rubenstein; directed by Tom Holland; teleplay by Tom Holland. See **B96**.

CAST: Dean Stockwell, Bronson Pinchot.

MUSICAL ADAPTATIONS

GC1. *Carrie*. Musical adaptation. Produced by Friedrich Kurz and the Royal Shakespeare Company association with White Cap Productions. Book by Lawrence D. Cohen; music by Michael Gore; lyrics by Dean Pitchford; directed by Terry Hands; chorographed by Debbie Allen. English opening, Stratford-Upon-Avon, February 18, 1988. American opening, Virginia Theater, New York City, May 12, 1988; closed May 15, 1988. See **A1**.

CAST: Barbara Wood [London], Betty Buckley [New York], Linzi Hateley, Charlotte D'Amboise, Paul Gygnell, Gene Anthony Ray, Darlene Love, Sally Anne Triplett.

SECONDARY SOURCES AND REVIEWS:

1. "*Annie* It Ain't," in *USA Today* (February 22, 1988): .
2. Barnes, Clive. "Musical *Carrie* Soars on Blood, Guts, and Gore," in *New York Post* (May 13, 1988): .
3. Barnes, Clive. *New York Post* (December 29, 1988): .
4. "*Carrie* Proves Costly Failure," in *New York Post* (May 17, 1988): .
5. "*Carrie* to be Musical," in *Castle Rock: The Stephen King Newsletter* 2:4 (April 1986): 6.
6. "*Carrie* to Open at Virginia Theater," in *Castle Rock: The Stephen King Newsletter* 4:3 (March, 1988): .
7. Cziraky, Dan. "Buckets of Talent Wasted in *Carrie*," in *Castle Rock: The Stephen King Newsletter* 4:8 (August, 1988): 6, 10.
8. Ebron, Betty Lou. "Apple Sauce," in *New York Daily News* (March, 1988): .
9. Foster, Tim. "*Carrie* as a Musical," in *Castle Rock: The Stephen King Newsletter* 4:2 (February 1988): .
10. Goden, Craig. "Black and White and Read All Over—*Carrie* on Broadway," in *Castle Rock: The Stephen King Newsletter* 4:7 (July, 1988): .
11. Henry, William A. III. "The Biggest All-Time Flop Ever—*Carrie*'s $7 Million Close Shows Why Musicals Are Like Dinosaurs," in *Time* (May 30, 1988): .
12. Henry, William A. III. "Getting All Fired Up Over Nothing," in *Time* (May 23, 1988): .
13. Holden, Stephen. *New York Times* (May 8, 1988): II, 5.

14. Kroll, Jack. "Shakespeare to Stephen King: The Sins of *Carrie,*" in *Newsweek* (May 23, 1988): .
15. "Name Game," in *USA Today* (March 22, 1988): .
16. Maychick, Diana. "Warming Up for *Carrie,*" in *New York Post* (May 12, 1988): .
17. Mills, Richard. "Musical *Carrie* Is a Strange Spectacle," in *Castle Rock: The Stephen King Newsletter* 4:4 (April 1988): .
18. Munster, Bill. "You Read the Book, Saw the Movie, But What About the Show," in *Castle Rock: The Stephen King Newsletter* 4:7 (July, 1988): 6, 7.
19. O'Haire, Patricia. "Stage Fright," in *New York Daily News* (May 8, 1988): .
20. Osborne, Brian. "More *Carrie*-ing On," in *Castle Rock: The Stephen King Newsletter* 4:5/6 (May-June, 1988): 1, 7.
21. Rich, Frank. *New York Times* (May 13, 1988): III, 3.
22. Roura, Phil, and Tom Poster. "Buckley Comes on in *Carrie,*" in *New York Daily News* (March 29, 1988): .
23. Scapperotti, Dan R. "Stephen King Musical Lays Eggs on Broadway," in *Cinefantastique* 19 (1989): . Reprinted: *The Stephen King Companion,* edited by George Beahm. Kansas City, MO: Andrews & McMeel, September 1989, cloth, p. 174-175.
24. Spignesi, Stephen. "'Carrie: The Musical'—The Biggest Flop in Broadway History," in *The Complete Stephen King Encyclopedia.* Ann Arbor, MI: Popular Culture, Ink, May 1991, cloth, p. 556-558. Includes a "diary" of related events from November, 1985 through December 29, 1988.
25. *New York Daily News* (January 3, 1988): .
26. *New York Daily News* (May 13, 1988): .
27. *New York Times* (November, 1985): . An article announcing the Royal Shakespeare Company plans for production.
28. *New York Times* (May 17, 1988): III, 15. Review.
29. *Newsweek* (May 23, 1988): . A review with photographs.
30. "What a Carrie On," in *Castle Rock: The Stephen King Newsletter* 4:5/6 (May/June, 1988): .
31. Williams, Jeannie. "Sneaks," in *USA Today* (May 5, 1988): .

STAGE PRODUCTIONS

GD1. ***Rage***. Blackburn Theater, Gloucester MA. March 30, 1989. Stageplay by Robert B. Parker and Joan Parker. Pearl Productions. See **A4**.

SECONDARY SOURCES AND REVIEWS:

1. Hartigan, Patti. "The Play's the Thing for the Parker Family," in *Castle Rock: The Stephen King Newsletter* 5:6 (June, 1989): 1, 12.
2. Lowell, Dave. "King Play Is Raging Success," in *Castle Rock: The Stephen King Newsletter* 5:5 (May, 1989): 4.
3. "World Premiere of 'Rage' Hits Community March 30: Robert B. Parker Sets Stage for Stephen King Novel," in *PR Newswire* (March 8, 1989): .

VIDEOCASSETTES

(Secondary Sources and Reviews herein refer to the videocassette version only)

GE1. *Carrie.* CBS/Fox Video, 1984. Beta, VHS, Laser, CED. 97 minutes. See **G1**.

SECONDARY SOURCES AND REVIEWS:

1. Arkush, A. *American Film* 9:10 (September, 1984): 66.
2. Barker, Clive. *American Film* 12:10 (September, 1987): 63.
3. Farber, J. *Video Review* 8:8 (November, 1987): 131.
4. Hoberman, J. *The Village Voice* 31:26 (July 1, 1986): 57.
5. Sarris, A., and T. Allen. *The Village Voice* 32:31 (August 4, 1987): 47.
6. Sikov, E. *Premiere* 3 (November, 1987): 94.

GE2. *Salem's Lot.* Warner Brothers, 1979. Edited videocassette version of television mini-series. Beta, VHS. See **GB1**.

GE3. *The Shining.* Warner Brothers/Hawk Films. VHS, Beta. 143 minutes. Rated R. See **G2**.

SECONDARY SOURCES AND REVIEWS:

1. Sarris, A., and T. Allen. *The Village Voice* 32:30 (July 28, 1987): 49.
2. Thomson, D. *American Film* 11:1 (October, 1985): 76.

GE4. *The Boogeyman.* Tantalus, 1982, 1984. VHS. 30 minutes. Produced, directed, written, and edited by Jeffrey C. Schiro. Based on "The Boogeyman" (*Night Shift*). See **B19** and **GE13**.

CAST: Michael Reid, Bert Linder, Terence Brady, Mindy Silverman, Jerome Bynder, Bobby Persicheth, Michael Dagostino.

SECONDARY SOURCES AND REVIEWS:

1. Collings, Michael R. *Castle Rock: The Stephen King Newsletter* 1:9 (September, 1985): 4. A letter-review.
2. Frank, Janrae. "Stephen King's *Night Shift:* Student Shorts of Stephen King Tales Headed for Videocassette Release," in *Cinefantastique* 15:3 (July, 1985): 12.
3. Sallee, Wayne Allen. "It's Really Only a Game," in *Castle Rock: The Stephen King Newsletter* 2:4 (April, 1986): 2.

GE5. *Creepshow*. Warner Home Video, 1982. VHS, Beta, CED. 120 minutes. Rated R. See **GE5**.

SECONDARY SOURCES AND REVIEWS:

1. Dauphin, E. *Creem* 14:11 (April, 1983): 47.
2. Hogan, D. J. "My Dribble Cup Runneth Over," in *Cinefantastique* 13:4 (April/May, 1983): 56.
3. Minton, L. *McCall's* 110:5 (February, 1983): 128.
4. *Sight and Sound* 52:1 (Winter, 1982/1983): 76.

GE6. ***Christine.*** Columbia Pictures, 1983. Beta, VHS, Laser, CED. 110 minutes. See **G4**.

GE7. ***Cujo***. Warner Communications, Taft Entertainment, 1983. Beta, VHS, CED. 120 minutes. See **G5**.

GE8. ***Dead Zone.*** Paramount Pictures, 1983. Beta, VHS, Laser, CED. 103 minutes. See **G6**.

GE9. ***The Woman in the Room.*** Darkwoods, 1983. Granite Entertainment, Canoga Park, CA. Produced by Gregopary Melton; directed by Frank Darabont; screenplay by Frank Darabont. VHS, Beta. 30 minutes. See **B41** and **GE13**.

CAST: Michael Cornelison, Dee Croxton, Brian Libby, Bob Brunson, George Russell

SECONDARY SOURCES AND REVIEWS:

1. Collings, Michael R. *Castle Rock: The Stephen King Newsletter* 1:9 (September, 1985): 4. A letter-review.
2. Frank, Janrae. "Stephen King's *Night Shift*: Student Shorts of Stephen King Tales Headed for Videocassette Release," in *Cinefantastique* 15:3 (July, 1985): 12.
3. Sallee, Wayne Allen. "It's Really Only a Game," in *Castle Rock: The Stephen King Newsletter* 2:4 (April, 1986): 2.

GE10. ***Cat's Eye***. MGM/United Artists, 1984. Beta/VHS. 94 minutes. See **G9**.

GE11. ***Children of the Corn.*** New World Pictures, 1984. Beta, VHS, Laser, CED. 93 minutes. See **G7**.

GE12. ***Firestarter.*** Universal Pictures, 1984. Beta, VHS, CED. 115 minutes. See **G8**.

GE13. ***Night Shift Collection.*** Granite Entertainment Group, Canoga Park CA. Includes *The Boogeyman* and *The Woman in the Room*. See **GE4**, **GE9**.

SECONDARY SOURCES AND REVIEWS:

1. *Fangoria* No. 52 (1986): .

GE14. ***Stephen King's Silver Bullet.*** Paramount Pictures. 1986. VHS, Beta. 95 minutes. See **G10**.

GE15. ***Tales from the Darkside.*** Laurel, 1985 (?). VHS, 70 minutes. See **GB2**.

EPISODES: "The Word Processor of the Gods," from a story by Stephen King; "Slippage," by David Patrick Kelly; "D'Jinn, No Chaser," by Charles Levin.

GE16. ***Maximum Overdrive.*** Karl-Lorimer Home Video, December 1986. See **G11**.

GE17. ***Stand By Me.*** RCS/Columbia Pictures Home Video, March 1987. VHS, Beta. 87 minutes. See **G12**.

GE18. ***The Last Rung on the Ladder.*** Talisman Productions, 1987. Produced by James Cole; directed by James Cole and Dan Thron; screenplay by James Cole and Dan Thron. 12 minutes, 30 seconds. See **B39**.

CAST: Adam Houhoulis, Melissa Whelden, Nat Wordell, Agam Howes. Student film, not available on videocassette.

SECONDARY SOURCES AND REVIEWS:

1. Blue, Tyson. "SK Flicks Not Found at a Theatre Near You," in *Castle Rock: The Stephen King Newsletter* 5:1 (January, 1989): 1, 8.
2. Cole, James. "The Good and Bad of Film Adaptation," in *Castle Rock: The Stephen King Newsletter* 4:9 (September, 1988): 1, 6.
3. Spignesi, Stephen J. "Student Cinema Focuses on Stephen King: 'The Last Rung on the Ladder' and 'The Lawnmower Man,'" in *The Complete Stephen King Encyclopedia*. Ann Arbor, MI: Popular Culture, Ink, May 1991, cloth, p. 602-605.

GE19. ***The Lawnmower Man.*** June 1987. New York University Student film production. Produced by Jim Gonis; directed by Jim Gonis; script by Mike DeLuca. 12 minutes. See **G22**.

CAST: E. D. Phillips, Andy Parks, Helen Hanft, Tony Di Sante, Robert Tossberg, Neil Schimmel.

SECONDARY SOURCES AND REVIEWS:

1. Blue, Tyson. "SK Flicks Not Found at a Theatre Near You," in *Castle Rock: The Stephen King Newsletter* 5:1 (January, 1989): 1, 8.
3. Spignesi, Stephen J. "Student Cinema Focuses on Stephen King: 'The Last Rung on the Ladder' and 'The Lawnmower Man,'" in *The Complete Stephen King Encyclopedia*. Ann Arbor, MI: Popular Culture, Ink, May 1991, cloth, p. 602-605.

GE20. ***Return to 'Salem's Lot.*** 1987. Project based loosely on King's characters, but without any participation by King.

GE21. ***Creepshow 2.*** New World Pictures, 1989. VHS. 92 minutes. Rated R. See **G13**.

GE22. ***The Running Man.*** Taft, 1989. VHS. Rated: R. See **G14**.

GE23. ***Pet Sematary.*** Paramount, 1989. VHS. 103 minutes. Rated: R. See **G15**.

SECONDARY SOURCES AND REVIEWS:

1. McCullaugh, Jim. "Horror Video: September Is Horror Month," in *Billboard Magazine* 101:38 (September 23, 1989): 54.

GE24. ***Tales from the Darkside: The Movie.*** Paramount, 1990. VHS. 93 minutes. Includes King's "The Cat From Hell." See **G16**.

SECONDARY SOURCES AND REVIEWS:

1. Collins, Max Allan. "Mystery Seen," in *Mystery Scene* No. 26 (June, 1990): 50.

GE25. ***Stephen King's Nightshift Collection***. Karl James Associates. Directed by John Woodward and Jack Garrett. 1989. 45 minutes. No rating.

EPISODES: "Disciples of the Crow" (1983); "The Night Waiter" (1987—student film).

GE26. ***Stephen King's Graveyard Shift.*** Paramount. June (?) 1991. 89 minutes. See **G17**.

GE27. ***Misery.*** Castle Rock Entertainment, with Nelson Entertainment, 1990. 107 minutes. See **G18**.

SECONDARY SOURCES AND REVIEWS:

1. Forer, Bruce. *Entertainment Weekly* No. 77 (August 2, 1991): 64.
2. "Sun Screening," in *Entertainment Weekly* No. 77 (August 2, 1991): 67. Notes that *Misery* is no. 1 on the rental charts for the previous week, moving up from #3.

GE28. ***Stephen King's Golden Years***. Produced in two formats: SP, 2-hour speed, two tapes, $29.95; and EP, 6-hour speed, one tape, $19.95. Both include a conclusion never broadcast. See **GB8**.

GE29. ***Stephen King's Sleepwalkers***. Columbia Tristar Home Video, 89 minutes, 1992. Rating: R. See **G19**.

GE30. ***The Lawnmower Man***. New Line Cinema, 1992. Director's cut; unrated. See **G22**.

GE31. ***The Dark Half***. Orion Home Video, 1993. 122 minutes. Rating: R. See **G20**.

GE32. ***Needful Things***. New Line Home Video/Columbia Tristar Home Video, 1994. 121 minutes. Rating: R. See **G21**.

GE33. ***The Tommyknockers***. Vidmark, 1993. 120 minutes. Rating: R. See **GB9**.

GE34. ***Stephen King's The Stand***. Republic Pictures; Greengrass Productions, 1994. Four cassettes. Also available in LASERDISC box set, which includes "The Making of *The Stand*." See **GB10**.

H.

AUDIO ADAPTATIONS OF KING MATERIALS

For general information on audiocassette adaptations, plus backgrounds to King's involvement with such projects, see the following:

Beahm, George, ed. *The Stephen King Companion*. Kansas City, MO: Andrews and McMeel, September 1989, cloth, p. 126-135.
Blue, Tyson. "King of Cassette: Reading SK by Ear," in *Castle Rock: The Stephen King Newsletter* 2:3 (March, 1986): 1, 5.

H1. ***The Ballad of the Flexible Bullet*,** produced by Recorded Books, Clinton, MD. Read by Frank Muller. #85330. 2 cassettes; reading time 3 hours. An unabridged recording. See **B78**.

H2. ***The Author Talks: Stephen King*,** produced by Recorded Books, Clinton, MD. #87380. 1 Cassette; reading time, 1 hour. A profile, interview, and reading of "Mrs. Todd's Shortcut." See **B77**.

H3. ***"Apt Pupil," from Different Seasons*,** produced by Recorded Books, Clinton, MD, 1984. Read by Frank Muller. #84065. 5 cassettes; reading time, 7½ hours. Unabridged recording. See **B62**.

H4. ***"The Body," from Different Seasons*,** produced by Recorded Books, Clinton, MD, 1984. Read by Frank Muller. #84064. 4 Cassettes; reading time, 6 hours. Unabridged recording. See **B63**.

H5. ***"The Breathing Method," from Different Seasons*,** produced by Recorded Books, Clinton, MD, 1984. Read by Frank Muller. #85230. 3 cassettes; running time, 4½ hours. Unabridged recording. See **B64**.

H6. ***"The Mist*,"** produced by ZBS Productions, Fort Edward NY, 1984. Directed by Bill Raymond. Adapted by M. Fulton. Musical score by Tim Clark. One cassette; reading time, 90 minutes. 3-D sound. See **B50**.

b. as: *"The Mist in 3-D Sound."* Simon & Shuster, May 1986. 90-minute adaptation.
c. Released on CD, digitally remastered from audiocassette.

SECONDARY SOURCES AND REVIEWS:

1. Barron, Neil. "King Between Your Ears," in *Fantasy Review* No. 76 (February, 1985): 16-17.

2. Beahm, George. "'The Mist' on Audiocassette: A Sound Idea," in *The Stephen King Companion,* edited by George Beahm. Kansas City, MO: Andrews & McMeel, September 1989, cloth, p. 131-133.
3. Blue, Tyson. "Review: 'The Mist' in 3-D Sound," in *Castle Rock: The Stephen King Newsletter* 2:7 (July, 1986): 5.
4. *Publishers Weekly* (April 4, 1986): 41-42.
5. *Publishers Weekly* (July 3, 1987): 38.
6. *Quill & Quire* 52 (September, 1986): 78.
7. *Time* 128 (July 21, 1986): 71.
8. *Washington Post Book World* 17 (February 22, 1987): 11.

H7. ***"Rita Hayworth & Shawshank Redemption," from Different Seasons***, produced by Recorded Books, Clinton, MD, 1984. Read by Frank Muller. #84063. 3 cassettes; reading time, 4½ hours. Unabridged recording. See **B61**.

H8. ***Best Stories from Stephen King***, produced by Book-of-the-Month Records, 1985. 19 cassettes. Various readers.

H9. ***"The Mist," from Skeleton Crew***, produced by Recorded Books, Clinton, MD, 1985. Read by Frank Muller. #85230. 3 cassettes; running time, 4½ hours. Unabridged recording. See **B50**.

H10. ***Skeleton Crew, (Book One)***, produced by Recorded Books, Clinton, MD, 1985. Read by Frank Miller. #85210. 6 cassettes; reading time, 9 hours. Unabridged recording. See **A28**.

CONTENTS: "The Raft"; "The Reaper's Image"; "The Monkey"; "Cain Rose Up"; "The Jaunt"; "Beachworld"; "Survivor Type"; "Morning Deliveries"; "Big Wheels"; "For Owen"; "The Man Who Wouldn't Shake Hands"; "The Reach"; "Uncle Otto's Truck."

H11. ***Skeleton Crew, (Book Two)***, produced by Recorded Books, Clinton, MD, 1985. Read by Frank Miller. #85220. 5 cassettes; reading time, 7½ hours. Unabridged recordings. See **A28**.

CONTENTS: "Mrs. Todd's Shortcut"; "The Wedding Gig"; "Nona"; "Paranoid: A Chant"; "Here There Be Tygers"; "The Ballad of the Flexible Bullet"; "Gramma."

H12. ***Stories from Night Shift***, produced by Warner Audio, 1985. Directed by Stuart Leigh. Read by Colin Fox. 2 cassettes. See **A6**.

H13. ***Thinner***, produced by Listening for Pleasure, Ltd., Downsview, Ontario, Canada, 1985. Two cassettes; 2½ hours. Text abridged by Sue Dawson. Read by Paul Sorvino. See **A27**.

SECONDARY SOURCES AND REVIEWS:

1. Beahm, George. "'Thinner' on Audiocassette," in *The Stephen King Companion*, edited by George Beahm. Kansas City, MO: Andrews & McMeel, September 1989, cloth, p. 134-135.
2. *Publishers Weekly* (July 3, 1987): 38.
3. *Science Fiction Chronicle* 7 (September, 1986): 42.
4. *Washington Post Book World* 16 (October 26, 1986): 10.

H14. ***Stephen King on The Larry King Live Show***, produced by Lion recordings. April 10, 1986. Playing time: 1½ hours. Tape of television/ radio interview.

H15. ***"Gramma,"*** produced by Audio Books/Random House, 1986, 1988. 1 cassette. 100 minutes. Read by Gale Garnett. Unabridged recording. See **B76**.

SECONDARY SOURCES AND REVIEWS:

1. *Publishers Weekly* (July 3, 1987): 36.

H16. ***"The Monkey,"*** produced by Warner Audio, New York, Summer 1986, 1988. 1 cassette. Read by David Purdham. Unabridged recording. See **B48**.

SECONDARY SOURCES AND REVIEWS:

1. *Publishers Weekly* (July 3, 1987): 36-37.

H17. ***"Mrs. Todd's Shortcut,"*** produced by Warner Audio, New York, Summer 1986. 1 cassette. Read by David Purdham. Unabridged recording. See **B77**.

H18. ***Night Shift,*** produced by Warner Audio, New York, 1986. Directed by Stuart Leigh. Read by Colin Fox. Set of 6 cassettes. See **A6**.

b. abridged as: *Night Shift*, produced by Sound Editions/Random House, 1988. 2 Cassettes. 130 minutes. Read by Colin Fox.

CONTENTS: "Strawberry Spring," "The Boogeyman," "Graveyard Shift," "The Man Who Loved Flowers," "One for the Road," "The Last Rung on the Ladder," "I Know What You Need," "Jerusalem's Lot," "I Am the Doorway."

SECONDARY SOURCES AND REVIEWS:

1. *Publishers Weekly* 231 (July 3, 1987): 38.
2. *School Library Journal* 32 (August, 1986): 24.

H19. ***The Stand,*** produced by Books on Tape, 1987. 2,070 minutes. Read by Grover Gardner. See **A5**.

SECONDARY SOURCES AND REVIEWS:

1. *Audio Video Review Digest, 1989 Cumulation,* edited by Susan L. Stetler. Detroit: Gale Research, 1990, cloth, p. 619.
2. *Library Journal* 114 (March 15, 1989): 100.

H20. ***The Dark Tower: The Gunslinger,*** produced by New Audio Library, July 1988. 4 cassettes; 6 hours, 18 minutes reading time. Read by Stephen King. Unabridged recordings. See **A17**.

SECONDARY SOURCES AND REVIEWS:

1. Blue, Tyson. "Dark Tower Tape Reviewed," in *Castle Rock: The Stephen King Newsletter* 4:8 (August, 1988): 5.

H21. ***The Dark Tower II: The Drawing of the Three,*** produced by New Audio Library, 1988. 8 cassettes. Read by Stephen King. 720 minutes. Unabridged recordings. See **A34**.

SECONDARY SOURCES AND REVIEWS:

1. *AudioVideo Review Digest, 1989 Cumulation,* edited by Susan L. Stetler. Detroit: Gale Research, 1990, cloth, p. 619.
2. Blue, Tyson. "Dark Tower II Audio Tapes Released," in *Castle Rock: The Stephen King Newsletter* 5:3 (March, 1989): 2, 6.
3. *Booklist* 85 (June 15, 1989): 1841.
4. *Publishers Weekly* 236 (March 3, 1989): 76.

H22. ***Prime Evil: A Taste of Blood,*** from *Prime Evil,* edited by Douglas E. Winter. New York: Simon and Schuster Audio Works, 1988, 1989. 2 cassettes; 150 minutes reading time. Read by Ed Begley. Unabridged recordings.

COMMENTS: Includes King's "Night Flier" (see **B89**) and two other stories. First of a series of audiocassettes based on Winter's collections.

SECONDARY SOURCES AND COMMENTS:

1. *AudioVideo Review Digest, 1989 Cumulation,* edited by Susan L. Stetler. Detroit: Gale Research, 1990, cloth, p. 619.
2. *Audio Video Review Digest* 2:3 (December, 1990): 155, 255.
3. *Locus* 22 (April, 1989): 13.
4. *Washington Post Book World* 20 (February 11, 1990): 11.

H23. ***The Stand,*** produced by Louise Braille Productions, Victoria, Australia, 1988. An audio-book for the handicapped. See **A5**.

SECONDARY SOURCES AND REVIEWS:

1. *Library Journal* 114 (March 14, 1989): 100. (?)

H24. ***The Shining,*** produced by Louise Braille Productions, Victoria, Australia, 1988. An audio-book for the handicapped. See **A3**.

H25. ***The Dark Half,*** produced by Hodder & Stoughton, London, October 19, 1989. Read by Stephen King. One cassette; 6 minutes. See **A39**.

H26. ***One Past Midnight: "The Langoliers,"*** produced by Penguin/High Bridge Audio, November 1990. Read by Willem Dafoe. See **B96**.

SECONDARY SOURCES AND REVIEWS:

1. Bauers, Sandy. *Wilson Library Journal* 65:8 (April, 1991): 71-72.
2. *Publishers Weekly* 238:6 (February 1, 1991): 45.

H27. ***Two Past Midnight: "Secret Window, Secret Garden,"*** produced by Penguin/High Bridge Audio. Read by James Wood. See **B97**.

SECONDARY SOURCES AND REVIEWS:

1. *Publishers Weekly* 238:25 (June 7, 1991): 44.

H28. ***Three Past Midnight: "The Library Policeman,"*** produced by Penguin/High Bridge Audio. Read by Ken Howard. May, 1991. See **B98**.

SECONDARY SOURCES AND REVIEWS:

1. Cheuse, Alan. *Forbes* 148:12 (November 25, 1991): F44.
2. Hiett, John. *Library Journal* 116:12 (July, 1991): 154.

H29. ***Four Past Midnight: "The Sun Dog,"*** produced by Penguin/High Bridge Audio, 1991. See **B99**.

SECONDARY SOURCES AND REVIEWS:

1. Annichiario, Mark. *Library Journal* 116:14 (September 1, 1991): 250.

H30. ***Needful Things, Part I: Grand Opening Celebration,*** produced by New American Library, September 30, 1991. Read by Stephen King. Six cassettes, 9 hours, $29.95. See **A44**.

b. Boxed set, with Parts II and III.
c. St. Paul, MN: Penguin-Highbridge Audio, 1991.

SECONDARY SOURCES AND REVIEWS:

1. Cheuse, Alan. *Forbes* 149:6 (March 16, 1992): S24.

H31. ***Needful Things, Part II: Sale of the Century,*** produced by New American Library, September 30, 1991. Read by Stephen King. Six cassettes, 9 hours, $29.95. See **A44**.

b. Boxed set, with Parts II and III.
c. St. Paul, MN: Penguin-Highbridge Audio, 1991.

H32. ***Needful Things, Part III: Everything Must Go,*** produced by New American Library, September 30, 1991. Read by Stephen King. Six cassettes, 9 hours, $29.95. See **A44**.

b. Boxed set, with Parts II and III.
c. St. Paul, MN: Penguin-Highbridge Audio, 1991.

H33. ***Needful Things, Parts I, II, III***. Produced by New American Library, September 30, 1991. Read by Stephen King. Eighteen cassettes, 27 hours, $89.85. See **A44**.

b. St. Paul, MN: Penguin-Highbridge Audio, 1991, $49.95.

H34. ***The Waste Lands: The Dark Tower III***. Produced by Penguin-Highbridge Audio, St. Paul, MN, 1991. Read by Stephen King. Twelve tapes, 18 hours. See **A43**.

SECONDARY SOURCES AND REVIEWS:

1. Smith, Kristen L. *Library Journal* 117:3 (February 15, 1991): 220.

H35. ***Gerald's Game***. Produced by Penguin-Highbridge Audio, St. Paul, MN, 1992. Read by Lindsay Crouse. Twelve cassettes; unabridged, 13 hours. See **A45**.

SECONDARY SOURCES AND REVIEWS:

1. Pober, Stanley. *Library Journal* 117:16 (October 1, 1992): 132.

H36. ***"The Revelations of 'Becka Paulson," in I Shudder at Your Touch***. 1992. See **B79**.

SECONDARY SOURCES AND REVIEWS:

1. Annichiarico, Mark. *Library Journal* 117:19 (November 15, 1992): 124.

H37. ***Dolores Claiborne***. Produced by Penguin-Highbridge Audio, St. Paul, MN, 1992. Read by Frances Sternhagen. Six cassettes, 9 hours. See **A46**.

SECONDARY SOURCES AND REVIEWS:

1. Annichiarico, Mark. *Library Journal* 118:1 (January, 1993): 186.
2. *Publishers Weekly* 239:53 (December 7, 1992): 28.

H38. ***Nightmares & Dreamscapes: I***. Produced by Penguin-Highbridge Audio, St. Paul, MN, 1993. Read by Tim Curry, Whoopi Goldberg, Stephen J.

Gould, Stephen King, Tabitha King, Rob Lowe, Robert B. Parker, Yardley Smith. Eight cassettes, 9½ hours. See **A47**.

CONTENTS: "Suffer the Little Children," "Rainy Season," "The House on Maple Street."

SECONDARY SOURCES AND REVIEWS:

1. Vignovich, Ray. *Library Journal* 119:1 (January, 1994): 186+.

H39. *Nightmares & Dreamscapes: II*. Produced by Penguin-Highbridge Audio, St. Paul, MN, 1994. Read by Stephen King, Kathy Bates, Tim Curry, Matthew Broderick, David Cronenberg, Jerry Garcia, Eve Beglarian. Eight cassettes, 9 hours. See **A47**.

CONTENTS: "Chattery Teeth," "The Moving Finger," "Home Delivery," "Sneakers."

SECONDARY SOURCES AND REVIEWS:

1. *Publishers Weekly* 241:14 (April 4, 1994): 32.

H40. *Night Shift, Vol. 1*. Produced by Bantam Doubleday Dell Audio, New York, 1994. Read by John Glover. Four cassettes. See **A6**.

CONTENTS: "The Bogeyman," "I Know What You Need," "Strawberry Spring," "The Woman in the Room," "Battleground."

H41. *Graveyard Shift and Other Tales from Night Shift* [Night Shift, Vol. II]. Produced by Bantam Doubleday Dell Audio, New York, 1994. Read by John Glover. Three cassettes, 205 minutes. See **A6**.

H42. *Insomnia*. Produced by Penguin-Highbridge Audio, St. Paul, MN, 1994. Read by Eli Wallach. Twenty-one cassettes, unabridged text, 26 hours. See **A48**.

H43. *Nightmares & Dreamscapes: III*. Produced by Penguin-Highbridge Audio, St. Paul, MN, November 1994. Read by Stephen King, Gary Sinise, Frank Muller, Joe Morton, Dominic Cuskern, Grace Slick, Joe Mategna. Eight cassettes, 9 hours. See **A47**.

CONTENTS: "The Night Flier," "It Grows on You," "You Know They Got a Hell of a Band," "The Ten O'Clock People," "The Fifth Quarter," "The Beggar and the Diamond."

H44. *Rose Madder*. Produced by Penguin-Highbridge Audio, St. Paul, MN, 1995. See **A49**.

MISCELLANEOUS AUDIO ADAPTATIONS

HB1. **"The Monkey,"** radio adaptation. October 31, Halloween Night, 1985. *The 1985 Halloween Broadcast for UNICEF*. By Dennis Etchison. See **B48**.

COMMENTS: Special segment that included Etchison's "The Night Man," Richard Matheson's "The Children of Noah," William F. Nolan's "The Party," and the King story.

HB2. ***The Mist***. Computer game. Mindscape Software. Mindscape, Inc., Northbridge, IL. See **B50**.

HB3. **Soundtrack for *Stand By Me*.** See **G12**.

HB4. **Soundtrack for *Maximum Overdrive*,** music by AD/DC. See **G11**.

PART TWO

SECONDARY SOURCES

I.

SECONDARY SOURCES

BOOKS AND BOOK-LENGTH STUDIES

The year 1982 saw the publication of two seminal studies of Stephen King's work: Tim Underwood and Chuck Miller issued an anthology of critical essays, *Fear Itself: The Horror Fiction of Stephen King*; and Douglas E. Winter published *Stephen King* in the Starmont Reader's Guides to Contemporary Science Fiction and Fantasy Authors series. By the end of 1995, those volumes will have been augmented by over fifty additional studies, ranging from narrowly focused single-author works to collections of essays and pictorial overviews of television and film adaptations, including Stephen J. Spignesi's monumental encyclopedia of all things King. At this point, the studies available encompass everything from fan-oriented appreciations to careful examinations of King's place within specific literary and academic traditions. Generalized discussions and evaluations of book-length critical works devoted to King include the following:

Barron, Neil, ed. *Horror Literature: A Reader's Guide*. GARLAND REFERENCE LIBRARY OF THE HUMANITIES, Vol. 1220. New York: Garland Publishing, 1990.

Beahm, George. *The Stephen King Companion*. Kansas City, MO: Andrews and McMeel, September 1989.

Blue, Tyson. "Book List," in *Castle Rock: The Stephen King Newsletter* 2:10 (October, 1986): 4, 8.

Blue, Tyson. "Books Offer Something for Everyone at Christmas," in *Courier Herald* [Dublin, GA] (December 14, 1985): .

Blue, Tyson. "Research Material on King Abounds," in *Macon* [Georgia] *Telegraph and News* "Books/The Arts" (May 3, 1987): 10E, 14E.

Collings, Michael R. *The Annotated Guide to Stephen King: A Primary and Secondary Bibliography of the Works of America's Premier Horror Writer*. STARMONT REFERENCE GUIDE, No. 8. Mercer Island, WA: Starmont House, 1986.

Collings, Michael R. *The Stephen King Phenomenon*. Mercer Island, WA: Starmont House, 1987.

Gaul, Lou. "Hey, Film Fans! It's Time to Hit Books Again," in *Burlington County Times* [New Jersey] (November 28, 1985): B1, B4.

Harris, Ian. "SK Critics Criticized," in *Castle Rock: The Stephen King Newsletter* 2:2 (February, 1986): 3.

Spignesi, Stephen J. *The Shape Under The Sheet: The Complete Stephen King Encyclopedia*. Ann Arbor, MI: Popular Culture, Ink., May 1991, cloth, p. 673-677.

Wolfe, Gary K. "Strange Invaders: An Essay-Review," in *Modern Fiction Studies* 32:1 (Spring 1986): 133-151.

I1. THE NOVELS OF STEPHEN KING

I1. ***The Novels of Stephen King: Teacher's Manual,*** by Edward J. Zagorski. New York: Education Department, New American Library, 1981, 46 p., paper. A pamphlet, then free upon request from NAL. [teacher's manual]

CONTENTS: "*Carrie*"; "*Salem's Lot*"; "*The Shining*"; "*The Stand*"; "*The Dead Zone*"; "*Firestarter*"; "*Night Shift*"; "*Frankenstein*, *Dracula*, and *Dr. Jekyll and Mr. Hyde*."

COMMENTS: The guide is directed toward teaching King's work in secondary schools and colleges. Although limited in scope, it does provide plot synopses for major novels through 1981, followed by discussion questions and suggested classroom activities.

I2. FEAR ITSELF

I2. ***Fear Itself: The Horror Fiction of Stephen King,*** edited by Tim Underwood and Chuck Miller. San Francisco, CA, Columbia, PA: Underwood-Miller, 1982, 255 p., cloth. Limited signed edition. [anthology of critical essays]

CONTENTS: "Introduction—Meeting Stevie," by Peter Straub; "Foreword—On Becoming a Brand Name," by Stephen King; "Cinderella's Revenge-Twists on Fairy Tale and Mythic Themes in the Work of Stephen King," by Chelsea Quinn Yarbro; "Horror Springs in the Fiction of Stephen King," by Don Herron; "Horror Hits a High," by Fritz Leiber; "The Movies and Mr. King," by Bill Warren; "Stephen King: Horror and Humanity for Our Time," by Deborah L. Notkin; "The Grey Arena," by Charles L. Grant; "King and the Literary Tradition of Horror and the Supernatural," by Ben P. Indick; "The Marsten House in *'Salem's Lot*," by Alan Ryan; "The Night Journeys of Stephen King," by Douglas E. Winter; "Stephen King: A Bibliography," by Marty Ketchum, Daniel J. H. Levack, and Jeff Levin; "Afterword," by George A. Romero; Notes on the Contributors.

REPRINTS:

ab. San Francisco, CA, Columbia, PA: Underwood-Miller, 1982, 255 p., cloth. Trade edition.
ac. as: *Fear Itself: The Early Works of Stephen King*. Novato, CA, Lancaster, PA: Underwood-Miller, 1993, 239 p., trade paper.
b. New York: A Plume Book, New American Library, June 1984, 277 p., trade paper.
bb. New York: A Signet Book, New American Library, 286 , p., mass-market paper.
c. London & Sydney: Pan Books, 1990, 255 p., paper.

SECONDARY SOURCES AND REVIEWS:

1. Anders, Smiley. "Fear Itself," in *Morning Advocate* [Baton Rouge, LA] (May 15, 1983): . As microfiche: *NewsBank: Literature* 9 (June, 1983): Fiche 98, G12.
2. *Choice* 20 (March, 1983): 985.
3. Eng, Steve. "Fantasy Writers Focus of Study," in *The Tennessean Sunday Bookcase* (January 23, 1983): 4F.
4. *Fantasy Review* 7 (January, 1984): 53.
5. Graham, Mark. "Critics Dissect Horror of Stephen King's Work," by Mark Graham, in *Rocky Mountain News* [Denver, CO]: .
6. *Kliatt Young Adult Paperback Guide* 20 (Winter, 1986): 24.
7. *Library Journal* 108 (March 1, 1983): 500.
8. *Voice of Youth Advocates* 6 (April, 1983): 57.
9. *West Coast Review of Books* 9 (March, 1983): 45.

I3. STEPHEN KING

I3. ***Stephen King,*** by Douglas E. Winter. STARMONT READER'S GUIDE, No. 16. Series Editor, Roger Schlobin. Mercer Island, WA: Starmont House, October 1982, 128 p., cloth [issued simultaneously in trade paperback]. [critique]

CONTENTS: "Foreword," by Winter; "Chronology"; "Introduction: Do the Dead Sing?"; "*Carrie*"; "*'Salem's Lot*"; "*The Shining*"; "*The Stand* and *The Dark Tower*"; "*The Dead Zone*"; "*Firestarter*"; "*The Mist*"; "*Cujo*"; "*Different Seasons, Christine*...and Other Stories"; "Primary Bibliography"; "Secondary Bibliography"; Index.

The Book was substantially revised as *Stephen King: The Art of Darkness* (see **I5**).

REPRINTS:

b. San Bernardino, CA: The Borgo Press, 1982, 128 p., cloth.
c. excerpted in: *Contemporary Literary Criticism, Volume 37,* edited by Daniel G. Marowski. Detroit, MI: Gale Research Co., 1986, cloth, p. 200-201. Review of *The Stand*.

SECONDARY SOURCES AND REVIEWS:

1. *Choice* 20 (March, 1983): 992.
2. Eng, Steve. "Fantasy Writers Focus of Study," in *The Tennessean Sunday Bookcase* (January 23, 1983): 4F.
3. *The Magazine of Fantasy & Science Fiction* 32 (Spring, 1986): 148.

I4. ENTERPRISE INCIDENTS PRESENTS STEPHEN KING

I4. ***Enterprise Incidents Presents Stephen King***, by James Van Hise. Tampa, FL: New Media, 1984, 58 p., trade paper. [critique]

CONTENTS: "The Stephen King Review"; "Steve Bissette Illustrated Story"; "Uncollected Short Fiction"; "Egyptian Graffiti"; "Stephen King One of a Kinds."

I5. STEPHEN KING: THE ART OF DARKNESS

I5. *Stephen King: The Art of Darkness,* by Douglas E. Winter. New York: NAL Books, New American Library, November 1984, xix+252 p., cloth. [critique]

CONTENTS: "Foreword"; "Chronology"; "Introduction: Do the Dead Sing?"; "Notes Toward a Biography: Living with the Boogeyman"; "*Carrie*"; "'*Salem's Lot*"; "*The Shining*"; "*The Stand*"; "*The Dark Tower: The Gunslinger*"; "*The Dead Zone*"; "*Firestarter*"; "*The Mist*"; "*Cujo*"; "*Different Seasons*"; "*Creepshow*"; "*Christine, Cycle of the Werewolf*"; "*Pet Sematary*"; "*The Talisman*"; "...Always More Tales"; Appendix A: "Short Fiction"; Appendix B: "Motion Picture and Television Adaptations"; "Notes"; "A Stephen King Bibliography"; Index.

COMMENTS: A substantial reworking of Winter's original monograph for the Starmont Reader's Guides series (see **I3**).

REPRINTS:

b. *Stephen King: The Art of Darkness*, expanded and updated ed. New York: A Plume Book, New American Library, June 1986, xx+297 p., trade paper. New contents include: "*Night Shift, Skeleton Crew,* and Other Stories"; "Appendix A: "The Bachman Books."

bb. New York: A Signet Book, New American Library, December 1986, xxi+327 p., mass-market paper.

c. Sevenoaks, Kent: New English Library, 1989, xxi+327 p., mass-market paper.

SECONDARY SOURCES AND REVIEWS:

1. Blue, Tyson. "King Biography Published in Revised Edition," by Tyson Blue, in *The Courier Herald* [Dublin, GA]: .
2. Blue, Tyson. "Review: *Stephen King: The Art of Darkness*" in *Castle Rock: The Stephen King Newsletter* 2:7 (July, 1986): 11.
3. *Book World* 14 (December 23, 1984): 11.
4. *Book World* 16 (June 22, 1986): 12.
5. *Fangoria* No. 45 (1985): .
6. *Fantasy Mongers* 13 (Winter 1984/1985): 5.
7. *Fantasy Review* 8 (March, 1985): 15.
8. Grooms, Roger. "A Bit of Light Shed on Master of Darkness," in *Cincinnati Enquirer* (November 25, 1984): . As microfiche: *Newsbank: Literature* 11 (December, 1984): Fiche 62, E8.
9. Johnson, Eric. *Library Journal* 109 (November 15, 1984): 2151.
10. *Kliatt Young Adult Paperback Book Guide* 21 (Spring, 1987): 27.
11. *Library Journal* 109 (November 15, 1984): 2151.
12. *The Magazine of Fantasy & Science Fiction* 32 (Spring, 1986): 135.

13. Neilson, Keith. "King Gets Compatible Critic," in *Fantasy Review* 77 (March, 1985): 15-16.
14. *Science Fiction Chronicle* 8 (April, 1987): 38.
15. *Science Fiction Review* 15 (November, 1986): 45.
16. *Voice of Youth Advocates* 8 (April, 1985): 70.
17. *West Coast Review of Books* 10 (November, 1984): 34.

I6. DISCOVERING STEPHEN KING

I6. *Discovering Stephen King*, edited by Darrell Schweitzer. STARMONT STUDIES IN LITERARY CRITICISM, No. 8. Mercer Island, WA: Starmont House, 1985, 219 p., cloth. [anthology of critical essays]

CONTENTS: "Introduction," by Schweitzer; "What Makes Him So *Scary?*," by Ben P. Indick; "Has Success Spoiled Stephen King?," by Alan Warren; "The Biggest Horror Fan of the All," by Don Herron; "Stephen King's American Gothic," by Gary William Crawford; "The Early Tales: Stephen King and *Startling Mystery Stories*," by Chet Williamson; "Stephen King and Peter Straub: Fear and Friendship," by Bernadette Bosky; "*The Stand*: Science Fiction into Fantasy," by Michael R. Collings; "Stephen King with a Twist: The E.C. Influence," Debra Stump; "*Cycle of the Werewolf* and the Moral Tradition of Horror," by Randall Larson; "Stephen King and the Lovecraft Mythos," by Robert M. Price; "Three by Bachman," by Don D'Ammassa; "A Matter of Choice: King's *Cujo* and Malamud's *The Natural*," by Debra Stump; "The Ultimate Horror: The Dead Child in Stephen King's Stories and Novels," by Leonard Heldreth; "Collecting Stephen King," by Darrell Schweitzer; "Synopses of Stephen King's Fiction," by Sanford Z. Meschkow (with additions by Darrell Schweitzer, Michael R. Collings, and Ben Indick); "Stephen King: A Bibliography," by Marshall Tymn; "Contributors"; "Index."

REPRINTS:

ab. Mercer Island, WA: Starmont House, 1985, 219 p., trade paper.
b. San Bernardino, CA: Borgo Press, 1985, 219 p., cloth.

SECONDARY SOURCES AND REVIEWS:

1. Bertin, Eddy C. *SF Gids* ["SF Guide"] 91 (November, 1986): . [Dutch]
2. *Choice* 23 (March, 1986): 1060.
3. *Fantasy Review* 9 (May, 1986): 135.
4. Reed, Glenn. "King Congeries," in *Fantasy Review* 91 (May, 1986): 29.
5. *Science Fiction Chronicle* 7 (March, 1986): 37.

I7. STEPHEN KING AS RICHARD BACHMAN

I7. ***Stephen King as Richard Bachman,*** by Michael R. Collings. STARMONT STUDIES IN LITERARY CRITICISM, No. 10. Mercer Island, WA: Starmont House, 1985, 168 p., cloth. [critique]

CONTENTS: 1. "A History for Richard Bachman"; 2. "Genre, Theme, and Image in Richard Bachman"; 3. "*Rage*"; 4. "*The Long Walk*"; 5. "*Roadwork*"; 6. "*The Running Man*"; 7. "*Thinner*"; 8. "Speculations"; Appendix—"The Bachman Novels, Synopses"; List of Works Cited; Index.

REPRINTS:

ab. Mercer Island, WA: Starmont House, 1985, 168 p., trade paper.
ac. Mercer Island, WA: Starmont House, January 1986, 168 p., cloth. Second printing.
ad. Mercer Island, WA: Starmont House, January 1986, 168 p., trade paper. Second printing.
b. San Bernardino, CA: Borgo Press, 1985, 168 p., cloth.
c. excerpted as: "Collings Studies King," in *Castle Rock: The Stephen King Newsletter* 1:6 (June 1985): 8-9. Excerpts from Chapter 2.
d. excerpted and revised as: *King Versus Koontz: Style and* Invasion," in *Footsteps VIII* (November, 1986): 32-42, 45.
e. excerpted in: *Contemporary Literary Criticism, Volume 37,* edited by Daniel G. Marowski. Detroit, MI: Gale Research Co., 1986, cloth, p. 207-208.

SECONDARY SOURCES AND REVIEWS:

1. Barron, Neil, ed. *Horror Literature: A Reader's Guide*. New York: Garland Publishing, 1990, cloth, p. 403.
2. Barron, Neil. "Starmont King Series" in *Fantasy Review* 8 (December, 1985): 26.
3. *Beacham's Popular Fiction: 1950-Present, American and British*, edited by Walter Beacham. Washington, DC: Beacham, 1986, cloth.
4. Bertin, Eddy. *SF-Gids* 60 (January, 1986): 29-30.
5. *Bibliographic Index* (April 1986): 119.
6. Blue, Tyson. "Book List," in *Castle Rock* 2:10 (October, 1986): 4+.
7. Blue, Tyson. "Research Material on King Abounds," in *Macon Telegraph and News* [Macon, GA] (May 3, 1987): 6.
8. *Booklist* 82 (October 15, 1985): 304.
9. Elkins, Charles. "Space: Special projects and Critical Endeavors," in *SFRA Newsletter* (September, 1986): 21-22.
10. Gaul, Lou. "Hey, Film Fans, It's Time To Hit the Books Again," in *Burlington County Times* [New Jersey] (November 28, 1985): B1+.

11. Gaul, Lou. "King Giving Pen a Rest," in *Burlington County Times* [New Jersey] (November 5, 1986): 19.
12. Gaul, Lou. "Stephen King—A Fire Starter," in *Daily Intelligencer/ Montgomery County Record* (August 19, 1985): .
13. Graham, Mark. "Revealing Work Examines King-Bachman Connection," in *Rocky Mountain Daily News* [Denver, CO] (September 15, 1985): .
14. Hall, Hal W., and Geraldine Hutchins. *Science Fiction and Fantasy Research Index, Volume 6.* San Bernardino, CA: Borgo Press, 1986.
15. Harris, Ian. "Arnold Who?" in *Castle Rock: The Stephen King Newsletter* (June 1986): 3.
16. [Hokenson, Jan]. *Fantasy Review* (October, 1985): 37.
17. *Literary Criticism Register* (November, 1985): 6862; and (April/May, 1986): 3030.
18. *The Magazine of Fantasy & Science Fiction* 32 (Spring, 1986): 135.
19. Myers, Greg. *Comic Buyers Guide* (December 17, 1985): .
20. *SF Chronicle* 7 (Fall, 1986): 36.
21. Siegel, Mark. *Choice* 23 (December, 1985): 602.
22. Tymn, Marshall. *The Year's Scholarship in Science Fiction, Fantasy, and Horror Literature*, in *Extrapolation* (Summer, 1986): 147.
23. *Weinberg Books Catalogue* (October 1985): .
24. Wolfe, Gary K. "Strange Invaders: A Review," in *Modern Fiction Studies* 32:1 (Spring, 1986): 133-151.

I8. THE SHORTER WORKS OF STEPHEN KING

I8. ***The Shorter Works of Stephen King,*** by Michael R. Collings and David A. Engebretson. STARMONT STUDIES IN LITERARY CRITICISM, No. 9. Mercer Island, WA: Starmont House, June 1985, 202 p., cloth. [critique]

CONTENTS: "Foreword," by Collings and Engebretson; "Abbreviations"; "Chronology," by Collings and Engebretson; 1. "The Early Uncollected Stories," by Collings; 2. "*Night Shift*," by Engebretson; 3. "*Different Seasons,*" by Engebretson; 4."*The Dark Tower,*" by Collings; 5. "*Creepshow*," by Engebretson; 6. "*Skeleton Crew*," by Collings; 7. "The Later Uncollected Stories," by Collings; Checklist; List of Works Cited; Index.

COMMENTS: The study provides brief bibliographical notations for each story included, followed by a short plot outline and a survey of critical or interpretive readings.

REPRINTS:

ab. Mercer Island, WA: Starmont House, June 1985, 202 p., trade paper.
b. San Bernardino, CA: Borgo Press, 1985, 202 p., cloth.

SECONDARY SOURCES AND REVIEWS:

1. Barron, Neil, ed. *Horror Literature: A Reader's Guide*. New York: Garland Publishing, 1990, cloth, p. 403.
2. Beacham, Walter, ed. *Beacham's Popular Fiction: 1950-Present, American and British*. Washington, DC: Beacham, 1986.
3. Bertin, Eddy. *SF-Gids* 60 (January, 1986): 30-31.
4. *Bibliographic Index* (April 1986): 118.
5. Blue, Tyson. *The Unseen King*. Mercer Island, WA: Starmont House, 1989.
6. Gaul, Lou. "Hey, Film Fans, It's Time to Hit the Books Again," in *Burlington County Times* [New Jersey] (November 28, 1985): B1+.
7. Hall, Hal W. and Geraldine Hutchins. *Science Fiction and Fantasy Research Index, Volume 6*. San Bernardino, CA: Borgo Press, 1986.
8. [Hokenson, Jan]. *Fantasy Review* (October, 1985): 37.
9. Kaminsky, S. M. *Choice* 23 (March, 1986): 119.
10. Kober, Karl D. *Fantasy Review* 9 (May 1986): 29.
11. *Literary Criticism Register* (November, 1985): 6861.
12. *Literary Criticism Register* (April/May, 1986): 3029.
13. *Magazine of Fantasy & Science Fiction* 32 (Spring, 1986): 135.
14. Myers, Greg. *Comics Buyers Guide* (December 17, 1985): .
15. *Science Fiction Chronicle* 7 (May 1986): 37.
16. Tymn, Marshall. *The Year's Scholarship in Science Fiction, Fantasy and Horror Literature*. *Extrapolation* (Summer, 1986): 147.
17. Wolfe, Gary K. "Strange Invaders: An Essay-Review." *Modern Fiction Studies* 32:1 (Spring, 1986): 133-151.

I9. THE MANY FACETS OF STEPHEN KING

I9. ***The Many Facets of Stephen King,*** by Michael R. Collings. STARMONT STUDIES IN LITERARY CRITICISM, No. 11. Mercer Island, WA: Starmont House, 1985, 190 p., cloth. [critique]

CONTENTS: Foreword; List of Abbreviations; 1. "Chronology and Criticism"; 2. "The Search for a Form"; 3. "Along the Main Stream"; 4. "The Twilight Lands"; 5. "'Ghosties and Ghoulies'"; 6. "One in Every Garage"; 7. "Exploring Tangential Worlds"; "8. "And Beyond." CHECKLIST: Primary Works: 1. Books; 2. Collections; 3. Short Fiction and Poetry; 4. Non-Fiction and Criticism; 5. Film Versions of King's Works; Secondary Works: 1. Criticism and Reviews; 2. Interviews and Profiles. List of Works Cited. Index.

COMMENTS: *Many Facets* provides a thematic study of King's novels, from *Carrie* through the Philtrum Press edition of *The Eyes of the Dragon,* with pre-publication references to *It, Misery, Tommyknockers,* and the trade edition of *The Eyes of the Dragon*. Also includes a checklist of primary and secondary works, later expanded into *The Annotated Guide to Stephen King*.

REPRINTS:

ab. Mercer Island, WA: Starmont House, 1985, 190 p., trade paper.
b. San Bernardino, CA: Borgo Press, 1985, 190 p., cloth.

SECONDARY SOURCES AND REVIEWS:

1. Barron, Neil. *Horror Literature: A Reader's Guide.* New York: Garland Publishing Co., 1990, cloth, p. 403.
2. Beacham, Walter. *Beacham's Popular Fiction: 1950-Present, American and British.* Washington DC: Beacham, 1986.
3. Bertin, Eddy C. *SF-Gids* 81 (January, 1986): .
4. Bertin, Eddy C. *SF-Gids* 78 (August, 1987): .
5. *Bibliographic Index* (August 1986): 102.
6. Hall, Hal W., and Jan Swanbeck. *Science Fiction and Fantasy Research Index, Volume 7.* San Bernardino, CA: Borgo Press, 1987.
7. *Literary Criticism Register* (July, 1986): 3741.
8. *Literary Criticism Register* (August/September, 1986): 4418.
9. Sanders, Joe. *Fantasy Review* 9 (May 1986): 28.
10. Walker, David. "Writings About Stephen King Almost as Prolific As His Books." *El Paso Herald-Post* [Texas] (November 10, 1986): C4.
11. Wiater, Stanley. "The Stephen King Phenomenon." *The Valley Advocate* [Massachusetts] (July 21, 1986): 30.

I10. As Novas Zonas da Morte

I10. ***As Novas Zonas da Morte: Uma Introduçao à Obra de Stephen King***, by Pedro Garcia Rosado. Porta, Portugal: Fantasporto, 1985, 47 p., paper. [Portuguese-language critique]

I11. Kingdom of Fear

I11. ***Kingdom of Fear: The World of Stephen King***, edited by Tim Underwood and Chuck Miller. San Francisco, CA, Columbia, PA: Underwood-Miller, April 1986, 267 p., cloth. Limited edition of 500 numbered copies, signed by 13 contributors (excluding King). [critical anthology]

CONTENTS: "The Horror Writer and the Ten Bears: Foreword," by Stephen King; "Stephen King's Horror Has a Healing Power: Foreword," by Andrew M. Greeley; "Monsters in Our Midst: Introduction," by Robert Bloch; "A Girl Named Carrie: Introduction," by Bill Thompson; "Welcome to Room 217: Introduction," by Ramsey Campbell; "Thanks to the Crypt-Keeper: Introduction," by Whitley Strieber; "Fantasy as Commodity and Myth: Introduction," by Leslie Fiedler; "Surviving the Ride," by Clive Barker; "Two Selections from Harlan Ellison's Watching," by Harlan Ellison; "The Unexpected and the Inevitable," by Michael McDowell; "The Good Fabric: Of Night Shifts and Sleketon Crews," by William F. Nolan; "The Life and Death of Richard Bachman: Stephen King's Doppelgänger," by Stephen P. Brown; "King: The Good, the Bad and the Academic," by Don Herron; "Stephen King Goes to the Movies," by Chuck Miller; "King as a Writer for Children," by Ben P. Indick; "The Mind's a Monkey: Character and Psychology in Stephen King's Recent Fiction," by Bernadette Bosky; "King's Charactes: The Main(e) Heat," by Thomas F. Monteleone; "The Skull Beneath the Skin," by Tim Underwood.

COMMENTS: The anthology presents a broad overview of responses to King's fictions, with initial emphasis on evaluations and appreciations by his fellow writers.

REPRINTS:

ab. San Francisco, CA, Columbia, PA: Underwood-Miller, 1986, 267 p., trade hardcover.
b. New York: A Plume Book, New American Library, September, 1986, 270 p., trade paper.
bb. New York: A Signet Book, New American Library, October 1987, 316 p., mass-market paper.
c. Sevenoaks, Kent: New English Library, 1987, 283 p., paper.

SECONDARY SOURCES AND REVIEWS:

1. *Book World* 16 (September 14, 1986): 12.
2. Blue, Tyson. *Castle Rock: The Stephen King Newsletter* 2:5 (May, 1986): 2.
3. Blue, Tyson. "Stephen King Fans Will Enjoy *Kingdom of Fear*," in *Macon Telegraph & News* [GA] (November 9, 1986): .
4. Penny, Susan. *School Library Journal* 33 (January, 1987): 92.
5. *Science Fiction Chronicle* 8 (December, 1986): 49.
6. *School Library Journal* 33 (January, 1987): 92.
7. Zacharias, Gary. "Seventeen Essays on Stephen King's Horror," in *Fantasy Review* 9 (November, 1986): 38.

I12. THE FILMS OF STEPHEN KING

I12. ***The Films of Stephen King***, by Michael R. Collings. STARMONT STUDIES IN LITERARY CRITICISM, No. 12. Mercer Island, WA: Starmont House, July 1986, 201 p., cloth. [film critique]

CONTENTS: Foreword; Abbreviations; 1. "Novel Versus Film"; 2. "On the Nature of Horror"; 3. "*Carrie*"; 4. "*Salem's Lot*"; 5. "*The Shining*"; 6. "*Creepshow*"; 7. "*Cujo*"; 8. "*Dead Zone*"; 9. "*Christine*"; 10. "*Children of the Corn*"; 11. "*Firestarter*"; 12. "*Cat's Eye*"; 13. "*Silver Bullet*"; 14. "Short Features"; 15. "Films in Production"; "Filmography"; "Works Cited and Consulted"; Index.

COMMENTS: Viewer-response criticism and backgrounds to the adaptations, with particular attention to King's original narratives. No illustrations or photographs in the English edition.

REPRINTS:

ab. Mercer Island, WA: Starmont House, July 1986, 201 p., trade paper.
b. San Bernardino, CA: Borgo Press, 1986, 201 p., cloth.
c. expanded as: *Stephen King und Seine Filme*. HEYNE FILMBIBLIOTHEK, 112. Translated by Norbert Stresau. München: Wilhelm Heyne Verlag, 1987, 288 p., paper. Illustrated with stills from the films. New contents for this edition include chapters on *Maximum Overdrive* and *Stand By Me*.

SECONDARY SOURCES AND REVIEWS:

1. Barron, Neil. "A Critical Survey of Fantastic Literature and Film Scholarship in 1987," in *Science Fiction & Fantasy Book Review Annual*, edited by Robert A. Collins and Robert Latham. Westport, CT: Meckler, 1988, cloth, p. 51-76 (esp. 69).
2. Barron, Neil. *Horror Literature: A Reader's Guide*. New York: Garland Publishing, 1990, cloth, p. 441.
3. Bertin, Eddy C. *SF-Gids* 81 (January, 1986): .
4. Bertin, Eddy C. *SF-Gids* (October, 1986): .
5. *Fantasy Review* 9 (October, 1986): 31.
6. Hall, Hal W., and Jan Swanbeck. *Science Fiction and Fantasy Research Index, Volume 7*. San Bernardino, CA: Borgo Press, 1987.
7. Kaminsky, S. M. *Choice* 24 (December, 1986): 206.
8. Klossner, Michael. *Science Fiction & Fantasy Book Review Annual*, edited by Robert A Collins and Robert Latham. Westport, CT: Meckler, 1988, cloth, p. 398. Review of *Stephen King Goes to Hollywood*, by Jeff Conner.
9. Landon, Brooks. *Extrapolation* (Summer, 1987): 174-176.
10. *Literary Criticism Register* (March, 1986): 7.
11. Sorel, Claire. "Notes de Lecture." *Starfix* (December, 1986): 80. French-language publication.

I13. STEPHEN KING: AT THE MOVIES

I13. ***Stephen King: At the Movies,*** by Jessie Horsting. New York: Starlog Press [distributed by New American Library], August 1986, 112 p., paper. Illustrated with stills and photographs. [film critique]

CONTENTS: "Introduction," by Horsting; "Who is This Guy Stephen King?—And Why Do They Make All Those Movies?"; "Carrie"; "The Shining"; "Creepshow"; "The Dead Zone"; "Christine"; "Cujo"; "Firestarter"; "Children of the Corn"; "Cat's Eye"; "Silver Bullet"; "Maximum Overdrive"; "Stand by Me"; "Salem's Lot"; "The Word Processor of the Gods"; "Gramma"; "Night Shift"; "Why the Children Don't Look Like Their Parents," by Harlan Ellison; "Film Credits"; "Films on Video."

REPRINTS:

b. as: *Stephen King und Seine Filme*. Bergisch Gladbach, West Germany: Bastei-Lübbe Verlag (Paperback 71200), 1987, p., paper. Translated by Harro Christensen and Helmut W. Pesch. [German]

SECONDARY SOURCES AND REVIEWS:

1. Blue, Tyson. *Castle Rock: The Stephen King Newsletter* 2:10 (October, 1986): 6.
2. Blue, Tyson. "Book Review: *Stephen King at the Movies*," in *Castle Rock: The Stephen King Newsletter* 2:12/3:1 (December, 1986/January, 1987): 6.
3. Bourget, Jean-Louis. "Notes de Lecture," in *Starfix* (December, 1986): 80. French-language publication.
4. Leonard, Stephanie. "Books on SK Films Similar," in *Castle Rock: The Stephen King Newsletter* 3:9 (September, 1987): 1, 5.

I14. THE ANNOTATED GUIDE TO STEPHEN KING

I14. ***The Annotated Guide to Stephen King: A Primary and Secondary Bibliography of the Works of America's Premier Horror Writer***, by Michael R. Collings. STARMONT REFERENCE GUIDE, No. 8. Mercer Island, WA: Starmont House, October 1986, 176 p., cloth. [bibliography]

CONTENTS: "Foreword"; "List of Abbreviations." PART ONE: PRIMARY BIBLIOGRAPHY—A. "Book-Length Fiction"; B. "Collections of King's Fictions"; C. "Short Fiction and Poetry"; D. "Non-Fiction, Criticism, and Reviews"; "E. "The Audio-Visual King".

PART TWO: SECONDARY BIBLIOGRAPHY—F. "Bibliographic Studies"; G. "Book-Length Critical Studies and Newsletters"; "H. "Selected Critical Articles, Reviews, and Interviews"; "List of Works Cited."

COMMENTS: Includes brief annotations for all of King's novels and stories to 1986, and major secondary works as well, indicating relevant critical or interpretive directions.

REPRINTS:

ab. Mercer Island, WA: Starmont House, October 1986, 176 p., trade paper.
b. San Bernardino, CA: Borgo Press, 1986, 176 p., cloth.

SECONDARY SOURCES AND REVIEWS:

1. *American Reference Books Annual* 19 (1988): 471.
2. Barron, Neil. *Horror Literature: A Reader's Guide*. New York: Garland Publishing, 1990, cloth, p. 401-402.
3. Blue, Tyson. "Rounding Up Books on King," in *Castle Rock: The Stephen King Newsletter* (June 1987): 6.

4. Blue, Tyson. "Two Collings' Books on SK Reviewed," in *Castle Rock The Stephen King Newsletter* (June 1986): 7.
5. Dziemianowicz, Stefan R. "Keys to the King-dom," in *Fantasy Review* (December, 1986): 44.
6. Gaul, Lou. "Some Gift Possibilities....," in *Burlington County Times* [New Jersey] (December 4, 1986): 19
7. Hall, Hal W., and Jan Swanbeck. *Science Fiction and Fantasy Research Index, Volume. 7.* San Bernardino, CA: Borgo Press, 1987.
8. Leonard, Stephanie. "New Books of Interest," in *Castle Rock: The Stephen King Newsletter* (June, 1987): 7; and (July, 1987): 7.
9. Leonard, Stephanie. *Castle Rock: The Stephen King Newsletter* (December, 1986/January, 1987): 2.

I15. THE STEPHEN KING PHENOMENON

I15. ***The Stephen King Phenomenon,*** by Michael R. Collings. STARMONT STUDIES IN LITERARY CRITICISM, No. 14. Mercer Island, WA: Starmont House, 1987, 144 p., cloth. Original paintings by Harvey Cusworth. Later printings with various covers, including pink cover with black ink, parchment cover with black and brown ink. [critique]

CONTENTS: "You, Stephen King," poem by Collings; 1. "A Concatenation of Monsters: Stephen King's *IT*"; 2. "A Bestselling Bestseller"; "3. "King and the Critics"; "Trucks," painting by Harvey Cusworth; 4. "Artists and Illustrators"; "The Woman in the Room," painting by Harvey Cusworth; 5. "Collecting Stephen King"; 6. "Beginnings: 'King's Garbage Truck'"; Appendix, "Some Notes on Foreign Publications"; Works Cited and Consulted; Index.

COMMENTS: In addition to critical perspectives on *IT*, *Phenomenon* includes tabulations of every appearance of King's novels on national bestsellers lists from August 1976 through August 1986; notations for leading illustrators of King's works; and synopses of the installments for King's college column at UMO, "King's Garbage Truck."

REPRINTS:

ab. Mercer Island, WA: Starmont House, 1987, 144 p., trade paper.
b. San Bernardino, CA: Borgo Press, 1987, 144 p., cloth.

SECONDARY SOURCES AND REVIEWS:

1. Barron, Neil. *Horror Literature: A Reader's Guide*. New York: Garland Publishing, 1990, cloth, p. 402.
2. Bertin, Eddy C. *SF-Gids* 81 (January, 1986): .
3. Blue, Tyson. "Two Collings' Books on SF Reviewed," in *Castle Rock: The Stephen King Newsletter* (June, 1987): 7.
4. Gaul, Lou. "Still the Horror King," in *Daily Intelligencer/Montgomery County Record* (April 23, 1987): 23.
5. Koehling, Joseph. "The Stephen King Phenomenon," in *Laird's Horn* [McArthur High School, Lawton, OK] 1:4 (January, 1989): 1+.

6. Leonard, Stephanie. "New Book of Interest," in *Castle Rock: The Stephen King Newsletter* (June, 1987): 7; and (July 1987): 7.
7. Leonard, Stephanie. *Castle Rock: The Stephen King Newsletter* (June, 1987): 2.
8. *Literary Criticism Register* (March, 1987): 2322.
9. Moore, J. T. *Science Fiction and Fantasy Book Review Annual 1988*, edited by Robert A. Collins and Robert Latham. Westport, CT: Meckler, 1988, cloth, p. 397-398.
10. Ott, Bill. *Booklist* (June 15, 1987): 1554.
11. *Peptalk* (April 14, 1987): 2.
12. Schneider, Martin. *Fantasy Review* (May, 1987): 35.
13. Tymn, Marshall. *The Year's Scholarship in Fantastic Literature 1987*, in *Extrapolation* (Fall, 1988): 264-265.
14. Vance, G. Warlock. *Extrapolation* (Spring, 1988): 84-87.

I16. STEPHEN KING GOES TO HOLLYWOOD

I16. ***Stephen King Goes to Hollywood: A Lavishly Illustrated Guide to All the Films Based on Stephen King's Fiction,*** by Jeff Conner, produced by Tim Underwood and Chuck Miller. New York: NAL Books, New American Library, August 1987, xv+144 p., cloth. [film critique]

REPRINTS:

ab. New York: A NAL Book, New American Library, 1987, 144 p., limited edition hardcover. 26 copies signed by author, in slipcase.
ac. New York: A Plume Book, New American Library, 1987, 144 p., trade paper.

SECONDARY SOURCES AND REVIEWS:

1. *Booklist* 84 (February 15, 1988): 38.
2. Klossner, Michael. "King vs. Moguls," in *SFRA Newsletter* No. 156 (March, 1988): 14. Reprinted: *Science Fiction & Fantasy Book Review Annual,* edited by Robert A. Collins and Robert Latham. Westport, CT: Meckler, 1988, cloth, p. 398.
3. Leonard, Stephanie. "Books on SK Films Similar," in *Castle Rock: The Stephen King Newsletter* 3:9 (September, 1987): 1, 5.
4. Stroby, W. C. "King's Work on Screen Examined," in *Asbury Park Press* [Neptune, NJ] (October 18, 1987): . As microfiche: *News-bank Literature Index* 13 (November, 1987): Fiche 50, B13.
5. *West Coast Review of Books* 13:5 (1988): 40.

I17. THE GOTHIC WORLD OF STEPHEN KING

I17. ***The Gothic World of Stephen King: Landscape of Nightmares,*** edited by Gary Hoppenstand and Ray B. Browne. Bowling Green, OH: Bowling Green State University Popular Press, December 1987, 143 p., cloth. [anthology of criticism]

CONTENTS: "Introduction: The Horror of It All: Stephen King and the Landscape of the American Nightmare," by Gary Hoppenstand and Ray B. Browne; "Blood, Eroticism, and the Vampire in Twentieth-Century Popular Literature," by Carol A. Senf; "Of Mad Dogs and Firestarters—The Incomparable Stephen King," by Garyn G. Roberts; "Reading Between the Lines: Stephen King and Allegory," by Bernard J. Gallagher; "A Blind Date with Disaster: Adolescent Revolt in the Fiction of Stephen King," by Tom Newhouse; "Freaks: The Grotesque as Metaphor in the Works of Stephen King," by Vernon Hyles; "Viewing 'The Body': King's Portrait of the Artist as Survivor," by Leonard Heldreth; "Stephen King's Creation of Horror in *'Salem's Lot*: A Prolegomenon Towards a New Hermeneutic of the Gothic Novel," by James E. Hicks; "Love and Death in the American Car: Stephen King's Auto-Erotic Horror," by Linda C. Badley; "*The Dark Tower*: Stephen King's Gothic Western," by James Egan; "Taking Stephen King Seriously: Reflections on a Decade of Best-Sellers," by Samuel Schuman; "A Dream of New Life: Stephen King's *Pet Sematary* as a Variant of *Frankenstein*," by Mary Ferguson Pharr; "Stephen King's *Pet Sematary*: Hawthorne's Woods Revisited," by Tony Magistrale; "'Oz the Gweat and Tewwible' and 'The Other Side': The Theme of Death in *Pet Sematary* and *Jitterbug Perfume*," by Natalie Schroeder. Contributors.

REPRINTS:

ab. Bowling Green, OH: Bowling Green State University Popular Press, December 1987, 143 p., trade paper.

SECONDARY SOURCES AND REVIEWS:

1. Barron, Neil. "Why Is Stephen King So Popular," in *SFRA Newsletter* No. 181 (October, 1989): 16. Reprinted: *Science Fiction & Fantasy Book Review Annual 1989*, edited by Robert A. Collins and Robert Latham. Westport, CT: Meckler, 1990, cloth, p. 520-521.
2. Barron, Neil. "A Critical Survey of Fantastic Literature and Film Scholarship in 1988," in *Science Fiction & Fantasy Book Review Annual, 1989*, edited by Robert A. Collins and Robert Latham. Westport, CT: Meckler, 1990, cloth, p. 110-138 (esp. p. 122-123).
3. Blue, Tyson. *Castle Rock: The Stephen King Newsletter* 4:7 (July, 1988): 1, 3, 9.
4. *Bookwatch* 9 (August, 1988): 6.
5. Rose, Kelly. "Essays Examine SK's Contribution to Academics," in *Castle Rock: The Stephen King Newsletter* 3:7 (July, 1987): 3, 5.
6. [White, Sarah J.] "Not for Everyone," in *Castle Rock: The Stephen King Newsletter* 4:5-6 (May-June, 1988): 4.

I18. STEPHEN KING: THE FIRST DECADE

I18. ***Stephen King: The First Decade,* Carrie *to* Pet Sematary,** by Joseph Reino. TWAYNE'S UNITED STATES AUTHORS SERIES (TUSAS 531), edited by Warren French. Boston: Twayne Publishers, February 1988, 162 p., cloth. [critique]

CONTENTS: "About the Author"; "Preface"; "Chronology"; 1. "Cinderella Hero/Cinderella Heroine"; 2. "The Dracula Myth: Shadow and Substance"; 3. "Strange Powers of Dangerous Potential"; 4. "One Touch of Horror Makes the Whole World Kin"; 5. "Two Terror Tales of a Town"; 6. "Impossible Cars and Improbable Cats"; 7. "*Night Shift*: Harbinger of Bad News"; 8. "Fantasies of Summer and Fall"; 9. "Metaphor as a Mask for Terror: A Final Estimate"; "Notes and References," "Selected Bibliography," "Index."

SECONDARY SOURCES AND REVIEWS:

1. Barron, Neil. "A Critical Survey of Fantastic Literature and Film Scholarship in 1988," in *Science Fiction & Fantasy Book Review Annual, 1989,* edited by Robert A. Collins and Robert Latham. Westport, CT: Meckler, 1990, cloth, p. 110-138 (esp. p. 123).
2. Barron, Neil. "Why Is Stephen King So Popular?" in *SFRA Newsletter* No. 181 (October, 1989): 16-17. Reprinted: *Science Fiction & Fantasy Book Review Annual, 1989,* edited by Robert A. Collins and Robert Latham. Westport, CT: Meckler, 1990, cloth, p. 521, 550.
3. *Booklist* 84 (February 15, 1988): 965.

I19. LANDSCAPE OF FEAR

I19. ***Landscape of Fear: Stephen King's American Gothic,*** by Tony Magistrale, with an annotated bibliography compiled by Marshall B. Tymn. Bowling Green, OH: Bowling Green State University Popular Press, 15 March 1988, 131 p., cloth. Published simultaneously in trade paperback. [critique]

CONTENTS: "Preface," by Magistrale; "Introduction," by Kenneth S. Wagner; 1. "Toward an American Gothic: Stephen King and the Romance Tradition"; 2. "'Crumbling Castles of Sand': The Social Landscape of King's Fictions"; 3. "Motorized Monsters: The Betrayal of Technology"; 4. "'Barriers Not Meant to Be Broken': Dark Journeys of the Soul"; 5. "Inherited Haunts: Stephen King's Terrible Children"; 6. "In Flight to Freedom: The Voyage to Selfhood and Survival"; 7. "Conclusions and Clowns: *It* as Summary and Recapitulation"; References Cited; Selected Bibliography—"Stephen King: A Guide to Scholarship, 1980-1987," compiled by Marshall B. Tymn. Index.

COMMENTS: A carefully constructed thematic analysis of King's major fictions. Magistrale's academic approach is well-modulated for readers; his scholarship supports his arguments without becoming self-assertive or obscure. Throughout the text, references to King's use of image, theme, motif, or symbol are used to illuminate readings of the text rather than as an end in themselves.

SECONDARY SOURCES AND REVIEWS:

1. Barron, Neil. "A Critical Survey of Fantastic Literature and Film Scholarship in 1988," in *Science Fiction & Fantasy Book Review Annual, 1989,* edited by Robert A. Collins and Robert Latham. Westport, CT: Meckler, 1990, cloty, p. 110-138 (esp. p. 122-123).
2. Blue, Tyson. "Book Review: *Landscape of Fear: Stephen King's American Gothic,*" in *Castle Rock: The Stephen King Newsletter* 4:7 (July, 1988): 1, 3, 9.
3. *Choice* 26 (November, 1988): 490.
4. Collings, Michael R. *Mystery Scene* No. 24 (January, 1990): 94.
5. Reesman, Jeanne Campbell. *Science Fiction & Fantasy Book Review Annual, 1989,* edited by Robert A. Collins and Robert Latham. Westport, CT: Meckler, 1990, cloth, p. 536.

I20. BARE BONES

I20. ***Bare Bones: Conversations on Terror with Stephen King***, edited by Tim Underwood and Chuck Miller. Los Angeles, CA, Columbia, PA: Underwood-Miller, 1988, 259 p., cloth. Limited edition of 1,000 copies, numbered. A compilation of interviews with King from 1979 through 1987. [interviews]

CONTENTS: 1. "Skeletons in the Closet"; 2. "Building Nightmares"; 3. "Terror Ink"; 4. "Hollywood Horrors"; 5. "Partners in Fear"; 6."Dancing in the Dark"; 7. "The Bad Seed."

REPRINTS:

ab. Los Angeles, CA, Columbia, PA: Underwood-Miller, 1988, 259 p., limited edition, lettered A-ZZ, bound in leather.
ac. Los Angeles, CA, Columbia, PA: Underwood-Miller, 1988, 259 p., presentation copies, 100 copies.
b. New York: McGraw-Hill, 1988, x+211 p., cloth.
c. New York: Warner Books, 1989, July 1989, x+211 p., trade paper.
d. as: *Angst. Gespräche Über das Unheimliche mit Stephen King*. Linkenheim, Germany: Edition Phantasia, 1989. Translated by Joachim Körber. 330 numbered copies, of which 30 are numbered I-XXX. [German]
e. London: New English Library, 1989, 217 p., cloth.
eb. London: New English Library, 1990, 217 p., paper.

SECONDARY SOURCES AND REVIEWS:

1. Barron, Neil. "A Critical Survey of Fantastic Literature and Film Scholarship in 1988," in *Science Fiction & Fantasy Book Review Annual, 1989,* edited by Robert A. Collins and Robert Latham. Westport, CT: Meckler, 1990, cloth, p. 110-138 (esp. p. 123).
2. Blue, Tyson. "Book Review: *Bare Bones: Conversations on Terror with Stephen King,*" in *Castle Rock: The Stephen King Newsletter* 4:7 (July, 1988): 1, 3, 9.

3. *Book Report* 8 (November, 1989): 56.
4. *Book World* 19 (September 17, 1989): 12.
5. *Booklist* 84 (May, 1988): 1566.
6. Dziemianowicz, Stefan. *Science Fiction & Fantasy Book Review Annual, 1989,* edited by Robert A. Collins and Robert Latham. Westport, CT: Meckler, 1990, cloth, p. 565.
7. Gilbert, John. *Fear* No. 6 (May/June, 1989): 44.
8. Hoffman, Barry. "*Bare Bones*: A Disquieting Look at Stephen King," in *Castle Rock: The Stephen King Newsletter* 4:10 (October, 1988): 7.
9. Holman, Curt. "Horrors: New Books Fall Short of Mark," in *Nashville Banner* [TN] (August, 1988): . As microfiche: *Newsbank Literature Index* 15 (September, 1988): Fiche 102, D5.
10. *Kirkus Reviews* 56 (May 15, 1988): 756.
11. *Kliatt Paperback Book Guide* 24 (January, 1990): 25.
12. *Review of Books* 14:1 (1988): 55.
13. Schweitzer, Darrell. "Anthology of New Horror Tales: Interviews with Stephen King," in *Philadelphia Inquirer* (July 24, 1988): . As microfiche: *Newsbank Literature Index* 15 (September, 1988): Fiche 102, D4.
14. Stuttaford, Genevieve. *Publishers Weekly* 233:15 (April 15, 1988): 66.
15. Walsh, Jay. "King Facts Entertaining But Repetitive," in *Lansing State Journal* [MI] (July 3, 1988): . As microfiche: *Newsbank Literature Index* 15 (September, 1988): Fiche 102, D3.
16. *West Coast Review of Books* 14:1 (1988): 55.

I21. REIGN OF FEAR

I21. ***Reign of Fear: Fiction and Film of Stephen King***, edited by Don Herron. Los Angeles, CA, Columbia, PA: Underwood-Miller, June 1988, xv+254 p., cloth. Limited edition, 500 copies, signed by 17 contributors (excluding King). [anthology of criticism]

CONTENTS: "Stephen King and Jo Fletcher—Interview"; "Foreword," by Dennis Etchison; "Digging It: Introduction," by Whoopi Goldberg; "King of the Comics? Introduction," by Marv Wolfman; "In Providence: Introduction," by Frank Belknap Long; "Stephen King and the American Dream: Alienation, Competition, and Community in *Rage* and *The Long Walk*," by Burton Hatlen; "When Company Drops In," by Charles Willeford; "The Cycles (Tricycles and Hogs) of Horror," by J. N. Williamson; "The Glass-Eyed Dragon," by L. Sprague de Camp; "The Big Producer," by Thomas Tessier; "The King and His Minions: Thoughts of a *Twilight Zone* Reviewer," by Thomas M. Disch; "Snowbound in the Overlook Hotel," by Guy N. Smith; "By Crouch End, in the Isles," by Peter Tremayne; "'Reach Out and Touch Some Thing': The Blurbs and Stephen King," by Stanley Wiater; "The Movies and Mr. King: Part II," by Bill Warren; "'Come Out Here and Take Your Medicine!' King and Drugs," by Ben P. Indick, R.Ph.; "Horror Without Limits: Looking into *The Mist*," by Dennis Rickard; "Fear and the Future: Stephen King as a Science Fiction

Writer," by Darrell Schweitzer; "Summation," by Don Herron. "About the Authors."

COMMENTS: An uneven collection, *Reign* ranges from a reprint of Whoopi Goldberg's *LA Times* pop-review of *IT*, to Burton Hatlen's long and carefully argued analytical essay. Herron's "Summation" is damning in its harsh, at times cynical and snide critiques of King's works since 1986—particularly *IT*, concluding the collection on a disquieting note. The collection seems directed toward no single audience; although some passages are enlightening and useful, others remain on the level of background or personal response.

REPRINTS:

ab. as: *Reign of Fear: The Fiction and the Films of Stephen King*. Novato, CA, Lancaster, PA: Underwood-Miller, 1992, xv+254 p., trade paper.
b. excerpted as: "Reach Out and Touch Some Thing: Blurbs and Stephen King," by Stanley Wiater, in *Castle Rock: The Stephen King Newsletter* 4:7 (July, 1988): 1, 8, 11-12.
c. excerpted as: "Fear and the Future: Stephen King as a Science Fiction Writer," by Darrell Schweitzer, in *Castle Rock: The Stephen King Newsletter* 3:11/4:1 (December, 1987/January, 1988): 1, 6-8.
d. as: *Reign of Fear: Fiction and Film of Stephen King (1982-1989)*. London: Pan Books, 1991, xv+254 p., paper.

SECONDARY SOURCES AND REVIEWS:

1. Collings, Michael R. *Mystery Scene* No. 24 (January, 1990): 94-95.

I22. THE UNSEEN KING

I22. ***The Unseen King,*** by Tyson Blue. STARMONT STUDIES IN LITERARY CRITICISM, No. 26. Mercer Island, WA: Starmont House, 1989, viii+200 p., cloth. [critique]

CONTENTS: "Introduction"; 1. "Childhood and Other Early Work"; 2. "The Maine Campus Years"; 3. "Early Uncollected Short Stories"; 4. "The 'True' Limiteds"; 5. "'The Plant': The Rarest King"; 6. "The Poetry of Stephen King"; 7. "Later Uncollected Stories"; 8. "Screenplays"; "Conclusion: Under the Wire"; "List of Works Cited and Consulted"; "Index.

COMMENTS: With his connections to *Castle Rock: The Stephen King Newsletter* and his apparent access to King's files, Blue is uniquely qualified to study the "unseen King"—those works of limited availability that nonetheless shed light on King's career and development. *The Unseen King* incorporates a wealth of bibliographical and critical information about little-known stories, articles, poems. The study is carefully constructed and well indexed, facilitating its use as a reference guide.

REPRINTS:

ab. Mercer Island, WA: Starmont House, 1989, viii+200 p., trade paper.
b. San Bernardino, CA: The Borgo Press, 1989, viii+200 p., cloth.

SECONDARY SOURCES AND REVIEWS:

1. Collings, Michael R. *Mystery Scene* No. 24 (January, 1990): 95.
2. Foster, Tim. "New King Book Set," in *Castle Rock: The Stephen King Newsletter* 3:8 (August, 1987): 3.
3. Graham, Mark. "Getting a Peek at Even More King Works," in *The Blood Review: The Journal of Horror Criticism* 1:1 (October 1989): 54, 59, 63.
4. Spruce, Christopher. "'*Unseen King*' Finally Is Seen," in *Castle Rock: The Stephen King Newsletter* 5:5 (May, 1989): 2-3.

I23. FEAST OF FEAR

I23. ***Feast of Fear: Conversations with Stephen King***, edited by Tim Underwood and Chuck Miller. Novato, CA, Lancaster, PA: Underwood-Miller, August 1989, x+282 p., cloth. Limited edition; 500 numbered copies. A companion volume to *Bare Bones*; a compilation of 47 interviews. [interviews]

CONTENTS: 1. "Genesis"; 2. "Early Years"; 3. "A Brand Name is Born"; 4. "Going Hollywood"; 5. "Scream Partners"; 6. "Highway to Horror"; "7. "Personal Demons"; 8. "Beyond the Brand Name"; 9. "Recent Years"; 10. "Has Success Spoiled Stephen King?"

COMMENTS: A handsomely produced specialty-press volume, *Feast of Fear* collects interviews with King ranging from his first published comments on *Carrie* (1973) to materials published 16 years later. Much like the earlier companion volume, *Bare Bones, Feast* provides insight into King's personality and temperament, his interests, his concerns as writer and as personality. The interviews—some as short as a page, others extending for twenty pages and more—allow the reader to discover through King's own words what is important to him. Unfortunately, the volume is not indexed, making it less useful as a reference tool.

REPRINTS:

b. New York: McGraw-Hill Book Co., 1989, x+282 p., cloth.
c. New York: Carroll & Graf, 1992, x+282 p., cloth.
d. New York: Warner Books, 1993, x+282 p., trade paper.

SECONDARY SOURCES AND REVIEWS:

1. Beaulieu, Janet C. "'Feast of Fear' Gets Behind the Scenes, Tells the Reader What Stephen King Thinks," in *Bangor Daily News* "Books in Review" (November 14, 1989): . As microfiche: *Newsbank Literature Index* 16 (December, 1989): Fiche 126, A6.

2. Collings, Michael R. *Mystery Scene* No. 24 (January, 1990): 95.
3. *Locus* 23 (November, 1989): 58.

I24. THE STEPHEN KING COMPANION

I24. ***The Stephen King Companion***, edited by George Beahm. Kansas City, MO: Andrew and McMeel, September 1989, xiv+363 p., trade paper. [bio-bibliography and criticism]

CONTENTS: Acknowledgments. PART ONE: THE REAL WORLD OF STEPHEN KING. "Chronology"; "The Long, Strange Trip of Stephen King: An Overview"; "The *Playboy* Interview," conducted by Eric Norden; "An Evening with Stephen King"; "Rocking in the Dead Zone!"; "Stephen King as Breckinridge Elkins?," by Donald M. Grant; "Stephen King Trivia"; "A Writer in Her Own Right: Tabitha King"; "The House That Horror Built."

PART TWO: THE UNREAL WORLD OF STEPHEN KING. "Fans"; "Book Publishing"; "Audio Publishing"; "Critics"; "Writing."

PART THREE: A LOOK AT THE BOOKS. "*The Bachman Books*"; "*Carrie*"; "*Creepshow*"; "*Cujo*"; "*Danse Macabre*"; "*The Dark Tower*"; "*The Dead Zone*"; "*Different Seasons*"; "*The Eyes of the Dragon*"; "*Firestarter*"; "Harlan Ellison's Watching"; "*It*"; "ID," by Charles McGrath; "*Misery*"; "*Night Shift*"; "*Pet Sematary*"; "*'Salem's Lot*"; "*The Shining*"; "*Skeleton Crew*"; "*The Stand*"; "*The Talisman*"; "*The Tommyknockers*"; "The Unpublished Novels"; "The Unpublished Work"; "The Dark Dreame: An Interview with Douglas E. Winter." APPENDICES: 1. "Books in Print"; 2. "Books About King"; 3. "Filmography and Videography"; 4. "Audiocassettes"; 5. "Book Collectibles by Stephen King: A Price Guide," by George Beahm with Barry R. Levin; 6. "Resources"; "Afterword," "About the Editor"

COMMENTS: Individual chapters contain essays, interviews, profiles, comments, and reviews by King, Joan H. Smith, Terry Steel, Michael R. Collings, Christopher Spruce, Clive Barker, Harlan Ellison, Dan R. Scapperotti, Berni Wrightson, Michael Whelan, Joe Bob Briggs, Nye Willden, and William Goldstein. The *Companion* is a flexible, accessible introduction to King and his works, designed for the casual reader rather than for the scholar or the fan. With Winter's *Art of Darkness*, it is an indispensible adjunct for anyone interested in simply reading more about King.

REPRINTS:

ab. Kansas City, MO: Andrew and McMeel, October, 1989, xiv+363 p., trade paper. Second printing, incorporating some additions and changes.
ac. Kansas City, MO: Andrew and McMeel, 1995, p., trade paper. Revised.
b Hampton, VA: GB Publishing, October 1989, xiv+363 p., cloth. Limited edition: 1000 copies, signed by editor, in dust jacket.
bb. Hampton, VA: GB Publishing, October 1989, xiv+363 p., cloth. Limited edition, 250 numbered copies, signed by editor and multiple contributors. Issued in conjunction with a special edition of *Grimoire,* edited by

George Beahm (GB Publishing, 1990 [see I31]), and including materials by Clive Barker, Roger Zelazny, Timothy O'Shaughnessy, and items deleted from the *Companion* because of lack of space.

bc. Hampton, VA: GB Publishing, October 1989, xiv+363 p., cloth. Contributor's copies.

c. London: Macdonald, 1990, xiv+363 p., cloth.

d. London: Futura, 1991, xv+539 p., paper.

e. Book-of-the-Month Club edition.

f. Quality Paperback Book Club edition.

SECONDARY SOURCES AND REVIEWS:

1. *American Reference Books Annual* 21 (1990): 487.
2. Barron, Neil. *Library Journal* 114:18 (November 1, 1989): 84.
3. Beahm, George. "Why I Wrote *The Stephen King Companion,*" in *The Shape Under the Sheet: The Complete Stephen King Encyclipedia,* by Stephen J. Spignesi. Ann Arbor, MI: Popular Culture, Ink, May 1991, cloth, p. 680-682.
4. Bleiler, Everett F. *Washington Post Book World* 108 (December 23, 1984): BW11.
5. Blue,Tyson. "King Book Companion Has Strengths, Faults," in *The Blood Review: Journal of Horror Criticism* 1:2 (January, 1990): 56.
6. *Book Report* 8 (March 1990): 48.
7. Collings, Michael R. *Mystery Scene* No. 24 (January, 1990): 95-96.
8. de Lint, Charles. "Night Journeys—Reviews of Horror: Installment #9," in *Mystery Scene* No. 24 (January, 1990): 87.
9. *Locus* 23 (November, 1989): 40.
10. *Locus* 24 (March, 1990): 63.
11. Olson, Ray. "*The Stephen King Companion,*" in *Booklist* 86 (October 1, 1989): 254.
12. Paget, Anne. *School Library Journal* 35:16 (December, 1989): 129.
13. *Reference & Research Book News* 5 (June, 1990): 35.
14. *Small Press* 8 (August 1990): 40.
15. Streitfeld, David. "Long Live the King," in *Washington Post Book World* (August 20, 1989): 15.
16. *West Coast Review of Books* 15:3 (1990): 42.

I25. THE MORAL VOYAGES OF STEPHEN KING

I25. ***The Moral Voyages of Stephen King***, by Anthony Magistrale. STARMONT STUDIES IN LITERARY CRITICISM, No. 25. Mercer Island, WA: Starmont House, 1989, vi+157 p., cloth. Published simultaneously in trade paperback. [critique]

CONTENTS: "Introduction"; "Chapter 1—Moral Collapse: Character, Setting, Free Will and Tragic Designs."

PART ONE: "When Good and Evil Collide." "Chapter 2—The Devil in the Machine: Technological Boogeymen"; "Chapter 3—The Fall from Grace: Sexuality and the Corruption of Innocence"; "Chapter 4—The

Shape Evil Takes: Hawthorne's Woods Revisited"; "Chapter 5—The Divine and the Damned: Tom Cullen and Trashcan Man."

PART TWO: "And Those Who Are Left to Tell the Tale." "Chapter 6—Speculations from the Locker Room: Male-Bonding and Non-Traditional Families"; "Chapter 7—Giving Birth to Salvation: The Mystery of Motherhood"; "Chapter 8—Portraits of the Artist: The Writer as Survivor."

"Works Cited"; "Selected Bibliography"; Index.

COMMENTS: "My goal in writing this book was to continue the advance of [the] emerging corpus of critical labors by presenting a still more focused approach. I have deliverately narrowed my scope to an examination of several of [King's] paramount literary themes and philosophical concerns"—p. iv.

REPRINTS:

ab. Mercer Island, WA: Starmont House, 1989, vi+157 p., trade paper.
b. San Bernardino, CA: The Borgo Press, 1989, vi+157 p., cloth.

I26. DAS STEPHEN KING BUCH

I26. ***Das Stephen King Buch***, herausgegeben von Joachim Körber. München: Wilhelm Heyne Verlag, 1989, 604 p., paper. [German-language critical anthology]

CONTENTS: "Vorwort." TEIL I: KING ÜBER KING—"Einige autobiographicische Anmerkungen" by Stephen King; "Ein Vortrag in der Billerica Library" by King; "Warum Ich 'Richard Bachman' war" by King.

TEIL 2: DIE BESTEN GESCHICHTEN VON STEPHEN KING—"Der Sensenmann" ["The Reaper's Image"]; "Das Schreckgespenst" ["The Boogeyman"]; "Die Höllenkatze" ["The Cat from Hell"]; "Die Kiste" ["The Crate"]; "Der Überlebenstyp" ["Survivor Type"]; "Der Floß" ["The Raft"]; "Der Gesang der Toten" ["Do the Dead Sing?"]; "Popsy."

TEIL 3: DIE INTERVIEWS—"Stephen King" by Charles Platt; "Stephen King, Peter Straub und die Suche nach dem Talisman" by Douglas E. Winter; "Das *Playboy*-Interview mit Stephen King" by Eric Norden.

TEIL 4: PROMINENTE KOLLEGEN ÜBER STEPHEN KING—"Mein Freund Stevie" ["Meeting Stevie"] by Peter Straub; "Willkommen in Zimmer 217" ["Welcome to Room 217"] by Ramsey Campbell; "Die Fahrt überleben" ["Surviving the Ride"] by Clive Barker.

TEIL 5: DAS WERK VON STEPHEN KING—"Zur Einführung: Warum leser wir phantastische Geschichten?" by King; "Wie macht er uns nur solche Angst?" by Ben P. Indick; "Die graue Arena" by Charles L. Grant; "Das Marstenhaus in "Salem's Lot" by Alan Ryan; "Kurzarbeit für die Nachtschicht" ["Short work for the night shift"] by Heiko Langhans; "Horror ohne Grenzen: Ein Blick in den Nebel" ["Horror Without Limits: Looking into The Mist"] by Dennis Rickard; "Wie man 'es' liest" ["How One Reads *It*"—"Digging It"] by Whoopi Goldberg; "Angst und Freundschaft: Stephen King und Peter Straub" by Bernadette Bosky; "King als

Schriftsteller für Jugendliche" by Ben P. Indick; "Der Drache mit den gläsernen Augen" ["The Glass-eyed Dragon"] by L. Sprague de Camp; "Der Mythos vom Dunklen Turm" ["The Mythos of the Dark Tower"] by Joachim Körber; "King als 'Richard Bachman'" ["King as Richard Bachman"] by Hans Joachim Alpers; "Crouch End, auf den Inseln" ["In Crouch End, On the Isles"] by Peter Tremayne; "Notizen aus der Toten Zone: Die Romane von Stephen King" ["Notes from the Dead Zone: The Novels of Stephen King"] by Joachim Körber.

TEIL 6: STEPHEN KING UND DIE FILME—"Horror vom Feinsten" ["Horror Hits a High"] by Fritz Leiber; "Horror in Hollywood oder Wie aus guten Romanen miese Filme werden" ["Horror in Hollywood, or how poor films are made from good novels "] by Norbert Stresau; "Maximum Overdrive: Stephen King als Regisseur" ["Maximum Overdrive: Stephen King as Director"] by Michael R. Collings.

TEIL 7: DATEN ZU STEPHEN KING—"Bibliographie der Veröffentlichungen von Stephen King" by Joachim Körber; "Filmographie" by Norbert Stresau. "Quellenverzeichnis" ["List of sources"]. "Über die Authoren" ["About the Authors"]

COMMENTS: This over-sized paperback anthology provides a solid introduction to King. It balances primary with secondary works, short stories with critical essays.

I27. LA PAURA

I27. ***La Paura, il Mistero l'Orrore dal Romanza Gotico a Stephen King***, by Carlo Bordoni. Chieti, Italy: M. Solfanelli, 1989, 145 p., paper? [Italian-language critique]

I28. THE STEPHEN KING QUIZ BOOK

I28. ***The Stephen King Quiz Book,*** by Stephen Spignesi. New York: A Signet Book, Penguin Books, August 1990, xvii+203 p., mass-market paper. [trivia book]

CONTENTS: Introduction. "I. The Life and Times of Stephen King"; "II. 'Page One'"; "III. The Novels"; "IV. The Shorter Collected Works" [*Night Shift, Different Seasons, Skeleton Crew*]; "V. The Shorter Uncollected Works"; "VI. The Bachman Books"; "VII. The *Dark Tower Books*"; "VIII. "The *Creepshow* Quizzes"; "IX. The Later Short Stories"; "X. Miscellaneous Quizzes"; "Epilogue—The Stephen King 'Show No Mercy and Take No Prisoners' Quiz"; The Answers; Bibliography.

COMMENTS: Each of the 107 individual quizzes included asks from ten to fifty trivia questions designed to test the readers' awareness of King's fictions. See Also **I39** for the second book in the series.

REPRINTS:

b. London: New English Library, 1991, xvii+203 p., paper.

I29. STEPHEN KING AND CLIVE BARKER

I29. ***Stephen King and Clive Barker: The Illustrated Masters of the Macabre,*** by James Van Hise. Las Vegas, NV: Pioneer Books, 1990, 146 p., trade paper. [critical anthology]

CONTENTS: STEPHEN KING—"The Man and the Writer"; "The Stephen King Interview: 'Secrets of Stephen King,'" by Stanley Wiater; "The Long Forms: Novels"; "Bachman Books"; "The Short Form: Short Stories"; "The Short Form: Uncollected"; "Non-Fiction: Danse Macabre"; "Media Mayhem: Film and Television."

CLIVE BARKER—"The Clive Barker Interview" by Bob Strauss; "Naughty Bits" by Cliff Burns; "Books of Blood" by Gus Meyer and James Van Hise; "The Novels"; "Flickering Frights: Film" by Bob Strauss.

COMMENTS: An updating of the earlier *Enterprise Incidents Presents Stephen King* [see I4], the book provides brief reviews of all of King's fictions and films. The volume also contains a number of black-and-white graphics as well as contributions by Kevin Mangold, Bob Strauss, Phil Gardner.

I30. STEPHEN KING: MAN AND ARTIST

I30. ***Stephen King: Man and Artist,*** by Carroll F. Terrell, illustrated by Kenny Ray Linkhaus. Orono, ME: Northern Lights Publishing Company, December 1990, 274 p., cloth. [criticism]

CONTENTS: Prologue: "The Human Condition." PART ONE: THE DIVINE AFFLATUS—"The Artist at Mid-Career"; "From Student to Teacher"; "From Celebrity to Phenomenon"; "The Mind of the Artist."

PART TWO: THE DISENCHANTMENT OF THE WORLD—"The Reductionist Orthodoxies of Science"; "The Reductionist Orthodoxies of Philosophy"; "The Reductionist Orthodoxies of Religion."

PART THREE: THE REENCHANTMENT OF THE WORLD—"Quest for an Absolute"; "The Mystic Way"; "The Mystic Moment."

PART FOUR: YOUTH IN A WORLD OF MONSTERS—"The Body"; *The Talisman*"; "*It*"; Epilogue: Works Mentioned in the Text.

COMMENTS: Terrell compares King favorably with major figures in Western literary history, including Chaucer, Dante, Shakespeare, Dickens, Pushkin, Twain, Pound, Sartre, and Camus; and at the same time suggests King's importance as observer, chronicler, and interpreter of late twentieth-century American society. The text draws on Terrell's expertise as scholar and critic as well as on his experiences as King's professor at UMO.

REPRINTS:

ab. Orono, ME: Northern Lights Publishing Company, December 1990, 274 p., cloth. A signed, numbered, limited edition of 75 copies.

ac. Orono, ME: Northern Lights Publishing Company, 1991, 159 p., paper?. Revised.

SECONDARY SOURCES AND REVIEWS:

1. Collings, Michael R. Review incorporated as dust-jacket text on the book.

I31. GRIMOIRE

I31. *Grimoire*, edited by George Beahm. Williamsburg, VA: GB Publishing, 1990, 64 p., paper. Included material received too late for *The Stephen King Companion* (see **I24bb**). [anthology]

I32. THE SHINING READER

I32. ***The Shining Reader***, edited by Anthony Magistrale. STARMONT STUDIES IN LITERARY CRITICISM, No. 30. Mercer Island, WA: Starmont House, 1991, xii+220 p., cloth. [critical anthology]

CONTENTS: "Introduction," by Magistrale. PART I: *The Shining as Text*. "Once, Out of Nature: The Topiary," by Michael N. Stanton; "Wendy Torrence, One of King's Women: A Typology of King's Female Characters," by Jackie Eller; "Jack's Nightmare at the Overlook: The American Dream Inverted," by Patricia Ferreira; "The 'Masked Author Strikes Again': Writing and Dying in Stephen King's *The Shining*," by Mary Jane Dickerson; "The Collapse of Family and Language in Stephen King's *The Shining*," by Alan Cohen; "The Redrum of Time: A Meditation of Francisco Goya's 'Saturn Devouring His Children' and Stephen King's *The Shining*," by Greg Weller.

PART II: *The Shining*'s Literary Tradition. "Good and Evil in Stephen King's *The Shining*," by Burton Hatlen; "The Red Death's Sway: Setting and Character in Poe's 'The Masque of the Red Death' and King's *The Shining*," by Leonard Mustazza; "Stephen King and the Tradition of American Naturalism in *The Shining*," by Jeanne Campbell Reesman; "Canaries in a Gilded Cage: Mental and Marital Decline in *McTeague* and *The Shining*," by Brian Kent; "Shakespeare in 58 Chapters: *The Shining* as Classical Tragedy," by Tony Magistrale; "The Dark Side of Childhood: *The 500 Hats of Bartholomew Cubbins* and *The Shining*," by Vernon Hyles.

PART III: *The Shining* as Film. "Kubrick's or King's—Whose *Shining* Is It?" by James Smith; "'Orders From the House': Kubrick's *The Shining* and Kafka's 'The Metamorphosis,'" by Mark Madigan; "Kubrick's *The Shining*: The Specters and the Critics," by James Hala. Index.

REPRINTS:

ab. Mercer Island, WA: Starmont House, 1991, xii+220 p., trade paper.
b. San Bernardino, CA: The Borgo Press, 1991, xii+220 p., cloth.

I33. THE SHAPE UNDER THE SHEET

I33. ***The Shape Under the Sheet: The Complete Stephen King Encyclopedia,*** by Stephen J. Spignesi. Ann Arbor, MI: Popular Culture, Ink, 24 May 1991, xx+780 p., hardcover. [critical anthology]

ANALYTICAL TABLE OF CONTENTS [all features by Spignesi, unless otherwise noted]: "Contents Classified"; "Foreword by Publisher," by Tom Schultheiss. Introduction: "Part 1—How Ryan O'Neal and Shelley Long Convinced Me to Lease A Copier; or, What Are John Ford and Woody Allen Doing in a Book About Stephen King"; "Part 2—A Kiss in the Dark"; "Part 3—Summing Up"; "Acknowledgments."

PART I: "THE SHAPE TAKES FORM—An Introduction to Stephen King and His Works." "The Shape Under the Sheet" [poem]; "'The Shape Under the Sheet': A Look at Stephen King's Seminal Metaphor and His 'Ten Bears' List of Personal Fears"; "Postcards from the Dark Side of the Moon: A Bare-Bones Biographical Profile."

PART II: "'I WRITE FEARSOMES'—Inside Stephen King." "The Stars and Stephen King"; "He Is Legend: An Interview with Richard Matheson"; "'King of Horror': *Time* Looks at the Stephen King Phenomenon," by Stefan Kanfer; "The Novelist Sounds Off"; "A 1990 Update to 'King of Horror'"; "'A Sense of the Ridiculous': An Interview with Stephen King's Personal Secretary, Shirley Sonderegger"; "'Growing Up with the Boogeyman: An Exclusive Interview with Stephen King's Brother, David King"; "A Eulogy for 'Huffy'"; "A Look at 'Dave's Rag'"; "A Talk with Stephen King's *True* First Collaborator, Chris Chesley"; "Genius," by Chris Chesley [short story]; "The Mission Boy," by Chris Chesley [short story].

PART III: "YERRR NNNUMBER WHUNNNN FAYUNNNN: Stephen King Fans, Conventions & Collectors." "The Find," by Barry Hoffman [short story]; "From Casual to Fanatic: The Three Levels of Stephen King Fandom"; "The Un-'Convention'-al Stephen King"; "A Visit to the Overlook Connection: An Interview with Dave Hinchberger"; "Stephen King Collector Editions: An Interview with Michael J. Autrey"; "Lost in the Time Tunnel: An Interview with Craig Goden"; "'A Possible Fairy Tale': Stephen King's 1970 Anti-War Essay," by Stephen King.

PART IV: "A VISIT TO CASTLE ROCK—A Look at the Stephen King Newsletter." "An Introduction to *Castle Rock, The Stephen King Newsletter*"; "Living in Castle Rock: An Interview with Stephanie Leonard, Founding Editor of *Castle Rock: The Stephen King Newsletter*"; A *Castle Rock* Autopsy, January 1985-December 1989"; "*Castle Schlock*: The Stephen King Parody Newsletter"; "'Character Assassination': A King Parody," by Ray Rexer.

PART V: "HORRORS LARGE AND SMALL—Stephen King's 'Strange and Wonderful Land.'" "An Index to the First Lines of Stephen King's Novels, Short Stories, and Poetry"; "Title/First Line Cross Index." PUBLISHED WORKS, 1974-1990. "Chronological Index to Published Works by Stephen King/Richard Bachman, 1974-1990"; "Alphabetical Index to Published Works by Stephen King/Richard Bachman, 1974-1990";

"A Look at *Danse Macabre,* Stephen King's Only Book-Length Work of Non-Fiction"; "'Steve Rose Up: Rick Hautala Remembers His First Time," by Rick Hautala. UNPUBLISHED & UNCOLLECTED WORKS. "Chronological index to Unpublished & Uncollected Works by Stephen King"; "Alphabetical Index to Unpublished & Uncollected Works by Stephen King"; "Kenny Ray Linkhaus." MOTION PICTURE ADAPTATIONS. "What a Long, Strange Trip It's Been: An Interview with Jessie Horsting"; "'Misery' Update"; "Chronological Index to Motion Picture Adaptations of Stephen King's Works"; "Alphabetical Index to Motion Picture Adaptations of Stephen King's Works"; "'Carrie: The Musical': The Biggest Flop in Broadway History"; "A Stop at the Marsten House: An Interview with Tobe Hooper"; "Dog (and Cat) Days: An Interview with Lewis Teague"; "'Death Scenes': Going to the Movies with Steve King," by Chris Chesley; "The King of Bowling: An Introduction to 'Pinfall'"; "Student Cinema Focuses on Stephen King: 'The Last Rung on the Ladder' and 'The Lawnmower Man'"; "It Is the Tale *And* He Who Tells It: A Review of 'Misery' (The movie)," by George Beahm; "The Art of Adaptation: A Synoptic Comparison of 'IT' and *IT*." MISCELLANEOUS FORMATS: SPOKEN WORD RECORDINGS & POETRY. "The Audio King: The Audiotape Versions of Stephen King's Works," by George Beahm; "The Radiating Pencils of His Bones: The Poetry of Stephen King," by Michael R. Collings; "You, Stephen King," by Michael R. Collings [poem]. A STROLL AMONG THE HEADSTONES: A GUIDED TOUR. "The Dread Zone: My Scariest Stephen King Moments," by Tyson Blue; "Tyson Blue's Top Ten Stephen King Novels and Short Stories"; "How King Kills: A Gory Guide to the Killer King"; "Page Number Key to Master Codes Cited in Character Indexes"; "An Index to Characters in the Novels of Stephen King"; "An Index to Characters in the Bachman Novels"; "An Index to Characters in Uncollected Short Stories."

PART VI: "BENEATH THE SHEET—Commentary on King's 'Marketable Obsession.'" "'He Who Tells It': An Annotated Bibliography of Books & Articles About Stephen King and His Work"; "A Gathering of Kings: A Valuable Addition to the Stephen King Bibliography"; "*The Stephen King Companion*: Author George Beahm Discusses His King Volume"; "Why I Wrote *The Stephen King Companion,*"by George Beahm; "*The Stephen King Companion*"; "George Beahm's Top Ten"; "'And His Kingdom Was Full of Darkness': An Interview with Douglas E. Winter"; "Taking Notice of 'The Noticer': An Interview with J. N. Williamson"; "Presenting Stephen King: An Interview with James Van Hise"; "On the Trail of the Boogeyman: An Interview with Stanley Wiater"; "Stan Wiater's 'Top 5'"; "The Toucher," by Stanley Wiater [short story]; "His Father's Son: An Interview with Richard Christian Matheson"; "One Live Guy: An Interview with Ray Garton"; "Texas Horrors: A Talk with Joe Lansdale"; "'In the Light': An Interview with Robert R. McCammon"; "Joseph Payne Brennan: A Living Legend Is Dead"; "Joseph Payne Brennan: The Nature of the Man," by Donald M. Grant; "Canavan's Back Yard," by Joseph Payne Brennan [short story].

PART VII: "IN A REGION WITH NO PROPER NAME—The Hidden Horrors of Stephen King." "The Unwritten King: Stories Stephen King Has Thought of, But Just Hasn't Written Down (Yet)"; "The Unfinished King: *The Stephen King Notebook*." ILLUSTRATIONS.

COMMENTS: The long-awaited volume provides an abundance of King-related information, arranged in interviews, indices, appreciations, reviews of books, stories, films, etc. Spignesi has incorporated every facet of King's published output (and a number of unpublished pieces), with cross-referencing and multiple tables of contents for easy access. The collection was originally to have included King's "Before the Play," the excised prologue to *The Shining*.

REPRINTS:

b. excerpted in: *Midnight Graffitti* (Spring, 1989): .
c. Overlook Connection, 1991?, slipcased, signed (by various contributors), numbered, limited edition of 350 copies, with 50 presentation copies.

SECONDARY SOURCES AND REVIEWS:

1. Hoffman, Barry. "An Interview About Stephen King with Stephen Spignesi," in *Mystery Scene* No. 27 (October, 1990): 94-98.

I34. THE STEPHEN KING STORY

I34. ***The Stephen King Story,*** by George Beahm. Kansas City, MO: Andrews & McMeel, October 1991, 291 p., cloth. [critique]

CONTENTS: Introduction, by Michael R. Collings; Introduction, by Carroll F. Terrell. "The Early Years (1947-1966)"; "Literary Apprenticeship (1966-1973)"; "The Doubleday Days (1975-1978)"; "The Shape of Things to Come (1979-1983)": Bestsellasaurus Rex (1984-1991)." Appendices: Footnotes, Selected bibliography, Index.

COMMENTS: The volume is designed to supplement Beahm's earlier *The Stephen King Companion,* providing not only research resources but discussions of the relationship between King's life and his works. Not intended as an exposé, *The Stephen King Story* focuses how understanding biographical backgrounds provides depth to reading his fictions.

REPRINTS:

ab. Kansas City, MO: Andrews & McMeel, 1992, 326 p., trade paper. Revised and updated.
b. Williamsburg, VA: GB Publishing, 1991, cloth. Limited edition, numbered and signed by Beahm. Less than 1,000 copies.
bb. Williamsburg, VA: GB Publishing, 1991, cloth. Deluxe limited edition. 250 numbered copies, signed by Beahm, Kenny Ray Linkhaus, Michael R. Collings, Chris Chesley, and Carroll Terrell.
bc. Williamsburg, VA: GB Publishing, 1991, cloth. Lettered state of 26 copies, specially bound.
c. London: Little, Brown, 1993, 372 p., cloth.
d. London: Warner Books, 1994, 421 p., paper.

I35. KONPURITO SUTIVUN KINGU

I35. ***Konpurito Sutivun Kingu***, by Seiji Okuzawa and Kenji Kazama. Tokyo: Byakuya-shobo, 1991, 479 p., paper. [Japanese-language critique]

I36. THE DARK DESCENT

I36. ***The Dark Descent: Essays Defining Stephen King's Horrorscape,*** edited by Tony Magistrale. CONTRIBUTIONS TO THE STUDY OF SCIENCE FICTION AND FANTASY, No. 48. New York: Greenwood Press, 1992, xix+227 p., cloth. [critical anthology]

CONTENTS: "Foreword: The King and I," by Joseph A. Citro; Acknowledgments; Stephen King Chronology; 1. "Defining Stephen King's Horrorscope: An Introduction," by Tony Magistrale; 2. "The Masks of the Goddess: The Unfolding of the Female Archetype in Stephen King's *Carrie*," by Greg Weller; 3. "Partners in the *Danse*: Women in Stephen King's Fiction," by Mary Pharr; 4. "Complex, Archetype, and Primal Fear: King's Use of Fairy Tales in *The Shining*," by Ronald T. Curran; 5. "The Three Genres of *The Stand*," by Edwin F. Casebeer; 6. "Some Ways of Reading *The Dead Zone*," by Michael N. Stanton; 7. "Fear and Pity: Tragic Horror in King's *Pet Sematary*," by Leonard Mustazza; 8. "The Mythic Journey in 'The Body'," by Arthur W. Biddle; 9. "'Everybody Pays... Even for Things They Didn't Do': Stephen King's Pay-out in the Bachman Novels," by James F. Smith; 10. "Science, Politics, and the Epic Imagination: *The Talisman*," by Tony Magistrale; 11. "A Clockwork Evil: Guilt and Coincidence in 'The Monkey'," by Gene Doty; 12. "Playing the Heavy: Weight, Appetite, and Embodiment in Three Novels by Stephen King," by Bernadette Lynn Bosky; 13. "Riddle Game: Stephen King's Metafictive Dialogue," by Jeanne Campbell Reesman; 14. "Stephen King Reading William Faulkner: Memory, Desire, and Time in the Making of *It*," by Mary Jane Dickerson; 15. "'The Face of Mr. Flip': Homophobia in the Horror of Stephen King," by Douglas Keesey; 16. "Reading, Writing, and Interpreting: Stephen King's *Misery*," by Lauri Berkenkamp; A Stephen King Bibliography; Index; About the Contributors.

COMMENTS: The collection includes essays from fifteen authors, each academically oriented, each focusing on a specific major King novel from *Carrie* through *Misery*. The articles approach King's writing from a variety of directions: feminist, Jungian, etc. Includes a bibliography.

I37. STEPHEN KING: THE SECOND DECADE

I37. ***Stephen King: The Second Decade*—Danse Macabre *to* The Dark Half,** by Tony Magistrale. TWAYNE UNITED STATES AUTHORS SERIES (TUSAS 599). New York: Twayne Publishers, 1992, xiii+188 p., cloth. [critique]

COMMENTS: A continuation of Joseph Reino's earlier volume for the Twayne series (see **I18**). Includes an updated bibliography.

I38. STEPHEN KING AND CLIVE BARKER II

I38. ***Stephen King and Clive Barker: Masters of the Macabre II,*** by James Van Hise. Las Vegas, NV: Pioneer Books, 1992, 143 p., trade paper. [critical anthology]

I39. THE SECOND STEPHEN KING QUIZ BOOK

I39. ***The Second Stephen King Quiz Book***, by Stephen J. Spignesi. New York: A Signet Book, Penguin Books, 1992, 253 p., paper. [trivia book]

See also **I28** for the first book in the series.

I40. A CASEBOOK ON THE STAND

I40. ***A Casebook on The Stand***, edited by Tony Magistrale. STARMONT STUDIES IN LITERARY CRITICISM, No. 38. Mercer Island, WA: Starmont House, 1992, xii+210 p., cloth. [critical anthology]

CONTENTS: Introduction; 1. "'Almost Better': Surviving the Plague in Stephen King's *The Stand*," by Mary Pharr; 2. "'I Think the Government Stinks!': Stephen King's *Stand* on Politics," by Douglas Keesey; 3. "Stephen King and His Readers: A Dirty, Compelling Romance," by Brian Kent; 4. "The 'Power of Blackness' in *The Stand*," by Leonard Cassuto; 5. "Repaying Service with Pain: The Role of God in *The Stand*," by Leonard Mustazza; 6. "Free Will and Sexual Choice in *The Stand*," by Tony Magistrale; 7. "Choice, Sacrifice, Destiny, and Nature in *The Stand*," by Bernadette Lynn Bosky; 8. "Dark Streets and Bright Dreams: Rationalism, Technology, and 'Impossible Knowledge' in Stephen King's *The Stand*," by Michael A. Morrison; 9. "Dialogue Within the Archetypal Community of *The Stand*," by Ed Casebeer; 10. "Beyond Armageddon: Stephen King's *The Stand* and the Post Catastrophic World in Speculative Fiction," by Steven Kagle; Notes; Works Cited, Index.

COMMENTS: This was the last of a series of Starmont House anthologies focusing on individual novels by Stephen King, and was one of the last Starmont House books published (the company folded in February 1993). The editor's name is given as Anthony Magistrale on the front cover.

REPRINTS:

ab. Mercer Island, WA: Starmont House, 1992, xii+210 p., trade paper.
b. San Bernardino, CA: The Borgo Press, 1993, xii+210 p., cloth.

I41. STEPHEN KING, MASTER OF HORROR

I41. ***Stephen King, Master of Horror***, by Anne Saidman. Minneapolis, MN: Lerner Publications, 1992, 56 p., cloth. [young adult critique]

I42. THE FILMS OF STEPHEN KING [LLOYD]

I42. ***The Films of Stephen King***, by Ann Lloyd. London: Brown, 1993, 96 p., trade paper. [film critique]

REPRINTS:

b. New York: St. Martin's Press, 1993, 96 p., cloth.
bb. New York: St. Martin's Press, 1993, 96 p., trade paper.

I43. STEPHEN KING'S AMERICA

I43. ***Stephen King's America***, by Jonathan P. Davis. Bowling Green, OH: Bowling Green State University Popular Press, 1994, 183 p., cloth. [critique]

CONTENTS: Foreword. PART ONE: Stephen King and the Horror Genre. PART TWO: Stephen King's America: "Traversing King's American Terrain"; "I. The Struggle for Personal Morality in America"; "II. Childhood and the Rites of Passage"; "III. Technology: America's Sweetheart"; "IV. Caught in the Machine of American Capitalism"; "V. Autonomy Versus Societal Conformity in America"; "VI. Survival in a Despairing World"; "Epilogue: The End of the Journey."

PART THREE: The Interviews. "Author's Note"; "I. Tony Magistrale, University of Vermont"; "II. Carroll Terrell, University of Maine at Orono"; "III. Burton Hatlen, University of Maine at Orono"; "IV. Gary Hoppenstand, Michigan State University." Works Cited. Index.

I44. STEPHEN KING [KEYISHIAN]

I44. ***Stephen King***, by Amy Keyishian and Marjorie Keyishian. New York: Chelsea House, 1995, 127 p., cloth. [critique]

REPRINTS:

ab. New York: Chelsea House, 1995, 127 p., trade paper.

I45. THE WORK OF STEPHEN KING

I45. ***The Work of Stephen King,*** by Michael R. Collings. BIBLIOGRAPHIES OF MODERN AUTHORS SERIES, No. 25. Series editor, Boden Clarke. San Bernardino, CA: Borgo Press, January 1996, 480 p., cloth. [bibliography]

CONTENTS: "Introduction: Not so Much To Tell, As To Let the Story Flow Through"; A Stephen King Chronology.

BIBLIOGRAPHY: A. Books; B. Short Fiction, Including Published Excerpts from Longer Works; C. Short Nonfiction; D. Poetry; E. Screenplays; F. Public and Screen Appearances; G. Visual Adaptations; H. Audio Adaptations; I. Secondary Sources: Books and Book-Length Studies; J. Secondary Sources: Newsletters; K. Secondary Sources: Bibliographies and Filmographies; L. Secondary Sources: Profiles and Bio-Bibliographical Sketches; M. Secondary Sources: Interviews; N. Secondary Sources: Scholarly Essays; O. Secondary Sources: Popular and News Magazines; P. Secondary Sources: Media Magazines, Specialty Magazines, Fan Publications; Q. Secondary Sources: *Castle Rock: The Stephen King Newsletter*; R. Secondary Sources: Newspaper Articles; S. Secondary Sources: Professional and Trade Journals; T. Secondary Sources: Selected Reviews of King Works; U. Stephen King Archives; V. Unpublished Works; W. Secondary Sources: Parodies, Pastiches, etc.; X. Honors and Awards; Y. Miscellanea. Quoth the Critics. Indexes.

A much reworked and expanded version of *The Annotated Guide to Stephen King* (see **I14**).

REPRINTS:

ab. San Bernardino, CA: Borgo Press, January 1996, 480 p., trade paper.

DISSERTATIONS AND THESES

IB1. ***Anatomy of a Best Seller: Form, Style, and Symbol in Stephen King's* The Stand**, by Fran Miller Rathburn. M.A. Thesis, Stephen F. Austin State University, 1981, i+75 p. See **A5**.

IB2. ***An Examination of Archetypes Pertaining to the Earth Mother Found in Selected Works of Twentieth-Century Short Fiction***, by Clair Juenell Kemp. M.A. Thesis, Mankato State University, 1983, 139 p. One of the three works covered is King's "Children of the Corn" (see **B31**).

IB3. ***Phobic Pressure Points in Poe: The Nineteenth-Century Reader and His Fears***, by Michael Lawrence Burduck. Ph.D. Dissertation, University of Mississippi, 1984, v+179 p. Burduck credits King with generating the phrase "phobic pressure points."

IB4. ***Traduction et Étude Critique d'un Conte de Stephen King: La Calandre***, par Bernard Marc Cabanne. M.A. Thesis, San Jose State University, 1984, xii+32 p.

IB5. ***American Holocaust Novels: (John Hersey, Leon Uris, Flannery O'Connor, Stephen King)***, by Audrey Wolff Chanen. Ph.D. Dissertation, University of Iowa, 1987, 172 p.

IB6. ***Three Sources of Fear in the Works of Stephen King***, by Mark Putnam. M.A. Thesis, Ohio State University, 1987, iv+91 p.

IB7. ***Horror: Landscape Change in Stephen King's Work***, by Jill Greer Rosenfeld. A.B. (Honors) Thesis, Harvard University, 1989, 100 p.

IB8. ***Stephen King's Family Frights***, by Dana H. Peterson. M.A. Thesis, University of South Florida, 1990, iv+73 p.

IB9. ***Fiction in the Secondary Classroom***, by Daniel Patrick Campora. M.Ed. Thesis, University of Toledo, 1990, iii+48 p. King's work is used as an example of the kinds of materials that can be used effectively in classroom teaching.

IB10. ***The Shining: Supernatural Thriller and/or Psychological Horror***, by Gloria J. LeMay. M.L.A. Thesis, University of South Florida, 1991, vii+74 p. See **A3**.

IB11. ***Stanley Kubrick's Post-Structural Vision of Horror***, by David Stephan. M.A. Thesis, University of South Florida, 1991, vi+38 p. Focuses specifically on Kubrick's adaptation of King's *The Shining* (see **A3** and **G2**).

IB12. ***Stephen King: Twentieth-Century Society and Politics***, by Cheryl L. Metz. M.A. Thesis, James Madison University, 1992, 57 p.

IB13. ***Stephen King: Literatura Real***, por Vicente Antonio Casañ Onsurse. M.A. Thesis, West Virginia University, 1992, iv+68 p.

IB14. ***All the King's Children: The Role of the Child in Stephen King's Novels***, by Betina S. Jones. M.A. Thesis, University of North Carolina at Wilmington, 1993, v+65 p.

IB15. ***Standing by the Body: A Look at Cinematic Adaptation***, by Leslie Jo Kennedy. M.S. Thesis, Texas Tech University, 1993, ii+41 p. Focuses on the adaption of King's story "The Body" into the motion picture, *Stand by Me* (see **B63** and **G12**).

IB16. ***The Origins of Modern Horror***, by Tara M. Hively. A.B. (Honors) Thesis, Rollins College, 1994, 97 p. One of the major authors covered is King.

IB17. ***Family Survival: Domestic Ideology and Destructive Paternity in the Horror Fictions of Stephen King***, by Joe M. Abbott, Jr. Ph.D. Dissertation, University of Southern California, 1994, v+249 p.

MISCELLANEOUS MONOGRAPHS

IC1. ***God Is in a Hurry***, by Marjorie Lewis Lloyd. Washington, DC: Review and Herald Publishing Associates, 1976, 64 p., paper. The autobiography of a Seventh Day Adventist, with references to the author's interest in Stephen King works.

J.

SECONDARY SOURCES

NEWSLETTERS

J1. ***Castle Rock: The Stephen King Newsletter***. Founding editor, Stephanie Leonard; Editor (1989), Christopher Spruce. P.O. Box 8060, Bangor, ME 04401. Published monthly January 1985 through December 1989; in newspaper format after May 1985; final issue, 1989. See also **Section Q** for a complete listing of original pieces published in this magazine.

SECONDARY SOURCES AND REVIEWS:

1. "Magazine Madness," in *The Blood Review: The Journal of Horror Criticism* 1:1 (October 1989): 3. Notes that *Castle Rock: The Stephen King Newsletter* will cease publication with the December 1989 issue.
2. Spignesi, Stephen J. "*Castle Rock* Autopsy," in *The Complete Stephen King Encyclopedia*. Ann Arbor, MI: Popular Culture, Ink, May 1991, cloth, p. 101-126.
3. Spignesi, Stephen J. "An Introduction to *Castle Rock, The Stephen King Newsletter,*" in *The Complete Stephen King Encyclopedia*. Ann Arbor, MI: Popular Culture, Ink, May 1991, cloth, p. 95-96.
4. Spignesi, Stephen J. "Living in Castle Rock: An Interview with Stephanie Leonard, the Founding Editor of *Castle Rock: The Stephen King Newsletter,*" in *The Complete Stephen King Encyclopedia*. Ann Arbor, MI: Popular Culture, Ink, May 1991, cloth, p. 97-100.

J2. ***Castle Schlock: The Stephen King Parody Newsletter***, edited by Ray Rexer. 'Wray Wreckser' publisher. 506 N. Powell. Essexville, MI 48732.

Five issues published, 1986-1989

SECONDARY SOURCES AND REVIEWS:

1. Rexer, Ray. "*Castle Schlock*: A Brief History," in *The Shape Under the Sheet: The Complete Stephen King Encyclopedia,* by Stephen J. Spignesi. Ann Arbor, MI: Popular Culture, Ink., May 1991, p. 127-129.

2. Spignesi, Stephen J. "Castle Schlock: An Abundance of Schlock," in *The Shape Under the Sheet: The Complete Stephen King Encyclopedia,* by Stephen J. Spignesi. Ann Arbor, MI: Popular Culture, Ink., May 1991, p. 129-130. Includes summaries of all five issues.

J3. *King's Crypt*, edited by Tom Simon and Bill Geohegan. 706 S. Fairfax Street, Alexandria, VA 22314.

Published monthly, beginning July 1985. 8 1/2" X 11" format.

J4. ***The Overlook Connection,*** edited by Dave Hinchberger. P.O. Box 526, Woodstock, GA 30188; (404) 926-1762. Includes materials on recent publications in conjunction with items (by King and others) for sale.

J5. ***Stephen King Krant*** 13:13 (October 13, 1986). Edited by 'B. Stoker.' Utrecht, Netherlands: Luitingh/Veen. [Dutch]

SELECTED CONTENTS:

"Angst voor Superflu is Groot" ["Fear of the Superflu is Great"], dateline: Arnette, TX: 6. Article about the outbreak of superflu, with excerpts from *De Beproeving* ["*The Stand*"] and a cartoon strip of Trashcan Man blowing up the oil refinery.

"Autowijzer Christine in Japanese Jas": 5. Article about the opening of the film adaptation of *Christine* in Japan.

"Boek van King Bijna uit de Handel" ["Books by King Almost off the Market"]: 5. Review of *Dodenwake* ["*Pet Sematary*"] and *Christine*.

"Chamberlain Rampgebied" ["Chamberlain Disaster Area"], dateline: Chamberlain, ME: 6. Article covering the "schoolfeest" at Ewen Gymnasium in Chamberlain, with excerpts from *Carrie*.

"De Kunst van het Geiezelen" ["The Art of Shiver/Gruesome/Creepy"], by Arnold Kaufman: 4. A psychologist's assessment of horror, based on discussions of *Die Beproevung* ["*The Stand*"], *Dodelijk Dilemma* ["*The Dead Zone*"], and *Duistere Krachten* ["*Skeleton Crew*"].

"Doodsbange Schrijver Opgespoord" ["Deathly afraid writer spurred on"]: 2. Interview with Ben Mears on an isolated island in Lapland—overview of *Bezeten Stad* ["*Salem's Lot*"].

"Door King in Cel" [full title: "Officier Asks Six Months in a Cell for Dealer: Throw King Into Cell"], by Fred Kanton: 5. Report of drug dealings by Edwin S. King, with references to *Ogen van Vuur* ["Eyes of Fire"—"*Firestarter*"].

"'Het' Forceert Doorbraak: Optimisme over akkord inzake wapenbeheersing na leziung van nieuwe Stephen King" ["*It* Forces Breakthrough: Optimism over arms control sinks after reading of the new Stephen King"]: 1. Reagan and Gorbachov take a break from arms negotiations to discuss *It*.

"Interview met Stephen King" [Full title: "The Master on His Words: Interview with Stephen King"]: 7.

"Jongeen vermist in Epe" [full title: "Search Warrant Delivered at Six O'Clock Results in Boy Missing in Epe"]: 5. A boy missing for some hours is found; his excuse for not answering calls of searchers is that he had begun reading *De Talisman* ["*The Talisman*"] and simply couldn't break away until he had finished the book: "It was so spellbinding. It shocked me that I had read so long."

"King in Beeld" ["King in Pictures"], by Henk Penseel: 3-4. Overview of films adapted from King's stories.

"Kooktip—Kalkoen à la Abigail" ["Cooking Tip—Turkey à la Abigail"]: 2. Recipe based on King's *De Beproeving* ["*The Stand*"].

"Leer King Kennen" ["Get to Know King"]: 6. Order form from Luitingh, listing all of King's available titles.

"Lees Deestelijk, Griezel Geestelijk": 8. Full-page listing of Luitingh's Dutch translations, with cover photographs for seventeen volumes of King translations.

"Musikaal huiveren bij Brabants Orkest" ["Musical Shivers by Brabant Orchestra"], by the *King Krant* art editor: 2. Review of a new symphony by Willem Telraam, called *Trucks*; includes passages from "Ik Weet Wat Je Wilt" ["I Know What You Want"].

"Operatie Thatcher Geslaagd": 1. Discussion of Margaret Thatcher's operation, Reagan, and Gorbachev, and *It*.

"Passagiers bus slaags" ["Passengers Come to Blows"], by Staff writer: 4. Report of a fight on a busload of Hague vacationers on the way to Hertogenbosch, with references to *De Satanskinderen* ["Satan's Children"—"*Night Shift*"].

"Roman King als Toneelstuk," ["King Novel as Stageplay"]: 2. Discussion of *Het Beest Cujo*, a play set to open on October 15, 1986, in Amsterdam; includes excerpts from *Cujo* and a short cartoon strip featuring King and an Odie-like dog.

"Televisie King Channel": 2. The day's program for the King television channel, including a documentary on the Schwarzwald, a children's program called "Ik zag twee monsters ["I Saw Two Monsters"], and the third segment in an American miniseries, *Salem's Lot*.

"Vakantiegangers Opgelucht" [Full title: "Travel Organization Pulling Their Hair; Publishers Capture a Blow from That"]: 5. Article about a trip to Costa Brava, with references to *4x Stephen King* ["*The Bachman Books*"].

COMMENTS: An 8-page mock-newsletter produced by King's Dutch publisher as advertising for his novels. The newsletter includes articles based on each King book available through Luitingh/Veen, often incorporating world figures such as Mikhail Gorbachev or Margaret Thatcher and their imagined connections with King's novels. It includes interviews, cartoons, and advertisements for other books, films, and such items as "King"-brand peppermint lozenges—interspersed with sidebar excerpts from King's novels and stories.

J6. *Privately Printed,* edited by George Beahm. March, 1990- .

"*Privately Printed* is an informal, infrequent newsletter of limited circulation *not* available by subscription. Distributed to friends, correspondents, book dealers, critics, select publishers, and bibliographers with a professional interest in Stephen King." The newsletter is not connected in any way with King or his staff.

K.

SECONDARY SOURCES

BIBLIOGRAPHIES AND FILMOGRAPHIES

K1. *Science Fiction and Fantasy Authors: A Bibliography of First Printings of Their Fiction,* by L. W. Currey. Boston: G. K. Hall, 1979, cloth, p. 277. [bibliography]

K2. **"Stephen King: A Bibliography,"** compiled by Marty Ketchum, Daniel J. Levack, and Jeff Levin, in *Fear Itself: The Horror Fiction of Stephen King*, edited by Tim Underwood and Chuck Miller. San Francisco, CA, and Lancaster, PA: Underwood-Miller, 1982, cloth, p. . See also **I2.** [bibliography]

K3. **"Primary Bibliography,"** compiled by Douglas E. Winter, in *Stephen King*. STARMONT READER'S GUIDE, No. 12. Mercer Island, WA: Starmont House, October 1982, cloth, p. 111-118. See also **I3.** [bibliography]

K4. **"Secondary Bibliography,"** compiled by Douglas E. Winter, in *Stephen King*. STARMONT READER'S GUIDE, No. 12. Mercer Island, WA: Starmont House, October 1982, cloth, p. 119-124. See also **I3.** [bibliography]

K5. **"A Stephen King Bibliography,"** compiled by Douglas E. Winter, in *Stephen King: The Art of Darkness*. New York: New American Library, November 1984, cloth, p. 215-241. See also **I5.** [bibliography]

K6. **"Stephen King in the Lowlands: An Annotated Bibliography of His Works as Published in the Netherlands (Holland and Belgium),"** by Eddy C. Bertin, in *SF Gids* [*SF Guide*] (December, 1984): . [Dutch]. [bibliography]

b. updated as: "Stephen King in the Lowlands," in *Castle Rock: The Stephen King Newsletter* 1:11 (November, 1985): 7-8. Translated by Bertin and updated to July 1985.

K7. **"Stephen King,"** compiled by Owen Haskell. Providence, RI: 1985. [bibliography of fiction, first printings, etc.]

K8. **"Stephen King: A Bibliography,"** compiled by Marshall Tymn, in *Discovering Stephen King*, edited by Darrell Schweitzer. STARMONT STUDIES IN LITERARY CRITICISM, No. 8. Mercer Island, WA: Starmont House, 1985, cloth, p. 205-209. See also **I6.** [bibliography]

K9. **"Checklist—Stephen King: Short Fiction and Poetry,"** compiled by Michael R. Collings, in *The Shorter Works of Stephen King*. STARMONT STUDIES IN LITERARY CRITICISM, No. 9. Mercer Island, WA: Starmont House, June 1985, cloth, p. 187-193. See also **I8.** [bibliography]

K10. **"Stephen King Bibliography,"** compiled by Stephanie Leonard, in *Castle Rock: The Stephen King Newsletter* (June 1985): 6-7. [bibliography]

K11. **"Stephen King Bibliography,"** compiled by Stephanie Leonard, in *Castle Rock: The Stephen King Newsletter* (July 1985): 4, 7. [bibliography]

K12. **"Checklist,"** compiled by Michael R. Collings, in *The Many Facets of Stephen King*. STARMONT STUDIES IN LITERARY CRITICISM, No. 11. Mercer Island, WA: Starmont House, 1986, cloth, p. 142-186. See also **I9.** [bibliography]

K13. **"Filmography,"** compiled by Michael R. Collings, in *The Films of Stephen King*. STARMONT STUDIES IN LITERARY CRITICISM, No. 12. Mercer Island, WA: Starmont House, July 1986, cloth, p. 167-188. See also **I12.** [filmography]

K14. **"Film Credits,"** compiled by Jesse Horsting, in *Stephen King at the Movies*. New York: Starlog, A Signet Book New American Library, August 1986, paper, p. 102-110. See also **I13**. [filmography]

K15. **"King, Stephen,"** compiled by Charles N. Brown and William G. Contento, in *Science Fiction in Print: 1985*. Oakland, CA: Locus Press, 1986, cloth, p. 35-36. [bibliography]

K16. **"Filmographie,"** compiled by Michael R. Collings, in *Stephen King und Seine Filme*. HEYNE FILMBIBLIOTHEK, 112. Translated by Norbert Stresau. München: Heyne Verlag, 1987, paper, p. 266-275. See also **I12c.** [filmography]

K17. ***The Annotated Guide to Stephen King: A Primary and Secondary Bibliography of the Works of America's Premier Horror Writer***, by Michael R. Collings. STARMONT REFERENCE GUIDE, No. 8. Mercer Island, WA: Starmont House, October 1986, 179 p., cloth. Published simultaneously in trade paper. See also **I14**. [bibliography]

b. San Bernardino, CA: Borgo Press, 1986, 179 p., cloth.

CONTENTS: "Foreword"; "List of Abbreviations."

PART ONE: PRIMARY BIBLIOGRAPHY. A. "Book-Length Fiction"; B. "Collections of King's Fictions"; C. "Short Fiction and Poetry"; D. "Non-Fiction, Criticism, and Reviews"; E. "The Audio-Visual King."

PART TWO: SECONDARY BIBLIOGRAPHY. F. "Bibliographic Studies"; "Book-Length Critical Studies and Newsletters"; H. "Selected Critical Articles, Reviews, and Interviews." "List of Works Cited."

K18. **"SK Paperback Bibliography Compiled,"** by Wayne Rhodes, in *Castle Rock: The Stephen King Newsletter* 3:2 (January, 1987): 3, 8. [bibliography]

Descriptive bibliography of all cover states for paperback editions through 1986.

K19. **"Update on SK Paperback Bibliography,"** by Wayne Rhodes, in *Castle Rock: The Stephen King Newsletter* 3:10 (October, 1987): 8. Addendum to **K18**.

K20. **"Stephen King: A Guide to Scholarship, 1980-1987,"** compiled by Marshall Tymn, in *Landscape of Fear: Stephen King's American Gothic,* by Tony Magistrale. Bowling Green OH: Bowling Green State University Popular Press, March 15, 1988, cloth/paper, p. 125-129. See also **I19**. [bibliography]

K21. **[Title unknown],** by Stefano Massaron, in *Febbre Gialla* (May, 1988): . [Italian]. [bibliography]

K22. **"Selected Bibliography,"** compiled by Joseph Reino, in *Stephen King: The First Decade,* Carrie *to* Pet Sematary. Boston: G. K. Hall, 1988, paper, p. 151-156. See also **I18.** Covers only 1974-1984. [bibliography]

K23. **"Stephen King,"** by Carl Rollyson, in *Critical Survey of Mystery and Detective Fiction,* Vol. 3, edited by Frank N. Magill. Englewood Cliffs, NJ: Salem Press, 1988, cloth, p. 989. [bibliography]

K24. **"List of Works Cited and Consulted,"** by Tyson Blue, in *The Unseen King,* by Tyson Blue. STARMONT STUDIES IN LITERARY CRITICISM, No. 26. Mercer Island, WA: Starmont House, 1989, cloth, p. 181-188. See also **I22**. [bibliography]

K25. **"Horror's Heaviest Hitter: Fifteen Titles on Tape Make Stephen King a One-Man Scarefest,"** by Frank Lovece, in *Video Magazine* 13:5 (August, 1989): 45+ [5-page article]. [filmography].

K26. **"Appendices,"** compiled by George Beahm, in *The Stephen King Companion,* edited by George Beahm. Kansas City, MO: Andrew and McMeel, September 1989, paper, p. 320-359. See also **I24.** [bibliography]

CONTENTS: 1. "Books in Print"; 2. "Books about King"; 3. "Filmography and Videography"; 4. "Audiocassettes"; 5. "Book Collectibles by Stephen King: A Price Guide," by George Beahm with Barry R. Levin; 6. "Resources."

K27. **"Selected Bibliography,"** compiled by Anthony Magistrale, in *The Moral Voyages of Stephen King*. STARMONT STUDIES IN LITERARY CRITICISM, No. 25. Mercer Island, WA: Starmont House, 1989, cloth, p. 125-153. See **I24.** [bibliography]

K28. **"King, Stephen (Edwin) 1947- (Richard Bachman),"** in *Something About the Author, Volume 55,* edited by Anne Commire. Detroit, MI: Gale Research, 1989, cloth, p. 61-76. [bibliography]

K29. **"Bibliographie der Veröffentlichungen von Stephen King,"** compiled by Joachim Körber, in *Das Stephen King Buch,* edited by Joachim Körber. München: Wilhelm Heyne Verlag, 1989, paper, p. 539-588. See also **I26**. [German-language bibliography]

CONTENTS: ERSTER TEIL: ORIGINALAUSGABEN ["Part One: Original Editions"]—"1. Selbständige Veröffentlichungen" ["Books and Chapbooks"]; "2. Unselbständige Veröffentlichungen" [Articles, stories, reviews, poetry]; "3. Interviews."

ZWEITER TEIL: DEUTSCHE AUSGABEN ["Part Two: German Editions"]-"1. Selbständige Veröffentlichungen"; "2. Unselbständige Veröffentlichungen"; 3. "Interviews."

K30. **"Filmographie,"** compiled by Norbert Stresau, in *Das Stephen King Buch,* edited by Joachim Körber. München: Wilhelm Heyne Verlag, 1989, paper, p. 598-597. See also **I26**. [German-language filmography]

CONTENTS: "I. Langfilme" ["Feature Films"]; "II. Kurzfilme" ["Short Films"]; "III. Projekte" ["Projects"].

K31. **"A Stephen King Bibliography,"** compiled by Stephen Spignesi, in *The Stephen King Quiz Book*. New York: A Signet Book, New American Library, August 1990, paper, p. 191-203. Gives source and date of first appearances. See also **I28**. [bibliography]

CONTENTS: "Part One-Novels and Collections"; "Part Two-Short Stories and Novellas"; "Other Books of Interest" [Secondary Sources]; "Addresses of Sources."

K32. **"Stephen King: Bibliography,"** compiled by Marsha De Filippo, in *The Magazine of Fantasy & Science Fiction* 79:6 (December, 1990): 56-60. [bibliography]

CONTENTS: "Novels by Stephen King"; "Also by Stephen King"; "Under the pseudonym 'Richard Bachman'"; "Anthologies andother publications containing work by Stephen King"; "Magazine [sic] and newspapers containing fiction and non-fiction by King"; "Other sources of information about King"

K33. ***The Shape Under the Sheet: The Complete Stephen King Encyclopedia,*** by Stephen J. Spignesi. Ann Arbor, MI: Popular Culture, Ink., May 1991, cloth, p. 152-542. Annotated bibliography of primary works. See also **I33**. [bibliography]

K34. **"'He Who Tells It': An Annotated Bibliography of Books & Articles About Stephen King and His Work,"** by Stephen J. Spignesi, in *The Shape Under the Sheet: The Complete Stephen King Encyclopedia,* by Stephen J. Spignesi. Ann Arbor, MI: Popular Culture, Ink., May 1991, cloth, p. 673-678. Annotated bibliography of secondary materials. See also **I33**. [bibliography]

K35. ***The Dark Descent: Essays Defining Stephen King's Horrorscape,*** edited by Anthony Magistrale. New York: Greenwood Press, 1992, cloth, p. 213-220. See also **I36**. [bibliography]

K36. ***Stephen King: The Second Decade*-Danse Macabre *to* The Dark Half**, by Anthony Magistrale. New York: Twayne Publishers, 1992, cloth, p. . See also **I37**. [bibliography]

K37. ***The Work of Stephen King: An Annotated Bibliography & Guide***, by Michael R. Collings. BIBLIOGRAPHIES OF MODERN AUTHORS, No. 25. Series editor, Boden Clarke. San Bernardino CA: Borgo Press, 1996, 480 p., cloth. See also **I45**. [bibliography]

b. San Bernardino CA: Borgo Press, 1996, 480 p., trade paper.

L.

SECONDARY SOURCES

PROFILES AND BIO-BIBLIOGRAPHICAL SKETCHES

L1. **"King, Stephen 1947- ,"** in *Contemporary Authors, Volumes 61-64,* edited by Cynthia R. Fadool. Detroit, MI: Gale Research, 1976, cloth, p. 300. [profile]

L2. **"King, Stephen 1947-,"** in *Something About the Author, Volume 9,* edited by Anne Commire. Detroit, MI: Gale Research, 1976, cloth, p. 126. [profile]

L3. **"Stephen King,"** in *Who's Who in Horror and Fantasy Fiction,* by Mike Ashley. London: Elm Tree Books, 1977, cloth, p. 187. [profile]

ab. New York: Taplinger Publishing Co., 1978, cloth, p. 107.

L4. **"King, Stephen Edwin,"** in *Who's Who in America, 40th edition, 1978-1979*. Wilmette, IL: Marquis Who's Who, 1978, cloth, p. . [profile]

L5. **"King, Stephen,"** by John Clute, in *The Encyclopedia of Science Fiction: An Illustrated A to Z,* edited by Peter Nicholls and John Clute. London: Granada, 1979, cloth, p. 330. [profile]

ab. *The Science Fiction Encyclopedia,* edited by Peter Nicholls and John Clute. Garden City, NY: Doubleday & Co., 1979, cloth, p. 330.

L6. **"King, Stephen,"** by Jeff Rovin, in *The Fantasy Almanac*. New York: E. P. Dutton, 1979, paper, p. 158. [profile]

L7. **"Living with the Boogeyman,"** by Tabitha King, in *Murderess, Ink.*, edited by Dilys Winn. New York: Bell, 1979, trade paper, p. 176-177. A profile of King by his wife, focusing on his family and personality. [profile]

L8. **"Stephen King,"** by R. Reginald, in *Science Fiction and Fantasy Literature, Volume 2: Contemporary Science Fiction Authors II*. Detroit, MI: Gale Research Co., 1979, cloth, p. 961. [profile]

L9. **"King, Stephen,"** in *Biography Index, Volume 11* (September 1976-August 1979). New York: H. W. Wilson Co., 1980, cloth. [index to profiles]

L10. **"King, Stephen Edwin,"** in *Who's Who in America, 41st Edition, 1980-1981, Volume 1.* Wilmette, IL: Marquis Who's Who, 1980, cloth, p. 1840. [profile]

L11. **"King, Stephen (Edwin) 1947-,"** by Peter M. Gareffa, in *Contemporary Authors, New Revision Series, Volume 1,* edited by Ann Evory. Detroit, MI: Gale Research, 1980, cloth, p. 333-336. [profile and reviews of selected books]

L12. **"Stephen King,"** in *Contemporary Literary Criticism, Volume 12, Young Adult Literature*, edited by Dedria Bryfonski. Detroit, MI: Gale Research Co., 1980, p. 309-311, cloth. [collection of critical excerpts]

L13. **[Title unknown],** in *Dictionary of Literary Biography Yearbook, 1980.* Detroit, MI: Gale Research, 1980, cloth, p. . [profile]

L14. **"King, Stephen,"** in *Current Biography* 42:10 (October, 1981): 31-33. [profile]

L15. **"King, Stephen [Edwin],"** in *Current Biography Yearbook, 1981*, edited by Charles Moritz. New York: H. W. Wilson Co., 1981, cloth, p. 252-255. An updated version of L14. [profile]

L16. **"King, Stephen,"** by Philip Kopper, in *1981 Britannica Book of the Year,* "Biographies." Chicago: Encyclopedia Britannica, Inc., 1981, cloth, p. 82. [profile]

L17. **"Stephen King,"** by Keith Neilson, in *Critical Survey of Short Fiction, Current Writers, Volume 7,* edited by Frank N. Magill. Englewood Cliffs, NJ: Salem Press, 1981, cloth, p. 2662. [profile]

L18. **"Stephen King,"** by Mark Harris, in *Dictionary of Literary Biography Yearbook, 1980*, edited by Karen L. Rood, Jean W. Ross, and Richard Ziegfeld. Detroit, MI: Gale Research Co., 1981, cloth, p. 226-234. [profile, bio-criticism, and bibliographical survey]

L19. **[Title unknown],** in *The New York Times Biographical Service: A Compilation of Current Biographical Information of General Interest, Volume 12.* New York: Arno Press, 1981, cloth. [profile]

L20. **"The King of the Macabre at Home,"** by Michael J. Bandler, in *Parents* (January, 1982): . [profile with photos]

L21. **"The Once and Future King,"** by David McDonnell, in *Prevue* (April/May, 1982): . [profile]

L22. **"King, Stephen Edwin,"** in *Who's Who in America, 42nd edition, 1982-1983, Volume 1.* Wilmette, IL: Marquis Who's Who, 1982, cloth, p. 1814. [profile]

L23. ***A Reader's Guide to Fantasy,*** by Baird Searles, Beth Meacham, and Michael Franklin. New York: Facts on File, 1982, cloth, p. 62-63, 74, 153, 160, 161. [profile; esp. p. 62-63]

L24. **"The Thrills, Chills, and Skills of Stephen King,"** by Andrea Thompson, in *McCall's* (February, 1983): 74-75. [profile]

L25. **"King, Stephen,"** in *Biography Index, Volume 12* (September 1979-August 1982). New York: H. W. Wilson Co., 1983, cloth. [index to profiles].

L26. **"King, Stephen,"** in *The Writers Directory, 1984-86.* Chicago: St. James Press, 1983, cloth, p. 541. [profile]

L27. **"Stephen King,"** by Charles Platt, in *Dream Makers II.* New York: Berkley Books, 1983, paper, p. 273-284. [profile and interview]

L28. **"Stephen King,"** in *Contemporary Literary Criticism, Volume 26*, edited by Jean C. Stine. Detroit, MI: Gale Research Co., 1983, cloth, p. 234-244. [critical excerpts]

L29. **"King, Stephen,"** in *Biography Index, Volume 13* (September 1982-August 1984). [index to profiles]

L30. **King, Stephen Edwin,"** in *Who's Who in America, 43rd Edition, 1984-1985, Volume 1.* Wilmette, IL: Marquis Who's Who, 1984, cloth, p. 1785. [profile]

L31. **[Title unknown],** in *Science Fiction Sourcebook,* edited by David Wingrove. New York: Van Nostrand Reinhold, 1984, cloth, p. . [profile]

L32. **"King, Stephen,"** in *Biography and Genealogy Master Index, 1981-1985 Cumulation, Volume 3,* edited by Barbara McNeil. Detroit, MI: Gale Research Co., 1985, 2324 p., cloth. [index to profiles]

L33. **"Stephen King,"** by Richard Bleiler, in *Supernatural Fiction Writers: Fantasy and Horror, Volume II*, edited by E. F. Bleiler. New York: Charles Scribner's Sons, 1985, cloth, p. 1037-1044. [profile with numerous indexed references]

L34. **[Title unknown],** in *Picture Week* [Time-Life] (September 29, 1986): . [short profile with 3 photographs]

L35. **"King of Horror: The Master of Pop Dread Writes On and On and On,"** by Stefan Kanfer, in *Time* 128:14 (October 6, 1986): 74-78.

b. *Tribune Review* [Greensburg, PA] (November 2, 1986): .
c. as microfiche: *NewsBank Names in the News* 9 (December, 1986): Fiche 83, F5-F9.
d. *The Shape Under the Sheet: The Complete Stephen King Encyclopedia,* by Stephen J. Spignesi. Ann Arbor, MI: Popular Culture, Ink., May 1991, cloth, p. 17-23.

L36. **"Stephen King, 1947- ,"** by Richard E. Meyer, in *Beacham's Popular Fiction in America, Volume 2,* edited by Walton Beacham. Washington, DC: Beacham Publishing, November 1986, cloth, p. 747-758. [profile, plus critical overviews of the major novels]

L37. **"King, Stephen,"** by Don Herron, in *The Penguin Encyclopedia of Horror and the Supernatural,* edited by Jack Sullivan. New York: Viking, 1986, cloth, p. 243-246. [bio-critical profile]

L38. **"King, Stephen,"** in *Biography Index, Volume 14* (September 1984-August 1986). [index to profiles]

L39. **"Stephen (Edwin) King,"** in *Contemporary Literary Criticism, Volume 37,* edited by Daniel G. Markowski. Detroit, MI: Gale Research Co., 1986, cloth, p. 197-208. [critical excerpts]

L40. **"King, Stephen Edwin,"** in *Who's Who in America, 44th edition, 1986-1987, Volume 1.* Wilmette, IL: Marquis Who's Who, Macmillan Directory Division, November 1986, cloth, p. 1530. [profile]

L41. **"King, Stephen,"** in *The Writers Directory, 1986-88.* Chicago: St. James Press, 1986, cloth, p. 526. [profile]

L42. **"King, Stephen,"** in *1987 Motion Picture Almanac, 58th Edition,* edited by Richard Gertner. New York: Quigley, 1987, cloth, p. 146. [profile]

L43. **"King, Stephen,"** in *Academic American Encyclopedia, Volume 12.* Danbury, CT: Grollier, 1987, cloth, p. 81. [profile]

L44. **"King, Stephen [Edwin] (1947-),"** in *Benét's Readers Encyclopedia, Third Edition.* New York: Harper & Row, 1987, cloth, p. 530. [profile]

L45. **"King, Stephen Edwin,"** in *International Who's Who, 1987-1988, 51st ed.* London: Europa Publications, 1987, cloth, p. 785. [profile]

L46. ***Science Fiction and Fantasy Reference Index, 1978-1985,*** edited by H. W. Hall. Detroit, MI: Gale Research, 1987, 2 vol., cloth. [numerous indexed references]

L47. **"Stephen King,"** in *Dream Makers: Science Fiction and Fantasy Writers at Work,* by Charles Platt. New and revised edition. New York: Frederick Ungar Publishing Co., 1987, cloth, p. 261-271. [profile]

L48. ***Supernatural Fiction for Teens: 500 Good Paperbacks to Read for Wonderment, Fear, and Fun,*** by Cosette N. Kies. Littleton, CO: Libraries Unlimited, 1987, paper, p. 42-43. [annotated references to King novels]

L49. **"King, Stephen Edwin,"** in *Who's Who in U.S. Writers, Editors & Poets: A Biographical Directory,* edited by Curt Johnson. Highland Park, IL: December Press, 1987, cloth, p. 228. [bio-bibliography]

L50. **"Stephen King, Author, Dons a Publisher's Hat,"** by E. McDowell, in *New York Times Biographical Service* (January 1988): 100. [profile]

L51. **"King, Stephen,"** in *1988 Motion Picture Almanac, 59th Edition,* edited by Richard Gertner. New York: Quigley, 1988, cloth, p. 143. [profile]

L52. **"King, Stephen,** in *Biography Index, Volume 15* (September 1985-August 1988): . [index to profiles]

L53. **"King, Stephen,"** by Barbara Perkins, *World Book Enclyclopedia, Volume 11, 1988 edition.* Chicago: World Book, 1988, cloth, p. 323. [encyclopedia entry]

L54. **"King, Stephen,"** in *Books for College Libraries: A Core Collection of 50,000 Titles, 3rd ed.* Chicago: American Library Association, 1988, cloth. Listings for *Danse Macabre* [item #2.75] and *'Salem's Lot* [item #2.13115].

L55. **"King, Stephen,"** in *The Writers Directory, 1988-90, Eighth Edition.* Chicago: St. James Press, 1988, cloth, p. 529. [profile]

L56. **"King, Stephen Edwin,"** in *International Who's Who, 1988-1989, 52nd edition.* London: Europa Publications, 1988, cloth, p. 805. [profile]

L57. **"King, Stephen Edwin,"** in *Who's Who in Entertainment, First Edition, 1988-1989.* Wilmette, IL: Marquis Who's Who, 1988, cloth. [bio-bibliography]

L58. **"King, Stephen [Edwin],"** by Mike Ashley, in *The New Encyclopedia of Science Fiction,* edited by James Gunn. New York: Viking, 1988, cloth, p. 256. [profile]

L59. **"King, Stephen Edwin,"** in *Who's Who in U.S. Writers, Editors & Poets: A Biographical Directory, 1988*, edited by Curt Johnson and Frank Nipp. Highland Park, IL: December Press, 1988, cloth, p. 289. [bio-bibliography]

L60. **[Title unknown],** in *New York Times Biographical Service* 19 (1988): . [profile]

L61. ***Horror: A Conoisseur's Guide to Literature and Film,*** by Leonard Wolf. New York: Facts on File, 1989, cloth, p. 37, 42, 121, 122, 168, 196. References to *Carrie* (novel); *Carrie* (film); *Children of the Corn* (film); *It*; and *The Shining* (film). [criticism]

L62. **"King, Stephen,"** in *1989 Motion Picture Almanac, 60th Edition,* edited by Jane Klain. New York: Quigley, 1989, cloth, p. 170. [profile]

L63. **"King, Stephen (1947-),"** in *Something About the Author, Volume 55,* edited by Anne Commire. Detroit, MI: Gale Research, 1989, cloth, p. 61-76. [profile, biography, criticism, and bibliography]

L64. **"King, Stephen (1947-),"** in *World Book Encyclopedia, Volume 11, 1989 Edition*. Chicago: World Book, Inc., 1989, cloth, p. 323. [profile]

L65. **"King, Stephen,"** in *International Authors and Writers Who's Who, Eleventh Edition*, edited by Ernest Kay. Cambridge: International Biographical Centre, 1989, cloth, p. 469. [profile]

L66. **"King, Stephen Edwin,"** in *International Who's Who, 1989-1990, 53ed edition*. London: Europa Publication, 1989, cloth, p. 835. [profile]

L67. **"King, Stephen Edwin,"** in *Who's Who in American 45th edition, 1988-1989, Volume 1*. Wilmette, IL: Marquis Who's Who, 1989, cloth, p. 1693. [profile]

L68. **[Title unknown],** in *Authors and Artists for Young People, Volume 1*. Detroit, MI: Gale Research, 1989, cloth. p. . [profile]

L69. **[Title unknown],** in *Cyclopedia of World Authors II*, edited by Frank N. Magill. Englewood Cliffs, NJ: Salem Press, 1989, cloth, p. . [profile]

L70. **"King, Stephen Edwin,"** in *Who's Who in Writers, Editors & Poets: United States & Canada, 1989-1990*, edited by Curt Johnson and Frank Nipp. Highland Park, IL: December Press, 1989, cloth, p. 279. [bio-bibliography]

L71. **[Title unknown],** in *Bestsellers: Books and Authors in the News* 90:1 (1990): . [profile]

L72. **"King, Stephen,"** in *1990 Motion Picture Almanac, 61st Edition*, edited by Jane Klain. New York: Quigley, 1990, cloth, p. 177. [profile]

L73. **"King, Stephen,"** in *Biography and Genealogy Master Index, 1986-1990 Cumulation, Volume 2*, edited by Barbara McNeil. Detroit, MI: Gale Research, 1990, cloth, p. . [index to profiles]

L74. **"Stephen King,"** in *Earl Blackwell's Celebrity Register, 1990*, compiled by Celebrity Services International, Inc. Detroit, MI: Gale Research, 1990, cloth, p. 235. [profile]

L75. **"King, Stephen Edwin,"** in *International Who's Who 1990-1991, 54th edition*. London: Europa Publication, 1990, cloth, p. 851-852. [profile]

L76. **"King, Stephen Edwin,"** in *Who's Who in America, 46th Edition, 1990-1991, Volume 1*. Wilmette, IL: Marquis Who's Who, 1990, cloth, p. 1792. [profile]

L77. **"King, Stephen,"** in *The Writers Directory, 1990-92, Ninth Edition*. Chicago: St. James Press, 1990, cloth, p. 554. [profile]

L78. **"Horror King, Stephen King,"** by Stephen Spignesi, in *Cinefantastique* 21:4 (February, 1991): 18-19, 61. [profile]

L79. **"Stephen King,"** in *Masters of Darkness III,* edited by Dennis Etchison. New York: Tor, A Tom Doherty Associates Book, May 1991, paper, p. 326-327. [profile]

L80. **"King, Stephen,"** in *1991 Motion Picture Almanac, 62nd Edition,* edited by Barry Monush. New York: Quigley, 1991, cloth, p. 176-177. [profile]

L81. **"King, Stephen,"** in *Biography and Genealogy Master Index, 1991 Cumulation*, edited by Barbara McNeil. Detroit, MI: Gale Research, 1991, cloth, p. . [index to profiles]

L82. **"Postcards from the Dark Side of the Moon: a Bare-Bones Biographical Profile,"** by Stephen J. Spignesi, in *The Shape Under the Sheet: The Complete Stephen King Encyclopedia.* Ann Arbor, MI: Popular Culture, Ink., May 1991, cloth, p. 5-10. [profile]

L83. **"King, Stephen,"** in *International Authors and Writers Who's Who, Twelfth Edition*, edited by Ernest Kay. Cambridge: International Biographical Centre, 1991, cloth, p. 468. [profile]

L84. **"King, Stephen,"** in *The Writers Directory, 1992-94, Tenth Edition.* Chicago: St. James Press, 1991, cloth, p. 545. [profile]

L85. ***Supernatural Fiction for Teens: More Than 1300 Good Paperbacks to Read for Wonderment, Fear, and Fun,*** *2d Edition*, by Cosette N. Kies. Englewood, CO: Libraries Unlimited, 1992, paper, p. 93-94. [annotated references to King novels]

L86. **"King, Stephen (1947-),"** in *The Encyclopedia of Science Fiction*, Second Edition, edited by John Clute and Peter Nicholls. London: Orbit, 1993, cloth, p. 666-667. [profile and critique]

b. New York: St. Martin's Press, 1993, cloth, p. 666-667.
bb. New York: St. Martin's Press, 1995, trade paper, p. 666-667.

L87. **"King, Stephen, 1946- ,"** in *Webster's New World Encyclopedia, College Edition*. New York: Prentice Hall, 1993, cloth, p. 587. [profile]

L88. **"King, Stephen,"** in *The Writers Directory, 1994-96, Eleventh Edition*, edited by Miranda H. Ferrara and George W. Schmidt. Detroit: St. James Press, 1994, cloth, p. 686. [profile]

L89. **"King, Stephen Edwin (1947-),"** in *Larousse Dictionary of Writers*, edited by Rosemary Goring. Edinburgh & New York: Larousse, 1994, cloth, p. 529. [profile]

L90. **"King, Stephen Edwin,"** in *Who's Who in America 1996*, 50th Edition. New Providence, NJ: Marquis Who's Who, 1995, cloth, Volume 1 (A-K), p. 2260. [profile]

L91. "**King, Stephen (1947-),**" in *The Oxford Companion to American Literature, Sixth Edition*, edited by James D. Hart, with revisions and additions by Phillip W. Leininger. New York, Oxford: Oxford University Press, 1995, cloth, p. 349. [profile]

L92. "**King, Stephen (Edwin),**" in *Merriam-Webster's Encyclopedia of Literature*. Springfield, MA: Merriam-Webster, 1995, cloth, p. 633. [profile]

L93. "**King, Stephen,**" in *The Writers Directory, 1996-98, Twelfth Edition*, edited by Miranda H. Ferrara. Detroit: St. James Press, 1996, cloth, p. 824-825. [profile]

M.

SECONDARY SOURCES

INTERVIEWS

For general information on King's appearances on radio and television interview shows, see:

Brooks, Dr. Barry M. "Stephen King on Television," in *Castle Rock: The Stephen King Newsletter* 2:11 (November, 1986): 5, 6.
Brooks, Dr. Barry M. "Stephen King on TV and Radio (New Listings)," in *Castle Rock: The Stephen King Newsletter* 3:1 (December, 1986-January, 1987): 13.

PRINT INTERVIEWS

M1. **"Hampden Teacher Hits Jackpot with New Book,"** conducted by David Bright, in *Bangor Daily News* [Bangor, ME] (May 25, 1973): . King's first interview; discussion of *Carrie*.

b. *Feast of Fear: Conversations with Stephen King*, edited by Tim Underwood and Chuck Miller. Novato, CA: Underwood-Miller, August 1989, cloth, p. 1-3. [See **I23**].

M2. **"Biographical Notes,"** in *Doubleday Books Publicity Department,* (September 15, 1973).

M3. **"Lisbon Graduate's Novel Published, Another Slated,"** conducted by Connie Footman, in *Lewiston Daily Sun* [Maine] (April 2, 1974): .

b. *Feast of Fear: Conversations with Stephen King*, edited by Tim Underwood and Chuck Miller. Novato, CA: Underwood-Miller, August 1989, cloth, p. 3-5. [See **I23**].

M4. **"Random Notes—An Interview with Stephen King,"** in *Cavalier* (August, 1974): .

M5. **[Title unknown],** *Sunday Telegraph* [Portland, ME] (October 31, 1976).

M6. **"Stephen King,"** conducted by John F. Baker, in *Publishers Weekly* 211 (January 17, 1977): 12-13.

M7. **"Stephen King's Silver-Lined Prose,"** conducted by Emmett Meara, in *Bangor Daily News* [Bangor, ME] (February 12, 1977): .

b. *Feast of Fear: Conversations with Stephen King*, edited by Tim Underwood and Chuck Miller. Novato, CA: Underwood-Miller, August 1989, cloth, p. 5-6. [See **I23**].

M8. **"Stephen King Makes Millions by Scaring Hell out of 3 Million Readers,"** conducted by Frank Sleeper, in *People Weekly* 7 (March 7, 1977): 61-62.

M9. **[Title unknown],** in *New York Post* (March 12, 1977): .

M10. **[Title unknown],** *Maine Campus* [University of Maine, Orono] (April, 1977): .

M11. **[Title unknown],** *Lewiston Journal* [Maine] (April 2, 1977): .

M12. **[Title unknown],** *New Hampshire* (April 26, 1977): .

M13. **"Witches and Aspirin,"** conducted by Mel Allen, in *Writer's Digest* 57:6 (June, 1977): 61-62.

M14. **[Title unknown],** *Chicago Daily News* (July 7, 1977): .

M15. **[Title unknown],** *New York Times Book Review* (August, 1977): .

M16. **"King of the Occult,"** conducted by Lois Lowry, in *Down East Magazine* (November, 1977).

M17. **"Horror Teller,"** in *Horizon* (February, 1978): .

M18. **[Title unknown],** *The Maine Campus* (September 8, 1978): .

M19. **"A Talk with Stephen King,"** conducted by Leonore Fleischer, in *Washington Post Book World* (October 1, 1978): .

M20. **[Title unknown],** *Sky* (November, 1978): .

M21. **[Title unknown],** *Shreveport Journal* (November 24, 1978): .

M22. **"Interview...Stephen King,"** conducted by Dan Weaver, in *The Literary Guild Monthly Selection Magazine* (December, 1978): .

M23. **"Stephen King on *Carrie, The Shining,* Etc.,"** conducted by Peter S. Perakos, in *Cinefantastique* 1:8 (Winter, 1978): 12-15.

b. *Feast of Fear: Conversations with Stephen King*, edited by Tim Underwood and Chuck Miller. Novato, CA: Underwood-Miller, August 1989, cloth, p. 63-70. [See **I23**].

M24. **"King of the Night,"** conducted by David Chute, in *Take One* (January, 1979): 33-38.

b. *Feast of Fear: Conversations with Stephen King*, edited by Tim Underwood and Chuck Miller. Novato, CA: Underwood-Miller, August 1989, cloth, p. 71-80. [See **I23**].

M25. **"Scaring People All the Way to the Bank,"** conducted by Charlotte Phelan, in *Houston Post* (February 25, 1979): .

b. *Feast of Fear: Conversations with Stephen King*, edited by Tim Underwood and Chuck Miller. Novato, CA: Underwood-Miller, August 1989, cloth, p. 9-10. [See **I23**].

M26. **[Title unknown],** *Morning Star Telegraph* (February 25, 1979): .

M27. **[Title unknown],** *Milwaukee Sentinel* [Wisconsin] (February 28, 1979): .

M28. **[Title unknown],** *St. Petersburg Times* [Florida] (March 4, 1979): .

M29. **"The Man Who Writes Nightmares,"** conducted by Mel Allen, in *Yankee* (March, 1979).

b. *Bare Bones: Conversations on Terror with Stephen King*, edited by Tim Underwood and Chuck Miller. San Francisco, CA: Underwood-Miller, 1988; New York: McGraw-Hill, 1988, p. 63-68. [See **I20**].

M30. **"The Night Shifter,"** conducted by Stephen Jones, in *Fantasy Media* [England] (March, 1979): .

b. *Bare Bones: Conversations on Terror with Stephen King*, edited by Tim Underwood and Chuck Miller. San Francisco, CA: Underwood-Miller, 1988; New York: McGraw-Hill, 1988, p. 117-119. [See **I20**].

M31. **[Title unknown],** *Middlesex News* [Massachusetts] (April 8, 1979): .

M32. **"Carrie's Mom and Danny's Dad,"** conducted by Monty Clinch, in *Ms. London* [England] (April 9, 1979): 10. Bio-critical article with interview, appearing just after the British publication of *The Stand*.

M33. **[Title unknown],** *Cleveland Press* [Ohio] (April 12, 1979): .

M34. **"Steve King's *The Stand*,"** conducted by Burton Hatlen, in *Kennebec* [University of Maine, Augusta] (April, 1979): .

M35. **"Shine of the Times: An Interview with Stephen King,"** conducted by Marty Ketchum, Pat Cadigan, and Lewis Shiner, in *Shayol* 1:3 (Summer, 1979): 43-46.

b. *Bare Bones: Conversations on Terror with Stephen King*, edited by Tim Underwood and Chuck Miller. San Francisco, CA: Underwood-Miller, 1988; New York: McGraw-Hill, 1988, p. 119-123. [See **I20**].

M36. **[Title unknown],** *Sunday Telegraph* [Portland, ME] (July 29, 1979): .

M37. **[Title unknown],** *Rochester Democrat and Chronicle* [New York] (August 26, 1979): .

M38. **[Title unknown],** *Washington Post* (August 26, 1979): .

M39. **"Visions of the Holocaust,"** conducted by Joseph McLellan, in *Washington Post* "Style," (August 30, 1979): F1.

M40. **[Title unknown],** *Patriot Ledger* [Quincy, MA] (August 31, 1979): .

M41. **[Title unknown],** *Pittsburgh Press* (September 6, 1979): .

M42. **"He Brings Life to Dead Issues,"** conducted by Christopher Evans, in *Minneapolis Star* [Minnesota] (September 8, 1979): .

b. *Bare Bones: Conversations on Terror with Stephen King*, edited by Tim Underwood and Chuck Miller. San Francisco, CA: Underwood-Miller, 1988; New York: McGraw-Hill, 1988, p. 90-92. [See **I20**].

M43. **[Title unknown],** *New American* [Baltimore, MD] (September 16, 1979): .

M44. **[Title unknown],** *Woodlands* [Houston, TX] (September 19, 1979): .

M45. **[Title unknown],** *Lincoln Star* (September 20, 1979): .

M46. **[Title unknown],** *Daily Nebraskan* (September 21, 1979): .

M47. **"Stephen King: Behind the Best Sellers,"** by Carol Lawson, in *New York Times Book Review* (September 23, 1979): 42.

M48. **[Title unknown],** *New York Daily News* (September 23, 1979): .

M49. **[Title unknown],** *Los Angeles Herald Examiner* (September 26, 1979): .

M50. **[Title unknown],** *Detroit News* (September 26, 1979): .

M51. **"Eyeglasses for the Mind,"** conducted by George Christian, in *Houston Chronicle* [Houston, TX] (September 30, 1979): .

b. *Feast of Fear: Conversations with Stephen King*, edited by Tim Underwood and Chuck Miller. Novato, CA: Underwood-Miller, August 1989, cloth, p. 34-38. [See **I23**].

M52. **[Title unknown],** *Houston Post* [Houston, TX] (September 30, 1979): .

M53. **[Title unknown],** *Boston Herald American* (September, 1979): .

M54. **[Title unknown],** *Burlington Free Press* [Vermont] (October 1, 1979): .

M55. **[Title unknown],** *Peninsula Times Tribune* (October 2, 1979): .

M56. **[Title unknown],** *Phoenix Arizona Gazeteer* (October 12, 1979): .

M57. **[Title unknown],** *Beaver County Times* [Pennsylvania] (October 14, 1979): .

M58. **[Title unknown],** *Contra Costa Times* [California] (October 14, 1979): .

M59. **[Title unknown],** *New Kensington Valley News Dispatch* (October 23, 1979): .

M60. **[Title unknown],** *North Hills News Record* (October 26, 1979): .

M61. **[Title unknown],** *Kennebec Journal* (October 27, 1979): .

M62. **[Title unknown],** *Lakeland Florida Ledger* (October 28, 1979): .

M63. **[Title unknown],** *Sunday Telegram* [Portland, OR] (October 28, 1979): .

M64. **"It *Is* You, Mr. King...Isn't It?"** conducted by Jery Harkavy, in *Portland Press Herald* (October 31, 1979): .

b. *Feast of Fear: Conversations with Stephen King*, edited by Tim Underwood and Chuck Miller. Novato, CA: Underwood-Miller, August 1989, cloth, p. 39-40. [See **I23**].

M65. **"Interview with Stephen King,"** conducted by Stanley Wiater and Peter Straub, 1979 World Fantasy Convention, Providence, Rhode Island, October 1979.

b. as: "Halloween Made for Horror Writers," in *Springfield Morning Union* [Springfield, MA] (October 31, 1979): .
c. *Fangoria* no. 6 (June 1980): .
d. as part of: "Three Interviews with Stephen King and Peter Straub," "Partners in Fear," *Bare Bones: Conversations on Terror with Stephen King*, edited by Tim Underwood and Chuck Miller. San Francisco, CA: Underwood-Miller, 1988; New York: McGraw-Hill, 1988, p. 153-160. [See **I20**].

M66. **[Title unknown],** *Portland Press Herald* [Portland, ME] (October 31, 1979): .

M67. **"An Interview with Stephen King,"** in *Waldenbooks Newsletter* (October, 1979): .

M68. **"Watching *'Salem's Lot*—With the King,"** conducted by Chris Palmer, in *Bangor Daily News* [Maine] (November 17, 1979): .

b. *Feast of Fear: Conversations with Stephen King*, edited by Tim Underwood and Chuck Miller. Novato, CA: Underwood-Miller, August 1989, cloth, p. 80-82. [See **I23**].

M69. **[Title unknown],** *Lewiston Daily Sun* [Maine] (January 10, 1980): .

M70. **[Title unknown],** *Tennesean* [Maine] (January 10, 1980): .

M71. **"Who's Afraid of Stephen (Carrie) King?"** conducted by Carrie Carmichael, in *Family Weekly* (January 16, 1980): 14. Photo-illustrated interview.

M72. **"Flix,"** conducted by Bhob [Robert] Stewart, in *Heavy Metal* (January, 1980): 7, 79-84; (February, 1980): 7, 53-55; and (March, 1980): 7, 80-83. Concentrates on film adaptations of *Carrie*, *'Salem's Lot*, and *The Shining*.

b. *Bare Bones: Conversations on Terror with Stephen King*, edited by Tim Underwood and Chuck Miller. San Francisco, CA: Underwood-Miller, 1988; New York: McGraw-Hill, 1988, p. 125-137. [See **I20**].

M73. **"An Interview with Stephen King,"** conducted by Paul Janeczko, in *English Journal* 69 (February, 1980): 1-10.

b. *Bare Bones: Conversations on Terror with Stephen King*, edited by Tim Underwood and Chuck Miller. San Francisco, CA: Underwood-Miller, 1988; New York: McGraw-Hill, 1988, p. 76-79. [See **I20**].

M74. **"Catching Up with the Rapidly Rising Star of Author Stephen King: Thoughts on Books, Films, and What Went Wrong on *The Shining*,"** conducted by Paul Gagne, in *Cinefantastique* 10:4 (Spring, 1980): .

b. revised in: *Feast of Fear: Conversations with Stephen King*, edited by Tim Underwood and Chuck Miller. Novato, CA: Underwood-Miller, August 1989, cloth, p. 90-108. [See **I23**].

M75. **"Interview with Stephen King,"** conducted by Paul R. Gagne, in *Famous Monsters* no. 162 (April, 1980): ; and no. 164 (June, 1980): .

b. *Cinefantastique* 10:4 (Spring 1981): ; and 14:2 (December/January, 1983/1984): .

c. revised in: *Feast of Fear: Conversations with Stephen King*, edited by Tim Underwood and Chuck Miller. Novato, CA: Underwood-Miller, August 1989, cloth, p. 90-108. [See **I23**].

M76. **"Fright King's World Grips Convention-Goers,"** conducted by Tom Wood, in *Nashville Tennesseean* (May 5, 1980): .

b. *Feast of Fear: Conversations with Stephen King*, edited by Tim Underwood and Chuck Miller. Novato, CA: Underwood-Miller, August 1989, cloth, p. 82-83. [See **I23**].

M77. **"Riding the Crest of the Horror Craze,"** conducted by William Wilson, in *New York Times Magazine* (May 11, 1980): 42-43.

M78. **"Interview with Stephen King: A Frank Conversation with the Author of *Carrie*,"** conducted by Richard Rothenstein, in *Pub* (May, 1980): 31-34, 98.

M79. **"The King of Horror Novels,"** conducted by David Chute, in *The Boston Phoenix* (June 17, 1980): .

b. *Feast of Fear: Conversations with Stephen King*, edited by Tim Underwood and Chuck Miller. Novato, CA: Underwood-Miller, August 1989, cloth, p. 83-87. [See **I23**].

M80. **"Stephen King and George Romero: Collaboration in Terror,"** conducted by Stanley Wiater, in *Fangoria* No. 6 (June, 1980): .

b. *Bloody Best of Fangoria* (1982): 28-29.
c. *Feast of Fear: Conversations with Stephen King*, edited by Tim Underwood and Chuck Miller. Novato, CA: Underwood-Miller, August 1989, cloth, p. 124-128. [See **I23**].

M81. **"The Dark Beyond the Door: Walking (Nervously) into Stephen King's World,"** conducted by Freff, in *Tomb of Dracula* No. 4 (June, 1980): 43-44; and no. 5 (July 1980): 60-63. The article concentrates on King as a person: family, interests, religious backgrounds.

b. *Bare Bones: Conversations on Terror with Stephen King*, edited by Tim Underwood and Chuck Miller. San Francisco, CA: Underwood-Miller, 1988; New York: McGraw-Hill, 1988, p. 137-142. [See **I20**].

M82. **"Interview with Stephen King,"** by Paul R. Gagne, in *Cinefantastique* 10:1 (Summer, 1980): .

b. excerpted in: *Feast of Fear: Conversations with Stephen King*, edited by Tim Underwood and Chuck Miller. Novato, CA: Underwood-Miller, August 1989, cloth, p. 128-129. [See **I23**].

M83. **[Title unknown],** *Boston Herald American* (August 3, 1980): .

M84. **"Stephen King Is Cashing In,"** conducted by Randi Henderson, in *The Baltimore Sun* (August 26, 1980): .

b. *Bare Bones: Conversations on Terror with Stephen King*, edited by Tim Underwood and Chuck Miller. San Francisco, CA: Underwood-Miller, 1988; New York: McGraw-Hill, 1988, p. 191-192. [See **I20**].

M85. **"Interview with Stephen King,"** conducted by Michael Kilgore, in *The Tampa Tribune* (August 31, 1980): .

b. *Bare Bones: Conversations on Terror with Stephen King*, edited by Tim Underwood and Chuck Miller. San Francisco, CA: Underwood-Miller, 1988; New York: McGraw-Hill, 1988, p. 101-111. [See **I20**].

M86. **"Ask Them Yourself,"** in *Family Weekly* (September 7, 1980.

M87. **[Title unknown],** *Canton Ohio Repository* (September 9, 1980): .

M88. **[Title unknown],** *Bowling Green News* [Kentucky] (September 14, 1980): .

M89. **"From Textbook to Checkbook,"** by Robert W. Wells, in *Milwaukee Journal* (September 15, 1980): .

b. *Feast of Fear: Conversations with Stephen King*, edited by Tim Underwood and Chuck Miller. Novato, CA: Underwood-Miller, August 1989, cloth, p. 6-8. [See **I23**].

M90. **[Title unknown],** *Fort Lauderdale News/Sun Sentinel* (September 28, 1980): .

M91. **[Title unknown],** *Chronicle Telegram* (October 3, 1980): .

M92. **[Title unknown],** *St. Cloud Times* [Minnesota] (October 3, 1980): .

M93. **[Title unknown],** *The Blade* [Toledo, OH] (October 5, 1980): .

M94. **[Title unknown],** *Sunday Star* [Toronto, Canada] (October 5, 1980): .

M95. **[Title unknown],** *Vermont Free Press* (October 8, 1980): .

M96. **"Five Bestselling Writers Recall Their First Novels,"** conducted by Stella Dong, in *Publishers Weekly* (October 10, 1980): .

M97. **[Title unknown],** *Abilene Reporter* (October 10, 1980): .

M98. **[Title unknown],** *Boston Globe* (October 10, 1980): .

M99. **[Title unknown],** *Primos Times* [Pennsylvania] (October 11, 1980): .

M100. **[Title unknown],** *Saginaw Michigan News* (October 11, 1980): .

M101. **"Steve King on Baseball,"** conducted by Bob Haskell, in *Bangor Daily News* [Maine] (October 16, 1980):

b. in *Feast of Fear: Conversations with Stephen King*, edited by Tim Underwood and Chuck Miller. Novato, CA: Underwood-Miller, August 1989, cloth, p. 226-227. [See **I23**].

M102. **Horror Panel, I-II,** moderated by Dick Cavett. New York, WNET, October 30-31, 1980. New York: Journal Graphics, Inc. Panel discussion with George Romero, Stephen King, Peter Straub, and Ira Levin.

M103. **[Title unknown],** *East/West* (October, 1980): .

M104. **[Title unknown],** *The Red and Black* [University of Georgia] (November 7, 1980): .

M105. **[Title unknown],** *Iowa City Press* [Iowa] (November 15, 1980): .

M106. **"Some Words with Stephen King,"** conducted by Douglas E. Winter, in *Fantasy Newsletter* (November, 1980): .

b. *Stephen King: The Art of Darkness,* by Douglas E. Winter. New York: New American Library, 1984, paper, p. .

M107. **"Stephen King's Court of Horror,"** conducted by Abe Peck, in *Rolling Stone College Papers* No. 3 (Winter, 1980): .

b. *Bare Bones: Conversations on Terror with Stephen King*, edited by Tim Underwood and Chuck Miller. San Francisco, CA: Underwood-Miller, 1988; New York: McGraw-Hill, 1988, p. 93-101. [See **I20**].

M108. **"Interview: Stephen King,"** in *Infinity Cubed* No. 5 (1980): .

M109. **"A Mild Down-Easter Discovers Terror is the Ticket,"** in *People Weekly* 14 (December 29, 1980-January 5, 1981): 53-54.

M110. **"Interview: Stephen King,"** conducted by Martha Thomases and Robert Tebbel, in *High Times* 65 (January, 1981): 37-41, 94-97.

b. *Bare Bones: Conversations on Terror with Stephen King*, edited by Tim Underwood and Chuck Miller. San Francisco, CA: Underwood-Miller, 1988; New York: McGraw-Hill, 1988, p. 198-210. [See **I20**].

M111. **[Title unknown],** *American Way* (February, 1981): .

M112. **"An Interview with Stephen King,"** conducted by Joyce Lynch Dewes Moore, in *Mystery* (March, 1981): 6.

b. *Bare Bones: Conversations on Terror with Stephen King*, edited by Tim Underwood and Chuck Miller. San Francisco, CA: Underwood-Miller, 1988; New York: McGraw-Hill, 1988, p. 68-76. [See **I20**].

M113. **"Dark Stars Rising" [Interview with Stephen King and Peter Straub],** conducted by Stanley Wiater, 1980 World Fantasy Convention, Baltimore, MD; in *Valley Advocate* [Hatfield, MA] (April 8, 1981): . See also **R14**.

b. as part of: "Three Interviews with Stephen King and Peter Straub," "Partners in Fear," *Bare Bones: Conversations on Terror with Stephen King*, edited by Tim Underwood and Chuck Miller. San Francisco, CA: Underwood-Miller, 1988; New York: McGraw-Hill, 1988, p. 161-171. [See **I20**].

M114. **"Stephen King: I Like to Go for the Jugular,"** conducted by Charles L. Grant, in *Twilight Zone Magazine* 1:1 (April, 1981): 18-23.

b. *Feast of Fear: Conversations with Stephen King*, edited by Tim Underwood and Chuck Miller. Novato, CA: Underwood-Miller, August 1989, cloth, p. 10-22. [See **I23**].

M115. "The Rest of the King," conducted by Bhob [Robert] Stewart, in *Starship* 18:1 (Spring, 1981): 45-46. Continuation of Stewart's *Heavy Metal* interview, with emphasis on King's pre-*Carrie* materials. Some inaccuracies appear in the discussion because of King's need to preserve the "BACHMAN" pseudonym.

b. *Feast of Fear: Conversations with Stephen King*, edited by Tim Underwood and Chuck Miller. Novato, CA: Underwood-Miller, August 1989, cloth, p. 31-34. [See **I23**].

M116. "Just Your Average Guy," [Interview with Stephen King and Peter Straub], conducted by Stanley Wiater, 1980 World Fantasy Convention, Baltimore, MD. Published in *Valley Advocate* [Hatfield, MA] (May 27, 1981): . [See **R15**].

b. as part of: "Three Interviews with Stephen King and Peter Straub," "Partners in Fear," *Bare Bones: Conversations on Terror with Stephen King*, edited by Tim Underwood and Chuck Miller. San Francisco, CA: Underwood-Miller, 1988; New York: McGraw-Hill, 1988, p. 161-171. [See **I20**].

M117. "The Kings of Horror," conducted by David D. Duncan and others, in *Oui* (August, 1981): 66-69, 88, 118-119. Interviews with King (p. 67-68), Brian de Palma, George A. Romero, John Carpenter, and David Cronenberg.

M118. [Title unknown], *Sun-Tattler* [Hollywood, FL] (September 17, 1981): .

M119. [Title unknown], *Portland Press Herald* [Maine] (September, 1981): .

M120. "The Healthy Power of a Good Scream," conducted by Sheila Weller, in *Self* (September, 1981): . According to Winter, this "interview" is composed of excerpted passages from *Danse Macabre* [*Art*, 304].

M121. "Interview with Stephen King and Peter Straub," conducted by Stanley Wiater, 1980 World Fantasy Convention, Baltimore, MD; in *Valley Advocate* [Hatfield, MA] (October 31, 1981): . [See **R32**].

b. as part of: "Three Interviews with Stephen King and Peter Straub," "Partners in Fear," *Bare Bones: Conversations on Terror with Stephen King*, edited by Tim Underwood and Chuck Miller. San Francisco, CA: Underwood-Miller, 1988; New York: McGraw-Hill, 1988, p. 161-171. [See **I20**].

M122. "The King of the Macabre at Home," conducted by Michael J. Bandler, in *Parents Magazine* 57 (January 1982): 68+ [5-page interview].

b. *Feast of Fear: Conversations with Stephen King*, edited by Tim Underwood and Chuck Miller. Novato, CA: Underwood-Miller, August 1989, cloth, p. 221-226. [See **I23**].

M123. **"Interview with Stephen King,"** conducted by Paul R. Gagne, in *Cinefantastique* 12:2/3 (April 1982): ; and 13:1 (September-October, 1982): .

b. *The Zombies That Ate Pittsburgh: The Films of George A. Romero.* by Paul R. Gagne. New York: Dodd, Mead, 1987, cloth, p. .

c. *Feast of Fear: Conversations with Stephen King*, edited by Tim Underwood and Chuck Miller. Novato, CA: Underwood-Miller, August 1989, cloth, p. 129-142. [See **I23**].

M124. **"*Penthouse* Interview: Stephen King,"** conducted by Bob Spitz, in *Penthouse* (April, 1982): 120-126, 160. Refers to King's having "just finished" *IT*.

b. *Bare Bones: Conversations on Terror with Stephen King*, edited by Tim Underwood and Chuck Miller. San Francisco, CA: Underwood-Miller, 1988; New York: McGraw-Hill, 1988, p. 181-191. [See **I20**].

M125. **"King's Gruesome Ideas Are Dead Serious,"** conducted by Mei-Mei Chan, in *USA Today* (October 14, 1982): .

M126. **"Novelist Loves His Nightmares,"** conducted by Jack Matthews, in *Detroit Free Press* [Michgan] (November 12, 1982): .

b. *Bare Bones: Conversations on Terror with Stephen King*, edited by Tim Underwood and Chuck Miller. San Francisco, CA: Underwood-Miller, 1988; New York: McGraw-Hill, 1988, p. 211-212. [See **I20**].

M127. **"Has Success Spoiled Stephen King? Naaah,"** by Pat Cadigan, Marty Ketchum, and Arnie Fenner, in *Shayol* 1:6 (Winter, 1982): 17-19.

b. *Feast of Fear: Conversations with Stephen King*, edited by Tim Underwood and Chuck Miller. Novato, CA: Underwood-Miller, August 1989, cloth, p. 1-3. [See **I23**].

M128. **"The King of Terror,"** conducted by Keith Bellows, in *Sourcebook: The Magazine for Seniors* (1982): 33. Interview conducted in conjunction with King's "My High School Horrors."

b. *Bare Bones: Conversations on Terror with Stephen King*, edited by Tim Underwood and Chuck Miller. San Francisco, CA: Underwood-Miller, 1988; New York: McGraw-Hill, 1988, p. 88-90. [See **I20**].

M129. **"Interview with Stephen King and George Romero,"** conducted by Jessie Horsting and Michael Stein, in *Fantastic Films* 32 (February, 1983): .

b. incorporated into: *Feast of Fear: Conversations with Stephen King*, edited by Tim Underwood and Chuck Miller. Novato, CA: Underwood-Miller, August 1989, cloth, p. 169-176. [See **I23**].

M130. **"Some Words with Stephen King,"** by Douglas E. Winter, in *Fantasy Review* 6:2 (February, 1983): 11-14.

M131. **"Would You Buy a Haunted Car from This Man?"** conducted by Edwin Pouncey, in *Sounds* [England] (May 21, 1983): 22-23. Interview-article in conjunction with King's stay in England.

b. *Bare Bones: Conversations on Terror with Stephen King*, edited by Tim Underwood and Chuck Miller. San Francisco, CA: Underwood-Miller, 1988; New York: McGraw-Hill, 1988, p. 56-62. [See **I20**].

M132. **"The *Playboy* Interview: Stephen King,"** conducted by Eric Norden, in *Playboy* (June, 1983): 62-85+.

b. *Bare Bones: Conversations on Terror with Stephen King*, edited by Tim Underwood and Chuck Miller. San Francisco, CA: Underwood-Miller, 1988; New York: McGraw-Hill, 1988, p. 24-56. [See **I20**].

c. *The Stephen King Companion*, edited by George Beahm. Kansas City, MO: Andrews and McMeel, September 1989, p. 19-45.

d. as: "Das *Playboy*-Interview mit Stephen King," in *Das Stephen King Buch*. München: Wilhelm Heyne Verlag, 1989, p. 247-286. Translated by Joachim Körber. [German]

M133. **"Stephen King's Ransom,"** in *Esquire* (August, 1983): .

M134. **"A *Starburst* Interview with Stephen King,"** conducted by Adam Pirani and Alan McKenzie, in *Starburst* [England] (September, 1983): 16-19.

M135. **"Horror Writer Stephen King Is Afraid There's Something Awful Under His Bed,"** conducted by Michael Hanlon, in *Toronto Star* (October 5, 1983): .

b. *Feast of Fear: Conversations with Stephen King*, edited by Tim Underwood and Chuck Miller. Novato, CA: Underwood-Miller, August 1989, cloth, p. 217-221. [See **I23**].

M136. **"Wie Lebt und Arbeitet ein Horror-schriftsteller?"** ["How Does a Horror Writer Live and Write"], in *Carrie*. Bergisch Gladbach, West Germany: Bastei-Lübbe Verlag (Paperback 28111), 1983. Translator unknown. [German]

b. abridged version in: *Carrie*. Bergisch Gladbach, West Germany: Bastei-Lübbe Verlag (TB13121), 1987, paper, p. . [German]

M137. **"Yet Another Interview with Stephen King,"** conducted by David Pettus, in *Fan Plus* (1983): .

b. *Castle Rock: The Stephen King Newsletter* 1:12 (December, 1985): 6.

M138. **"Horror and the Limits of Violence: A Forum of Interviews,"** conducted by Douglas E. Winter, in *Shadowings: The Reader's Guide to Horror Fiction, 1981-1982,* edited by Douglas E. Winter. STARMONT STUDIES IN LITERARY CRITICISM #1. Mercer Island, WA: Starmont House, 1983, cloth, p. 125-134. Participants include King, Suzy McKee Charnas, John

Coyne, Dennis Etchison, David Morrell, Alan Ryan, and Chelsea Quinn Yarbro.

M139. **"Stephen King,"** by Charles Platt, in *Dream Makers II*. New York: Berkley Books, 1983, paper, p. 273-284.

ab. *Dream Makers: Science Fiction and Fantasy Writers at Work,* by Charles Platt. New and revised edition. New York: Ungar, 1987, cloth, p. 261-271.

b. as: "Stephen King," in *Das Stephen King Buch*. München: Wilhelm Heyne Verlag, 1989, p. 221-222. Translated by Joachim Körber. [German]

M140. **"Stephen King: With *Cujo, The Dead Zone*, and *Christine*, He Just Might Be the Most Bankable Name in Hollywood,"** conducted by Paul Gagne, in *Cinefantastique* 14:2 (December, 1983/January, 1984): 4-5. King discusses the films named, plus plans for *Cycle of the Werewolf, The Talisman, Skeleton Crew, It,* and others.

b. incorporated into: *Feast of Fear: Conversations with Stephen King*, edited by Tim Underwood and Chuck Miller. Novato, CA: Underwood-Miller, August 1989, cloth, p. 90-108. [See **I23**].

M141. **"The King/George Conversation,"** conducted by Tony Crawley, in *Starburst* no. 54-55 (1983):

b. incorporated into: *Feast of Fear: Conversations with Stephen King*, edited by Tim Underwood and Chuck Miller. Novato, CA: Underwood-Miller, August 1989, cloth, p. 142-169. [See **I23**].

M142. **"Stephen and Tabitha King,"** conducted by Rodney Labbe and Brian Robitaille, in *Ubris II* No. 1 (1984): 45-48. Interview with King and his wife published in the University of Maine, Orono, literary magazine. Reminiscences from their experiences as students at UMO in the late sixties.

M143. **"Stephen King Takes a Stand for Records,"** conducted by Joel Denver, in *Radio & Records* (February 24, 1984): .

b. *Bare Bones: Conversations on Terror with Stephen King*, edited by Tim Underwood and Chuck Miller. San Francisco, CA: Underwood-Miller, 1988; New York: McGraw-Hill, 1988, p. 193-197. [See **I20**].

M144. **"Stephen King Talks About *Christine*,"** conducted by Randy Lofficier, in *Twilight Zone Magazine* 3:6 (February, 1984): 73-74.

b. *Feast of Fear: Conversations with Stephen King*, edited by Tim Underwood and Chuck Miller. Novato, CA: Underwood-Miller, August 1989, cloth, p. 59-62. [See **I23**].

M145. **"Stephen King: Horror in a Secular Age,"** conducted by William Robertson, in *Miami Herald* [Florida] (March 25, 1984): . [See **R34**].

b. as microfiche: *Newsbank: Literature* 10 (April, 1983): Fiche 74, D10-D13.

c. *Feast of Fear: Conversations with Stephen King*, edited by Tim Underwood and Chuck Miller. Novato, CA: Underwood-Miller, August 1989, cloth, p. 231-238. [See **I23**].

M146. [Title unknown], in *Science Fiction Times* No. 4 (April, 1984): . Translated by Marcel Bieger and Andreas Decker. [German]

M147. "The Stephen King Interview," Conducted by David Sherman, in *Fangoria* No. 35 (April, 1984); and No. 36 (July, 1984): .

b. *Feast of Fear: Conversations with Stephen King*, edited by Tim Underwood and Chuck Miller. Novato, CA: Underwood-Miller, August 1989, cloth, p. 47-59. [See **I23**].

M148. "A Coupl'a Authors Sittin' Around Talkin'," conducted by William Goldstein, in *Publishers Weekly* (May, 11, 1984): .

b. *The Stephen King Companion,* by George Beahm. Kansas City, MO: Andrews and McMeel, September 1989, paper, p. 283-287.

M149. "Träume Zwischen Himmel und Erde" ["Dreams Between Heaven and Earth"], conducted by Margarete von Schwarzkopf, in *Die Welt* (September 9, 1984): . [German]

M150. "Horror Partners," conducted by Stanley Wiater and Roger Anker, 1984 World Fantasy Convention: Ottowa, Canada; in *Valley Advocate* [Hatfield, MA] (October 31, 1984): .

b. *Fangoria* No. 42 (February 1985): ; and No. 43 (March 1985): 10-13.

c. *The Bloody Best of Fangoria* Vol. 5 (1986): .

d. as part of: "Three Interviews with Stephen King and Peter Straub," "Partners in Fear," *Bare Bones: Conversations on Terror with Stephen King*, edited by Tim Underwood and Chuck Miller. San Francisco, CA: Underwood-Miller, 1988; New York: McGraw-Hill, 1988, p. 171-180. [See **I20**].

M151. "Stephen King's Art of Darkness," conducted by Douglas E. Winter, in *Fantasy Review* (November, 1984): 8-15. Interview with King at the International Conference on the Fantastic in the Arts, March 1984, Boca Raton FL. Some audience questions as well.

M152. "The 'King' of Horror Is a Gentle Giant," in *Cinema* No. 79 (1984): . Translator unknown. [German]

M153. "Peter Straub and Stephen King Team Up for Fear," conducted by Michael Small, in *People Weekly* 23 (January 28, 1985): 50-52.

M154. "Stephen King, Peter Straub, and the Quest for *The Talisman*," conducted by Douglas E. Winter, in *Twilight Zone Magazine* (February, 1985): 62-68.

b. as: "Stephen King, Peter Straub, und die Suche nach dem Talisman," in *Das Stephen King Buch*. München: Wilhelm Heyne Verlag, 1989, p. 223-246. Translated by Joachim Körber. [German]

M155. **[Title unknown],** in *Fangoria* No. 42 (February, 1985): . King/Straub interview on *The Talisman*.

M156. **[Title unknown]**, in *Fangoria* No. 43 (March, 1985): . King/Straub interview, part two.

M157. **"I'd Really Like to Write a Rock 'n' Roll Novel,"** conducted by Craig Modderno, in *USA Today* (May 10, 1985): . King's responses to film adaptations to date.

b. as: "Topic: Horrors!" in *Bare Bones: Conversations on Terror with Stephen King*, edited by Tim Underwood and Chuck Miller. San Francisco, CA: Underwood-Miller, 1988; New York: McGraw-Hill, 1988, p. 142-145. [See **I20**].

M158. **"King's Eye: An Author's-Eye-View of Scriptwriting, Working for Dino De Laurentiis, and Horror,"** conducted by Tim Hewitt, in *Cinefantastique* 15:2 (May, 1985): 9-11. Interview focusing on the creation and filming of *Cat's Eye*.

b. as: "Interview with Stephen King," *Bare Bones: Conversations on Terror with Stephen King*, edited by Tim Underwood and Chuck Miller. San Francisco, CA: Underwood-Miller, 1988; New York: McGraw-Hill, 1988, p. 145-151. [See **I20**].

M159. **"From Doug Winter: *The Faces of Fear*,"** conducted by Douglas E. Winter, in *Castle Rock* 1:5 (May, 1985): 7.

b. excerpted in: *Twilight Zone Magazine* (February, 1986): .
c. excerpted in: *Gallery* (January 1986): .
d. *Faces of Fear: Encounters with the Creators of Modern Horror Fiction*, edited by Douglas Winter. New York: Berkley Books, November 1985, paper, p. .

M160. **"King's Eye,"** in *Cinefantastique* (May, 1985): .

M161. **"King-Size Interview,"** conducted by Charles L. Grant, in *Monsterland* No. 2 (May, 1985): 27-30; and No. 3 (June, 1985): .

b. as: "Interview with Stephen King," *Bare Bones: Conversations on Terror with Stephen King*, edited by Tim Underwood and Chuck Miller. San Francisco, CA: Underwood-Miller, 1988; New York: McGraw-Hill, 1988, p. 79-88. [See **I20**].

M162. **"King of Horror Steps Behind the Camera,"** in *Dallas Morning News* [Texas] (July 28, 1985): .

M163. **"Interview with King,"** conducted by Peter Strupp, in *King's Crypt* (August, 1985): . Prepared press-release interview in conjunction with publication of *Skeleton Crew*.

M164. **"Stephen King Turns Director,"** conducted by James Calloway, in *News and Observer* [Raleigh, NC] (September 1, 1985): . Discussion of *Maximum Overdrive*.

b. as microfiche: *NewsBank Film and Television* 12 (September, 1985): Fiche 28, A6-A8.

M165. **[Title unknown],** in *The State* [Columbia, SC] (September 2, 1985): . Discussion of *Maximum Overdrive*.

M166. **[Title unknown],** in *The Courier Herald* [Dublin, GA] (September 28, 1985): . Discussion of *Maximum Overdrive*.

M167. **"Stephen King,"** in *Charlotte Observer* [North Carolina] (September 29, 1985): . Discussion of *Maximum Overdrive*.

b. as microfiche: *NewsBank Film and Television* 12 (October, 1985): Fiche 40, F6-F7.

M168. **[Title unknown],** in *The Salt Lake Tribune* [Salt Lake City, UT] (October 3, 1985): . Discussion of *Maximum Overdrive*.

M169. **[Title unknown],** in *Wilmington Morning Star* (October 3, 1985): . Discussion of *Maximum Overdrive*.

M170. **[Title unknown],** in *Dallas Morning News* [Texas] (October 8, 1985): . Discussion of *Maximum Overdrive*.

M171. **[Title unknown],** in *USA Weekend* (October 25-27, 1985): . Discussion of *Maximum Overdrive*.

M172. **[Title unknown],** in *Chicago Tribune* (October 27, 1985): . Discussion of *Maximum Overdrive*.

M173. **[Title unknown],** in *Newsday* (October 31, 1985): . Discussion of *Maximum Overdrive*.

M174. **"Stephen King on Overdrive and on Pet Sematary and on Capturing the Spirit,"** conducted by Robert H. Martin, in *Fangoria* No. 48 (October, 1985): 10-12, 64.

M175. **"S.K. Interviewed on *Overdrive* Movie Set,"** conducted by Tyson Blue, in *Castle Rock: The Stephen King Newsletter* 1:11 (November, 1985): 1, 4-6. Recorded on September 21, 1985, King's birthday.

M176. **"Cosmo Talks to Stephen King: Heavyweight Horror Writer,"** conducted by T. N. Murari, in *Cosmopolitan* 199 (December, 1985): 112, 117.

b. *Feast of Fear: Conversations with Stephen King*, edited by Tim Underwood and Chuck Miller. Novato, CA: Underwood-Miller, August 1989, cloth, p. 238-240. [See **I23**].

M177. "New Adventures in the Scream Trade: A Non-Stop King Takes on TV," conducted by Ben Herndon, in *Twilight Zone Magazine* 5:5 (December, 1985): 6A-7A. Discusses the influence of Rod Serling's *Twilight Zone* on King, and comments on *Creepshow* and *Cat's Eye*.

b. *Feast of Fear: Conversations with Stephen King*, edited by Tim Underwood and Chuck Miller. Novato, CA: Underwood-Miller, August 1989, cloth, p. 87-89. [See **I23**].

M178. "Interview with Stephen King," conducted by Peter Strupp, in *Science Fiction Review* No. 56 (1985): 32.

M179. "Stephen King," conducted by Douglas E. Winter, in *Faces of Fear: Encounters with the Creators of Modern Horror*, edited by Douglas E. Winter. New York: Berkley Books, November 1985, paper, p. 235-257.

M180. "Stephen King," conducted by Mick Farren, in *Interview* 15:2 (February, 1986): 68+ [3-page interview].

b. *Feast of Fear: Conversations with Stephen King*, edited by Tim Underwood and Chuck Miller. Novato, CA: Underwood-Miller, August 1989, cloth, p. 240-247. [See **I23**].

M181. "Talking Terror," by Douglas E. Winter, in *Twilight Zone Magazine* (February, 1986): 16-22. Incorporates several G. K. Potter illustrations from the limited *Skeleton Crew*.

M182. [Title unknown], in *Andy Warhol's Interview* (February, 1986): .

M183. "I Am a Hick, and This Is Where I Feel at Home," conducted by Elaine Landa, in *Inside* [Orono High School, Orono, ME] 5:4 (April 4, 1986): .

b. *Feast of Fear: Conversations with Stephen King*, edited by Tim Underwood and Chuck Miller. Novato, CA: Underwood-Miller, August 1989, cloth, p. 249-259. [See **I23**].

M184. "Die Neuen Formen Des Schreckens," conducted by Silvia Bizio, in *Die Tageszeitung* (May 2, 1986): . Translated from Italian; translator unknown. [German]

M185. "Stephen King: The Maximum Overdrive Interview," conducted by Stanley Wiater, in *Prevue* 64 (May-July, 1986): .

b. *Valley Advocate* (July 21, 1986):

c. *Feast of Fear: Conversations with Stephen King*, edited by Tim Underwood and Chuck Miller. Novato, CA: Underwood-Miller, August 1989, cloth, p. 181-192. [See **I23**].

M186. "King of the Road," conducted by Darrell Ewing and Dennis Myers, in *American Film* 11:8 (June, 1986): 44-47. King as director, including comments on film adaptations of *The Shining, Dead Zone, Maximum Overdrive,* and *Firestarter*.

b. *Feast of Fear: Conversations with Stephen King*, edited by Tim Underwood and Chuck Miller. Novato, CA: Underwood-Miller, August 1989, cloth, p. 108-111. [See **I23**].

M187. "The Director Is King," conducted by Stephen Schaefer, in *Film Comment* 22 (June, 1986): 2.

b. *Feast of Fear: Conversations with Stephen King*, edited by Tim Underwood and Chuck Miller. Novato, CA: Underwood-Miller, August 1989, cloth, p. 179-181. [See **I23**].

M188. "Midas with the Common Touch: Why Hasn't Success Spoiled Stephen King?" conducted by Edgar Allen Beem, in *The Maine Times* [Topsham, ME] 18:40 (July 11, 1986): . [See **R65**].

b. as microfiche: *NewsBank Literature* 13 (August, 1986): Fiche 15, G5-G9.
c. as microfiche: *NewsBank Names in the News* 9 (August, 1986): Fiche 12, G7-G11.
d. *Feast of Fear: Conversations with Stephen King*, edited by Tim Underwood and Chuck Miller. Novato, CA: Underwood-Miller, August 1989, cloth, p. 274-282. [See **I23**].

M189. "The Steevie Jeebies," in *Atlanta Journal-Constitution* [Georgia] (July 20, 1986): .

M190. "Shockmeister: King Takes a Run at Directing," by Tyson Blue, in *Orange County Register* (July 20, 1986): .

M191. [Title unknown], conducted by Marilyn Beck, in *Orange County Register* (July 20, 1986): .

M192. "King's at Helm of 'Overdrive'," by Glen Lovell, in *San Jose Mercury News* [California] (July 23, 1986): .

b. as microfiche: *NewsBank: Film and Television* 13 (August, 1986): Fiche 13, G13-G14.

M193. "An Insight on Stephen King," conducted by Burckett in *Fun* [Puget Sound, WA] (July 24, 1986): .

M194. "Directing New Experience for Stephen King," in *Macon Telegraph and News* [Macon, GA] (July 25, 1986): .

M195. **"King in Overdrive,"** conducted by Stephen Schaefer, in *Boston Herald* (July 27. 1986).

b. incorporated into: *Feast of Fear: Conversations with Stephen King*, edited by Tim Underwood and Chuck Miller. Novato, CA: Underwood-Miller, August 1989, cloth, p. 192-203. [See **I23**].

M196. **"Reviews of 'Maximum Overdrive' Don't Faze Author-Turned-Director,"** conducted by Philip Wuntch, in *Dallas Morning News* [Texas] (July 28, 1986): .

b. as microfiche: *NewsBank: Film and Television* 13 (August, 1986): Fiche 14, A5-A6.

M197. **"When King Meets King,"** in *New York Post* (July 28, 1986): .

M198. **"Full Throttle with Stephen King,"** by Burckett, in *New Times*, "Valley News and Arts Journal" [Phoenix, AZ] (July 30-August 5, 1986): . [See **R76**].

M199. **"King of Horror Finds Directing Unnerving,"** conducted by Calvin Ahlgren, in *San Francisco Chronicle* (July , 1986): .

b. as microfiche: *NewsBank: Film and Television* 13 (August, 1986): Fiche 14, D8-D9.

M200. **[Title unknown],** conducted by Robert Strauss, in *Chicago Sun-Times* (July, 1986): .

b. incorporated into: *Feast of Fear: Conversations with Stephen King*, edited by Tim Underwood and Chuck Miller. Novato, CA: Underwood-Miller, August 1989, cloth, p. 203-215. [See **I23**].

M201. **"Prince of Darkness: Q&A with Stephen King,"** in *MA Free Weekly* (August 1, 1986): I, 10.

M202. **"King of Horror: His Career's in 'Overdrive' as He Directs His First Film,"** conducted by G. Wayne Miller, in *Providence Sunday Journal* [Rhode Island] (August 3, 1986): I, 1-I3. [See **R77**].

b. as microfiche: *NewsBank: Film and Television* 13 (August, 1986): Fiche 14, A1-A4.

c. as microfiche: *NewsBank Names in the News* 9 (August, 1986): Fiche 12, G3-G6.

M203. **[Title unknown],** in *The Star* (August 19, 1986): .

M204. **"Horror Stories Have Staying Power,"** conducted by Loukia Louka, in *Maryland Coast Dispatch* (August 8, 1986): 11, 73+.

M205. **"The Roots of Terror,"** conducted by E. Seidner, in *Macleans* 99 (August 11, 1986): 6-7.

M206. **"Best-Selling Writer Stephen King Takes a Stab at Directing,"** in *Ft. Worth Star* (August 24, 1986): .

M207. **"Who Is This Guy Stephen King?—And Why Do They Make All Those Movies?"** by Jessie Horsting, in *Stephen King at the Movies*. New York: Starlog/Signet, August 1986, paper, p. 6-11.

b. *Fangoria* No. 56 (August, 1986): .

c. *Feast of Fear: Conversations with Stephen King*, edited by Tim Underwood and Chuck Miller. Novato, CA: Underwood-Miller, August 1989, cloth, p. 111-124. [See **I23**].

M208. **[Title unknown],** in *Fangoria* No. 56 (August, 1986): . Discussion of *Maximum Overdrive*.

M209. **[Title unknown],** in *Rave Reviews* 2 (August-September, 1986): .

M210. **"Horror and the Limitations of Violence,"** conducted by Douglas Winter, in *American Fantasy* 2:1 (Fall, 1986): . Short interviews with King, Dennis Etchison, and others.

M211. **"The Novelist Sounds Off,"** conducted by Cathy Booth, in *Time* 128:4 (October 6, 1986): 80. Sidebar to Stefan Kanfer's "King of Horror."

M212. **[Title unknown],** by Stephen Schaefer, in *Men's Guide to Fashion* 2:9 (October, 1986): .

b. incorporated into: *Feast of Fear: Conversations with Stephen King*, edited by Tim Underwood and Chuck Miller. Novato, CA: Underwood-Miller, August 1989, cloth, p. 192-203. [See **I23**].

M213. **"De Meester aan Het Woord: Interview met Stephen King,"** in *Stephen King Krant* 13:13 (October 13, 1986): 7. Interview in a King mock-newspaper issued as publicity for the Dutch translations of King's works. [Dutch]

M214. **"Stephen King Takes a Vacation,"** conducted by Edward Gross, in *Fangoria* No. 58 (October, 1986): .

b. *The Bloody Best of Fangoria* Vol. 6 (1987): .

M215. **"Stephen King: 1981 Interview,"** conducted by Bill Munster, in *Footsteps VII* (November 1986): 28-31.

b. *Feast of Fear: Conversations with Stephen King*, edited by Tim Underwood and Chuck Miller. Novato, CA: Underwood-Miller, August 1989, cloth, p. 40-43. [See **I23**].

M216. **[Title unknown],** by Robert Strauss, in *Monsterland* 15 (December, 1986): .

b. incorporated into: *Feast of Fear: Conversations with Stephen King*, edited by Tim Underwood and Chuck Miller. Novato, CA: Underwood-Miller, August 1989, cloth, p. 203-215. [See **I23**].

M217. "The Truth About 'IT': America's Ghostmaster General Discusses Halloween, Childhood, and His Newest 'Monster' Bestseller," conducted by Tyson Blue, in *Twilight Zone Magazine* 5:6 (December, 1986): 48-49.

M218. "He's the Undisputed King of the Macabre," conducted by Stacey A. Chase, in *Sun Times* [Lowell, MA] (March 8, 1987): .

b. as microfiche: *NewsBank Names in the News* 9 (April, 1987): Fiche 190, F13-G1.

M219. [Title unknown], in *Capital Mazaginze* [England] (March 26, 1987): .

M220. "The West Interview: Stephen King," conducted by D. C. Denison, in *West Magazine, San Jose Mercury News* [California] (July 19, 1987):

b. *Feast of Fear: Conversations with Stephen King*, edited by Tim Underwood and Chuck Miller. Novato, CA: Underwood-Miller, August 1989, cloth, p. 265-268. [See **I23**].

M221. [Title unknown], in *Boston Globe Magazine* (August 2, 1987): . One-page question-and-answer interview.

M222. [Title unknown], conducted by Marthayne Pelegrimas, in *Thin Ice* 1 (October, 1987): .

M223. "WB Celebrates Halloween with an Exclusive Interview with the Scaremaster Himself...Stephen King!" in *WB* [Waldenbooks publication] 145 (November, 1987): .

b. *The Stephen King Companion,* by George Beahm. Kansas City, MO: Andrews and McMeel, September 1989, paper, p. 290-295. [See **I24**].

M224. "Stephen King: The Limits of Fear," conducted by Jo Fletcher, in *Knave* 19:5 (1987): .

b. excerpted as: "Stephen King and Jo Fletcher—Introduction," in *Reign of Fear: Fiction and Film of Stephen King,* edited by Don Herron. Los Angeles, California: Underwood-Miller, June 1988, 254 p., cloth, p. vii-xv.

c. *Feast of Fear: Conversations with Stephen King*, edited by Tim Underwood and Chuck Miller. Novato, CA: Underwood-Miller, August 1989, cloth, p. 258-265. [See **I23**].

M225. "Interview with Stephen King," conducted by Ed Gorman, in *Mystery Scene* No. 10 (July, 1987): 4-5.

b. *Feast of Fear: Conversations with Stephen King*, edited by Tim Underwood and Chuck Miller. Novato, CA: Underwood-Miller, August 1989, cloth, p. 268-272. [See **I23**].

M226. **"If You're Scared Silly, Then Stephen King is Happy,"** conducted by Julie Washington, in *Cleveland Plain Dealer* [Ohio] (January 31, 1988) . [See **R107**].

b. *Castle Rock: The Stephen King Newsletter* 4:4 (April, 1988): 11.

SECONDARY SOURCES AND REVIEWS:

1. Spignesi, Stephen. "The Unwritten King: Stories Stephen King Has Thought Of, But Just Hasn't Written Down (Yet)," in *The Shape Under the Sheet: The Complete Stephen King Encyclopedia*. Ann Arbor, MI: Popular Culture, Ink., May 1991, cloth, p. 773-775.

M227. **[Title unknown],** in *Publishers Weekly* (February 19, 1988): . Discussion of *The Dark Tower* tapes.

M228. **"Stephen King: Der Meister des Grauens,"** conducted by Harry Doherty, in *Metal Hammer* No. 3 (March, 1988): . Translator unknown. [German]

M229. **"A Bloody Mary and a Monster Steak with Stephen King: Over Dinner, the Writer Confesses His Tricks and Treats,"** by Bryan Miller, in *New York Times* 138 (October 26, 1988): 17. [National edition].

b. as: "Eating Out with Stephen King: Writer Eats Steak Before It Eats Him," by Bryan Miller, in *New York Times* (October 26, 1988): C1. [Late edition].

M230. **[Title unknown],** in *The Ram* [Fordham University] (December 3, 1988): .

M231. **"'Gunslinger' Stalks Darkness in Human Spirit,'** in *Bangor Daily News* [Bangor, ME] (January 10, 1989): .

b. as microfiche: *NewsBank Literature* 16 (February, 1989): Fiche 19, B4-B5.

M232. **"He Has the Last Word on What's Scary,"** conducted by Martin Booe, in *Los Angeles Herald Examiner* (January 31, 1989): .

b. *Feast of Fear: Conversations with Stephen King*, edited by Tim Underwood and Chuck Miller. Novato, CA: Underwood-Miller, August 1989, cloth, p. 272-274. [See **I23**].

M233. **"Stephen King, 41,"** conducted by David Bright, in *Portland Monthly* [Maine] (1989): .

b. *Castle Rock: The Stephen King Newsletter* 5:1 (January, 1989): 1, 5.

M234. **"King Digs Horror in 'Pet Sematary,'"** conducted by Stephen Schaefer, in *Boston Herald* (April 16, 1989): .

b. as microfiche: *NewsBank: Names in the News* 11 (May, 1989): Fiche 134, C1-C3.
c. as microfiche: *NewsBank: Film and Television* 16 (June, 1989): Fiche 65, A10-A12.

M235. **"Unearthing the Origins of King's 'Pet Sematary,'"** conducted by Diana Maychick, in *New York Post* (April 16, 1989): .

b. as microfiche: *NewsBank: Names in the News* 11 (May, 1989): Fiche 134, C4-C5.
c. as microfiche: *NewsBank: Film and Television* 16 (May, 1989): Fiche 53, B2-B3.

M236. **"In 'Pet Sematary,' Stephen King Replays the Horror on Film,"** conducted by Donna Rosenthal, in *New York Daily News* (April 17, 1989):

b. as microfiche: *NewsBank Film and Television* 16 (May, 1989): Fiche 53, A14-A15.

M237. **"Mein Horror in Jedem Hotel"** ["My Horror in Every Hotel"], conducted by Cristel Vollmer, in *Bild Zeitung* (April 20, 1989): . Translator unknown. [German]

M238. **"Stephen King Philosophizes from the Grave,"** conducted by Stephen Schaefer, in *Record* [Hackensack, NJ] (April 21, 1989:): .

b. as microfiche: *NewsBank Literature* 16 (June, 1989): Fiche 58, G9-G10.
c. as microfiche: *NewsBank Names in the News* 11 (July, 1989): Fiche 203, C13-C14.

M239. **"Master of Ghouls Fears Loss of a Child,"** conducted by Candace Burke-Block, in *Washington Times* [D.C.] (May 9, 1989): .

b. as microfiche: *NewsBank Film and Television* 16 (June, 1989): Fiche 65, A13.

M240. **"Interview with Stephen King,"** by Paul R. Gagne, in *Feast of Fear: Conversations with Stephen King*, edited by Tim Underwood and Chuck Miller. Novato, CA: Underwood-Miller, August 1989, cloth, p. 176-178. [See **I23**].

M241. **"Interview with Stephen King,"** by Paul R. Gagne, in *Feast of Fear: Conversations with Stephen King*, edited by Tim Underwood and Chuck Miller. Novato, CA: Underwood-Miller, August 1989, cloth, p. 215-216. [See **I23**].

M242. **"SK Discusses Making of *Maximum Overdrive*,"** conducted by Tyson Blue, in *Castle Rock: The Stephen King Newsletter* 2:9 (September, 1989): 1, 4-5.

M243. **"Occupation: Offending,"** conducted by Irv Slifkin, in *Philadelphia Inquirer* (October 12, 1989): .

b. as microfiche: *NewsBank: Names in the News* 11 (November, 1989): Fiche 315, D10-D11.

M244. **"Stephen King: Bogeyman as Family Man,"** by Gail Caldwell, in *Boston Globe* (April 15, 1990): [2-page article]. Discusses King's one-minute scene for the American Repertory Theater benefit, incorporating God, a sitcom, and a six-pack of beer.

b. as microfiche: *NewsBank Literature* 17 (May, 1990): Fiche 48, A5-7.
c. as microfiche: *NewsBank: Names in the News* 12 (May, 1990): Fiche 139, E9-E11.

M245. **"King Working on Book He Believes Could Be His Best,"** by Lynn Flewelling, in *Bangor Daily News* [Maine] (September 11, 1990): .

b. as microfiche: *NewsBank Literature* (October, 1990): Fiche 103, A13.
c. as microfiche: *NewsBank Names in the News* 12 (October, 1990): Fiche 272, B9.

M246. **"Horror Master Stephen King Gets Spooked,"** [no author listed] in *Boston Herald* (October 29, 1990): .

b. as microfiche: *NewsBank Literature* (November, 1990): Fiche 112, D6.
c. as microfiche: *NewsBank: Names in the News* 12 (December, 1990): Fiche 309, G4.

M247. **"Stephen King,"** conducted by A.T., in *W.B.: Waldenbooks' News, Reviews & Exclusive Interviews with Today's Hottest Authors* No. 10 (November/December, 1989): . Interview on *The Dark Half.*

M248. **"The Stephen King Interview: 'Secrets of Stephen King,'"** conducted by Stanley Wiater, in *Stephen King and Clive Barker: The Illustrated Guide to the Masters of the Macabre,* by James Van Hise. Las Vegas, NV: Pioneer Books, 1990, paper, p. 15-22.

M249. **"On Moviemaking with Dino DeLaurentiis: King Looks Back on the Painful Association That Cost Him His Reputation and Almost His Soul,"** conducted by Gary Wood, in *Cinefantastique* 21:4 (February, 1991): 40-41.

NON-PRINT INTERVIEWS

MB1. **"Interview with Stephen King,"** radio interview conducted by Richard Wolinsky and Lawrence Davidson, KPFA-FM. Berkeley, CA (September 8, 1979).

b. transcribed in: *Feast of Fear: Conversations with Stephen King*, edited by Tim Underwood and Chuck Miller. Novato, CA: Underwood-Miller, August 1989, cloth, p. 22-31. [See **I23**].

MB2. Television interview, on *The David Letterman Show* (August 18, 1980). 9 minutes. Discussion of *Firestarter* novel.

MB3. Television interview, on *The Merv Griffin Show* (September 19, 1980). 3 minutes. Discussion of *Firestarter* novel.

MB4. Panel Discussion, on *The Dick Cavett Show* (October 30, 31, 1980). 1 hour. [Other panelists: George A. Romero, Ira Levin, Peter Straub].

MB5. Television interview, on *The Mike Douglas Show* (February, 1981). 10 minutes. [Originally taped, October, 1980].

MB6. Television interview, conducted by Mike Leavitt, on *More* [Boston] (April 9, 1981). 7 minutes.

MB7. Television interview, conducted by Gene Shalitt, on *Today Show* [NBC] (April 14, 1981). 5 minutes. Discussion of *Danse Macabre*.

MB8. Television interview, on *Today Show* [NBC], (October 30, 1981). 5 minutes. Interview with King and George A. Romero on the set of *Creepshow*.

MB9. Television interview, conducted by Jack Perkins, on *NBC Magazine* (November 27, 1981). 11 minutes.

MB10. Television interview, on *The David Letterman Show* (April 1, 1982). 10 minutes. Discussion of *Creepshow*.

MB11. Television interview, on *CBS Morning News* (May 3, 1982). 4 minutes. Discussion of *Creepshow*.

MB12. Television interview, conducted by Earle Ziff, on *Star-TV* (May, 1982). Discussions of *Danse Macabre*, *'Salem's Lot*, *The Shining*.

MB13. Television interview, conducted by Bryant Gumbel, on *Today Show* [NBC] (August 13, 1982). 5 minutes. Discussion of *Creepshow*, *Different Seasons*.

MB14. "Creepshow's Creepy Secrets," on *Evening Magazine* [Boston] (October 29, 1982). 7 minutes. On-set interview with King, George A. Romero, and Tom Savini.

MB15. "Horror Movies & Books," panel moderated by Studs Terkel and Calvin Trillan, on *Nightcap* [Arts Channel] (December, 1982). 27 minutes. Panel included King, George A. Romero, and Tom Savini; also clips from *Creepshow*.

MB16. "Stephen King: An Alumnus in Profile," on *UMO Magzine* [University of Maine, Orono], WABI-TV [Bangor, ME] (February 20, 1983). 30 minutes.

MB17. "An Evening with Stephen King," at Billerica Public Library, Billerica, MA, on local cable television (April 22, 1983). 90 minutes.

MB18. Television interview, on *Live on 4* [Boston] (July 28, 1983). 4 minutes. Clips from *Cujo*, *The Shining*.

MB19. Television interview, conducted by Joan Lunden, on *Good Morning America* (August 15, 1983). 8 minutes. Discussion of *Cujo*.

MB20. Television interview, conducted by Pat Collins, on *CBS Morning News* (September 2, 1983). 4 minutes. Discussion of *Cujo*.

MB21. Radio interview, conducted by Matt Schaffer, on WBCN-FM [Boston] (October 31, 1983). 25 minutes.

b. rebroadcast July 7, 1985.
c. transcribed in: *Bare Bones: Conversations on Terror with Stephen King*, edited by Tim Underwood and Chuck Miller. San Francisco, CA: Underwood-Miller, 1988; New York: McGraw-Hill, 1988, p. 111-116. [See **I20**].

MB22. Television interview, on *Entertainment Tonight* (December 7, 1983). 2 minutes. Discussion of *Christine* film.

MB23. Television interview, on *Entertainment Tonight* (December 19, 1983). 3 minutes. Interview in King's Maine home.

MB24. "The Book Business Interview," television interview conducted by Ted Koppel, ABC News *Nightline* (January 13, 1984).

b. *Feast of Fear: Conversations with Stephen King*, edited by Tim Underwood and Chuck Miller. Novato, CA: Underwood-Miller, August 1989, cloth, p. 229-231. [See **I23**].

MB25. Television interview, by Joan Lunden, on *Good Morning America* (March 13, 1984). 5 minutes. Discussion of *Pet Sematary* (novel) and *Children of the Corn*.

MB26. Television interview, on *CBS Evening News* (March 23, 1984). 1 minute.

MB27. Television interview, on *CBS Morning News* (May 9, 1984). 6 minutes. Interview from King's Maine home.

MB28. Television interview, on *The Movie Channel* (October, 1984). Interview before and after showing of *Creepshow*.

MB29. Television interview, on *The Movie Channel* (October, 1984). Interview before and after showing of *Dead Zone*.

MB30. Television interview, on *The Movie Channel* (October, 1984). Interview before and after showing of *Salem's Lot*.

MB31. Television interview, on *The Movie Channel* (October, 1984). Interview before and after showing of *Cujo*.

MB32. Television interview, conducted by Joan Lunden, on *Good Morning America* (April 12, 1985). 4 minutes. Discussion of *Cat's Eye* and the Bachman novels.

MB33. Television interview, on CNN (April 12, 1985).

MB34. Television interview, on *Seeing Starts* [Boston] (May 24, 1985). 6 1/2 minutes. Discussion of *Cat's Eye*.

MB35. Television interview, on *Entertainment This Week* (September 22, 1985). 3 minutes. On the set of *Maximum Overdrive*.

MB36. Television interview, conducted by Maria Shriver, on *Good Morning America* (November 22, 1985). Discussion of *Maximum Overdrive* and "RICHARD BACHMAN."

MB37. Television interview, on *Good Morning America* (December, 1985).

MB38. Television interview, on *Live at Five* (December, 1985).

MB39. "Stephen King on *The Larry King Live Show*," television interview on *The Larry King Show* (April 10, 1986). 35 minutes.

MB40. "Stephen King on *The Larry King Live Show*," radio interview on *The Larry King Show* (April 10, 1986). 35 minutes.

MB41. Television interview, on *ABC Evening News* [Bangor, ME] June, 1986). 3.2 minutes. King speaking out against the anti-pornography referendum.

MB42. "Attack of the Summer Movies," on *MTV* (June 23-27, 1986). 5 minutes. Clips from interviews with King.

MB43. "Stephen King Meets the Ghost of Truman Capote," conducted by Charles Laguidara, on WBCN-FM [Boston] (June 24, 1986). 15 minutes.

MB44. Radio Interview, conducted by Bob Haskell, WCBN [Boston], June 24, 1986. Interview about the Red Sox.

MB45. MTV Guest VJ, on *MTV* (June 27, 1986). 60 minutes. King plays his ten favorite music videos.

MB46. Television interview, on local channels, Bangor, ME (July 6, 1986). 4 minutes. King's response to winning the Red-Sox bet with Bob Haskell.

MB47. Television interview, on *Show Biz Today* (July 16-17, 1986). Two-part interview on *Maximum Overdrive*.

MB48. Television interview, on *Take Two* [CNN] (July 17, 1986). Discussion of *Maximum Overdrive*.

MB49. Radio interview, on WITS [San Francisco] (July 17, 1986). 35 minutes. Morning show with studio audience.

MB50. Television interview, on *The Ed Busch TV Talk Show* [Dallas-Fort Worth, TX] (July 20, 1986). 24 minutes.

MB51. Radio interview, on WNEW-FM [New York] (July 24, 1986). 35 minutes.

MB52. Television interview, on *CBS Morning News* (July 25, 1986). 6.5 minutes. Discussion of *Maximum Overdrive*.

MB53. "Lunch with Soupy," radio interview conducted by Soupy Sales, on WNBC [New York] (July 25, 1986). 30 minutes. Discussion of *Maximum Overdrive*.

MB54. Television interview, on *Entertainment Tonight* (July 25, 1986). Discussion of *Maximum Overdrive*.

MB55. Television interview, conducted by Matt Lowrey, on *Evening Magazine* [Boston] (August 18, 1986). 6 minutes.

MB56. "The Source," radio interview conducted by Bill Vitko, on WCXL/WKQA [Peoria, Illinois] (August 24, 1986). 13 minutes. Comments on *Maximum Overdrive*, *Stand by Me*, and *IT*.

MB57. "*Stand by Me*: The Inside Story," on *HBO Behind the Scenes* (September, 1986).

MB58. "Stephen King's World of Horror," syndicated (October 25, 1986). 60 minutes.

MB59. Television interview, conducted by Ted Koppel, on *Nightline* [ABC] (January 13, 1987). 10 minutes.

MB60. "All Things Considered," interview/panel, on *PBS Radio Show* (April 1988). A panel of writers, including King, were asked how they would approach a sequel to *Gone with the Wind*. King answered that he probably wouldn't try to write one.

MB61. "Wie Schrijft Die Blijft" ["He Who Writes Will Be Remembered"], television interview conducted by Martin Coenen (1989). For transmission on Belgian television as part of a series of monthly literary programs.

SECONDARY SOURCES AND REVIEWS:

1. Spignesi, Stephen. "Maximum Overdrive," in *The Shape Under the Sheet: The Complete Stephen King Encyclopedia*. Ann Arbor, MI: Popular Culture, Ink, May 1991, cloth, p. 590.

MB62. "King Fear," conducted by Diane Sawyer. "Prime Time Live," ABC (August 23, 1990).

MB63. Television Interview, on CNN (October 31, 1990). Discussion of horror in America and of the release of *Graveyard Shift* film.

MB63. Television interview, 1991. Interview in conjunction with broadcast of *Sometimes They Come Back*, made-for-television film.

N.

SECONDARY SOURCES

SCHOLARLY ESSAYS

N1. **"Stephen King's *Carrie*—A Universal Fairy Tale,"** by Alex E. Alexander, in *Journal of Popular Culture* (Fall, 1979): 282-288.

b. excerpted: *Contemporary Literary Criticism, Volume 26*, edited by Jean C. Stine. Detroit, MI: Gale Research Co., 1983, cloth, p. 234-236.

N2. **"*Carrie:* Book and Film,"** by Leigh A. Ehlers, in *Ideas of Order in Literature and Film,* edited by Peter Rupert and others. Tallahassee, FL: University Presses of Florida, 1980, cloth, p. 39-50.

b. *Literature Film Quarterly* (Spring, 1981): 32-39.

N3. **"*The Dead Zone*,"** by Keith Neilson, in *Magill's Literary Annual 1980, Volume 1,* edited by Frank N. Magill. Englewood Cliffs, NJ: Salem Press, 1980, cloth, p. 205-209.

N4. **"Understanding Kubrick: *The Shining*,"** by Anthony F. Macklin, in *Journal of Popular Film and Television* 9:2 (Summer, 1981): 93-95.

Relates *The Shining* to Kubrick's earlier films.

N5. **"Carrie on Screaming,"** by Michael A. Morrison, in *Times Educational Supplement* (August 21, 1981): 18.

Intelligent analysis of the conflict between literary pretentiousness and colloquial tone in *Stephen King's Danse Macabre*.

b. excerpted: *Contemporary Literary Criticism, Volume 37,* edited by Daniel G. Markowski. Detroit, MI: Gale Research Co., 1986, cloth, p. 199-200.

N6. **"Apocalypse and the Popular Imagination: Stephen King's *The Stand*,"** by Leonard Cheever, in *RE: Artes Liberales* 8 (Fall, 1981): .

N7. **"The Door Ajar: Structure and Convention in Horror Films That Would Terrify,"** by W. H. Rockett, in *Journal of Popular Film and Television* (Fall, 1981): 130-136.

Rejects King's theories as expressed in *Stephen King's Danse Macabre*.

N8. **"The Shining: Ted Kramer Has a Nightmare,"** by Greg Keeler, in *Journal of Popular Film and Television* (Winter, 1981): 2-8.

Comparison of *Kramer vs. Kramer* and *The Shining* as studies of disintegrating family units, one exploring the rational, the other the unconscious and irrational.

N9. **"The Night Journeys of Stephen King,"** by Douglas E. Winter, in *Fantasy Newsletter* (1981): .

b. *Fear Itself: The Horror Fiction of Stephen King*, edited by Tim Underwood and Chuck Miller. San Francisco, CA: Underwood-Miller, 1982, cloth, p. 183-229. [See **I2**].

c. as: "Von Carrie bis Christine-Stephen King, der Meister des Makabren" ["From *Carrie* to *Christine*—Stephen King, the Master of the Macabre"], in *Das Jahr des Werwolfs* ["*The Cycle of the Werewolf*"]. Bergish Gladbach, West Germany: Bastei-Lübbe Verlag (TB 28135), 1985, p. . Translated and edited by Helmut W. Pesch. [German]

N10. "***Carrie***" [film], by Janet Lorenz, in *Magill's Survey of Cinema, 2nd Series, Volume 1,* edited by Frank N. Magill. Englewood Cliffs, NJ: Salem Press, 1981, cloth, p. 408-411.

N11. "***Danse Macabre*,"** by Michael Adams, in *Magill's Literary Annual, Book of 1981, Volume 1,* edited by Frank N. Magill. Englewood Cliffs, NJ: Salem Press, 1982, cloth, p. 171-174.

N12. **"The Modern Masters, 1920-1980,"** by Gary William Crawford, in *Horror Literature: A Core Collection and Reference Guide,* edited by Marshall Tymn. New York: R. R. Bowker, 1981, paper, p. 325-327.

Entries for *Carrie*, *The Dead Zone*, *Firestarter*, *Night Shift*, *'Salem's Lot*, *The Shining*, and *The Stand*.

N13. "***The Shining*,"** by Frances M. Malpezzi and William M. Clements, in *Magill's Survey of Cinema, 2nd Series, Volume 5*, edited by Frank N. Magill. Englewood Cliffs, NJ: Salem Press, 1981, cloth, p. 2175-2178.

Critique of the film adaptation, focusing on Kubrick's attempts to expand horror as genre.

N14. "***The Shining***" [film], by John Willis, in *Screen World 1981, Volume 32.* New York: Crown Publishers, 1981, cloth, p. 44. List of production crew and cast, with six stills.

N15. **"Master of Postliterate Prose,"** by Paul Gray, in *Time* 120:9 (August 20, 1982): 20.

King's fictions as an "echo chamber of pop culture."

b. excerpted: *Contemporary Literary Criticism, Volume 26*, edited by Jean C. Stine. Detroit, MI: Gale Research Co., 1983, cloth, p. 242-243.

N16. **"Return of the Curse of the Son of Mr. King: Book Two,"** by David J. Schow, in *Whispers* no. 17/18 (August, 1982): 49-56.

Critical study of film adaptations of *Carrie*, *'Salem's Lot*, and *The Shining*.

N17. **"Family Life and Leisure Culture in *The Shining*,"** by Stephen Snyder, in *Film Criticism* 7:1 (Fall, 1982): 4-14.

N18. **"*Dracula* and '*Salem's Lot*: Why the Monsters Won't Die,"** by Robert Lidston, in *West Virginia Philological Papers* 28 (1982): .

N19. **"Introduction—Meeting Stevie,"** by Peter Straub, in *Fear Itself: The Horror Fiction of Stephen King,* edited by Tim Underwood and Chuck Miller. San Francisco, CA: Underwood-Miller, 1982, cloth, p. 7-13. [See **I2**].

N20. **"Cinderella's Revenge-Twists on Fairy Tale and Mythic Themes in the Work of Stephen King,"** by Chelsea Quinn Yarbro, in *Fear Itself: The Horror Fiction of Stephen King,* edited by Tim Underwood and Chuck Miller. San Francisco, CA: Underwood-Miller, 1982, cloth, p. 45-55. [See **I2**].

N21. **"Horror Springs in the Fiction of Stephen King,"** by Don Herron, in *Fear Itself: The Horror Fiction of Stephen King,* edited by Tim Underwood and Chuck Miller. San Francisco, CA: Underwood-Miller, 1982, cloth, p. 57-82. [See **I2**].

N22. **"The Movies and Mr. King,"** by Bill Warren, in *Fear Itself: The Horror Fiction of Stephen King,* edited by Tim Underwood and Chuck Miller. San Francisco, CA: Underwood-Miller, 1982, cloth, p. 105-128. [See **I2**].

N23. **"Stephen King: Horror and Humanity for Our Time,"** by Deborah L. Notkin, in *Fear Itself: The Horror Fiction of Stephen King,* edited by Tim Underwood and Chuck Miller. San Francisco, CA: Underwood-Miller, 1982, cloth, p. 131-142. [See **I2**.]

N24. **"The Grey Arena,"** by Charles L. Grant, in *Fear Itself: The Horror Fiction of Stephen King,* edited by Tim Underwood and Chuck Miller. San Francisco, CA: Underwood-Miller, 1982, cloth, p. 145-151. [See **I2**.]

N25. **"King and the Literary Tradition of Horror and the Supernatural,"** by Ben P. Indick, in *Fear Itself: The Horror Fiction of Stephen King,* edited by Tim Underwood and Chuck Miller. San Francisco, CA: Underwood-Miller, 1982, cloth, p. 153-167. [See **I2**].

N26. **"The Marsten House in '*Salem's Lot*,"** by Alan Ryan, in *Fear Itself: The Horror Fiction of Stephen King,* edited by Tim Underwood and Chuck

Miller. San Francisco, CA: Underwood-Miller, 1982, cloth, p. 169-180. [See **I2**].

N27. "**Afterword,**" by George A. Romero, in *Fear Itself: The Horror Fiction of Stephen King,* edited by Tim Underwood and Chuck Miller. San Francisco, CA: Underwood-Miller, 1982, cloth, p. 247-251. [See **I2**].

N28. "***Danse Macabre,***" by Michael Adams, in *Magill's Literary Annual, 1982, Volume 1,* edited by Frank N. Magill. Englewood Cliffs, NJ: Salem Press, 1982, cloth, p. .

N29. "***The Shining:* Remembrance of Things Forgotten,**" by Thomas Allen Nelson, in *Kubrick: Inside a Film Artist's Maze.* Bloomington IN: Indiana University Press, 1982, paper, p. 197-231.

Discussion of King's novel in the context of Kubrick's film (p. 199-202).

N30. "**Stephen King,**" by Charles Platt, in *Dream Makers: The Uncommon Men and Women Who Write Science Fiction, Volume II.* New York: Berkley, June 1983, trade paper, p. 273-284.

Extensive essay based on interviews with King.

b. New York: Ungar Publishing Co., 1987, cloth, p. . Revised.

N31. "**Antidetection Gothic and Detective Conventions in the Fiction of Stephen King,**" by James Egan, in *Clues: A Journal of Detection* 5:1 (Summer, 1983): 131-146.

Demonstrates how King combines Gothic and detective fiction.

b. excerpted: *Contemporary Literary Criticism, Volume 37,* edited by Daniel G. Marowski. Detroit, MI: Gale Research Co., 1986, cloth, p. 201-203.

N32. "**Lovecraft's Influence on Stephen King,**" by Sam Gafford, in *Crypt of Cthulhu* (Yuletide, 1983): .

N33. "**The Art of Darkness,**" by Douglas E. Winter, in *Shadowings*, edited by Douglas E. Winter. Mercer Island, WA: Starmont House, 1983, cloth, p. 3-23.

Overview of horror fiction in 1981 and 1982, with section on King opening the discussion.

N34. ***The Best, Worst, and Most Unusual Horror Films***, by Darrell Moore. Skokie, IL: Publications International, 1983, cloth, p. 93, 128.

Articles on *Carrie* and *The Shining*.

N35. "*Carrie*," by Keith Neilson, in *Survey of Modern Fantasy Literature, Volume 5,* edited by Frank N. Magill. Englewood Cliffs, NJ: Salem Press, 1983, cloth, p. 197-202.

Critical survey focusing on the novel as science fiction in form and content, horror in atmosphere and evocation of destruction rising from petty causes.

N36. "*Creepshow,*" [film], by John Willis, in *Screen World 1983, Volume 34.* New York: Crown Publishers, 1983, cloth, p. 114. Production crew and cast.

N37. "*The Dead Zone,*" by Christine Watson, in *Survey of Modern Fantasy Literature, Volume 1,* edited by Frank N. Magill. Englewood Cliffs, NJ: Salem Press, 1983, cloth, p. 350-354.

N38. "*Different Seasons,*" by Keith Neilson, in *Magill's Literary Annual 1983, Volume 1,* edited by Frank N. Magill. Englewood Cliffs, NJ: Salem Press, 1983, cloth, p. .

N39. "**Fantasy Versus Horror,**" by Roger C. Schlobin, in *Survey of Modern Fantasy Literature, Volume 5,* edited by Frank N. Magill. Englewood Cliffs, NJ: Salem Press, 1983, cloth, p. 2259-2264.

N40. "*Firestarter,*" by Keith Neilson, in *Survey of Modern Fantasy Literature, Volume 2,* edited by Frank N. Magill. Englewood Cliffs, NJ: Salem Press, 1983, cloth, p. 553-556.

N41. *A Literary Symbiosis: Science Fiction/Fantasy Mystery,* by Hazel Beasley Pierce. CONTRIBUTIONS TO THE STUDY OF SCIENCE FICTION AND FANTASY, No. 6. Series editor, Marshall Tymn. Westport, CT: Greenwood Press, 1983, cloth, p. 221.

N42. "**The Mad Dog and Maine,**" by Burton Hatlen, in *Shadowings,* edited by Douglas E. Winter. Mercer Island, WA: Starmont House, 1983, cloth, p. 33-38.

Analysis of the importance of Maine settings and characters in *Cujo*.

N43. "**The Mist,**" by Keith Neilson, in *Survey of Modern Fantasy Literature,* edited by Frank N. Magill. Englewood Cliffs, NJ: Salem Press, 1983: 1040-1043.

Critical overview of the story, calling it a minor masterpiece within the genre.

N44. "*Night Shift,*" by Keith Neilson, in *Survey of Modern Fantasy Literature, Volume 3,* edited by Frank N. Magill. Englewood Cliffs, NJ: Salem Press, 1983, cloth, p. 116-1120.

Discussions of "Graveyard Shift," "Sometimes They Come Back," and "Children of the Corn."

N45. **"The Remaking of Zero: Beginning at the End,"** by Gary K. Wolfe, in *The End of the World,* edited by Eric S. Rabkin, Martin H. Greenberg, and Joseph Olander. Carbondale, IL: Southern Illinois University Press, 1983, cloth, 1-19 (esp. p. 14).

N46. **"*'Salem's Lot*,"** by Christine Watson, in *Survey of Modern Fantasy Literature, Volume 3,* edited by Frank N. Magill. Englewood Cliffs, NJ: Salem Press, 1983, cloth, p. 1350-1354.

King's novel as homage to *Dracula*.

N47. **"*The Shining*,"** by Keith Neilson, in *Survey of Modern Fantasy Literature, Volume 3,* edited by Frank N. Magill. Englewood Cliffs, NJ: Salem Press, 1983, cloth, p. 1402-1406.

N48. ***The Shape of Rage: The Films of David Cronenberg***, edited by Piers Handling. Toronto, Canada: General Publishing Company, 1983, cloth, p. .

References to *The Dead Zone*.

b. New York: Zoetrope, 1983.

N49. **"*The Stand*,"** by Mary Ferguson, in *Survey of Modern Fantasy Literature, Volume IV,* edited by Frank Magill. Englewood Cliffs, NJ: Salem Press, 1983, cloth, p. 1801-1806.

Critical analysis of *The Stand* as Gothic, popular epic, and apocalyptic literature.

N50. **"Stephen King in Context,"** by Joseph R. Patrouch, Jr., in *Patterns of the Fantastic,* edited by Donald M. Hassler. Mercer Island, WA: Starmont House, 1983, cloth, p. 5-10.

Carrie as SF novel published as horror; King's success stems from his ability to cross genres.

b. excerpted: *Contemporary Literary Criticism, Volume 12,* edited by Daniel G. Markowski. Detroit, MI: Gale Research Co., 1986, cloth, p. 204-205.

N51. **[Title unknown],** by D. A. Cook, in *Literature Film Quarterly* 12:1 (January, 1984): 2+.

Discussion of economic exploitation as theme in the film version of *The Shining*.

N52. **[Title unknown],** by C. Hoile, in *Literature Film Quarterly* 12:1 (January, 1984): 5+.

Freud and Betelheim as sources for the visual imagery in the film version of *The Shining*.

N53. **"Stephen King's Vietnam Allegory: An Interpretation of 'Children of the Corn,'"** by Anthony S. Magistrale. Presented to the International Conference on the Fantastic in the Arts, March 1984, Boca Raton, Florida; in *Footsteps V* (April, 1985): 61-65.

King's characters represent American adults during the Vietnam crisis. In reponses to the Conference panel, King denied any conscious attempt at creating allegory in the story.

b. *Cuyahoga Review* (Spring/Summer, 1984): 61-66.

N54. **"Fantasy as Commodity, Pornography, Camp, and Myth,"** by Leslie Fiedler, in *Fantasy Review* (June, 1984): 6-9, 42.

Guest-of-Honor Address at the Conference on the Fantastic in the Arts, March 1984.

b. as: "Fantasy as Commodity and Myth: Introduction," in *Kingdom of Fear: The World of Stephen King*, edited by Tim Underwood and Chuck Miller. Columbia, PA: Underwood-Miller, 1986, cloth, p. 47-52. [See **I11**].

N55. **"Apocalypticism in the Fiction of Stephen King,"** by James Egan, in *Extrapolation* 25:3 (Fall, 1984): 214-227.

Scholarly study of biblical apocalypse in *Carrie, The Stand,* and "The Mist."

N56. **"Stephen King's Art of Darkness: The First Decade,"** by Douglas E. Winter, in *Fantasy Review* No. 73 (November, 1984): 8-15.

N57. **"Stephen King in the Lowlands: An Annotated Bibliography of His Works as Published in the Netherlands (Holland and Belgium),"** by Eddy C. Bertin, in *SF Gids* ["SF Guide"] (December, 1984): . [Dutch]

b. *Castle Rock: The Stephen King Newsletter* 1:11 (November, 1985): 7-8. Translated by Bertin and updated to July 1985.

N58. **"Urban Gothic: From Transylvania to the South Bronx,"** by S. Rudin, in *Extrapolation* 25 (1984): .

N59. "***Christine***" [film], by John Willis, in *Screen World 1984, Volume 35*. New York: Crown Publishers, 1984, cloth, p. 95. List of cast and crew for film.

N60. "***Christine,***" by Dan Kilbourne, in *Magill's Cinema Annual 1984*, edited by Frank N. Magill. Englewood Cliffs, NJ: Salem Press, 1984, cloth, p. .

N61. "***Cujo***" [film], by John Willis, in *Screen World 1984, Volume 35*. New York: Crown Publishers, 1984, cloth, p. 113. List of cast and crew for film.

N62. "*The Dead Zone*" [film], by John Willis, in *Screen World 1984, Volume 35*. New York: Crown Publishers, 1984, cloth, p. 76-77. List of production and cast, with seven stills.

N63. "***Different Seasons*,**" by Keith Neilson, in *Magill's Literary Annual, Book of 1983, Volume 1,* edited by Frank N Magill. Englewood Cliffs, NJ: Salem Press, 1984, cloth, p. 189-193.

N64. **"The Bosom Serpent: Folk Lore and Popular Art,"** by Harold Schechter, in *The Georgia Review* (Spring, 1985): .

b. *Castle Rock: The Stephen King Newsletter* 2:2 (February, 1986): 3, 5; and 2:3 (March, 1986): 6-7.

N65. **"Inherited Haunts: Stephen King's Terrible Children,"** by Anthony S. Magistrale, in *Extrapolation* 26:1 (Spring, 1985): 43-49.

b. *Landscape of Fear: Stephen King's American Gothic*. Bowling Green, OH: Bowling Green State University Popular Press, 1988, cloth/paper, p. 73-89. [See **I19**].

N66. **"The Destruction and Re-Creation of the Human Community in Stephen King's *The Stand*,"** by Burton Hatlen. Presented to the International Conference on the Fantastic in the Arts, March 1984, Boca Raton, Florida. In *Footsteps V* (April, 1985): 56-60.

N67. **"Introduction,"** by Darrell Schweitzer, in *Discovering Stephen King*, edited by Darrell Schweitzer. STARMONT STUDIES IN LITERARY CRITICISM, No. 8. Mercer Island, WA: Starmont House, 1985, cloth, p. 5-7. [See **I6**].

N68. **"What Makes Him So *Scary?*,"** by Ben P. Indick, in *Discovering Stephen King,* edited by Darrell Schweitzer. STARMONT STUDIES IN LITERARY CRITICISM, No. 8. Mercer Island, WA: Starmont House, 1985, cloth, p. 9-14. [See **I6**].

N69. **"Has Success Spoiled Stephen King?"** by Alan Warren, in *Discovering Stephen King,* edited by Darrell Schweitzer. STARMONT STUDIES IN LITERARY CRITICISM, No. 8. Mercer Island, WA: Starmont House, 1985, cloth, p. 15-25. [See **I6**].

N70. **"The Biggest Horror Fan of them All,"** by Don Herron, in *Discovering Stephen King,* edited by Darrell Schweitzer. STARMONT STUDIES IN LITERARY CRITICISM, No. 8. Mercer Island, WA: Starmont House, 1985, cloth, p. 26-40. [See **I6**].

N71. **"Stephen King's American Gothic,"** by Gary William Crawford, in *Discovering Stephen King,* edited by Darrell Schweitzer. STARMONT STUDIES IN LITERARY CRITICISM, No. 8. Mercer Island, WA: Starmont House, 1985, cloth, p. 41-46. [See **I6**].

Relates King to American Gothic from Charles Brockden Brown through Lovecraft and Leiber; King shows "the nightmare of our idealistic civilization."

N72. **"The Early Tales: Stephen King and *Startling Mystery Stories*,"** by Chet Williamson, in *Discovering Stephen King,* edited by Darrell Schweitzer. STARMONT STUDIES IN LITERARY CRITICISM, No. 8. Mercer Island, WA: Starmont House, 1985, cloth, p. 46-54. [See **I6**].

N73. **"Stephen King and Peter Straub: Fear and Friendship,"** by Bernadette Bosky, in *Discovering Stephen King,* edited by Darrell Schweitzer. STARMONT STUDIES IN LITERARY CRITICISM, No. 8. Mercer Island, WA: Starmont House, 1985, cloth, p. 55-82. [See **I6**].

N74. **"*The Stand*: Science Fiction Into Fantasy,"** by Michael R. Collings, in *Discovering Stephen King,* edited by Darrell Schweitzer. STARMONT STUDIES IN LITERARY CRITICISM, No. 8. Mercer Island, WA: Starmont House, 1985, cloth, p. 83-90. [See **I6**].

Originally presented as part of the King panel at the International Conference on the Fantastic in the Arts, Boca Raton, Florida, March 1984, with King in attendance.

N75. **"Stephen King with a Twist: The E.C. Influence,"** Debra Stump, in *Discovering Stephen King,* edited by Darrell Schweitzer. STARMONT STUDIES IN LITERARY CRITICISM, No. 8. Mercer Island, WA: Starmont House, 1985, cloth, p. 91-101. [See **I6**].

N76. **"*Cycle of the Werewolf* and the Moral Tradition of Horror,"** by Randall Larson, in *Discovering Stephen King,* edited by Darrell Schweitzer. STARMONT STUDIES IN LITERARY CRITICISM, No. 8. Mercer Island, WA: Starmont House, 1985, cloth, p. 102-108. [See **I6**].

N77. **"Stephen King and the Lovecraft Mythos,"** by Robert M. Price, in *Discovering Stephen King,* edited by Darrell Schweitzer. STARMONT STUDIES IN LITERARY CRITICISM, No. 8. Mercer Island, WA: Starmont House, 1985, cloth, p. 109-122. [See **I6**].

N78. **"Three by Bachman,"** by Don D'Ammassa, in *Discovering Stephen King,* edited by Darrell Schweitzer. STARMONT STUDIES IN LITERARY CRITICISM, No. 8. Mercer Island, WA: Starmont House, 1985, cloth, p. 123-130. [See **I6**].

Analyses of *The Long Walk*, *The Running Man*, and *Thinner*.

N79. **"A Matter of Choice: King's *Cujo* and Malamud's *The Natural*,"** by Debra Stump, in *Discovering Stephen King,* edited by Darrell Schweitzer. STARMONT STUDIES IN LITERARY CRITICISM, No. 8. Mercer Island, WA: Starmont House, 1985, cloth, p. 131-140. [See **I6**].

N80. **"The Ultimate Horror: The Dead Child in Stephen King's Stories and Novels,"** by Leonard Heldreth, in *Discovering Stephen King,* edited by

Darrell Schweitzer. STARMONT STUDIES IN LITERARY CRITICISM, No. 8. Mercer Island, WA: Starmont House, 1985, cloth, p. 141-152. [See **I6**].

N81. **"Collecting Stephen King,"** by Darrell Schweitzer, in *Discovering Stephen King,* edited by Darrell Schweitzer. STARMONT STUDIES IN LITERARY CRITICISM, No. 8. Mercer Island, WA: Starmont House, 1985, cloth, p. 153-164. [See **I6**].

N82. **"Synopses of Stephen King's Fiction,"** by Sanford Z. Meschkow (with additions by Darrell Schweitzer, Michael R. Collings, and Ben Indick), in *Discovering Stephen King,* edited by Darrell Schweitzer. STARMONT STUDIES IN LITERARY CRITICISM, No. 8. Mercer Island, WA: Starmont House, 1985, cloth, p. 165-204. [See **I6**].

N83. **"Stephen King: A Bibliography,"** by Marshall Tymn, in *Discovering Stephen King,* edited by Darrell Schweitzer. STARMONT STUDIES IN LITERARY CRITICISM, No. 8. Mercer Island, WA: Starmont House, 1985, cloth, p. 205-209. [See **I6**].

N84. **"Introduction,"** by Darrell Schweitzer, in *Discovering Modern Horror Fiction, Volume I,* edited by Darrell Schweitzer. STARMONT STUDIES IN LITERARY CRITICISM, No. 4. Mercer Island, WA: Starmont House, July 1985, cloth/paper, p. 5-8.

N85. **"Jonathan Carroll: Galen to Vienna to the World,"** by Edna Stumpf, in *Discovering Modern Horror Fiction, Volume I,* edited by Darrell Schweitzer. STARMONT STUDIES IN LITERARY CRITICISM, No. 4. Mercer Island, WA: Starmont House, July 1985, cloth/paper, p. 129-134 (esp. p. 131, 133).

N86. **"Stephen King as an Epic Writer,"** by Ben P. Indick, in *Discovering Modern Horror Fiction, Volume I,* edited by Darrell Schweitzer. STARMONT STUDIES IN LITERARY CRITICISM, No. 4. Mercer Island, WA: Starmont House, July 1985, cloth/paper, p. 56-67.

N87. **"T.E.D. Klein,"** by Robert M. Price, in *Discovering Modern Horror Fiction, Volume I,* edited by Darrell Schweitzer. STARMONT STUDIES IN LITERARY CRITICISM, No. 4. Mercer Island, WA: Starmont House, July 1985, cloth/paper, p. 68-85 (esp. p. 75, 80).

Discussion of "The Mist."

N88. **"Crumbling Castles of Sand: The Social Landscapes of Stephen King's Gothic Vision,"** by Tony Magistrale, in *Journal of Popular Literature* 1 (1985): 45-59.

b. *Landscape of Fear: Stephen King's American Gothic.* Bowling Green, OH: Bowling Green State University Popular Press, 1988, cloth/paper, p. 23-40. [See **I19**].

N89. **"Fandom: Its Value to the Professional,"** by Marion Zimmer Bradley, in *Inside Outer Space: Science Fiction Professionals Look at Their Craft*, edited by Sharon Jarvis. New York: Ungar, 1985, cloth, p. 69-86.

N90. **"The Glorious Past, Erratic Present, and Questionable Future of the Speciality Presses,"** by Stuart David Schiff, in *Inside Outer Space: Science Fiction Professionals Look at Their Craft*, edited by Sharon Jarvis. New York: Ungar, 1985, cloth, 37-51.

References to King's limited editions.

N91. "***Firestarter*,**" in *Magill's Cinema Annual, 1985: A Survey of 1984 Films*, edited by Frank N. Magill. Englewood Cliffs, NJ: Salem, 1985, cloth, p. 519.

N92. "***Carrie*,**" by Jay Robert Nash and Stanley Ralph Ross, in *The Motion Picture Guide, 1927-1983, Vol II*. Chicago: Cinebooks, 1985, cloth, p. 364.

N93. "***Christine*,**" by Jay Robert Nash and Stanley Ralph Ross, in *The Motion Picture Guide, 1927-1983, Vol II*. Chicago: Cinebooks, 1985, cloth, p. 422.

N94. "***Creepshow*,**" by Jay Robert Nash and Stanley Ralph Ross, in *The Motion Picture Guide, 1927-1983, Vol II*. Chicago: Cinebooks, 1985, cloth, p. 512.

N95. "***Cujo*,**" by Jay Robert Nash and Stanley Ralph Ross, in *The Motion Picture Guide, 1927-1983, Vol II*. Chicago: Cinebooks, 1985, cloth, p. 535.

N96. "***The Dead Zone*,**" by Jay Robert Nash and Stanley Ralph Ross, in *The Motion Picture Guide, 1927-1983, Vol II*. Chicago: Cinebooks, 1985, cloth, p. 594-595.

N97. **"Strange Invaders: An Essay-Review,"** by Gary K. Wolfe, in *Modern Fiction Studies* 32:1 (Spring 1986): 133-151.

Discussion of the current state of horror-criticism, with emphasis on works about King.

N98. **"A Girl Named Carrie: Introduction,"** by Bill Thompson, in *Kingdom of Fear: The World of Stephen King*, edited by Tim Underwood and Chuck Miller. Columbia, PA: Underwood-Miller, 1986, cloth, p. 29-34. [See **I11**].

N99. **"The Good Fabric: Of Night Shifts and Skeleton Crews,"** by William F. Nolan, in *Kingdom of Fear: The World of Stephen King*, edited by Tim Underwood and Chuck Miller. Columbia, PA: Underwood-Miller, 1986, cloth, p. 99-106. [See **I11**].

N100. **"King as a Writer for Children,"** by Ben P. Indick, in *Kingdom of Fear: The World of Stephen King*, edited by Tim Underwood and Chuck Miller. Columbia, PA: Underwood-Miller, 1986, cloth, p. 189-205. [See **I11**].

N101. **"King: The Good, the Bad and the Academic,"** by Don Herron, in *Kingdom of Fear: The World of Stephen King*, edited by Tim Underwood and Chuck Miller. Columbia, PA: Underwood-Miller, 1986, cloth, p. 129-157. [See **I11**].

N102. **"King's Characters: The Main(e) Heat,"** by Thomas F. Monteleone, in *Kingdom of Fear: The World of Stephen King*, edited by Tim Underwood and Chuck Miller. Columbia, PA: Underwood-Miller, 1986, cloth, p. 241-251. [See **I11**].

N103. **"The Life and Death of Richard Bachman: Stephen King's Doppelgänger,"** by Stephen P. Brown, in *Kingdom of Fear: The World of Stephen King*, edited by Tim Underwood and Chuck Miller. Columbia, PA: Underwood-Miller, 1986, cloth, p. 109-126. [See **I11**].

N104. **"The Mind's a Monkey: Character and Psychology in Stephen King's Recent Fiction,"** by Bernadette Bosky, in *Kingdom of Fear: The World of Stephen King*, edited by Tim Underwood and Chuck Miller. Columbia, PA: Underwood-Miller, 1986, cloth, p. 209-238. [See **I11**].

Analysis of King based on the contention that character is the most important element in horror fiction.

N105. **"Monsters in Our Midst: Introduction,"** by Robert Bloch, in *Kingdom of Fear: The World of Stephen King*, edited by Tim Underwood and Chuck Miller. Columbia, PA: Underwood-Miller, 1986, cloth, p. 23-27. [See **I11**].

King is a monster—but then also are all writers of Dark Fantasy, whose works reflect childhood questions of identity, reality, and terror.

N106. **"The Skull Beneath the Skin,"** by Tim Underwood, in *Kingdom of Fear: The World of Stephen King*, edited by Tim Underwood and Chuck Miller. Columbia, PA: Underwood-Miller, 1986, cloth, p. 255-267. [See **I11**].

N107. **"Stephen King Goes to the Movies,"** by Chuck Miller, in *Kingdom of Fear: The World of Stephen King*, edited by Tim Underwood and Chuck Miller. Columbia, PA: Underwood-Miller, 1986, cloth, p. 161-186. [See **I11**].

N108. **"Stephen King's Horror Has a Healing Power: Foreword,"** by Andrew M. Greeley, in *Kingdom of Fear: The World of Stephen King*, edited by Tim Underwood and Chuck Miller. Columbia, PA: Underwood-Miller, 1986, cloth, p. 21-22. [See **I11**].

N109. **"Thanks to the Crypt-Keeper: Introduction,"** by Whitley Strieber, in *Kingdom of Fear: The World of Stephen King*, edited by Tim Underwood and Chuck Miller. Columbia, PA: Underwood-Miller, 1986, cloth, p. 41-45. [See **I11**].

N110. **"The Unexpected and the Inevitable,"** by Michael McDowell, in *Kingdom of Fear: The World of Stephen King*, edited by Tim Underwood and Chuck Miller. Columbia, PA: Underwood-Miller, 1986, cloth, p. 83-95. [See **I11**].

b. excerpted: *Castle Rock: The Stephen King Newsletter* 2:4 (April, 1986): 1, 3-4, 6.

N111. **"Welcome to Room 217: Introduction,"** by Ramsey Campbell, in *Kingdom of Fear: The World of Stephen King*, edited by Tim Underwood and Chuck Miller. Columbia, PA: Underwood-Miller, 1986, cloth, p. 35-40. [See **I11**].

N112. **"'A Single Powerful Spectacle': Stephen King's Gothic Melodrama,"** by James Egan, in *Extrapolation* 21:2 (Spring, 1986): 62-75.

Sex, violence, and horror in melodrama, and King's permutations on those conventions.

N113. **"*IT*: Stephen King's Comprehensive Masterpiece,"** by Michael R. Collings, in *Castle Rock: The Stephen King Newsletter* 2:7 (July, 1986): 1, 4-6.

b. *The Stephen King Phenomenon*, by Michael R. Collings. Mercer Island, WA: Starmont House, March 1987, cloth, p. 13-25. [See **I15**]. Updated.

SECONDARY SOURCES AND REVIEWS:

1. Johnson, Kimball, Letter, in *Castle Rock: The Stephen King Newsletter* 3:11 (December, 1986/January, 1987): 7.

N114. **"The Bestselling Bestseller: King and the Lists,"** by Michael R. Collings, in *Castle Rock: The Stephen King Newsletter* 2:10 (October, 1986): 1, 3.

b. *The Stephen King Phenomenon*, by Michael R. Collings. Mercer Island, WA; Starmont House, 1987, cloth/paper, p. 36-50. [See **I15**]. Updated.

N115. **"The Funhouse of Fear,"** by Douglas E. Winter, in *Fantasy Review* No. 95 (October, 1986): 15-16.

On the nature of horror, with frequent references to King's work.

N116. **"Stephen King: Alienation, Competition and Community in *Rage* and *The Long Walk*,"** by Burton Hatlen, presented to the Maine Writers and Publishers Alliance, College of the Atlantic, Bar Harbor, ME (November 8, 1986).

N117. **"King Versus Koontz: Style and *Invasion*,"** by Michael R. Collings, in *Footsteps VII* (November, 1986): 32-42, 45.

Stylistic analysis of similarities between King's *The Shining* and Dean R. Koontz's pseudonymous *Invasion* (as AARON WOLFE), in light of previous suggestions that King might have written the novel. Revision of "Speculations" chapter from *Stephen King as Richard Bachman*, emphasizing Koontz's authorship of *Invasion* by "Aaron Wolfe."

N118. **"'Come and Play with Us': The Play Metaphor in Kubrick's *The Shining*,"** by Larry W. Caldwell and Samuel J. Umland, in *Literature/Film Quarterly* 14:2 (1986): 106-111.

N119. **"Stephen King—A Modern Interpretation of the Frankenstein Myth,"** by Carol Senf, in *Science Fiction: A Review of Speculative Literature* 8:3 (1986): 65-73.

N120. ***The Living and the Undead: From Stoker's* Dracula *to Romero's* Dawn of the Dead,"** by Gregory A. Waller. Urbana, IL: University of Illinois Press, November 1986, cloth, p. .

Critical overview of the Dracula motif, with references to King's work.

SECONDARY SOURCES AND REVIEWS:

1. Heldreth, Leonard G. "Extraordinary Vampire Survey," in *Fantasy Review* No. 92 (June 1986): 28. Comments on Waller's references to King's retelling of the Dracula tale.

N121. **"The Artist as Demon in Mary Shelley, Stevenson, Walpole, Stoker, and King,"** by Mary McGuire, in *Gothic* n.s. 1 (1986): 1-5.

N122. **"Stephen King and the Tradition of American Gothic,"** by Kenneth Gibbs, in *Gothic* n.s. 1 (1986): 6-14.

N123. **"*The Shining*,"** by Julia Meyers, in *Masterplots II: American Fiction Series, Volume 4,* edited by Frank N. Magill. Englewood Cliffs, NJ: Salem Press, 1986, cloth, p. 1407-1410.

N124. **"*The Stand*,"** by Julia Meyers, in *Masterplots II: American Fiction Series, Volume 4,* edited by Frank N. Magill. Englewood Cliffs, NJ: Salem Press, 1986, cloth, p. 1532-1535.

N125. **"Stephen King,"** by Michael R. Collings, in *Contemporary Literary Criticism, Volume 26,* edited by Jean C. Stine. Detroit, MI: Gale Research Co., 1986, cloth, p. 207-208. Excerpt from *Stephen King as Richard Bachman,* p. 9-29. See **I7**.

N126. ***The Secrets of Writing Popular Fiction,*** by Stanley Wiater. Cincinnati, OH: Writer's Digest, 1986?, cloth, p. .

N127. **"Geschichten aus dem Dunkel: Über des Phänomen des Schriftstellers, Drehbuchautors und Filmregisseurs Stephen King"** ["Tales from the Dark: Concerning the Phenomenon of Writers, Screenwriters, and Film Directors for Stephen King Films"], by Willy Loderhose, in *Katzenauge* ["*Cat's Eye*"]. Bergisch Gladbach, West Germany: Bastei-Lübbe Verlag, 1986, paper?, p. .

b. *Trucks*. Bergish Gladbach, West Germany: Bastei-Lübbe Verlag, 1986, paper, p. .

N128. **"Katzenauge: Wie es zu der Verfilmung Kam"** ["Cat's Eye: How It Came to Be Filmed"], by Willy Loderhose, in *Katzenauge* ["*Cat's Eye*"]. Bergisch Gladbach, West Germany: Bastei-Lübbe Verlag, 1986, paper?, p. .

N129. **"Trucks: Bermerkungen zur Verfilmung"** ["Trucks: Comments on the Filming"], by Willy Loderhose, in *Katzenauge* ["*Cat's Eye*"]. Bergisch Gladbach, West Germany: Bastei-Lübbe Verlag, 1986, paper?, p. .

N130. **"Kinder des Zorns—Bemerkungen zur Entstehung des Films"** ["Children of Anger: Comments on the Film"], by Willy Loderhose, in *Katzenauge* ["*Cat's Eye*"]. Bergisch Gladbach, West Germany: Bastei-Lübbe Verlag, 1986, paper?, p. .

N131. **"*The Shining* as Lichtung: Kubrick's Film, Heidegger's Clearing,"** by Howard Pearce, in *Forms of the Fantastic: Selected Essays from the Third International Conference on the Fantastic in Literature and Film*, edited by Jan Hokenson and Howard Pearce. CONTRIBUTIONS TO THE STUDY OF SCIENCE FICTION AND FANTASY, No. 20. Westport, CT: Greenwood Press, 1986, cloth, p. 49-57.

N132. ***How to Write Tales of Horror, Fantasy, and Science Fiction,*** by J. N. Williamson. Cincinnati, OH: Writer's Digest, March 1987, cloth, p. .

N133. **"Teaching Critical Analysis Writing Using Stephen King's *Danse Macabre*,"** by Michael Begg, in *English Journal* 76:3 (March, 1987): 72-74.

N134. ***Do You Believe in Magic? The Second Coming of the '60s Generation,*** by Anne Gottlieb. New York: Times Books, 1987, cloth/paper, p. .

SECONDARY SOURCES AND REVIEWS:

1. Spruce, Sarah. "Back in the 60's Again," in *Castle Rock: The Stephen King Newsletter* 3:10 (October, 1987): 3.

N135. **"Some Notes on *It*,"** by Faye Ringel, in *Castle Rock: The Stephen King Newsletter* 3:9 (September, 1987): 1, 4.

N136. **"The Automobile Motif: Stephen King's Most Frequent Villain,"** by Mark Graham, in *Castle Rock: The Stephen King Newsletter* 3:11 (November, 1987): 3, 5-6, 8.

N137. **"Stephen King, Sci-Fi, and *The Tommyknockers*,"** by Michael R. Collings, in *Castle Rock: The Stephen King Newsletter* 3:11 (November, 1987): 1, 4-5.

N138. **"Stephen King,"** in *Anatomy of Wonder: A Critical Guide to Science Fiction, 3rd edition,* edited by Neil Barron. New York: R. R. Bowker, 1987, cloth, p. 651.

N139. **"The Marvelous Horror Thriller"** [Chapter Three], in *The Delights of Terror: An Aesthetics of the Tale of Terror,* by Terry Heller. Urbana, IL: University of Illinois Press, September 1987, cloth/paper, p. 45-46.

Discusses "The Mangler."

N140. **"Introduction,"** by Gregory A. Waller, in *American Horrors: Essays on the Modern American Horror Film,* edited by Gregory A. Waller. Urbana, IL: University of Illinois Press, 1987, cloth/paper, p. 1-14 (esp. 2, 10).

N141. **"More Dark Dreams: Some Notes on the Recent Horror Film,"** by Charles Derry, in *American Horrors: Essays on the Modern American Horror Film,* edited by Gregory A. Waller. Urbana, IL: University of Illinois Press, 1987, cloth/paper, p. 162-174.

Notes that even films based on King properties were not commercially successful.

N142. **"A Blind Date with Disaster: Adolescent Revolt in the Fiction of Stephen King,"** by Tom Newhouse, in *The Gothic World of Stephen King: Landscape of Nightmares,* edited by Gary Hoppenstand and Ray B. Browne. Bowling Green, OH: Bowling Green State University Popular Press, December 1987, cloth, p. 49-55. [See **I17**].

N143. **"Blood, Eroticism, and the Vampire in Twentieth-Century Popular Literature,"** by Carol A. Senf, in *The Gothic World of Stephen King: Landscape of Nightmares,* edited by Gary Hoppenstand and Ray B. Browne. Bowling Green, OH: Bowling Green State University Popular Press, December 1987, cloth, p. 20-30. [See **I17**].

N144. **"*The Dark Tower*: Stephen King's Gothic Western,"** by James Egan, in *The Gothic World of Stephen King: Landscape of Nightmares,* edited by Gary Hoppenstand and Ray B. Browne. Bowling Green, OH: Bowling Green State University Popular Press, December 1987, cloth, p. 95-106. [See **I17**].

N145. **"A Dream of New Life: Stephen King's *Pet Sematary* as a Variant of *Frankenstein*,"** by Mary Ferguson Pharr, in *The Gothic World of Stephen King: Landscape of Nightmares,* edited by Gary Hoppenstand and Ray B. Browne. Bowling Green, OH: Bowling Green State University Popular Press, December 1987, cloth, p. 115-125. [See **I17**].

N146. **"Freaks: The Grotesque as Metaphor in the Works of Stephen King,"** by Vernon Hyles, in *The Gothic World of Stephen King: Landscape of Nightmares,* edited by Gary Hoppenstand and Ray B. Browne. Bowling Green, OH: Bowling Green State University Popular Press, December 1987, cloth, p. 56-63. [See **I17**].

N147. **"Introduction: The Horror of It All: Stephen King and the Landscape of the American Nightmare,"** by Gary Hoppenstand and Ray B. Browne, in *The Gothic World of Stephen King: Landscape of Nightmares,* edited by Gary Hoppenstand and Ray B. Browne. Bowling Green, OH: Bowling Green State University Popular Press, December 1987, cloth, p. 1-19. [See **I17**].

N148. **"Love and Death in the American Car: Stephen King's Auto-Erotic Horror,"** by Linda C. Badley, in *The Gothic World of Stephen King: Landscape of Nightmares,* edited by Gary Hoppenstand and Ray B. Browne. Bowling Green, OH: Bowling Green State University Popular Press, December 1987, cloth, p. 84-94. [See **I17**].

N149. **"Of Mad Dogs and Firestarters—The Incomparable Stephen King,"** by Garyn G. Roberts, in *The Gothic World of Stephen King: Landscape of Nightmares,* edited by Gary Hoppenstand and Ray B. Browne. Bowling Green, OH: Bowling Green State University Popular Press, December 1987, cloth, p. 31-36. [See **I17**].

N150. **"'Oz the Gweat and Tewwible' and 'The Other Side': The Theme of Death in *Pet Sematary* and *Jutterbug Perfume*,"** by Natalie Schroeder, in *The Gothic World of Stephen King: Landscape of Nightmares,* edited by Gary Hoppenstand and Ray B. Browne. Bowling Green, OH: Bowling Green State University Popular Press, December 1987, cloth, p. 135-141. [See **I17**].

N151. **"Reading Between the Lines: Stephen King and Allegory,"** by Bernard J. Gallagher, in *The Gothic World of Stephen King: Landscape of Nightmares,* edited by Gary Hoppenstand and Ray B. Browne. Bowling Green, OH: Bowling Green State University Popular Press, December 1987, cloth, p. 37-48. [See **I17**].

N152. **"Stephen King's Creation of Horror in *'Salem's Lot*: A Prolegomenon Towards a New Hermeneutic of the Gothic Novel,"** by James E. Hicks, in *The Gothic World of Stephen King: Landscape of Nightmares,* edited by Gary Hoppenstand and Ray B. Browne. Bowling Green, OH: Bowling Green State University Popular Press, December 1987, cloth, p. 75-83. [See **I17**].

N153. **"Stephen King's *Pet Sematary*: Hawthorne's Woods Revisited,"** by Tony Magistrale, in *The Gothic World of Stephen King: Landscape of Nightmares,* edited by Gary Hoppenstand and Ray B. Browne. Bowling Green, OH: Bowling Green State University Popular Press, December 1987, cloth, p. 126-134. [See **I17**].

N154. **"Taking Stephen King Seriously: Reflections on a Decade of Best-Sellers,"** by Samuel Schuman, in *The Gothic World of Stephen King: Landscape of Nightmares,* edited by Gary Hoppenstand and Ray B. Browne. Bowling Green, OH: Bowling Green State University Popular Press, December 1987, cloth, p. 107-114. [See **I17**].

N155. **"Viewing 'The Body': King's Portrait of the Artist as Survivor,"** by Leonard Heldreth, in *The Gothic World of Stephen King: Landscape of Nightmares,* edited by Gary Hoppenstand and Ray B. Browne. Bowling Green, OH: Bowling Green State University Popular Press, December 1987, cloth, p. 64-74. [See **I17**].

N156. **"Breaking Up Isn't Hard to Do: Stephen King, Christopher Lasch, and Psychic Fragmentation,"** by Bernard J. Gallagher, in *Journal of American Culture* 10 (Winter, 1987): 59-67.

N157. **"Filling the Niche: Fantasy and Science Fiction in Contemporary Horror,"** by Michael R. Collings, in *Intersections: Fantasy and Science Fiction—Selected Essays from the Seventh Eaton Conference,* edited by George Slusser and Eric S. Rabkin. Carbondale, IL: Southern Illinois University Press, 1987, cloth, p. 48-54.

On the nature of horror, with references to King.

N158. **"The Gestation of Genres: Literature, Fiction, Romance, Science Fiction, Fantasy...,"** by Samuel R. Delany, in *Intersections: Fantasy and Science Fiction,* edited by George E. Slusser and Eric S. Rabkin. Carbondale, IL: Southern Illinois University Press, 1987, cloth, p. 63-73.

King's debt to science fiction as genre.

N159. **"Homecomings: Fantasy and Horror,"** by Celeste Pernicone, in *Intersections: Fantasy and Science Fiction,* edited by George E. Slusser and Eric S. Rabkin. Carbondale, IL: Southern Illinois University Press, 1987, cloth, p. 171-180.

Reference to *Carrie*: "Fantasy stories summon up friends....Horror stories summon fiends" (p. 178).

N160. **"Victorian Urban Gothic: The First Modern Fantastic Literature,"** by Kathleen Spencer, in *Intersections: Fantasy and Science Fiction,* edited by George E. Slusser and Eric S. Rabkin. Carbondale, IL: Southern Illinois University Press, 1987, cloth, p. 87-96.

King's novels as mediating between science fiction and fantasy (p. 90-91).

N161. **"*Maximum Overdrive*,"** in *Magill's Cinema Annual, 1987: A Survey of the Films of 1986,* edited by Frank N. Magill. Englewood Cliffs, NJ: Salem Press, 1987, cloth, p. 497.

N162. "*Stand By Me*," by Norman Carson, in *Magill's Cinema Annual, 1987: A Survey of the Films of 1986*, edited by Frank N. Magill. Englewood Cliffs, NJ: Salem Press, 1987, cloth, p. 413-417.

N163. **"Bibliography for Remade World Literature: Backgrounds, Criticism, and Fiction,"** compiled by Paul Brians, Thomas P. Dunn, Marshall Tymn, and Carl B. Yoke, in *Phoenix from the Ashes: The Literature of the Remade World,* edited by Carl B. Yoke. CONTRIBUTIONS TO THE STUDY OF SCIENCE FICTION AND FANTASY, No. 30. Series editor, Marshall Tymn. Westport, CT: Greenwood Press, 1987, cloth, p. 207-231.

The Stand as King's contribution to literature of the remade world (p. 223).

N164. "*The Shining*," by Jay Robert Nash and Stanley Ralph Ross, in *The Motion Picture Guide, 1927-1983, Vol VII.* Chicago: Cinebooks, 1987, cloth, p. 2886.

N165. ***The Zombies That Ate Pittsburgh: The Films of George A. Romero***, by Paul R. Gagne. New York: Dodd, Mead, 1987, paper, p. .

Study of Romero and his work, with a chapter on *Creepshow*.

b. excerpted: *Cinefantastique* (September-October, 1986): .
c. excerpted as: "King and Romero: The Filming of *Creepshow*," in *Castle Rock: The Stephen King Newsletter* 3:3 (March, 1987): 1, 6-7, 12.
d. excerpted as: "The Zombies that Ate Pittsburgh, Part II," in *Castle Rock: The Stephen King Newsletter* 3:4 (April/May, 1987): 1, 6-7, 10.

N166. **"The Big Producer,"** by Thomas Tessier, in *Reign of Fear: Fiction and Film of Stephen King,* edited by Don Herron. Los Angeles: Underwood-Miller, June 1988, cloth, p. 69-78. [See **I21**].

N167. **"By Crouch End, in the Isles,"** by Peter Tremayne, in *Reign of Fear: Fiction and Film of Stephen King,* edited by Don Herron. Los Angeles: Underwood-Miller, June 1988, cloth, p. 99-108. [See **I21**].

N168. **"'Come Out Here and Take Your Medicine': King and Drugs,"** by Ben P. Indick, in *Reign of Fear: Fiction and Film of Stephen King,* edited by Don Herron. Los Angeles: Underwood-Miller, June 1988, cloth, p. 149-176. [See **I21**].

N169. **"The Cycles (Tricycles and Hogs) of Horror,"** by J. N. Williamson, in *Reign of Fear: Fiction and Film of Stephen King,* edited by Don Herron. Los Angeles: Underwood-Miller, June 1988, cloth, p. 57-62. [See **I21**].

N170. **"Foreword,"** by Dennis Etchison, in *Reign of Fear: Fiction and Film of Stephen King,* edited by Don Herron. Los Angeles: Underwood-Miller, June 1988, cloth, p. 1-6. [See **I21**].

N171. **"The Glass-Eyed Dragon,"** by L. Sprague de Camp, in *Reign of Fear: Fiction and Film of Stephen King,* edited by Don Herron. Los Angeles: Underwood-Miller, June 1988, cloth, p. 63-68. [See **I21**].

N172. **"Horror Without Limits: Looking into *The Mist*,"** by Dennis Rickard, in *Reign of Fear: Fiction and Film of Stephen King,* edited by Don Herron. Los Angeles: Underwood-Miller, June 1988, cloth, p. 177-192. [See **I21**].

N173. **"In Providence: Introduction,"** by Frank Belknap Long, in *Reign of Fear: Fiction and Film of Stephen King,* edited by Don Herron. Los Angeles: Underwood-Miller, June 1988, cloth, p. 15-18. [See **I21**].

N174. **"The King and His Minions: Thoughts of a *Twilight Zone* Reviewer,"** by Thomas M. Disch, in *Reign of Fear: Fiction and Film of Stephen King,* edited by Don Herron. Los Angeles: Underwood-Miller, 1988, cloth, p. 79-92. [See **I21**].

N175. **"King of the Comics?: Introduction,"** by Marv Wolfman, in *Reign of Fear: Fiction and Film of Stephen King,* edited by Don Herron. Los Angeles: Underwood-Miller, June 1988, cloth, p. 11-14. [See **I21**].

N176. **"The Movies and Mr. King, Part II,"** by Bill Warren, in *Reign of Fear: Fiction and Film of Stephen King,* edited by Don Herron. Los Angeles: Underwood-Miller, June 1988, cloth, p. 123-148. [See **I21**].

N177. **"'Reach Out and Touch Some Thing': Blurbs and Stephen King,"** by Stanley Wiater, in *Reign of Fear: Fiction and Film of Stephen King,* edited by Don Herron. Los Angeles: Underwood-Miller, June 1988, cloth, p. 109-122. [See **I21**].

b. *Castle Rock: The Stephen King Newsletter* 4:7 (July, 1988): 1, 8, 11-12.

N178. **"Snowbound in the Overlook,"** by Guy N. Smith, in *Reign of Fear: Fiction and Film of Stephen King,* edited by Don Herron. Los Angeles: Underwood-Miller, June 1988, cloth, p. 93-98. [See **I21**].

N179. **"Stephen King and the American Dream: Alienation, Competition, and Community in *Rage* and *The Long Walk*,"** by Burton Hatlen, in *Reign of Fear: Fiction and Film of Stephen King,* edited by Don Herron. Los Angeles: Underwood-Miller, June 1988, cloth, p. 19-50. [See **I21**].

N180. **"Summation,"** by Don Herron, in *Reign of Fear: Fiction and Film of Stephen King,* edited by Don Herron. Los Angeles: Underwood-Miller, June 1988, cloth, p. 209-240. [See **I21**].

N181. **"When Company Drops In,"** by Charles Willeford, in *Reign of Fear: Fiction and Film of Stephen King,* edited by Don Herron. Los Angeles: Underwood-Miller, June 1988, cloth, p. 51-56. [See **I21**].

N182. **"'The Road Laid Its Mark on You': Jack's Metamorphosis in *The Talisman* (or, Beyond Boy-Wonderdom),"** by Jack Slay, Jr., in *Castle Rock: The Stephen King Newsletter* 4:7 (July, 1988): 1, 4-5.

Characterization in *The Talisman*.

N183. **"Technohorror: The Dystopian Vision of Stephen King,"** by James Egan, in *Extrapolation* 29:2 (Summer, 1988): 140-152.

On King's relationship with dystopian literature.

N184. **"H. P. Lovecraft and Those Tommyknockers,"** by Ben Indick, in *Castle Rock: The Stephen King Newsletter* 4:8 (August, 1988): 4, 12.

Analytical comparison of King's novel and Lovecraft's *The Colour Out of Space*.

N185. **"Questions for Analysis" and "Commentary,"** by Rise B. Axelrod and Charles R. Cooper, in *The St. Martin's Guide to Writing*, Shorter Second Edition. New York: St. Martin's Press, 1988, paper, p. 296-298.

Discussion of King's article, "Why We Crave Horror Movies."

N186. **"Introduction,"** by David G. Hartwell, in *The Dark Descent*, edited by David G. Hartwell. New York: Tor, October 1988, cloth, p. 1-11.

References to King and his role in the evolution of contemporary horror fiction.

N187. **Headnote to "The Reach,"** by David G. Hartwell, in *The Dark Descent*, edited by David G. Hartwell. New York: Tor, October 1988, cloth, p. 15.

"The Reach" is often considered King's best short story, "a work of unusual subtlety and sentiment, a ghost story of love and death, a virtuoso performance in which the horror is distanced but underpins the whole."

N188. **Headnote to "The Monkey,"** by David G. Hartwell, in *The Dark Descent*, edited by David G. Hartwell. New York: Tor, October 1988, cloth, p. 382.

N189. **Headnote to "Crouch End,"** by David G. Hartwell, in *The Dark Descent*, edited by David G. Hartwell. New York: Tor, October 1988, cloth, p. 690.

"This story is the closest King approaches, except in the odd, surreal 'Big Wheels,' and perhaps in 'Mrs. Todd's Shortcut' to a concern with alterations in base or concensus reality."

N190. **"Stephen King and Modern Horror,"** by I. D. Breque, in *Europe-Revue Litteraire Menouelle* 66:707 (1988): 97-104.

N191. **"Stephen King: *'Salem's Lot*,"** by Al Sarrantonio, in *Horror: 100 Best Books*, edited by Stephen Jones and Kim Newman. London: Xanadu, 1988, cloth, p. 161-162. Limited edition (300 copies), and trade edition.

N192. **"Stephen King: *The Shining*,"** by Peter Straub, in *Horror: 100 Best Books*, edited by Stephen Jones and Kim Newman. London: Xanadu, 1988, cloth, p. 171-172. Limited edition (300 copies) and trade edition.

N193. **"The Year in Horror, 1987,"** by Michael A. Morrison, in *Science Fiction & Fantasy Book Review Annual 1988*, edited by Robert A. Collins and Robert Latham. Westport, CT: Meckler, 1988, cloth, p. 21-36.

Includes a discussion of *Misery* (p. 26-27, 35) and *The Tommyknockers* (p. 30-31).

N194. **"A Critical Survey of Fantastic Literature and Film Scholarship in 1987,"** by Neil Barron, in *Science Fiction & Fantasy Book Review Annual*, edited by Robert A. Collins and Robert Latham. Westport, CT: Meckler, 1988, cloth, p. 51-76.

Discussion of the King-criticism "cottage industry" (p. 65) and studies of King's films (69).

N195. **"The Realities of Unreal Worlds: King's *The Dead Zone*, Schmidt's *Kensho*, and Lem's *Solaris*,"** by Patrick D. Murphy, in *Spectrum of the Fantastic: Selected Essays from the Sixth International Conference on the Fantastic in the Arts*, edited by Donald Palumbo. CONTRIBUTIONS TO THE STUDY OF SCIENCE FICTION AND FANTASY, Number 31. Series editor, Marshall Tymn. Westport, CT: Greenwood Press, 1988, cloth, p. 175-183.

N196. **"*Creepshow 2*,"** in *Magill's Cinema Annual, 1988: A Survey of the Films of 1987*, edited by Frank N. Magill. Englewood Cliffs, NJ: Salem Press, 1988, cloth, p. 398.

N197. **"Stephen King,"** by Carl Rollyson, in *Critical Survey of Mystery and Detective Fiction*, edited by Frank N. Magill. Englewood Cliffs, NJ: Salem Press, 1988, cloth, Vol. 3, p. 985-989.

N198. **"Dean R. Koontz and Stephen King: Style, *Invasion*, and an Aesthetics of Horror Fiction,"** by Michael R. Collings, in *Sudden Fear: The Horror and Dark Suspense Fiction of Dean R. Koontz*, edited by Bill Munster. STARMONT STUDIES IN LITERARY CRITICISM, No. 24. Mercer Island, WA: Starmont House, 1988, cloth, p. 45-65.

N199. **"Interview with Dean R. Koontz,"** conducted by Bill Munster, in *Sudden Fear: The Horror and Dark Suspense Fiction of Dean R. Koontz*, edited by Bill Munster. STARMONT STUDIES IN LITERARY CRITICISM, No. 24. Mercer Island, WA: Starmont House, 1988, cloth, p. 5-31 (esp. p. 19, 22).

N200. **"Dean R. Koontz's *Twilight Eyes*: Art and Artifact,"** by Michael R. Collings, in *Sudden Fear: The Horror and Dark Suspense Fiction of Dean R. Koontz*, edited by Bill Munster. STARMONT STUDIES IN LITERARY CRITICISM, No. 24. Mercer Island, WA: Starmont House, 1988, cloth, p. 145-154 (esp. p. 146-147).

N201. **"Stephen King: Things That Go Bump in the Night,"** by Andrew M. Greeley, in *God in Popular Culture*, by Andrew M. Greeley. Chicago: Thomas More, 1988, cloth, p. 211-220.

N202. **"The Playing Fields of Eden,"** by Frank McConnell, in *Mindscapes: The Geographies of Imagined Worlds,* edited by George E. Slusser and Eric S. Rabkin. Carbondale, IL: Southern Illinois University Press, 1989, cloth, p. 78-87.

N203. **"Native Sons: Regionalism in the Work of Nathaniel Hawthorne and Stephen King,"** by Tony Magistrale, in *The Journal of the Fantastic in the Arts* 2:1 (Spring, 1989): 76-86.

N204. **"Rising Like Old Corpses: Stephen King and the Horrors of Time-Past,"** by Leonard G. Heldreth, in *The Journal of the Fantastic in the Arts* 2:1 (Spring, 1989): 5-14.

N205. **"Acorns to Oaks: Explorations of Theme, Image, and Characterization in the Early Works of Stephen King, Part I,"** by Michael R. Collings, in *Castle Rock: The Stephen King Newsletter* 5:8 (August, 1989): 1, 8.

Analytical discussion of "Slade," the early poems, and other works; originally presented as Academic Guest of Honor Address, Horrorfest '89, May 1989.

N206. ***Harlan Ellison's Watching***, by Harlan Ellison. Los Angeles: Underwood-Miller, 1989, cloth, p. 172-174, 182, 185, 250, 253, 435-436. Limited, signed edition and trade edition.

Ellison's often trenchant, always characteristically direct essays include references to *Carrie* (p. 172-174), "Children of the Corn" (p. 182), *Christine* (172, 182), *Creepshow* (185), *Cujo* (172, 182), *Cycle of the Werewolf* (250), *The Dark Tower* (172), *The Dead Zone* (172), *Different Seasons* (172), *Firestarter* (172-173), "Gramma" (253), *Night Shift* (172, 182), "The Plant" (172), *The Running Man* (435-436), *'Salem's Lot* (182), *The Shining* (172, 184-185), *Silver Bullet* (250-251), and *The Tommyknockers* (436). Among other things, he discusses resemblances in plot between a Robert Sheckley short story and *The Running Man* as an indication of King's ability to translate elements of stories and films he might have read or seen years before into uniquely personal narratives.

N207. **"Acorns to Oaks: Explorations of Theme, Image, and Characterization in the Early Works of Stephen King, Part II,"** by Michael R. Collings, in *Castle Rock: The Stephen King Newsletter* 5:9/10 (September/October, 1989): 3, 10.

Analytical discussion of "Slade," the early poems, and other works; presented as Academic Guest of Honor Address, Horrorfest '89, May 1989]

N208. **"Clive Barker on Stephen King, Horror, and E.C. Comics,"** in *The Stephen King Companion,* edited by George Beahm. Kansas City, MO: Andrews & McMeel, September 1989, cloth, p. 144-145.

Barker's interview is drawn from his responses on *The Larry King Show*, May 6, 1987 and October 11, 1988.

N209. **"Introducing Stephen King,"** by Kelly Powell, in *The Stephen King Companion,* edited by George Beahm. Kansas City, MO: Andrews & McMeel, September 1989, cloth, p. 49-50.

Kelly's introductory statement for King's "Virginia Beach Lecture"; Kelly focuses on episodes of censorship against King's novels in school libraries across the country.

N210. **"Stephen King and the Critics: A Personal Perspective,"** by Michael R. Collings, in *The Stephen King Companion*, edited by George Beahm. Kansas City, MO: Andrews & McMeel, September 1989, cloth, p. 139-140.

N211. **"Hooked on Horror: Why Rational American Readers are Obsessed with Scaring Themselves Silly,"** by Marshall Blonsky, in *The Blood Review: Journal of Horror Criticism* 1:1 (October, 1989): 70-72.

N212. ***Horror: A Connoisseur's Guide to Literature and Film***, by Leonard Wolf. New York: Facts on File, 1989, cloth, p. .

N213. **"Kurzarbeit für die Nachtschicht"** ["Short Work for the Night Shift"], by Heiko Langhans, in *Das Stephen King Buch*, edited by Joachim Körber. München, West Germany: Wilhelm Heyne Verlag, 1989, paper, p. .

N214. **"Der Mythos vom Dunklen Turm"** ["The Mythos of the Dark Tower"], by Joachim Körber, in *Das Stephen King Buch*, edited by Joachim Körber. München, West Germany: Wilhelm Heyne Verlag, 1989, paper, p.

N215. **"King als 'Richard Bachman'"** ["King as Richard Bachman"], by Hans Joachim Alpers, in *Das Stephen King Buch*, edited by Joachim Körber. München, West Germany: Wilhelm Heyne Verlag, 1989, paper, p. .

N216. **"Notizen aus der Toten Zone: Die Romane von Stephen King"** ["Notes from the Dead Zone: The Novels of Stephen King"], by Joachim Körber, in *Das Stephen King Buch*, edited by Joachim Körber. München, West Germany: Wilhelm Heyne Verlag, 1989, paper, p. .

N217. **"Language, Modes of Seeing, and Magic—The Covenant of Stephen King,"** by Joseph Grixti, in *Terrors of Uncertainty*. London: Routledge, 1989, cloth, p. 45-74.

N218. **"Terror Writing by the Formerly Terrified: A Look at Stephen King,"** by L. C. Tree, in *Psychoanalytic Study of the Child* 44 (1989): 369-390.

N219. **"Sacral Parodies in the Fiction of Stephen King,"** by James Egan, in *Journal of Popular Culture* 23:3 (Winter 1990): 125-141.

N220. **"The Year in Horror, 1988,"** by Stefan Dziemianowicz, with Michael A. Morrison, in *Science Fiction & Fantasy Book Review Annual, 1989,* edited by Robert A. Collins and Robert Latham. Westport, CT: Meckler, 1990, cloth, p. 69-92.

N221. **"Stephen King,"** by Algis Budrys, in *The Magazine of Fantasy & Science Fiction* 79:6 (December, 1990): 44-55. Trade edition. A special Stephen King issue.

ab. *The Magazine of Fantasy & Science Fiction* 79:6 (December, 1990): 44-56. Limited edition, signed on back cover by King.

N222. **"Pet Sematary,"** by James M. Welsh, in *Magill's Cinema Annual, 1990: A Survey of the Films of 1989,* edited by Frank N. Magill. Englewood Cliffs, NJ: Salem Press, 1990, cloth, p. 271-274.

N223. **"Pet Sematary,"** by James Mulay, in *The Motion Picture Guide, 1990 Annual.* Evanston, IL: Cinebooks, 1990, cloth, p. 175-176.

N224. **"Stephen King: Powers of Horror,"** by Clare Hanson, in *American Horror Fiction: From Brockden Brown to Stephen King*, edited by Brian Docherty. New York: St. Martin's Press, 1990, cloth, p. 135-154.

N225. **"Bringing the Holocaust Home: The Freudian Dynamics of Kubrick's *The Shining*,"** by Geoffrey Cocks, in *Psychoanalytic Review* 78:1 (Spring, 1991): 103-125.

N226. **"Canaries in a Gilded Cage: Mental and Marital Decline in *McTeague* and *The Shining*,"** by Brian Kent, in *The Shining Reader,* edited by Anthony Magistrale. Mercer Island, WA: Starmont House, 1991, cloth, p. 139-154. [See **I32**].

N227. **"The Collapse of Family and Language in Stephen King's *The Shining*,"** by Alan Cohen, in *The Shining Reader,* edited by Anthony Magistrale. Mercer Island, WA: Starmont House, 1991, cloth, p. 47-60. [See **I32**].

N228. **"The Dark Side of Childhood: *The 500 Hats of Bartholomew Cubbins* and *The Shining*,"** by Vernon Hyles, in *The Shining Reader,* edited by Anthony Magistrale. Mercer Island, WA: Starmont House, 1991, cloth, p. 169-178. [See **I32**].

N229. **"Good and Evil in Stephen King's *The Shining*,"** by Burton Hatlen, in *The Shining Reader,* edited by Anthony Magistrale. Mercer Island, WA: Starmont House, 1991, cloth, p. 81-104. [See **I32**].

N230. **"Jack's Nightmare at the Overlook: The American Dream Inverted,"** by Patricia Ferreira, in *The Shining Reader,* edited by Anthony Magistrale. Mercer Island, WA: Starmont House, 1991, cloth, p. 23-32. [See **I32**].

N231. **"Kubrick's or King's—Whose *Shining* Is It?"** by James Smith, in *The Shining Reader,* edited by Anthony Magistrale. Mercer Island, WA: Starmont House, 1991, cloth, p. 181-192. [See **I32**].

N232. **"Kubrick's *The Shining:* The Specters and the Critics,"** by James Hala, in *The Shining Reader*, edited by Anthony Magistrale. Mercer Island, WA: Starmont House, 1991, cloth, p. 203-216. [See **I32**].

N233. **"The 'Masked Author Strikes Again': Writing and Dying in Stephen King's *The Shining*,"** by Mary Jane Dickerson, in *The Shining Reader*, edited by Anthony Magistrale. Mercer Island, WA: Starmont House, 1991, cloth, p. 33-46. [See **I32**].

N234. **"Once, Out of Nature: The Topiary,"** by Michael N. Stanton, in *The Shining Reader*, edited by Anthony Magistrale. Mercer Island, WA: Starmont House, 1991, cloth, p. 3-10. [See **I32**].

N235. **"'Orders from the House': Kubrick's *The Shining* and Kafka's 'The Metamorphosis,'"** by Mark Madigan, in *The Shining Reader*, edited by Anthony Magistrale. Mercer Island, WA: Starmont House, 1991, cloth, p. 193-202. [See **I32**].

N236. **"The Red Death's Sway: Setting and Character in Poe's 'The Masque of the Red Death' and King's *The Shining*,"** by Leonard Mustazza, in *The Shining Reader*, edited by Anthony Magistrale. Mercer Island, WA: Starmont House, 1991, cloth, p. 105-120. [See **I32**].

N237. **"The Redrum of Time: A Meditation on Francisco Goya's 'Saturn Devouring His Children' and Stephen King's *The Shining*,"** by Greg Weller, in *The Shining Reader*, edited by Anthony Magistrale. Mercer Island, WA: Starmont House, 1991, cloth, p. 61-78. [See **I32**].

N238. **"Shakespeare in 58 Chapters: *The Shining* as Classical Tragedy,"** by Tony Magistrale, in *The Shining Reader*, edited by Anthony Magistrale. Mercer Island, WA: Starmont House, 1991, cloth, p. 155-168. [See **I32**].

N239. **"Stephen King and the Tradition of American Naturalism in *The Shining*,"** by Jeanne Campbell Reesman, in *The Shining Reader*, edited by Anthony Magistrale. Mercer Island, WA: Starmont House, 1991, cloth, p. 121-138. [See **I32**].

N240. **"Wendy Torrance, One of King's Women: A Typology of King's Female Characters,"** by Jackie Eller, in *The Shining Reader*, edited by Anthony Magistrale. Mercer Island, WA: Starmont House, 1991, cloth, p. 11-22. [See **I32**].

N241. **"Considering *The Stands*,"** by Michael R. Collings, in *Gauntlet* No. 2 (April 1991): 179-188.

Argues from internal evidence that there may have been more overt censorship in excision made to the original version of *The Stand* than King admits to in his introduction to the 1990 Doubleday unexpurgated version.

b. *Gauntlet 2*, edited by Barry Hoffman. Baltimore: Borderlands Press, May 1991, cloth, 129-134.

N242. **"The Radiating Pencils of His Bones: The Poetry of Stephen King,"** by Michael R. Collings, in *The Shape Under the Sheet: The Complete Stephen King Encyclopedia,* by Stephen J. Spignesi. Ann Arbor, MI: Popular Culture, Ink., May 1991, cloth, p. 627-632.

N243. **"How the Real Returns and Answers: Beyond Pet Sematary,"** by Slavoj Zizek, in *Looking Awry: An Introduction to Jacques Lacan Through Popular Culture.* Cambridge, Massachusetts: The MIT Press, 1991, cloth, p. 23-26.

Discussion of *Pet Sematary* as a "kind of perverted *Antigone*...."

N244. **"Digging Up Stories with Stephen King,"** by W. C. Stroby, in *Writer's Digest* 72:3 (March, 1992): 22-27.

N245. **"Born of *Misery*: Stephen King's (En)gendered Text,"** by Sharon Delmendo, in *Styles of Creation: Aesthetic Technique and the Creation of Fictional Worlds*, edited by George E. Slusser and Eric S. Rabkin. Athens, GA: University of Georgia Press, 1992, cloth, p. 172-180.

N246. **"Foreword: The King and I,"** by Joseph A. Citro, in *The Dark Descent: Essays Defining Stephen King's Horrorscape,* edited by Tony Magistrale. CONTRIBUTIONS TO THE STUDY OF SCIENCE FICTION AND FANTASY, No. 48. New York: Greenwood Press, 1992, cloth, p. xi-xiv. [See **I36**].

N247. **"Defining Stephen King's Horrorscope: An Introduction,"** by Tony Magistrale, in *The Dark Descent: Essays Defining Stephen King's Horrorscape,* edited by Tony Magistrale. CONTRIBUTIONS TO THE STUDY OF SCIENCE FICTION AND FANTASY, No. 48. New York: Greenwood Press, 1992, cloth, p. 1-4. [See **I36**].

N248. **"The Masks of the Goddess: The Unfolding of the Female Archetype in Stephen King's *Carrie*,"** by Greg Weller, in *The Dark Descent: Essays Defining Stephen King's Horrorscape,* edited by Tony Magistrale. CONTRIBUTIONS TO THE STUDY OF SCIENCE FICTION AND FANTASY, No. 48. New York: Greenwood Press, 1992, cloth, p. 5-17. [See **I36**].

N249. **"Partners in the *Danse*: Women in Stephen King's Fiction,"** by Mary Pharr, in *The Dark Descent: Essays Defining Stephen King's Horrorscape,* edited by Tony Magistrale. CONTRIBUTIONS TO THE STUDY OF SCIENCE FICTION AND FANTASY, No. 48. New York: Greenwood Press, 1992, cloth, p. 19-32. [See **I36**].

N250. **"Complex, Archetype, and Primal Fear: King's Use of Fairy Tales in *The Shining*,"** by Ronald T. Curran, in *The Dark Descent: Essays Defining Stephen King's Horrorscape,* edited by Tony Magistrale. CONTRIBUTIONS TO THE STUDY OF SCIENCE FICTION AND FANTASY, No. 48. New York: Greenwood Press, 1992, cloth, p. 33-46. [See **I36**].

N251. **"The Three Genres of *The Stand*,"** by Edwin F. Casebeer, in *The Dark Descent: Essays Defining Stephen King's Horrorscape,* edited by Tony Magistrale. CONTRIBUTIONS TO THE STUDY OF SCIENCE FICTION AND

FANTASY, No. 48. New York: Greenwood Press, 1992, cloth, p. 47-59. [See **I36**].

N252. **"Some Ways of Reading *The Dead Zone*,"** by Michael N. Stanton, in *The Dark Descent: Essays Defining Stephen King's Horrorscape,* edited by Tony Magistrale. CONTRIBUTIONS TO THE STUDY OF SCIENCE FICTION AND FANTASY, No. 48. New York: Greenwood Press, 1992, cloth, p. 61-72. [See **I36**].

N253. **"Fear and Pity: Tragic Horror in King's *Pet Sematary*,"** by Leonard Mustazza, in *The Dark Descent: Essays Defining Stephen King's Horrorscape,* edited by Tony Magistrale. CONTRIBUTIONS TO THE STUDY OF SCIENCE FICTION AND FANTASY, No. 48. New York: Greenwood Press, 1992, cloth, p. 73-82. [See **I36**].

N254. **"The Mythic Journey in 'The Body',"** by Arthur W. Biddle, in *The Dark Descent: Essays Defining Stephen King's Horrorscape,* edited by Tony Magistrale. CONTRIBUTIONS TO THE STUDY OF SCIENCE FICTION AND FANTASY, No. 48. New York: Greenwood Press, 1992, cloth, p. 83-97. [See **I36**].

N255. **"'Everybody Pays...Even for Things They Didn't Do': Stephen King's Pay-out in the Bachman Novels,"** by James F. Smith, in *The Dark Descent: Essays Defining Stephen King's Horrorscape,* edited by Tony Magistrale. CONTRIBUTIONS TO THE STUDY OF SCIENCE FICTION AND FANTASY, No. 48. New York: Greenwood Press, 1992, cloth, p. 99-112. [See **I36**].

N256. **"Science, Politics, and the Epic Imagination: *The Talisman*,"** by Tony Magistrale, in *The Dark Descent: Essays Defining Stephen King's Horrorscape,* edited by Tony Magistrale. CONTRIBUTIONS TO THE STUDY OF SCIENCE FICTION AND FANTASY, No. 48. New York: Greenwood Press, 1992, cloth, p. 113-127. [See **I36**].

N257. **"A Clockwork Evil: Guilt and Coincidence in 'The Monkey',"** by Gene Doty, in *The Dark Descent: Essays Defining Stephen King's Horrorscape,* edited by Tony Magistrale. CONTRIBUTIONS TO THE STUDY OF SCIENCE FICTION AND FANTASY, No. 48. New York: Greenwood Press, 1992, cloth, p. 129-136. [See **I36**].

N258. **"Playing the Heavy: Weight, Appetite, and Embodiment in Three Novels by Stephen King,"** by Bernadette Lynn Bosky, in *The Dark Descent: Essays Defining Stephen King's Horrorscape,* edited by Tony Magistrale. CONTRIBUTIONS TO THE STUDY OF SCIENCE FICTION AND FANTASY, No. 48. New York: Greenwood Press, 1992, cloth, p. 137-156. [See **I36**].

N259. **"Riddle Game: Stephen King's Metafictive Dialogue,"** by Jeanne Campbell Reesman, in *The Dark Descent: Essays Defining Stephen King's Horrorscape,* edited by Tony Magistrale. CONTRIBUTIONS TO THE STUDY OF SCIENCE FICTION AND FANTASY, No. 48. New York: Greenwood Press, 1992, cloth, p. 157-170. [See **I36**].

N260. **"Stephen King Reading William Faulkner: Memory, Desire, and Time in the Making of *IT*,"** by Mary Jane Dickerson, in *The Dark Descent: Essays Defining Stephen King's Horrorscape,* edited by Tony Magistrale. CONTRIBUTIONS TO THE STUDY OF SCIENCE FICTION AND FANTASY, No. 48. New York: Greenwood Press, 1992, cloth, p. 171-186. [See **I36**].

N261. **"'The Face of Mr. Flip': Homophobia in the Horror of Stephen King,"** by Douglas Keesey, in *The Dark Descent: Essays Defining Stephen King's Horrorscape,* edited by Tony Magistrale. CONTRIBUTIONS TO THE STUDY OF SCIENCE FICTION AND FANTASY, No. 48. New York: Greenwood Press, 1992, cloth, p. 187-201. [See **I36**].

N262. **"Reading, Writing, and Interpreting: Stephen King's *Misery*,"** by Lauri Berkenkamp, in *The Dark Descent: Essays Defining Stephen King's Horrorscape,* edited by Tony Magistrale. CONTRIBUTIONS TO THE STUDY OF SCIENCE FICTION AND FANTASY, No. 48. New York: Greenwood Press, 1992, cloth, p. 203-211. [See **I36**].

N263. **"'Almost Better': Surviving the Plague in Stephen King's *The Stand*,"** by Mary Pharr, in *A Casebook on The Stand*, edited by Tony Magistrale. STARMONT STUDIES IN LITERARY CRITICISM, No. 38. Mercer Island, WA: Starmont House, 1992, cloth, p. 1-19. [See **I40**].

N264. **"'I Think the Government Stinks!': Stephen King's *Stand* on Politics,"** by Douglas Keesey, in *A Casebook on The Stand*, edited by Tony Magistrale. STARMONT STUDIES IN LITERARY CRITICISM, No. 38. Mercer Island, WA: Starmont House, 1992, cloth, p. 21-36. [See **I40**].

N265. **"Stephen King and His Readers: A Dirty, Compelling Romance,"** by Brian Kent, in *A Casebook on The Stand*, edited by Tony Magistrale. STARMONT STUDIES IN LITERARY CRITICISM, No. 38. Mercer Island, WA: Starmont House, 1992, cloth, p. 37-67. [See **I40**].

N266. **"The 'Power of Blackness' in *The Stand*,"** by Leonard Cassuto, in *A Casebook on The Stand*, edited by Tony Magistrale. STARMONT STUDIES IN LITERARY CRITICISM, No. 38. Mercer Island, WA: Starmont House, 1992, cloth, p. 69-88. [See **I40**].

N267. **"Repaying Service with Pain: The Role of God in *The Stand*,"** by Leonard Mustazza, in *A Casebook on The Stand*, edited by Tony Magistrale. STARMONT STUDIES IN LITERARY CRITICISM, No. 38. Mercer Island, WA: Starmont House, 1992, cloth, p. 89-108. [See **I40**].

N268. **"Free Will and Sexual Choice in *The Stand*,"** by Tony Magistrale, in *A Casebook on The Stand*, edited by Tony Magistrale. STARMONT STUDIES IN LITERARY CRITICISM, No. 38. Mercer Island, WA: Starmont House, 1992, cloth, p. 109-122. [See **I40**].

N269. **"Choice, Sacrifice, Destiny, and Nature in *The Stand*,"** by Bernadette Lynn Bosky, in *A Casebook on The Stand*, edited by Tony Magistrale. STARMONT STUDIES IN LITERARY CRITICISM, No. 38. Mercer Island, WA: Starmont House, 1992, cloth, p. 123-142. [See **I40**].

N270. **"Dark Streets and Bright Dreams: Rationalism, Technology, and 'Impossible Knowledge' in Stephen King's *The Stand*,"** by Michael A. Morrison, in *A Casebook on The Stand*, edited by Tony Magistrale. STARMONT STUDIES IN LITERARY CRITICISM, No. 38. Mercer Island, WA: Starmont House, 1992, cloth, p. 143-171. [See **I40**].

N271. **"Dialogue Within the Archetypal Community of *The Stand*,"** by Ed Casebeer, in *A Casebook on The Stand*, edited by Tony Magistrale. STARMONT STUDIES IN LITERARY CRITICISM, No. 38. Mercer Island, WA: Starmont House, 1992, cloth, p. 173-187. [See **I40**].

N272. **"Beyond Armageddon: Stephen King's *The Stand* and the Post Catastrophic World in Speculative Fiction,"** by Steven Kagle, in *A Casebook on The Stand*, edited by Tony Magistrale. STARMONT STUDIES IN LITERARY CRITICISM, No. 38. Mercer Island, WA: Starmont House, 1992, cloth, p. 189-202. [See **I40**].

N273. **"Art Versus Madness in Stephen King's *Misery*,"** by Tony Magistrale, in *The Celebration of the Fantastic: Selected Papers from the Tenth Anniversary Conference on the Fantastic in the Arts*, edited by Donald E. Morse, Marshall B. Tymn, and Csilla Bertha. CONTRIBUTIONS TO THE STUDY OF SCIENCE FICTION AND FANTASY, No. 49. Westport, CT: Greenwood Press, 1992, cloth, p. 271-278.

O.

SECONDARY SOURCES

POPULAR AND NEWS MAGAZINES

O1. **"Carrie's Mom and Danny's Dad,"** by Monty Clinch, in *Ms. London* [England] (April 9, 1979): 10. Bio-critical article appearing just after the British publication of *The Stand*.

O2. **"The Scare Movies,"** by James Horwitz, in *Cosmopolitan* (September, 1979): .

O3. **"Stephen King: Taking You Blindfolded to the Cliff Edge,"** by Alexander Stuart, in *19* [England] (March, 1980): 66-67. Introductory photo-illustrated article following the publication of *The Stand* in England.

O4. **"Devolution,"** by Pauline Kael, *The New Yorker* (June 8, 1980): 130-147.

O5. **"Checking In: Stephen King,"** in *Boston Magazine* (October, 1980): .

O6. **"Stephen King's Appeal to Youth,"** by Sanford Phippen, in *Maine Life* (December, 1980): .

O7. **"When Is Television Too Scary for Children,"** by Katie Leishman, in *TV Guide* (January 10, 1981): 5-8. Uses the film version of *'Salem's Lot* as an opening for discussing children's fears and television.

O8. **"A Master of the Macabre,"** by Michelle Slung, in *The New Republic* 184:8 (February 21, 1981): 38-39.

b. expanded as: "In the Matter of Stephen King," in *Armchair Detective* (Spring, 1981): 147-149.
c. excerpted in: *Contemporary Literary Criticism, Volume 26,* edited by Jean C. Stine. Detroit, MI: Gale Research Co., 1983, cloth, p. 237-238.
d. *Castle Rock: The Stephen King Newsletter* 1:9 (September, 1985): 5, 7.

O9. **"*Creepshow*: The Dawn of a Living Horror Comedy,"** by Ron Hansen, in *Esquire* (January, 1982): 72-73, 76. Concentrates on the comic-book antecedents of the film as it exhibits the sense of absolute good and evil one perceives as a child.

b. excerpted in: *Contemporary Literary Criticism, Volume 26,* edited by Jean C. Stine. Detroit, MI: Gale Research Co., 1983, cloth, p,. 239-240.

O10. **"Stephen King: A Change of Season,"** by Ethrane Wimbey, in *Maine's Regional Writers*. Newport News, VA: GB Publishing, 1982, paper?, p. 65.

O11. **"The Thrills, Chills and Skills of Stephen King: Yikes!,"** by Andrea Thompson, in *McCall's* (February, 1873): 74-75.

O12. **"American Gothic,"** by Richard Raynor, in *Time Out* [England] (May 27-June 2, 1983): 16-17. Discussion of King a cultural indicator.

O13. **"Inside Moves,"** in *Esquire* (August, 1983): . King's move from Doubleday to Viking, with photographs.

O14. **"Wrought Iron,"** by Terry Steel, in *Fine Homebuilding* (October/November, 1983): .

b. *The Stephen King Companion,* ed. by George Beahm. Kansas City, MO: Andrews & McMeel, September 1989, cloth, p. 82-87.

O15. **"Giving Hollywood the Chills: Stephen King's Scary Bestsellers Become Hot Film Properties,"** by Richard Zoglin, in *Time* (January 9, 1984): 56. On forthcoming film properties.

O16. **"*Firestarter*'s Premier Was a Critical Fizzle,"** by Cable Neuhaus, in *People Weekly* (May 28, 1984): 64. Photo-essay; the film's premier in Bangor, ME.

O17. **"Iza Azbranjenih Vrata,"** by Aleksandar Zicik, in *Intervju* (September 28, 1984): 32-34. [Serbo-Croatian]

O18. **[Title unknown],** in *Money* (September, 1984): . With photographs: King and Straub and their use of computers in writing.

O19. **"Picks & Pans,"** in *People Weekly* (December 24-31, 1984): 18. Note on *The Talisman*: "In horror fiction, two heads are better than one only if they're on the same body."

O20. **"An Unstoppable Thriller King,"** by Penelope Wang and Kim Foltz, in *Newsweek* 105 (June 10, 1985): 62-63.

O21. **"Stephen King's Torrent of Horror,"** in *USA Today* (July 11, 1985): 2D.

O22. **"Eyeglasses of the Rich and Famous,"** in *PM Magazine* (July 30, 1985):

O23. **[Title unknown],** in *USA Today* (August 25, 1985): . King's scariest movies.

O24. **"Prince of Darkness: In His Reign of Best-Selling Terror, Author Stephen King Remains Absolute Master of the Scary Story,"** by Constance Adler, in *Philadelphia Magazine* 76 (August, 1985): 85+ [3 pages]. Criticism and interpretation of *Skeleton Crew*, *The Talisman*, and *Thinner*.

O25. **"Fraidy-Cat?"** in *TV Guide* (September 7-September 13, 1985): . Note about Barrett Oliver's role in *Gramma*.

O26. **"Newsmakers,"** in *Time* (September 9, 1985): .

O27. **"People,"** by Guy D. Garcia, in *Time* 126 (September 9, 1985): 63. References to King and *Maximum Overdrive*.

O28. **"Porn Ban Fails in Maine,"** in *Newsweek* (June 23, 1986): 33. King's involvement in defeating an anti-pornography measure in 1986.

O29. **"One Picture Is Worth a Million Words,"** by Susin Shapiro, in *Daily News Magazine* [New York] (July 13, 1986): 8-13. Overview of King and his works.

b. as microfiche: *NewsBank: Film and Television* 13 (August, 1986): Fiche 14, D10-D12.

O30. **"Stephen King: Horror Iperrealista,"** by Roberto Duiz, in *Lui* (July-August, 1986): 108-109. Discussion of films from *Carrie* through *Dead Zone*. [Italian]

O31. **"King Comments on How Bobby Ewing Will Return,"** in *TV Guide* (August 30, 1986): .

O32. **"King of Horror,"** by Robert Hunt, in *St. Louis Magazine* (August, 1986): 40-41. Overview to King's films and non-fiction.

O33. **"The Child of Flower Children, Actor River Phoenix Rises from a Strange Past to Bloom in *Stand By Me*,"** by Susan Reed and James Grant, in *People Weekly* 26:13 (September 26, 1986): 73-74.

O34. **"King of Horror: The Master of Pop Dread Writes on—and on—and on—,"** by Stefan Kanfer, in *Time* 128:14 (October 6, 1986): 74-78.

b. *Tribune Review* [Greensburg, PA] (November 2, 1986): .
c. as microfiche: *NewsBank Names in the News* 9 (December, 1986): Fiche 83, F5-F9.
d. *The Shape Under the Sheet: The Complete Stephen King Encyclopedia*, by Stephen J. Spignesi. Ann Arbor, MI: Popular Culture, Ink., May 1991, cloth, p. 17-23.

O35. **"The October Selection: *IT*,"** by Gloria Norris, in *Book-of-the-Month Club News* (October, 1986): 2, 4.

O36. **"The Pleasure of the Subtext: Stephen King's Id-Life Crisis,"** by Andrew Klavan, in *Village Voice* (March 3, 1987): 46.

O37. **"Meet the New (Stephen) King of Horror, Briton Clive Barker,"** by Andrea Chambers, in *People Weekly* 27 (June 15, 1987): 87-88.

O38. **[Title unknown],** in *People Weekly* (September 24, 1987): . On celebrity doodles, including one by King.

O39. **[Title unknown],** by C. McGuigan and J. Huck, in *Newsweek* 110:23 (December 7, 1987): 84. Discussion of *The Running Man* film.

O40. **Editor's Column,** in *Archaeology* (March/April, 1988): . Discussion of "powers of supernatural vision" in *The Dead Zone*.

O41. **[Title unknown],** by Stefano Massaron, in *Febbre Gialla* (May, 1988): . [Italian]

O42. **"The Voices of Maine,"** in *Down East Magazine* (January, 1989): .

O43. **"Mr. King Meets the Comics,"** by Gary D. Robinson, in *Amazing Heroes* No. 151 (1989?): .

b. *Castle Rock: The Stephen King Newsletter* 5:5 (May, 1989): 3, 8.

O44. **"Stephen King,"** by Andrew Davidson, in *Marketing* (March 16, 1989): 30+ [2 pages].

O45. **"Author as Star,"** in *The Economist* 310:7594 (March 18, 1989): 97. King's financial state.

O46. **"Counting Pretty Ponies: Barbara Kruger and Stephen King Make Book,"** by Susan Tallman, in *Arts Magazine* 63 (March, 1989): 19-20.

O47. **"Specials,"** in *T.V. Guide* (September 9, 1989): 6. Brief announcement of plans for an ABC six-hour mini-series based on *IT*.

O48. **"SK Brings Hollywood to Maine,"** in *Maine Magazine* (September/October, 1989): . Includes cover photo.

O49. **"The Student King,"** in *Maine* [University of Maine Alumnus Magazine] (Fall, 1989): .

O50. **"Dismember Mama: The Mass Media is Turning us into a Nation of Ghouls,"** by Hal Crowther, in *Port Folio Magazine* [Virginia] (November 27, 1990): 5-6.

O51. **"Master of Horror and Money,"** by John W. Porter, in *Maine Sunday Telegram* [Portland, ME] (December 23, 1990): [2 pages].

b. *Newsbank Literature Index* (January 1991): Fiche 4, C12-13.

P.

SECONDARY SOURCES

MEDIA MAGAZINES, SPECIALTY MAGAZINES, FAN PUBLICATIONS

P1. **"De Palma Has the Power,"** by Mike Childs and Alan Jones, in *Cinefantastique* (Summer, 1977): .

P2. **"The Shining,"** by Jim Alberton and Peter S. Perakos, in *Cinefantastique* 7:3/4 (1978): .

P3. **"*'Salem's Lot*: Filming Horror for Television,"** by Bill Kelley, in *Cinefantastique* 9:2 (Winter, 1979): .

P4. **"Kubrick's Shining,"** by Richard T. Jameson, in *Film Comment* 16:4 (July/August, 1980): 28-32.

P5. **"A New Definition for Ultimate Horror: *The Shining*,"** by Jim Wynorski, in *Fangoria* (August, 1980): .

P6. **"Photographing Stanley Kubrick's *The Shining:* An Interview with John Alcott,"** by Herb Lightman, in *American Cinematographer* (August, 1980): 760.

P7. **"The Steadicam and *The Shining*,"** by Garrett Brown, in *American Cinematographer* (August, 1980): 786. Technology in Kubrick's film.

P8. **"Horror Hits a High,"** by Fritz Leiber, in *Locus* (1980): .

b. *Fantasy Newsletter* (1980): .
c. *Fear Itself: The Horror Fiction of Stephen King,* edited by Tim Underwood and Chuck Miller. San Francisco, CA: Underwood-Miller, 1982, cloth, p. 85-103. See **I2.**

P9. **"On the Set of *'Salem's Lot*,"** by Susan Casey, in *Fangoria* No. 4 (1980): 38-41, 45. Preview of the television mini-series, based on comments by cast members, producer, director, set designer, and others. Includes stills from the film.

P10. **"The Shining,"** by Phil Edwards, in *Starburst* [England] (1980): 24-27.

P11. **"The Overlook Hotel,"** by Paul Mayersberg, in *Sight and Sound* (Winter, 1980/1981): 54-57.

P12. **"The 'Film Script as Novel' Scam,"** by Michael Goodwin, in *Boulevards* (January, 1981): .

P13. **"King of the Macabre,"** by R. G. Pushkar, in *American Way* (February, 1981): .

P14. **"Kubrick and *The Shining*,"** by P. L. Titterington, in *Sight and Sound* [England] 50:2 (Spring, 1981): 117-121. The film as an allegorical interpretation of American culture and communication.

P15. **"Stephen King: The King of the Beasties,"** in *Chiller* (November, 1981):

P16. **"Frank Belknap Long on Literature, Lovecraft, and the Golden Age of 'Weird Tales,'"** by Tom Collins, in *Twilight Zone Magazine* (January, 1982): 13-19. References to King as modern writer contributing much to the genre.

P17. **[Title Unknown],** by Paul R. Gagne, in *Cinefantastique* 12:1 (February, 1982): 6. Pre-release overview of *Creepshow*.

P18. **"*Creepshow*: Five Jolting Tales of Horror! from Stephen King and George Romero,"** by Paul Gagne, in *Cinefantastique* 12:2/3 (April, 1982): 16+. Discussion of story outlines.

P19. **"*Creepshow*: The First Look Inside George Romero's New Bestiary,"** by David McDonnell and John Sayers, in *Mediascene Prevue* (May, 1982): 61-63.

P20. **"Fritz Weaver and *Creepshow*,"** by Ed Naha, in *Fangoria* (May, 1982): 43.

P21. **"Front Row Seats at the *Creepshow*,"** by Ed Naha, in *Twilight Zone Magazine* (May, 1982): 46-50.

P22. **[Title unknown],** in *American Fantasy* 1:2 (May, 1982): . On the release of *the Dark Tower*.

P23. **[Title unknown],** by D. Chute, in *Film Comment* 18:5 (September/ October, 1982): 13+. *Creepshow* and E.C. horror comics.

P24. **"Are These the Scariest Men in America?"** in *Cinefantastique* 13:1 (September/October, 1982): .

P25. **"*Creepshow*: It's an $8 Million Comic Book, from George Romero and Friends,"** by Paul Gagne, in *Cinefantastique* 13:1 (September/October, 1982): 17-35.

P26. **"A Casual Chat with Mr. George A. Romero,"** by Robert H. [Bob] Martin, in *Fangoria* (October, 1982): . On *Creepshow*, with stills from the film.

P27. **"Stephen King's Scary Monsters Live Right Next Door,"** by Toby Goldstein, in *Creem* (October, 1982): [1 page]. With photos.

P28. **[Title Unknown],** by Paul R. Gagne, in *Cinefantastique* 13:2/3 (November/December, 1982): 10+. Backgrounds to production of *Creepshow*.

P29. **"*Dead Zone*: David Cronenberg to Direct Stephen King's Chilling ESP Saga for Dino DeLaurentiis,"** by Tim Lucas, in *Cinefantastique* 13:3/4 (November/December, 1982): .

P30. **"Of Roaches and Snakes,"** by David Everitt, in *Fangoria* No. 20 (1982): 13-16.

P31. **"On (and Off) the Set of *Creepshow*: Tom Savini at Work; Stephen King at Home,"** by Robert H. [Bob] Martin, in *Fangoria* No. 20 (1982): 40-43. King's work with *Creepshow* and plans for other projects.

P32. **"Stephen King and George Romero: Collaboration in Terror,"** by Stanley Wiater, in *Bloody Best of Fangoria* (1982): 28-29. On *Creepshow* and *Children of the Corn*, with backgrounds for both films.

P33. **"Stephen King: Living in 'Constant Deadly Terror,'"** by Dan Christensen, in *Bloody Best of Fangoria* (1982): 30-33. King's reactions to Kubrick's filming of *The Shining*.

P34. **"King on ''Salem's Lot,'"** in *Bloody Best of Fangoria* (1982): 31. Sidebar to Christensen's "Stephen King: Living in 'Constant, Deadly Terror.'"

P35. **"King on 'The Dead Zone,'"** in *Bloody Best of Fangoria* (1982): 33. Sidebar to Christensen's "Stephen King: Living in 'Constant, Deadly Terror.'"

P36. **"Stephen King: The Shadow Exploded,"** by Pete Scott, in *Dark Horizons* No. 25 (1982): .

P37. **"I Want My Cake!: Thoughts on *Creepshow* and E.C. Comics,"** by Douglas E. Winter, in *Fantasy Newsletter* (February 1983).

b. *Shadowings*, edited by Douglas E. Winter. Mercer Island, WA: Starmont House, 1983, cloth/paper, p. 135-138. Revised.

P38. **"Romero, King Bring Back the Gory Glory Days of E.C. Comics,"** by David J. Hogan, in *Cinefantastique* 13:4 (April/May, 1983): .

P39. **"Would You Buy a Haunted Car from This Man,"** by Edwin Pouncey, in *Sounds* (May 21 1983): 22.

P40. **"From Niagara-on-the-Lake, Ontario,"** by Michael Tuchman, in *Film Comment* 19:3 (May-June, 1983): . Interview with Cronenberg on filming *Dead Zone*.

P41. **"*Dead Zone:* David Cronenberg Shuns the Auteur Route to Adapt Stephen King's ESP Novel to the Screen,"** by Tim Lucas, in *Cinefantastique* 13:5 (June/July, 1983): 17. Discussion with Cronenberg about adapting King's novel.

P42. **"Stephen King Signs Books in Britain,"** in *Locus* (August, 1983): .

P43. **"King Signs at London's 'Forbidden Planet,'"** in *Science Fiction Chronicle* (August, 1983): 3.

P44. **"John Carpenter's *Christine*: Bringing Stephen King's Best Seller to the Screen,"** by Bill Kelley, in *Cinefantastique* 13:6/14:1 (September, 1983): 8.

P45. **"On the Set of *Dead Zone*,"** by James Vernier, in *Twilight Zone Magazine* (December, 1983): 55. Comparison of King and Cronenberg in their approaches to horror.

P46. **"A Talk with David Cronenberg,"** by James Vernier, in *Twilight Zone Magazine* (December, 1983): 56-58.

P47. **"Zeroing in on the *Dead Zone*,"** by James Vernier, in *Twilight Zone Magazine* (December, 1983): 52-54.

P48. **"*Christine*: Stephen King and John Carpenter Take a Joy Ride into Terror,"** by Kim Johnson, in *Mediascene Prevue* (1983): 24-26.

P49. **"Keith Gordon and Christine,"** by Robert H. [Bob] Martin, in *Fangoria* No. 32 (1983): 19-22.

P50. **"Richard Kobritz and Christine,"** by Robert H. [Bob] Martin, in *Fangoria* No. 32 (1983): 14-17.

P51. **"David Cronenberg's *The Dead Zone*: Horror Film Auteur David Cronenberg Takes a Brief Hiatus in Stephen King Territory,"** by Tim Lucas, in *Cinefantastique* 14:2 (December, 1983/January, 1984): 24-31, 60-61.

P52. **"King and Cronenberg: The Best of Both Worlds,"** by David J. Hogan, in *Cinefantastique* 14:2 (December, 1983/January, 1984): 51+.

P53. **"Stephen King: With *Cujo*, *The Dead Zone*, and *Christine*, He Just Might Be the Most Bankable Name in Hollywood,"** by Paul R. Gagne, in *Cinefantastique* 14:2 (December, 1983-January, 1984): 4-5.

P54. **"*Christine*,"** by James Vernier, in *Twilight Zone Magazine* (February, 1984): 69-74.

P55. **"On the Set of *Firestarter*: Exclusive Scoop! It's Not a Horror Picture,"** by Robert H. [Bob] Martin, in *Fangoria* No. 35 (April, 1984): 56-59.

P56. **"Stephen King's Children of the Corn,"** by David Everitt, in *Fangoria* No. 35 (April, 1984): 42-45.

P57. **"Firestarter: E. T.'s Drew Barrymore Gets Scary as the Title Character in Stephen King's Best-seller,"** by David J. Hogan, in *Cinefantastique* 14:3 (May, 1984): 28-30.

P58. **"King of Rock & Roll,"** in *Locus* (May, 1984): 50.

P59. **"Reflection and Desire: *The Shining*,"** by Allen Brodsky, in *Cinemacabre* (Summer, 1984): [9 pages]. On Kubrick's *The Shining*.

P60. **"*Firestarter*,"** by David J. Hogan, in *Cinefantastique* 14:4/5 (September, 1984): 16-25.

P61. **"Gary Zeller,"** by Dan Scapperotti, in *Cinefantastique* 14:4/5 (September, 1984): 22. On special effects for *Firestarter*.

P62. **[Title unknown],** in *The Ecphorizer* [Sunnyvale, CA] (December, 1984): . Relationship of *Pet Sematary* to King's earlier works.

P63. **"Episode Guide: *Tales from the Darkside*,"** in *Starburst* 80 (1984): 19-22. References to "The Word Processor of the Gods," listing scriptwriter, director, and cast.

P64. **"Harlan Ellison's Watching—Part One: In Which We Shuffle Through the Embers,"** by Harlan Ellison, in *The Magazine of Fantasy & Science Fiction* (1984): .

b. *Castle Rock: The Stephen King Newsletter* 2:2 (February, 1986): 1, 7.
c. as: "Two Selections from Harlan Ellison's Watching," in *Kingdom of Fear: The World of Stephen King*, edited by Tim Underwood and Chuck Miller. Columbia, PA: Underwood-Miller, 1986, cloth, p. 67-80. See **I11**.
d. as: Why the Children Don't Look Like Their Parents," in *Stephen King at the Movies*, by Jessie Horsting. New York: Starlog/Signet, August 1986, paper, p. 96-101. See **I13**.
e. as: "Harlan Ellison's Watching," in *The Stephen King Companion*, edited by George Beahm. Kansas City, MO: Andrews and McMeel, September 1989, cloth, p. 225-234. See **I24**.

P65. **"Harlan Ellison's Watching—Part Two: In Which We Discover Why the Children Don't Look Like Their Parents,"** by Harlan Ellison, in *The Magazine of Fantasy & Science Fiction* (1984): .

b. *Castle Rock: The Stephen King Newsletter* 2:2 (February, 1986): 1, 4, 6.
c. as: "Two Selections from Harlan Ellison's Watching," in *Kingdom of Fear: The World of Stephen King*, edited by Tim Underwood and Chuck

Miller. Columbia, PA: Underwood-Miller, 1986, cloth, p. 67-80. See **I11**.

d. as: "Why the Children Don't Look Like Their Parents," in *Stephen King at the Movies*, by Jessie Horsting. New York: Starlog/Signet, August 1986, paper, p. 96-101. See **I13**.

e. as: "Harlan Ellison's Watching," in *The Stephen King Companion*, edited by George Beahm. Kansas City, MO: Andrews and McMeel, September 1989, cloth, p. 225-234. See **I24**.

P66. **"Mark Lester Directs *Firestarter*,"** by Robert H. [Bob] Martin, in *Fangoria* 36 (1984): 12-15.

P67. **[Title unknown]**, in *Cinefantastique* 15:1 (January, 1985): 18. On *Silver Bullet*.

P68. **"King Rejects Book Club Offer for *The Talisman*,"** in *Science Fiction Chronicle* 6:4 (January, 1985): 4.

P69. **"Tales from the Darkside,"** by Dan Scapperotti, in *Cinefantastique* (January, 1985): 15, 52. References to King's "The Word Processor of the Gods."

P70. **"Stephen King Admits Pseudonym,"** in *Locus* 18:3 (March, 1985): 5.

P71. **"Weinberg Gets Last Laugh,"** by Robert A. Collins, in *Fantasy Review* (March, 1985): 15. Notes listings by Weinberg and Currey of the Bachman books under King's name in 1984.

P72. **"An Interview with Douglas E. Winter,"** by Bill Munster, in *Footsteps V* (April, 1985): 66-75. On the writing of *Art of Darkness* and Winter's friendship with King.

P73. **"Strawberry Spring: Stephen King's Gothic Universe,"** by Mary Ferguson, in *Footsteps V* (April, 1985): 50-55.

P74. **"Barron Confesses,"** by Neil Barron, in *Fantasy Review* (May, 1985): 34. Acknowledgement that the "John Wilson" review was a hoax; Barron suggested the idea and Charles Platt wrote the "Helen Purcell" review.

P75. **"Mea Maxima Culpa,"** by Neil Barron. Mimeographed letter, May 21, 1985. Explanation of the "John Wilson" hoax: "Reviews of imaginary books have a long if not honorable tradition," including Lem's *A Perfect Vacuum*. As of May 21, Barron had received sixteen responses to the review of *Love Lessons*, attributed pseudonymously to King.

b. *Fantasy Review* (June, 1985): 44.

P76. **"Cat's Eye: Horror Master Stephen King Blends Stories from *Night Shift* with a Dash of Macabre Humor,"** by Tim Hewitt, in *Cinefantastique* 15:2 (May, 1985): 9-11.

P77. **"Lawyer Threatens"** [letter], by Arthur E. Greene, in *Fantasy Review* (May, 1985): 11, 34. A strongly worded response on King's part—through his lawyer—to the Wilson hoax-reviews.

P78. **"Silver Bullet,"** by Tim Hewitt, in *Cinfantastique* 15:2 (May, 1985): 12.

P79. **"Stephen King Admits Richard Bachman Alias,"** in *Science Fiction Chronicle* 6:7 (April, 1985): 5.

P80. **"The Night of the Horror King,"** by Ray Ellis and Katalin Ellis, in *Cinefantastique* 15:2 (May, 1985): 20. Discussion of King's participation in the Third Annual World Drive-in Movie Festival and Custom Car Rally in Dallas.

P81. **"We Are Hoaxed by Gabby Snatch,"** by Robert A. Collins, in *Fantasy Review* (May, 1985): 11. Identifies the "John Wilson" hoax and introduces letters from King and his attorney.

P82. **[Letter to Neil Barron],** by James Van Hise, June 1, 1985. Negative response to the hoax review in *Fantasy Review*, pointing to the longevity of such hoaxes.

b. *Fantasy Review* (June, 1985): 44.
c. *King's Crypt* (July, 1985): .

P83. **"A Director's Eye View of Stephen King's *Cat's Eye,"*** by Jessie Horsting, in *Fantastic Films* (June, 1985): 20-21, 42. Pre-release interview-article based on discussions with Lewis Teague, director of *Cat's Eye*.

P84. **"King as Bachman Update,"** in *Science Fiction Chronicle* 6:9 (June, 1985): 5.

P85. **"Stephen King's *Cat's Eye*,"** by Bob Strauss, in *Monsterland* (June, 1985): 55-57, 66. Interview-article with Candy Clark, Drew Barrymore's mother in "The General."

P86. **"Not King But Koontz,"** by Stephen Brown, in *Fantasy Review* 81 (July, 1985): 6. Identifies the author of *Invasion*, by "Aaron Wolfe."

P87. **"King/Bachman Again: Who Said What, When?"** by Robert Weinberg, in *Fantasy Review* (August, 1985): 4, 6. Reasserts Weinberg's claim to have documented King's "Bachman" pseudonym in 1984.

P88. **"Stephen King,"** in Science Fiction Book Club brochure (August 1985). Lists eleven books available through the SFBC, including *Creepshow*.

P89. **"Unauthorized Stephen King Videotapes Released,"** in *Science Fiction Chronicle* 6:11 (August, 1985): 4.

P90. **"Cat and Dog: Lewis Teague's Stephen King Novels,"** by Robin Wood, in *Action* 2 (Fall, 1985): 39-45.

P91. **"Introducing 'Richard Bachman,'"** by Pat Chase, in *Writers at Large* (1985?): .

b. *Castle Rock: The Stephen King Newsletter* 1:10 (October, 1985): 5, 8.

P92. **"An Artist's Profile: Stephen Gervais,"** by Roger Anker, in *Fantasy Review* 84 (October, 1985): 8-11. Includes photographs of Gervais's illustrations for the limited edition of *Christine*.

P93. **"Brown Versus Weinberg"** [letter], by Stephen Brown, in *Fantasy Review* 84 (October, 1985): . Discussion of who should receive credit for "discovering" Richard Bachman's true identity.

P94. **"John Coyne: A Profile,"** by Douglas E. Winter in *Fantasy Review* (October, 1985): 12-14, 33. King's increasing visibility as a personage might work to his disadvantage.

P95. **"Now Re-Entering 'The Twilight Zone,'"** by Lee Goldberg, in *Starlog* 99 (October, 1985): 38-40. References to King's stories being used as the bases for scripts on the television series, specifically "Gramma."

P96. **"Stephen King's *Cycle of the Werewolf* Becomes *Silver Bullet* for the Silver Screen,"** by Sharon Williams, in *Fantastic Films* (October, 1985): 20-22. Interview-article with Dan Attias, director of *Silver Bullet*.

P97. **"Stephen King's *Cat's Eye*,"** by Tim Hewitt, in *Cinefantastique* 15:4 (October, 1985): 34-39.

P98. **"Twilight Zone,"** by Max Rebeaux, in *Cinefantastique* 15:4 (October, 1985): 13, 53. References to the teleplay *Gramma*.

P99. **"100 Most Important People in Science Fiction/Fantasy,"** by Anthony Timpone, in *Starlog* No. 100 (November, 1985): 44.

P100. **"On Specialty Presses: The State of the Art,"** by Jack L. Chalker, in *Fantasy Review* 85 (November, 1985): 11-12, 40. Disparaging assessment of Philtrum press and the production of *The Eyes of the Dragon*.

P101. **[Title unknown],** in *Home Viewer* (December, 1985): . Overview of King stories available on videocassette.

P102. **"50% of the Cycle: Berni Wrightson,"** by Bill Munster, in *Footsteps VI* (December, 1985): 47-54.

P103. **"Real Tube Terror: The Secretaries Were Afraid to Type 'Gramma,'"** by Ben Herndon, in *Twilight Zone Magazine* (December, 1985): 10A-11A. Article based on Ellison's comments about writing the teleplay for "Gramma."

P104. **"TZ Terror,"** by F. Paul Wilson, in *Twilight Zone Magazine* (December, 1985): 112-113. Reference to King in article about New England as the seat of modern horror.

P105. **[Title unknown],** by Don Pettus, in *Fan Plus* 2:2 (1985): . Discussion of King.

P106. **"A Gift to Frighten: The Films of Stephen King,"** by Don Minifie, in *Films & Filming* No. 369 (1985): .

P107. **"Interview with a Werewolf,"** by Robert H. [Bob] Martin, in *Fangoria* No. 44 (1985): 41-44. Interview-article with Everett McGill, who played "Reverend Lowe" in *Silver Bullet*.

P108. **"George Romero on *Day of the Dead* and *Pet Sematary*,"** by Robert H. [Bob] Martin, in *Fangoria* No. 48 (1985): 43-47.

P109. **"Stephen King's *Silver Bullet*,"** by David Everitt, in *Fangoria* No. 48 (1985): 30-32. Interview-article based on discussions with director Daniel Attias.

P110. ***Your Movie Guide to Horror Video Tapes and Discs***, by Tim Lucas and the editors of *Video Times*. Publications International, 1985, paper. Multiple references to film adaptations of King's works.

P111. **Announcement of the Starmont Series,** by Eddy C. Bertin, in *SF Gid* [Belgium] (January, 1986): . [Dutch].

P112. **"Stephen King's *Carrie* Coming to Broadway,"** in *Science Fiction Chronicle* 7:4 (January, 1986): 6.

P113. **"Surviving the Ride,"** by Clive Barker, in *Fantasy Review* 87 (January, 1986): 6-8.

b. *Kingdom of Fear: The World of Stephen King*, edited by Tim Underwood and Chuck Miller. Columbia, PA: Underwood-Miller, 1986, cloth, p. 55-63. See **I13.**

c. *Clive Barker's Shadows in Eden*, by Clive Barker. Novato, CA, Lancaster, PA: Underwood-Miller, 1991, cloth, p. 69-76.

P114. **"And Now a Stephen King Newsletter—*Castle Rock*,"** by Adam Rogers, in *Twilight Zone Magazine* (February, 1986): 97.

P115. **"Collecting Stephen King: For Feverish Collectors—A Cautionary Tale,"** by Douglas E. Winter, in *Twilight Zone Magazine* (February, 1986): 32-33, 97.

P116. **"David and Goliath,"** by Tim Sullivan, in *Fantasy Review* 88 (February, 1986): 39-40. Defense of Chalker in the Chalker-King debate over specialty publishing.

P117. **"In the Twilight Zone: Unnatural Forces,"** by Michael Blaine, in *Twilight Zone Magazine* (February, 1986): 6-7. Comments on King, "Richard Bachman," and "John Swithen."

P118. **"King Goes into Overdrive,"** by Tyson Blue, in *Twilight Zone Magazine* (February, 1986): 30-31.

P119. **"On Specialty Presses: Criticism and Other Matters,"** by Jack L. Chalker, in *Fantasy Review* (March, 1986): 13-14. Response to King's criticism of Chalker's earlier article.

P120. **"Overdrive,"** by Tim Hewitt, in *Cinefantastique* 16:1 (March, 1986): 9. Discussion of King's directorial debut.

P121. **"The Twilight Zone,"** by Ben Herndon, in *Cinefantastique* (March, 1986): 22-23, 58-59. Discussion of Ellison's teleplay for "Gramma."

P122. **"*The Vivisector*: Scary Stuff,"** by Darrell Schweitzer, in *Science Fiction Review* (Spring, 1986): . Analysis of the shift in horror from short fiction to novel; *Skeleton Crew* is an exception.

b. *Castle Rock: The Stephen King Newsletter* 2:4 (April, 1986): 7.

P123. **"King Klips,"** by Stephanie Leonard, in *Castle Rock: The Stephen King Newsletter* 2:2 (February, 1986): 2. Update on recent publications by and about King.

P124. **"And Now, the Publisher's Apprentice,"** by Stephanie Leonard, in *Fantasy Review* 91 (May, 1986): 40. King's secretary's rejoinder to Jack Chalker's articles on King, Philtrum Press, and *The Eyes of the Dragon*.

P125. **"The Editor's Notebook: Read the Letters First, Friends,"** by Robert A. Collins, in *Fantasy Review* (May, 1986): 4. Collins's response to the King/Chalker controversy over *The Eyes of the Dragon*.

P126. **"The 'Eyes' Have It,"** by Walnum Clayton, in *Fantasy Review* (May, 1986): 40. Defense of King's position in the Chalker-King debate over specialty presses.

P127. **"The Director Is King,"** by Stephan Schaefer, in *Film Comment* 22 (May/June, 1986): 2.

P128. **"Stephen King Shifts into High Gear on the Highway to Hell-Driving Horror,"** by Stanley Wiater, in *Mediascene Prevue* (May/July, 1986): 52-55, 71. Overview of *Maximum Overdrive*.

P129. **[Title unknown],** in *Fangoria* (September, 1986): . Discussion of *Stand by Me*.

P130. **"The Funhouse of Fear,"** by Douglas E. Winter, in *Fantasy Review* No. 95 (October, 1986): 15-16. Critical discussion of the nature of horror, with frequent references to King's work.

P131. **"Scream Press *Skeleton Crew*,"** in *Locus* 19:10 (October, 1986): 4.

P132. **"Stand by Stephen King,"** by S. P. Somtow, in *Fantasy Review* No. 95 (October, 1986): 11, 16.

P133. **"King Versus Koontz: Style and *Invasion*,"** by Michael R. Collings, in *Footsteps VII* (November, 1986): 32-42, 45. Stylistic analysis of similarities between King's *The Shining* and Dean R. Koontz's pseudonymous *Invasion* (as "Aaron Wolfe"), in light of previous suggestions that King might have written the novel. Revision of "Speculations" chapter from *Stephen King as Richard Bachman*, empahasizing Koontz's authorship of *Invasion* by "Aaron Wolfe."

P134. **"Amy Irving's DePalma Days,"** by Anthony Timpone, in *Fangoria* 52 (1986): 46-47.

P135. **"Monster Invasion—Stephen King's 'Night Shift' Videos,"** by Anthony Timpone, in *Fangoria* 52 (1986): 12. On the Granite Entertainment Group release of *The Boogeyman* and *The Woman in the Room.*

P136. **"Horror in Print: Dennis Etchison,"** by Roger Anker, in *Fangoria* 52 (1986): 62-65. Discussion of the *Children of the Corn* and the radio and audiocassette versions of "The Mist."

P137. **"King on Directing *Maximum Overdrive* for Dino De Laurentiis,"** by Joseph Treadway, in *Cinefantastique* 17:2 (March, 1987): 49.

P138. **"The Fantasy Worlds of Stephen King,"** in *Gateways 5* [Canada] (August, 1987): . Compares King's fictional worlds and suggests appropriate game-playing for each.

P139. **[Title unknown],** by D. Scapperotti, in *Cinefantastique* 17:5 (September, 1987): 17. On *The Running Man* film.

P140. **[Title unknown],** by Tim Hewitt, in *Cinefantastique* 16:4/5 (October, 1987): 96. On *Maximum Overdrive.*

P141. **"The Subotsky-King Connection,"** by Alan Jones, in *Cinefantastique* 16:4/5 (October, 1987): 101. On *Maximum Overdrive.*

P142. **[Title unknown],** in *Fangoria* (December, 1987): . On *The Running Man.*

P143. **[Title unknown],** in *Starlog* (December, 1987): . On *The Running Man.*

P144. **"Stephen King: The Quantel Philosophy,"** by James Fadden, in *Back Stage* 29:20 (May, 13, 1988): 12B+ [3 pages].

P145. **"King's English,"** by Tyson Blue, in *Twilight Zone Magazine* (August, 1988): .

P146. **"Stephen King: The Dark Tower Mythology,"** by Paddy McKillop, in *Fear: Fantasy and Science Fiction* No. 2 (September, 1988): .

P147. **"Stephen King: 1989, the Year in Preview,"** by Tyson Blue, in *Midnight Graffiti* (Spring, 1989): .

P148. **"Mr. King Meets the Comics,"** by Gary D. Robinson, in *Amazing Heroes* No. 151 (1989): . Discussion of references to King in national comics.

b. *Castle Rock: The Stephen King Newsletter* 5:5 (May, 1989): 3, 8.

P149. **"An Interview with Richard Christian Matheson,"** by Clifford Brooks, in *The Scream Factory* 3 (Summer, 1989): 33-36 (esp. p. 34). Matheson comments on the excellences of King's style.

P150. **"The Maine Man,"** by Paddy McKillop, in *Fear: Fantasy and Science Fiction* No. 8 (August, 1989): 8-10. Pictorial essay on Bangor, ME locations important in King's fictions.

P151. **"Horror's Heaviest Hitter: Fifteen Titles on Tape Make Stephen King a One-Man Scarefest,"** by Frank Lovece, in *Video Magazine* 13:5 (August, 1989): 46+ [5 pages].

P152. **"Horror Video: September Is Horror Month,"** by Jim McCullaugh, in *Billboard Magazine* 101:38 (September 23, 1989): 54. On the videocassette of *Pet Sematary*.

P153. **"Twenty Who Defined the Decade,"** by Brad Darrach, in *People Weekly* 32 (Fall, 1989): 90.

P154. **"Resting in Pieces: *Pet Sematary* Offers Grounds for Intense Horror Scenes,"** by Michael R. Collings, in *The Blood Review: The Journal of Horror Criticism* 1:1 (October 1989): 46-49.

P155. **"Coming Soon to a Bookshelf Near You,"** in *The Blood Review: The Journal of Horror Criticism* 1:1 (October 1989): 4-9 (esp. 6-7). Overview of King's future publication projects.

P156. **"Hooked on Horror: Why Rational American Readers are Obsessed with Scaring Themselves Silly,"** by Marshall Blonsky, in *The Blood Review: The Journal of Horror Criticism* 1:1 (October 1989): 70-72.

P157. **"Stephen King on *Pet Sematary*,"** in *The Blood Review: The Journal of Horror Criticism* 1:1 (October 1989): 49. On the genesis of *Pet Sematary*, with excerpts from a King interview.

P158. **"Stephen King: At Home with Horror,"** by Jim McCullaugh, in *Music Plus Video Guide* 4:5 (October/November, 1989): 5. Overview of King's recent films.

P159. **"King's Tale of Mystery & Intrigue—And That's Just His Contract,"** by Charles Kipps, in *Variety* (1989?): .

b. *Mystery Scene* No. 24 (January, 1990): 81.

P160. "***Mystery Scene* Horror Bestseller List,**" in *Mystery Scene* No. 24 (January, 1990): 96. Includes *The Dark Half* and *My Pretty Pony*.

P161. "**1989: The Year in Horror,**" by David B. Silva, in *The Blood Review: Journal of Horror Criticism* 1:2 (January, 1990): 14-16. Reference to King and Koontz as having "transcended the genre."

P162. "**Needful Kings,**" by Tyson Blue, in *The Blood Review: Journal of Horror Criticism* 1:2 (January, 1990): 11.

P163. "**Stephen King Strikes Back!**" by Gary Wood, in *Cinefantastique* 20:3 (January, 1990): . On *Pet Sematary* film.

P164. "**Stephen King Sold to Las Vegas Resident for $46,**" by Tyson Blue, in *Horrorfest Press* No. 2 (Spring, 1990): 4, 17.

P165. "**German Horrors Made in U.S.,**" by Uwe Luserke and Carsten Kuhr, in *Mystery Scene* No. 26 (June, 1990): 76.

P166. "**An Interview About Stephen King with Stephen Spignesi,**" conducted by Barry Hoffman, in *Mystery Scene* No. 27 (October, 1990): 94-98.

P167. "**Stephen King,**" by Algis Budrys, in *The Magazine of Fantasy & Science Fiction* (Special Stephen King Issue) 79:6 (December, 1990): 44-55. Trade edition.

ab. *The Magazine of Fantasy & Science Fiction* (Special Stephen King Issue) 79:6 (December, 1990): 44-56. Limited edition, signed on back cover by King.

P168. "**Misery: To Splatter, or Not to Splatter, Rob Reiner Sounds as Tortured as Lady Macbeth,**" by Gary Wood, in *Cinefantastique* 21:4 (February, 1991): 16-22.

P169. "**Horror King, Stephen King,**" by Stephen Spignesi, in *Cinefantastique* 21:4 (February, 1991): 18-19, 61.

P170. "**Rob Reiner on Stephen King: Putting Horror in Its Place—,**" by Gary Wood, in *Cinefantastique* 21:4 (February, 1991): 21.

P171. "**Hard Hitting Makeup Effects,**" by Gary Wood, in *Cinefantastique* 21:4 (February, 1991): 23.

P172. "**King's Ransom: Other Writers Get Paid to Keep a Finger on the Pulse of America; Stephen King Gets Paid Millions to Rip Its Heart Out,**" by Richard Panek, in *Inc.* 8:5 (February, 1991): 29-31.

P173. "**Stephen King: On Movie Making with Dino DeLaurentiis,**" by Gary Wood, in *Cinefantastique* 21:4 (February, 1991): 40-41.

P174. **"Shooting It in Maine: Bangor's Own Best-Selling Author Has Been a Boon to the State's Filmmaking Economy,"** by Gary Wood, in *Cinefantastique* 21:4 (February, 1991): 45.

P175. **"Stephen King: Spawn of Satan,"** by Howard Wornom, in *Gauntlet* No. 2 (April, 1991): 173-178.

b. *Gauntlet 2*, edited by Barry Hoffman. Baltimore, MD: Borderlands Press, May 1991, cloth, p. 125-128.

P176. **"Considering *The Stands*,"** by Michael R. Collings, in *Gauntlet* No. 2 (April 1991): 179-188. Argues from internal evidence that there may have been more overt censorship of the original version of *The Stand* than King admits to in his introduction to the 1990 Doubleday unexpurgated version.

b. *Gauntlet 2*, edited by Barry Hoffman. Baltimore: Borderlands Press, May 1991, cloth, p. 129-134.

P177. **"News on King,"** by George Beahm, in *Gauntlet* No. 2 (April, 1991): 187-194.

b. as: "Stephen King News," in *Gauntlet 2*, edited by Barry Hoffman. Baltimore: Borderlands Press, May 1991, cloth, p. 135-142.

P178. **"Buying Without Fear: A Buyers Guide to King Collectibles,"** by George Beahm, in *Gauntlet* No. 2 (April, 1991): 195-198.

P179. **"The Stephen King Influence,"** by Stephen Spignesi, in *Gauntlet* No. 2 (April, 1991): 199-204.

b. *Gauntlet 2*, edited by Barry Hoffman. Baltimore: Borderlands Press, May 1991, cloth, p. 143-148.

P180. **"Needful Kings,"** by Tyson Blue, in *From the Tunnel* (May, 1991): 3. Discussion of *Misery, Needful Things, The Stephen King Encyclopedia,* and other projects.

P181. **"The 1991 Poll: Which of These Three Authors Is the Scariest?—Stephen King, Dean R. Koontz, or Thomas Harris,"** in *Entertainment Weekly* (June 7, 1991): 24. Poll indicated that King received 66% of the vote, Koontz 3%, and Harris 2%. King was featured on cover.

Q.

SECONDARY SOURCES

CASTLE ROCK: THE STEPHEN KING NEWSLETTER (1985-1989)

This listing includes only items initially appearing in *Castle Rock: The Stephen King Newsletter;* primary entries for reprinted materials from other sources will appear in the appropriate sections of this bibliography. For a full discussion of each issue of *Castle Rock*, see Stephen J. Spignesi, *The Shape Under the Sheet: The Complete Stephen King Encyclopedia*. Ann Arbor, MI: Popular Culture, Ink., May 1991, cloth, p. 95-126.

Q1. **"'Shining' at the Overlook,"** by Teresa Bagnato, in *Castle Rock: The Stephen King Newsletter* 1:2 (February, 1985): 7-8; and 1:3 (March, 1985): 7-8, 10; and 1:5 (May, 1985): 2. Account of a stay at the Stanley Hotel.

Q2. **"Collecting Stephen King,"** by George Beahm, in *Castle Rock: The Stephen King Newsletter* 1:5 (May, 1985): 3, 7.

Q3. **"Death Notice: Richard Bachman,"** in *Castle Rock: The Stephen King Newsletter* 1:5 (May, 1985): 2.

Q4. **"An Evening with Stephen King at Amherst,"** by Sheryl Mayer, in *Castle Rock: The Stephen King Newsletter* 1:5 (May 1985): 1, 6. Report on King's lecture at the University of Massachusetts.

Q5. **"The Real Beginning of The Real Bachman,"** by Stephen Brown, in *Castle Rock: The Stephen King Newsletter* 1:5 (May, 1985): 2, 8.

Q6. **"Some Reflections on Specialty Publishing,"** by Donald M. Grant, in *Castle Rock: The Stephen King Newsletter* 1:5 (May, 1985): 6-7.

Q7. **"Stephen King as Breckinridge Elkins,"** by Donald M. Grant, in *Castle Rock: The Stephen King Newsletter* 1:5 (May, 1985): 5-6. King celebrity roast at Roger Williams College, Rhode Island.

b. *The Stephen King Companion,* ed. George Beahm. Kansas City, MO: Andrews & McMeel, September 1989, cloth, p. 64-67. See **I24**.

Q8. **"Collings Studies Stephen King,"** by Michael R. Collings, in *Castle Rock: The Stephen King Newsletter* 1:6 (June, 1985): 8-9. Pre-publication excerpt from *Stephen King as Richard Bachman*, Chapter II. See **I7**.

b. *Stephen King as Richard Bachman*, by Michael R. Collings. STARMONT STUDIES IN LITERARY CRITICISM, No. 10. Mercer Island, WA: Starmont House, 1985, cloth, p. 9-19. See **I7**.

Q9. **"Editor's Column,"** by Stephanie Leonard, in *Castle Rock: The Stephen King Newsletter* 1:6 (June, 1985): 2.

Q10. **"Fantasy Review Article Is a Hoax!"** in *Castle Rock: The Stephen King Newsletter* 1:6 (June, 1985): 12. Refutation of various reports about pseudonymous King publications.

Q11. **"Stephen King Bibliography, Parts I and II,"** by Stephanie Leonard, in *Castle Rock: The Stephen King Newsletter* 1:6 (June, 1985): 6-7.

Q12. **"Book Dealers Respond to Grant on Limiteds,"** by Martin Last, Richard Spelman, Chuck Miller, Robert Weinberg, Phyllis Weinberg, and L. W. Currey, in *Castle Rock: The Stephen King Newsletter* 1:7 (July, 1985): 3, 5.

Q13. **"Editor's Column,"** by Stephanie Leonard, in *Castle Rock: The Stephen King Newsletter* 1:7 (July, 1985): 6.

Q14. **"Straub Talks About *Talisman*,"** by Peter Straub, in *Castle Rock: The Stephen King Newsletter* 1:7 (July, 1985): 1, 3.

Q15. **"WZON Offers Movie Role,"** in *Castle Rock: The Stephen King Newsletter* 1:7 (July, 1985): 1, 5.

Q16. **"Designing *The Eyes of the Dragon*,"** by Michael Alpert, in *Castle Rock: The Stephen King Newsletter* 1:8 (August, 1985): 1, 4, 6. Extensive discussion of how *The Eyes of the Dragon* was produced.

Q17. **"Goshgarian Finds the Real Stephen King,"** by Gary Goshgarian, in *Castle Rock: The Stephen King Newsletter* 1:8 (August, 1985): . Address presented to the Hartford College of Woman, April 24, 1985.

Q18. **"Starmont House Adds Three Volumes to SK Studies,"** [by Stephanie Leonard], in *Castle Rock: The Stephen King Newsletter* 1:8 (August, 1985): 1. Publication announcement for the Starmont series: *Discovering Stephen King*, *Stephen King as Richard Bachman*, *The Shorter Works of Stephen King*, *The Stephen King Concordance*, *The Films of Stephen King*, and *The Stephen King Phenomenon*.

Q19. **"Editor's Column,"** by Stephanie Leonard, in *Castle Rock: The Stephen King Newsletter* 1:9 (September, 1985): 4.

Q20. **"King Is Dead. Long Live the Kings,"** by Erskine Carter, in *Castle Rock: The Stephen King Newsletter* 1:9 (September, 1985): 6. Satirical pastiche of *Pet Sematary* written in King's style and couched as an interview with Stephanie Leonard.

Q21. **"My First Science Fiction Convention,"** by Alberta Dudley, in *Castle Rock: The Stephen King Newsletter* 1:9 (September, 1985): 2. Prices for King collectibles listed and assessed.

Q22. **"Searching for Richard Bachman,"** by Frank Norulak, in *Castle Rock: The Stephen King Newsletter* 1:9 (September, 1985): 3.

Q23. **"Editor's Column,"** by Stephanie Leonard, in *Castle Rock: The Stephen King Newsletter* 1:10 (October, 1985): 6.

Q24. **"Erskine Carter's Stephen King Primer,"** by Erskine Carter, in *Castle Rock: The Stephen King Newsletter* 1:10 (October, 1985): 5. Listing of key names and ideas from *'Salem's Lot* and *The Shining*.

Q25. **"Games Highlight King's Terror,"** by Stephanie Leonard, in *Castle Rock: The Stephen King Newsletter* 1:10 (October, 1985): 1. Discussion of computer game based on "The Mist."

Q26. **"How I Found Uncle Otto's Truck,"** by Richard McIntosh, in *Castle Rock: The Stephen King Newsletter* 1:10 (October, 1985): 3. Finding the truck that inspired King's story.

Q27. **"Questions Asked Most Often of S.K.,"** by Stephanie Leonard, in *Castle Rock: The Stephen King Newsletter* 1:10 (October, 1985): 1, 2.

Q28. **"Stephen King Fan or Fanatic,"** by Judith R. Behunin, in *Castle Rock: The Stephen King Newsletter* 1:10 (October, 1985): 5, 6. Appreciation of King as romantic and romancer.

Q29. **"How SK Has Changed Our Lives,"** by Kent Daniel Benkowski, in *Castle Rock: The Stephen King Newsletter* 1:11 (November, 1985): 1-2. Discussion of how King has altered American publishing and American society.

Q30. **"Reader's Pick: *The Stand*,"** by Diane Cousins, in *Castle Rock: The Stephen King Newsletter* 1:11 (November, 1985): 1, 2.

Q31. **"*Overdrive* Movie Set Relaxed,"** by Tyson Blue, in *Castle Rock: The Stephen King Newsletter* 1:11 (November, 1985): 3. Backgrounds to filming *Maximum Overdrive*, derived from on-set interview.

Q32. **"Editor's Column,"** by Stephanie Leonard, in *Castle Rock: The Stephen King Newsletter* 1:12 (December, 1985): 2.

Q33. **"Points from Don,"** by Donald M. Grant, in *Castle Rock: The Stephen King Newsletter* 1:12 (December, 1985): 2.

Q34. **"Putting Richard to Rest,"** by Wayne Allen Sallee, in *Castle Rock: The Stephen King Newsletter* 1:12 (December, 1985): 5.

Q35. **"Silver Bullet: Another Opinion,"** by Michael R. Collings, in *Castle Rock: The Stephen King Newsletter* 1:12 (December, 1985): 3.

b. *The Films of Stephen King*, by Michael R. Collings. Mercer Island WA: Starmont House, July 1986, cloth/paper, p. 137-146.

Q36. **"Stephen King: The Critic's Non-Choice,"** by Christopher Spruce, in *Castle Rock: The Stephen King Newsletter* 1:12 (December, 1985): 1, 4. Critique of King's critics.

Q37. **"The Blurbs of Stephen King,"** by Stephanie Leonard, in *Castle Rock* 2:1 (January, 1986): 2. On King's endorsements on novel covers, including Stuart Applebaum's comment that King is "One of the great Blurb-meisters...."

Q38. **"'Bullet' is SK's Best Screenplay,"** by Tyson Blue, in *Castle Rock: The Stephen King Newsletter* 2:1 (January, 1986): 6. Cogent analysis of the difficulties King's screenplay met with critics and viewers.

Q39. **"Editor's Column,"** by Stephanie Leonard, in *Castle Rock: The Stephen King Newsletter* 2:1 (January, 1986): 2.

Q40. **"Kids Love SK; Parents Don't,"** by Bill Munster, in *Castle Rock: The Stephen King Newsletter* 2:1 (January, 1986): 5. Response to students' and parents' attitudes toward King.

Q41. **"World Fantasy Convention Classy Again,"** by Bud White, in *Castle Rock: The Stephen King Newsletter* 2:1 (January, 1986): 1, 3. Discussion of King collectibles at the WFC.

Q42. **"Editor's Column,"** by Stephanie Leonard, in *Castle Rock: The Stephen King Newsletter* 2:2 (February, 1986): 2.

Q43. **"The King Goes On,"** by Judith Behunin, in *Castle Rock: The Stephen King Newsletter* 2:2 (February, 1986): 5-6. Appreciation of the Bachman novels, *Silver Bullet*, and King in general.

Q44. **"King Klips,"** by Stephanie Leonard, in *Castle Rock: The Stephen King Newsletter* 2:2 (February, 1986): 2. Update on recent publications by and about King.

Q45. **"SK Critics Criticized,"** by Ian Harris, in *Castle Rock: The Stephen King Newsletter* 2:2 (February, 1986): 3. Assessment of Don Herron, Douglas E. Winter, and Michael R. Collings as critics.

Q46. **"'The Stanley' Shines On,"** by Gary Taylor, in *Castle Rock: The Stephen King Newsletter* 2:2 (February 1986): 1, 4. On the inspiration for King's Overlook Hotel.

Q47. **"Uncut Edition of *The Stand* to be Published by Doubleday,"** in *Castle Rock: The Stephen King Newsletter* 2:2 (February, 1986): 1, 4.

Q48. "***Carrie* to Be Musical,"** in *Castle Rock: The Stephen King Newsletter* 2:3 (March, 1986): 6.

Q49. **"Editor's Column,"** by Stephanie Leonard, in *Castle Rock: The Stephen King Newsletter* 2:3 (March, 1986): 2.

Q50. **"Gramma Update,"** by Tyson Blue, in *Castle Rock: The Stephen King Newsletter* 2:3 (March, 1986): 4. On the *Twilight Zone* production of "Gramma."

Q51. **"King of Cassette: Reading SK by Ear,"** by Tyson Blue, in *Castle Rock: The Stephen King Newsletter* 2:3 (March, 1986): 1, 5. Evaluations of audiocassette adaptations of King's stories.

Q52. "***Carrie* to be Musical,"** [by Stephanie Leonard], in *Castle Rock: The Stephen King Newsletter* 2:4 (April 1986): 6.

Q53. **"Editor's Column,"** by Stephanie Leonard, in *Castle Rock: The Stephen King Newsletter* 2:4 (April, 1986): 2, 8.

Q54. **"Stephen King's Religious Vision,"** by Robert J. Hutchinson, in *Castle Rock: The Stephen King Newsletter* 2:4 (April, 1986): 6, 8.

Q55. **"Celebrating a Mystery Weekend at Mohonk,"** by Naomi King, in *Castle Rock: The Stephen King Newsletter* 2:5 (May, 1986): 1, 8. King's daughter's account of a mystery weekend with King, Tabitha King, Gahan Wilson, and others.

Q56. **"Editor's Column,"** by Stephanie Leonard, in *Castle Rock: The Stephen King Newsletter* 2:5 (May, 1986): 2, 8.

Q57. **"Searching for S.K.,"** by Dan McMillan, in *Castle Rock: The Stephen King Newsletter* 2:5 (May, 1986): 3, 8. King collectibles; *Maximum Overdrive*.

Q58. **"SK's Literary Agent Discusses Friend and Client,"** interview with Kirby McCauley, conducted by Christopher Spruce, in *Castle Rock: The Stephen King Newsletter* 2:5 (May, 1986): 1, 7.

Q59. **"Stephen King, One; Updike, Zip,"** by Tyson Blue, in *Castle Rock: The Stephen King Newsletter* 2:5 (May, 1986): 6, 8. Evaluation of King according to "literary" standards.

Q60. **"Arnold Who?"** by Ian Harris, in *Castle Rock: The Stephen King Newsletter* 2:6 (June, 1986): 2. Discussion of casting in the film version of *The Running Man*.

Q61. **"Darabont Responds to Sallee's Critique of His Film,"** by Frank Darabont, in *Castle Rock: The Stephen King Newsletter* 2:6 (June, 1986): 7.

Q62. **"Editor's Column,"** by Stephanie Leonard, in *Castle Rock: The Stephen King Newsletter* 2:6 (June, 1986): 2, 8.

Q63. **"If I Could Re-Cast *The Stand*,"** by Kathy Lathrop, with Christine Furru, in *Castle Rock: The Stephen King Newsletter* 2:6 (June, 1986): 6. Response to Edward De George's casting suggestions, arguing for Judd Hirsch as Stu Redman, Rosanna Arquette as Frannie Goldsmith, Armand Assante as Randall Flagg, Joan Collins as Nadine Cross, and Whoopi Goldberg as Mother Abigail.

Q64. **"On Hidden Treasures,"** by Bud White, in *Castle Rock: The Stephen King Newsletter* 2:6 (June, 1986): 5-6. On the trade in limited editions.

Q65. **"The Plant: The Unseen King,"** by Tyson Blue, in *Castle Rock: The Stephen King Newsletter* 2:6 (June, 1986): 1, 3. Overview and critique of "The Plant."

b. incorporated into: *The Unseen King*, by Tyson Blue. Mercer Island, WA: Starmont House, 1989, cloth. See **I22.**

Q66. **"Sallee Reconsiders 'Woman in the Room,'"** by Wayne Allen Sallee, in *Castle Rock: The Stephen King Newsletter* 2:6 (June, 1986): 8.

Q67. **"The States of the Jackets,"** by Stephanie Leonard, in *Castle Rock: The Stephen King Newsletter* 2:6 (June, 1986): 8. Discussion of variant dustjackets for *'Salem's Lot*.

Q68. **"Editor's Column,"** by Stephanie Leonard, in *Castle Rock: The Stephen King Newsletter* 2:7 (July, 1986): 2, 5.

Q69. **"IT: Stephen King's Comprehensive Masterpiece,"** by Michael R. Collings, in *Castle Rock: The Stephen King Newsletter,* 2:7 (July, 1986): 1, 4-6.

b. revised in: *The Stephen King Phenomenon*, by Michael R. Collings. Mercer Island, WA: Starmont House, March 1987, cloth, p. 13-25. See **I15**.

SECONDARY SOURCES AND REVIEWS:

1. Johnson, Kimball, Letter, in *Castle Rock: The Stephen King Newsletter* 3:11 (December, 1986/January, 1987): 7.

Q70. **"One More Time, Wayne,"** by Frank Darabont, in *Castle Rock: The Stephen King Newsletter* 2:7 (July, 1986): 2. Response to Sallee's reconsideration of *The Woman in the Room* [film].

Q71. **"One Stormy Friday Night with Stephen King,"** by Doris McClelland, in *Castle Rock: The Stephen King Newsletter* 2:7 (July, 1986): 6-7. Anecdotal response to reading *Skeleton Crew* on a "dark and stormy night."

Q72. **"The Situation Over Here,"** by Andrew Wolczyk, in *Castle Rock: The Stephen King Newsletter* 2:7 (July, 1986): 3, 5. On the difficulty of locating King's novels in England.

Q73. **"SK 'Lists' Set for Syndication,"** in *Castle Rock: The Stephen King Newsletter* 2:7 (July, 1986): 12.

Q74. **"SK Items Dominate West Coast Book Auction,"** by F. Lennox Campello, in *Castle Rock: The Stephen King Newsletter* 2:7 (July, 1986): 10. Resource for King collectors, listing prices paid at the California Book Auction Gallery Sale, May, 1986, in San Francisco.

Q75. **"Stephen King at the Movies,"** by Stephanie Leonard, in *Castle Rock: The Stephen King Newsletter* 2:7 (July, 1986): 3. Preview essay about Jessee Horsting's *Stephen King at the Movies* See. **I13.**

Q76. **"Stephen King Helps Spearhead Censorship Referendum Defeat,"** by Christopher Spruce, in *Castle Rock: The Stephen King Newsletter* 2:7 (July, 1986): 12.

b. *The Stephen King Companion,* ed. George Beahm. Kansas City, MO: Andrews & McMeel, September 1989, cloth, p. 141-143. See **I24.**

Q77. **"Stephen King in Boxer Shorts? Don't Hold Your Breath,"** [by Stephanie Leonard], in *Castle Rock* 2:7 (July, 1986): 7. Update on King-Haskell Boston Red Sox bet.

Q78. **"Stephen King on Videocassette,"** by Tyson Blue, in *Castle Rock: The Stephen King Newsletter* 2:7 (July, 1986): 8-9.

Q79. **"In Search of the Pets Sematary,"** by Terrie Bagnato, in *Castle Rock: The Stephen King Newsletter* 2:8 (August, 1986): 1, 3, 6. On locating the original for King's Pet Sematary, in Orrington, Maine.

Q80. **"Index to Back Issues of *Castle Rock*,"** in *Castle Rock: The Stephen King Newsletter* 2:8 (August, 1986): 5, 8.

Q81. **"Person, Persona,"** by Ken Shipley, in *Castle Rock: The Stephen King Newsletter*, 2:8 (August, 1986): 6. Discussion of public King versus private King.

Q82. **"Popular SK Taken as Serious Literature,"** by Pat Chase, in *Castle Rock: The Stephen King Newsletter* 2:8 (August, 1986): 4, 5. Critical comparison between King and Faulkner, King and Poe; written as a term paper for an English literature class.

Q83. **"SK Character Poll Results,"** by Thomas Cattrysse, in *Castle Rock: The Stephen King Newsletter* 2:8 (August, 1986):

Q84. **"Unanthologized Short Stories: The Unseen King, II,"** by Tyson Blue, in *Castle Rock: The Stephen King Newsletter* 2:8 (August, 1986): 8.

Q85. **"What's It Like Being the Daughter of SK,"** by Naomi King, in *Castle Rock: The Stephen King Newsletter* 2:8 (August, 1986): 3.

Q86. **"Why and How to Teach Stephen King,"** by Bill Munster, in *Castle Rock: The Stephen King Newsletter* 2:8 (August, 1986): 1, 4. Teaching *'Salem's Lot* in connection with *Beowulf* and *Sir Gawain and the Green Knight*.

Q87. **"The Austin Book and Paper Show,"** by Amy Edwards, in *Castle Rock: The Stephen King Newsletter* 2:9 (September, 1986): 2. Reference to King collectibles.

Q88. **"Baseball Poem is by SK,"** in *Castle Rock: The Stephen King Newsletter* 2:9 (September, 1986): 8. Identification of King as author of "Brooklyn August."

Q89. **"Editor's Column,"** by Stephanie Leonard, in *Castle Rock: The Stephen King Newsletter* 2:9 (September, 1986): 2.

Q90. **"Joe Bob Briggs Says SK Is Jordy,"** by Joe Bob Briggs [pseud.], in *Castle Rock: The Stephen King Newsletter* 2:9 (September, 1986): 3.

Q91. **"The Bestselling Bestseller: King and the Lists,"** by Michael R. Collings, in *Castle Rock: The Stephen King Newsletter* 2:10 (October, 1986): 1, 3.

b. updated in: *The Stephen King Phenomenon*, by Michael R. Collings. Mercer Island, WA: Starmont House, 1987, cloth/paper, p. 36-50. See **I15**.

Q92. **"Book List,"** by Tyson Blue, in *Castle Rock: The Stephen King Newsletter* 2:10 (October, 1986): 4, 8. Listing of critical studies of King's works.

Q93. **"Editor's Column,"** by Stephanie Leonard, in *Castle Rock: The Stephen King Newsletter* 2:10 (October, 1986): 2.

Q94. **"OBSESSION: The True Confessions of an SK Collector,"** in *Castle Rock: The Stephen King Newsletter* 2:10 (October, 1986): 7, 8.

Q95. **"Stephen King and the Stars (Up There),"** by J. N. Williamson, in *Castle Rock: The Stephen King Newsletter* 2:10 (October, 1986): 3. Essay on Astrology and Stephen King.

Q96. **"The Stephen King Phenomenon,"** in *Castle Rock: The Stephen King Newsletter* 2:10 (October, 1986): 4, 10. Listing of critical works discussing King.

Q97. **"Editor's Column,"** by Stephanie Leonard, in *Castle Rock: The Stephen King Newsletter* 2:11 (November, 1986): 2.

Q98. **"New King Cassettes,"** by Tyson Blue, in *Castle Rock: The Stephen King Newsletter* 2:11 (November, 1986): 4.

Q99. **"Stephen King on Television,"** by Dr. Barry M. Brooks, in *Castle Rock: The Stephen King Newsletter* 2:11 (November, 1986): 5, 6. Listing of King's appearances on televisio and radio, 1980-1986.

Q100. **"Who's On First?"** by Barbara Doty Larkin, in *Castle Rock: The Stephen King Newsletter* 2:11 (November, 1986): 1, 3. Difficulties in talking about King's *IT* with those who don't understand the pronoun usage.

Q101. **"World Sci-Fi Con: A Report for Castle Rock,"** by Ken Cobb, in *Castle Rock: The Stephen King Newsletter* 2:11 (November, 1986): 7. Collectibles available at the World Science Fiction convention.

Q102. **"*Creepshow II*,"** in *Castle Rock: The Stephen King Newsletter* 3:1 (December, 1986-January, 1987): 11-12.

Q103. **"Finally, SK Story Filmed in Bangor,"** by Christopher Spruce, in *Castle Rock: The Stephen King Newsletter* 3:1 (December, 1986-January, 1987): 11-12. Filming of a segment of *Creepshow II*.

Q104. **"Kings Deliver UM Lectures,"** by Sarah W. Spruce, in *Castle Rock: The Stephen King Newsletter* 3:1 (December, 1986-January, 1987): 1, 12. Report on Stephen and Tabitha King lectures at the University of Maine.

Q105. **"Running Man Still Unmade,"** by Christopher Spruce, in *Castle Rock: The Stephen King Newsletter* 3:1 (December, 1986-January, 1987): 13. Update on filming of *The Running Man*.

Q106. **"Stephen King on TV and Radio (New Listings),"** by Dr. Barry M. Brooks, in *Castle Rock: The Stephen King Newsletter* 3:1 (December, 1986-January, 1987): 13. Addendum to **N301**.

Q107. **"Two Versions of *The Shining*,"** by Ian Harris, in *Castle Rock: The Stephen King Newsletter* 3:1 (December, 1986-January, 1987): 14-15.

Q108. **"Finding the Dead Zone,"** by Sheryl and Richard Weilgosh, in *Castle Rock: The Stephen King Newsletter* 3:2 (February, 1987): 1, 7. Travelogue on the locations for the *Dead Zone* film.

Q109. **"*The Dark Tower II: The Drawing of the Three*,"** by Donald M. Grant, in *Castle Rock: The Stephen King Newsletter* 3:2 (February, 1987): 1, 8. Pre-publication description and announcement of *The Dark Tower II*.

Q110. **"Editor's Column,"** by Stephanie Leonard, in *Castle Rock: The Stephen King Newsletter* 3:2 (February, 1987): 2, 8.

Q111. **"The Exit: An Homage to Stephen King—Castle Rock Exit 5 Miles,"** by Dan P. McMillan, in *Castle Rock: The Stephen King Newsletter* 3:2 (February, 1987): 6.

Q112. **"And Where He Stops, Nobody Knows,"** by Julie Knox, in *Castle Rock: The Stephen King Newsletter* 3:3 (March, 1987): 4.

Q113. **"Editing *Eyes*: An Interview with Deborah Brodie,"** by Tyson Blue, in *Castle Rock: The Stephen King Newsletter* 3:3 (March, 1987): 5, 8.

Q114. **"Editor's Column,"** by Stephanie Leonard, in *Castle Rock: The Stephen King Newsletter* 3:3 (March, 1987): 2, 4.

Q115. **"Stephen King Items *Very* Collectible,"** by F. Lennox Campello, in *Castle Rock: The Stephen King Newsletter* 3:3 (March, 1987): 8.

Q116. **"Editor's Column,"** by Stephanie Leonard, in *Castle Rock: The Stephen King Newsletter* 3:4 (April 1987): 2.

Q117. **"Mystification in King,"** by Chris Thomson, in *Castle Rock: The Stephen King Newsletter* 3:4 (April, 1987): 12. Discussion of errors and inconsistencies in King's short fiction.

Q118. **"Editor's Column,"** by Stephanie Leonard, in *Castle Rock: The Stephen King Newsletter* 3:5 (May, 1987): .

Q119. **"About the Filmmakers: Some *Creepshow II* Notes,"** in *Castle Rock: The Stephen King Newsletter* 3:6 (June, 1987): 1, 6.

Q120. **"The Art of Movie Poster Collecting,"** by Stephanie Leonard, in *Castle Rock: The Stephen King Newsletter* 3:6 (June, 1987): 3.

Q121. **"Editor's Column,"** by Stephanie Leonard, in *Castle Rock: The Stephen King Newsletter* 3:6 (June, 1987): 3.

Q122. **"*The Eyes of the Dragon*: New King, Old King,"** by Mark Freeman, in *Castle Rock: The Stephen King Newsletter* 3:6 (June, 1987): 5.

Q123. **"Goden on Posters,"** by Craig Goden, in *Castle Rock: The Stephen King Newsletter* 3:6 (June, 1987): 3.

Q124. **"King Discusses His Creepy Craft,"** by Tiffany Vail, in *Castle Rock: The Stephen King Newsletter* 3:6 (June, 1987): 6.

Q125. **"Mystification in SK Continued or Points to Ponder in King: Part II,"** by Chris Thomson, in *Castle Rock: The Stephen King Newsletter* 3:6 (June, 1987): 10, 12. Addenda to **Q117.**

Q126. **"Nearly All of SK's Books Under One Roof: The 20th Annual California International Bookfair,"** by F. Lennox Campello, in *Castle Rock: The Stephen King Newsletter* 3:6 (June, 1987): 8, 9.

Q127. **"Will Stephen King's Work Survive?"** by Darrell Schweitzer, in *Castle Rock: The Stephen King Newsletter* 3:6 (June, 1987): 1, 4.

Q128. **"The Young and Restless: Trendy and Sharp Focus on SK,"** by Trendy Sharp, in *Castle Rock: The Stephen King Newsletter* 3:6 (June, 1987): 10, 12. Letter-essay on King's influence on young readers.

Q129. **"Editor's Column,"** by Stephanie Leonard, in *Castle Rock: The Stephen King Newsletter* 3:7 (July, 1987): 2.

Q130. **"The Growing Optimism of Stephen King: Bachman's Pessimism Gets Thinner,"** by Michael Pepper, in *Castle Rock: The Stephen King Newsletter* 3:7 (July, 1987) 1, 4. Excerpt from senior English thesis.

Q131. **"Objects in This Mirror are Closer Than They Appear,"** by Gerry Whetter, in *Castle Rock: The Stephen King Newsletter* 3:7 (July, 1987): 4. Reader-response to *Stand by Me*.

Q132. **"On Becoming a Stephen King Fan,"** by Karen L. Jackson, in *Castle Rock: The Stephen King Newsletter* 3:7 (July, 1987): 3.

Q133. **"Rounding Up Books on King,"** by Tyson Blue, in *Castle Rock: The Stephen King Newsletter* 3:7 (July, 1987): 6.

Q134. **"A Book on Stephen King in the Netherlands,"** by Eddy C. Bertin, in *Castle Rock: The Stephen King Newsletter* 3:8 (August, 1987): 7, 8. Announcement of plans for *Het Stephen King Boek: De Griezelige Werelden Van Stephen King*. The publisher subsequently declined to pursue the book any further.

Q135. **"Co-Miser-A-Ting with Stephen King,"** by Tabitha King, in *Castle Rock: The Stephen King Newsletter* 3:8 (August, 1987): 1, 5. On reader responses to *Misery*.

Q136. **"Editor's Column,"** by Stephanie Leonard, in *Castle Rock: The Stephen King Newsletter* 3:8 (August, 1987): 2.

Q137. **"More on Flagg/Gunslinger Connection,"** by Mark Freeman, in *Castle Rock: The Stephen King Newsletter* 3:8 (August, 1987): 3. Analysis of character in *The Eyes of the Dragon* and *The Dark Tower*.

Q138. **"The World of Horror: Writing Up Bad Dreams,"** by Dory L. Wethington, in *Castle Rock: The Stephen King Newsletter* 3:8 (August, 1987): 6.

Q139. **"Editor's Column,"** by Stephanie Leonard, in *Castle Rock: The Stephen King Newsletter* 3:9 (September, 1987): 2.

Q140. **"*IT* in the Netherlands; or, The Rape of Stephen King,"** by Eddy C. Bertin, in *Castle Rock: The Stephen King Newsletter* 3:9 (September, 1987): 7. Critique of the Dutch translation, noting that the version is reduced to about 50% of the original text.

Q141. **"King Class a Small Success,"** by Karl D. Kober, in *Castle Rock: The Stephen King Newsletter* 3:9 (September, 1987): 3, 5. Report on results of course in "The Masters of Modern Horror" at Coastline College, Huntington Beach, CA.

Q142. **"A KING-size Remedy That Worked!"** by David M. Lowell, in *Castle Rock: The Stephen King Newsletter* 3:9 (September, 1987): 3. Reader-response essay on *Misery*.

Q143. **"SK's House Is a Tourist Hot Spot,"** by Stephanie Leonard, in *Castle Rock: The Stephen King Newsletter* 3:9 (September, 1987): 1, 4.

Q144. **Editor's Column,"** by Stephanie Leonard, in *Castle Rock: The Stephen King Newsletter* 3:10 (October, 1987): 2.

Q145. **"Misery on Stage?"** by Ian Harris, in *Castle Rock: The Stephen King Newsletter* 3:10 (October, 1987): 3, 6. Essay analyzing the possibility of adapting King's works for stage presentation.

Q146. **"Rocking On in SK's Rock and Roll Zone,"** by Hank Cheever, Jr., in *Castle Rock: The Stephen King Newsletter* 3:10 (October, 1987): 1, 4. On King's interest in Rock and Roll.

Q147. **"The Automobile Motif: Stephen King's Most Frequent Villain,"** by Mark Graham, in *Castle Rock: The Stephen King Newsletter* 3:11 (November, 1987): 3, 5-6, 8. Extensive analysis of automobiles as theme and symbol in King's work.

Q148. **"Editor's Column,"** by Stephanie Leonard, in *Castle Rock: The Stephen King Newsletter* 3:11 (November, 1987): 2.

Q149. **"A Few Thoughts on Why SK Should Review His Christmas Mailing List,"** by F. Lennox Campello, in *Castle Rock: The Stephen King Newsletter* 3:11 (November, 1987): 7. Note about the appearance of King's Christmas Greetings, "The Plant," on the collectors' market.

Q150. **"*IT* an ABC Mini-Series: I Shudder at the Thought,"** by Barry Hoffman, in *Castle Rock: The Stephen King Newsletter* 3:11 (November, 1987): 7-8. Discussion of the difficulty in translating King's materials to television, with emphasis on *IT*.

Q151. **"Stephen King, Sci-Fi, and *The Tommyknockers*,"** by Michael R. Collings, in *Castle Rock: The Stephen King Newsletter* 3:11 (November, 1987): 1, 4-5. Extensive analytical review-article relating *The Tommyknockers* to elements of King's earlier works.

Q152. **"Different Seasons II—A Look Back at the Five-Book Year,"** by Tyson Blue, in *Castle Rock: The Stephen King Newsletter* 3:12/4:1 (December, 1987-January 1988): 14. Thematic overview of *IT*, *The Eyes of the Dragon*, *Misery*, *The Drk Tower II: The Drawing of the Three*, and *The Tommyknockers*.

Q153. **"Editor's Column,"** by Stephanie Leonard, in *Castle Rock: The Stephen King Newsletter* 3:12/4:1 (December, 1987-January, 1988): 1.

Q154. **"Fear and the Future: King as a Science-Fiction Writer,"** by Darrell Schweitzer, in *Castle Rock: The Stephen King Newsletter* 3:12/4:1 (December, 1987-January, 1988): 1, 6-8.

b. *Reign of Fear: Fiction and Film of Stephen King,* edited by Don Herron. Los Angeles: Underwood-Miller, June 1988, cloth, p. 193-208.

Q155. **"The King/Roland Quest,"** by Estelle Ruiz, in *Castle Rock: The Stephen King Newsletter* 3:12/4:1 (December, 1987-January 1988): 3, 13. Discussion of Tarot correspondances in *the Dark Tower II: The Drawing of the Three.*

Q156. **"Tabitha King: Resisting the Star-Making Machinery,"** by Rodney Labbe, in *Castle Rock: The Stephen King Newsletter* 3:12/4:1 (December, 1987-January 1988): 5, 10. Profile of King's wife, with references to King.

Q157. **"'Carrie' as Musical,"** by Tim Foster, in *Castle Rock: The Stephen King Newsletter* 4:2 (February, 1988): 2.

Q158. **"Editor's Column,"** by Stephanie Leonard, in *Castle Rock: The Stephen King Newsletter* 4:2 (February, 1988): 2, 5.

Q159. **"Having a Wonderful Time,"** by Dory L. Wethington, in *Castle Rock: The Stephen King Newsletter* 4:2 (February, 1988): 1, 5.

Q160. **"*The Running Man* and Stephen King: Not a Bad Film,"** by Michael R. Collings, in *Castle Rock: The Stephen King Newsletter* 4:2 (February, 1988): 1, 4. Discussion of changes from King's text to film adaptation.

Q161. **"*The Running Man* and Stephen King:*The Running Man* is Fundamentally Dishonest,"** by Darrell Schweitzer, in *Castle Rock: The Stephen King Newsletter* 4:2 (February, 1988): 1, 4.

Q162. **"'Carrie' to Open at the Virginia Theater,"** in *Castle Rock: The Stephen King Newsletter* 4:3 (March, 1988): 5.

Q163. **"Editor's Column,"** by Stephanie Leonard, in *Castle Rock: The Stephen King Newsletter* 4:3 (March, 1988): 2.

Q164. **"*Observations from the Terminator: The Dark Side of Fandom,*"** by Tyson Blue, in *Castle Rock: The Stephen King Newsletter* 4:3 (March, 1988): 1, 4, 5.

Q165. **"Profile: R. Bradley Trent of Oklahoma City,"** by Stephanie Leonard, in *Castle Rock: The Stephen King Newsletter* 4:3 (March, 1988): 3.

Q166. **"Queen for a Day with King in Cleveland,"** by Jeanne Zulkowski, in *Castle Rock: The Stephen King Newsletter* 4:3 (March, 1988): 6.

Q167. **"Report from River Oaks,"** by William R. Wilson, in *Castle Rock: The Stephen King Newsletter* 4:3 (March, 1988): 6. Reader-response to a King/Robertson autograph session.

Q168. **"SK Criticized for References to Blacks,"** by Kima R. Hicks, in *Castle Rock: The Stephen King Newsletter* 4:3 (March, 1988): 1.

Q169. **"SK's Rock 'n' Roll Zone for Sale,"** by Hank Cheever, Jr., in *Castle Rock: The Stephen King Newsletter* 4:3 (March, 1988): 3. Announcement that King's radio station, WZON, is for sale.

Q170. **"Whitney Museum Planning Limited,"** in *Castle Rock: The Stephen King Newsletter* 4:3 (March, 1988): 2. Announcement of plans for *My Pretty Pony*.

Q171. **"...And the Critics be Damned,"** by Barry Hoffman, in *Castle Rock: The Stephen King Newsletter* 4:4 (April, 1988): 8. Comments on King films and film reviewers.

Q172. **"Editor's Column,"** by Stephanie Leonard, in *Castle Rock: The Stephen King Newsletter* 4:4 (April, 1988): 2.

Q173. **"He Can Turn the Page, But He Can't Turn Back,"** by Mike Cummins, in *Castle Rock: The Stephen King Newsletter* 4:4 (April, 1988): 9. On being a King "addict."

Q174. **"*Nightmares* Publication Set for Fall,"** in *Castle Rock: The Stephen King Newsletter* 4:4 (April, 1988): 3.

Q175. **"The Power of the Unseen,"** by Tim Murphy, in *Castle Rock: The Stephen King Newsletter* 4:4 (April, 1988): 3, 4. Discussion of film adaptations of King's works, and why those films fail.

Q176. **"Printing Error Explained,"** by Tyson Blue, in *Castle Rock: The Stephen King Newsletter* 4:4 (April, 1988): 9. Article on the "Permissions to Come" page in *The Tommyknockers*.

Q177. **"SK Read *Gunslinger* Tapped for June,"** by Tyson Blue, in *Castle Rock: The Stephen King Newsletter* 4:4 (April, 1988): 1, 5.

Q178. **"Thanks for the Memories, SK: Houston Book Signing,"** by Del Rhea Watson, in *Castle Rock: The Stephen King Newsletter* 4:4 (April, 1988): 2, 8.

Q179. **"Years 'n Fears: A Look Backward,"** by Tyson Blue, in *Castle Rock: The Stephen King Newsletter* 4:4 (April, 1988): 4, 12. Reminiscences on first reading King.

Q180. **"Before the Brand Name,"** by Philip Wilson, in *Castle Rock: The Stephen King Newsletter* 4:5-6 (May-June, 1988): 4. Survey of early reviews of *Carrie*.

Q181. **"Editor's Column,"** by Stephanie Leonard, in *Castle Rock: The Stephen King Newsletter* 4:5-6 (May-June, 1988): 2.

Q182. **"Lost in Derry,"** in *Castle Rock: The Stephen King Newsletter* 4:5-6 (May-June, 1988): 1, 6-7.

Q183. **"Observations from the Terminator: The Dark Side of Fandom: Part II,"** by Tyson Blue, in *Castle Rock: The Stephen King Newsletter* 4:5-6 (May-June, 1988): 3, 9.

Q184. **"Oh Goodie...They Might Have Fallen,"** by Barry Hoffman, in *Castle Rock: The Stephen King Newsletter* 4:5-6 (May-June, 1988): 8-9. Critique of King's critics.

Q185. **"Editor's Column,"** by Stephanie Leonard, in *Castle Rock: The Stephen King Newsletter* 4:7 (July, 1988): 2, 5.

Q186. **"Horrorfest Convention Lists Appearances,"** by Tim Foster, in *Castle Rock: The Stephen King Newsletter* 4:7 (July, 1988): 6, 12.

Q187. **"King's Kids...Less than Meets the Eye,"** by Barry Hoffman, in *Castle Rock: The Stephen King Newsletter* 4:7 (July, 1988): 3. Analysis of children as characters in *IT*.

Q188. **"The Arrival of a Limited,"** by Tom Draheim, in *Castle Rock: The Stephen King Newsletter* 4:8 (August, 1988): 1, 3.

Q189. **"Editor's Column,"** by Stephanie Leonard, in *Castle Rock: The Stephen King Newsletter* 4:8 (August, 1988): 2.

Q190. **"H. P. Lovecraft and Those Tommyknockers,"** by Ben Indick, in *Castle Rock: The Stephen King Newsletter* 4:8 (August, 1988): 4, 12. Analytical comparison of King's novel and Lovecraft's *The Colour Out of Space*.

Q191. **"SK Book Banned in Virginia,"** in *Castle Rock: The Stephen King Newsletter* 4:8 (August, 1988): 5. On the banning of *'Salem's Lot* by the Goochland, VA school board.

Q192. **"S.K.'s *Pet Sematary* Scheduled for Maine Production,"** by Hank Cheever, Jr., in *Castle Rock: The Stephen King Newsletter* 4:8 (August, 1988): 1.

Q193. **"Collector's News,"** by Tyson Blue, in *Castle Rock: The Stephen King Newsletter* 4:9 (September, 1988):5.

Q194. **"Editor's Column,"** by Stephanie Leonard, in *Castle Rock: The Stephen King Newsletter* 4:9 (September, 1988): 2.

Q195. **"The Good and Bad of Film Adaptation,"** by James Cole, in *Castle Rock: The Stephen King Newsletter* 4:9 (September, 1988): 1, 6. Reminiscences of filming a version of King's "The Last Rung on the Ladder."

Q196. **"From Richard to Stephen to Richard: How Richard Matheson Influenced the Work of Both Stephen King and Richard Christian Matheson,"** by Stephen Spignesi, in *Castle Rock: The Stephen King Newsletter* 4:9 (September, 1988): 1, 4. Pre-publication excerpt from *The Shape Under the Sheet: The Complete Stephen King Encyclopedia*.

Q197. **"Audio-Cassette News,"** by Tyson Blue, in *Castle Rock: The Stephen King Newsletter* 4:10 (October, 1988): 5.

Q198. **"Blue Updates *Unseen King*,"** by Tyson Blue, in *Castle Rock: The Stephen King Newsletter* 4:10 (October, 1988): 8.

Q199. **"Editor's Column,"** by Stephanie Leonard, in *Castle Rock: The Stephen King Newsletter* 4:10 (October, 1988): 2.

Q200. **"How I Spent My Summer Vacation; or, A Stephen King Fan's Study in Frustration,"** by Judee Gardner, in *Castle Rock: The Stephen King Newsletter* 4:10 (October, 1988): 6.

Q201. **"King's Characters: The Good, the Bad, and the Badder,"** by Barry Hoffman, in *Castle Rock: The Stephen King Newsletter* 4:10 (October, 1988): 3. Analytical discussion; King's villains are his most memorable characters.

Q202. **"'Pet Sematary' Finally Converted to Celluloid,"** by Christopher Spruce, in *Castle Rock: The Stephen King Newsletter* 4:10 (October, 1988): 1, 6

Q203. **"Stephen King's WZON Rocks On,"** in *Castle Rock: The Stephen King Newsletter* 4:10 (October, 1988): 3. Announcement that the radio station will not be sold, will run commercial-free, and will retain its rock-and-roll format.

Q204. **"Sure Glad the Book Wasn't 'Cujo,'"** by Sherwood Springer, in *Castle Rock: The Stephen King Newsletter* 4:10 (October, 1988): 1, 6.

Q205. **"Editor's Column,"** by Stephanie Leonard, in *Castle Rock: The Stephen King Newsletter* 4:11 (November, 1988): 2.

Q206. **"Interview with Robert R. McCammon,"** by Jodi Strissel, in *Castle Rock: The Stephen King Newsletter* 4:11 (November, 1988): 6. References to King's influence on McCammon.

Q207. **"Mount Hope: 'The Most Beautiful Cemetery'—A Visit to the Set of *Pet Sematary* in Pictures,"** [by Christopher Spruce], in *Castle Rock: The Stephen King Newsletter* 4:11 (November, 1988): 4, 5.

Q208. ***"Pet Sematary* Film Crews Visit Bangor,"** by Christopher Spruce, in *Castle Rock: The Stephen King Newsletter* 4:11 (November, 1988): 1, 7.

Q209. **"SK Wins Stoker Award,"** by Jodi Strissel, in *Castle Rock: The Stephen King Newsletter* 4:11 (November, 1988): 3.

Q210. **"Stranger Than Fiction?"** by Dory L. Wethington, in *Castle Rock: The Stephen King Newsletter* 4:12 (December, 1988): 8.

Q211. **"References to SK Found in Unusual Books,"** by Daniel W. Hayes, in *Castle Rock: The Stephen King Newsletter* 4:12 (December, 1988): 12.

Q212. **"Editor's Column,"** by Christopher Spruce in *Castle Rock: The Stephen King Newsletter* 5:1 (January, 1989): 1, 2.

Q213. **"More Info Released on Dark Tower II,"** by Tyson Blue, in *Castle Rock: The Stephen King Newsletter* 5:1 (January, 1989): 7.

Q214. **"Happy New Year: SK Inks New Four Book Contract,"** by Christopher Spruce, in *Castle Rock: The Stephen King Newsletter* 5:2 (February, 1989): 1.

Q215. **"Editor's Column,"** by Christopher Spruce, in *Castle Rock: The Stephen King Newsletter* 5:3 (March, 1989): 2.

Q216. **"Interview: Talking Horror Fiction with Rick Hautala, Part I,"** by David M. Lowell, in *Castle Rock: The Stephen King Newsletter* 5:3 (March, 1989): 3. On King as a student at the University of Maine, Orono.

Q217. **"Belgian TV Interview Provides Insights to SK,"** by Christopher Spruce, in *Castle Rock: The Stephen King Newsletter* 5:4 (April, 1989): 3, 10.

Q218. **"Editor's Column,"** by Christopher Spruce, in *Castle Rock: The Stephen King Newsletter* 5:4 (April, 1989): 2, 5.

Q219. **"*My Pretty Pony*: An Odd Couple Produces a Work of Art,"** by Ben Indick, in *Castle Rock: The Stephen King Newsletter* 5:4 (April, 1989): 1, 9.

Q220. **"Opening Night: No Glitz, Just the Jitters,"** by T. J. Tremble, in *Castle Rock: The Stephen King Newsletter* 5:4 (April, 1989): 1, 12. On the opening night of *Pet Sematary* film.

Q221. **"Spignesi Updates SK Encyclopedia,"** by Stephen J. Spignesi, in *Castle Rock: The Stephen King Newsletter* 5:4 (April, 1989): 3.

Q222. **"Talking Horror with Rick Hautala, Part 2,"** by David Lowell, in *Castle Rock: The Stephen King Newsletter* 5:4 (April, 1989): 11. Frequent references to Hautala's friendship with King.

Q223. **"Editor's Column,"** by Christopher Spruce, in *Castle Rock: The Stephen King Newsletter* 5:5 (May, 1989): 2, 11.

Q224. **"God of Blood and Fire,"** by Gary D. Robinson, in *Castle Rock: The Stephen King Newsletter* 5:6 (June, 1989): 3, 12. Critical discussion of the image of God in King's works.

Q225. **"Horrorfest Plans Finalized,"** by Tim Foster, in *Castle Rock: The Stephen King Newsletter* 5:5 (May, 1989): 8.

Q226. **"Editor's Column,"** by Christopher Spruce, in *Castle Rock: The Stephen King Newsletter* 5:6 (June, 1989): 2.

Q227. **"One Fan's Night in Pasadena,"** by Suzanne Biddinger, in *Castle Rock: The Stephen King Newsletter* 5:6 (June, 1989): 1, 12. On King's appearance at the Pasadena Public Library.

Q228. **"The Play's the Thing for the Parker Family,"** by Patti Hartigan, in *Castle Rock: The Stephen King Newsletter* 5:6 (June, 1989): 1, 12. On adaptation of King's *Rage* as a stage play.

Q229. **"Censorship Rears Its Ugly Head...Again,"** by Barry Hoffman, in *Castle Rock: The Stephen King Newsletter* 5:7 (July, 1989): 3.

Q230. **"'Companion' Book Nears Publication,"** by Tyson Blue, in *Castle Rock: The Stephen King Newsletter* 5:7 (July, 1989): 2. Pre-publication announcement of Beahm, *The Stephen King Companion*.

Q231. **"Editor's Column,"** by Christopher Spruce, in *Castle Rock: The Stephen King Newsletter* 5:7 (July, 1989): 2.

Q232. **"Horrorfest '89: Bill and Bud's Excellent Adventure,"** by W. F. Roberts and Marcelo Mathew Martinez, in *Castle Rock: The Stephen King Newsletter* 5:7 (July, 1989): 5.

Q233. **"Lullabye Haven: A Fairy Tale in Which a Gander Can Indeed Become a Cooked Goose,"** by Gillian Ewing, in *Castle Rock: The Stephen King Newsletter* 5:7 (July, 1989): 6-7. Parable on censorship; focus on King's works.

Q234. **"More Than 300 Attend Horrorfest,"** by Tyson Blue, in *Castle Rock: The Stephen King Newsletter* 5:7 (July, 1989): 1, 9.

Q235. **"Mr. Norman's Longcut: The Horror After the Fest,"** by Ray Rexer, in *Castle Rock: The Stephen King Newsletter* 5:7 (July, 1989): 1, 4.

Q236. **"The Organizer Offers His Account,"** by Ken Morgan, in *Castle Rock: The Stephen King Newsletter* 5:7 (July, 1989): 1, 9.

Q237. **"Page after Page after Page of Garbage,"** in *Castle Rock: The Stephen King Newsletter* 5:7 (July, 1989): 3. Attempts to remove *Cujo* from Fayetteville AS school library shelves.

Q238. **"Stanley Uris: World's Smallest Adult,"** by Michael Moses, in *Castle Rock: The Stephen King Newsletter* 5:7 (July, 1989): 3, 10-11. Student essay (Pepperdine University) on the depths of King's characterization in *IT*.

Q239. **"Acorns to Oaks: Explorations of Theme, Image, and Characterization in the Early Works of Stephen King, Part I,"** by Michael R. Collings, in *Castle Rock: The Stephen King Newsletter* 5:8 (August, 1989): 1, 8. Analytical discussion of "Slade," the early poems, and other works; presented as Guest of Honor Address, Horrorfest '89, May 1989.

Q240. **"Beahm Updates the Stephen King Companion,"** by George Beahm, in *Castle Rock: The Stephen King Newsletter* 5:8 (August, 1989): 7.

Q241. **"Editor's Column,"** by Christopher Spruce, in *Castle Rock: The Stephen King Newsletter* 5:8 (August, 1989): 2.

Q242. **"Letters to CR,"** in *Castle Rock: The Stephen King Newsletter* 5:8 (August, 1989): 2.

Q243. **"Acorns to Oaks: Explorations of Theme, Image, and Characterization in the Early Works of Stephen King, Part II,"** by Michael R. Collings, in *Castle Rock: The Stephen King Newsletter* 5:9-10 (September-October, 1989): 3, 10. Analytical discussion of "Slade," the early poems, and other works; presented as Guest of Honor Address, Horrorfest '89, May 1989.

Q244. **"Bill and Steve—Two of a Kind,"** by Mark Graham, in *Castle Rock: The Stephen King Newsletter* 5:9-10 (September-October, 1989): 4, 9. Essay comparing the popular appeal of and genre choices made by William Shakespeare and Stephen King.

Q245. **"I Wouldn't Tease 'Em If I Didn't Love 'Em,"** interview with Ray Rexer, conducted by Barry Hoffman, in *Castle Rock: The Stephen King Newsletter* 5:9-10 (September-October, 1989): 8. Comments on the genesis of *Castle Schlock*.

Q246. **"Editor's Column,"** in *Castle Rock: The Stephen King Newsletter* 5:11 (November, 1989): .

Q247. **"Letters to CR,"** in *Castle Rock: The Stephen King Newsletter* 5:11 (November, 1989): .

Q248. **"Some SK Soundtracks Are More Than Background Music,"** by Wayne Rhodes, in *Castle Rock: The Stephen King Newsletter* 5:11 (November, 1989): .

Q249. **"Here's An Unusual King Collectible,"** by Ben P. Indick, in *Castle Rock: The Stephen King Newsletter* 5:11 (November, 1989): .

Q250. **"An Interview with *New Blood*'s Chris Lacher,"** conducted by Barry Hoffman, in *Castle Rock: The Stephen King Newsletter* 5:11 (November, 1989): .

Q251. **"More Videos of SK Works Released,"** by Tyson Blue, in *Castle Rock: The Stephen King Newsletter* 5:11 (November, 1989): .

Q252. **"*Castle Rock* and the Stephen King Experience,"** by Tom Draheim, in *Castle Rock: The Stephen King Newsletter* 5:12 (December, 1989): .

Q253. **"A Concordance to Stephen King's First Published Short Story, 'I Was a Teenage Grave Robber,'"** by Stephen J. Spignesi, in *Castle Rock: The Stephen King Newsletter* 5:12 (December, 1989): .

b. *The Shape Under the Sheet: The Complete Stephen King Encyclopedia*. Ann Arbor, MI: Popular Culture, Ink, May 1991, cloth, p. 472-474.

Q254. **"Cut Adrift in a Plagiarized Raft,"** by Wayne Rhodes, in *Castle Rock: The Stephen King Newsletter* 5:12 (December, 1989): .

Q255. **"DT Books Make Dutch Appearance,"** by Eddy C. Bertin, in *Castle Rock: The Stephen King Newsletter* 5:12 (December, 1989): .

Q256. **"Editor's Column,"** by Christopher Spruce, in *Castle Rock: The Stephen King Newsletter* 5:12 (December, 1989): .

Q257. **"An Interview with *Gauntlet*'s Barry Hoffman,"** conducted by Richard Chizmar, in *Castle Rock: The Stephen King Newsletter* 5:12 (December, 1989): .

Q258. **"Just in the Nick of Time,"** conducted by Barry Hoffman, in *Castle Rock: The Stephen King Newsletter* 5:12 (December, 1989): . Interview with Chris Spruce, *Castle Rock* editor.

Q259. **"The Last Rat Swims; Or, A Farewell to the *Rock*,"** by Tyson Blue, in *Castle Rock: The Stephen King Newsletter* 5:12 (December, 1989): .

Q260. **"Letters to *CR*,"** in *Castle Rock: The Stephen King Newsletter* 5:12 (December, 1989): .

R.

SECONDARY SOURCES

NEWSPAPER ARTICLES

R1. **"3 Durham Lads Publishing Bright Hometown Newspaper,"** by Don Hansen, in *Record* [Brunswick, ME] (April 23, 1959): .

b. *The Shape Under the Sheet: The Complete Stephen King Encyclopedia,* by Stephen J. Spignesi. Ann Arbor, MI: Popular Culture, Ink., May 1991, cloth, p. 41.

R2. **"Author Finds Haunt in Fleet,"** in *Fleet News* [England] (October 7, 1977).

R3. **"Where the Conscious Meets the Subconscious,"** by Leslie Cannon, in *Cincinnati Enquirer* (April 6, 1978): .

R4. **"King: Sailing Uncharted Seas,"** by Judith P. Harris, in *Houston Chronicle* (October 7, 1979): .

R5. **"Kubrick: Critics Be Damned,"** by John Hofsess, in *Soho News* [New York] (May 28, 1980): .

R6. **"King's *Shining*—Very Bright,"** by Stanley Wiater, in *The Valley Advocate* [Hatfield, MA] (June 25, 1980): .

R7. **"Stricken a la King,"** by Curt Suplee, in *Washington Post* (August 26, 1980): .

R8. **"A Story Fired with Imagination, Protest,"** by John Barkham, in *Philadelphia Inquirer* (August 31, 1980): .

R9. **"The Magnificent Revels of Stephen King,"** by John Podhoretz, in *Wall Street Journal* (September 4, 1980): .

R10. **"Master of Horror Stephen King: The Scariest Man Alive?"** in *Los Angeles Herald Examiner* (September 7, 1980): .

b. *Newsbank Literature Index* 2:8 (1980/1981): G11.

R11. **"Stephen King Thinks It's Fun to 'Get the Reader,'"** by Tim Grobaty, in *Watertown Daily Times* (September 18, 1980): .

R12. **"The Horror Is as Much Political as Biological,"** by Michael J. Bandler, in *Newsday* [Long Island, NY] (October 19, 1980): .

R13. **"Reign of Horror,"** by David Chute, in *Boston Phoenix* (December 9, 1980): .

R14. **"Dark Stars Rising,"** by Stanley Wiater, in *The Valley Advocate* [Hatfield, MA] (April 8, 1981): . See **M113**.

R15. **"Just Your Average Guy,"** by Stanley Wiater, in *The Valley Advocate* [Hatfield, MA] (May 27, 1981). See **M116**.

R16. **"A Bestseller That Foams at the Mouth,"** by Melissa Mia Hall, in *Fort Worth Star-Telegram* (August 23, 1981): .

R17. **"A Few Kind Words about Book Blurbs,"** by Curt Suplee, in *Washington Post* (January 17, 1982): .

R18. **"Una Charla Con el Rey del Terror,"** by Silvia Licha, in *El Nuevo Dia Domingo* [Puerto Rico] (March 14, 1982): 10-11. Spanish-language overview of King and his work.

R19. **"King Keeps Writing and Bucks Keep Rolling In,"** by Helen Dudar, in *Chicago Tribune* (August 22, 1982): .

b. *NewsBank: Literature* 18 (1982/1983): G11.

R20. **"Fitting Author Stephen King to the Charles Dickens' Mold,"** by John Rolfe, in *Maine Sunday Telegram* (September 19, 1982): .

R21. **"King of the Creeps,"** by John Boonstra, in *Hartford Advocate* (October 27, 1982): .

R22. **"King's New Book Advance—$1.00,"** in *Locus* (January, 1983): .

R23. **"Search for Terror Is Worth King's Ransom,"** by Manny Cruz, in *The Daily Californian* [El Cajon, CA] (January, 1983): .

b. *Castle Rock: The Stephen King Newsletter* 1:9 (September, 1985): 3, 7.

R24. **"Hands Across the Border,"** by Donald Chase, in *Los Angeles Times* (March 13, 1983): "Calendar," 20.

R25. **"A Bumper Crop of Killing,"** by Carolyn See, in *Los Angeles Times* (May 8, 1983).

R26. **"G. B. Shaw Has Been the R_x for Rex,"** by Robert Mann, in *Los Angeles Times* 102 (June 9, 1983): "View," 1. References to King in an article on Rex Harrison.

R27. **"A Mania for the Macabre,"** by Eloise de Pina, in *Boston Globe* (July 21, 1983): .

R28. **"Two Terror Titans Team Up,"** by Richard Rothenstein, in *Daily News* [New York] (October 14, 1984):

b. as microfiche: *Newsbank: Literature* 11 (November, 1984): Fiche 45, G10-G11.

R29. **"Dark Doings in King Country,"** by Edward Kline, in *Wall Street Journal* (October 28, 1983): .

R30. **"The (Stephen) King of Books,"** by Barry Boesch, in *Dallas Morning News* (October 29, 1984): .

b. as microfiche: *Newsbank: Literature* 11 (December, 1984): Fiche 58, B2-B3.

R31. **"America's Boogeyman Is Raising Hair Again, Including His Own,"** by Jack Garner, in *Rochester Democrat and Chronicle* [New York] (October 30, 1983): .

b. as microfiche: *Newsbank: Literature* 10 (December, 1983): Fiche 44, E11-E12.

R32. **"Interview with Stephen King and Peter Straub,"** by Stanley Wiater, in *The Valley Advocate* [Hatfield, MA] (October 31, 1984): . On King and Straub at the World Fantasy Convention. See **M121.**

R33. **"David Keith: On Fire Over Stephen King,"** by Bart Mills, in *Los Angeles Times* 102 (November 20, 1983): C39.

R34. **"Stephen King: Horror in a Secular Age,"** by William Robertson, in *Miami Herald* [Florida] (March 25, 1984): . See **M145.**

b. as microfiche: *Newsbank: Literature* 10 (April, 1983): Fiche 74, D10-D13.

R35. **"Stephen King,"** by Clarus Backes, in *Denver Post* (April 1, 1984): .

b. as microfiche: *Newsbank: Literature* 10 (May, 1983): Fiche 83, E4-E5.

R36. **"Morkets Mester"** ["Master of Darkness"], by Tom Engelend, in *Aftenposten* [Norway] (April 14, 1984). Extensive special Easter article on King and his books available in Norway. [Norwegian]

R37. **"The King of Horror,"** by Leo Seligsohn, in *Newsday* [Long Island, NY] (May 6, 1984): . Survey of film adaptations to date.

b. as microfiche: *NewsBank: Film and Television* 10 (June, 1984): Fiche 111, C14-D1.

R38. **"Handshake Seals Film Deal for *Pet Sematary*,"** by Aljean Harmetz, in *New Orleans Times Picayune* (July 4, 1984): E12.

R39. **"Kindred Spirits: Horror Pros Stephen King and Peter Straub Put Their Skills Together for a Best Seller,"** by Michael Kernan, in *Washington Post* 107 (November 27, 1984): C1.

R40. **"A Girl's Dream Comes True in Mansion Fit for Kings,"** by Joan H. Smith, in *Bangor Daily News* (December 8, 1984): .

b. *The Stephen King Companion,* ed. by George Beahm. Kansas City, MO: Andrews & McMeel, September 1989, cloth, p. 76-81.

R41. **"American Notes,"** by C. Hitchens, in *The Times Literary Supplement* No. 4219 (1984): .

R42. **"When Buying Rare Books, Remember: Go for Stephen King, Not Galsworthy,"** by Mark Zieman, in *Wall Street Journal* (January 14, 1985): 19 [E], 15 [W]. Discussion of the growing market in King collectibles.

R43. **"Pseudonym Kept Five King Novels a Mystery,"** by Joan Smith, in *Bangor Daily News* (February 9, 1985): 1-2. Public announcement of King's pen name.

R44. **[Title unknown]** by Stanley Wiater, in *The Springfield Morning Union* [Springfield, MA] (April 2, 1985); . On King at the University of Massachusetts.

R45. **"Stephen King, Shining Through,"** by Stephen Brown, in *Washington Post* (April 9, 1985): C1, C4. Identification of "Richard Bachman" as King's pseudonym.

R46. **"The Works of Richard Bachman,"** by Stephen Brown, in *Washington Post* (April 9, 1985): C4. Plot summaries, publishing histories, and brief criticism of the Bachman novels.

R47. **"King's Too Fast for His Own Good,"** in *Los Angeles Daily News* (April 11, 1985): .

R48. **"Writer King Is the Attraction of His Homogenized Movies,"** in *Altanta Journal-Constitution* [Georgia] (April 21, 1985): .

b. as microfiche: *NewsBank: Film and Television* 11 (May, 1985): Fiche 112, G5.

R49. **"Secretly Hidden Behind the Pen Name of Richard Bachman Was Stephen King,"** by Stephen P. Brown, in *New York Daily News* (May 19, 1985):

b. *Newsbank: Literature* 11 (June, 1985): Fiche 110, A1-A2.

R50. **"Stephen King: A Fire Starter,"** by Lou Gaul, in *Daily Intelligencer/Montgomery County Record* (August 19, 1985): 12. Discussion of King's films, *The Bachman Books,* and the musical version of *Carrie.*

R51. "***Tales from the Darkside*: The Word Processor of the Gods,"** Public Information Sheet. Lexington Broadcasting Services, [1985?]. Publicity packet giving backgrounds to the series and to the adaptation of King's story.

R52. **"Pay Is Better,"** in *Providence Journal* [Rhode Island] (September 3, 1985): .

b. *Seattle Post-Intelligencer* (September 3, 1985): .
c. *Castle Rock: The Stephen King Newsletter* 1:10 (October, 1985): 6.

R53. **"Stephen King's *The Woman in the Room*,"** in *Variety* (September 19, 1985): . Announcement for the Los Angeles PBS premier of Frank Darabont film; cites King.

R54. **"The Titan of Terror: King Trades His Pen for One-Time Director's Chair,"** by Jo Ann Rhetts, in *Escondido Times-Advocate* [California] (October 3, 1985): 30. News profile from the *Overdrive* set in Wilmington NC.

R55. **"Horrifying Duo: King and Romero,"** by Deborah Cauldfield, in *Los Angeles Times* (October 27, 1982): .

b. *Newsbank: Film and Television* 50 (December, 1982): B7.

R56. **"King of Horror Tries His Hand at Moviemaking,"** by Frank Hunter, in *St. Louis Globe Democrat* [Missouri] (November 6/7, 1985):

b. *Newsbank: Film and Television* 53 (December, 1985): F9-F10.

R57. **"Novelist Loves His Nightmares,"** by Jack Matthews, in *Detroit Free Press* (November 12, 1985):

b. *Newsbank: Literature* (December, 1985): Fiche 43: E10-E11.

R58. **"Probing the Mystery of Richard Bachman,"** by R. L. Day, in *Telegraph and News* [Macon, GA] : .

b. *Castle Rock: The Stephen King Newsletter* 2:4 (April, 1986): 3.

R59. **"True Horror Stories Take the Fun out of Fear,"** by Rick Thomas, in *Telegraph and News* [Macon, GA] (1986?): . Editorial comparing the pleasure of reading horror fiction with the fear and frustration of confronting "real" horrors: poisoned Tylenol capsules or bombs in city streets.

b. *Castle Rock: The Stephen King Newsletter* 2:4 (April, 1986): 6.

R60. **"King Klips,"** by Stephanie Leonard, in *Castle Rock: The Stephen King Newsletter* 2:2 (February, 1986): 2. Update on recent publications by and about King.

R61. **"The Candid Careers of Woody and Joan,"** in *USA Today* (April 21, 1986): .

R62. **[Title unknown],** in *USA Today* (May 20, 1986): . Article on King's challenge to Bangor sportswriter Bob Haskell's column criticizing the Boston Red Sox during the 1986; the article ends with a bet on the team's standings by July 1, the loser to eat a chicken dinner on the lawn of the *Bangor Daily News* office in his underwear. King won.

b. *Newark Star Ledger* (May 20, 1986): .

R63. **"'Emperor of Spook' Terrorizes through Book and Film Markets,"** by Steven K. Kent, in *The Universe* [Brigham Young University, Provo, UT] (June 25, 1986): 3.

R64. **"Reiner Directs Comedy About Kids,"** by United Press International, in *Dallas Times Herald* (July 4, 1986): .

b. *Castle Rock: The Stephen King Newsletter*, 2:9 (September, 1986): 1.

R65. **"Midas with the Common Touch: Why Hasn't Success Spoiled Stephen King,"** by Edgar Allen Beem, in *The Maine Times* [Topsham, ME] Vol. 18. no. 40 (July 11, 1986): . See **M188**.

R66. **"Stephen King: On the Dark Side with the Horror Master,"** by Steven Beeber, in [Atlanta, GA]: (July 19, 1986): 15A-16A.

R67. **"Shockmeister: Stephen King Takes a Run at Directing,"** in *The Orange County Register* [Santa Ana, CA] (July 20, 1986): H1, H2.

R68. **[Title unknown],** in *Reporter Dispatch* (July 22, 1986): . On *Return to 'Salem's Lot*.

R69. **[Column],** by Marilyn Beck, in *Bakersfield Californian* (July 22, 1986): .

R70. **"The King of Horror: The Author of *Carrie* and *The Shining* Takes a Stab at Film Directing,"** by Lewis Beale, in *The Press-Enterprise* [Riverside, CA] (July 24, 1986): F-5.

R71. **"King: Doctor of Dementia Has Directorial Debut,"** by Scott Williams, in *The Red and White* [University of Georgia] (July 24, 1986): .

R72. **"Directing New Experience for Stephen King,"** by Tyson Blue, in *Macon Telegraph and News* [Macon, GA] (July 25, 1986): .

R73. **"Mastering Mayhem in the Screen,"** in *San Francisco Chronicle* (July 25, 1986): .

R74. **"King of Horror Finds Directing Unnerving,"** by Calvin Ahlgren, in *San Francisco Chronicle* "Datebook" (July 27, 1986): 25.

R75. **"SK Takes on the Ratings Board,"** in *San Francisco Chronicle* (July 28, 1986): . Discussion of rating for *Maximum Overdrive*.

R76. **"Full Throttle with Stephen King,"** by Burckett, in *New Times*, "Valley News and Arts Journal" [Phoenix, AZ] (July 30-August 5, 1986): 79, 83-84. See **M198**.

R77. **"King of Horror: His Career's in 'Overdrive' as He Directs His First Film,"** by G. Wayne Miller, in *Providence Sunday Journal* [Rhode Island] (August 3, 1986): I1-I3. See **M202**.

R78. **[Title unknown],** in *Chicago Tribune* (August 17, 1986): . Discussion of *Stand By Me*, with an interview with Rob Reiner.

R79. **"Surprising Thing That Makes Stephen King's Blood Run Cold,"** in *Star* (August 19, 1986): .

R80. **"Duck Stumbles But Fly Takes off at Box Office,"** by David T. Friendly, in *Los Angeles Times* (August 28, 1986): Part VI, 7. Reference to *Stand By Me* as summer sleeper.

R81. **"Record Manuscript Price: Stephen King's Notebook Brings $2500 at World SF Con Charity Auction for Wellman,"** by Don Thompson, in *Comics Buyers Guide* (September 26, 1986): .

R82. **"King Fans Wait in Line for More Fright Flicks,"** by Lou Gaul, in *Burlington County Times*, "What's Happening" [New Jersey] (October 3, 1986): 13. References to several King films, King novels, and critical studies about King.

R83. **"Horror's Master Keeps the Blood Boiling,"** by Billy Turner, in *Clarion-Ledger* [Jackson, MO] (October 5, 1986): .

b. as microfiche: *Newsbank Literature Index* 13 (November, 1986): Fiche 37, F1-F2.

R84. **[Title Unknown],** by Bob Haskell, in *The Bangor Daily News* (October 8, 1986): . Article about vandalism at King's home.

R85. **"Filming Begins Locally in Horror Epic,"** by T. J. Tremble, in *Bangor Daily News* [Bangor, ME] (October 29, 1986): 9. Filming of *Creepshow II* episode with Barbara Eden.

R86. **"A Night with the Master of Terror; And We Don't Mean Stephen King,"** by Francine Schwadel, in *The Wall Street Journal* (October 31, 1986): 31 [W], 35 [E]. Article on Edgar Allan Poe.

R87. **"King Giving Pen a Rest,"** by Lou Gaul, in *Burlington County Times* [NJ] "Entertainment" (November 5, 1986): 19.

R88. **"Stephen King,"** by Edward Gross, in *The Island-Ear* (November 11, 1986): 14-15.

R89. **"Some Gift Possibilities...,"** by Lou Gaul, in *Burlington Country Times* "Entertainment" [New Jersey] (December 4, 1986): 19.

R90. **"A King-Size Fairy Tale,"** in *USA Today* (December 8, 1986): . Announcement of *The Eyes of the Dragon*.

R91. **"Everything Old Is New Again at Dodge,"** by Debbie Seaman, in *Adweek* (1986?): .

b. *Castle Rock: The Stephen King Newsletter* 3:2 (January, 1987): 3.

R92. **[Title unknown],** in *The Oregonian* [Portland, OR] (March 15, 1987): . On the King limited editions.

R93. **[Title unknown],** in *Chicago Sun-Times* (March 30, 1987): . Reference to King's inclusion in the *World Book Encyclopedia*.

R94. **"The Horror, The Horror,"** by Stanley Wiater, in *Valley Advocate* [Amherst MA]: .

b. *Castle Rock: The Stephen King Newsletter* 3:3 (March, 1987): 9.

R95. **"Who Knows What Lurks on Your Bookshelves; It Could Be Valuable,"** by Julie Penn, in *Las Vegas Sun* (1987): .

b. *Castle Rock: The Stephen King Newsletter* 3:3 (March, 1987): 3.

R96. **"Still the Horror King,"** by Lou Gaul, in *Burlington County Times* "Entertainment" [NewJersey] (April 23, 1987): 23.

R97. **"In Praise of Horror—And Those Who Frighten Us,"** by Lynn Beck, in *Las Vegas Sun* (1987): .

b. *Castle Rock: The Stephen King Newsletter* 3:4 (April/May, 1987): 10.

R98. **"Stephen King's No. 1 Fans,"** by David Streitfield, in *Washington Post* "Style" (May 8, 1987): .

b. *Castle Rock: The Stephen King Newsletter* 3:8 (August, 1987): 1, 4.

R99. **"Kubrick's 'Shining' Secret,"** by Bill Blakemore, in *Washington Post* (July 12, 1987): .

R100. **[Title Unknown],** in *Los Angeles Times* (August 19, 1987): . On celebrity doodles, including one by King.

R101. **"King's 'Other' Publishers Well-Kept Collectors' Secret,"** by Garrett Condon, in *Hartford Courant* [Connecticut] (August 28, 1987): .

b. as microfiche: *NewsBank Names in the News* 9 (September, 1987): Fiche 325, F10-F11.

c. *Castle Rock: The Stephen King Newsletter* 3:12/4:1 (December, 1987-January 1988): 9, 12.

R102. **"Stephen King, Come On Down,"** in *The Gwinnet Daily News* (September, 1987): .

R103. **"To This Dedicated Fan, King Is a Prince,"** in *Dallas Times Herald* (1987): .

b. *Castle Rock: The Stephen King Newsletter* 3:12/4:1 (December, 1987-January, 1988): 11.

R104. **"Stephen King, Author, Dons a Publisher's Hat,"** by Edwin McDowell, in *New York Times* 137 (January 23, 1988): 13 [N], 11 [L]. On the production of Robertson's *The Ideal, Genuine Man* by King's Philtrum Press.

R105. **[Column],** by John Blades in *Chicago Tribune* (January 24, 1988): Sect. 14, 3.

R106. **"A Real Life Firestarter,"** in *Examiner* (January 26, 1988): . Reference to King's novel as lead-in for article.

R107. **"If You're Scared Silly, Then Stephen King Is Happy,"** by Julie Washington, in *Cleveland Plain Dealer* [Ohio] (January 31, 1988): . Report on the King/Robertson book signing. See **M226**.

b. *Castle Rock: The Stephen King Newsletter* 4:4 (April, 1988): 11.

R108. **[Title unknown],** in *Houston Chronicle* (January, 1988): .

R109. **"King Turns Publisher with 'Ideal' Book,"** by Michael Spies, in *Houston Chronicle* (February 3, 1988): . Discussion of Philtrum Press's edition of Don Robertson's *Ideal, Genuine Man*.

b. as microfiche: *Newsbank Literature* 15 (March, 1988): Fiche 31, A6-A7.

R110. **"Stephen King's Novel 'Christine' Focus of Suit Alleging Literary Piracy,"** by Jeanne Curran, in *Bangor Daily News* (February 18, 1988): . Discussion of suit brought by Edward J. Glanzmann of Pennsylvania, claiming that King and Columbia Pictures pirated an idea submitted in 1974 about an indestructible Corvette that is used for murder. The articles notes that this is Glanzmann's second suit, the first (1987) having been dismissed.

b. as microfiche: *Newsbank Literature* 15 (March, 1988): Fiche 28, B7.

R111. **"Cedar Falls Students Tell Why They Like Stephen King,"** by Jackie Young, Don Haugh, and Jamie Dietsch, in *The Courier* [Waterloo, Iowa]: . Two award-winning student essays responding to King's influence on young readers.

b. *Castle Rock: The Stephen King Newsletter* 4:2 (February, 1988): 6.

R112. **[Column]**, by Cynthia Vann, in *Chicago Tribune* (March 30, 1988): Sect. 5, 1. On the pressures of King's public life.

R113. **"Stephen King Is Basis for Class,"** by Daniel Miller, in *Amherst Bulletin* [MA] (1988): . Overview of Stanley Wiater's class, "The Dark Visions of Stephen King," for the University of Massachusetts Division of Continuing Education.

b. *Castle Rock: The Stephen King Newsletter* 4:8 (April, 1988): 6.

R114. **[Title unknown]**, in *Columbus Dispatch* (May 15, 1988): . King's participation in a PBS radio panel discussing how various writers would tackle writing a sequel to *Gone with the Wind*.

R115. **"Stephen King First Editions are Hot Stuff,"** by Wayne Curtis, in *Wall Street Journal* (May 24, 1988): 36 [Eastern], 32 [Western].

R116. **"Librarians in Stephen King's Home State of Maine Say...,"** by Kim Clark, in *Wall Street Journal* (August 25, 1988): 19. Disappearance of King's books from New England libraries.

R117. **[Title unknown]**, in *Boston Globe* (September 1, 1988): . Article on banning books; references to King's novels.

R118. **[Title unknown]**, in *Bangor Daily News* [Bangor, ME] (September 2, 1988): . Announcement that WZON is going commercial-free.

R119. **[Title unknown]**, in *Bangor Daily News* [Bangor, ME] (September 19, 1988): . King 23rd in *Forbes'* list of America's wealthiest entertainers.

R120. **"On Location: Maine's Not Profiting from Hollywood As Much As It Might,"** by Robert McKibben, in *Maine Times* [Topsham, ME] (September 23, 1988): .

b. as microfiche: *NewsBank: Film and Television* 15 (October, 1988): Fiche 159, D11-D13.

R121. **"Pet Sematary: Movie-making Next Door Can Really Change Scenes,"** by Anne Hyde Degan, in *Maine Sunday Telegram* [Portland, ME] (October 2, 1988): 10E-11E, 13E.

b. as microfiche: *NewsBank: Film and Television* 15 (October, 1988): Fiche 159, D8-D10.
c. *Castle Rock: The Stephen King Newsletter* 4:12 (December, 1988): 6, 7.

R122. **"'Pet Sematary' Continues King Tradition,"** by Greg Gadberry, in *Maine Sunday Telegram* [Portland, ME] (October 2, 1988): 11E.

R123. **"A Bloody Mary and a Monster Steak with Stephen King: Over Dinner, the Writer Confesses His Tricks and Treats,"** by Bryan Miller, in *New York Times* 138 (October 26, 1988): 17 [N].

b. as: "Eating Out with Stephen King: Writer Eats Steak Before It Eats Him," by Bryan Miller. *New York Times* [L] (October 26, 1988): C1 [L].

R124. **"The Sightings: Have You Seen Stephen King Today,"** by Cynthia Vann, in *Hartford Courant* (January 8, 1989): .

R125. **"A Monster of a Deal for Stephen King,"** by Edwin McDowell, in *The New York Times*, "Living Arts Pages" Vol. 138 (January 11, 1989): B3 [National edition], C22 [Late edition].

R126. **[Title unknown],** *Los Angeles Herald Examiner* (January 30, 1989): . Announcement of four-book sale.

R127. **"The Stephen King Phenomenon,"** by Josh Moehling, in *The Laird's Horn* [MacArthur High School, Lawton, OK] 1:4 (January, 1989): 1, 4. Results of telephone interview with Michael R. Collings; King's influence on student readers.

R128. **[Title unknown],** by David Streitfeld, in *Washington Post Book World* (February 24, 1989): 15.

R129. **"World Premier of 'Rage' Hits Community March 30,"** in *PR Newswire* (March 8, 1989).

R130. **"Book Notes,"** in *New York Times* (March 22, 1989): III, 25. Announcement of Stephen King library to be made available through the Book-of-the-Month Club, 1990.

R131. **[Title unknown],** in *Bangor Daily News* [Bangor, ME] (April 11, 1989): . Coverage of the premier of *Pet Sematary* film.

R132. **"Dress Rehearsal for Death,"** in *New York Daily News* (April 17, 1989): . On *Pet Sematary* film.

R133. **"On Stage,"** in *New York Times* (May 5, 1989): . Musical *Carrie* to become an album.

R134. **"Kentucky Hostage Crisis Sounded Familiar to King,"** by Douglas Kesseli, in *Bangor Daily News* [Bangor, ME] (September 20, 1989): . Notes connections between King's *Rage* and a McKee, Kentucky, student named Dustin Pierce, who held eleven students hostage for eght hours.

b. as microfiche: *Newsbank Literature* 16 (November, 1989): Fiche 112, F11.

c. as microfiche: *NewsBank: Names in the News* 11 (October, 1989): Fiche 290, F6.

R135. **"King's Tale of Mystery—And That's Just His Contract,"** by Charles Kipps, in *Variety* 337:8 (November 29, 1989): 3.

b. *Mystery Scene* No. 24 (January, 1990): 81.

R136. **"Odd, Isn't It, That History's Most Developed Society Has a Deep Craving for Gore,"** by George F. Will, in *Philadelphia Inquirer* (December 11, 1989): .

R137. **"DSL Deals King Vid Series to Good Times, HG,"** by Tom Bierbaum, in *Variety* 338:4 (January 31, 1990): 59. Sale of King videos by DSL Entertainment to Good Times Home Video and Harmony Gold.

R138. **"King Horrifies His Audience: Author Jams Dark City Hall,"** in *Portland Press Herald* [Maine] March 7, 1990): .

b. as microfiche: *NewsBank: Literature* 17 (April, 1990): Fiche 38, D2. King's appearance at the Portland Public Library Centennial celebration.

R139. **"Doubleday Pulls Out All the Stops for Reissue of Stephen King Novel,"** *The Wall Street Journal* (May 8, 1990): B7.

R140. **"'Misery's' Company Loves a Good Time: Filming the Stephen King Thriller is Serious Business with Time Out for a Laugh,"** by Betsy Sharkey, in *The New York Times* 139 (June 17, 1990): H13.

R141. **"Horror Writer Revisits State in 'Misery,'"** by Mark Graham, in *Rocky Mountain News* [Denver, CO] (November 29, 1990): .

b. as microfiche: *NewsBank: Film and Television* 18 (January, 1991): Fiche 5, E5.

S.

SECONDARY SOURCES

ARTICLES IN PROFESSIONAL AND TRADE JOURNALS

S1. **"Stephen King,"** by John F. Baker, in *Publishers Weekly* (January 17, 1977): .

S2. **"The Consolations of Terror,"** by Roz Kaveney, in *Books & Bookmen* (November, 1981): .

S3. **"Stephen King Target of $200,000 Promotion at NAL,"** by Stella Dong, in *Publishers Weekly* 2:21 (June 11, 1982): 43-44.

S4. **"Collecting the Works of Stephen King,"** by Peter Schneider, in *AB Bookman's Weekly* (October 24, 1983): 2709-2711.

S5. **"Science Fiction and Fantasy: An Overview,"** by Roy A. Squires, in *AB Bookman's Weekly* (October 24, 1983): 2662-2698. Summary of Science Fiction/Fantasy collecting, with references to King.

S6. **"Stephen King Tells Library Audience: 'I'm Warped,'"** in *American Libraries* 14 (July-August, 1983): 489. On King's appearance at the Billerica, MA, library in 1983.

S7. **"King-Straub on Spielberg's Plate,"** in *Publishers Weekly* (January 27, 1984): .

S8. **"King as Partner,"** in *Publishers Weekly* (January 29, 1984): .

S9. **"502,000 Copies of *Talisman* Shipped in One Day,"** by Madalynne Reuter, in *Publishers Weekly* (October 26, 1984): 25-26. Details of Viking's unprecedented handling of the book.

S10. **"*The Talisman* and the Clubs,"** by Paul S. Nathan, in *Publishers Weekly* (November 23, 1984): 28. On King's decision not to sell the novel to book clubs; the role of clubs in publishing.

S11. **"Trade News: Bachman Revealed to be Stephen King Alias,"** by Joann Davis, in *Publishers Weekly* 2:27 (March 22, 1985): 43. Publishing data for *Thinner*.

S12. **"The Man Who Wouldn't Be King,"** by Leonore Fleischer, in *Publishers Weekly* (August 2, 1985): . Reports that King is not "Aaron Wolfe."

S13. **"Helping Hand,"** by Paul S. Nathan, in *Publishers Weekly* (August 30, 1985): 403. On King's aid in getting Michael Kimball's *Firewater Pond* published.

S14. **"Big Bucks,"** by Leonore Fleischer, in *Publishers Weekly,* (September 6, 1985): 69. Response to King's $10 million advance for two novels.

S15. **"Early Stephen King,"** by Daniel F. McGrath, in *Publishers Weekly* (January 17, 1986): 10. Discussion of collectible King first editions.

S16. **"The Unknown King,"** by Chuck Miller, in *West Coast Review of Books* 13:3 (1986): . On rare King books.

S17. **"Talk of the Trade,"** by Leonore Fleischer, in *Publishers Weekly* (October 17, 1986): 65. Announcement that King's Philtrum Press will publish Don Robertson's *The Genuine, Ideal Man*.

S18. **"If You Like Stephen King—Then You'd Like—,"** in *The Unabashed Librarian* No. 65 (1987): 3.

S19. **"Talk of the Trade,"** by Leonore Fleischer, in *Publishers Weekly* (January 22, 1988): . Reference to King's announced break in writing schedule.

S20. **"Stephen King Taped Readings Coming from NAL,"** in *Publishers Weekly* 2:33 (February 19, 1988): 55-56.

S21. **"Signet Binds *Misery* with Unique Double Cover,"** in *Publishers Weekly* 2:33 (May 6, 1988): 82.

S22. **"If You Like the Chills of Stephen King, Try These Authors—,"** in *The Unabashed Librarian* No. 75 (1990): 3.

S23. **"King of Horror: His Books Make Millions, But the Prolific Author Would Prefer to Be Recognized as Having Changed a Genre,"** by Bill Goldstein, in *Publishers Weekly*, 238:4 (January 24, 1991): 6.

T.

SECONDARY SOURCES

SELECTED REVIEWS OF KING WORKS

For more complete listings of reviews, see the "Secondary Sources and Reviews" sections under entries for individual books, novels, and stories.

T1. **"Alumnus Publishes Symbolic Novel, Shows Promise,"** by Burton Hatlen, in *The Maine Campus* [University of Maine, Orono] (April 12, 1974): .

T2. **[Title unknown],** by Elizabeth Hall, in *Psychology Today* 9 (September, 1975): 76. On *Carrie*.

b. excerpted in: *Contemporary Literary Criticism, Volume 12, Young Adult Literature,* edited by Dedria Bryfonski. Detroit: Gale Research Company, 1980, cloth, p. 309.

T3. **"*'Salem's Lot* Critiques American Civilization,"** by Burton Hatlen, in *The Maine Campus* [University of Maine, Orono] (December 12, 1975):.

T4. **"Carrie and Sally and Leatherface Among the Film Buffs,"** by Roger Greenspun, in *Film Comment* 13, no. 1 (January/February, 1977): 16.

T5. **"Ten Ways to Write a Gothic,"** by Jack Sullivan, in *New York Times Book Review* (February 20, 1977): 8.

b. excerpted in: *Contemporary Literary Criticism, Volume 12, Young Adult Literature,* edited by Dedria Bryfonski. Detroit: Gale Research Company, 1980, cloth, p. 309-310.

T6. **"Something Nasty in the Tub,"** by Richard R. Lingeman, in *New York Times* (March 1, 1977): 35.

T7. **"Steve King's Third Novel Shines On,"** by Burton Hatlen, in *The Maine Campus* [University of Maine, Orono] (April 1, 1977): .

T8. **"Novels and Stories,"** by Michael Mewshaw, in *New York Times Book Review* (March 26, 1978): 13, 23. On *Night Shift*.

b. excerpted in: *Contemporary Literary Criticism, Volume 12, Young Adult Literature,* edited by Dedria Bryfonski. Detroit: Gale Research Company, 1980, cloth, p. 310.

T9. **[Title Unknown]**, by Bruce Kawin, in *Take One* (May, 1978): 7. Review of *The Fury*; references to Alfred Hitchcock's influence in Brian DePalma's *Carrie*.

T10. **"The Supernatural Con Man vs. the Hymn-Singing Mother,"** by Linda B. Osbourne, in *Washington Post* (November 23, 1978): .

T11. **"No Sympathy for the Devil,"** by Anne Collins, in *Maclean's Magazine* 91 (December 18, 1978): 51.

b. excerpted in: *Contemporary Literature Criticism, Volume 12, Young Adult Literature,* edited by Dedria Bryfonski. Detroit: Gale Research Company, 1980, cloth, p. 311.

T12. **"Genre Items,"** by Martin Levin, in *New York Times Book Review* (February 4, 1979): 15. Negative review of *The Stand* as disgusting and occult.

T13. **"A Stunning Storyteller,"** by Jeff Frane, in *Seattle Times Magazine* (February 4, 1979): .

T14. **"Steve King's *The Stand*,"** by Burton Hatlen, in *Kennebec* (April, 1979): .

T15. **"Gift of Sight: Visions from a Nether World,"** by Dick Roraback, in *Los Angeles Times Book Review* (August 26, 1979): .

T16. **"Vision of the Holocaust,"** by Joseph McLellan, in *Washington Post* (August 30, 1979): .

T17. **"Behind the Best Sellers: Stephen King,"** by Carol Lawson, in *New York Times Book Review* (September 23, 1979): 42. Written when *The Dead Zone* reached the bestseller lists, the piece provides background to King's career.

T18. **"Stanley Kubrick's Horror Show,"** by Jack Kroll, in *Newsweek* 95:21 (May 26, 1980): 96-99.

T19. **"On Books: The Best of 1979,"** by Charles N. Brown, in *Isaac Asimov's Science Fiction Magazine* 7 (May, 1980): 17. Lists *The Dead Zone* as among the best novels of 1979.

T20. **"Red Herrings and Refusals,"** by Richard Schickel, in *Time* 115:22 (June 2, 1980): 69. On *The Shining* film: Kubrick's *The Shining* is made from King's "pulpy haunted house novel." The film uses "false clues and red herrings" because Kubrick rejects the supernatural explanations at the heart of the novel.

T21. **"The Dulling,"** by Stanley Kaufman, in *New Republic* 182:24 (June 14, 1980): 26-27.

T22. **"Kubrick Goes Gothic,"** by Harlan Kennedy, in *American Film* 5:8 (June, 1980): 49.

T23. **"Stephen King Strikes Again,"** by Bill Granger, in *Chicago Tribune Book World* (August 24, 1980): .

T24. **"Hot Moppet,"** by Michael Demarest, in *Time* 116 (September 15, 1980): K12, K18. Review of *Firestarter*.

T25. **"King's *Firestarter*: It's Hot Stuff, All Right,"** by Algis Budrys, in *Chicago Sun-Times* (September 21, 1980): .

T26. **"American Thrillers: *Firestarter, Brass Diamonds, Brain 2000*,"** by Paul Stuewe, in *Quill and Quire* 46 (October, 1980): p. 40-41.

b. excerpted in: *Contemporary Literary Criticism, Volume 26,* edited by Jean C. Stine. Detroit: Gale Research Company, 1983, cloth, p.237.

T27. **"*Dark Forces* Anthology of Horror,"** by Mark Graham, in *Rocky Mountain News* (October 5, 1980): 32. On "The Mist."

T28. **"Stephen King Gets Eminent,"** by Walter Kendrick, in *The Village Voice* 26:18 (April 29-May 5, 1981): p. 45. Extremely negative review of *Danse Macabre*.

b. excerpted in: *Contemporary Literary Criticism, Volume 37,* edited by Daniel G. Marowski. Detroit: Gale Research Company, 1986, cloth, p. 197-198.

T29. **"Stephen King's Car: Repossessed by the Devil,"** by Algis Budrys, in *Chicago Sun-Times* (May 3, 1981): .

T30. **"The Wolf-Mask of Horror, As Lifted by Stephen King,"** by Algis Budrys, in *Chicago Sun-Times* (May 3, 1981): .

T31. **"Scare Tactics,"** by Michelle Slung, in *New York Times Book Review* 86 (May 10, 1981): 15, 27. On *Danse Macabre*.

b. excerpted in: *Contemporary Literary Criticism, Volume 37,* edited by Daniel G. Marowski. Detroit: Gale Research Company, 1986, cloth, p. 198-199.

T32. **"A Shabby Dog Story from Stephen King,"** by L. J. Davis, in *Chicago Tribune Book World* (August 16, 1981): .

T33. **"Mad Dogs...and Englishmen,"** by Michael Bishop, in *Washington Post Book World* 11 (August 23, 1981): 1-2.

b. as: "The Saint Bernard That Becomes an Engine of Madness and Death," in *San Francisco Chronicle Review* (September 20, 1981): .

c. excerpted in: *Contemporary Literary Criticism, Volume 26,* edited by Jean C. Stine. Detroit: Gale Research Company, 1983, cloth, p. 238-239.

T34. **"Beware of the Dog,"** by Jean Strouse, in *Newsweek* 98 (August 31, 1981): 64. Review of *Cujo*.

T35. **"A Doggy New Novel from Stephen King,"** by Algis Budrys, in *Chicago Sun-Times Book Week* (September 6, 1981): .

T36. **"King's Latest a Shaggy Rabid Dog Story,"** by Thomas Thompson, in *Los Angeles Times* (September 6, 1981): .

b. as: "*Cujo*: Tale About a Mad Dog Ought to Be Put to Sleep," in *Baltimore News American* (September 6, 1981): .

T37. **"King Gives Second-Best Horror Effort in *Cujo*,"** by David Chute, in *Los Angeles Herald Examiner* (September 9, 1981): .

T38. **"King's *Cujo*: 'Nope, Nothing Wrong Here,'"** by Douglas E. Winter, in *Fantasy Newsletter* (November, 1981): 9-11.

b. incorporated into: *Stephen King*. STARMONT READER'S GUIDE, No. 16. Mercer Island, WA: Starmont House, October 1982, cloth/paper, p. 90-96. See **I3**.

T39. **"*Dark Tower* Shows King in Different Light,"** by Mark Graham, in *Rocky Mountain News* (August 1, 1982): . On *The Dark Tower: The Gunslinger*.

T40. **"Stephen King's Quartet,"** by Thomas Gifford, in *Washington Post Book World* 12 (August 22, 1982): 1-2. Generally positive review of *Different Seasons'* "elemental story values, broad strokes."

b. excerpted in *Contemporary Literary Criticism, Volume 26*, edited by Jean C. Stine. Detroit: Gale Research Company, 1983, cloth, p. 240-241.

T41. **"Stephen King: Making Burgers with the Best,"** by Kenneth Atchity, in *Los Angeles Times Book Review* (August 29, 1982): 7.

b. excerpted in: *Contemporary Literary Criticism Volume 26*, edited by Jean C. Stine. Detroit: Gale Research Company, 1983, cloth, p. 241.

T42. **"Horror Writer's Holiday,"** by Alan Cheuse, in *New York Times Book Review* (August 29, 1982): 10, 17. [Review of *Different Seasons*.]

b. excerpted in: *Contemporary Literary Criticism, Volume 26,* edited by Jean C. Stine. Detroit: Gale Research Company, 1983, cloth, p. 242.

T43. **"*Locus* Looks at More Books,"** by Jeff Frane, in *Locus* (August, 1982): .

T44. **"Stephen King Departs from Horror,"** by Desmond Ryan, in *Cleveland Plain Dealer* (September 26, 1982): .

T45. **"Behind the Bestsellers: Stephen King,"** by Edwin McDowell, in *New York Times Book Review* (September 27, 1981): 40. Overview of King's career following *Cujo*'s appearance on the *New York Times* bestsellers list.

T46. **"Jolly Contempt,"** by Richard Corliss, in *Time* 120:21 (November 22, 1982): 108-110. On *Creepshow*.

b. excerpted in: *Contemporary Literary Criticism, Volume 26,* edited by Jean C. Stine. Detroit: Gale Research Company, 1983, cloth, p. 243.

T47. **"The Roaches Did It,"** by David Ansen, in *Newsweek* 100:21 (November 22, 1982): 118A. On *Creepshow*.

b. excerpted in *Contemporary Literary Criticism, Volume 26,* edited by Jean C. Stine. Detroit: Gale Research Company, 1983, cloth, p. 243.

T48. **"Stephen King's *Creepshow*: The Aesthetics of Gross-Out,"** by Michael Sragow, in *Rolling Stone* 383 (November 25, 1982): 48, 54. Negative review of film; the film's importance is as a cultural indicator.

b. excerpted in: *Contemporary Literary Criticism, Volume 26,* edited by Jean C. Stine. Detroit: Gale Research Company, 1983, cloth, p. 243-4.

T49. **"Fantasy Writers Focus of Study,"** by Steve Eng, in *The Tennessean Sunday Bookcase* (January 23, 1983): . Review of Underwood and Miller's *Fear Itself,* and of Winter's *Stephen King*.

T50. ***"The Dark Tower: The Gunslinger,"*** by Larry D. Woods, in *Science Fiction & Fantasy Book Review* [Science Fiction Research Association] (January/February, 1983): 28-29. *The Dark Tower* is brilliant but incomplete, "storytelling with a vengeance."

T51. **"Different Seasons,"** by Glenn Reed, in *Science Fiction & Fantasy Book Review* [Science Fiction Research Association] (January/February, 1983): 29-30.

T52. **"Books,"** by Algis Budrys, in *The Magazine of Fantasy & Science Fiction* (February, 1983): .

T53. **"Different Writers on *Different Seasons*,"** by Charles L. Grant, David Morrell, Alan Ryan, and Douglas E. Winter, in *Fantasy Newsletter* (February, 1983): .

b. in: *Shadowings: The Reader's Guide to Horror Fiction, 1981-1982,* edited by Douglas E. Winter. STARMONT STUDIES IN LITERARY CRITICISM, No. 1. Mercer Island, WA: Starmont House, 1983, cloth/paper, p. 38-43.

T54. **"Standing by Jericho,"** by Steve Gallagher, in *Science Fiction Review* 12:1 (February, 1983): 35-36. On *The Long Walk* before King acknowledged authorship.

b. excerpted in: *Contemporary Literary Criticism, Volume 37,* edited by Daniel G. Marowski. Detroit: Gale Research Company, 1986, cloth, p. 201.

T55. **"Stephen King's *Christine*: ...Where Innocence Peels Away Like Burnt Rubber and Death Rides Shotgun,"** by Douglas E. Winter, in *Fantasy Newsletter* (February, 1983): .

T56. **"*Christine* Is Demon for Punishment,"** by Dave Barry, in *Philadelphia Inquirer* (March 27, 1983): .

T57. **"The Other Woman Was a Car,"** by Phillipe Van Rjndt, in *New York Times Book Review* 88 (April 3, 1983): 12. Review of *Christine*: King's "clear, precise style" leads from the known and understandable to the unknown and terrifying.

T58. **"King Drives at Horror with Less-Than-Usual Fury,"** by Peter Gorner, in *Chicago Tribune* (April 6, 1983): .

T59. **"Horror Master Tells Motor-Vating Tale,"** by Randy Chandler, in *Atlanta Journal-Constitution* (April 17, 1983): .

T60. **"*Locus* Looks at More Books,"** by Dan Chow, in *Locus* (April, 1983): .

T61. **"My Dribble Cup Runneth Over,"** by D. J. Hogan, in *Cinefantastique* 13:4 (April/May, 1983): 56. On *Creepshow* film and videocassette.

T62. **"King of High-School Horror,"** by Gene Lyons, in *Newsweek* 101 (May 2, 1983): 76.

T63. **"The Future in Words,"** by Edward Bryant, in *Mile High Futures* (May, 1983; January, 1984): 18-20. On *Pet Sematary* and the Land of Enchantment edition of *Cycle of the Werewolf*.

T64. **"High Suspense,"** by Marilyn Stasio, in *Penthouse* (July, 1983): 56. Review of *Christine*: the first half of the novel shows King being self-indulgent, but the second half brilliantly unites his themes and images.

T65. **"*Christine*,"** by Peter J. Pautz, in *Science Fiction & Fantasy Book Review* [Science Fiction Research Association] 16 (July-August, 1983): 35. The novel is flawed but worth reading; King takes chances and creates a sense of horror embedded in reality.

T66. **[Title unknown],** by Frank Ward, in *Library Journal* 108 (October 15, 1983): 1973. On *Pet Sematary*: while the action is incrementally suspenseful and effective, characters remain too distant, never engaging the readers' empathy.

T67. **"Something Lurks in Ludlow,"** by Anne Gottlieb, in *New York Times Book Review* 88 (November 6, 1983): p. 15. On *Pet Sematary*.

b. excerpted in: *Contemporary Literary Criticism, Volume 37,* edited by Daniel G. Marowski. Detroit: Gale Research Company, 1986, cloth, p. 203.

T68. **[Title unknown],** by Douglas E. Winter, in *Washington Post Book World* 13 (November 13, 1983): 1. On *Pet Sematary*.

b. excerpted in: *Contemporary Literary Criticism, Volume 37,* edited by Daniel G. Marowski. Detroit: Gale Research Company, 1986, cloth, p. 203-204.

T69. **"Macabre Master,"** by Mark Graham, in *Rocky Mountain News* [Denver, CO] (December 4, 1983): 38M. On *Pet Sematary* and limited edition *Cycle of the Werewolf*.

T70. **"*Pet Sematary*: Opposing Views...Finest Horror Ever Written,"** by Michael A. Morrison, in *Fantasy Review* 65 (January, 1984): 49.

T71. **"*Pet Sematary*: Opposing Views...Flawed, Unsatisfying,"** by Michael E. Stamm, in *Fantasy Review* 64 (January, 1984): 49.

T72. **"Pet Sematary,"** by Mary Helene Rosenbaum, in *Christian Century* 101 (March 21-28, 1984): 316. Review concentrating on religious motifs.

T73. **"Good News for Horror Buffs,"** by Mark Graham, in *Rocky Mountain News* [Denver, CO] (May 11, 1984): 15W. On Douglas E. Winter's *Shadowings*.

T74. **"Firestarter,"** by Ralph Novak, in *People Weekly* (May 28, 1984): 12. On the film: it never "quite catches fire."

T75. **"Footsteps in the Dark,"** by Bill Munster, in *Footsteps IV* (Summer, 1984): 76-79. On *'Salem's Lot* and *Firestarter*.

T76. **"Boo! Ha-Ha, You Sap!"** by Ken Tucker, in *The Village Voice* 29:43 (October 23, 1984): 53. Negative review of *the Talisman*.

b. excerpted in: *Contemporary Literary Criticism, Volume 37,* edited by Daniel G. Marowski. *Detroit:* Gale Research Company, 1986, cloth, p. 205.

T77. **"Fit for a King,"** by Mark Graham, in *Rocky Mountain News* [Denver, CO] (December 23, 1984): 26M. On *Thinner*; incorporates reasons for believing the novel is by King.

T78. **"The Titans of Terror,"** by Charles Leerhsen, in *Newsweek* (December 24, 1984): 61-62. On *The Talisman,* which reads "like a novelization of a film."

T79. "*Stephen King: The Art of Darkness*" [by Douglas E. Winter], in *Fantasy Mongers* 13 (Winter 1984/1985): 5.

T80. **"Vigorous, Messy, Untidy—And Compulsively Readable,"** by Joe Sanders, in *Fantasy Review* 76 (February, 1985): 17-18. On *The Talisman*.

T81. **"'Bachman' Indeed Reads Like Stephen King,"** by Neil Barron, in *Fantasy Review* 77 (March, 1985): 15. On *Thinner*.

T82. **"King Gets Compatible Critic,"** by Keith Neilson, in *Fantasy Review* 77 (March, 1985): 15-16. On Douglas E. Winter's *Stephen King: The Art of Darkness*.

T83. **"The King of Bump in the Night,"** by Will Cortland, in *Dodge Adventurer* (Spring, 1985): 17-18. Review of King's writings through *The Talisman*.

b. as: "The Adventurer Looks at Stephen King," in *Castle Rock: The Stephen King Newsletter* 1:6 (June, 1985): 11.

T84. **"Horrormonger Stephen King on Screen,"** by Julie Salamon, in *Wall Street Journal* (April 25, 1985): 34. Review of *Cat's Eye*: the films elicits "approving howls of laughter" but not of horror.

T85. **"Another Pseudonymous King Book?"** by "Helen Purcell" [i.e., Charles Platt], in *Fantasy Review* 78 (April, 1985): 31-32. Review of *Love Lessons*, by "John Wilson"—purportedly by King. The review identifies this erotic novel published in 1974 as an early King item to be reprinted in a limited edition by Pinetree Press. The novel, the pseudonym, and the press were inventions of Neil Barron and Charles Platt; the review was inserted into *Fantasy Review* as a means of testing its readership, but instead drew heavy fire from King and others, leading to retractions by Barron and *Fantasy Review*.

T86. **"King Recycles a Chilling Tale,"** by Jeanne Klein, in *Seattle Post-Intelligencer* (May 6, 1985): .

T87. **"Beach Blanket Books: *Skeleton Crew*,"** by Peter Nicholls, in *Washington Post Book World* (June 16, 1985): 1, 13.

b. excerpted in: *Contemporary Literary Criticism, Volume 37,* edited by Daniel G. Marowski. Detroit: Gale Research Company, 1986, cloth, p. 206-207.

T88. **"Multiple Shivers from a Champion of the Game,"** by Chuck Moss, in *The Detroit News* (June 16, 1985): p. 2K.

b. excerpted in: *Contemporary Literary Criticism, Volume 37,* edited by Daniel G. Marowski. Detroit: Gale Research Company, 1986, cloth, p. 207-208.

T89. **"King Collection Worth Waiting For,"** by Michael R. Collings, in *Fantasy Review* 80 (June, 1985): 22.

T90. **"Privately Printed Fantasy King's Best,"** by Charles de Lint, in *Fantasy Review* 81 (July, 1985): 19. On *The Eyes of the Dragon* (Philtrum edition).

T91. **"Beyond Stephen King: Read Them Only If You Dare,"** by Marijo Duncan, in *Voice of Youth Advocates* 8 (August,1985): 181.

T92. **[Title unknown].** Review of *Tales by Moonlight*, edited by Jessica Amanda Salmonson; Introduction by King, in *Fangoria* (August 1985): .

T93. **"Revealing Work Examines King-Bachman Connection,"** by Mark Graham, in *Rocky Mountain News* (September 15, 1985): 33M. Review of Collings's *Stephen King as Richard Bachman*.

T94. **"Hey, Film Fans! It's Time to Hit Books Again,"** by Lou Gaul, in *Burlington County Times* [New Jersey] (November 28, 1985): B1, B4. Reviews of *Discovering Stephen King*, *Stephen King as Richard Bachman, Discovering Modern Horror Fiction*, *The Shorter works of Stephen King*, and *The Bachman Books*.

T95. **"*Discovering Modern Horror*,"** by Greg W. Meyers, in *Comics Buyers Guide* (December 27, 1985): .

T96. **"*The Shorter Works of Stephen King*, "** by Greg W. Meyers, in *Comics Buyers Guide* (December 27, 1985): .

T97. **"*Stephen King as Richard Bachman*, "** by Greg W. Meyers, in *Comics Buyers Guide* (December 27, 1985): .

T98. **"Considered Interviews,"** by Michael R. Collings, in *Fantasy Review* 86 (December, 1985): 25. On Winter's *Faces of Fear*.

T99. **"Nightmare Library,"** by David Sherman, in *Fangoria* 44 (1985): 39-40. Review of *The Talisman*: if not the best, at least the most important horror novel of the year, a "serious, highly entertaining book."

T100. **"Review of *Faces of Fear: Encounters with the Creators of Modern Horror*"** [by Winter], by Tyson Blue, in *Castle Rock: The Stephen King Newsletter* 2:2, (February, 1986): 2.

T101. **"Strange Invaders: An Essay-Review,"** by Gary K. Wolfe, in *Modern Fiction Studies* 32:1 (Spring 1986): 133-151. Review-essay on the current state of horror-criticism, with emphasis on works about King.

T102. **"Horror Delightfully Discussed,"** by J. T. Moore, in *Fantasy Review* 90 (April, 1986): 32. On Schweitzer's *Discovering Hodern Horror Fiction I*.

T103. **"King Congeries,"** by Glenn Reed, in *Fantasy Review* 91 (May, 1986): 29. On Schweitzer's *Discovering Stephen King*.

T104. **"King Study Seems Incomplete,"** by Joe Sanders, in *Fantasy Review* 91 (May, 1986): 28. On Collings's *The Many Facets of Stephen King*.

T105. **"A Necessity for King Scholars,"** by Karl D. Kober, in *Fantasy Review* 91 (May, 1986): 29. On Collings and Engebretson's *The Shorter Works of Stephen King*.

T106. **"Review: *Stephen King: The Art of Darkness*"** [by Douglas E. Winter], review by Tyson Blue, in *Castle Rock: The Stephen King Newsletter* 2:7 (July, 1986): 11.

T107. **"Horror 'Wonderland,'"** by Judy Kimberly, in *Fantasy Review* 93 (July/August, 1986): 28-29. Review of *IT*.

T108. **"And Along the Way, They All Grow Up,"** by Kathleen Carroll, in *Daily News* [New York] (August 8, 1986): 3. Positive review of the film *Stand by Me*—three stars awarded: "It's coming of age theme is hardly original. But 'Stand by Me' turns out to be a very special movie, an exuberant Boy's Life adveunture yarn that also succeeds in exposing the bruised feelings and bitter frustrations of four boisterous adolescents."

T109. **"At the Movies: Rob Reiner Films Unusual Teen Drama,"** by Stephen Holden, in *New York Times* 135 (August 8, 1986): C8.

T110. **"Film: Rob Reiner's *Stand by Me*,"** by Walter Goodman, in *New York Times* 135 (August 8, 1986): C10.

T111. **"*Stand by Me*—A Corny Kids' Caper,"** by Rex Reed, in *New York Post* (August 8, 1986): 22.

T112. **"Horror and Fantasy: Stephen Kings und Peter Straubs *Der Talisman*,"** by Norbert Schachtsiek-Freitag, in *Frankfurter Rundschau* [Frankfurt, West Germany] (August 12, 1986): . Review-essay on theme, characterization, and structure in *The Talisman*.

T113. **"More Evil Than a 15-Foot Spider,"** by Walter Wager, in *New York Times Book Review* 91 (August 24, 1986): VII, 9. Harshly critical review of *It*.

T114. **"An Encounter with the Horror King,"** by John Podhoretz, in *Washington* [D.C.] *Times* (August 25, 1986): . Negative parody-review of *IT*. Podhoretz argues that the novel "repeats the author's time-worn formulas, ensuring its blockbuster success."

b. as: "Stopping 'It' Before It's Too Late," in *Insight* (August 25, 1986): 68-69.

c. as: "An Encounter with the Horror King," *Newsbank Literature Index* 13 (September, 1986): Fiche 23, A14-B1.

T115. **"Literature or Pop Fiction? What's the Difference, Eh?"** by Ken Tucker, in *Birmingham News* [Alabama] (August 31, 1986): . Review-article in defense of *IT*.

b. as microfiche: *Newsbank Literature Index* 13 (December, 1986): Fiche 45, B2-B4.

T116. **"The Specter of Death Shadows Stephen King's 'It,'"** by Dean R. Koontz, in *San Jose Mercury News* [California] (August 31, 1986): .

b. as microfiche: *Newsbank Literature Index* 13 (October, 1986): Fiche 30, G8.

T117. **"The Creature That Refused to Die,"** by David Gates, in *Newsweek* 108:9 (September 1, 1986): 84. Negative review of *IT* as pretentious, overwritten, "vague and heavy-handed at the same time."

T118. **"What Is Death, What Is Goofy?"** by David Brooks, in *Insight* (September 1, 1986): 57. Positive review of *Stand By Me*, "a powerful, affecting and completely original movie."

T119. **"A Growing Film Canon,"** by Michael Klossner, in *Fantasy Review* 95 (October, 1986): 31. On Collings's *The Films of Stephen King*.

T120. **"Stephen King Fans Will Enjoy *Kingdom of Fear*,"** by Tyson Blue, in *Macon Telegraph & News* [Macon, GA] (November 9, 1986): .

T121. **"Gulp!"** by Thomas R. Edwards, in *The New York Review of Books* (December 18, 1986): 58-59.

T122. **"Keys to the King-dom,"** by Stefan R. Dziemianowicz, in *Fantasy Review* 97 (December, 1986): 44. On Collings's *The Annotated Guide to Stephen King*.

T123. **"Book Review: *Stephen King at the Movies*,"** by Tyson Blue, in *The Stephen King Newsletter* 2:12/3:1 (December, 1986/January, 1987): 6.

T124. **"Stephen King's Fairy Tale Come True,"** by Mark Graham, in *Rocky Mountain News* [Denver, CO] (February 7, 1987): 33-M. On *The Eyes of the Dragon*.

T125. **"Research Material on King Abounds,"** by Tyson Blue, in *Telegraph and News*, "Books/The Arts" [Macon, GA] (May 3, 1987): 10E, 14E. Review of Collings's *The Annotated Guide to Stephen King* and *Stephen King as Richard Bachman*; Winter's *Stephen King: The Art of Darkness*; *Fear Itself*, *Kingdom of Fear*, *Discovering Stephen King*, and others.

T126. **"Stephen King Bares His Soul (Maybe) in 'Misery,'"** by Algis Budrys, in *Chicago Sun Times* (June 21, 1987): . Discussion of popular literature, comparing King with "Chuck Dickens," "Eddie Poe," and "Blarney Bill Shakespeare," each writing what the people want to hear.

b. as microfiche: *Newsbank Literature Index* 14 (August,1987): Fiche 20, B13-B14.

T127. **"King Shares 'Misery,' and Reader Grimaces,"** by Mark Graham, in *Rocky Mountain News* [Denver, CO] (June 21, 1987): 28-M.

T128. **"A New Conquest for King Bibliophiles,"** by Steve Paul, in *Kansas City Star* [Missouri] (July 7, 1987): .

b. as microfiche: *Newsbank Literature Index* 14 (July, 1987): Fiche 7, B11.

T129. **"The Films of Stephen King,"** by Brooks Landon, in *Extrapolation* (Summer, 1987): 164-176.

T130. **"Essays Examine SK's Contribution to Academics,"** by Kelly Rose, in *Castle Rock: The Stephen King Newsletter* 3:7 (July, 1987): 3, 5. On Hoppenstand and Browne's *The Gothic World of Stephen King: Landscape of Nightmares*, here referred to as *Journey into Horror*.

T131. **"Nearly a 'Swan Song' but Not Quite,"** by J. T. Moore, in *Fantasy Review* 103 (July, 1987): 52-53. Review of Robert McCammon's *Swan Song*, as not as good as King's *The Stand* but better than the King/Straub *The Talisman*.

T132. **"Review: *Masques II*"** [edited by J. N. Williamson], by Tyson Blue, in *Castle Rock: The Stephen King Newsletter* 3:8 (August, 1987): 3. Review contains references to King's "Popsy."

T133. **"Books on SK Films Similar,"** by Stephanie Leonard, in *Castle Rock: The Stephen King Newsletter* 3:9 (September, 1987): 1, 5. Comparative review of Horsting's *Stephen King at the Movies* and Conner's *Stephen King Goes to Hollywood*.

T134. **"Book Review: *The New Adventures of Sherlock Holmes*"** [edited by Martin H. Greenberg and Carol-Lynn Rössel Waugh], by Mark Graham, in *Castle Rock: The Stephen King Newsletter* 3:10 (October, 1987): 7.

T135. **"Sherlock Celebration,"** by Mark Graham, in *Rocky Mountain News* [Denver, CO] (November 1, 1987): 38-M. Review of *The New Adventures of Sherlock Holmes*.

T136. **"Horror Turns to Disgust: Stephen King Lets Us Down When He Holds Human Spirit in Low Regard,"** by Daryl Frazell, in *St. Petersburg Times* [Florida] (December 6, 1987): .

b. as microfiche: *Newsbank Literature Index* (January, 1988): Fiche 8, C9.

T137. **"'Tommyknockers' Finds Stephen King at His Scary Best,"** by Marianne Dougherty, in *Pittsburgh Press* (December 12, 1987): .

b. as microfiche: *Newsbank Literature Index* (January, 1988): Fiche 8, D1.

T138. **"Stephen King as Nerd's Best Friend,"** by Arend Flick, in *The Book Review/Los Angeles Times* (December 20, 1987): B1, B13.

T139. **"Horrors Red,"** by Al Sarrantonio, in *Mystery Scene* No. 10 (1987): 35-36. On *Misery*.

T140. **"King Epic Complex, Incongruous,"** by Mark Graham, in *Rocky Mountain News* [Denver, CO] (February 1, 1988): 53. On *The Tommyknockers*.

T141. **"Book Review: *The Dark Descent*"** [edited by David C. Hartwell], by Tyson Blue, in *Castle Rock: The Stephen King Newsletter* 4:2 (February, 1988): 7.

T142. **"King vs. Moguls,"** by Michael Klossner, in *SFRA Newsletter* 156 (March, 1988): 14. On Conner's *Stephen King Goes to Hollywood*.

b. *Science Fiction & Fantasy Book Review Annual*, edited by Robert A. Collins and Robert Latham. Westport, CT: Meckler, 1988, cloth, p. 398.

T143. ***"The Stephen King Phenomenon"*** [by Collings], by G. Warlock Vance, in *Extrapolation* 29:1 (Spring, 1988): 86-87.

T144. **"Book Review: *The Door to December*"** [by Dean R. Koontz], by George Hamilton, in *Castle Rock: The Stephen King Newsletter* 4:5-6 (May-June, 1988): 5. References to King's *Firestarter*.

T145. **"New Book Compares Koontz and SK,"** by Tyson Blue, in *Castle Rock: The Stephen King Newsletter* 4:5-6 (May-June, 1988): 10, 12. Review of Bill Munster's *Sudden Fear* (STARMONT STUDIES IN LITERARY CRITICISM, No. 24. Mercer Island, WA: Starmont House, 1988), with multiple references to King.

T146. **"Review of *The Gothic World of Stephen King: Landscape of Nightmares*"** [edited by Hoppenstand and Brown], by Sarah J. White, in *Castle Rock: The Stephen King Newsletter* 4:5-6 (May-June, 1988): 4.

T147. **"Schweitzer on TK, SK, and Science Fiction,"** by Darrell Schweitzer in *Castle Rock: The Stephen King Newsletter* 4:5-6 (May-June, 1988): 9. On *The Tommyknockers*.

T148. **"Black and White and Read All Over: *Carrie* on Broadway,"** by Craig Goden, in *Castle Rock: The Stephen King Newsletter* 4:7 (July, 1988): 7. On the New York Broadway production of *Carrie* musical.

T149. **"Book Review: *The Gothic World of Stephen King: Landscape of Nightmares*"** [edited by Hoppenstand and Browne], by Tyson Blue, in *Castle Rock: The Stephen King Newsletter* 4:7 (July, 1988): 1, 3, 9.

T150. **"Book Review: *Landscape of Fear: Stephen King's American Gothic*"** [by Tony Magistrale], by Tyson Blue, in *Castle Rock: The Stephen King Newsletter* 4:7 (July, 1988): 1, 3, 9.

T151. **"Book Review: *Stephen King: The First Decade,* Carrie *to* Pet Sematary"** [by Reino], by Tyson Blue, in *Castle Rock: The Stephen King Newsletter* 4:7 (July, 1988): 1, 3, 9.

T152. **"Book Review: *Bare Bones: Conversations on Terror with Stephen King*"** [edited by Underwood and Miller], by Tyson Blue, in *Castle Rock: The Stephen King Newsletter* 4:7 (July, 1988): 1, 3, 9.

T153. **"'Night Flier' Tops Horror Stories,"** by Tyson Blue, in *Castle Rock: The Stephen King Newsletter* 4:7 (July, 1988): 5, 9. Review of Douglas E. Winter's *Prime Evil*, containing King's "Night Flier."

T154. **"SK Contributions are Worth Reading,"** by Tyson Blue, in *Castle Rock: The Stephen King Newsletter* 4:8 (August, 1988): 3, 5. Review of Winter's *Night Visions 5*, containing King's "The Reploids," "Sneakers," and "Dedication."

T155. **"Philtrum Press' Second Book: *The Ideal, Genuine Man*, by Don Robertson,"** by Ben Indick, in *Castle Rock: The Stephen King Newsletter* 4:8 (August, 1988): 10. Review of Robertson's novel, with frequent mention of King's involvement in the production.

T156. **"*Bare Bones*: A Disquieting Look at Stephen King,"** by Barry Hoffman, in *Castle Rock: The Stephen King Newsletter* 4:10 (October, 1988): 7.

T157. **"Of New Frontiers and Gargoyles,"** by Tyson Blue, in *Castle Rock: The Stephen King Newsletter* 4:10 (October, 1988): 3. On *Nightmares in the Sky*.

T158. **"Horrors Red,"** by Al Sarrantonio, in *Mystery Scene* No. 14 (1988): 48. On *The Tommyknockers*.

T159. ***"The Dark Tower II: The Drawing of the Three*,"** by Charles de Lint, in *Science Fiction & Fantasy Book Review Annual,* edited by Robert A. Collins and Robert Latham. Westport, CT: Meckler, 1988, cloth, p. 226-227.

T160. ***"The Tommyknockers,"*** by Michael R. Collings, in *Science Fiction & Fantasy Book Review Annual,* edited by Robert A. Collins and Robert Latham. Westport, CT: Meckler, 1988, cloth, p. 228-229.

T161. ***"The Stephen King Phenomenon"*** [by Michael Collings], by J. T. Moore, in *Science Fiction & Fantasy Book Review Annual,* edited by Robert A. Collins and Robert Latham. Westport, CT: Meckler, 1988, cloth, p. 397-398.

T162. **"Stephen King,"** by David Isaacson, in *American Reference Books Annual, 1988, Volume 19,* edited by Bohdan S. Wynar. Englewood, CO: Libraries Unlimited, 1988, cloth, p. 471, Item #1181. On Collings's *The Annotated Guide to Stephen King*.

T163. **"King Excels in Quest for Dark Tower,"** by Janet C. Beaulieu, in *Bangor Daily News* [Bangor, ME] (January 10, 1989): .

b. as microfiche: *Newsbank Literature* 16 (February, 1989): Fiche 19, B6-B7.

c. *Castle Rock: The Stephen King Newsletter* 5:3 (March, 1989): 1, 6.

T164. **"Short Subjects: Recent Short Fiction of Stephen King,"** by Ben P. Indick, in *Castle Rock: The Stephen King Newsletter* 5:1 (January, 1989): 3, 4. On "Popsy." "Reploids," "Sneakers," "Dedication," "The Night Flier," "The Doctor's Case."

T165. **"McCammon Makes Werewolf Grand in Its 'Hour,'"** by Mark Graham, in *Rocky Mountain News* [Denver, CO] (March 26, 1989): 25-M. On *The Dark Tower II: The Drawing of the Three*.

T166. **"New Cormier Novel Garners SK Praise,"** by Mark Graham, in *Rocky Mountain News* [Denver, CO] (1989?): . On *Fade*, by Robert Cormier, with frequent references to King.

b. *Castle Rock: The Stephen King Newsletter* 5:3 (March, 1989): 5.

T167. **"SK Story Featured in Grant Anthology,"** by Tyson Blue, in *Castle Rock: The Stephen King Newsletter* 5:4 (April, 1989): 10. On Charles L. Grant's *The Best of Shadows*, including King's "The Man Who Would Not Shake Hands."

T168. **"*Pet Sematary* Doesn't Draw Raves in Boston,"** by Tom Draheim, in *Boston Globe* (1989?): .

b. *Castle Rock: The Stephen King Newsletter* 5:6 (June, 1989): 1, 12.

T169. **"A Cadillac for King's Used Car Lot,"** by Ben P. Indick, in *Castle Rock: The Stephen King Newsletter* 5:5 (May, 1989): 8. Review of *Dolan's Cadillac*.

T170. **"Do You Know Where Your Kid Is Tonight?"** by Christopher Spruce, in *Castle Rock: The Stephen King Newsletter* 5:5. (May, 1989): 1, 12. On the *Pet Sematary* film.

T171. **"Long-Awaited Horror Collection Arrives,"** by Mark Graham, in *Rocky Mountain News* [Denver, CO] (July 9, 1989): 25-M. On Skipp and Spectre's *Book of the Dead*.

T172. **"Hale, Hale the Maniac's All Here,"** by Tyson Blue, in *Castle Rock: The Stephen King Newsletter* 5:8 (August, 1989): 3. On Charles L. Grant's *In a Dark Dream*, with references to King.

T173. **"SK's Tale the Tamest in *Book of the Dead*,"** by Tyson Blue, in *Castle Rock: The Stephen King Newsletter* 5:8 (August, 1989): 3, 6, 8. Review including references to "Night Flier."

T174. **[Letter],** by Gerry de la Ree, in *Castle Rock: The Stephen King Newsletter* 5:9-10 (September-October, 1989): 9. Letter review criticizing the format and appearance of the limited *My Pretty Pony*.

T175. **"Danger Within: New King Novel Hits Close to Home,"** by William D. Gagliani, in *Milwaukee Journal* (October 22, 1989): .

b. as microfiche: *Newsbank Literature* 16 (November, 1989): Fiche 112, G4

T176. **"Venturing a Bit into the Magical,"** by Douglas E. Winter, in *Washington* [D.C.] *Times* (November, 1989): . On *The Dark Half* and *My Pretty Pony*.

b. as microfiche: *Newsbank Literature* 16 (December, 1989): Fiche 126, A11.

T177. **"Urban Thrills: Reviews of Short Horror and Contemporary Fantasy Fiction,"** by Charles de Lint, in *Short Form* 1:3/4 (1989): 56-70. Includes *Misery* on the "Best of the Year" list.

T178. **"Night Journeys—Reviews of Horror: Installment #9,"** by Charles de Lint, in *Mystery Scene* No. 224 (January, 1990): 87-88. On George Beahm's *The Stephen King Companion* and King's *The Dark Half.*

T179. **"Short Story Is Something New for King,"** by Gene Williams, in *Plain Dealer* [Cleveland, OH] (April 22, 1990): . Negative review of *My Pretty Pony*, criticizing it for its cost, its pretentiousness, and its obscurity. Williams suggests readers would be better rewarded by spending far less and buying King's newspaper account of his son's Little League game.

b. as: microfiche: *Newsbank Literature Index* (May, 1990-August, 1990): Fiche 48, A10.

T180. **"King's Restoration Strengthens 'The Stand,'"** by Gregory N. Krolczyk, in *Sun* [Baltimore, MD] (May 6, 1990): .

b. as microfiche: *Newsbank Literature Index* (May, 1990-August, 1990): Fiche 59, D9.

T181. **"The King's Last 'Stand' Is a Winner,"** by Chuck Moss, in *Detroit News* (May 9, 1990): .

b. as microfiche: *Newsbank Literature Index* (May, 1990-August, 1990): Fiche 59, D10.

T182. **"Armageddon: Complete and Uncut,"** by Robert Kiely, in *New York Times Book Review* (May 13, 1990): 3. Full-page review article.

T183. **"King's 1978 Cult Classic Refurbished, Improved,"** by James P. Girard, in *Wichita Eagle* (June 10, 1990): .

b. as microfiche: *Newsbank Literature Index* (May, 1990): Fiche 71, D14-E1.

T184. **"The Writer and His Shadow,"** by J. T. Moore, in *SFRA Newsletter* No. 182 (November, 1990): 38-39. Discusses King's trilogy of works about writers and writing: *Misery*, *The Dark Half*, and "Secret Window, Secret Garden."

U.

SECONDARY SOURCES

STEPHEN KING ARCHIVES UNIVERSITY OF MAINE, ORONO

For a full discussion of the King materials available through the Special Collections Library at University of Maine, Orono, see Beahm, *The Stephen King Companion*, p. 297-300.

U1. **"The Aftermath."** Unpublished novel-length manuscript.

U2. **"And Sometimes They Come Back."**

U3. **"Blaze."** Unpublished novel manuscript.

U4. **"The Boogeyman."**

U5. ***Carrie*.** Typescript ms.; second draft; third draft; final galley; foundry copy.

U6. ***Christine*.** Typescript ms.

U7. ***Cujo*.** Typescript ms.; galley.

U8. **"Gulch."** Unpublished essay.

U9. ***The Dead Zone*.** Original ms.; photocopy of typescript.

U10. ***Firestarter*.** Foundry proof.

U11. **"The Ledge."**

U12. **"The Monkey."**

U13. ***Night Shift*.** Original typescript; second ms. copy; final galley; foundry proof.

U14. **"Paranoid: A Chant."**

U15. ***Pet Sematary*.** Typescript ms.; galley.

U16. **"Second Coming."** Original version of *'Salem's Lot*.

U17. ***The Shining.*** Original ms.; final galley; foundry proof; typescript, "The Shine."

U18. ***Skeleton Crew.*** Photocopy of typescript.

U19. ***The Stand.*** Original typescript; second draft; final galley; foundry proof.

U20. **"Sword in the Darkness."** Unpublished mainstream novel manuscript.

U21. ***The Talisman.*** Photocopy of typescript.

U22. **"Time in a Glass That Ran."** Unpublished story; originally called "The Last of Her."

U23. **"Your Kind of Place."** Unpublished essay.

U24. **Miscellaneous correspondance.**

V.

UNPUBLISHED WORKS

Many of King's early unpublished materials are discussed at various places in the following studies:

Beahm, George. *The Stephen King Companion*. Kansas City, MO: Andrews and McMeel, September 1989.
Collings, Michael R. *The Annotated Guide to Stephen King: A Primary and Secondary Bibliography of the Works of America's Premier Horror Writer*. Mercer Island, WA: Starmont House, October 1986.
Collings, Michael R. *The Many Facets of Stephen King*. Mercer Island, WA: Starmont House, 1986.
Spignesi, Stephen J. *The Shape Under the Sheet: The Complete Stephen King Encyclopedia*. Ann Arbor, MI: Popular Culture, Ink., May 1991, cloth, 780 p.
Winter, Douglas E. *Stephen King: The Art of Darkness*. New York: New American Library, November 1984.

UNPUBLISHED NOVELS

V1. **"The Aftermath."** Written when King was 16.

V2. **"Blaze."** Manuscript. Written around 1970, heavily influenced by Steinbeck's *Of Mice and Men*, with elements of supernatural horror and the ghost story overlaid.

V3. **"Sword in the Darkness."** Also called *Babylon Here*. Early attempt, predating *Carrie*.

V4. **"The Cannibals."** Completed manuscript [*Fear Itself* 268].

V5. **"The Corner."** Incomplete.

V6. **"Milkman."** Incomplete. Two short stories for *Skeleton Crew* were taken from this manucscript: "Morning Deliveries (Milkman #1)" and "Big Wheels: A Tale of the Laundry Game (Milkman #2)."

V7. **"Welcome to Clearwater."** Incomplete.

V8. **"The Doors."** Incomplete. A passage of prose identified as a portion of this "unpublished, unfinished, unscheduled, and previously unknown novel" included in the ms. notebook King donated for a charity auction for the benefit of Manly Wade Wellman's widow.

UNPUBLISHED SHORT FICTION

VB1. **"Squad D,"** for *The Last Dangerous Visions,* edited by Harlan Ellison.

With its references to the Vietnam War, the story seems dated; in spite of content, however, it is a touching tale, with sufficient supernatural incursions to satisfy King's fans and deep enough awareness of human pains to make it ring psychologically. Ellison has indicated in his interview in Beahm's *The Stephen King Companion* that the story would need extensive revision at this point to appear in the anthology.

SECONDARY SOURCES AND REVIEWS:

1. Beahm, George. *The Stephen King Companion.* Kansas City, MO: Andrews & McMeel, 1989, cloth, p. 153.
2. Collings, Michael R. "Squad D," in *The Shorter Works of Stephen King*, by Michael R. Collings and David A. Engebretson. Mercer Island, WA: Starmont House, 1985, cloth, p. 184-184.
3. Spignesi, Stephen J. "Squad D," in *The Shape Under the Sheet: The Complete Stephen King Encyclopedia.* Ann Arbor, MI: Popular Culture Ink, May 1991, cloth, p. 541.
4. Winter, Douglas E. *The Art of Darkness.* New York: New American Library, November 1984, cloth.

VB2. **"Keyholes,"** opening segment of an unfinished, unpublished short story. Handwritten pages contained in a notebook donated to the American Repertory Theater Benefit Auction, May 1, 1988.

VB3. **"An Evening at God's,"** signed manuscript of one-minute play, written for the American Repertory Theater. Manuscript auctioned April 23, 1990.

SECONDARY SOURCES AND REVIEWS:

1. Caldwell, Gail. "Stephen King: Boogeyman as Family Man," in *Boston Sunday Globe* (April 15, 1990): . As microfiche: *NewsBank:Literature* 17 (May, 1990): Fiche 48, A5-7. As microfiche: *NewsBank: Names in the News* 12 (May, 1990): Fiche 139, E9-E11.
2. Spignesi, Stephen J. "An Evening at God's," in *The Shape Under the Sheet: The Complete Stephen King Encyclopedia.* Ann Arbor, MI: Popular Culture Ink, May 1991, cloth, p. 537-537.

W.

PARODIES, PASTICHES, ETC.

CARTOONS ABOUT STEPHEN KING

W1. **Cartoon,** by Vic Runtz, in *Bangor Daily News* [Bangor, ME] (1983): .

b. *Here Today*. Bangor, ME: Bangor Publishing, 1983, p. .
c. *Castle Rock: The Stephen King Newsletter* 1:4 (April, 1985): 9.

W2. **"Bloom County,"** by Berke Breathed, 1984.

b. *Castle Rock: The Stephen King Newsletter* 1:2 (February, 1985): [1].

W3. **Cartoon,** by Diane Mayo, in *Murder at the Big Store*. New York: St. Martin's Press, 1984, p. .

b. *Castle Rock: The Stephen King Newsletter* 1:8 (August, 1985): 3.

W4. **"An Ordinary Day at the Word Processor,"** in *Castle Rock: The Stephen King Newsletter* 1:1 (January, 1985): [2].

W5. **Cartoon,** in *Castle Rock: The Stephen King Newsletter* 1:2 (February, 1985): 7.

W6. **"cpl kev,"** by K. D. Bark, in *Stars & Stripes* (1985): .

b. *Castle Rock: The Stephen King Newsletter* 1:7 (July, 1985): 6.

W7. ***Spider-Man*** (August, 1985): .

b. *Castle Rock: The Stephen King Newsletter* 2:2 (February, 1986): 2.

W8. **"Cheeverwood,"** by Michael Frye, in *Washington Post* (1985): .

b. *Castle Rock: The Stephen King Newsletter* 2:8 (August, 1986): 2.

W9. **Cartoon,** by Rurik Tyler.

b. *Castle Rock: The Stephen King Newsletter* 1:9 (September, 1985): 3.

W10. **"Downtown,"** by Tim Owen, Universal Press Syndicate, 1985.

b. *Castle Rock: The Stephen King Newsletter* 2:10 (October, 1985): 2.

W11. ***Web of Spiderman*** 1:7 (October, 1985): .

b. *Castle Rock: The Stephen King Newsletter* 2:2 (February, 1986): 2.

W12. ***Captain America*** (November, 1985): .

b. *Castle Rock: The Stephen King Newsletter* 2:2 (February, 1986): 2.

W13. **"Cheeverwood,"** by Michael Frye, in *Washington Post* (1985): .

b. *Castle Rock: The Stephen King Newsletter* 2:8 (August, 1986): 2.

W14. **"Bloom County,"** by Berke Breathed, in *Washington Post* (1985): .

b. *Castle Rock: The Stephen King Newsletter* 1:11 (November, 1985): 2.

W15. **"The Blue Beetle"** (1985): .

b. *Castle Rock: The Stephen King Newsletter* 2:2 (February, 1986): 2.

W16. **"Fear Stalks the Henhouse, and Her Name Is Helen,"** by T. O. Sylvester, in *San Francisco Chronicle* (1985): .

b. *Castle Rock: The Stephen King Newsletter* 2:5 (May, 1986): 2.

W17. **"Pigsfeet,"** by Alan Vitello, in *The Rocky Mountain Collegian* [Fort Collins, CO], 1985: .

b. *Castle Rock: The Stephen King Newsletter* 2:12 (December, 1985): 2.

W18. **"That's Jake,"** by Jake Vest, Tribune Media Services, 1985.

b. *Castle Rock: The Stephen King Newsletter* 2:12 (December, 1985): 7.

W19. **"The Quigmans,"** by Nickerson, in *Los Angeles Times* Syndicate, 1986.

b. *Castle Rock: The Stephen King Newsletter* 2:6 (June, 1986): 2.

W20. **Cartoon,** by Rich Pine, in *Castle Rock: The Stephen King Newsletter* 2:9 (September, 1986): 2.

W21. **"Cobwebs,"** by Gorrell and Brookins, Asterisk Features, Peterborough, NH, 1986.

b. *Castle Rock: The Stephen King Newsletter* 2:10 (October, 1986): 2.

W22. **"Gumdrop,"** by Scott. United Features Syndicate, Inc., 1986.

b. *Castle Rock: The Stephen King Newsletter* 4:3 (March, 1988): 2.

W23. "Willy 'n Ethel," by Joe Martin.

b. *Castle Rock: The Stephen King Newsletter* 3:1 (December, 1986/January, 1987): 3.

W24. "Crock," by Bill Rechin and Don Wilder, 1987.

b. *Castle Rock: The Stephen King Newsletter* 3:6 (June, 1987): 2.

W25. "Funky Winkerbean," by Tom Batiuk, 1987.

b. *Castle Rock: The Stephen King Newsletter* 3:7 (July, 1987): 2.

W26. Cartoon, by Vojtko, in *Sunday Magazine of the Milwaukee Journal.*

b. *Castle Rock: The Stephen King Newsletter* 3:7 (July, 1987): 2.

W27. "The Quigmans," by Nickerson, in *Los Angeles Times*, 1987.

b. *Castle Rock: The Stephen King Newsletter* 3:10 (October, 1987): 2.

W28. "Get Well Soon," by Leslie Murray, Near North Graphics [Illinois]. Get-well card.

b. *Castle Rock: The Stephen King Newsletter* 3:11/4:1 (December, 1987/ January, 1988): 2. Cartoon greeting-card of a nurse with "Wilkes" written on the pocket. Text: "Get well soon / Or I will break every bone in your body."

W29. "Hartland," by Rich Torrey, 1987.

b. *Castle Rock: The Stephen King Newsletter* 4:2 (February, 1988): 2.

W30. "Gorge," by Paul Williams, 1988.

b. *Castle Rock: The Stephen King Newsletter* 4:3 (February, 1988): 2.

W31. "Out of Line," by Mort Gerberg, in *Publishers Weekly* (March 11, 1988):.

b. *Castle Rock: The Stephen King Newsletter* 4:5-6 (May-June, 1988): 2.

W32. "Arlo and Janice" (March 27, 1988): . Shows character reading *The Tommyknockers*.

W33. "Fishpaper," by Carl Hennicke, in *The Targum* [Rutgers University], 1988.

b. *Castle Rock: The Stephen King Newsletter* 4:7 (July, 1988): 2.

W34. Cartoon, by Gorrell, in *Richmond News Leader,* 1988.

b. *Castle Rock: The Stephen King Newsletter* 4:8 (August, 1988): 2.

W35. **Cartoon,** by Mark Cullum, in *The Birmingham News* (1988): .

b. *Castle Rock: The Stephen King Newsletter* 4:11 (November, 1988): 2.

W36. **"Bizarro,"** by Piraro, in *San Francisco Chronicle* (1989)

b. *Castle Rock: The Stephen King Newsletter* 5:3 (March, 1989): 2.

W37. **"Out of Line,"** by Mort Gerberg, in *Publishers Weekly* (January 25, 1991): .

b. *The Shape Under the Sheet: The Complete Stephen King Encyclopedia,* by Stephen J. Spignesi. Ann Arbor, MI: Popular Culture, Ink., May 1991, cloth, p. 30.

W38. **"Jump Start,"** by Robb Armstrong. Reprinted in *The Shape Under the Sheet: The Complete Stephen King Encyclopedia,* by Stephen J. Spignesi. Ann Arbor, MI: Popular Culture, Ink., May 1991, cloth, p. 622.

CONTESTS, QUIZZES, AND PUZZLES

WB1. **"Trivia Quiz,"** in *Castle Rock: The Stephen King Newsletter* 1:1 (January, 1985): 2.

WB2. **"Puzzle,"** in *Castle Rock: The Stephen King Newsletter* 1:1 (January, 1985): 5. Find-the-word puzzle.

WB3. **"Cat Contest,"** in *Castle Rock: The Stephen King Newsletter* 1:5 (May, 1985): 8.

WB4. **"King Krosswords,"** by Beth Ann Myers, in *Castle Rock: The Stephen King Newsletter* 1:6 (June, 1985): 9.

WB5. **"The Past and Future King's a Horror Show Scramble,"** by T. Vern Jones, in *Castle Rock: The Stephen King Newsletter* 1:10 (October, 1985): 6.

WB6. **"Seven Titles of Novels and/or Short Stories in Magazines by Stephen King,"** in *Castle Rock: The Stephen King Newsletter* 1:12 (December, 1985): 8. Anagrams.

WB7. **"Trivia,"** in *Castle Rock: The Stephen King Newsletter* 2:1 (January, 1986): 5.

WB8. **"Crew Quiz,"** in *Castle Rock: The Stephen King Newsletter* 2:3 (March, 1986): 7.

WB9. **"Crew Quiz,"** in *Castle Rock: The Stephen King Newsletter* 2:4 (April, 1986): 7.

WB10. **"Lathrop Trivia Quiz,"** by Kathy Lathrop, in *Castle Rock: The Stephen King Newsletter* 2:5 (May, 1986): 2.

WB11. **"Trivia Quiz,"** by Andrew Wolczyk, in *Castle Rock: The Stephen King Newsletter* 2:7 (July, 1986): 7.

WB12. **"Stephen King Scream Contest,"** in *Fangoria* (August, 1986): .

WB13. **"A Novel Contest,"** by Naomi King, in *Castle Rock: The Stephen King Newsletter* 2:9 (September, 1986): 3, 8.

WB14. **"Seek and Find: Short Stories by Stephen King,"** by Michael Hardy, in *Castle Rock: The Stephen King Newsletter* 3:4 (April-May, 1987): 14. "Hidden name" puzzle.

WB15. **"All of Us Would-Be Writers, #1: Characterization in the Work of Stephen King,"** by Julie Knox, in *Castle Rock: The Stephen King Newsletter* 3:7 (July, 1987): 8. Quiz.

WB16. **"Castle Rock, Maine: Just the Facts,"** by Julie Knox, in *Castle Rock: The Stephen King Newsletter* 3:9 (September, 1987): 3, 6. Quiz based on Castle Rock locales and characters.

WB17. **"Sinister Synonyms and Creepy Cliches: A Puzzle,"** by J. N. Williamson and David Taylor, in *Castle Rock: The Stephen King Newsletter* 3:9 (September, 1987): 6. Crossword puzzle with King-based clues.

WB18. **"Mrs. Todd's Newest Shortcut: An SK Word-Find Game,"** by Lela Marie de la Garza, in *Castle Rock: The Stephen King Newsletter* 3:10 (October, 1987): 6. Short story with 28 King titles embedded into the text.

WB19. **"Can You Hack It on the Skeleton Crew?"** by David Taylor and J. N. Williamson, in *Castle Rock: The Stephen King Newsletter* 3:11/4:1 (December, 1987/January, 1988): 12. Crossword puzzle with clues drawn from *Skeleton Crew*.

WB20. **"Stephen King's Women in Cinema,"** by Flo Stanton, in *Castle Rock: The Stephen King Newsletter* 4:2 (February, 1988): 7. Quiz.

WB21. **"King Crossword,"** by Phil Dickinson, in *Castle Rock: The Stephen King Newsletter* 4:4 (April, 1988): 11.

WB22. **"Kingy Kingies,"** by Lela Marie de la Garza, in *Castle Rock: The Stephen King Newsletter* 4:4 (April, 1988): 8.

WB23. **"King Krossword,"** by Phil Dickinson, in *Castle Rock: The Stephen King Newsletter* 4:8 (August, 1988): 11.

WB24. **"Thicket from Hell,"** by Ray Rexer, in *Castle Rock: The Stephen King Newsletter* 4:9 (September, 1988): 5. Short story containing 30 embedded and punning King titles.

WB25. **"King Klues,"** by Rob Edmiston, in *Castle Rock: The Stephen King Newsletter* 4:12 (December, 1988): 5. Quiz.

WB26. **"King Krossword,"** by Phil Dickinson, in *Castle Rock: The Stephen King Newsletter* 4:12 (December, 1988): 5.

WB27. **"Middle Name Quiz,"** by Ray Rexer, in *Castle Rock: The Stephen King Newsletter* 5:2 (February, 1989): 9.

WB28. **"Last Words Quiz,"** by Ray Rexer, in *Castle Rock: The Stephen King Newsletter* 5:4 (April, 1989): 5.

PARODIES AND SATIRES

WC1. **"The Shiner,"** by Larry Siegel, in *Mad* No. 221 (March 1981): 4-10.

WC2. **Parody Letter,** in "Letters to the Editor," in *National Lampoon* (September, 1981): .

b. *The Stephen King Companion,* edited by George Beahm. Kansas City, MO: Andrews & McMeel, September 1989, cloth, p. 12.

WC3. **Parody Letter,** in "Letters to the Editor," *National Lampoon* (July 1983):.

b. *The Stephen King Companion,* edited by George Beahm. Kansas City, MO: Andrews & McMeel, September 1989, cloth, p. 12.

WC4. **"Eggboiler,"** by Paul Proch and Charles Kaufman, in *National Lampoon* (May, 1984): 32-37, 48, 54, 70. Parody of *Firestarter.*

WC5. ***When Good Things Happen to Bad People,*** by Alan Robbins. p. 634. Includes a lampoon of King.

WC6. **[Title unknown],** in *Not Necessarily the News* (October, 1985): . Parody of King films.

WC7. **"25 Most Irritating People of 1985,"** in *People Parody* (Winter, 1985): .

WC8. **"CRACKED Interviews Stephen Kink,"** in *Cracked* 221 (August, 1986): . References to "Stephen Kink" and his pen name, "Richard Backwash."

WC9. **"*HE*,"** by Dan Jenkins, in *Dallas-Times Herald* (December 14, 1986): . Parody of *IT*.

WC10. **"*ID*,"** by Charles McGrath, in *The New Yorker* 62 (December 29, 1986): 24-26.

b. *The Stephen King Companion,* by George Beahm. Kansas City, MO: Andrews and McMeel, September 1989, paper, p. 239-244.

WC11. **"Stand But Me,"** by Dick Debartolo, illustrated by Mort Drucker, in *Mad* No. 269 (March, 1987): . Parody of *Stand By Me*.

WC12. **"The Dark Bard of New Hampshire,"** by Michael Berry, in *The San Francisco Chronicle* (1988?): . Parody review of the works of "Rex Stephens."

b. *Castle Rock: The Stephen King Newsletter* 4:9 (September, 1988): 3.

WC13. **"A Plethora of Fall Pulp,"** by Wayne Saroyan, in *San Francisco Chronicle Sunday Punch* (October 2, 1988): . Parody review of *It's-It*, by "Stephen King."

WC14. **"The Adventures of Friend and I: The Search for Stephen King Chapter 111: Children of the Cabbage,"** in *Threshold of Reality 3*. Queens Village, NY: Maintech Publications, 1989?, paper, p. .

WC15. **"Children of King: A Closet Screenplay,"** by Ben P. Indick, in *Castle Rock: The Stephen King Newsletter* 5:4 (April, 1989): 4, 11, 12.

WC16. **"You Can Write Like Stephen King!"** by Doug Martin, illustrated by Peter Mulligan, in *Cracked* No. 4 (April, 1989): . Satirical flow-chart.

WC17. **"Return of the Wind: How Other Authors May Have Treated the Sequel,"** by Elliot Krieger, in *Providence Journal-Bulletin,* "Sunday Journal Magazine" [Providence, RI] (1989?): . Opening paragraphs of *Tarrie*, by Stephen King—how King would have written a sequel to *Gone with the Wind.* Other titles include *The Wind Also Rises,* by Ernest Hemingway; *Fiddle-dee-dumb,* by Ogden Nash; *One Hundred Years of Scarlitude,* by Gabriel García Márquez; and *The Armies of the Wind,* by Norman Mailer.

b. *The Blood Review: The Journal of Horror Criticism* 1:1 (October 1989): 36.

WC18. **"Collecting Horror: Or at Least as Much as You Can Stand,"** by Ed Bryant, in *The Blood Review: The Journal of Horror Criticism* 1:1 (October 1989): 10. Parody essay reporting the existence of a wreath of human hair, fashioned from the hair collected from the shower drain at the Stanley Hotel following King's stay there while writing *The Shining*. "Comes with a letter of Provenance ($7,500)."

WC19. **"Mad's Video Reviews: 'Misery,'"** by Stan Hart, in *Mad* No. 304 (July, 1991): 37. Two-frame parody of the film.

PASTICHES AND OTHER FICTION

WD1. **"The Man Who Would Not Be King,"** by Stanley Wiater, in *Castle Rock* 2:6 (June, 1986): 1, 4-5. Pastiche short story based on King's men's club stories.

WD2. **"We've Been Expecting You,"** by Ken Richert, in *Castle Rock: The Stephen King Newsletter* 3:11/4:1 (December, 1987/January 1988): 1, 4, 14. Fantasy based on King's characters and locales.

WD3. **"The Wrath of Herb & Marge,"** by Paddy McKillop, in *Castle Rock: The Stephen King Newsletter* 5:8 (August, 1989): 4-5. Story incorporating multiple references to King's novels.

WD4. **"Stephen King Is Scaring Me,"** by Jonathan Floyd, in *Grue 2* ( ): 52-53. Fiction about the effects of King's stories on a fan.

POEMS AND STORIES ABOUT KING

WE1. **"To Stephen King,"** by Marie A. Asner. Des Moines, IA: CSS Publications of Des Moines, 1984. Poem.

b. *Castle Rock: The Stephen King Newsletter* 2:3 (March, 1986): 7.

WE2. **"The Man Who Read King,"** by John Pike, in *Castle Rock: The Stephen King Newsletter* 3:6 (June, 1987): 5. Poem.

WE3. **"You, Stephen King,"** by Michael R. Collings, in *The Stephen King Phenomenon*. Mercer Island, WA: Starmont House, 1987, cloth/paper, p. 11-12. Poem.

b. *The Shape Under the Sheet: The Complete Stephen King Encyclopedia*, by Stephen Spignesi. Ann Arbor, MI: Popular Culture, Ink, May 1991, cloth, p. 632.

WE4. **"Scarier Than King,"** by Julie Jackson Lusby, in *Castle Rock: The Stephen King Newsletter* 4:8 (April, 1988): 6. Poem.

WE5. **"Old Haunts,"** by Wayne Allen Sallee, in *Grue 2* (1989?): 62. Poem.

WE6. **"Character Assassination,"** by Ray Rexer, in *The Shape Under the Sheet: The Complete Stephen King Encyclopedia,* by Stephen J. Spignesi. Ann Arbor, MI: Popular Culture, Ink., May 1991, cloth, p. 131-135. Short story.

WE7. **"The Find,"** by Barry Hoffman, in *The Shape Under the Sheet: The Complete Stephen King Encyclopedia.,* by Stephen J. Spignesi. Ann Arbor, MI: Popular Culture, Ink., May 1991, cloth, p. 70. Short story.

WE8. **"The Shape Under the Sheet,"** by Stephen J. Spignesi, in *The Shape Under the Sheet: The Complete Stephen King Encyclopedia*, by Stephen J. Spignesi. Ann Arbor, MI: Popular Culture, Ink., May 1991, cloth, p. 2. Poem. "Dedicated—with thanks and admiration—to Stephen King."

CONFERENCES

WF1. **Horrorfest '89.** Organized by Ken Morgan. May 12-14, 1989, at the Stanley Hotel, in Estes Park, Colorado

GUESTS: Douglas E. Winter; Tyson Blue; Michael R. Collings; Bryan Moore; Paul David Anderson; Bryan Cooper; Gretta Anderson; Lisa W. Cantrell; Ray Rexer; Matthew J. Costello.

WF2. **Horrorfest '90.** Organized by Ken Morgan. Denver, CO, Spring 1990.

WF3. **Horrorfest '91.** Denver, CO.

MISCELLANEOUS SECONDARY ITEMS

WG1. ***The K. G. Stevens Slant on Celebrity Handwriting,*** by K. G. Stevens. Covina, CA: Tambra Publishing, 1985, cloth/paper. Includes an analysis of King's handwriting.

WG2. **"The Art of Stephen King,"** illustrations by various authors, in *Gauntlet: Exploring the Limits of Free Expression—Stephen King Special* No. 2 (April, 1991): .

ab. *Gauntlet 2*, edited by Barry Hoffmann. Baltimore: Borderlands Press, May, 1991, cloth, p. .

X.

HONORS AND AWARDS

X1. *School Library Journal* **Book List, 1974,** for *Carrie.*

X2. **Nebula Award Nomination, (Science Fiction Writers of America), 1977,** best novel category, for *The Shining.*

X3. **Hugo Award Nomination (World Science Fiction Convention), 1978,** best novel, for *The Shining.*

X4. **American Library Association's Best Books for Young Adults, 1978,** for *'Salem's Lot.*

X5. **Balrog Nomination (World Fantasy Award), 1979,** best novel category, for *The Stand.* Placed second.

X6. **Balrog Nomination (World Fantasy Award), 1979,** best collection category, for *Night Shift.* Placed second.

X7. **Hugo Award Nomination (World Science Fiction Convention), 1979,** best novel, for *The Stand.*

X8. **Guest of Honor, 5th World Fantasy Convention, 1979,** Providence, RI, October 12-14. Co-Guest-of-Honor with Frank Belknap Long.

X9. **Alumni Career Award, 1980,** University of Maine.

X10. **American Library Association's Best Books for Young Adults, 1981,** for *Firestarter.*

X11. **New York Public Library's Books for the Teen Age, 1981,** for *Firestarter.*

X12. **Hugo Award (World Science Fiction Convention), 1982,** best non-fiction book category, for *Danse Macabre.*

X13. **World Fantasy Award, 1982,** best short fiction category, for "Do the Dead Sing?"

X14. **Best Fiction Writer of the Year, 1982,** selected by *Us* Magazine.

X15. **New York Public Library's Books for the Teen Age, 1982,** for *Firestarter.*

X16. **New York Public Library's Books for the Teen Age, 1982,** for *Cujo*.

X17. **Roastee, Necon II**, 1982.

X17. **"Favorite Author," 1985,** Augusta County [GA] Patrons of the Library, National Library Week, April 14-21.

X18. **Listed, "100 Most Important People in Science Fiction/Fantasy," 1985**, in *Starlog* (November, 1985): .

X19. **Balrog Nomination (World Fantasy Award), 1985,** for *Pet Sematary*.

X20. **Balrog Nomination (World Fantasy Award), 1985,** for *The Talisman*.

X21. ***Esquire Register* Nomination, 1985.**

X22. **Golden Pen Award, 1986,** from the Young Adult Advisory Committee of the Spokane Public Library.

X23. **Bram Stoker Award [Horror Writers of America] 1988,** Best Novel category, for *Misery* (tied with Robert R. McCammon's *Swan Song*).

X24. **Recommendation (Horror Writers of America), 1989,** Best Novella category, for "Night Flier."

X25. **Bram Stoker Recommendation [Horror Writers of America], 1989,** Best Novella Category, for "Dedication."

X26. **Bram Stoker Award [Horror Writers of America], 1990**, best collection category, for *Four Past Midnight*.

X27. **World Fantasy Award, 1994**, best short fiction category, for "The Man in the Black Suit."

X28. **O. Henry Award, 1994, Best American Short Story**, for "The Man in the Black Suit."

Y.

MISCELLANEA

Y1. **Judge, 1977 World Fantasy Awards.**

Y2. **"Stephen King's Year of Fear: 1986 Calendar."** New York: New American Library, 1985. An annotated calendar, with King indicating important dates, birthdays, anniversaries (real and fictional).

SECONDARY SOURCES AND REVIEWS:

1. Collings, Michael R. *The Annotated Guide to Stephen King*. Mercer Island, WA: Starmont House, 1986, cloth, p. 90.

Y3. **Judge, The Tale of Terror or the Occult Contest,** sponsored by Signet Books and WBCN-FM. Winner: "The Toucher," by Stanley Wiater, in *The Boston Phoenix*.

b. *Castle Rock: The Stephen King Newsletter* 2:10 (October, 1986): 5-6.
c. *The Shape Under the Sheet: The Complete Stephen King Encyclopedia*, by Stephen J. Spignesi. Ann Arbor, MI: Popular Culture, Ink., May 1991, cloth, p. 724-726.

Y4. **Judge,** Ghost Story Contest, sponsored by Oxford University Press, 1987.

Y5. **Cartoon,** by Stephen King, in *Castle Rock: The Stephen King Newsletter* 3:11 (November, 1987): 2.

Y6. **Library of Congress Cataloging**. In the Library of Congress classification scheme, the author's main entry is "King, Stephen, 1947- ," his literature number is PS3561.I483, and his bibliography number is Z8464.47.

QUOTH THE CRITICS

GENERAL COMMENTS

"At his best, [King] puts everyone in touch with the nightmare anxieties of youth."—Michael Sragow.

"King is a fast, sometimes sloppy, always energetic writer who keys almost unerringly into contemporary character types who evoke our everyday compatriots and remind us of ourselves. King fabricates characters of utmost normality and then thrusts them into extraordinary circumstances, most often confronting the supernatural. Done well, it's a formula that really has to try to fail. King usually does well, and in so doing, has shaped and redefined the horror (oops...dark fantasy) market."—Edward Bryant.

"Stephen King [is] the most popular and and quite possibly the best supernatural story teller since Lovecraft...."—Mark Graham.

"When all the trappings are gone, King shows the difference between strength and tyranny, between persuasion and manipulation."—Chelsea Quinn Yarbro.

"A Lovecraft for our times. Ozzie and Harriet and Beaver and Wally with brain tumors, and things that eat people held back by fraying ropes in damp cellars."—Thomas Gifford.

"To find the secret of his success, you have to compare King to Twain, Poe—with a generous dash of Philip Roth and Will Rogers thrown in for added popular measure. King's stories tap the roots of myth buried in all our minds...."—Kenneth Atchity.

"Fact is, Stephen King *is* the Shakespeare of this age. He writes what the *people* want for entertainment, which is just what William Shakespeare did. If Shakespeare were alive today, no doubt he would win a Nobel prize. He's the best, right? Well, if we don't nuke the planet, my money says 300 years from now folks will be wondering why Steve didn't get one. Hell, he still might."—Mark Graham.

"—I think he has founded his own genre—and been followed into it by scores of other writers. He has not narrowed down, but rather has expanded the definition of what he is as a writer, to the point where he can say, as no one else can, that he has tried everything and made it work in some sense. I think in the end that may be Stephen King's greatest achievement; he is the first writer, ever, to have truly baffled the critics."—Algis Budrys.

Carrie (1974)

"*Carrie*...is folklore. It is a fairy tale and like the fairy tales of the Brothers Grimm and Afanas'ev in Russia, it feeds on universal myths, magic, ancient ways and the narrator's rich imagination. But *Carrie*'s narrator is far more sophisticated than the story tellers of the Grimms or Afanas'ev, and so is his audience. *Carrie*...is a universal fairy tale, folklore of the last quarter of the twentieth century."—Alex E. Alexander.

"The incongruity between terrible consequences and their seemingly trivial causes is a theme that runs throughout King's fiction. Petty mistakes, jealousies, and conflicts have enormous and awful results, consequences all out of proportion to the initial causes. Careless, casual malice, even well-intentioned blundering, can unleash forces which, once set in motion, cannot be stopped until they have worked out their terrible repercussions. That is, in fact, one of the basic tenets of horror fiction: the dark powers, be they supernatural or human in origin, need only the slightest provocation to break loose and wreak their terror."—Keith Neilson.

'Salem's Lot (1975)

"...the modern classic vampire novel...."—Douglas E. Winter.

"It is this certainty that good, despite the cost, will emerge triumphant over evil that keeps *'Salem's Lot* from becoming a morose, depressing book, just as it is King's insistence that horror is not ultimately gratuitous which keeps the book from being a meaningless one. If humanity does, indeed, as King suggests, foster its own monsters, then it is also capable of ridding itself of them and of emerging stronger from the ordeal."—Christine Watson.

The Shining (1977)

"For all the bloodshed presented in *The Shining*, the forces of 'good' do win—or at least survive, bruised and battered physically and emotionally, but intact in mind and body."—Keith Neilson

"...when all's said, the novel *works!* It makes one tremble in anticipation of the day when King gets it all together and writes a 'perfect' book."—Frederick Patten.

"King's creation of atmosphere is masterful."—Marc Laidlaw.

The Stand (1978)

"...An aerobics workout for every emotion known to mankind."—Will Cortland.

"Its detractors have suggested that it seems endless in reading...but length is a necessary aspect of an epic structure, and *The Stand* is truly popular epic."—Mary Ferguson.

"Of all King's work, the most clearly mythic in structure and intent is *The Stand*. Here King is using the post-catastrophic landscape as the setting for a final confrontation of Good and Evil."—Chelsea Quinn Yarbro.

"King does not profess to be a religious man, but in an age when most people believe evil to be the result of illness or error, King writes novels (especially *'Salem's Lot* and *The Stand*) showing evil in its darker and more ancient vitality."—Mark Harris.

NIGHT SHIFT (1978)

"The range and variety of the stories in *Night Shift* are impressive. The book is almost a catalog of contemporary dark fantasy subjects...."—Keith Neilson.

"At best King is simply himself, and when he loses consciousness of himself as a writer—the way an old tale-teller around the campfire occasionally will—he can be outstanding."—Mark Harris.

The Dead Zone (1980)

"Selflessness is not a virtue often espoused in literature these days, but pitting selflessness against the Neo-Nazi destruction in *The Dead Zone* shows how that choice must be clearly made by all of us one time or another, with or without the benefit of psychic insight."—Chelsea Quinn Yarbro.

"While Stephen King is most often pigeonholed as a horror specialist, many of his readers have long been of the opinion that he could function equally well outside that genre. *The Dead Zone* both confirms this belief and demonstrates its author's versatility, for despite attempts to group it with King's more frightening works, it is *not* a horror novel. Rather, it is a tragic novel...."—Christine Watson.

"In defense of *The Dead Zone* and King, it is a good read; in fact, it is a very good read, not impossible to put down, but putting it down is not something one does willingly."—John Gault.

FIRESTARTER (1980)

"Despite the pseudo-scientific hokum, a vital ingredient to *roman à la* King—*Firestarter*—a bestseller weeks before its official publication date—is the most realistic, even credible novel he has written."—Michael Demarest.

"Although Stephen King's meteoric rise has earned him a reputation as the best and most popular of contemporary 'horror story' authors, his writings, especially the novels, are a blend of several popular genres, and, with the possible exception of *The Stand* (1978), *Firestarter* offers the most complex and interesting mix. It is part horror novel, part science-fiction story, and part political intrigue adventure, with a climax that echoes the classic Western formula."—Keith Neilson.

"*Firestarter* is Stephen King at his best. It moves so fast that the end comes suddenly, yet the end is one of the best parts. Whatever you do, don't sneak a peak at the last page; it will be worth the wait."—Mark Graham.

"[*Firestarter*] is your advanced post-Watergate cynical American thriller with some eerie parapsychological twists, and it's been done so distinctively well that we'd better talk about genius rather than genre."—Paul Stuewe.

"THE MIST" (1980)

"In 'The Mist,' King adroitly combines a menagerie of the most extravagant and bizarre comic book/horror movie monsters with an intensely realistic setting and a collection of believable characters in conflict to produce one of his best and most viscerally scary, stories."—Keith Neilson.

"'The Mist' (almost a short novel) is by far the best supermarket-menaced-by-horrible-monsters story ever likely to be written, and some of the nastiest monsters are human...."—Peter Nicholls.

CUJO (1981)

"...*Cujo* is perhaps the best book [King] has yet written...."—Burton Hatlen.

"*Cujo* is as good as anything as Stephen King has written and by far his most unsettling novel."—Mark Graham.

"*Cujo* is...steeped in a reality that is as inescapable as it is frightening, emphasizing not only the role of horror fiction as the modern fairy tale but the importance of realism in creating effective horror fiction."—Douglas E. Winter.

DANSE MACABRE (1981)

"So after you have spent a few hours dancing with Stephen King, which will truly be a pleasure, he leaves you with countless hours of gratification, if no 'pleasant dreams.'"—Mark Graham.

DIFFERENT SEASONS (1982)

"Very few authors could have gotten away with a book like this one....Great novellas become critical classics and financial failures, yet *Different Seasons* is already a best seller because it comes from the pen of Stephen King. King won't let you down; it deserves to be there."—Mark Graham.

CHRISTINE (1983)

"King has become perhaps the most popular author in the United States, turning out books filled with horror, gore and the supernatural. No one has been able to achieve such wide acceptance while writing almost solely on such a narrow end of the literary spectrum. But King is different, and *Christine*, which ends the first decade of 'Kingdom' (*Carrie* was published in 1974), may be able to tell you why.

"Perhaps it is his ability to mix the ordinary with the extraordinary that accounts for his popularity. Maybe it is his insight into our innermost fears or the combination of the unknown with the horrors of modern technology, or the nostalgia which creeps through his stories and novels.

"Regardless of what it is, we are forced to believe in Christine and to care about what happens to those whose lives she interrupts, and we will continue to let King interrupt our lives for decades to come."—Mark Graham.

"At times genuinely frightening, but at 500 pages a bit long, *Christine* contains some of the best writing King has ever done; his teenage characters are superbly drawn and their dilemma is truly gripping."—*Publishers Weekly*.

PET SEMATARY (1983)

"Even though *Pet Sematary* flinches at the end, that does not deny the innate power of the balance of the novel. Incompletely realized as it is, I still think the book supports my view of the writer. It's stretching, pushing things to the limit, that causes the author to grow. It is only through experiments such as *Pet Sematary*, painful and difficult as they may be, that Stephen King will cross that hazy but undeniable line between good and great."—Edward Bryant.

"[*Pet Sematary* is King's] grimmest. Through its pages runs a taint of primal malevolence so strong that on each of the three nights it took me to read it, both my companion and I had nightmares. Reader, beware. This is a book for those who like to take their scare straight—with a chaser of despair."—Annie Gottlieb.

"*Pet Sematary* delivers, not simply for those who love a tale well told, but for those who like to think about what they read. Despite some faults...this book offers the rare exhilaration of being scared within the safe limits of art, and the opportunity to exercise our need, as rational beings, to grapple with the fact of our mortality."—Douglas E. Winter.

CYCLE OF THE WEREWOLF (1983)

"This 128-page tale is a howling success for horror fiction connoisseurs."—Jeannine E. Klein.

THE TALISMAN (1984)

"No longer trusting Hollywood to adapt their work, King and Straub combined their talents and wrote *The Talisman,* an immensely satisfying collaboration that has 'blockbuster movie' written all over it....The trip is long and arduous—more than 600 pages—but the reader never tires."—Dale Pollack.

"...the first half of *The Talisman* is concerned with scariness-through-simple-storytelling, King's trademark...."—Ken Tucker.

THINNER (1984)

"This is what Stephen King would write if Stephen King could really write."—Literary Guild member.

"If you are still not convinced that this book was written by the No. 1 writer in the genre of the strange and the supernatural, wait until the last page. If King didn't write the end of this little narrative, his doppelgänger did—which of course would be only appropriate."—Mark Graham.

SKELETON CREW (1985)

"'The Reach'...is often considered his best short story. It is a work of unusual subtlety and sentiment, a ghost story of love and death, a virtuoso performance in which the horror is distanced but underpins the whole."—David Hartwell.

"*Skeleton Crew* is a veritable cornucopia of the nasty, the horrible, the cruel, or the just plain unearthly."—Chuck Moss.

THE BACHMAN BOOKS (1985)

"This final characteristic is what fully differentiates the earlier Bachman novels from King's other works. They are insistently non-horrific; what horror they evoke is of a radically different order than vampires or ghosts or malevolent, sentient Plymouth Furies can create. More like *Cujo* than *The Shining*, they assert the actuality of horror within the commonplace."—Michael R. Collings.

IT (1986)

"*It* is another King triumph, balancing love and loss, innocence and age, good and evil."—Judy Kimberly.

"*It* is King's immortality ode. To his young enthusiasts he keeps saying, rather loudly, Don't ever change! even while he whispers to those who already have changed, The best is yet to be."—Thomas R. Edwards.

THE DARK TOWER II: THE DRAWING OF THE THREE (1987)

"On the strength of this installment, one can say that *The Dark Tower*, when completed, may well become the new epic against which all other serious fantasies are measured. It has a unique vision, combining King's strength at portraying real people and our recognizable world, with his growing assurance as a fantasist; and it's infused with an enthusiasm that cannot help but be conveyed to its readers."—Charles de Lint.

"There is power and passion in King's writing here. At one point this passion pours forth in a remarkable two-and-a-half page sentence that begins with the momentum of a steam engine and ends with that of a laser, leaving the reader breathless and admiring and envious of his skill."—Janet C. Beaulieu.

MISERY (1987)

"It's a first-rate Stephen King novel. If this book doesn't keep you up all night it's because you weren't paying attention. There isn't a speck of fantasy here, yet Annie Wilkes earns a place among the most extraordinary and believable monsters in all of literature.... Sure [King] has weaknesses.... So did Charles Dickens, the Stephen King of the 1880s.... Inevitably, the arbiters of literary fashion will mock his attempt at explaining the integrity of his kind of storytelling. But what does that matter? They might hurt King's feelings. They might reassure some deservedly insecure academic-literary writers. But they can't change one simple fact: King is telling America what to believe and what to care about, and America is listening."—Orson Scott Card.

"With *Misery,* King charts a new tack on his literary course, proving to his critics that it is his ability as a storyteller which has made him one of the bestselling authors in the history of literature, and not merely what he refers to his 'vampires, ghoulies, and slushy crawling things.' And those readers who can take this book, the literary equivalent of the Scream Machine or the Coney Island Cyclone—at least pre-insurance hikes—are in for the ride of their lives."—Tyson Blue.

"*Misery* is part character study, part exploration of the artistic impulse. It's the closest King has yet come to a 'literary' work. But mostly it's a compelling story, a wonderful adventure through an all-too-human conflict, encompassing territories dark and bright."—Charles de Lint.

"*Misery* most of all is about the writing of a book. It may be King's confession of the agony that goes into the making of all that money, of the writer's terror of staring into the gaping maw and wondering whether he has what it takes to plunge in."—Steve Paul.

THE TOMMYKNOCKERS (1987)

"*The Tommyknockers* meshes well with King's other novels, pushing the edges of his explorations a bit further while still retaining the flavor, the structure, the intensive characterization and imagination that are his strengths. At the same time, it confronts narratively the knotty issue of the relationships between science fiction and horror, between alien and monster, between the connotations of words such as 'spacecraft' and 'flying saucer.'"—Michael R. Collings.

"The appeal of horror in an age like ours is pretty obvious. But what seems to me to set King apart from some of his lesser colleagues is his credible exploration of *power* in his fiction—as something most of us don't have, secretly want, but probably could not use wisely if we were ever to get it."—Arend Flick.

"It is [King's] darkest vision yet, because it involves not just malevolent telepathy and rampaging technology—but also the townspeople's own acquiescence and even complicity in their own destruction."—Daryl Frazell.

"King proves himself in this novel to be a writer of formidable talent. 'The Tommyknockers' is taut and timely."—Marianne Dougherty.

MY PRETTY PONY (1989)

"The story is a charming fable of an old man's passing of a timepiece, and a lesson, to his favorite grandchild. This is the writer at his most avuncular, a bittersweet fiction, in which he takes our hands and walks us along toward that long, dark night ahead."—Douglas E. Winter.

THE DARK HALF (1989)

King "...analyzes the writer's natural duality, the very quality that begets creation. Between King's terse lines of prose lies an intriguing allegory for the creative process and, more importantly, for the special relationship a writer maintains with his pseudonym"—William D. Gagliani.

THE STAND: THE COMPLETE AND UNCUT EDITION (1990)

"The restored passages aren't just decoration; they do reinforce King's purpose. The new conclusion, showing what happens to Randall Flagg *after* Las Vegas, amplifies the dark ambiguity of King's apocalypse."—Joe Sanders.

"For those who aren't King fans, this can be a really grim journey through death and senseless destruction."—Sue Martin.

"What was the rest of the story? What was missing? The answer is: the heart of the book. The 'uncut' version of 'The Stand' is by far the richer novel."—Janet C. Beaulieu.

"'The Stand' has been hailed as Mr. King's greatest novel. 'The Stand: The Complete and Uncut Edition' should do nothing bu make that opinion unanimous. It is simply a superb work of truly epic proportions."—Gregory N. Krolczyk.

"*The Stand II* is not a ripoff, but a new and improved book. It's a fully realized work to the earlier one's outline."—Chuck Moss.

FOUR PAST MIDNIGHT (1990)

"Mr. King's recurring tactic of making the ordinary function in a bizarre way always hooks the child in us."—Andy Solomon.

"*Four Past Midnight* is true to form. The four longish novellas deal with various aspects of the supernatural, all in King's breezy, almost chatty style."—Alan Gottlieb.

"King's real strength is that he's a decent person in an exposed position. Internal evidence indicates the decency of the writer; it's in the tenderness of his good guys, the unhappiness of his bad guys, the hopefulness of his children. It's in the writer's honest refusal to deny that the universe is unspeakably dangerous, to deny that it kills. It's in the affection of the writer for his characters and their affection for one another, even when they occasionally display bad taste."—Edna Stumpf.

INDEX

1. PRIMARY WORKS

2. SECONDARY WORKS

3. AUTHORS OF SECONDARY WORKS AND MISCELLANEA